# The Fighting Ship of the Royal Navy

# The

## of the Royal Navy AD 897–1984

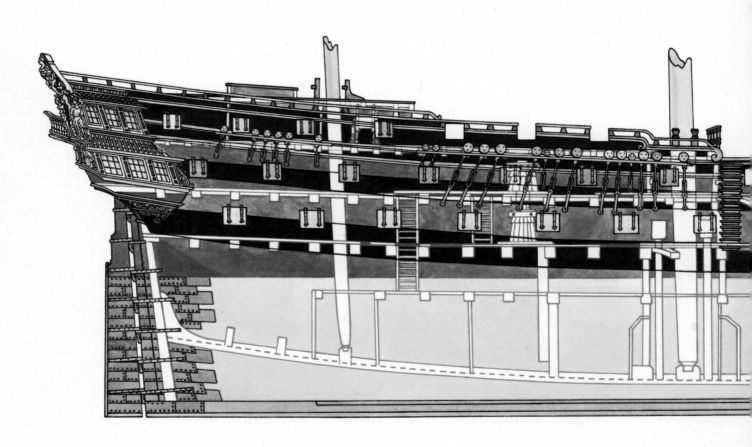

The classic ship of the line, a British seventy-four. This drawing was made from the draught of the Berwick of 1775. She fought the French at the Battle of Ushant in 1778, the Dutch at Doggerbank in 1781, and was in Lord Howe's fleet that finally relieved Gibraltar in 1782. In 1793 she was in Lord Hood's fleet at the capture of Toulon. Eighteen months later, still in the Mediterranean, she had the rare experience for a British ship of the line to be captured by the French. She was sailing under a jury rig, having been dismasted, when she was found by Admiral Martin's fleet and taken by three of his frigates. She fought for the French at Calder's action off Ferrol in 1805, and at Trafalgar in the same year was recaptured by the Achilles 74, but was wrecked in the storm that followed the battle.

# Fighting Ship

By E.H.H. Archibald

Illustrated by Ray Woodward

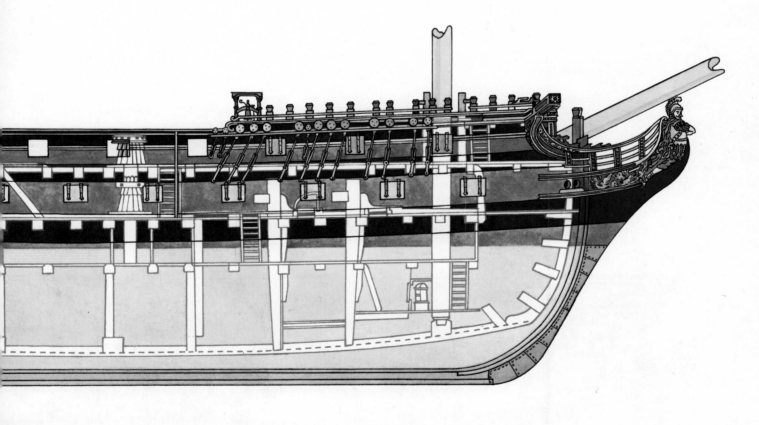

**MILITARY PRESS**

New York

Special technical advisor Bob Todd
Additional drawings by Clifford and Wendy Meadway

Originally published in two volumes
*The Wooden Fighting Ship in the Royal Navy AD 897–1860*, Blandford Press, 1968, Revised 1972
*The Metal Fighting Ship in the Royal Navy 1860–1970*, Blandford Press, 1971

This single-volume and revised edition first published in the U.K. in 1984
by Blandford Press Ltd., Link House, West Street, Poole, Dorset BH 15 1LL.
© 1984 E.H.H. Archibald

Reprinted with minor revisions 1987.
This 1987 edition published by
Military Press, distributed by Crown Publishers, Inc.,
225 Park Avenue South, New York, New York 10003

Printed by Toppan Printing Co. Singapore.

h g f e d c b a

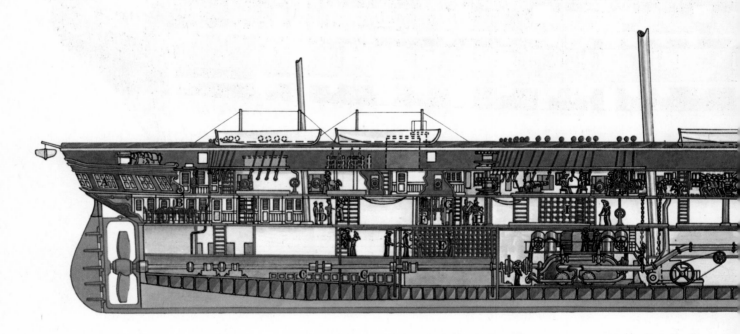

**WARRIOR 1860**
*This beautiful iron hull is still afloat at Hartlepool, and remains, with the GREAT BRITAIN, the finest monument to the Victorian marine engineers – who, with a seemingly effortless shrug, mocked with this ship the French efforts to threaten Britain's naval supremacy, with wooden hulls hung about with armour plates. When her restoration is completed she will go on show at Portsmouth.*

## Abbreviations, dates and dimensions

A.A.    Anti-aircraft guns
A/S    Anti-submarine weapons
B.L.    Breech-loading guns (some mentioned as B.L.R. but all were rifled)
D.P.    Dual-purpose guns (anti-ship and anti-aircraft)
M.L.    Muzzle-loading (smooth-bores)
M.L.R.    Muzzle-loaders rifled
P.D.R.    Pounder
Q.F.    Quick-firers

Dates given in both text and index are in nearly every case dates of launching.

Dimensions are expressed in feet and inches. Lengths where not marked o/a (overall) are between perpendiculars, that is, between the rudder-post and the bow end of the main-deck.

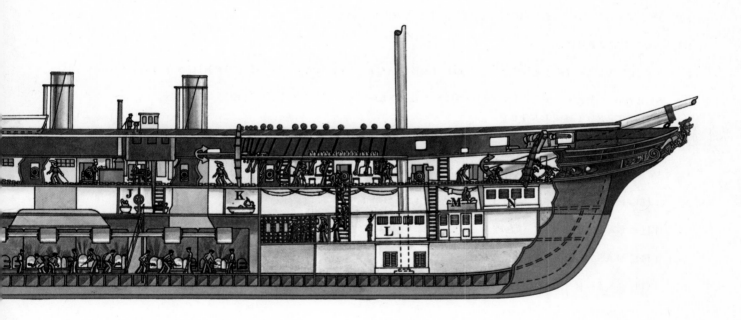

# Contents

*To attack with greater numbers from a larger, higher platform: King Alfred's lesson in tactics to the Danes.*

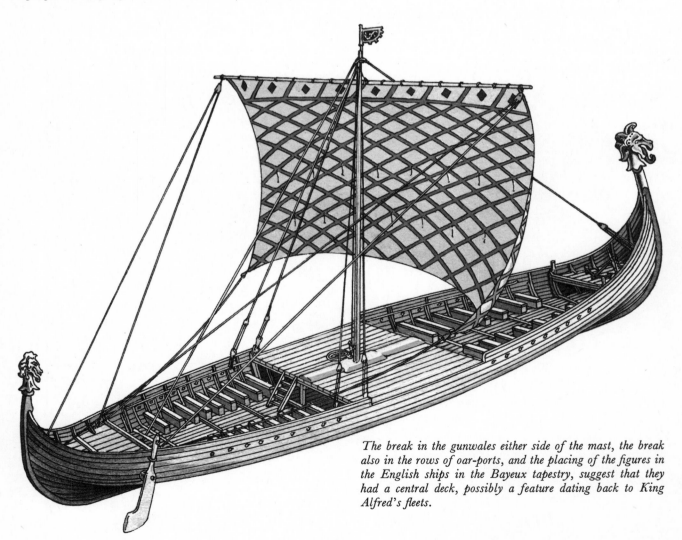

*The break in the gunwales either side of the mast, the break also in the rows of oar-ports, and the placing of the figures in the English ships in the Bayeux tapestry, suggest that they had a central deck, possibly a feature dating back to King Alfred's fleets.*

# 1

## Alfred the Great
## to William the Conqueror

The purpose of warship design is now and has always been to procure some advantage over the known qualities of the vessels of one's enemies, or potential enemies, or friends. The first conscious expression of this principle in England that we know of occurred in the year 897, when King Alfred ordered ships to be built to particular specifications which he believed would enable his navy to beat the squadrons of the marauding Danes. The new ships that the king ordered were to be larger and higher than the Danish ships, so that when they met in combat the English had the advantage of fighting from a higher platform in greater numbers, and the Danes were defeated. To keep their advantage the English would decline to land and fight on shore if they found the Danes already disembarked, but would stand off shore and wait for the Danes to put to sea and fight them. Alfred thus created a formidable navy and used it as an effective weapon against his enemies, but there was to be no continuity of organisation or service, nor could there have been in those chaotic times. As soon as the danger receded the ships were laid aside, and a new navy had to be created to meet a new threat. As for the Danes, many settled in the lands they had come to pillage and became respectable, so that this nuisance abated.

We do not know what Alfred's ships looked like, but the Saxon Chronicle does say that they were different in appearance from those of the Danes. Even so, apart from their size, it seems unlikely that they differed in more than styling and proportions, and their higher freeboard would give them a contrasting profile to the sleek Danish ships. But if we do not know the form or details of the English ships we do know something about the ships of the Danes and the other Scandinavian tribes. Two beautiful ships of this period have been discovered in Norway and restored, but they are both merchant ships, both shorter and proportionately broader in the beam than the long ships. The bigger of the two, the Gokstad ship, is 76 feet long and 17 feet broad amidships, clinker-built and decked close to her floor. There is provision for a single mast which carried a large square sail, and being a merchant ship she would have depended more on this than on her oars. There are sixteen oar ports a side, since her crew would normally be small. The long-boats which were the fighting ships, or drakkans, were enormous open rowing boats which, even allowing for poetic exaggeration, must have been up to 150 feet long, longer than the largest pleasure boats now plying on the Thames in the London area.

The size and shape of these ships were conditioned to their purpose, which in the ninth century was to transport a strong body of men as quickly as possible to the places that were to be attacked. The large crews made possible the manning of powerful banks of oars, thirty or forty a side, and these, unlike in a merchant ship, were the principal means of propulsion. They were especially important in the rivers which were the high roads through the lands they sailed to, and on whose banks were to be found the richest communities. There was a large square sail as well as the oars and the ships must have run well before the wind or on a broad reach. The long ships, though built for war, were not themselves weapons, like the ram-bowed Mediterranean galleys, nor did they carry weapons heavier than hand arms. Their armament was their men and they provided the transport and on occasion a platform to fight from. The crew had the comfort and amenities of an open rowing boat, though it seems reasonable to assume that they could rig an awning if they wanted to. But the men were used to hardships, both ashore and afloat; they were vigorous and mostly young, and there was the expectation of adventure, the chance of coming on a rich town, to fight and kill, to take what they wanted and destroy what they did not, and afterwards to celebrate with the wine and women of the place.

As a result of the Danish invasions in the late tenth and early eleventh centuries they gained political control in England, and the raids largely ceased. From this time on the role of the oared fighting ship became less and less important in northern waters, and the need for a bluffer cargo carrier increased.

There is no reason to believe, however, that the English and Norman ships in 1066 differed substantially from Alfred's. The Bayeux Tapestry, which records the Norman invasion and the events leading up to it, confirms this, but also makes a clear distinction between the Norman and English ships. In the former there is a continuous row of oar ports which indicates that their decks were flush from bow to stern. The English ships, on the other hand, have a break in the gunwale amidships where there are no oar ports, and the men standing in that area near the mast can be seen from their ankles up, while those behind the oar ports stand lower. This can surely only mean that the English ships had a deck amidships with a 6- to 8-foot clearance between the floor and deckhead. This must have been useful as a covered place for cargo or shelter, and in a fight the high deck would have been a useful vantage point. It is to be noted also that both Normans and Saxons lined the inside of the gunwales of their ships with their long oval topped shields, which protruded to give added protection against wind and spray. In the Saxon ships the shields amidships are outside the gunwales, which is evidence that there was something to prevent their going inside, such as a raised deck.

# 2

## The Normans to the Tudors

This is the period in England when the fighting ship as a separate design disappeared for over four hundred years in the largest type of vessel. These all came to be designed to the needs of commerce, and if they also had sometimes to be modified to take an army to war, this could be done. This does not mean that the oared warship entirely disappeared. Large double-ended rowing boats called balyngers were used in peace to fend off raids by the pirates who came to infest the Channel and other coastal waters; and in wartime they accompanied the fleet, which consisted mostly of sailing cogs, though also of some large-oared vessels.

If the English had abandoned the building of large specialised fighting ships it did not mean that they had abandoned fighting; far from it. It is, therefore, within the scope of this book to look at the merchant ships in which they fought and see how their design affected tactics. In any case, it was this type of ship that was to become the vehicle for Britain's naval supremacy over the world, though much modified, and much later. The chief pressure which forced a change in design was the need for the big double-ended ships to carry more cargo, but so long as they kept their banks of oars the deck could not be too high above the water-line or the oarsman could not work, nor could the ships be too broad in the beam as they would be too clumsy to row. Once, however, the oars were abandoned in the twelfth century the deck and sides of the ships could be raised to make room for a proper hold inside. The raising of the ships' centres of gravity meant that their beams had to be increased as well for stability and to keep their draught shallow for river work. At the same time their length had to be reduced, for long, wide, high ships with a single sail and a steering oar would have been too unhandy. They were still double-ended and clinker-built like the Viking ships, but they would not sail to weather as a replica of the Gokstad ship was able to do. They were called cogs.

By the thirteenth century, ships of this type that were impressed by the king in time of war began to be modified if they were expected to have to fight. This took the form of raised platforms with protective sides fore and aft called forecastles and sterncastles from which the bowmen could shoot down into the waist of an enemy ship, and these were followed by a topcastle at the head of the mast, which, however, could only have held a couple of warriors. These structures served no other purpose and were dismantled at the end of the charter. The ships were fought by soldiers as if they were little floating forts, which was really what they were. On the whole the men relied on their hand

3

The cog, a double ended sailing ship with a steering oar, developed in the twelfth and thirteenth centuries for trading, but here shown with a temporary forecastle, aftercastle and topcastle, as modified for war.

*The nef, being fitted with a rudder, was no longer double-ended, and here, as in the detail, the old high sternpost is retained which gave the chief support to the aftercastle, so that the tiller had to bow round it. This is an early type of the first half of the fourteenth century.*

arms, as the use of the great siege engines for throwing rocks would not have been practical; though some of the smaller catapults and slings were used on occasion. In 1217 when a French fleet under Eustace the Monk threatened Kent, the English purposely manœuvred to have the weather gauge, bore down on them and threw bags of quicklime over them. Under cover of this cloud of blinding powder they grappled, boarded and entered the French ships, winning a brilliant victory, with great slaughter.

This was a real naval battle of ships and movement, more so than the better remembered Battle of Sluys in 1340, which was Edward III's curtain-raiser to the Hundred Years War. The French fleet of about two hundred ships was drawn up in four lines, the ships of the first line at least were chained together side to side, a most unwieldy arrangement, reflecting an attitude of mind adapted only to land warfare on the part of the French commander. The English with a similar force attacked them from to windward and destroyed nearly all of them.

*In this nef, slightly later than the one on page 5, the sternpost is cut short below the rudder-head, so that support for the aftercastle comes from the raised gunwales, which soon became permanent structures for shelter and accommodation.*

By this time the English cog type ships were being built with rudders instead of using steering oars and were called nefs. This made a considerable difference in their appearance since they had now a distinctive bow and stern, but it made no material difference to their qualities as fighting ships. Another development was that the temporary castles, which had been growing in size, began in the mid-fourteenth century to become permanent structures, boarded in all round for cabins. This began with the sterncastle and was followed in the fifteenth century by the forecastle. When this happened the difference between a ship prepared for war and a merchant ship disappeared; they were equally fitted to play both roles as built. Indeed they had to fight to trade, for pirates were plentiful, and many merchants, who would not have thought of themselves as pirates were close to Chaucer's Shipman:

> *who of nyce conscience took no keep*
> *If that he faught, and hadde the hyer hond,*
> *By water he sent hem hoom to every lond.*

*An early fifteenth-century nef with solid castles, but as yet only one sail.*
*These ships were suitable without alteration for warlike or peaceful purposes.*

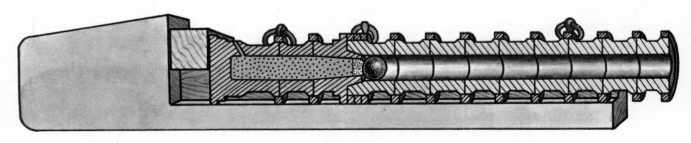

*A section of a wrought-iron breech-loading gun with a bobbin type barrel, early sixteenth century.*

# 3

## The Tudor Navy and the Gun

It was the use on shipboard of the heavy gun that forced the shipwrights to modify the design of ships intended for war, with the result that they could only be of practical use as fighting ships, being uneconomical if put to trade. By the same token, ships built for trade could no longer satisfactorily be adapted for war. This is a generalisation which was not true of all classes of ships, but it was true of ships of the largest size and force afloat at the end of the Tudor period, and it marks the end of the medieval dual purpose ship. Guns had been carried aboard ships since the fourteenth century, but they were at first of small size and only meant as man killing adjuncts to the hand arms. The opportunity for a change came with the rapid developments in the size and rig of the northern round ship, which at the beginning of the fifteenth century had one mast, one sail and one deck; and at the end of it had perhaps as many as three masts and a bowsprit, five sails and two decks, and these ships could bear guns heavy enough to cause damage to an opposing ship's structure and not just to her crew.

There were two types of large gun available, the cast bronze or brass muzzle-loader or the iron breech-loader, and before they invented a suitable gun-carriage and tackle for overcoming the loading problems of muzzle-loaders on board ship, the early naval guns of any size were iron breech-loaders. Because of the difficulty of heating iron to a sufficient temperature to pour into a mould, it had proved impossible for the medieval gun founders to cast them in iron. They therefore made them exactly as a cooper makes a barrel, with a faggot of wrought-iron bars fitting together to form a tube; this was the earliest and worst kind of iron gun. The bars were held in place by iron hoops sweated on round the outside, the joins between the bars being sealed with lead. The resulting

*A wrought-iron breech-loader with a bar-barrel, fifteenth to mid-sixteenth centuries.*

*Preparing a breech-loading bobbin-barrelled gun for firing.*
*The block and tackle shown are hypothetical, but the guns*
*must have been secured in some way.*

barrel was open at both ends, so a separate chamber was attached to one end to hold the powder. The whole contrivance had to be set in a stout timber cradle with a solid piece of timber behind the powder chamber which took the recoil and held the wedge, which in turn held the breech shut. The bar gun type of bombard was followed by an improved design at the end of the fifteenth century, whereby instead of a barrel of iron bars, a core of short lengths of wrought-iron tube was made, the ends of each being lipped like a cotton bobbin. As with the bar guns, the tubes were held together by broad iron bars, beaten round the barrel where the lips met. These guns were breech-loaded as before, but a big improvement on the bar guns though still a very rough instrument. Indeed the bar guns must have belched fire from other places than the barrel mouth and touchhole. The gun at Greenwich, which was salved from the king's ship *Mary Rose*, is of this type, and that ship sank off Portsmouth in 1545. It is 7 feet 6 inches long and has a bore of about 5 inches; there are rings on the barrel for moving it, but maybe also for a rope tackle to be attached to it as its wooden cradle was not solid on the deck. The gun at Woolwich on the other hand is of the bar type, as are those at the Tower of London. Both types used stone shot. In Madrid there are iron guns which combine the bar and bobbin techniques.

The size of ships' guns was partly governed by their weight; the really heavy guns had to be carried lower in the ship than the upper deck, and these took the form of

9

large brass or bronze muzzle-loaders on wheeled carriages, carried on the lower deck. In order to get the big guns working between decks it was necessary to pierce the ship's sides for gun-ports, and to devise a carriage and tackle so that the barrel mouth could be run in and out of the port for firing and loading. These guns might be 10 or 12 feet long and threw a stone or iron ball of up to 30 pounds. In design they differed hardly at all from the guns of the mid-nineteenth century, but they were lighter and thinner for their bore since the powder was then so bad that the barrels need be no more than eighty times the weight of the shot as against about four hundred times a century later. From the mid-sixteenth century the improvement in smelting processes made possible by the blast furnace made the casting of guns in iron possible. To their credit they were cheaper than bronze ones and the metal being harder they did not bruise themselves with their own shot, nor did their vents so easily wear out. On the other hand, when the barrel failed, it shattered like a bomb without warning, while the bronze barrels usually just gave a warning bulge; both the iron and bronze guns suffered too from honey-combing, making the inside of the barrels look like lump sugar. The iron guns were also despised by the gunners because they were of a coarse metal which could not be enriched by the elaborate decoration which embellished so many sixteenth- and seventeenth-century bronze pieces.

By the middle of the century all the larger units belonging to King Henry VIII had two tiers of heavy guns, with the old breech-loaders still continuing to be the main part of the upper-deck armament. The ships themselves were modelled on the most admired type of northern round ship, the carrack; the ships were up to 1000 tons, only twice as long as they were broad. Henry either built them in England or bought them from abroad, and although they were exactly similar to the largest merchant ships, they were too large and valuable, and too much modified, for gun platforms to be chartered out for trading in the summer, as the fifteenth-century English kings had done with their ships. In the winter they were laid up; so that the 'great ships' of the Tudor navy, because they were used exclusively for war, became separate and specialised fighting ships. The king was anxious to make his fleet an effective fighting force to beat the French, and was not only receptive to new ideas, but also designed some of the ships himself.

The Venetians had been trading with their galleys to England and the north European ports for many years, and it was they who developed from them a type of

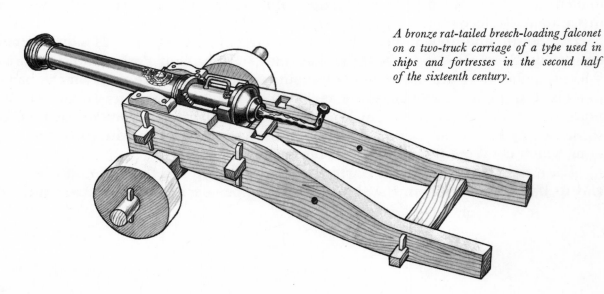

*A bronze rat-tailed breech-loading falconet on a two-truck carriage of a type used in ships and fortresses in the second half of the sixteenth century.*

sailing ship which the English were to adopt and turn into a world-beating warship. In these ships, the race-built galleons, the hull proportions lengthened to two and a half to three times the beam, and the towering superstructures, especially the forecastles, were reduced in size; all this in the interest of creating a faster and more weatherly ship. The Venetian ships appeared when Henry was enlarging his fleet in the first quarter of the century, and were admired and copied. Even so, it was to be many years before a full-scale maritime war was to prove or disprove the various schools of thought that existed on the effective composition of a fleet and how it should be used, so that the possibilities of the new race-built galleons were not generally appreciated at first, and indeed they were probably built to work with the galleys and galleasses, as they were in the Venetian navy.

The result was a mixture of types which reflected the conflict of ideas, for Henry's early experiences with the French convinced him that he should have in his fleet several large vessels of free movement, which at that time meant oared, as well as the smaller-oared vessels that traditionally accompanied the fleet. These were called galleasses, but according to the Anthony Anthony Rolls they did not much resemble their Mediterranean namesakes. They had square tucks, and English type superstructures, though much lower than the great ships; they also had beaks, a tier of guns along their upper decks and tiers of oars below, they were presumably long and lean in proportion. Apart from their ability to move without a wind, they were in all other respects inferior to

11

a great ship. They lacked the loftiness for boarding and their lower decks, instead of housing the heaviest tiers of guns, were full of oarsmen who could not fight and who, so far as the English were concerned, were extremely hard to recruit, since the English did not employ slaves, or send felons to the galleys as the French did. By the middle of the century, however, the large-oared warship was fast disappearing from the English service, probably because of the great improvement in sailing rigs, which would especially have benefited the galleon and galleass type of hull, so that the galleasses were probably rebuilt as sailing ships. By Queen Elizabeth's time the navy had only one left, and that seldom employed.

The argument as to what constituted the most effective sort of capital ship resolved itself into two main lines of thought. The first, supported by the traditionalists, the military-minded and the very able Sir Richard Hawkins, favoured the old type of carrack-built great ship. The second, passionately advocated by the hard core of seamen such as Drake, Raleigh and Sir Richard's father, Sir John Hawkins, were in favour of the race-built galleon. There is no doubt that in a close fight, and for boarding, the former type had all the advantages. From their high musket-proof superstructures her people could fire their light breech-loading pivot guns, hand guns and crossbows down on to the unprotected deck of the galleon, and even if the galleon's crews managed to swarm into her waist and clear it, the great ship's company could retire into the fore-castle and steerage and continue to harry them from there. These ships were even armed with light truck-mounted cannon of the murderer type, pointing across the waist

*An English great ship of the time of Henry VIII. She is of the floating fortress type which lost favour in the Elizabethan navy, but which the Spanish continued to build.*

for this purpose. The great ship needed a broad beam to carry her superstructure, and so be able also to carry more men and ordinance for her length. It was Alfred's theory again, more men on a higher platform; and in this case the enemy was the Spanish infantry, then the best in the world, who ran their ships on military lines and strongly favoured the great ship principle. The galleon, on the other hand, by her greatly superior sailing qualities, did not have to close, but could sit to weather of the great ship or off her quarter, knocking her about at a distance on her own terms. Admittedly, gunnery was a most inexact art and the bigger ship could take a lot of punishment, as well as serve it out. There was, however, one overriding disadvantage to the great ship types in an age of exploration and deep-water seafaring. They had been given a rig that should have let them sail on a wind, but their great superstructures baulked them, and their bluff bowed beamy hulls would not bite the water. They were leewardly, crank and unhandy; not at all the sort of ships in which the seamen of England cared to take the war to Spain and her empire. They therefore evolved the fast, handy big-gun warship, which lasted in principle entirely, and largely in form, until the coming of armour in the middle of the nineteenth century.

*In the English galleass of the time of Henry VIII, the broadside guns are carried above the banks of oars. The type disappears from the English lists early in Queen Elizabeth's reign, but they were the precursors of the race-built galleons.*

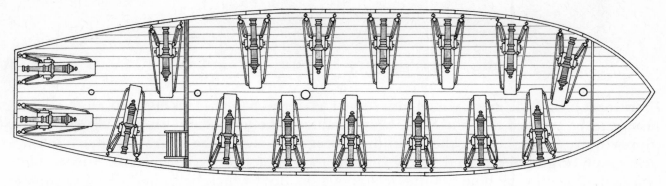

*Owing to the length of the guns and their carriages, it is suggested here that the tiers were staggered on the gun-deck and falls.*

4

# The Elizabethan Galleon

The high-water mark of Tudor ship design was the building of the queen's ships of the galleon type, of which the most admired model was the *Revenge*, Drake's favourite ship and the one that Raleigh held up as a shining example against the great ships of 'marvellous charge and fearefull cumber'. Indeed, she and her near sisters were very small for capital ships by the standards of even fifty years after he wrote. She was 100 feet on the gun-deck, with an overall length from beakhead to taffrail of about 120 feet, or roughly the same overall length as a present-day fast patrol boat. Her beam was 32 feet, a bluffer proportion than was usual later, but not far from the 100-foot gun-deck and 30-foot beam of the average eighteen-gun brig-sloop in the Nelsonic period. The Elizabethan galleons had a main armament of about twenty large truck-mounted muzzle-loading culverins, which were about 12 feet long and fired a ball weighing about 18 pounds. These were carried on the lower deck and a further battery of demi-cannon and demi-culverins were on the upper deck; these fired ball of about 10 pounds. In addition to all this, room was found to mount a further fifteen or so smaller carriage guns; all of them muzzle-loaders of bronze or brass. There was always a tendency for the English to over-gun their ships, but nothing afterwards approached this.

Elizabethan gunnery was cursed with a great variety of guns. In the same ship might be found the demi-cannon, cannon-perier, whole-culverin, demi-culverin, saker, minion and falcon, as well as a variety of lighter pivot guns. The result was that it was difficult to have a sufficient store of every type of shot when it was wanted so that by the end of the week's fighting with the Spanish Armada in the Channel in 1588, too many guns in the English ships stood around like scarecrows for want of shot. It must be supposed that the lower-deck batteries were staggered, otherwise with an internal beam of only about 28 feet and gun plus carriage lengths of about 14 feet, the guns must have recoiled on to each other. The deckhead must also have been very low for working such large pieces.

Unlike the older carrack-built ships, the galleons had a rather pronounced sheer, so to keep the weight low they had their lower gun-deck stepped down aft for the two sternmost broadside guns, which also served as stern-chasers. This enabled all the decks above to be stepped down as well, which reduced the top weight aft and also gave the opportunity for higher deckheads in the officers' quarters. The men were quartered on the lower or gun-decks, and below that there was at least a partial orlop-deck. This was a platform in the hold about 8 feet above the floor which held the cable and cabins for the boatswain, master gunner, carpenter, surgeon and storekeeper. In Elizabethan ships it would not have extended aft of the step in the deck above, and probably stopped short of the galley which was in the hold amidships. This awkward arrangement was a relic of medieval times, but in merchant ships it had been sensibly moved to the fo'c'sle; the navy followed suit in the seventeenth century. The total company of a galleon was about one hundred and fifty sailors, thirty gunners and seventy soldiers. The soldiers manned the guns as well as fought as infantry, and the sailors manned the guns and fought and sailed the ship as well. This was a flexible system which meant that the maximum fighting power was to be had from the crew; whereas in a Spanish ship the sailors were not armed and did not fight, the gunners only served the guns, and the soldiers did nothing but keep watch and ward and clean their equipment. In the fight their ship was turned into a fortress; not a nimble one, nor on the whole so powerfully gunned as the English galleons, but formidable all the same.

The moment of truth in the great ship versus galleon controversy came in 1591, when the *Revenge*, for reasons that need not concern us here, was trapped in the Azores

*How open are the decks of an Elizabethan race-built galleon. This one is as close as one can get to the* Ark Royal, *built privately to Sir Walter Raleigh's ideas, but bought from him by the State.*

*The* San Martin, *flagship of the Duke of Medina Sidonia, Captain-General of the Spanish Armada of 1588. She was the Spanish idea of a floating castle, with high gunwales and firing-steps, and her captain is issuing orders from a raised platform in the middle of the poop. There are even guns that train inwards across the waist.*

by a fleet of fifty-three Spanish warships and fought them for fifteen hours before she surrendered. It might have been supposed that she must have fought the action by keeping her enemies at a distance, but the accounts say that she was boarded a number of times and once by the Spanish flagship the *San Felipe*, a vessel three times her size. It must have been a desperate moment for the English and the enemy should have triumphed, but the terrible havoc that the *Revenge*'s lower guns continued to make in the hull of the Spaniard caused her to haul off. It is amazing that the *Revenge*'s crew, and through sickness less than a third of them were fit to even begin the action, could sustain their morale so long in the circumstances. In the end they had used up all their powder, which was another reason for not following up her commander's famous order to 'split me the ship Master Gunner'. During the action at least two, possibly four, Spanish ships were sunk by the *Revenge*'s guns, and in the storm that blew up after it sixteen more as well as the *Revenge* foundered, presumably because of gun damage.

This action took place three years after the great confrontation with the Spanish Armada. But indeed in the week's fighting up the Channel the English fleet made little impression on the Spanish, who kept excellent order while the English banged away at their heels. Only three ships were taken, and these because they became disabled and fell behind, and none were sunk. It was at the Battle of Gravelines, after the Spanish had been driven out of Calais Roads in disorder by the fireships, that they really suffered severely from the Anglo-Dutch guns, and after that the weather took over to destroy them. In 1602 the final lesson on the uselessness of the Mediterranean-type galley in northern waters was given to Frederigo Spinola, when he tried to bring his galleys to Flanders and lost eight out of a fleet of nine to Sir Robert Mansell's galleons, assisted by the Dutch. The galleys were not only smashed by the guns, but were rammed and sailed over.

*The* Sovereign of the Seas *of 1637. The biggest ship in the world at that date (see page 22), she was the first ship to mount 100 guns, have three flush decks, rig topgallant sails at her fore and mizzen, and a royal sail at the main.*

# 5

## Enlargements and Improvements under James I and Charles I

During the last years of Elizabeth's reign the English fighting ship was supreme in northern waters, both for itself and because of the people who handled it. The Spanish had fallen behind for backing the wrong set of ideas; the Dutch were only just beginning to find their sea legs and build warships on the lines of the English galleons, and the French were too busy with civil wars to attempt anything on the sea. For the English the first fifty years of the seventeenth century were comparatively uneventful at sea. Peace was made with Spain in 1604 and apart from two abortive expeditions to La Rochelle against the French, which were more military than naval, and a skirmish or two in the Civil War, the English ships had little to do. It was the increase in foreign trade in England and the Low Countries that set the straws in the wind for a commercial war between them, and it was the massacre in 1623 of the English traders by the Dutch at Amboyna that made this certain. But England's domestic affairs and the Civil War delayed an open clash for nearly thirty years, and when it came, in 1652–53, the Dutch were badly beaten.

All this was far away when James I came to the throne in 1603. He inherited a fine navy of forty-two ships, thirty of them of great or considerable force. James had nothing particularly in mind to do with them, but he was interested in his navy and conscious of the dignity it gave to his crown; so that when the idea of a super-ship was put to him, he was delighted. She was the brainchild of a master shipwright in the royal service called Phineas Pett, a member of an old shipbuilding family which continued to be famous throughout the century. He built a model in 1607 which he showed to his patron, old Nottingham, the lord admiral, who arranged for the king to see it, and James ordered Pett to put the ship in hand. She was to be 115 feet on the keel, which would mean about 135 feet on the gun-deck, and 43 feet in the beam and was the first English ship to be double planked. She was to be twice as big as the *Revenge*, and mount fifty-five carriage guns weighing in all over 83 tons, carried on three decks. She was built to the accompaniment of three courts of inquiry, the last presided over by the king himself, at which every informed opinion roundly condemned the design of the ship, the competence of the builder, as well as his honesty in choosing his materials. In spite of this Pett survived, for he was an inner member of the dishonest little clique that ran the navy; the Lord Admiral was his patron, and he was a retainer of Henry, Prince of Wales, who was enthusiastic about the ship.

The *Prince Royal*, as she was called, was floated out at Woolwich in 1610, after one

20

failure to do so had humbled Phineas Pett before his king. Success came with the following tide at two o'clock in the morning, and Phineas was comforted by the cheerful presence of Prince Henry, who rode over from Greenwich to be aboard for it. There are no draughts of her to show her internal arrangements; but there are a number of paintings of her, of which the authoritative ones are the two by Hendrik Cornelisz Vroom who painted her as she appeared on a visit to Flushing in 1613, and again in 1623. In the 1613 painting there are also two other large English warships which show the design trend of the time, and how the *Prince* was evolved. There had been a swing back from the extreme race-built galleon of the 1570s and 1580s, towards the great ship type. Not in the hull proportions, but in the lofty superstructures that towered fore and aft, made possible by the larger hulls. Sir Walter Raleigh, writing at this time, acknowledges the trend, and puts it down to a desire to improve the accommodation, 'The high charging of ships is it that brings them all ill qualities . . . for men may not expect the ease of many cabins and safety at once in sea-service . . . and albeit the marriners doe covet store of cabins, yet indeed they are but sluttish dens, that breed sickness in peace, serving to cover stealths, and in fight are dangerous to teare men with their splinters.'

To return to the two warships with the *Prince* at Flushing; the larger of the two has two decks with full tiers of guns on each. These have falls aft, and over the upper tier there is a third deck which forms the waist, and which bears no ordnance, but two guns aside are mounted on the same deck aft under the half-deck. What is remarkable is that the break of the half-deck and fo'c'sle is two decks high, and there is a quarter-deck abaft and above the half-deck. The other ship is similar except that the breaks of the half-decks and fo'c'sle are only one deck high and there are no guns on the third deck.

When Phineas Pett came to build the *Prince*, he gave her nearly 10 feet more beam than existing English warships, and length in proportion, so that he could increase the top weight without a dangerous loss of stability. She was built with all the decks and superstructures described in the larger of her two consorts at Flushing, but in addition the third deck was given complete tiers of guns, and another deck, presumably a light one, was built over the guns in the waist, joining the lower decks of the two superstructures. It is just possible, for we cannot see it clearly, that this deck did not cover the entire waist, but took the form of two platforms along the gunwales, as became the practice in the eighteenth century, but if this was so it was out of keeping with contemporary practice, and the full deck is the more likely. She thus had four decks, and, incredible as it may seem, she had gratings above this as a spar-deck. This was a light platform supported on stanchions, which was level with the half-deck and fo'c'sle deck, but as these also had gratings their height was raised also. The other English ships lack this, so the *Prince* may have started the fashion in the English navy.

It is not surprising that her rig was light by later standards, for she must have been top heavy and crank. She was rigged as a four-master, which was a little old fashioned by that date, and is shown at Flushing with the recent additions of topgallant sails at the main and fore, and square topsails at the mizzen and bonaventure-mizzen. These last required crossjack yards, to which the riggers had felt obliged to bend sails, a

*'A ship to fight for a Kingdom',* the Prince Royal, *55 guns of 1610.*
*The first three-decker, she was the greatest ship of her time (see page 21).*

practice soon dropped. The picture of her in 1623 shows her in her winter rig; no
topmasts on the mizzen and bonaventure-mizzen, and no topgallant masts on the main
and fore. There is provision for a sprit topmast, which was not in the 1613 picture, but
the mast is not stepped, and her spar-deck on the fo'c'sle has been removed; all of which
is evidence of a very tender sided ship. One other alteration is that her channels have
been brought down a deck in the case of main and fore from the upper to middle
gun-deck level. This was presumably because the tumblehome of the sides would give
the shrouds a better leverage from the middle deck, and this practice continued until
they went up again in the 1740s, and up again, in three-deckers to quarter-deck level
in 1794.

She was, of course, a prestige ship, a mighty galleon with the potential of a great
ship; indeed a 'ship to fight for a kingdom', as they said at the time, and she had no
sisters and no peers until Phineas Pett and his son Peter built the great *Sovereign of the
Seas* in 1637.

As the *Prince* was built to be the prestige ship of James I's navy, so the *Sovereign* was
to be of Charles I's. She was a good deal bigger again than the *Prince* and triple planked,

22

with a keel length of 127 feet and with a beam of 48 feet. In the 1670s her gun-deck was 167 feet 9 inches, but her keel had by then been lengthened to 135 feet 6 inches. Her total length from beakhead to taffrail was 234 feet, and it was 63 feet from the bottom of her keel to the top of her huge lantern, in which twelve men might stand together. It is interesting to compare these figures with the measurements of the last wooden three-decker to serve in a British fleet as a sea-going flagship, the *Victoria* of 1859. She was 289 feet from figurehead to taffrail, had a beam of 60 feet, and it was 72 feet from the base of her keel to her poop rail, a vastly larger ship.

The *Sovereign* had a lower profile than the *Prince* with, according to her portraits, only a single deck to the break of the fo'c'sle and half-decks, though she did have a roundhouse at the after end of the quarter-deck. As built she was given the gratings such as the *Prince* had and, surprisingly, light carriage guns (murderers) were mounted to fire across the waist from the half-deck, and down the half-deck from the quarter-deck. This was old-fashioned thinking of the great ship school, which advocated close action and boarding. She carried a hundred guns on three decks which were flush throughout the length of the ship without falls. These consisted on the gun-deck of twenty cannon drakes on the broadsides and eight demi-cannon drakes as stern- and bow-chasers; twenty-four culverin drakes with six culverins as chasers formed the middle-deck tiers, and on the upper broadsides were twenty-four demi-culverin drakes and four demi-culverins as chasers. The word drakes implies cannon of a lighter type than the full cannon. There were eight demi-culverin drakes in the fo'c'sle, six on the half-deck and two in the quarter-deck. Broadside guns were also carried for the first time on the half-deck, and there was even one per side on the quarter-deck. The long low

*The building of these little cruisers was probably the first instance of the building of a class of vessel to one draught, and certainly the first to have a class name; they were called* The 1st to the 10th Whelps.

beak permitted a battery of eight bow-chasers in the fo'c'sle. The rig was remarkable for including royal sails at the main and fore, and a topgallant sail at the mizzen. She was the only ship in the fleet to have these sails, and although the mizzen topgallant was revived in the second quarter of the eighteenth century, it was not until the 1780s that English naval ships began to use royals again. The sprit topmast is in evidence, which carried the jack and a small square sail. Its position at the end of the bowsprit was precarious, but before the fitting of fore stay-sails it was useful in getting the ship's head about when tacking.

Unlike the *Prince*, which was, in her first building, something of a freak, the *Sovereign* was the prototype for every English capital ship to be built until 1860, two hundred and forty-three years later. To study her is to understand in all but detail the ships that fought at Trafalgar in 1805, and served at the Crimea in 1854–55. The *Sovereign* would have looked a bit odd at Trafalgar, with her long beak, her partially open quarter-galleries and old-fashioned rig; but she still would have carried a hundred truck-mounted muzzle-loaders on three decks, just like the other three-deckers, and would have been a force to reckon with. In 1651 some of her superstructure was removed to improve her performance. In the shipwrights' recommendation to the Commissioners they say:

> 'First as to the Soveraigne wee conceive that to make her more serviceable than now shee is, the gratings and the upper-decke in the midshippe bee taken downe that the side lored to the upper edge of the ports in the midshippe, the upper state room to bee taken away, the forecastle to be lored to six foote high and the works abaft be taken down proportionably to the waist and answerable to the sheere of the worke fore and after, the halfe deck to be shortened as shall bee convenient, as alsoe the head to bee made shorter and soe fitted for the sea. And the galleryes to bee altered as may be comely and most convenient for service.'

She thus assumed her modern image. The one puzzling reference in this is to the 'upper-decke in the midshippe' and the 'side lored to the upper edge of the ports'. In the *Prince* this would be perfectly understandable, but neither the drawing by the elder Van de Velde, nor the contemporary Payne engraving, from which admittedly the former may wholly derive, really suggest that there was room for a deck over the guns and under the gratings as with the *Prince*. But it does seem that she had such a deck, so either Payne was wrong or perhaps it was added in the fourteen years before she was cut down. Whatever the answer it was certainly not true, as is still sometimes suggested, that it was the upper gun-deck that was taken down and that she was made into a two-decker. Other new buildings in Charles I's reign were, in the late 1620s, ten fourteen-gun ships obviously conceived as a class as they were named the *First* to the *Tenth Whelp* and were built to deal with the Dunkirk privateers which played havoc with English trade in the Channel during the French war. The name whelp might have become a famous generic name for a type of warship, but it did not come to pass, and foreign names like frigate, corvette and sloop were adopted. In the 1630s Charles also built ten two-deckers, besides the *Sovereign* and the rebuilding of the *Prince*, the Ship Money fleet.

# 6

## The Rates

From the time of Charles I until the 1850s the force of an English fighting ship was graded into six rates. Originally the rating was based on the number of men carried per ton, until 1677 when Pepys changed it to the number of men needed per gun. The number of men, and therefore a ship's rating depended on the number and weight of her guns, which in turn determined the size of her crew. Once a proper gun establishment had been defined (see page 347), it was no longer necessary to consider the number of men but merely rate the ships by the number of their guns. There is also a theory that in early days the word rate meant the rate at which a captain was paid, and this makes sense if one considers that captains of royal yachts were given a second-rate's pay. There were six rates in 1652, on the eve of the First Dutch War; ships with crews of over three hundred were called first-rates, over two hundred second-rates, over a hundred and fifty third-rates, and over a hundred fourth-rates, over fifty fifth-rates, and below that was the sixth-rate. The effective part of the fleet that was going to meet the Dutch, in what proved to be furious action, consisted on paper of three first-rates, of one hundred, eighty-five and sixty guns; seven third-rates of forty-six to forty guns and thirty-one fourth-rates of forty to thirty guns, but not all of these would have been fit for service. As a whole they were ship for ship larger and more powerfully armed than the Dutch ships, which proved a decisive factor in the war. The Dutch throughout the three wars built nothing larger than two-deckers, though the biggest carried over eighty guns. They were built full-bellied by English standards, so that they drew less in their shallow home waters, but it enabled them to place the ports of their lower tier over 4 feet above the water, whereas it might be as little as 3 feet in the English ships, whose fine underwater lines made them more inclined to plunge in a sea. The Dutch ships could carry provisions for four months instead of only ten weeks as for the English, which was to be important in the Third Dutch War when the English and French were blockading the Dutch coast. Because the Dutch ships had the lines and sailing performance of merchantmen, a fair proportion of their fleet consisted of temporarily converted Indiamen and large merchantmen, a practice to which the English did not resort. As the Dutch had been fighting the Spanish more continuously and much more recently than the English, they started the war more experienced in naval warfare; they also had a slight superiority in numbers of ships. Against this England had been engaged in a bloody civil war which had bequeathed to her a generation of unusually hardy and able soldiers whose Model Army was indeed a model of order and discipline to the world. When it came to a war at sea some of them exchanged their tents for a quarter-deck and brought their ideas with them. It took them a season to settle down, and the battles of 1652 were indecisive, but in 1653 the Dutch were routed at the Battle of Scheveningen and their great commander, Marten Tromp, was killed. The English success against the world's greatest maritime power owed much to a central and comparatively efficient administration, whereas the Dutch provinces each had their own administration, which supplied the ships and men for the common cause, but not often in common accord.

Cromwell as Lord Protector squeezed far more money out of the country for the navy than ever poor Charles had tried to do, besides cutting down the royal forests for his ships, with the result that by 1658 the Ship Money fleet of forty-two had risen to a Commonwealth fleet of one hundred and fifty-seven, seventy-three of these being fourth-rates and above.

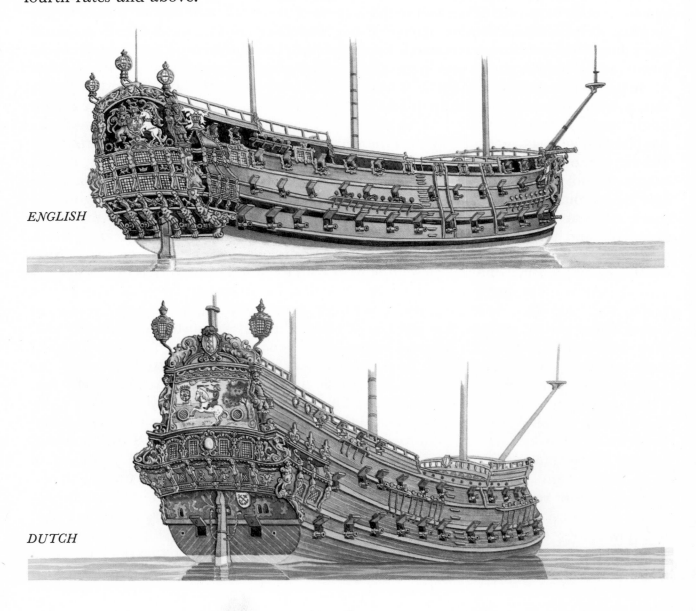

ENGLISH

DUTCH

# 7

## The Restoration

Charles II, on his return as king in 1660, became master of the finest fleet in Europe, which proceeded to underline its success in the First Dutch War by giving the same enemy fleet a shattering defeat in the first action of the second, the Battle of Lowestoft, 30 May 1665. The Dutch were driven off the North Sea for the rest of the year, and in those days fleets only commissioned for the summer. Their precious East India fleet was bottled up in Bergen and would have fallen a prize to the English squadron sent to take it, for they had unscrupulously bought the co-operation of the neutral king of Denmark, had not the governor of Bergen taken the Dutchmen's part, and between them the English were driven off.

The following year a new factor emerged which nearly led to England's undoing. The French by a heavy building programme in 1663–64 now appeared as a competing sea power, and it was thought that they were going to join the Dutch for the 1666 fighting season, which began in May. Charles foolishly split his fleet, sending two-thirds under Albemarle to watch for the Dutch, who had spent the year frantically enlarging their fleet, and a third under Prince Rupert to watch for the French. In fact, the French made no move, and when Albemarle met the Dutch on 1 June he was heavily out-numbered. It was the one big chance the Dutch had of inflicting a decisive defeat on

FRENCH

*The sterns of the English, Dutch and French ships of the seventeenth century were quite distinctive as those of about 1670 plainly show. This did not apply only to the galleries, but also in the case of the English to a round, instead of a square, tuck below them.*

the English fleet. After two days of fighting, in which Albemarle did most of the attacking, he decided to run west to join Rupert, and putting his damaged ships before him he set off in that admirable order that had saved him in the first two days.

It was now, however, that English losses occurred, for any crippled ship that fell behind was doomed. The most serious loss was the *Prince*, the rebuilt giant of 1610; she ran on the Galloper Sand, and Sir George Ayscue was given the sad distinction of being the only British flag officer ever to be captured in action. On the fourth day of this marathon of all fleet actions, Albemarle and Rupert, now together, and de Ruyter, fought each other to a standstill. It was a Dutch victory, but they were not elated: 'If we cannot defeat them divided, how will we fare with them united?' Six weeks later, on St James's Day, they had their answer in a severe defeat which left the English masters once again. Indeed the war would have ended with the Dutch in eclipse had not the English committed the crowning folly of at once demanding harsh peace terms at Breda in the spring of 1667, and at the same time deciding to save money and leave the fleet in ordinary. So de Ruyter sailed up the Medway on 9 June and stayed in Sheerness nearly a fortnight. The disaster to the English was more to their pride than to the fleet, which only lost six destroyed and the principal flagship captured, but the Dutch got better terms at Breda.

The battles of the Third Dutch War were fought in the same manner as the other two, but with more credit to the Dutch than to the Allies; for the French had joined the English. Though the four hard-fought fleet actions of 1672–73 were tactically drawn, they were a strategic defeat for the Allies who were trying to clear the way for an invasion; so that de Ruyter, outnumbered, won the war by denying the Allies the victory they needed, and by keeping the Dutch fleet in being.

The presence of the new French fleet in the Thames gave the English naval architects the opportunity to study their new ships, and they liked what they saw. French influence was nothing new, for Pepys regarded the Restoration fleet as 'Dunkirk built', i.e. with very fine underwater lines; yet the French two-deckers of 1663–64 were over 3 or 4 feet broader in the beam as well as being deeper in the hold than their English counterparts which made them better gun platforms and gave their lower ports 4 feet 6 inches clearance from the water. Sir Anthony Deane, the naval architect, instigated the building of similar two-deckers in the middle 1660s, his own *Resolution* 70 being the best remembered. Now again, in 1673, the French fashion proved a strong influence on English building. Charles II and his brother James visited a fine seventy-four called the *Superbe*, Deane measured her, and for some years her dimensions were the pattern for all English second- and third-rates. The end of Charles II's reign saw the navy in a sad state of neglect due to the meanness of Parliament, and an inquiry of 1684 stated that:

> 'The greatest part of the 30 new ships, without having ever been out of harbour, were let to sink into decay; and even their exterior appearance was rendered worse than had been usually seen upon the coming in of the Fleet after a battle. And several of the said Ships had been recently reported by the Navy Board to be in danger of sinking at their moorings. Some ships were become altogether irreparable.'

Charles himself had been the keenest sailor the country had ever had for a monarch, delighting in his yachts with his brother James, who had been a conscientious Lord High Admiral and a brave commander, and who knew as much about the fleet as any man in England. At Charles's death in February 1685 the fleet consisted of one hundred and seventy-nine vessels, one hundred and eight of them of the fourth-rate and above, and fifty-five of these of seventy guns and above.

It is from this time that regular ships' draughts exist. Among them are seven drawn by William Keltridge and dated 1684, though one has James II's cypher on it, showing that it was finished later. The first is of a fourth-rate of the largest size, and is 124 feet 6 inches on the gun-deck with a beam of 35 feet. She is a two-decker with eleven guns on each tier, and three aside on the quarter-deck. The height between decks 'planke to planke' is 5 feet 9 inches forward and 6 feet 6 inches aft. This does not take into account the beams which make her true deckheads very low indeed; she drew over 15 feet. The second is of a slightly smaller fourth-rate, similarly laid out, and the third of a fifth-rate of the largest dimensions. She is also a two-decker, mounting twenty guns on the gun-deck which is 103 feet 9 inches ('frome ye rabbit of the stem to ye rabbit of the sternpost'). On the upper-deck she mounts five guns aside under the quarter-deck and two aside under the fo'c'sle, but none in the waist; there are also two aside on the quarter-deck. The last four draughts are of sixth-rates. These all have one deck, of from 70 to 90 feet long to carry the guns (eight to ten a side), a quarter-deck with two to three aside, and a fo'c'sle; below the gun-deck is the hold. In the case of the fourth-rates the guns are specified as culverins on the gun-deck (12-pounders), 6-pounders on the upper-deck, and sakers on the quarter-deck (5½-pounders), which shows that the old names still held, but that the new ones based on the weight of ball were coming in.

## Fireships

The sixth-rates were also of the size suitable for adapting into fireships. These instruments of destruction were an idea as old as naval warfare, and though most alarming to see as they approached, those captains who kept cool heads usually saved their ships. As we have seen, Drake had a great success against the Spanish with his fireships, not for the destruction they did, but because the Spanish were panicked into leaving their anchorage, and drove out on the open sea never to return and some to destruction. Admiral Saunder's fleet, on the other hand, anchored in the confined waters of the St Lawrence off Quebec in 1759, survived two dangerous attacks by fireships and fire rafts from upstream, by the resolute action of the crews of his ships' boats in guiding the flaming vessels safely past.

The Dutch were fond of them and used them with some success in their wars with England. At Scheveningen in 1653 one of the best English ships, the *Andrew*, was nearly destroyed by one, and the *Henry* was grappled by two and had her sails set alight on the first day of the Four Days Fight in 1666, but survived. Their greatest success was the destruction of the *Royal James*, a first-rate and a flagship at the Battle of Solebay in 1672. The English did not seem to bother much with them during the Dutch wars, though Pepys mentions being very touched at Myngs's funeral when some of the dead admiral's seamen stopped Sir William Coventry, who was walking with Pepys, and

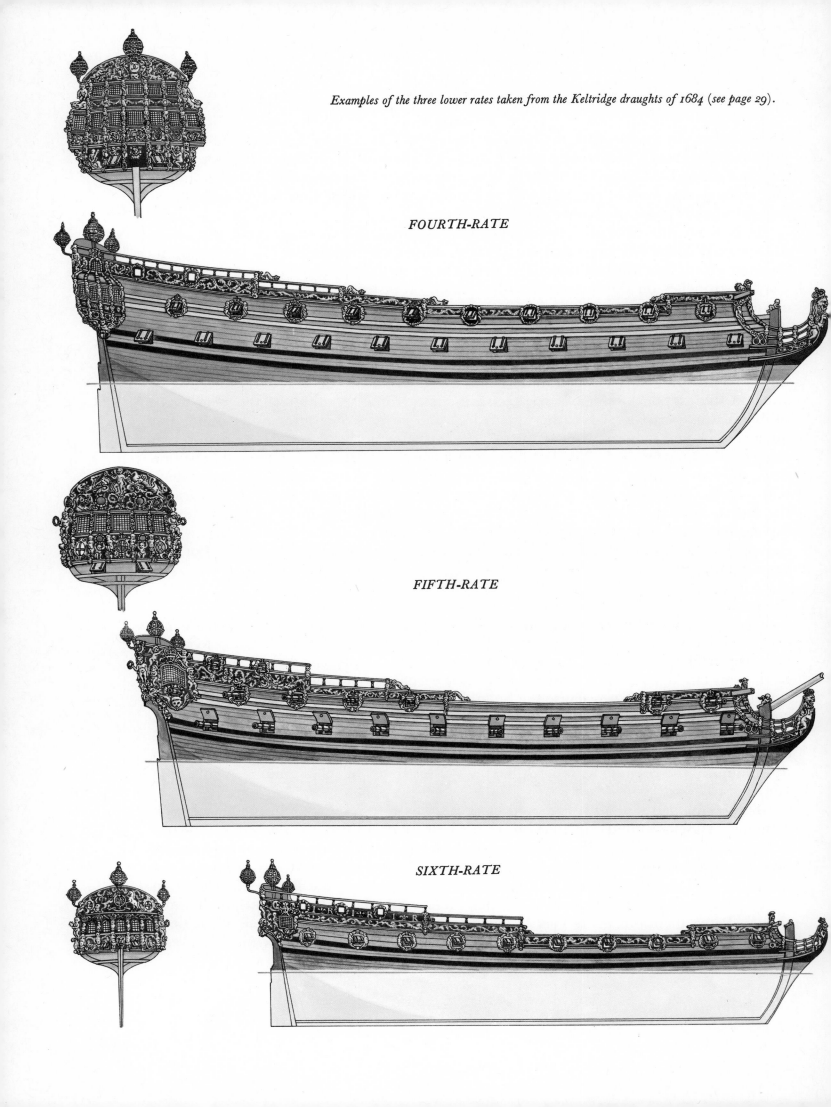

*Examples of the three lower rates taken from the Keltridge draughts of 1684 (see page 29).*

FOURTH-RATE

FIFTH-RATE

SIXTH-RATE

*A fireship: note how the ports hinge downwards, lest they closed while she burned.*

asked 'if you will please to get His Royal Highness to give us a fireship among us all ... (to) do what shall show our memory of our dead commander and of our revenge'.

In 1675 the English only had three fireships, but in 1688 the number had risen to twenty-six, and they were used successfully to destroy a large part of the French fleet which had taken refuge at La Hogue and near Cherbourg after the Battle of Barfleur in 1692. This sudden enthusiasm did not last, and the number had sunk to one in 1712 and remained around three until 1780, when there was a sudden jump to eighteen. After that war the number was halved and declined to nothing in the Napoleonic Wars.

How a fireship was fitted out depended on the type of vessel used, but they were basically small vessels filled with combustibles and explosive materials. The English eighteenth-century sixth-rates which were built or converted as fireships had a complete row of ports cut in their lower decks, where before there were only two or four for guns. These were hinged at the bottom so that they would stay open and serve to let air in to speed the burning rate, and also to let the flames out to do their worst. Their upper decks had their planking removed forward of the accommodation and altered to square sectioning that kept the barrels from moving in bad weather. Over this the quarter-deck and fo'c'sle were joined to keep out the wet. Large fireships built as such might have three decks, but the middle deck was again of square sections of timber and very close to the lower deck. More common were the smaller vessels built with two decks.

In fact, outside of attacks on anchorages, they were not very effective. The technique in a fleet action was to attack the enemy ship from to windward when she was either holding her wind or, better, disabled. As only large and important ships were worth the expenditure of a fireship, there was a good chance of being sunk by the enemy guns before she could grapple. If she was fired too soon she would burn out harmlessly, and if too late the crew of the target might ungrapple her and probably free themselves of her. It took a cool nerve and good judgment on the part of the fireship captain, who at the last moment escaped with his devoted crew in a small boat that they were towing, if it was still afloat. Fire ships were often converted to sloops in peace-time.

*A sectioned drawing of a fireship showing the stowage for the combustibles.*

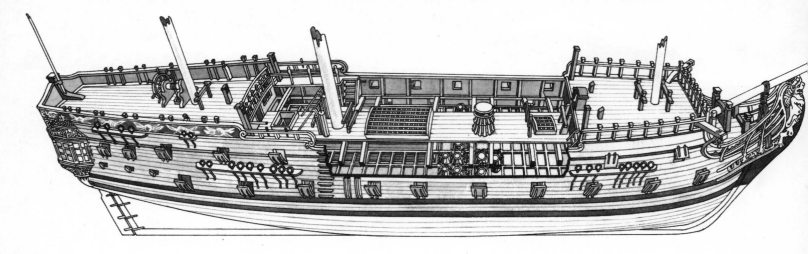

# 8

## The Fighting Ship
## in the Eighteenth Century

During the wars of the English and Spanish Successions, which covered the period 1689 to 1713, the English fleet emerged as the largest in the world with one hundred and thirty-one ships of the line on the books in 1714 which, combined with the Dutch, were too much for the French and Spanish, even though at the drawn Battle of Malaga of 1704 the opposing fleets had a parity of fifty-one ships of the line each. The expression 'ship of the line' first appears at this time because of the evolution of fighting tactics which involved manœuvring in the line of battle. The strength of the English fleet, which had a grand total of two hundred and forty-seven vessels in 1714 of all kinds, sank a little after the war, until it rose again in the mid-eighteenth century to three hundred and thirty-nine in 1748, though the increase was mainly in the smaller rates. The Seven Years War, 1756 to 1763, showed a marked increase. Of the line the number remained almost the same as in 1748 at one hundred and forty-one, but by now the fifty-gun ships were excluded, and there were twenty-four of them. The total of all vessels was four hundred and thirty-two. The struggles with France and Spain and Holland which started with the revolt in the American colonies required a further increase, so that by 1783 there were a hundred and seventy-four ships of the line on the list, which, with the rest totalled the huge figure of six hundred and seventeen vessels. It should be remembered that a fairly large proportion of the fleet was in various states of unfitness for sea, depending on time of peace and war and other factors; but in the late 1780s great efforts were made to put the fleet in order so that in 1790 ninety-three ships of the line were in the first state of repair out of a total of a hundred and forty-six, a proportion considered extremely high, though many of the older ships had been scrapped. Such a great armada required a great organisation, and the eighteenth-century navy provided the country with its largest industry and was the biggest employer of manpower, which was spread over the great dockyards at Deptford, Woolwich and Chatham on the Thames, and Portsmouth and Plymouth on the Channel.

### Eighteenth-century First-rates
The first-rate men-of-war were the biggest ships in the world from the early seventeenth century until the building of iron merchantmen in the second quarter of the nineteenth century, and were rightly regarded as one of the great marvels of their age. They were reserved almost exclusively for wearing the flags of the commanders-in-chief of the main

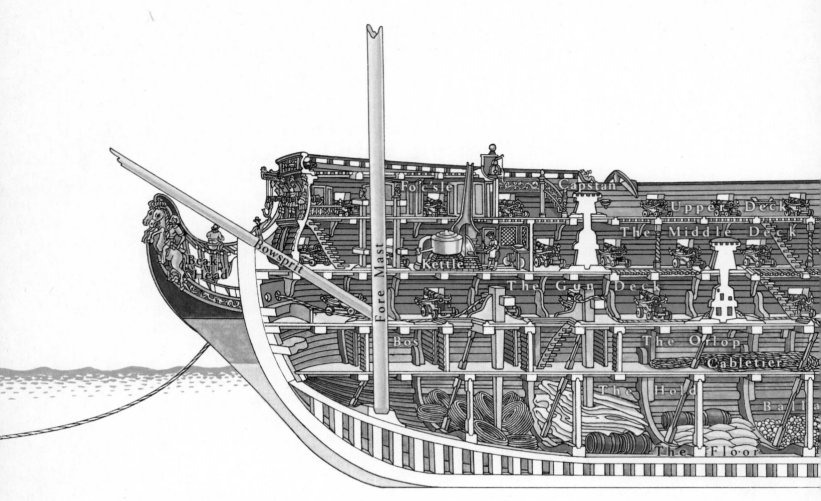

*A profile section of a first-rate of 1701. The layout
remained almost unchanged for over 200 years.*

fleets in home waters in wartime, and there was seldom more than one in commission
out of a possible half-dozen in existence. Admittedly, when old Sir John Norris commanded the Channel Fleet in 1741 there were three in commission, two as private ships,
and in 1795 both the *Queen Charlotte* and, for a time, the *Victory* also served as private
ships; but this was exceptional, and they all, right up to the very end in the 1860s,
confined their activities to European waters, never straying farther than the Baltic and
the Black Sea. In 1701 the first of the eighteenth-century first-rates, the *Royal Sovereign*,
was built by Fisher Harding. She showed an increase in size on the old *Royal Sovereign*,
originally Pett's *Sovereign of the Seas* of 1637, but not a great one; 174 feet 6 inches against
167 feet 9 inches on the gun-deck, and 50 feet in the beam against 48 feet in the older
ship.

There were two obvious differences between the first-rates built between 1700 and
1750 and the other three-deckers of the second- and third-rates, apart from their size.
They had a topgallant poop, or poop royal, which was divided into two little cabins for
the master and another officer. Previous first-rates usually had large flag lockers at the

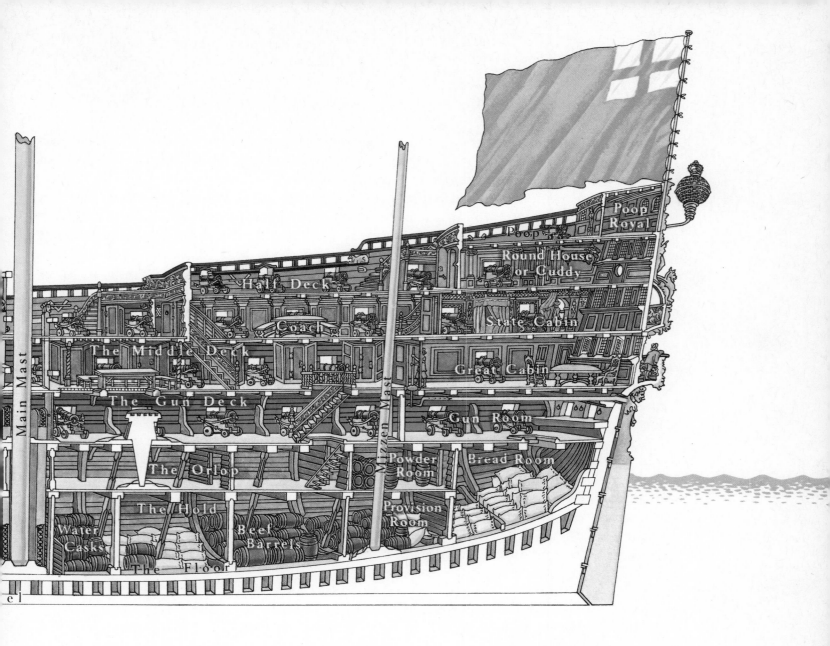

after end of the poop-deck which also provided cramped quarters for the trumpeters. The cabins in the topgallant poop started as a modest structure, with their stern lights peeping through the carvings, but by 1737, when the *Victory* was built, it had grown to a full coach, with a stern-walk and galleries. She had a gun-deck and four tiers of stern galleries above the water-line, a formidable sight. In 1744 this ship was lost on the Casquets off Guernsey in a storm at night with all hands, apparently due to a navigational error; the only first-rate ever to be lost in this sort of accident. The only other losses in this class of ship were the *Royal George* which sank at anchor at Spithead in 1782, and the *Queen Charlotte* which accidentally burnt off Leghorn in 1800. The *Royal George* was lost under the most extraordinary circumstances. She had been listed to port by running out her guns on that side and shifting weights so that she could repair a small damage under the water-line on the starboard side; in addition she was taking on stores from a hoy, naturally also on the port side. Crowded with visitors, many of them women and children, it was not noticed that the sills of the lower ports were getting dangerously close to the water as the stores piled up on the port side of her upper deck. In any case it would have been a difficult business to drag the 42-pounders up the canting-deck. As soon as the water began to lap in and add to the weight it was too late, and down she went with the loss of about nine hundred people.

The other noticeable distinction of early eighteenth-century first-rates was the profusion of decoration, which was natural for prestige ships of their importance. The amount of carving in the seventeenth century had steadily increased to include almost every visible deck fitting on and above the upper deck, as well as the beak and the stern galleries. This reached its apogee in the *Royal Sovereign* of 1701, which at the same time resulted in a large cut in the carving of future ships; for the scandal of the expense of her decorations, which included an allegorical scene, painted on panels set into the deckhead of the state cabin, induced their lordships to order that in future carving was to be confined to the beakhead and stern galleries, and anything further must be carried out in paint. This created considerable unemployment in the dockyards, and the wood-carvers sought employment where they could find it, which is why so many interiors of houses and churches decorated in the first thirty years of the eighteenth century show a wealth of fine baroque carving.

A less obvious feature of the first-rates which made them much more powerful than the other three-deckers was their armament. The difference of one hundred guns against ninety, or later ninety-eight, between the first- and second-rates may not seem much until it is realised that the mid-eighteenth-century first-rates, such as the *Royal George* of 1756, mounted 42-pounders on the lower gun-deck against a second-rate's 32s; 24-pounders on the middle deck against 18s, and 12-pounders apiece on the upper deck, though some second-rates had only 9s; late eighteenth-century ships of both classes had 18s. This is why the crew ratio had to be eight hundred and fifty men for first-rates against seven hundred and fifty for second-rates, and why the first-rates were not so often employed. The ordnance establishment of 1715 gives a choice of 32-pounders or 42-pounders for the gun-deck, but in fact the extra weight of the 42-pounder ball did not compensate for the slower rate of fire due to the greater weight of the guns. These were therefore exchanged in all ships by 1800, and a ship such as the present *Victory*, which had fought the Battle of St Vincent in 1797 with a lower battery of 42-pounders, fought at Trafalgar with 32-pounders. Ships rearmed in this way were rearmed with 18-pounders on the upper deck. The *Victory* is the biggest and the latest of the three first-rates built between 1756 and 1765, being 186 feet long on the gun-deck and 51 feet 10 inches in the beam, a considerable increase on the *Royal Sovereign* of 1701.

A further increase in size was on the way. The draught of the *Ville de Paris* (named after the French flagship captured at the Saints in 1782) of 1788, is for a ship of one hundred and ten guns, and she is 190 feet on the gun-deck, with a beam of 53 feet. It is interesting that this same draught was used for the *Hibernia* ten years later, but with 16 feet inserted in the centre section which gave her a gun-deck of 206 feet, and she was to mount one hundred and twenty guns. This lengthening, it was estimated, would raise her freeboard by $1\frac{1}{2}$ feet, so that the sills of her lower gun-ports would be a clear $6\frac{1}{2}$ feet above the water, or about twice the clearance of an equivalent ship of 1660. This was about the limit in size that wood alone and the traditional methods of construction could stand without the danger of serious hogging of the hull. To build bigger ships,

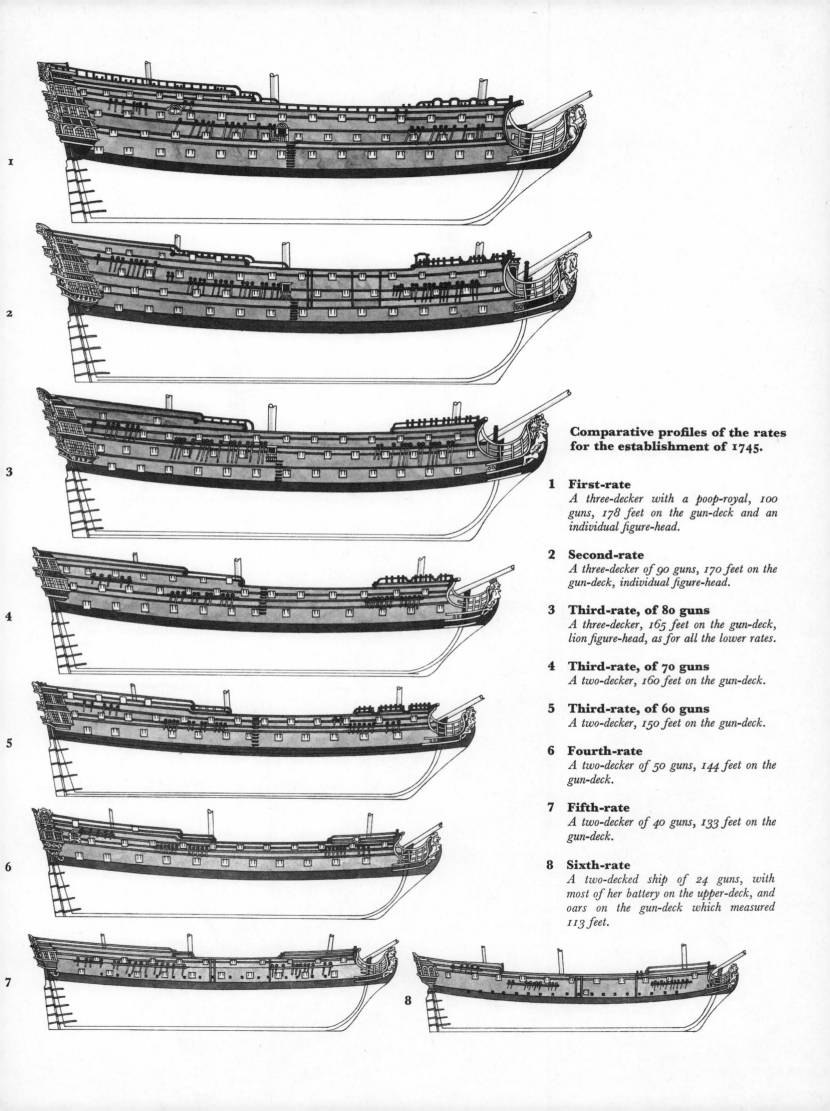

**Comparative profiles of the rates for the establishment of 1745.**

**1  First-rate**
*A three-decker with a poop-royal, 100 guns, 178 feet on the gun-deck and an individual figure-head.*

**2  Second-rate**
*A three-decker of 90 guns, 170 feet on the gun-deck, individual figure-head.*

**3  Third-rate, of 80 guns**
*A three-decker, 165 feet on the gun-deck, lion figure-head, as for all the lower rates.*

**4  Third-rate, of 70 guns**
*A two-decker, 160 feet on the gun-deck.*

**5  Third-rate, of 60 guns**
*A two-decker, 150 feet on the gun-deck.*

**6  Fourth-rate**
*A two-decker of 50 guns, 144 feet on the gun-deck.*

**7  Fifth-rate**
*A two-decker of 40 guns, 133 feet on the gun-deck.*

**8  Sixth-rate**
*A two-decked ship of 24 guns, with most of her battery on the upper-deck, and oars on the gun-deck which measured 113 feet.*

*The* Victory *of 1737, known as Balchen's* Victory *because she was wearing his flag when she was lost with all hands in 1744. In her short day she was the biggest ship in the world and the only English first-rate to have an open gallery to her poop-royal.*

*A first-rate of the Establishment of 1741. The chief improvement over the seventeenth-century ships is in the rigging. Reef-points and stay-sails have appeared, and the awkward sprit-topmast, though officially still retained for the first-rates, had all but disappeared.*

new ideas had to be introduced to stiffen the hulls which were the problems of the nineteenth-century surveyors. Nevertheless the degree to which design had frozen was remarkable, and shows how excellent it was. Not only was the *Victory* forty years old when she fought at Trafalgar as the principal flagship, but nearly fifty when she retired from active service; her draught, slightly amended in the upper works, was used for the proposed building of four second-rates in 1801. Two of them were completed; one was the *London* in 1810 and she served as Sir Edward Pellew's flagship in the Mediterranean in 1815; the other, the *Princess Charlotte*, was not launched until 1825, though admittedly she had collected the new round bow and stern over the years, and she was Sir Robert Stopford's flagship in the Mediterranean as late as the Syrian operations of 1840.

39

## Eighteenth-century Second-rates

The ninety-gun three-deckers which comprised the second-rate, until the increase to ninety-eight guns in the late 1770s, were the work-horse fleet flagships of the eighteenth century. They were cheaper to operate than the first-rates but very powerful, and at all the important fleet actions in the Mediterranean, the West Indies and off North America up to the French Revolutionary Wars, the flag was in a second-rate.

Something of the difference between their armament and a first-rate's has already been mentioned previously, and there was also the difference in size. They were generally about 165 feet on the gun-deck, or a little less for the first half of the century, and around 45 feet to a maximum of 48 feet in the beam. This was close to the seventeenth-century first-rates, some of which had survived into the eighteenth century to serve in the lower rate. By the third quarter of the century lengths had increased by 10 feet and beams by 2 feet. It needed the increase to ninety-eight guns to make a large increase in size necessary to take the extra two or four guns per deck. Indeed a late eighteenth-century ninety-eight gun ship, such as the *Ocean* with a 195-foot gun-deck, was over 10 feet longer than the *Victory*, and differed in armament from her, at the time of Trafalgar, only in having 18-pounders on the middle deck instead of 24-pounders.

In Queen Anne's navy there were thirteen second-rates, and the number remained fairly constant until the wars connected with the revolution in America, by the end of which, in 1783 there were nineteen, and this increased to twenty-one by the end of the century. Of this number only a few would be in commission even in wartime, and at the beginning of the Revolutionary Wars in 1793 the number was eight. In appearance and layout they closely resembled the first-rates except that they were never given topgallant poops, and the ones built in the early part of the century often had only quite modest coaches.

## Eighteenth-century Third-rates, the Three-decker Eighties

The notorious three-decker eighties are always held up as the example of how English warship design lagged behind the Continental. This was mainly due to a bellicose determination on the part of the English to fill their ships full of guns, and certainly the effect of putting three decks of too closely fitted guns into the smallest three-decker built proved unfortunate. Their narrow beam made them crank, and their lower tiers lay too near to the water. There is a famous letter from Admiral Mathews to the Duke of Newcastle, written after the drawn Battle of Toulon in February 1744, when the English had been unable to achieve more against the combined Franco-Spanish fleet than the capture of one Spanish sixty-four, in which he complains of his equipment: 'I have now but two ships of 90 and three of 80 guns that can make use of the lower tiers of guns if it blow a cap full of wind.' This meant that they could not fight with their heaviest batteries, the 32-pounders, and in the case of the eighties were reduced to the 12-pounders on their middle deck, 6-pounders on the upper and quarter-decks. In comparison the French two-decker seventy-fours had no such difficulty, and some carried 40-pounders on the gun-deck and 18-pounders on the upper. On the day of the battle there was a 'cap full of wind', so that the lower ports on the leeside of many English ships had to be kept shut, though some commanders contrived by desperate

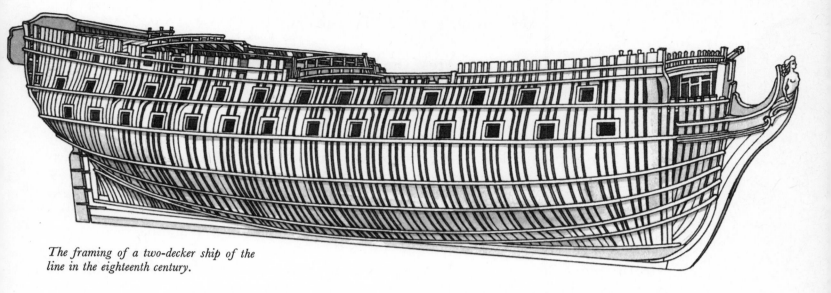

*The framing of a two-decker ship of the
line in the eighteenth century.*

measures to keep them open. Rear-Admiral Rowley, the third in command, in the *Barfleur*, a ninety gun second-rate, Mathew's letter continues, 'was obliged to run out his weather guns, to lash thirty tuns of water to windward, and to cut away his lee anchor before he could do it, the *Princess Caroline* (an eighty) took in water so fast, that her captain, whose conduct and behaviour proves him to be a very good officer, was obliged to skuttle the deck to vent the water; she took it in so fast'. That is to say, he tore up some of his lee-deck planking on the lower deck so that the water coming in through the ports could escape down into the bilge and be taken out by the pumps. 'As for the rest of them, they can scarce haul up a port; the *Chichester* hauled up but her two aftermost, but was obliged soon to lower them; as for the rest of her ports they were caulked in when she was fitted out, and have never been opened since, nor will they ever be, except in a Mill Pond.'

The dimensions of the *Chichester* show her to be 155 feet 6 inches on the gun-deck, and 43 feet 5 inches in the beam; almost the same as the old *Prince Royal* of 1610, but without her towering superstructures. The model of the *Chichester* shows her to have had no fo'c'sle at all, though there is a quarter-deck, and apparently no coach. In the model she mounts no guns in her waist, so that she was armed like a two-decker but with a deck joining the quarter-deck and fo'c'sle. The draughts of other three-decker eighties show them to have had at least a tiny coach, and though some have fo'c'sles, in others it is reduced to the forward bulkhead and a small platform. The *Chichester* was one of the early ones of 1706, which were originally designed as two-decker eighties, but were decked over the waist to strengthen them.

At the time that Mathews was writing there were seventeen on the list, but his words and the criticism of other naval officers such as Vernon had their effect, for after the war ended in 1748 most of these ships were scrapped or reduced to two-decker sixty-fours. The new three-decker eighties that were built up to 1757 were bigger and presumably better. The last, the *Princess Amelia*, was 165 feet on the gun-deck and 47 feet 3 inches in the beam. Like all those built after the gun establishment of 1740 she had 18-pounders on her middle deck and 9-pounders on her upper, her gun-deck continuing to carry 32-pounders.

41

## Eighteenth-century Third-rates, the Two-decker Eighties

Eighty guns was the limit a wooden two-decker, built on traditional lines, could mount without hogging or straining. The Dutch had built them successfully in the seventeenth century, and in the 1690s the English built thirteen of their own. The principle was good, but unfortunately they were built too light in their upper works and strained. In three further ships laid down the difficulty was dealt with by decking over the waist, so that they became three-deckers, but with their armament disposed like a two-decker; and this is really why the English began on their long and unlucky attachment to the eighty gun three-decker. Indeed, although the latter type ceased to be built in the late 1750s, the resumption of the building of two-decker eighties did not begin until the late 1780s.

In the meantime the navy had to rely on foreign prizes. The best-known of these was the *Foudroyant*, a magnificent French eighty which in 1758, as M. Duquesne's flagship, was fought to a standstill in a four and a half hours action with the *Monmouth* 64; which was very creditable since, apart from the disparity in the number of guns, the *Foudroyant* mounted 42- and 24-pounders against the *Monmouth*'s 24- and 12-pounders. The *Foudroyant* was added under her own name and became Rodney's flagship in the West Indies, and in the following war, from 1775 to 1782, was commanded by Captain John Jervis, who was knighted for capturing with her the brand-new French seventy-four *Pegase*. He was later to become one of our greatest naval officers, and Lord St Vincent. The ship was 180 feet 5 inches on the gun-deck and 50 feet 3 inches in the beam, and was considered all her active life to be the finest two-decker in the service.

The *Caesar* was the first of the new English two-decker eighties and was launched in 1793. The dimensions were much the same as the old *Foudroyant*'s, 181 feet on the gun-deck by 50 feet in the beam. A new *Foudroyant* was another built at the same time, and

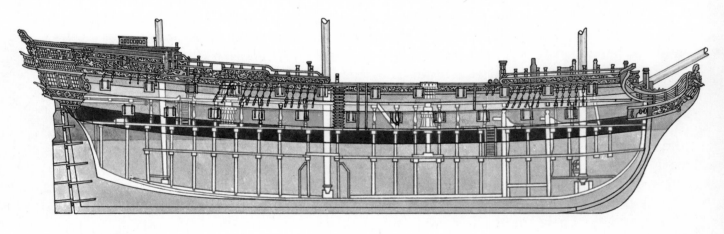

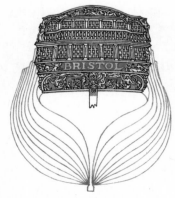

*A profile section and stern of a 50-gun ship of 1775, taken from the draught of the* Bristol *(see page 45).*

she became Nelson's flagship after the Battle of the Nile in 1798. On this occasion the *Franklin*, a new French eighty and their vice-admiral, was captured and turned out to be so notable a performer under sail that eight ships were built to her lines, one of them, the *Asia*, built in Bombay of teak and launched as late as 1824, was Codrington's flagship at the Battle of Navarino in 1827, when an Anglo-Franco-Russian fleet destroyed the Turkish-Egyptian one. The *Franklin* was added as the *Canopus* and became a great favourite in the service for half a century. Almost at the end of her active career, in 1847, she took part in a sailing trial off Lisbon in a squadron including some of the newest English liners, and beat them all, to the delight of nearly everybody present. One feature of the new eighties was that they carried their lower tier of guns high enough, and were deep enough in the hold, for the orlop-deck to become a proper deck instead of three platforms as before. The number of eighties built at the end of the eighteenth century and during the Revolutionary Wars was quite small, since building policy continued to concentrate on the seventy-four.

## Eighteenth-century Third-rates, the Seventies and Seventy-fours

The standard large two-decker until the middle of the eighteenth century was the seventy, of which at the end of Queen Anne's reign there were twenty-six, ten more than of the eighties. The 1716 gun establishment shows that they mounted 24-pounders on the gun-deck and 12-pounders on the upper. They sailed better than the three-decker eighties and could work their lower tiers in weather when the others had to close their lower ports. A typical seventy would be 151 feet on the gun-deck and 43 feet in the beam. In the late 1740s ships with that odd number of guns, seventy-four, began to appear in the lists. These ships, the seventy-fours, became the type of ship of the line, that was to endure the longest, of which by far the most were built, and which, in English hands, proved indeed to be 'the ship to fight for a kingdom'.

Those on the list in 1750 were there for several reasons; three were French, captured in 1747, and the largest of them the *Monarch* was no less than 174 feet 10 inches on the gun-deck and 47 feet 2 inches in the beam. One was an old ninety, the *Torbay* (ex *Neptune*), cut down a deck; she had been the second flagship at Mathew's action off Toulon in 1744. (Mathew's own ship, the *Namur*, was similarly treated, but was lost in the East Indies in 1749.) One only, the *Culloden*, had been built, at Deptford, and launched in 1747. She was quite small, only 161 feet 4 inches on the gun-deck with a 46 foot 4 inch beam; but she does prove, especially as another, the *Somerset*, was launched in 1748, that the English did not build seventy-fours just to copy the captured Frenchmen, though the increase was probably prompted by the urge to keep up with French policy; nor were those built in the late fifties up to the dimensions of the Frenchmen: it was the middle sixties before they approached a gun-deck of 170 feet. Around this figure it remained until a general lengthening was ordered for new ships in 1793, about 10 feet in the gun-deck and a foot in the beam. Of the great armada of these ships, the navy at the beginning of the Seven Years War in 1755 possessed only six, but seven fought at the Battle of Quiberon Bay in 1759, the largest number of any class of ship present, and by the end of the war in 1763 the number built was around forty. This figure was doubled by the end of the American Revolutionary War in 1783, when they nearly equalled the total number of ships in other rates of the line listed, and when it came to ships in commission the proportion was far higher. In 1800 the fleets in home waters contained of the line, three first-rates, fourteen second-rates, six third-rate eighties, a seventy-eight, a sixty-eight, fifteen sixty-fours and forty-one seventy-fours, five of them flagships. In the Mediterranean there were sixteen more and six in the West Indies.

The popularity and prestige of the large two-decker reached its peak during the French Revolutionary War when the British found that not only did they sail better than the stately three-decker, which they knew already, but that by superior gunnery and training their two-deckers could be a match for any enemy warship, even three-deckers of over one hundred guns. In the long Franco-Spanish wars that stretch from 1689 to 1815 the British never lost a three-decker in action, but the French lost three in battle and one, the *Commerce de Marseille* 120, taken at Toulon in 1793. The Spanish lost seven, all in action, and it is interesting to see that six of them fell to English two-deckers.

To take them in order: in 1782 the French *Ville de Paris* 104, their flagship at the Battle of the Saints, struck to the English three-decker *Barfleur* 98. At the Battle of St Vincent in 1797, two Spanish three-deckers, both flagships, were captured, the *Salvadore del Mundo* 112, by the *Victory* 100, and the *San Josef* 112, by the *Captain* 74, though other ships contributed. There was nothing above a seventy-four in Nelson's fleet at the Battle of the Nile when the great French flagship *L'Orient* 120 was destroyed. In 1801 a squadron under de Saumarez defeated a much stronger Spanish squadron, destroying two one-hundred-and-twelve-gun three-deckers, the *San Hermenegildo* and the *Real Carlos*, all the British ships were two-deckers. Three more enemy three-deckers, all Spanish, struck at Trafalgar. The *Santissima Trinidad* 136, the biggest ship in the world and a four-decker, struck to the *Prince* 98, but earlier in the action the captain of the *Africa* 74, seeing the great ship silent and apparently beaten, sent aboard a lieutenant to take the surrender. When this officer, Lieutenant John Smith, appeared on her quarter-deck he found that she had not struck; he therefore withdrew, unmolested. The *Santa Anna* 112 was taken by the *Royal Sovereign* 100, but was recaptured with her prize crew two days later. The third one, the *Rayo* 100, escaped from the main battle but was captured at anchor off Lucar by the *Donegal* 74 three days later. In 1806 during Duckworth's action the *Canopus* 80 drove ashore the *Imperial*, a French one-hundred-and-twenty-gun ship which became a total loss. Finally, Napoleon Bonaparte was sent to St Helena in the *Northumberland* 74 after he had surrendered to the captain of *Bellerophon* 74. For years the very words seventy-four were synonymous to the British public with an invincible naval supremacy.

## The Eighteenth-century Third-rates, the Sixties and Sixty-fours
The sixty-gun ships became sixty-fours in the 1740s which was made possible by the increase in size that allowed them to bear the extra two guns per deck. The sixty of the beginning of the century was 145 feet on the gun-deck and 38 feet in the beam, while one of the later sixty-fours of the 1780s measured 159 feet by 44 feet 4 inches. They remained ships of the line throughout their service in their original form, and were certainly fit to stand in it for the first half of the eighteenth century. There were sixty-

two of them on the list in 1762 against forty-seven seventies and seventy-fours. The older sixties carried 24-pounders on the lower deck, 9-pounders on the upper, and 6-pounders on the quarter-deck and fo'c'sle; the sixty-fours mounted 24s, 18s, and 9s. By the end of the century they had come to be thought rather light for the line and found employment as flagships on distant stations, convoy work, or even, after conversion, as troopers.

The most famous sixty was the *Centurion* of 1732. She was Commodore Anson's ship when he set out with a squadron to circumnavigate the world in 1740, and only she completed the journey, after wonderful adventures which included capturing the Spanish treasure ship *Nuestra Senora de Covadonga*. It took thirty carts to carry the treasure from Plymouth to London. The *Centurion* was reduced to a fifty-gun ship in 1746. In 1749 Commodore Augustus Keppel hoisted his broad pendant in her at the tender age of twenty-four to take a squadron to the Mediterranean where he was chiefly concerned with the Barbary pirates. Two years later the commodore called on the Dey of Algiers over some breach of treaty. The Dey asked him why his master had had the insolence to send an insignificant beardless youth to be his representative. 'Had my master supposed that wisdom was measured by the length of one's beard,' said Keppel, 'he would have sent your deyship a he goat.' This, however, was not well received, and Keppel had to remind the Dey that Algiers would be destroyed by his ships if anything happened to him.

The most famous sixty-four was the *Agamemnon*, Nelson's favourite command, in which he fought in the Mediterranean in the early years of the French Revolutionary Wars; it was a commission characteristically full of incident.

### Eighteenth-century Fourth-rates, the Fifties

The prestige of the fifty-gun ship remained high from the early seventeenth century when the *Prince Royal* 55 was the greatest ship in the world, until the 1860s saw the last of the great fifty-gun frigates. The dimensions of the ships serving at the beginning of the eighteenth century have already been described from Keltridge's draughts, and in the 1716 gun establishment they mounted 18-pounders on the lower deck, 9-pounders on the upper deck and 6-pounders on the quarter-deck and fo'c'sle. Although still listed as ships of the line, this was obviously insupportable, and by 1760 they had been dropped. Their usefulness remained particularly as flagships on foreign stations where large enemy vessels were unlikely to be met with and the fifty was the ideal size. At 146 feet on the gun-deck, with a 40-foot beam and a complement of 350, they were small enough to be reasonably inexpensive to maintain, yet big enough to carry a coach on the quarter-deck to accommodate the admiral and his secretaries. They also had, as two-deckers, the required presence for a flagship. They were in fact warships built more for peace than for war, and on the eve of the French Revolutionary Wars in 1790 six out of the seven flagships on foreign stations were fifties.

There are two stories about individual fifties which are worth retelling. Early in 1778 Vice-Admiral Clark Gayton was preparing to give up his post as commander-in-chief at Jamaica and return to England in his flagship, the *Antelope* 50. Two circumstances were causing comment. One was that the very large sum that the admiral had amassed from the sale of American prizes he had turned into the form of gold dollars which he was preparing to take with him, not trusting bills, for as he said, 'he knew nothing so valuable as money'. The second circumstance was the extreme age and rottenness of the *Antelope* which made it doubtful if either the admiral or his gold would ever reach England. But when it was suggested that he sent the money home in a frigate he said, 'No, my money and myself will take our passage in the same bottom, and if we are lost there will be an end of two bad things at once.' On the passage home they sighted a large ship and beat to quarters. The stranger would have been much the stronger even if the *Antelope*'s lower-deck guns had not been taken out before she sailed, to ease her. The admiral, who was unwell, took a chair on the quarter-deck, saying to his men that, 'he could not stand by them, but that he would sit and see them fight for as long as they pleased'. Fortunately the stranger turned out to be English and the *Antelope* reached home safely, collecting one more American prize on the way.

The other story is of a sterner occasion. At the Battle of the Nile in 1798 the *Leander* was the only fifty present and was the last one to play a full part with the liners in a fleet action. The French were anchored in line, but the *Peuple Souverain* had parted her cable and fallen out of the line. The *Leander* moved into the gap and her raking fire into the bows of the *Franklin* 80 on her port side and the stern of the *Aquilon* 74 greatly contributed to their surrender. After the victory Captain Thompson was publicly kissed by Nelson on the quarter-deck of the *Vanguard*, this being before the days of British phlegm, and the *Leander* was sent home with the dispatches. These were entrusted to Captain Berry who had been Nelson's flag captain during the campaign. Unfortunately she fell in with one of the two French ships of the line that had escaped from the battle, the *Genereux* 74, and was captured after a furious action lasting six and a half hours, at the end of which all the *Leander*'s masts had gone and she had lost ninety-two men killed and wounded. The *Genereux*'s casualties were two hundred and eighty-eight, and considering that her broadside weighed over twice that of the *Leander*'s, and that she carried over three times the crew, the British ship's performance was very creditable. The French captain made the most of this crumb of success from the French disasters in Egypt by promoting his prize to a seventy-four in his report to his superiors. He pillaged his prisoners and made the wounded seamen help refit the ship, and in general behaved rather worse than was usual; but when he tried to get the British to join the French navy, George Bannister, a seaman, gave him this reply: 'No, you damned French rascal; give us back our little ship and we'll fight you again till we sink.'

## Fifth-rates, the Forties and Forty-fours and Large Frigates

Just as the smallest class of three-decker was considered a failure, so the smallest of the two-deckers was equally unsuccessful. These suffered from the same defects, which were that they could not work their lower-deck guns in blowy weather and were heavy sailers compared to ships of similar force which carried their main batteries on one deck. In the early years of the century when the French and Spanish were still building small two-deckers the shortcomings of ours were not so apparent, but when they began to meet the large frigates that the French had in service during the War of Jenkins' Ear in the 1740s, which could out-sail them, and in rough weather out-gun them too, it was clearly time to make a change in the design of our large cruisers.

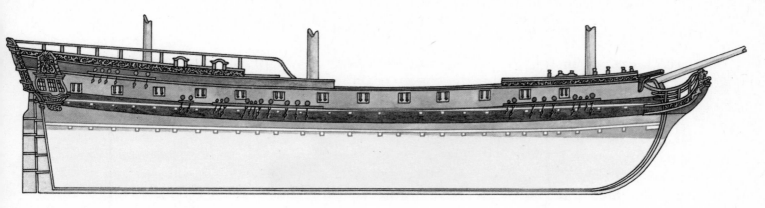

*The* Renommée, *one of the French frigates captured in 1747,
and which set a trend in cruiser design.*

The early eighteenth-century forties were only about 115 feet on the gun-deck and
31 feet in the beam. They carried 12-pounders on the gun-deck and 6-pounders on the
upper deck. In the second quarter of the century they increased in length to around
124 feet on the gun-deck and were rated up to forty-fours by the addition of guns on
the fo'c'sle. The weight of the metal was also increased in the 1743 gun establishment
to 18-pounders on the gun-deck and 9-pounders on the upper; the fo'c'sle guns were
6-pounders.

By 1760 no more ships of this type were being built, and the dockyards were beginning to build frigates of the type we had captured from the French in the previous war.
The word frigate has been bandied about in so many contexts that it must be made
clear that the word here means only a ship of two decks which carried a main armament
of twenty to fifty guns on her upper deck, quarter-deck and fo'c'sle, there being no
ports of any kind at gun-deck level.

The *Embuscade*, a French forty-gun frigate which was captured in 1746, was a fine
example. She carried twenty-eight 12-pounders on her upper deck, ten 6-pounders on
the quarter-deck and two on the fo'c'sle. She was able to do this since, by having no
gun-ports on her lower deck, the deck itself could be lowered to the level of, or just
below, the water-line. The upper deck in turn was lowered so that though there was
a fine freeboard to the gun-ports of about 8 feet, the deck was still low enough for the
ship to carry reasonably heavy guns on it, and more guns and spar-decks over it, without
making her crank. She was 132 feet 6 inches on the gun-deck (lower deck) and 36 feet
in the beam.

The first large English-built frigates were the *Pallas* and *Brilliant*, both thirty-sixes

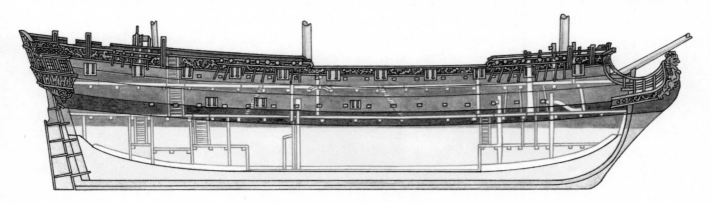

*The* Queenborough, *an example of the type of sixth-rate
of the Establishments of 1733, 1741, and 1745, which was
to be superseded by the frigate.*

and launched in 1757, so that the English were in no rush to build the new type; but some were ready in time for the Seven Years' War. They were 128 feet 4 inches on the gun-deck and 35 feet 11 inches in the beam. They went on calling the lower deck in frigates the gun-deck for another fifty years even though it carried no guns at all. The frigates were a great success, and one would have thought the discredited two-decker forty-fours would have vanished for ever; but in 1774 Their Lordships rediscovered some forgotten virtue in the type and ordered a whole new class of them, some twenty-five of which were built. The new two-decker forty-fours were a good deal larger than the previous ones of a generation before, about 140 feet on the gun-deck and 38 feet in the beam, and their guns were 18-pounders, 12-pounders, and a couple of 6-pounders on the fo'c'sle. They served at home and on the American station during the war of 1775 to 1783, but by the eve of the French Revolutionary Wars all thought of using them as fighting ships had gone, and those that were in commission operated as troop-ships, storeships or hospital ships. The one selected to become the hospital ship for the Channel Fleet was, naturally, the *Charon*.

The large frigate caught on rather slowly in England and there were only four thirty-sixes at the end of the Seven Years' War, and they carried a light armament of 12-pounders on the upper-deck and 6-pounders on the quarter-deck and fo'c'sle. Even at the end of the following war in 1783, the number was only seventeen thirty-sixes and seven thirty-eights, but the guns were now 18-pounders and 9-pounders. The French were by this time building forties with heavier guns than the *Embuscade*, and were soon to build forty-fours. The British followed suit in the Napoleonic Wars, but only in small numbers. A typical thirty-eight-gun frigate of 1795 was 148 feet on the lower deck and 40 feet in the beam; this was an increase of over 20 feet in length and these ships proved magnificently seaworthy and efficient instruments of naval warfare.

**The Smaller Fifth-rates**
These were the thirties, and at the beginning of the eighteenth century were of two types: those as drawn and previously described in the Keltridge draughts with their main battery on the gun-deck, and a few small guns on the upper deck, but with the waist kept clear, and the newer ones with a main battery of 6-pounders on the upper deck and eight 9-pounders on the lower or gun-deck, the other ports being row-ports and two loading ports. However, the building of the thirties ceased by the 1719 establishment, and until after the middle of the century there was no class of ships built for the navy between the twenties and the forties. The return of the small fifth-rate began with the building of a class of thirty-two-gun frigates similar to the *Renommée*, captured in 1747, though the draught for the first one, dated 1756, following the layout rather than the lines of the Frenchman, and was called the *Southampton*. They became the standard and most successful class of English frigates until the end of the French wars in 1815. At the height of the Revolutionary Wars there were sixty of them. At first they mounted 12-pounders on their upper-deck and 6-pounders on the quarter-deck and fo'c'sle, but the larger and later ones mounted 18-pounders instead of 12s, and from the 1770s onwards the 6-pounders tended to be replaced by the short-barrelled, heavy-shotted carronades. The *Southampton*'s lower-deck was 124 feet 4 inches long and

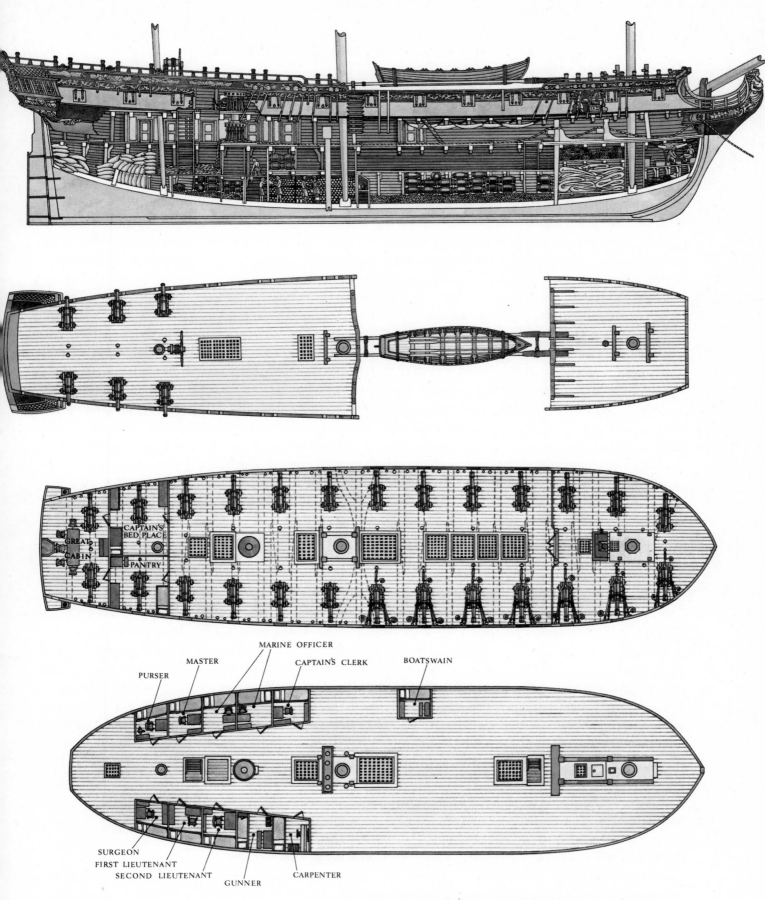

MARINE OFFICER

PURSER  MASTER  CAPTAIN'S CLERK  BOATSWAIN

GREAT CABIN  CAPTAIN'S BED PLACE  PANTRY

SURGEON
FIRST LIEUTENANT
SECOND LIEUTENANT  GUNNER  CARPENTER

*One of the first English frigates, the* Southampton, *launched in 1757.*

49

her beam 34 feet. By the middle 1790s the thirty-twos were being built 144 feet on the lower-deck and 39 feet in the beam.

There is no doubt that the thirty-twos and the larger frigates were the most popular commands. Properly handled they could take on any sort of merchantman, and foreign frigates of similar force. The smaller thirty-twos had a complement of two hundred and twenty, and the big forty-fours nearly three hundred. With such crews, and being handy under sail, they were found to be ideal for the harrying of enemy coasts, with cutting-out parties and raids. A good and lucky frigate captain could make himself rich on prize-money and the crew had their share too, so that he would not usually have to resort to the press gang like the captains of the liners, and might even pick and choose his crew.

**Eighteenth-century Sixth-rates**
The smaller the vessel the cheaper it is as a subject for experiments, so that there is some variety of type in this rate. The old type still in service in the early years of the eighteenth century was a single-decked ship of between twenty and thirty guns with plat-forms low in her hold and a quarter-deck and fo'c'sle. It was a layout that, without the quarter-deck and fo'c'sle, was to reappear in the last quarter of the century. A few were two-deckers with all their battery on the gun-deck and neither guns nor spar-decks on or above the upper deck; but the sixth-rate of the Establishments which they continued to build into the late 1750s was a two-decker with her main battery on her upper deck and the lower deck pierced for seventeen or eighteen row-ports a side. According to the Establishment there might be two, four or no gun-ports on the lower deck and there was always a loading-port a side. The guns were 9-pounders, and a late-built ship would be 107 feet on the lower deck and 29 feet in the beam.

The advantages of being able to manœuvre under oars was the same as offered by the outboard motor in a sailing yacht today, particularly in getting in and out of harbours in conditions adverse to sailing. On the other hand, the ports were close to the water, which made things uncomfortable by leaking, unless they were caulked. When it was decided to do away with the lower-deck ports in the middle fifties, lower the decks and generally conform to the frigate type, the row-ports were moved up a deck and appear between the guns on the upper deck. This meant much longer sweeps at an awkward angle, but quite a few vessels up to the twenty guns and some even larger continued to have row-ports well into the nineteenth century and, for instance, at least one Spanish two-decker fifty. With this type of sixth-rate came in the twenty-eight-gun frigate, only 107 feet on the gun-deck and with a 30 foot 4 inch beam; a useful cruiser with 9-pounders, whose number in the lists for the last quarter of the century fluctuated around thirty. The twenties and twenty-twos of the last half of the century were small frigates with 9-pounders, or carronades, but were only built in small numbers.

**Eighteenth-century Sloops, Gun-vessels and Corvettes**
The general term for a man-of-war, excluding cutters, of a force less than twenty guns was a sloop-of-war; the largest ones were ship-rigged and frigate-built, if not below

eighteens. Draughts of the first half of the eighteenth century show a reversion to the stepped deck in ships and brig-rigged sloops, with a fall aft for the commander's cabin, and a low poop. This fashion did not persist, and those that were not fully frigate-built were designed without spar-decks, carrying their guns on an open deck, with platforms in the hold where everyone and most things had to find a place. Some vessels of this type, which were called gun-vessels, were as long as twenty-gun frigates, say 118 feet, and might carry as many as twenty or more guns or carronades, but were not classed as sixth-rates because of their shallow build and poor accommodation; a sixth-rate being a captain's command. As stated the accommodation in the open-decked sloops was all below, with a 5-foot deckhead to the beams and even less below the platforms to the floor. These vessels appeared during the Revolutionary Wars at the end of the century and could carry a heavy battery into waters where the frigates could not go, but their shallow draught made them poor performers under sail, especially to windward, and very wet.

The smaller sloops were similar, all single-decked with platforms below, but did not necessarily suffer from the same defects in their underwater lines as the larger ones just described; in fact, most of them were quite long-legged. In the Revolutionary Wars they were built in great numbers. The draught of the *Columbine* of 1803 has over sixty names of other brigs to be built to her lines. She was to be armed with sixteen 32-pounder carronades and two 6-pounders, was 100 feet on the deck and 30 feet 6 inches in the

*A gun-brig of 1801. Over sixty were built to the draught of the* Columbine *alone, mostly in private yards.*

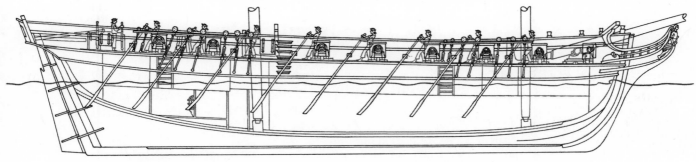

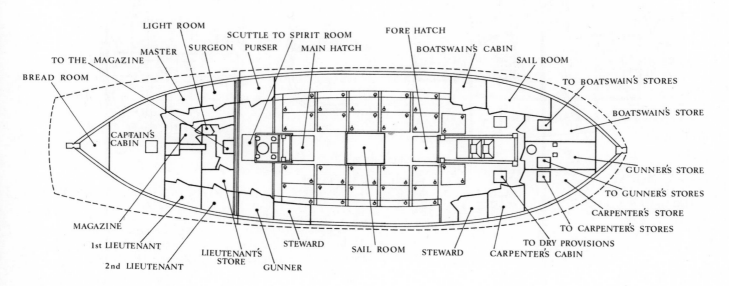

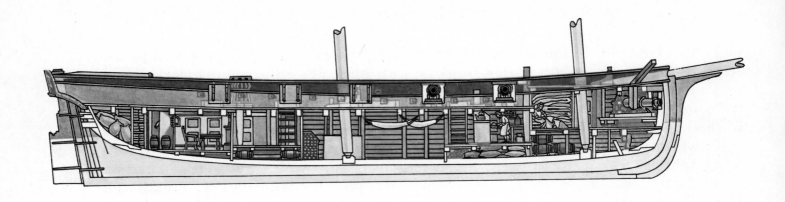

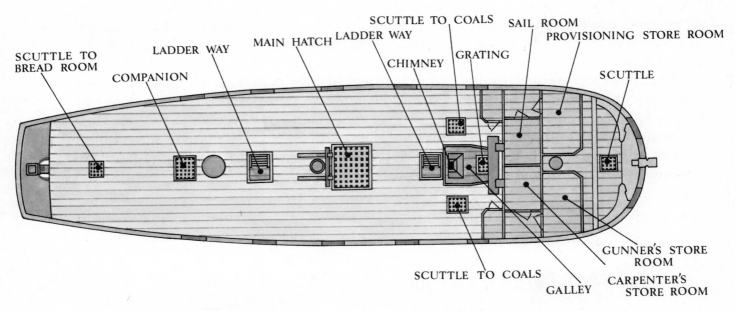

SCUTTLE TO BREAD ROOM

COMPANION

LADDER WAY

MAIN HATCH

LADDER WAY

SCUTTLE TO COALS

CHIMNEY

GRATING

SAIL ROOM

PROVISIONING STORE ROOM

SCUTTLE

SCUTTLE TO COALS

GALLEY

GUNNER'S STORE ROOM

CARPENTER'S STORE ROOM

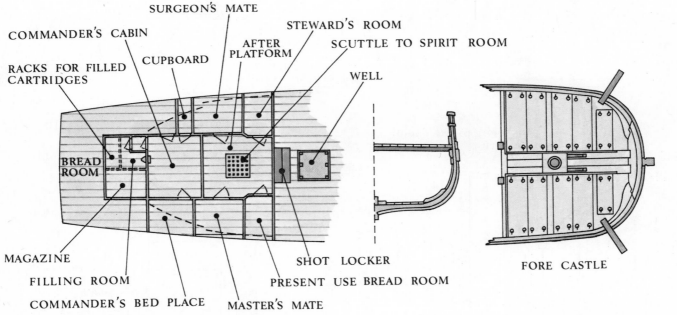

COMMANDER'S CABIN

RACKS FOR FILLED CARTRIDGES

SURGEON'S MATE

CUPBOARD

AFTER PLATFORM

STEWARD'S ROOM

SCUTTLE TO SPIRIT ROOM

WELL

BREAD ROOM

MAGAZINE

FILLING ROOM

COMMANDER'S BED PLACE

MASTER'S MATE

PRESENT USE BREAD ROOM

SHOT LOCKER

FORE CASTLE

*A gun-vessel of the 1794 class. Shallow-draught craft of this type appeared for hostilities only during the Napoleonic Wars, and in a steam-driven form during the Russian War of 1854–5.*

*A ketch-rigged bomb-vessel with her mortars (see page 54).*
Bottom right: *The classic type twin mortar bomb-ketch.*

beam, almost the same dimensions as the *Revenge* of 1575, though without her draught, and the *Columbine*'s broadside was more than half as heavy again. They were all tiller-steered and quite a few at the end of the eighteenth century had a double tiller, one above the deck and one under it. This gave an extra leverage when necessary, and in action a secondary and safer steering position.

Words have different uses at different times which makes it impossible only to indicate their meaning in one context. One word that came into English naval parlance during the Revolutionary Wars was 'corvette', which, though it had various civilian uses, in the French navy had always meant the same as we meant by sloop-of-war. Its introduction into the Royal Navy would seem unnecessary, except that by applying the word to the largest type of frigate-built sloop, it separated them for commands, the smallest sloops being lieutenants' commands, the larger sloops and the corvettes, commanders'. The sloops were armed with 6- or 4-pounders until the introduction of the carronade during the American War of Independence, after which this weapon increasingly monopolised the batteries which might increase the weight of their broadsides as much as five times, though this would only be effective at short range.

## Eighteenth-century Bomb-vessels

As in siege warfare on land, the lobbing of the large round explosive shells at sea was done by mortars, carried in the first half of the century in large ketches. This two-masted rig was preferred since there was less rigging to mask the mortars, which fired with a very high trajectory out of the centre of the bomb-vessels. These mortars, 13- or 10-inch bore, seem to have been common, were very short-barrelled chambered guns, and were mounted on revolving platforms on the centre line more or less amidships, usually two per bomb-vessel, but sometimes only one. This platform was strongly constructed to the floor of the hold and the ammunition kept in cupped shelves between the upright stanchions. The bombs also carried a broadside armament of about fourteen 4- or 6-pounders, and were about 90 feet on the deck with a 26-foot beam.

After the Seven Years' War, it was decided, presumably on sailing grounds, to build ship-rigged bombs. Possibly the first of these was the *Carcass*, which in 1773, stripped of her mortars, went with the *Racehorse* to probe for a north-east passage to the East, north of Russia, with the youthful Nelson aboard as a midshipman. This conversion of bombs in peace-time was very common, and there were never more than two or three on the

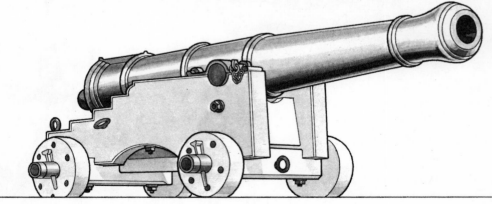

*A 32-pounder, the largest gun in service at the end of the eighteenth century.*

lists unless there was a war on, when there would suddenly be a dozen or more. They were, however, of a distinct design from the sloops, particularly in their deck layout. The mortars took up so much room amidships that though the deck in the ketches was flush, there was a complicated arrangement of stepped platforms below, and in the later ship-rigged bombs the decks were generally stepped aft, even to a stepped quarter-deck for a poop cabin. In the Revolutionary Wars a specialised type of bomb called a mortar-vessel was built. They were very shallow draught, just one deck and a hold, banks of oars and a fore and aft rig. Not many were built.

## Eighteenth-century Rig

The basic square rig layout of the ships hardly altered from that of the seventeenth century, but the fore and aft sails grew in both number and efficiency, as the improvements in the seaworthiness of the hulls permitted far more canvas to be carried. Improvements in rig started with the smaller types of vessel and progressed to the greatest, and the first big alteration was the replacement of the sprit-sail-topmast by the jib-boom. It is difficult to understand why, since triangular sails on the fore stay had been in use in small north European boats since the sixteenth century, this change had not come sooner. In the 1719 Establishment both the sprit-sail-topmast and the jib-boom appear together, but in practice the former was usually struck. Further stay-sails between the fore and main, and main and mizzen-masts, came in more slowly, though they had been known since the late seventeenth century. They were not appreciably used until after the Seven Years' War, but seem to have been firmly established in the American War of Independence. The development of the mizzen-sail was one of the major changes. Since the fifteenth century it had been a triangular sail on a lateen yard. The 1740s and 1750s saw the fore part of the sail cut off and laced down the mast. It would have been a logical development to cut off the yard at the mast too, but the great yard was regarded as a possible jury-mast, so remained, in the biggest ships at any rate, until the end of the century; smaller ships did cut it down in the third quarter of the century. The next innovation was the driver. This sail was an extension of the mizzen or spanker, and in its early form required its own little yard, hoisted to the peak, and a boom from the mast. For a time the two sails remained separate, and the driver might also be used, double-sheeted to the taffrail, as a square sail from the peak in light airs. Obviously the sensible thing was to combine the two into one large sail lashed to the driver-boom, which was the case in most ships by the end of the century, though the old loose-footed spanker was still used as well.

The upward pull exerted by the new head-sails made necessary the bob-stay. Its duties got heavier through the century, but dolphin-strikers were not fitted until 1794, with the flying jib-boom, for which staying over a dolphin-striker was essential. A useful guide to dating eighteenth-century ships of the line in paintings or models was the gradual raising of the channels to which the fore and main shrouds were brought, prompted by the storm damage they and the shrouds might suffer from being set too low, and because they masked the guns, which might also set the shrouds on fire. In three-deckers this meant a rise from the middle deck to the upper deck at the beginning of the century, and from the upper deck to quarter-deck in 1794. The mizzen-channels

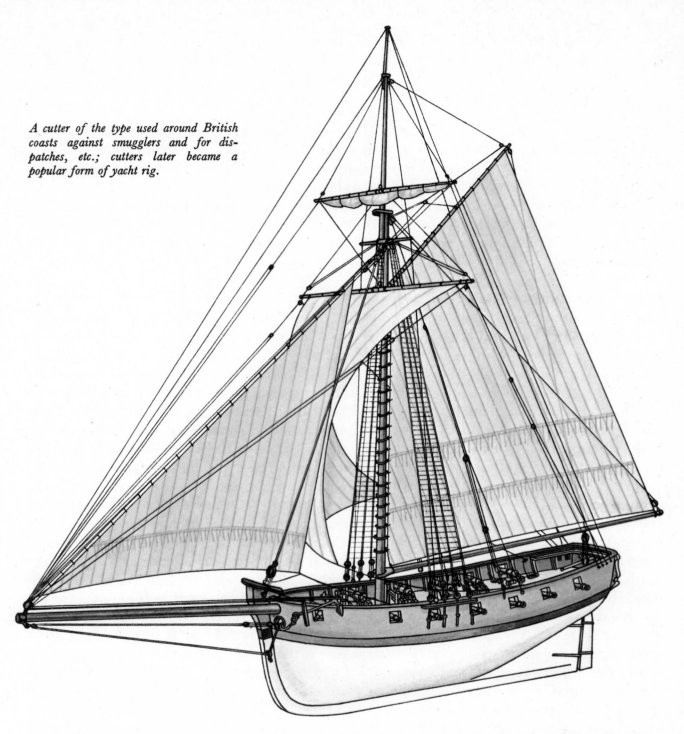

A cutter of the type used around British coasts against smugglers and for dispatches, etc.; cutters later became a popular form of yacht rig.

were moved up from quarter-deck to poop-deck level at the same time. In two-deckers the change was made about 1745 from the upper deck to the quarter-deck.

As the demand for more and larger lower-masts and bowsprits grew, the strain on the supply of large softwood trees made it necessary for the creation of what in the early eighteenth century was called the 'made mast' and later the 'built-up mast'. This took the form of large pieces of wood, in section like a round cake cut from the centre in eight wedges. The structure was bound together at intervals with rope woldings, or after 1800 with iron hoops, and made a stronger mast than a whole tree. The supply of timber for all purposes was a constant headache, and as regards the masts, nearly all were of white pine from America until the rebellion, when the English turned to the Baltic and the 'Riga' mast, of a stronger but heavier wood.

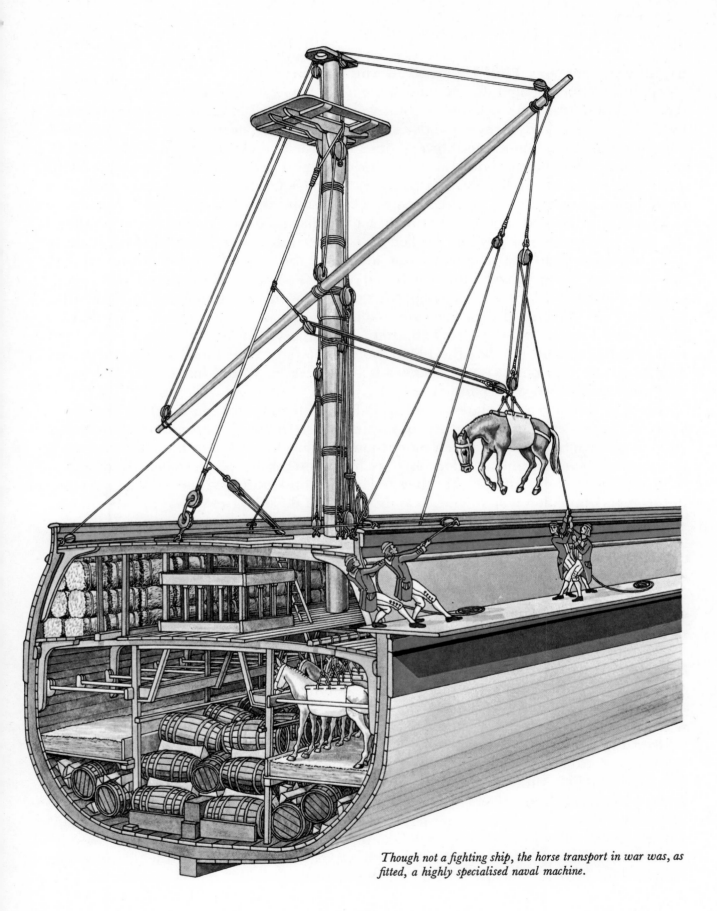

*Though not a fighting ship, the horse transport in war was, as fitted, a highly specialised naval machine.*

57

## Eighteenth-century Hull Decoration and Appearance

As has already been noted, the scandal of the *Royal Sovereign*'s decorations caused a sharp reduction in the carved work, but decorative painting, often in the form of gold trophies on a blue background, formed bands along the sides of the ships above the upper-deck guns, a practice that continued throughout the century, though dying a rapid death in the last ten years. Until about the 1780s the hulls and spars of naval ships were, with a few exceptions in small ships, not painted, but payed. The mixture for the sides was resin, pine varnish, tar, oil and red ochre. The bottom, which needed more protection against marine animals and plant growth, had similar mixtures, reinforced with tallow, sulphur, brimstone and possibly broken glass. The wales were black-pitched, making a double black band near the water-line for about the first forty years of the century, but thereafter were joined into one broad wale. The spars were payed with resin, varnish and tallow. Mixtures varied of course, but it would be interesting to know what Captain Peter Warren precisely meant when he noted in his log in the 1740s that he had given his ship a 'pease porridge bottom'. Inside, below decks the sides were painted red, it has been said, so that the blood would not show, but more to give fierce red mouths to the gun-ports. Later deckheads tended to be white, but earlier ones were probably natural wood or painted red.

So long as they used plates of mica, called then muscovy glass, which had been universal in the seventeenth century for glazing the stern windows, these remained small and could have hardly been much more than translucent; but with the change to glass in 1703 and the simultaneous adoption of sash windows the ship's stern became designed to let in so much light and air that they resembled conservatories. Indeed we know that in the years immediately following Trafalgar, Admiral Collingwood was an enthusiastic cultivator of potted plants in his cabin. The stern walk made a reappearance at the end of the seventeenth century as an open recess to the round house and even the great cabin, but settled down to one recessed and slightly overhanging gallery in two-deckers and two in three-deckers. The figureheads on the beaks were so universally the crowned lion for ships below the second-rate that the head was referred to as the 'lyon', and it was only after individual figureheads were generally authorised in the late 1750s that the word figurehead came back.

## Steering Improvements

In the seventeenth century the tiller entered the ship above the gun-deck level through a fairly wide port to allow it play, and was worked by a pole, called the whip-staff, which passed through the deck above, which itself formed the fulcrum. The men who worked the whip-staff, either on the upper deck in a two-decker, or the middle deck in a three-decker, could not see where the ship was going and received orders relayed from above. The position of the tiller flat made the gun-deck very wet in certain conditions, so a great improvement was to raise the rudder head through an opening in the underside of the counter, in a housing, to the deck above. A further great improvement harnessed the tiller to ropes from a wheel on the quarter-deck. The principle was the same as a capstan, and there is evidence that experiments were made with windlasses mounted athwartships before settling for the admirable double-wheel and drum.

## Sheathing

From the fifteenth century, when ships began to venture into warmer seas, there was a pressing need to protect the underwater parts of the hulls against the dreaded teredo or ship worm, which chewed its way into the timbers and could reduce the ship to a sinking condition in a few months. The Indians had been known to use hardened leather sheathing, and at least one Japanese ship was seen to be encased in iron; but in Europe the solution in general use up to the middle of the 1770s was to pay over the bottoms with stuff containing poisonous substances such as sulphur, and sometimes pulverised glass, and then seal it with a soft wood sheathing, also payed. The teredines were expected to feed on the sheathing, but died if they tried to get through to the oak. At the end of the voyage, or from time to time, the sheathing was stripped off and renewed. A more sophisticated process introduced in the early eighteenth century was to coat the bottom with pitch and cover this with brown paper; another coat of pitch went on this and a layer of hair was stuck to it; then the wooden sheathing was fixed by a vast number of broad-headed iron nails covering the whole surface. This use of an iron facing of nails called 'filling' was also applied and more widely to wooden anchor stocks, examples of which still survive. It was effective against the teredines, but laborious and expensive, and gave the vessels that had it a very rough bottom. Of course the ordinary wooden sheathing got very foul with weed. This was a trouble particularly felt by the English, who kept their ships at sea much of the time, while the French ships, which spent most of the time in port, could usually appear with clean bottoms when they did venture abroad. Lead sheathing was tried in the third quarter of the seventeenth century, but since it could not be fastened with lead nails, and since iron ones caused electrolytic reactions, it was abandoned. It was in any case very heavy. In 1671 Charles II, inspecting the *Phoenix*, building at Deptford, asked why lead sheathing was not used. He was told that the plank sheathing was to strengthen her. The king then observed that they might as well use sarsenet to strengthen her, adding, 'Lord have mercy on the men who depend on that sheathing if the ship be not strong enough herself without it.' The final answer was copper, but again the first ship that tried it in 1758 had iron fasteners and the same electrolytic trouble occurred. However, in the case of copper, copper nails could be used, and once this was done the ships were not only teredo-proof but presented a smooth, slightly poisonous, surface to the water which did not foul so quickly, and greatly improved a ship's sailing qualities.

## Signals

Although it is no part of the design of warships, the development of an articulate signals system in the late eighteenth and early nineteenth century was the most important advance in naval warfare for the period, and deserves some mention in the context of the story of the warship.

The first systematised signal code the navy had was that of Sir William Penn in the reign of James II. There had been signals by flag and gun before, but crude and few, and really the most useful one was the signal to call a council of war. This might occur at the height of the battle, as when Marten Tromp was killed at the Battle of Scheviningen in 1653 and the Dutch flag officers gathered round his body to decide

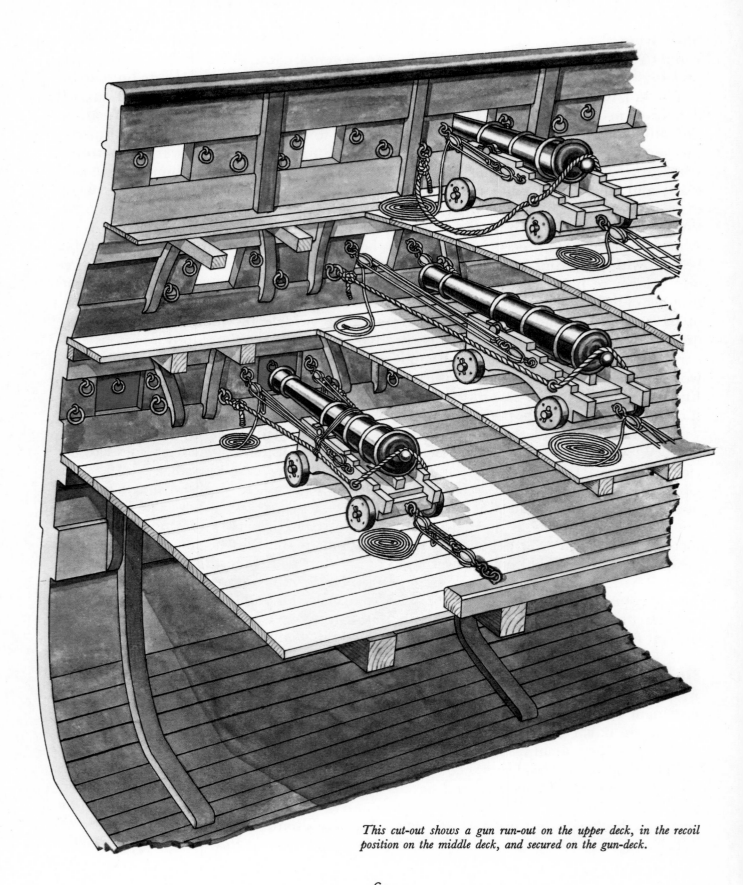

*This cut-out shows a gun run-out on the upper deck, in the recoil position on the middle deck, and secured on the gun-deck.*

60

From   Mark.Pellegrino@engelhard.com

Sent   Monday, May 15, 2006 8:38 pm

To   "Barbara J. Furze" <bj.furze@patmedia.net>

Cc   Pellegrino Linda <ivy_108@hotmail.com> , Mark Pellegrino
<Mark_Pellegrino@engelhard.com> , Michelle Terry
<MICH51692@AOL.COM> , Ron Pellegrino
<rpellegr@tampabay.rr.com>

Bcc

Subject   Re: New Address


So when's the housewarming party?  By the way, I'm sending this via Chennai/Madras India!

Love,

#1 Godson

Mark R. Pellegrino
Team Leader NJ Campus
Information Technologies
Engelhard Corporation
732-205-6974


**"Barbara J. Furze"**
**<bj.furze@patmedia.net>**

05/15/2006 09:11 PM

To "Pellegrino Linda" <ivy_108@hotmail.com>, "Mark
Pellegrino" <Mark_Pellegrino@engelhard.com>, "Ron
Pellegrino" <rpellegr@tampabay.rr.com>, "Michelle
Terry" <MICH51692@AOL.COM>

cc

Subject New Address


ANDY + MADDY
1-828-877-3650

Hello Everyone – I had forgotten how much work this moving stuff is but I'm finally here in
Flemington.  I'm up to my butt in boxes but all in all everything went pretty smoothly.  I wanted
everyone to have the new info.  I keep getting an e-mail failure on the address I have for
Pammie.  Ron – can you forward this to her and let me know what her e-mail address is now.
Thanks.

35 Joseph Drive
Flemington, NJ 08822
908-237-2468

what to do. One of the last councils of war at sea to decide the tactics of a coming sea fight must have been aboard the *Ajax* in December 1939, when Commodore Harwood summoned the captains of his other two cruisers aboard his flagship before engaging the *Admiral Graf Spee*.

The Stuart system, as of 1714, which continued up to the 1780s was for single flags, sometimes under a pendant, but only in one case two flags together, flown at various places in the rigging of the flagship to give a limited number of orders. All a private ship in the fleet could do was either to strike his main-topsail and place an ensign at the topgallant mast 'to speak with the Admiral' or put a union flag at the main-topmost backstay 'to discover danger'. Nearly all the signals were hoisted to the accompaniment of a gun.

A curiously small number of pure signal flags were used, the flags of command, the union, the ensigns and even the royal standard doubled for signal flags. One of the disadvantages of the system was that to make a code of over one hundred signals it was necessary to place flags in the yards, in the shrouds, and other places where they might not easily be seen, also the flagship had on occasion to strike her ensign, or even the flag of command to place a signal flag in their place.

In fog the admiral was down to eight gun signals, but at night there were fifteen possible signals, using set numbers of guns, and lanterns hoisted at various points. Loosing the topsails was the signal to weigh.

In the 1770s Captain Richard Kempenfelt developed the first numeral signal code,

*The 24-pounder Carronade (see page 63).*

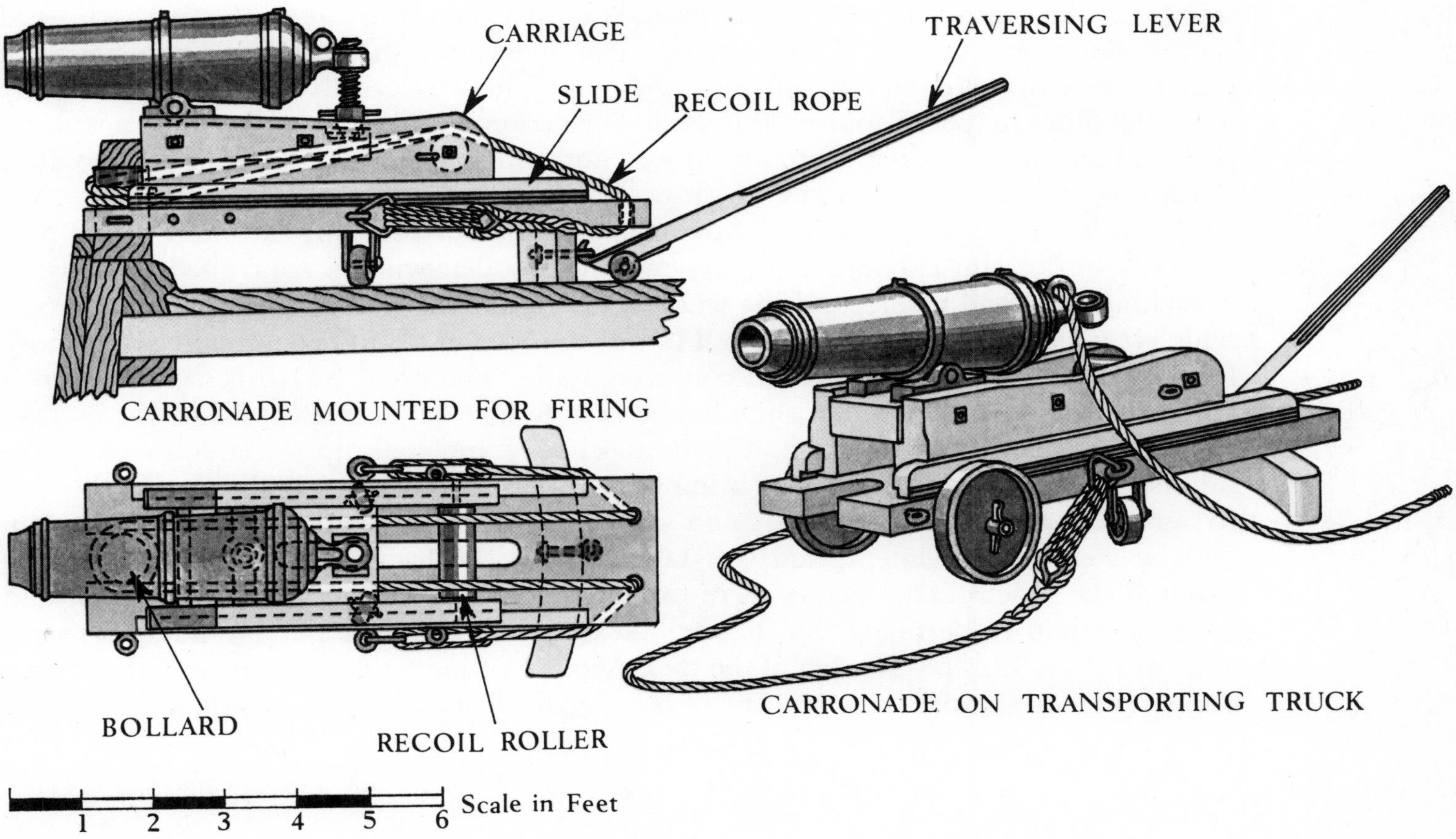

CARRIAGE

SLIDE    RECOIL ROPE

TRAVERSING LEVER

CARRONADE MOUNTED FOR FIRING

BOLLARD

RECOIL ROLLER

CARRONADE ON TRANSPORTING TRUCK

1  2  3  4  5  6    Scale in Feet

with hoists of more than one flag which read off as a number and corresponded to a given signal. As they were flown from the mast-heads they could be seen better and read off quicker. In a modified form Lord Howe used them in 1782, when they materially helped him get a convoy into Gibraltar in the face of a superior force of the enemy, which he was able to outmanoeuvre.

Still, however, this system did not permit ships to speak to each other, and it was Admiral Sir Home Popham's greatly extended numeral and alphabetical code of 1801 which permitted this and which was the basis for the modern naval code. It included firstly an alphabet to spell out words if necessary; secondly a code of words; and thirdly codes of sentences and of syllables; also codes for technical terms, provisions and stores, etc. It was in this code that Nelson made his famous signal before the Battle of Trafalgar.

## Eighteenth-century Naval Gunnery

The developments in this field, as in ship design, were confined on the whole to the improvements of existing types rather than the invention of new techniques. There was more system than formerly, and establishments of guns dated 1716, 1740, 1757, 1762 and 1792 defined the number and types of guns allotted to each rate. Except in the largest type of ship there was a general trend for cannon throwing increasingly heavy ball to be mounted, and this was not only due to the increase in the size of ships for the number of guns carried, but to a lesser degree to the improvement in the powder, which made a decrease in the length of the barrels justified, with a subsequent saving in weight. More important was the quality of the barrels. The English gun-founders had been acknowledged the best in Europe since the middle sixteenth century, and in the eighteenth the French were still sending people over to see how it was done. By the middle of the century Britain was embarked on her own iron age as the first industrial nation, and it was in the refinement of the iron metal that she excelled. These new iron guns were cast solid and bored out; they were now relatively safe and practically indestructible compared to the soft metalled bronze guns. They were also more accurate, though this was a relative term, and it was not until the early nineteenth century that the fitting of sights was thought worth while.

Even less change affected the carriage. The idea of perching two and a half tons of metal on an elm carriage with free-moving wooden wheels, controlled only by its breeching rope and tackle, and the whole set on a moving platform, sounds dangerous, which it sometimes was; but until well into the nineteenth century no really satisfactory form of slide to take up the recoil could be made. The great Swedish naval architect Chapman designed a wooden slide in the late eighteenth century, which was used in some French ships, but was found to be too heavy and took up too much room. The sailors in any case were used to securing most things with ropes, whether it was the ship to her anchors, or the masts, spars and sails in their places. The recoil of the gun when fired was extremely violent, and was taken up by the friction of the tackle running through the blocks. The tackles were brought to bolts on either side of the port, and great care had to be taken that neither tackle jammed or the gun would spin round and turn over. This positioning of the tackle bolts also made traverse-firing difficult and dangerous, for the different lengths of the tackles from gun to gunwale made for an uneven strain, and the gun tended to centre itself on firing. Some of the difficulties were overcome by the fitting of judiciously placed ring bolts and wedges to check the recoil. These and other ideas were successfully experimented with by Captain Sir Charles Douglas in the late 1770s and early 1780s. This enthusiast also perfected the goose-quill primer and the flintlock for cannon.

The one important eighteenth-century innovation in naval gunnery was the carronade, a type of gun invented by General Robert Melville in 1752 and made for the navy by Mr Gascoigne of the Scots firm of Carron, from 1779 the foremost among the improvers of iron gun-metal. The carronade was basically a short light-barrelled gun with a large bore. It threw its heavy ball, 32 or even 68 pounds, with a low initial velocity which at short range had a crushing effect more destructive than the swift passage of a ball at high velocity. Early carronades had trunnions and a carriage, but this was changed to lugs on to the bottom of the barrel, attached to a slide, with a worm screw at the breech to angle the barrel. There was a tackle from the slide to the gunwale and a heavy breeching to the carriage, but the use of a wooden slide was only possible with a moderate recoil. The carriage pivoted on a vertical bolt for traverse firing. Two men could work them, which was one of the main reasons why they were first adopted in bulk by the merchant service, but the navy adopted them too in the American War of Independence, when they formed a large proportion of the quarter-deck armament of the frigates, and nearly all the armament of many sloops and most gun-brigs of the French Revolutionary Wars. In an age devoted to close action, the heavy broadside that even quite small vessels armed with carronades could mount made them a popular weapon, but an entire battery of them could be disastrous; for, as several captains found to their cost, a superior sailing enemy with ordinary cannon could stand off out of range and batter them till they struck.

The French, who liked to stand off to lee and fire at the rigging, were slow to adopt the new gun; indeed their gunners, firing from an upward sloping deck, had worse recoil and running out problems with their cannon than the English, fighting to weather on a downwards sloping deck.

## Conclusions on the Eighteenth Century

The names of the Petts and Anthony Deane ring down to us from the seventeenth century because they created a new type of fighting ship; but the same cannot be said for the naval architects of the eighteenth century. Men like Ward, Stacy, Hayward, Locke, Allen and Slade were merely the improvers of basic designs, and the inheritors of principles which they found no reason to alter. The extent of their improvements made the difference between summer season operations only at the beginning of the century, and blockading the north-west coast of France in winter and summer, often in dreadful conditions off a lee shore, for years during the Revolutionary Wars at the end of the century. Indeed as early as 1759 Hawke, by keeping the seas off Brest into the autumn, finally caught de Conflans and destroyed him in Quiberon Bay, in November.

It is certainly true that the French designers were more scientific in their approach to hull design, and showed the way where English designers had perforce to follow. But though it might have been fashionable for some English naval officers to say that the best ships in the service were French prizes, certainly French officers could not have had the satisfaction to claim that the worst ships in their service were English prizes. For during the long French wars, from 1688 to 1815, the loss by capture and destruction in action of English ships of the line down to the fifties was twenty-seven, while the loss to the French was one hundred and seventy-eight. Added to this armada over the same period of time were seventy-eight Spaniards, thirty-three Dutch, twenty-three Danish, one Russian and a Turk, making a grand total of three hundred and fourteen. The French have the credit of accounting for twenty-six of the twenty-seven, the odd ship, a fifty, blew up in action with a Spanish seventy-four in 1747.

The score is even more impressive during the Revolutionary Wars from 1793 to 1815 the longest and hardest-fought naval wars of all time. The English loss of ships of the line, by capture a seventy-four in 1794, another in 1795, two more in 1801, and that was all; none were destroyed. Their enemies on the other hand lost one hundred and thirty-one captured and twenty-nine destroyed. So if the success was not due to the ships, it must have been due to the men and the system.

The excellence of the French ships did not extend to their material or their construction, which was generally inferior to the English, so that promising captures soon became unserviceable and had to be scrapped. A notable example of this was the *Commerce de Marseilles* 120, the biggest ship in the world when taken in 1793 at Toulon. She was found to be so badly constructed that she was not thought fit to bear her guns, and was turned into a trooper for two voyages before being broken up.

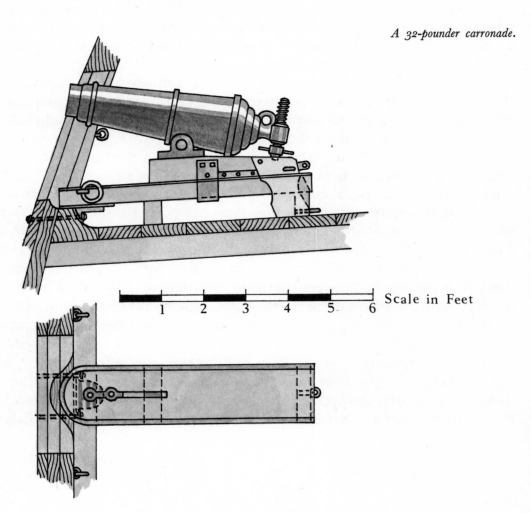

*A 32-pounder carronade.*

Scale in Feet

1  2  3  4  5  6

# 9

## The Nineteenth-century Wooden Battle Fleet

### Numbers in Commission 1814–70

As the Great War drew to a close the cumulative strength of the Royal Navy shows as over a thousand ship names in the Navy List. Although this list included all the hulks used for harbour duties and as prisons, there were still over nine hundred vessels of all kinds available for service, of which about six hundred and fifty were in commission at sea. Of this number between ninety and a hundred were ships of the line. Such a force of capital ships has never before or since been maintained at sea by any nation, and there were at least sixty more in reserve. The seventy-four was still the dominant type with over seventy in commission, none of the other rates reaching double figures.

After the war there was naturally a wholesale scrapping of the older ships, about half, and so long as the navy relied on sails alone the figure fluctuated between ninety and a hundred all told, with fifteen to twenty in commission and the rest in reserve or building. On the conversion to a steam assisted battle fleet in the early 1850s, the number dropped below the nineties and was little over sixty ten years later. Indeed by the second year of the Russian war, in 1855, when steam had become to be considered essential to the management of the fleets in action, only twenty-eight were completed and at sea, so that apart from the sixteen screw-liners building the other fifty liners that had not been converted were of little further use although it was thought necessary to keep some pure sailors in commission at home, and the Mediterranean fleet was mixed. The China station, where coaling stations were almost non-existent, saw the last of the purely sailing ship of the line when the *Ganges* 84 was ordered home in 1863.

With the arrival of the first ironclad in the 1860s, the disappearance of the wooden capital ship from the effective list was as rapid as the armoured ships could be built to replace them. The Mediterranean fleet had a wooden three-decker, the *Victoria* 121, until as late as 1867, and her final appearance was with the Channel Fleet in July of the same year when the queen reviewed the fleet with the Shah of Persia. The last of all to serve on an active sea-going commission was the *Rodney* 72, which was the flagship on the China station in 1868 and 1869 and paid off at Portsmouth on the morning of 27 April 1870.

### The Enemy

The foregoing figures must be taken in relation to the fleets of foreign powers, notably Russia and France, whose ambitions mounted with the years. In the year of Queen

Victoria's accession (1837) the Russians sent to sea a fleet of twenty-six sail of the line, while the British Channel Fleet had but seven, the rest being in the Mediterranean or other distant stations. Britain could have commissioned a dozen others at short notice which would have been too much for the Russians, never a first-class service, even when they were under the Empress Catherine's Scottish flag officers. However, had the Russians been joined by the French, a very serious situation could have arisen. The French had been building up their fleet and were beginning to dream again of wresting the naval crown from the British. Following their old practice of building bigger ships than the British for the equivalent rates, their one-hundred-and-twenty-gun ships of 1830 were 232 feet on the gun-deck, whereas the British were still around 205 feet. In 1839 they had twelve ships of the line in commission and twelve in ordinary; made up of six first-rates, three second-rates and fifteen third-rates, none mounting less than eighty guns. In fact, this threat from France never materialised, and when it came to fighting, it was against the Russians, with Anglo-French fleets commanded by British admirals.

## Nineteenth-century Developments

It was a matter of critical comment in early Victorian times that while Britain was leading engineering revolutions in many fields, particularly in land transport by

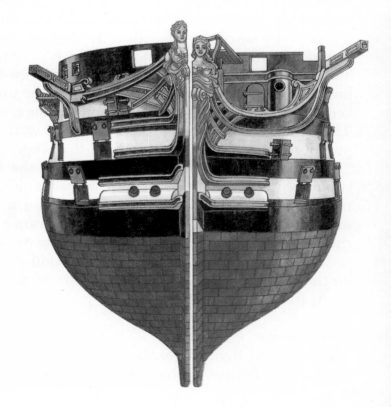

*The improved method of construction with diagonal framing to stiffen the hull, and the round bow and stern introduced towards the end of the Napoleonic Wars, compared to the old method.*

inventing the railway, developments in naval architecture, especially as regards the Royal Navy, appeared to be almost at a standstill. This stagnation was not only apparent but real, as will be seen by the choice of ships to go into commission. This was governed by the selection of the dozen or so ships of the line kept in the first reserve which formed a force which could quickly be put in commission for sea in an emergency, but also was the pool from which ships were commissioned to replace those coming home to pay off. These ships might be new or forty years old, like the *Hibernia* 104, launched in 1804, which went out as a flagship to the Mediterranean in 1845. A few of the liners converted to steam in the 1850s had been launched in time to fight at the end of the Napoleonic Wars.

The great stride forward was in the new method of framing perfected by Sir Robert Seppings and first tried in the *Tremendous* 74, in February 1811. In this ship additional frames were placed diagonally between the parallel frames and also between the parallel deck beams. These gave the whole structure much greater strength and rigidity. His system was generally applied to all new building when Sir Robert became Surveyor following Sir William Rule in 1813, and the initial benefit was that since the ships no longer worked so much in a sea, their planking did not open and they remained much drier inside. The long-term benefit was that hulls could be built much longer without hogging, and, when the time came, could bear the weight of boilers and

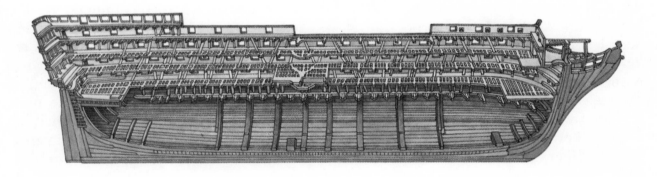

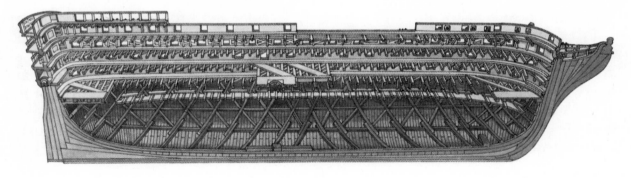

engines. The *Tremendous* was 170 feet on the gun-deck, while the biggest class of two-decker, built in the 1850s, was 250 feet. This increase in size compensated for the considerable increase in the weight of construction which made the early Seppings ships heavy sailers.

It was to improve the sailing performance that prompted Sir Robert Seppings's successor, Sir William Symonds, to change the underwater lines so that the ships had a sharper entry and a markedly steeper floor. They certainly sailed better, and a ship of the line would do about 13 knots, but they had a lively movement and would heel to the wind in a manner which made them less useful as gun platforms. The Symonds lee lurch was familiar to naval officers of the period. His two other major changes were to the designs of the bow and stern. The bows of eighteenth-century liners were framed up to the upper deck, the forward bulkhead between the upper deck and the fo'c'sle was square with round-houses and comparatively lightly built; this left the upper deck vulnerable to raking fire from ahead, and this was sorely felt by the *Victory* and *Royal Sovereign* as they slowly led their lines before a light breeze to break the Franco-Spanish line at Trafalgar. The new bow, called the round bow, was framed up to fo'c'sle level and there was a good solid bulwark above it.

Solid bulwarks for the poop-deck and fo'c'sle of liners appear in draughts dating from 1801, and for the poop alone a year or two earlier. They soon rose to be 6 feet high to give protection to those on the exposed decks. In ships without a poop-deck this led to a light bridge between the gunwales being necessary for conning the ship, a most exposed position.

To return to the dangers of raking fire a much worse vulnerability than the bow affected the stern, from ancient times the traditional living quarters of the officers. From the habitability point of view the old square stern had much to recommend it. The frames rose solid each side to poop level, but only up to the transom beams at upper-deck level in a two-decker, or middle-deck level in a three-decker. Above this rose the delightful tiers of sash windows and galleries which gave in plenty of light, and air if required, but would not stop a musket ball. Also, although of fairly light construction, their weight was mainly borne by the transom which caused straining of the main structure which could open up the seams of the planking and let in water in bad weather.

Another consideration was the extremely poor stern and chase fire of the eighteenth-century liner, which had at the most four ports opening dead astern, all at gun-deck level. This was because on the decks above even if guns were manhandled round and their barrels pushed through the stern windows, the structure could not have withstood the recoil, and if strengthened to take it, would have imposed an intolerable strain on the transom beams below it. With a built-up circular stern to poop-deck level pierced for an additional fourteen guns in two-deckers and sixteen in three-deckers, making twenty in all in the latter, a respectable stern and quarter-fire was possible. There were still the stern windows and galleries abaft the main structure, so beloved by naval officers, and these would have suffered severely from the blast of the ship's own guns. This was acceptable in the emergency of battle, but not for practice shooting. At the end of the eighteenth century an effort had been made to reduce the weight and increase the strength of the old type of stern by doing away with the open galleries and having

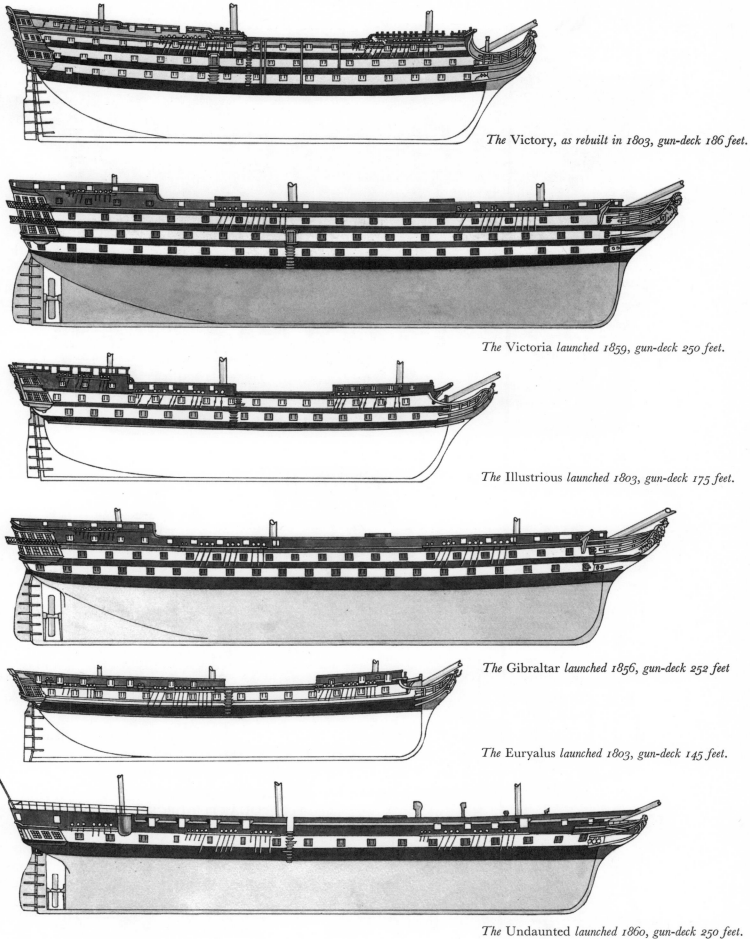

The Victory, *as rebuilt in 1803, gun-deck 186 feet.*

The Victoria *launched 1859, gun-deck 250 feet.*

The Illustrious *launched 1803, gun-deck 175 feet.*

The Gibraltar *launched 1856, gun-deck 252 feet*

The Euryalus *launched 1803, gun-deck 145 feet.*

The Undaunted *launched 1860, gun-deck 250 feet.*

Scale in Feet

0    20    40    60    80    100

*The increasing lengths of wooden hulls in the first half of the
nineteenth century was made possible by the added rigidity
introduced with the adoption of diagonal framing.*

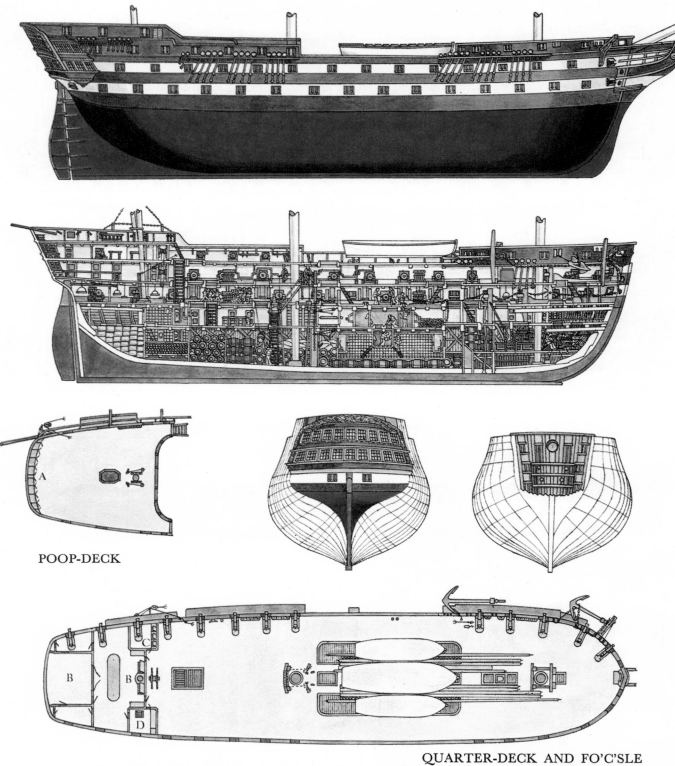

POOP-DECK

QUARTER-DECK AND FO'C'SLE

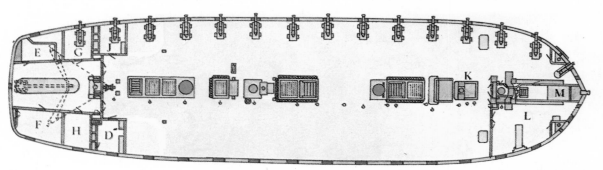

THE UPPER-DECK

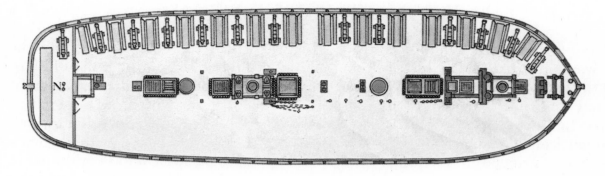

GUN-DECK

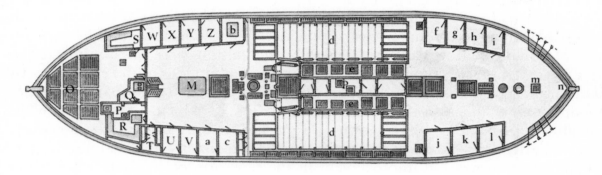

ORLOP-DECK

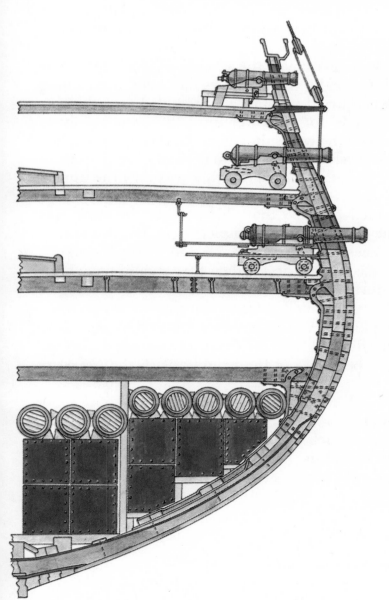

*The Vanguard of 1835, one of a class of eleven sailing two-deckers, the last to be designed without auxiliary steam propulsion, and in her case, one of several which were never converted.*

## KEY TO VANGUARD

| | | | |
|---|---|---|---|
| **A** | Colour lockers | **T** | Dispensary |
| **B** | Captain's apartments | **U** | Surgeon |
| **C** | Clerks office | **V** | Chaplain |
| **D** | Captains' steward | **W** | Purser |
| **E** | Master | **X** | 2nd Lieut. |
| **F** | Commander | **Y** | 3rd Lieut. |
| **G** | Captain of Marines | **Z** | 4th Lieut. |
| **H** | 1st Lieut. | **a** | 5th Lieut. |
| **I** | Ward room | **b** | 6th Lieut. |
| **J** | Ward room stewards | **c** | 1st Lieut. of Marines |
| **K** | Galley | **d** | Cable Tier |
| **L** | Sick berth | **e** | Sail room |
| **M** | Amputation table | **f** | Naval Instructor |
| **N** | Gun room | **g** | 2nd Lieut. of Marines |
| **O** | Gratings over Bread room | **h** | 3rd Lieut. of Marines |
| **P** | Magazine passage and Scuttle to Magazine | **i** | Marine store |
| | | **j** | Gunner |
| **Q** | Handing room | **k** | Carpenter |
| **R** | Captain's store room | **l** | Boatswain |
| **S** | Ward store room | **m** | Scuttle to Gunner's store |
| | | **n** | Stand for Arms |

complete rows of stern windows instead. This was called the closed stern, and the *Victory* was converted to one during her rebuilding of 1798 to 1803, which she still has.

By the end of the Napoleonic Wars the open gallery, by popular demand, had crept back, but Sir Robert Seppings followed up his built-up sterns with a series of extra-ordinary 'lighthouse' stern galleries, designed to facilitate the field of fire. Behind which were often iron hanging canopied stern walks, such as are associated with Regency houses, and continued in Victorian villas for decades. These stern walks continued in popularity in our capital ships and large cruisers until recent times, and only finally disappeared with the scrapping of the battleships *Queen Elizabeth* and *Warspite* after the Second World War. In 1827 a modified round stern, called the elliptical stern, in which the framing took on a much squarer form on the deck plan, was introduced by Captain Symonds. This refinement was adopted generally, and with it there was a return to the old style of quarter-gallery, though slightly bowed in the middle of the stern-line. In their final form the squared-off outer edge was modified so that the quarter-galleries curved round to the flatter line of the stern windows. The improvement in the chase fire made possible by the built-up bow was not so marked, mainly because the bowsprit, jib-booms and attendant spreaders and rigging made fire directly ahead almost impos-sible. There was, however, an improvement in the bow fire, particularly when a big 68-pounder was mounted on the fo'c'sles of the liners around 1850, with a slide-carriage designed to swivel on traversing-rings, and bear over wide angles on both sides of the fo'c'sle, which had enlarged ports.

Another considerable structural improvement was the closing of the waist. The gangway between the quarter-deck and fo'c'sle by the gunwales had been broadening until by the beginning of the nineteenth century it was just a large hole beamed across to carry the boats and spare yards. This hole got narrower until the surveyorship of Sir William Symonds in 1832, when he closed the waist altogether. In theory a complete tier of guns from quarter-deck to fo'c'sle was now possible, but partly for reasons of weight distribution, and more especially because a space on what was now the upper-most deck was needed for boats and spars, this was almost never done. It would have impeded the firing of truck-mounted guns so that this part of the deck was generally kept clear of guns, though some draughts show complete tiers. For this reason there are mid-nineteenth-century references to four-deckers instead of three-deckers, but if this is to be based on the number of complete decks, then they should have been called five-deckers, with their orlops. A further change introduced at the beginning of the century was the substitution of iron knees for wooden ones. This was made necessary by the acute shortage of timbers for the purpose which, if they were to have sufficient strength, had to be cut where the trunk divided and the grain of the wood curved, otherwise the knee would split. This had been one of the troubles with the *Commerce de Marseille*.

## The Nineteenth-century Rates to 1856

In 1816 there was a revision of the ratings, which had been in force since 1746. First-rates remained at one hundred guns and over, but the second-rate now included ships of eighty guns and above and the third-rate began at seventy guns. Previously the third-rate had covered any ship from sixty guns to eighty and had been by far the largest and most important rate in the battle fleet, but now was reduced more or less to the seventy-fours. The fourth-rate began at fifty guns, the fifth-rate at thirty-six guns and the sixth-rate at twenty-four guns. There was a scale of men attached to the gun list, and in 1856 a new list based on the number of men employed, with different scales for steamers and pure sailors was introduced, which cut out the number of guns altogether.

Advances in gunnery and the coming of steam power might reduce the number of guns a ship carried to the point when she dropped a rate, yet was a more powerful warship than before. Also the designation of a first-rate as being a ship of one hundred guns and above became a trifle nonsensical when the number rose to one hundred and thirty-one. Indeed there were even, as early as the Napoleonic Wars, proposals for four-deckers of one hundred and sixty or one hundred and seventy guns, such as Joseph Tucker's proposed ship to be called the *Duke of Kent*. She was not built because there was no requirement for such a ship which would have been most expensive to run, but at 221 feet on the gun-deck and 62 feet 5 inches in the beam she would have been much smaller than the last three-deckers to be built. The *Howe* of 1860, which was 266 feet on the gun-deck and 61 feet 1 inch in the beam, was to have been completed with only one hundred and twenty-one guns.

The tendency was for the gradual abandonment of the smaller rates of liner and an increase in proportion of the most powerful ships, particularly in the building of the two-decker first-rates in the early 1850s. Five ships actually completed as one-hundred-and-one-gun ships, and of the twenty-five or so others that were built, all except those few that were converted into armoured ships, completed as nineties or ninety-ones.

In 1830 there were sixteen first-rates, sixteen second-rates and fifty-seven third-rates. Still an all-sailing battle fleet in 1845, the proportion was twenty-seven first-rates, twenty-eight second-rates, all two-deckers, and forty-one third-rates. The last date worthy of comparison is 1855, during the Russian war, a year before rating by guns was dropped, when the first-rates remained at seventeen; the number of second-rates had increased to thirty-six, the third-rates had dropped to thirteen and the fourth-rate was back with sixty-gun liners, all in commission.

*A 32-pounder 45 cwt smooth-bore muzzle-loader of 1840, mounted on a Ferguson slide carriage.*

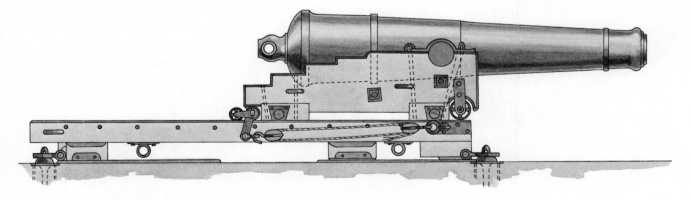

The paddle frigate Sidon of 1846. The painted ports on her paddle-boxes give an indication of how they reduced her main-deck armament. They were also vulnerable to cannon-shot.

A deck-plan of H.M.S. Sidon, showing the great awkward paddle-boxes, and the armament lay-out.

## Steam Power

In the spring of 1845 there were one hundred and thirteen steam vessels in the Navy List, but not one of them belonged to the battle fleet. This may seem remarkable when one considers the commercial success of the steam-ship by this date, there being already steam services operating to America and India. The *Comet* of 1822, which served as a tug and survey vessel in home waters, was the first steam vessel to serve the Royal Navy, but it was to be twenty-four years before the *Ajax* 60 was undocked in Cowes in 1846 to become the first steam-liner. She was screw-driven and powered by a four-cylinder horizontal engine of 450 horse-power by Maudsley, which was capable of driving her at 7 knots. Under sail her screw and funnel retracted, a device generally adopted.

The reason for the delay in giving steam power to the battle fleet was that it had to await the invention of the 'submarine propeller or archimedean screw', now known as the screw propeller. This was because paddle wheels would have meant doing away with at least one-quarter, perhaps a third, of the ship's broadside armament, and the machinery to drive them would have filled the entire centre section of the ship. In addition the paddles would have been extremely vulnerable to fire and would have impeded the ship's sailing performance when not in use. The screw propeller was first

*A steam-assisted first-rate of 1855, showing the ultimate development of the wooden liner.*

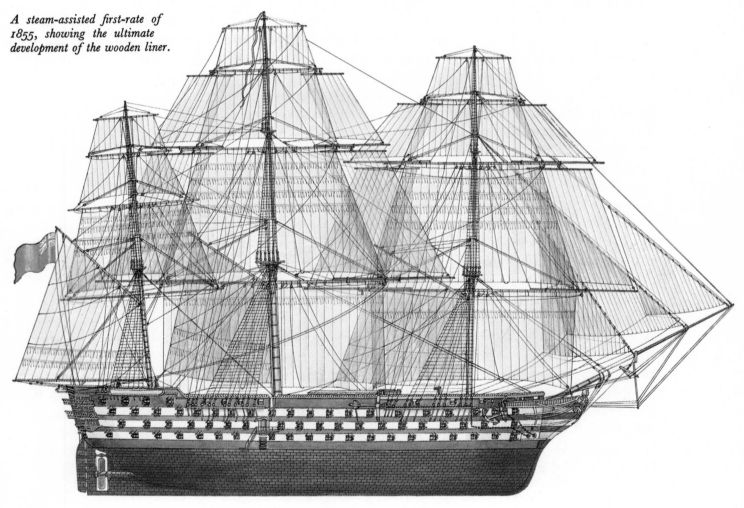

75

successfully tested in a vessel called the *Archimedes* in 1840, and Brunel first tried one in a big ship when he launched his iron steamer the *Great Britain* in 1843. About this time the Admiralty became convinced of the virtues of a free-moving battle fleet based on screw propulsion, and considering that the fate of the nation might be said to have hung on their policy regarding the battle fleet, then the decision to adopt it was not too tardy.

The *Ajax*'s 7 knots gave her no more than manœuvring power, but by the sixties the engines for two-deckers were rated up to 800 horse-power which gave them a useful steaming speed of about 12 knots, the last three-deckers had engines of 1,000 horse-power. The method of altering ships on the stocks, such as the two three-deckers *Duke of Wellington* and *Marlborough*, laid down as pure sailers, was to cut off the stern and launch it; then to lengthen the hull and install the engines and boilers; finally to drag the stern ashore and reattach it to the rest of the ship. It was recognised by the time of the Crimean War that all future fleet actions would be conducted under power.

## Armament of Nineteenth-century Ships of the Line

The old system, in force since the beginning of naval gunnery, of carrying a mixed armament with the greatest guns on the gun-deck and lighter ones above, had the disadvantage that several different sizes of shot and of powder charges had to be carried, and in action this might easily lead to confusion. In 1825 a Colonel Munro of the Royal Artillery submitted a proposal that a single calibre should be used for all guns, the necessary weight distribution being met by having shorter barrelled guns on the upper decks, and that this armament should be based on the 32-pounder.

This scheme was put into effect in the next few years, so that a three-decker's armament now consisted of truck-carriage mounted 32-pounders, weighing 56 cwt on the gun- and middle decks, 32-pounders of 40 cwt on the upper deck, and 32-pounders of 25 cwt, called gunnades, on the quarter-deck; the fo'c'sle had two guns of 25 cwt and two of 49 cwt. This uniformity was shortly afterwards disturbed, however, by a demand for a small number of very large chase-guns, so that 68-pounder 'millers' were added, two to each deck below the quarter-deck; later they were confined to the fo'c'sle and possibly the quarter-deck. There were some slight variations in different ships.

From the 1820s to the 1850s the French, bitterly jealous of British naval supremacy, were looking round for a weapon which would make up for their own natural short-comings and neutralise the British advantage. They pinned their hopes on M. Paixhan's shell-firing guns which he developed in the 1820s. Shell-firing from cannon as well as from mortars was not new; the French had experimented with it as far back as the beginning of the eighteenth century, and encouraging experiments were carried out by them in Napoleonic times. French ships were issued with a variety of tricky combustible projectiles before the end of the eighteenth century. The British, who had long used shell-firing mortars in their bomb-vessels for shore bombardments, regarded with distrust and distaste the idea of using shell in ship-to-ship engagements as being ungentlemanly and dangerous. Dangerous, that is to say, more to oneself from accidents in carrying them; a view that proved justified from the number of disasters to French ships from fires and explosions.

There were also limitations in the early days of shell-firing to the amount of charge that could safely be used and the ball itself being hollow was lighter for its size than a solid one, so that range and penetrating power were reduced. The effect of the explosion was also largely discounted, even though Sir Samuel Bentham, an inventive Englishman who joined Russian service, had proved, back in 1788, the effectiveness of the shell-firing gun, by destroying a Turkish squadron with them mounted in long-boats.

The attitude here, though watchful, was to leave things as they were until forced to make a change by a foreign power. So it was in 1837 when the French announced a general change to shell-firing guns that the British had also to introduce them, which was quickly done by boring out some of the 32-pounders to 8- or 10-inch calibre. So long as the shells were spherical a mixed armament of shell-firing and shot-firing guns was necessary because the shot had a better range. In the Russian war the *Duke of Wellington* 131, flagship of the Baltic fleet, had a mixed armament in the following distribution: gun-deck, ten 8-inch shell-firing and twenty-six 32-pounders (shot); middle deck, six 8-inch shell-firing and thirty 32-pounders; upper deck, thirty-eight 32-pounders; quarter-deck and fo'c'sle, twenty 32-pounders and one 68-pounder on a slide carriage and pivot mounting. A better arrangement, more generally adopted, was to have the whole of the gun-deck battery shell-firing and the batteries above shot-firing, the 32-pounders graded as before. There was a general introduction in the 1840s of the slide carriage pivoting on traversing-rings for the chase-guns, usually one in the bows and two at the stern; otherwise the truck carriage continued to be general, and was to continue to prevail in wooden-built ships until the last class of wooden corvettes paid off in the late 1880s.

There had been efforts to improve the truck carriage, the most significant of which was Captain Marshall's carriage by which the forepart of the carriage was removed and the weight taken by the barrel resting on a crutch attached to the gunwale. This crutch was hinged, the weight taken by one small truck wheel on the deck, and by moving this from side to side the gun could be laterally trained. Elevation still relied on the wooden quoin. The mounting was tested with 12-pounders aboard the *Prince Regent*, and the Marshall mounting proved itself by firing eight rounds in 7 minutes 44 seconds, manned by three men, against 9 minutes 6 seconds, for the normal truck-mounted gun manned by six men. As a result of this the system was approved for stern- and bow-chasers, but was never extended to the broadside guns, and it is doubtful whether it became general even for a short time for the chase-guns.

Although sights had been experimented with for many years, and some enthusiasts like Sir Philip Broke had fitted them at their own expense to their ships' guns, the navy did not take officially a very scientific interest in this subject until the second quarter of the century when it set up an experimental and training establishment in H.M.S. *Excellent* at Portsmouth under Captain Thomas Hastings in 1832, which he ruled for fifteen years. Initially no great strides could be taken to revolutionise naval gunnery so long as it depended on a cast, smooth-bore gun, firing spherical projectiles. It took the wrought-iron rifled gun of the 1860s firing cylindrical shells to achieve accuracy, range and penetrating power unheard of before.

## Fastening

It may be said that a ship is as strong as her fastening, and unfortunately it was in its fastening that a wooden hull was apt to be most vulnerable. Fastening meant in practice the nailing of the wooden parts together. Up to the 1780s this had been done with iron nails and trenails, after that copper nails were used under the copper sheathing and in the second quarter of the nineteenth century tinned iron came into use, but copper continued to dominate the underwater fastening of wooden hulls.

Of these materials iron was the strongest and had the virtue of fusing with the wood when it started to corrode. As corrosion advanced, however, the strength of the nail ebbed and the wood around it rotted. Copper was introduced because the iron nails under the copper sheathing, when it came in, caused electrolytic action between the two metals which damaged the sheathing. It was not so strong as iron, and since it did not corrode, or hardly at all, it did not grip so hard. Still, it was strong enough, and by not corroding it kept its strength and did not rot the wood around it. Its disadvantage was the expense of the copper, and a seventy-four-gun ship required 35 tons of copper just for her undersides. The hull above the sheathing therefore continued to be fastened with iron, but the tinning process cut down corrosion and gave a much longer life to nail and wood. Finally, there was the trenail, a wooden peg which was cheap and weak, but one would have thought harmless to the wood around it; not so—it was found that a trenail of one wood set into another wood caused rotting to both, and in the nineteenth century when so many different woods were in use for shipbuilding it was often impossible to avoid mixing woods.

## Accommodation

The deck layout of a typical two-decker to the early Victorian period does not differ greatly from the century before. The captain remained in the coach under the poop-deck, where he had a sitting-room, dining-room, two bedrooms, clerk's office and steward's pantry. Below him on the upper deck the wardroom remained in its traditional place, and along each side of it and, somewhat forward of it, were cabins for the commander (an innovation of the 1820s), the first, second and third lieutenants, the master, captain of marines and the captain's steward. The sick-berth was forward of the galley under the fo'c'sle. The gun-deck housed the men, who messed on folding tables between the guns, and slung their hammocks above them, while right aft was the midshipmen's gunroom. The orlop-deck, which was now quite flush with a good deckhead, housed, in addition to its traditional denizens (the surgeon, surgeon's mate, purser, carpenter, gunner and boatswain), the fourth, fifth and sixth lieutenants, the chaplain, naval instructor, first, second and third lieutenants of marines and the captain's clerks. Their cabins either faced each other across the surgery and amputation table two-thirds the way aft, or were well forward. Being on the fourth deck down without any forced ventilation, the air must have been pretty thick at times, though by the innovation of scuttles which were angled down through the timbers from gun-deck level, the inhabitants had some natural light and visual contact with the world outside. Another refinement was piped water through lead pipes from a cistern in the poop.

*The gun-deck of a late wooden ship of the line.*

# 10

## The Nineteenth-century Frigates and Other Cruising Vessels

In 1814 the Royal Navy had a round one hundred and thirty frigates in commission, of which ninety were of the larger classes of thirty-six and thirty-eight guns, and a dozen more were of forty or forty-four guns. This was a reversal of the pattern of ten years before when the thirty-twos, now down to twenty at sea, outnumbered all other classes. It was indeed the large frigate that was to take over the peace-time duties as flagships on distant stations, formerly the province of the two-decker sixty-fours and fifties. Already by 1814 two monster frigates the *Leander* and *Newcastle* had been commissioned and sent out to America to cope with the U.S. Navy's huge frigates which had been giving Britain such shocks. The *Leander* and *Newcastle* were built of pitch pine with their waists decked over and furnished with a complete tier of guns from poop to fo'c'sle, so that they were called double-banked frigates. On the draught the *Newcastle* has a coach and a double tier of stern galleries. It is most doubtful, however, if she was finished with a coach, since when she was on the American coast Commodore Sir George Collier, who was in the *Leander*, successfully passed off his ships as an American squadron, when they fell in with an American ship. The captain of this vessel, an English prize, came aboard the *Leander* in his own boat, saying to Sir George, whom he addressed as Commodore Decatur, that he knew his ship to be the *President* the moment he saw her, and Nick himself would not deceive him. When asked what ship the *Newcastle* was, he did not know, but accepted that she was the *Constitution*, saying only that she was not painted as she used to be. Having been pumped by Sir George, and communicating the pious hope that his squadron would do 'a tarnation share of mischief to the damned English sarpents, and play the devil's game with their rag of a flag', the Yankee took his leave with great apparent satisfaction; but when about to quit, the first lieutenant told him the truth of his situation, and on seeing Sir George come up in his uniform coat, he became almost frantic. The upshot of all this is that if the *Newcastle* did have a coach it would surely have been impossible to pass her off as the *Constitution*, which we know did not.

In one respect the *Leander* and *Newcastle* were small three-deckers without gun-ports on the lower deck, and they mounted fifty-eight guns and carronades, though since carronades did not count in the total until 1817 they were classed as fifties at that time. The advantages of this type of ship over equivalent two-deckers was the same as the frigates had always enjoyed. Compared to the draught of a late two-decker fifty, to be called the *Saturn*, of the same year, the dimensions of the *Newcastle* were 177 feet on the

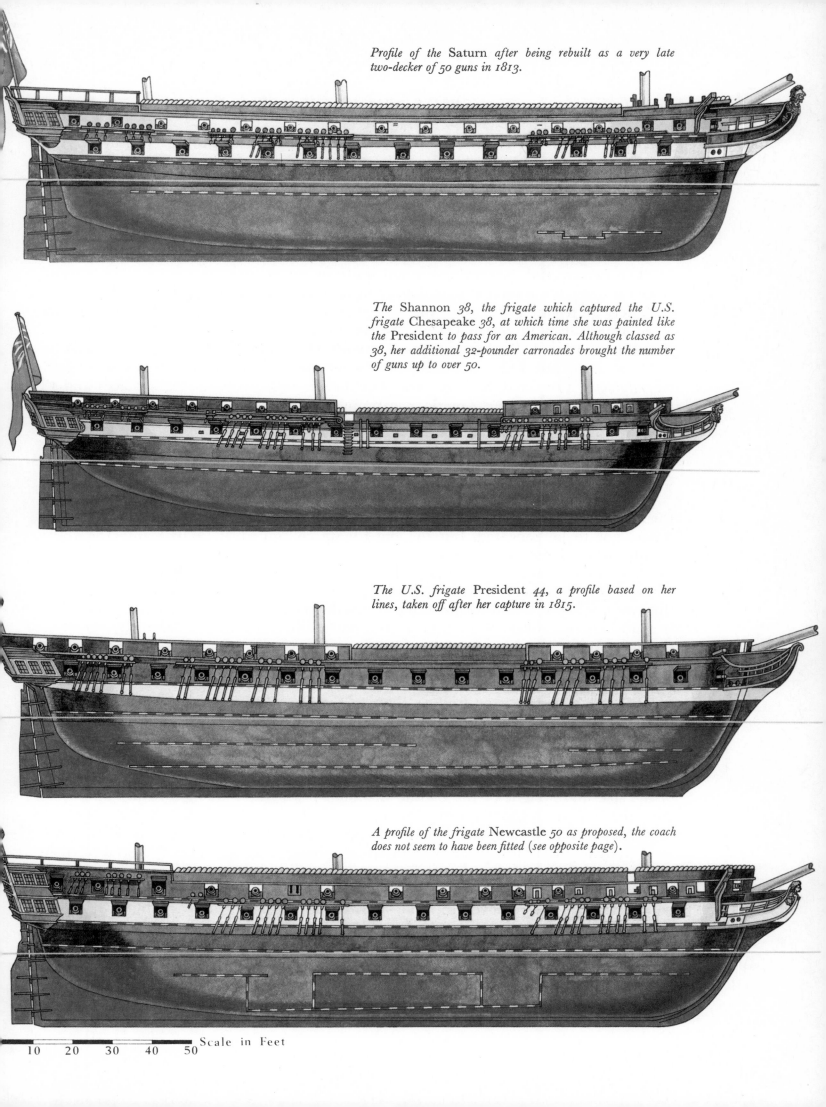

*Profile of the Saturn after being rebuilt as a very late two-decker of 50 guns in 1813.*

*The Shannon 38, the frigate which captured the U.S. frigate Chesapeake 38, at which time she was painted like the President to pass for an American. Although classed as 38, her additional 32-pounder carronades brought the number of guns up to over 50.*

*The U.S. frigate President 44, a profile based on her lines, taken off after her capture in 1815.*

*A profile of the frigate Newcastle 50 as proposed, the coach does not seem to have been fitted (see opposite page).*

Scale in Feet
10    20    30    40    50

gun-deck and 41 feet 11 inches in the beam, against 154 feet and 44 feet 4 inches, and the *Newcastle* carried her lower tier a good 9 feet above her water-line, while the *Saturn* could hardly manage 6.

Another advantage of the frigate type was that all the men lived on the lower deck where there were no guns, so that in the event of action there was much less to clear away on the deck above which carried the main battery. In two-deckers the crew lived on the gun-deck, so took longer to clear away.

The *Leander* and *Newcastle* were not built for the American war, as has been said, since the draughts are dated 1810, before Britain was much concerned with the potential of American frigates. One day when the two frigates were blockading Boston in 1814, some Americans went out in a fishing-boat to the *Leander* and asked permission to board, which was granted. During conversation with the commodore one said that 'You are a larger ship, but I do not think that your men are as stout as ours aboard the *Constitution*.' 'They may be very little, but their hearts are in the right place; and I'll thank you to inform the American captain, that if he will come out and meet the *Leander*, I will pledge my word and honour that no British ship shall be within twenty leagues; and further, if my ship mounts more guns than the *Constitution*, I will throw the additional guns overboard.' We do not know if the message was ever delivered, but the *Constitution* did not come out while the *Leander* was there and they never met.

In order to meet the sudden demand for very large frigates for the American war, three seventy-fours were razed down to flush-decked frigates. This was an emergency move, not to be repeated, but the big frigate continued to flourish into the 1860s, mostly 70 feet longer than the *Leander*.

A further feature of the nineteenth-century frigate establishment was the re-emergence of the small frigate of twenty-four or twenty-six guns. In calling them small, they were as big as a mid-eighteenth-century thirty-six, but as they carried 32-pounders instead of 12-pounders the weight of the battery had to be considered. By the 1830s the 32-pounder was in general use.

## Steam-Frigates

Steam came earlier to the frigates than to the liners, as a number of paddle-driven frigates were built alongside the pure sailors until screw propulsion was adopted. The first of them was a converted forty-six-gun sailing frigate called the *Penelope* which had originally been launched in 1829, and in 1842 was cut in two and lengthened from 152 feet on the lower deck to 215 feet 2 inches to take paddle machinery. An indication of the size and weight of the paddle machinery was the reduction in the number of guns that could be carried, forty-six to sixteen. Her engine was 650 horse-power and drove her at about 10 knots. Altogether eighteen wooden and one iron paddle-frigates were built in the 1840s, the last of them completing in 1852. They served a purpose, but suffered from the inordinate amount of space the machinery took up, and the paddles were a serious hindrance to their sailing powers. It was known, indeed, for the paddle vanes to be removed in some ships on occasion; also the armament of any of them never exceeded twenty-one guns and over half of them only mounted six. Most were broken up in 1864 but one at least lasted in service until 1870.

The first steam-frigates were paddlers, but the screw-frigates followed fast. The first, the *Amphion*, was converted during construction and launched in 1846. The screw system was so obviously better than the paddles that it is remarkable that the paddlers continued to be built at the same time as the screw-vessels. The machinery to drive the shaft was situated low in the hull and did not interfere with the main-deck battery, and the drag of the screw was overcome by raising it.

The screw-frigates were very large, most of them between 230 and 250 feet on the lower deck, and with a beam of about 50 feet; and two of the later ones, the *Mersey* and *Orlando*, were 300 feet on the lower deck with a 52-foot beam, the largest un-armoured wooden hulls ever built for the navy. They were completed in 1859 and 1861 respectively, but it was found that the strains of such a length were too great for the material. Altogether forty-five screw-frigates were built, and these wore the flag on many distant stations into the middle 1870s, the last one was the *Undaunted* which came home from the Far East at the end of 1878. The last wooden frigate of all to serve was the *Newcastle*, completed as late as 1874, and when she paid off in 1880 there disappeared from view the most splendid-looking type of masted ship ever built.

## Sailing Corvettes and Sloops

From the Napoleonic Wars until about 1860 a large share of the work of keeping what became known as the *Pax Britannica* was borne by the little ships of the navy, mostly the beautiful brig-rigged sloops and corvettes. These last, eighteen- or twenty-gun ships, were about 120 feet on the main-deck and 38 feet in the beam. They had two flush-decks and possibly nothing more above the battery, but they might have a quarter-deck, or even a complete deck with a well for the boats amidships, but with no guns on it; they were ship-rigged. The smaller eighteen- or sixteen-gun ship-sloops were about 113 feet on the main-deck and had a beam of about 31 feet; they were ship- or barque-rigged and sometimes had a tiny cabin aft on the main-deck, and a fo'c'sle. The lower deck would probably not be complete or flush. The brigs were laid out very much the same as those already described as serving in the late eighteenth century; the battery on an open deck, and the crew accommodated on the platforms below. They were 95 to 100 feet on the main-deck with a beam of about 32 feet. The armament of the early post-war sloops was largely based on the 32-pounder carronade, but this last was replaced in the 1830s with the 25-cwt 32-pounder gun, or gunnade, with possibly 6 feet long 18-pounders for chasers. When it came to the class below them, a large gun mounted on a slide carriage on the centre line amidships was preferred, with pivots and traversing-rings. There would be also two or four carronades, or later, from the 1840s, light guns of the same calibre.

They were usually called hermaphrodite brigs, because of their rig, which by the middle of the century was called brigantine. Sir William Symonds, the surveyor from 1832 to 1847, was particularly successful with what became known as the Symonite brigs. He had largely got his job as a result of the sailing qualities of a barque-rigged sloop which he designed, called the *Columbine*, which beat everyone else's in the sailing trials held in 1827.

In 1845 there were over sixty of these vessels in commission, but the steam-assisted

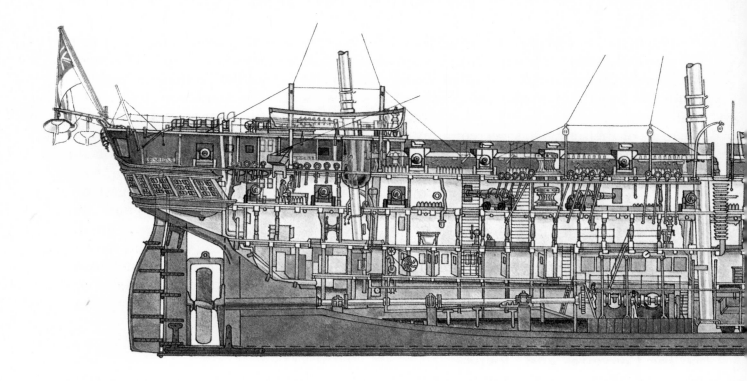

sloops were already, with over twenty in commission, gaining on the pure sailers, which disappeared from the oceans in the early 1860s.

## Nineteenth-century Rigging

The sail plans of the sailing navy were perfected in the years following the Napoleonic Wars. The most obvious modifications to the appearance of the plans were the dropping of the loose-footed spanker and the general adoption of a large single driver. To compensate for this more head-sails had to be set, so that the flying jib-boom became a permanent feature. The sprit-sail yard was retained as a spreader in the ships of the line until the fifties, but in frigates and below it was replaced by two separate spreaders, fitted with jaws to the bowsprit. Another improvement to the fore and aft sails was the use of loose-footed trysails set on small masts abaft the fore and mainmasts. The square sails were, from 1811, bent to jackstays below the yards instead of being lashed to them.

In 1830, when the Royal Navy was being forced to enlarge its ships to keep up with the French, people began to worry about the practical difficulties of handling the spars and sails which would have to increase proportionately with the hulls. In fact, the crews always managed, and smartness aloft, which became a fetish in the Victorian navy, reached a remarkable standard of efficiency never equalled before.

An indication of the increase in the size of the masts and yards may be seen by

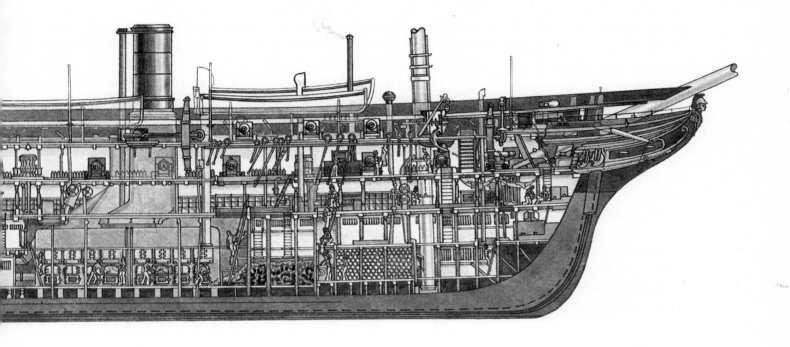

*The screw steam-frigate* Undaunted *of 1860, one of the last of a highly successful type of cruiser which had been evolved over a hundred years before (see pages 46–50 and 82).*

comparing some of these of the *Victory* 100 of 1765 with a one-hundred-and-twenty-gun ship of 1853:

|  | *'Victory', 1765* | *120-gun ship of 1853* |
|---|---|---|
| Mainmast | 94 feet 10 inches | 119 feet 8 inches |
| Main topmast | 57 feet 4 inches | 68 feet 1 inch |
| Main topgallantmast | 29 feet 1 inch | 34 feet 5 inches |
| Main yard | 86 feet 5 inches | 104 feet 4 inches |

The general policy of standardising fittings brought in by Sir William Symonds in the 1830s also affected masts and spars which were reduced to twenty establishments, where there had formerly been eighty-eight.

## The Wooden and Composite Screw-Corvettes

The difference between the screw-frigates and the screw-corvettes was not one of size, for some of the corvettes were larger than some of the frigates, but of layout. The frigates had a lower deck for accommodation, a main-deck which carried the main armament, and above that what was virtually a third deck, since the quarter-deck and fo'c'sle had been joined together, leaving only a well in the waist; this deck too carried a heavy broadside armament and chasers.

The corvettes were two-deck ships, the lower deck for accommodation and the main-deck for the battery which was out in the open. With the building of the *Eclipse* class of 1867, poops and fo'c'sles were added but these never met, or anything like, and nothing heavier than light quick-firers were ever mounted on them. The early corvettes built during or just after the Russian war of 1854–55 were about 195 feet on the main-deck and 38 feet in the beam. The next generation, the *Eclipse* class, were originally called sloops on the plans but were launched as corvettes, and were 212 feet on the main-deck and 36 feet in the beam; they had ram bows. The last wooden corvettes were the five ships of the *Amethyst* class of 1873–75. These were much easier on the eye than the ram-bowed type since they were given graceful knee-bows. They were 220 feet on the main-deck and 37 feet in the beam; their engines were around 350 horse-power, which gave a useful steaming speed of 13 knots, which was also their sailing speed. For armament they had twelve truck-mounted 64-pounder rifled-muzzle-loaders, and two more on slides as the bow- and stern-chasers. In their second commissions three of them had their truck-mounted broadside guns exchanged for ten slide-mounted guns of a lighter pattern. The early corvettes were all ship-rigged, but the last two classes, though with one exception built with ship-rigs, were all converted to barques for their second commissions.

Altogether thirty wooden and six composite corvettes were launched between 1854 and 1877, and with the launch of the *Sapphire* in September 1874 of the *Amethyst* class, wooden shipbuilding in the traditions begun in the Tudor navy came to an end.

It was fitting that the name ship of this class should close the chapter of their exploits with one last sea fight, which was with the Peruvian armoured turret ship *Huascar*. This vessel, a British-built armoured ship, was the major unit of the Peruvian navy, and in May 1877 she was seized during a revolution by the aspirant to the presidency. At first the British did not consider it their business, but when Pierolo, for that was the aspirant's name, began to stop British merchant ships, claiming government mail and seizing coal on an illegal bill drawn on the Peruvian treasury, it was time to take a hand. The Pacific flagship was the *Shah*, one of three very large iron-built unarmoured cruisers with a powerful armament. The other British warship in those waters at the time was the *Amethyst*, and the two ships intercepted the *Huascar* on 29 May. Admiral de Horsey demanded her surrender for piracy, but the 'President' haughtily refused to yield. In the resulting action the *Huascar*'s fire was naturally directed against the *Shah*, but the *Amethyst* also kept up a well-directed fire until de Horsey sent her to close the land on the Chilean side in case the *Huascar* should seek neutral sanctuary. In fact, she managed to get herself in the shallows before the town of Ilo where de Horsey could not follow and dared not fire for the houses. Although the *Huascar*'s upper works were badly damaged her armour was proof against British fire. She, on the other hand, mounted two 300-pounder Armstrong rifled-muzzle-loaders which would have destroyed the *Shah* if they had hit her in the right places. In fact, only some rigging was damaged. In the night the *Huascar* stole away and surrendered to the Peruvian squadron which was supposed to be in pursuit of her, but had not dared to take her on. Unaware of this, de Horsey had sent in a cutter with a Whitehead torpedo only to find the bird had flown. This was the last occasion when a British wooden warship with a broadside battery of muzzle-loading, truck-mounted guns was ever in action, and the only occasion when one was engaged with an armoured adversary.

Although this volume sets out to confine itself to the wooden navy, it is not reasonable to leave out the composite-built corvettes and smaller cruisers. This style of building was popular in the 1860s and 1870s until the coming in of mild steel hulls, but in the Royal Navy was not used in anything larger than the corvettes. The principle was to make the ship's frames of iron, but the keel, decks and planking were of wood. This gave a stronger and more rigid hull than a wooden-framed one, and in the hot and distant places where these ships spent their working lives the iron inside the wooden sheathing kept the temperature down below decks. One of the last composite corvette classes, the *Carolines*, were given an iron protective deck over their boilers and engines.

So far as the corvettes were concerned only one class was composite-built and this was the *Emerald* class of six, launched 1875–77. Apart from a slight difference in their underwater lines these ships were identical to the *Amethyst* class of wooden corvettes and proved magnificent sea-boats. One example of composite construction can be seen at Greenwich today, the merchant clipper *Cutty Sark*; a second, the sloop *Gannet*, is now lying in Fareham Creek awaiting a decision on her future.

## The Wooden and Composite Screw-Sloops

The old sailing sloops, because they were among the smallest of warships, might be ship-rigged, brig-rigged, or cutter-rigged; the rating was on force and the number of men carried, not on a design type. The scale for the screw-sloops was the same, but in their case their engines and boilers required them to be so big that three masts and a square rig was necessarily uniform. They were in fact scaled-down corvettes, and in 1875 any warship with more than one hundred, but less than two hundred officers and men was called a sloop.

No less than ninety-seven of these vessels went into service between the middle 1840s, when the first ones were being either built, converted from paddle sloops or from sailing sloops which had to be lengthened, until the last one was launched in May 1888. The distribution was fifty-seven wooden, thirty-nine composite and one experimental iron one, the latter built in 1846. They were generally barque-rigged, certainly all the later ones, and many classes were ram bowed. The large *Amazon* class of 1865–66 were the first to have poops and fo'c'sles. They measured 187 feet by 46 feet in the beam.

It is difficult to make any generalisation about armament when the type spans forty years, and at a time of big changes in gunnery. But it is possible to state that the early ones might have as many as seventeen smooth-bore 32-pounders, or a slightly smaller number which included a 68-pounder. In the middle 1860s the number had been reduced to four or six heavier guns such as the 7-inch rifled-muzzle-loader. This policy continued into the middle 1880s when the final armament was about ten 5-inch breech-loaders.

The sloops, being in between the corvette and gun-vessel classes, were apt to include features from either or both. Some sloops, for instance, had a complete lower deck like

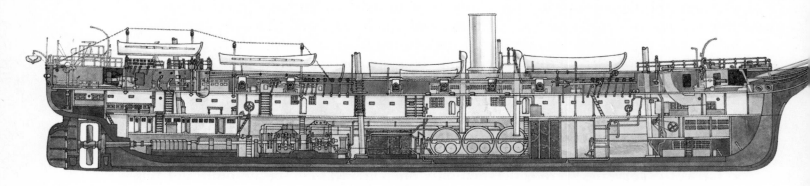

*H.M.S.* Amethyst, *the name ship of the last class of wooden corvettes to be built for the Navy. She was the last wooden cruiser of any kind to be built for the service; launched in 1873, she was ship-rigged.*

*H.M.S.* Niobe. *Launched in 1866, she was a ram-bowed wooden sloop with a fixed screw and a barque rig.*

H.M.S. Beacon, *launched 1867, the name ship of a class of composite built, twin-screw gun vessels built for service in China. They were shallow-draught, their two engines were taken from the hulls of unused and rotten Crimean gun boats. They were rigged as topsail schooners.*

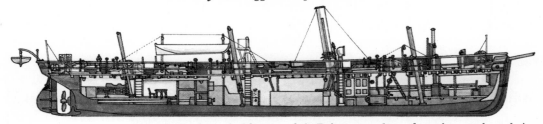

H.M.S. Tyrian *of 1861, one of the* Britomart *class of wooden gun boat designed as an improvement on the Crimean gun boats. She was rigged as a three-mast schooner, with some additional square sails on the foremast.*

H.M.S. ,Skylark, *one of the numerous Crimean gun boats. This one was launched in 1855 and is of the Dapper class. They had little 60 h.p. engines and originally a light schooner rig.*

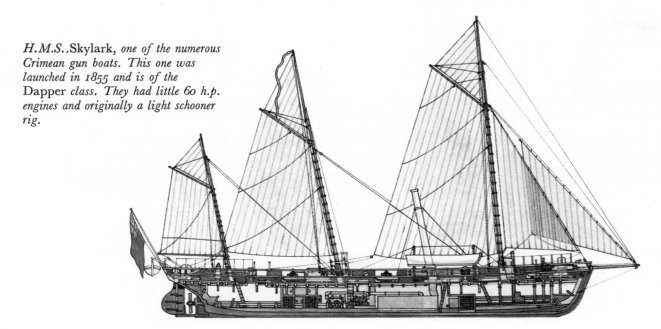

THE FIGHTING SHIP IN THE ROYAL NAVY

a corvette while others had it divided by the engine-room. Some had batteries mounted on the broadside and some on the centre line. In size they averaged about 170 feet between perpendiculars and 36 feet in the beam. Steaming speeds were about 10 knots.

## Steam Gun-vessels and Gunboats

As with the other sailing classes, the sailing gun-brigs became due for replacement by steam-assisted vessels in the 1850s. The gunboats took the place of the brigs as the smallest British ocean-going warships, and the gun-vessels were similarly employed, but were larger.

Six little screw-steamers of the *Arrow* class were already in service at the beginning of the Russian war of 1854 and proved so effective that the Admiralty decided to order a large number, specially designed for use against Russian shore bases and fortresses in the Baltic and Crimea. The views behind this move were firstly that the shallow waters to be found in the Baltic sometimes impeded large units of the fleet getting within effective range, and secondly that it was felt that a large number of small vessels, well dispersed and mounting one or two large-calibre guns, would be less vulnerable to the fire of the Russian shore batteries than a small number of big ships.

As a result the first classes of gunboats were designed not to replace the brigs but for specialised duties in the Baltic and Black Sea, duties which had once been the province of the old bomb-vessels. These Crimean gunboats, as they were called, were given an ugly, almost square-sectioned, flat-bottomed hull, with slab sides and a stem without a knee. In an effort to keep down the weights the masts were stepped in tabernacles on the upper deck, and the original intention was to give them a miserable sail-plan of three dipping lugsails, but this was altered to gaffs of about the same sail area. By the same token small 20, 40 or 60 horse-power engines were installed, giving about 6 to 8 knots. One tall, slender funnel between the boats on davits completed the profile. There were four classes of the Crimean gunboats, varying in rig and horse-power, and altogether no less than one hundred and fifty-six were ordered, though not all by any means were completed. Many were finished too late to take part in the war for which they were designed to fight.

The armament of the first class was intended to be two 68-pounders on slides, but this was increased to three. Later classes had 32-pounders, also mounted on slides, and 24-pounder howitzers on trucks. The howitzer was a short barrelled brass gun which was designed to lob shells at a high trajectory and at low velocity. The large guns were centre-mounted ordinarily but could be moved over the iron traversing-rings to pivots at either side in action. In small ships the effect of moving so great a weight made them heel, so that the angle to which the barrel could be elevated was reduced. One advantage of the light rig and small number of guns was that the crew need only number about thirty-five, and in practice in service might have only a couple of officers aboard, if attached to a ship of the line. This was just as well, for the engines, coal bunkers, magazines and water tanks took up a good two-thirds of the internal space. The officers lived on the platforms aft and the men forward; there was no hold.

After the war some of the Crimean gunboats were refitted with a heavier rig and sent out to distant stations on general service. Their peculiar shape made them lively in heavy weather when they had to be carefully watched, and the shallow draught with no hold meant stowage problems on long passages, but they could do their work well enough. In 1857 and 1860 two further classes based on the Crimean gunboats were built, but with conventionally shaped hulls. Also at this time (1855–60) four classes of the larger gun-vessels were built; and whereas the Crimean gunboat might be 108 feet long, these vessels were between 140 feet and 185 feet. They had proper holds and better accommodation. A typical armament was one 95-cwt 68-pounder rifled-muzzle-loader and four 24-pounder howitzers; all were barque-rigged.

There was then a pause until age and decay made replacements necessary. The three new classes built around 1870 were all shallow draught, twin-screw and of composite construction. With their twin-screws and shallow draughts they were all poor sailers, and were mainly intended for river work against the Chinese. A further four classes of gun-vessel with single-screws and conventional hulls were built for ocean-going service and were about 157 feet long with a beam of 29 feet 6 inches. They were all more heavily built than the gun-vessels of the 1850s to bear the 4½-ton 7-inch rifled-muzzle-loaders as well as the two 68-pounders; or instead of the muzzle-loaders, 64-pounder breech-loaders. The 7-inch was mounted between the funnel and the main-mast, the other two at the bow and stern. They served the Victorian navy until the end of the 1880s when they were replaced by steel third-class cruisers.

With the gunboats all the replacements of the Crimean classes were composite-built. The wooden Crimean boats had in any case lasted badly, having been built in a hurry and the later ones of green wood. The new programme began in 1867 with twenty-two vessels of shallow draught and with twin-screws, and twenty-one conventionally hulled and single-screw. These last were 125 feet between perpendiculars and 23 feet 5 inches in the beam; the twin-screw gunboats were about 30 feet longer. They were all given a barquentine rig and carried two 56-cwt 64-pounder muzzle-loaders and two 20-pounder breech-loading Armstrongs. Some of these in service in the late 1880s were given 5-inch and 4-inch breech-loaders; they could steam at 9 or 10 knots. Altogether one hundred and twenty gun-vessels and two hundred and sixty-two gun-boats were ordered for the navy between the 1850s and early 1880s.

## Gunboat Diplomacy

British gunboat diplomacy often served to prevent an ugly situation becoming much uglier and reflected the greatest credit on the British officers involved. Commander Sir Lambton Loraine Bart, for instance, who from 1871 to 1874 was on the North American station in command of the *Niobe*, strictly speaking a sloop. In 1874 an American ship called the *Virginians*, which unknown to her passengers had been illegally running arms from Haiti to Cuba, was stopped by a Spanish man-of-war on the high seas and taken into Santiago. No arms were found aboard, but the blood-thirsty departmental governor, aptly named General Burriel Lynch, had all aboard declared pirates and thrown into prison, and without informing his superiors and ignoring the protests of the British and American consuls began executing the prisoners after summary trials. On hearing what was going on, the *Niobe* was dispatched by the governor of Jamaica to stop the executions. When Sir Lambton appeared before Lynch he was defied, and so was forced to threaten to sink all the Spanish warships in the harbour. This stopped the executions, and Sir Lambton received the thanks of both Houses of Parliament and the freedom of the City of New York.

# 11

## The Coming of
## the Great Iron Frigate

### Rot in the Wooden Walls

At three o'clock in the afternoon of 23 November 1864, a fine new wooden three-decker sailed from Spithead for Malta on her first commission as flagship of the Mediterranean Fleet. Her name was *Victoria* and she was in every respect the most up-to-date wooden first-rate to go into service. She was also to be the last, and she left in her wake bitter criticism and controversy over the decision to send her out at all. Condemned in the papers and Parliament as a useless hulk and no fighting ship, it was claimed that her only role could be as a floating office-block for the admiral. 'It is not too much to say', commented *The Times* on 16 November, 'that if we were to have a war with France or America, the admiral on board the *Victoria* would have to decide between going into port or going to the bottom.'

What had happened to the prestige of the great wooden liners, which had stood so high ten years before during the war with Russia? Even five years before when the *Victoria* was launched by the Princess Royal she was the most modern and powerful warship afloat. The answer was the introduction of iron armour, from behind which one or two heavy shell-firing guns could knock the stately three-decker into a sinking shambles, a disaster which none of her one hundred and twenty-one guns could prevent.

The official reason for sending out the *Victoria* instead of an ironclad was one of health. Lord Clarence Paget, Secretary of the Admiralty, told his constituents in December that, 'you require to have a roomy well-ventilated ship, aboard of which you may put a vast number of supernumeraries – that is to say, the reinforcements which are constantly being added to the crews of that fleet. If you were to put them on board of armour-plated ships the men would, from want of ventilation, speedily become utterly useless, and have to go into hospital. And therefore, until we can find means of ventilating our armour-plated ships, we must be satisfied to have attached to our squadrons one or more of these large roomy ships.'

Forced-draught ventilation in any ship was nine years away, more in the navy, and certainly the early ironclads, with their frigate layout, were the least comfortable capital ships ever built in Britain. In fact, however, they did not prove especially unhealthy, even in hot climates. The *Caledonia* proved this when she joined the *Victoria* in the Mediterranean and was therefore thought suitable to supersede her, in 1867, as the first ironclad flagship. Ironically, her admiral was Lord Clarence Paget, who, however, suffered no hardship from the lack of ventilation, for a comfortable poop and handsome stern-walk were added to accommodate him.

93

# THE BATTLE-FLEET

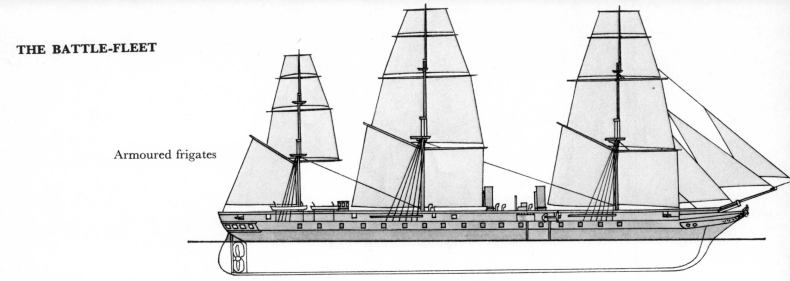

Armoured frigates

**WARRIOR 1860 and BLACK PRINCE 1861**
9,210 *tons* 380′ × 58½′ × 26′. Guns *First armament* (1861) 26 68-*pdrs. M.L.*, 10 110-*pdrs. B.L.*, 4 70-*pdrs. B.L. Second armament* (1867) 28 7″ *M.L.R.* (*BLACK PRINCE* 24 7″ *M.L.R.*), 4 8″ *M.L.R.* Main armour 4½″ *belt* (*sides*), 18″ *teak backing. Engines and speed Trunk; WARRIOR 5,267 h.p., BLACK PRINCE 5,770 h.p.; 13 knots under sail, 14 knots under steam.*

Armoured frigates

**RESISTANCE and DEFENCE, both 1861**
6,070 *tons* 280′ × 54′ × 25′. Guns *DEFENCE* 8 7″ *B.L.*, 10 68-*pdrs. M.L.*, 4 5″ *B.L. RESISTANCE* 6 7″ *B.L.*, 10 68-*pdrs. M.L.*, 2 32-*pdrs. M.L. Rearmed* (1867) 2 8″ *M.L.R.*, 14 7″ *M.L.R.* Main armour 4½″ *belt* (*sides*), 18″ *teak backing. Engines and speed Trunk; DEFENCE 2,540 h.p., RESISTANCE 2,430 h.p.; 10½ knots under sail, 11½ knots under steam. Remarks Painted with a white band like a wooden frigate in their first commission.*

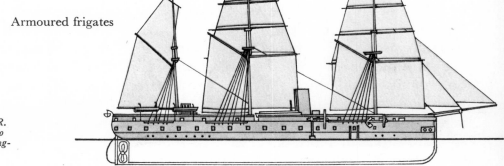

Armoured frigates

**HECTOR 1862 and VALIANT 1863**
6,700 *tons* 280′ × 56¼′ × 24¾′. Guns *HECTOR* 4 7″ *B.L.*, 20 68-*pdrs. M.L. Rearmed* (1867) 2 8″ *M.L.R.*, 16 7″ *M.L.R. VALIANT had the second armament only. Main armour 4½″ to 2½″ belt, 18″ teak backing. Engines and speed Return connecting-rod; HECTOR 3,260 h.p., VALIANT 3,560 h.p.; 10 knots under sail, 12½ knots under steam.*

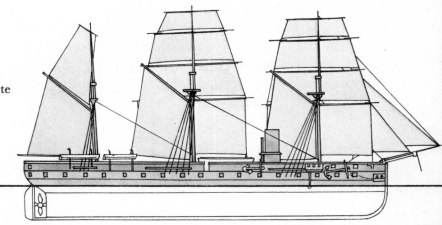

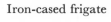

Iron-cased frigate

**ROYAL OAK 1862**
6,360 *tons* 273′ × 58¼′ × 24′. Guns (1863) 11 7″ *B.L.R.*, 24 68-*pdrs. M.L. Rearmed* (1867) 4 8″ *M.L.R.*, 20 7″ *M.L.R.* Main armour 4½″ *to* 3″ *belt. Engines and speed Return connecting rod; 3,000 h.p.; 13½ knots under sail, 12½ knots under steam, range 2,200 miles at 5 knots. Remarks First British wooden-hulled armoured ship.*

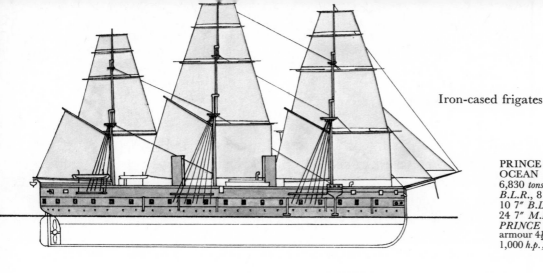

Iron-cased frigates

PRINCE CONSORT 1862, CALEDONIA 1862,
OCEAN 1863
6,830 *tons* 273′ × 58½′ × 26′. Guns *PRINCE CONSORT* 7 7″
*B.L.R.*, 8 100-*pdrs. M.L.*, 16 68-*pdrs. M.L. CALEDONIA*
10 7″ *B.L.R.*, 8 100-*pdrs. M.L.*, 12 68-*pdrs. M.L. OCEAN*
24 7″ *M.L.R. All rearmed* (1867) 4 8″ *M.L.R.*, 20 7″ *M.L.R.*
*PRINCE CONSORT* (1871) 7 9″ *M.L.R.*, 8 8″ *M.L.R.* Main
armour 4½″ *to* 3″ *belt. Engines and speed Return connecting rod;*
1,000 *h.p.*; 10 *to* 11½ *knots under sail*, 12½ *knots under steam.*

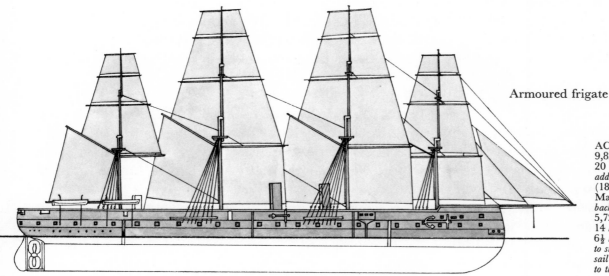

Armoured frigate

ACHILLES 1863
9,820 *tons* 380′ × 58½′ × 27½′. Guns (1864)
20 100-*pdrs. M.L.* (1865) 6 68-*pdrs. M.L.*
*added.* (1868) 22 7″ *M.L.R.*, 4 8″ *M.L.R.*
(1874) 14 9″ *M.L.R.*, 2 7″ *M.L.R.*
Main armour 4½″ *belt*, 18″ *teak*
*backing. Engines and speed Trunk;*
5,720 *h.p.*; *about* 13 *knots under sail and*
14 *knots under steam, range* 1,000 *miles at*
6½ *knots. Remarks The only British warship*
*to step four masts which carried the largest*
*sail area of any warship, she was reduced*
*to three masts in* 1865.

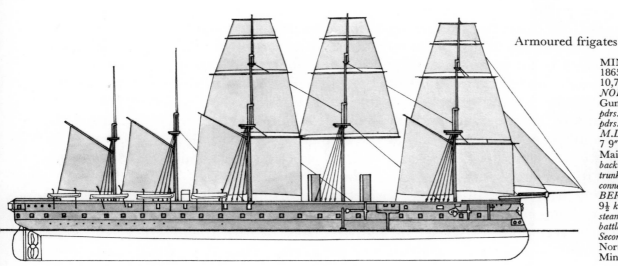

Armoured frigates

MINOTAUR 1863, AGINCOURT
1865, NORTHUMBERLAND 1866
10,700 *tons* 400′ × 59½′ × 27¾′.
*NORTHUMBERLAND* 10,780 *tons.*
Guns 4 9″ *M.L.R.*, 24 7″ *M.L.R.*, 8 24-
*pdrs.. M.L.* (1875) 17 9″ *M.L.R.*, 2 20-
*pdrs. NORTHUMBERLAND* 4 9″
*M.L.R.*, 22 8″ *M.L.R.*, 2 7″ *M.L.R.* (1875)
7 9″ *M.L.R.*, 20 8″ *M.L.R.*, 2 20-*pdrs.*
Main armour 5¾″ *to* 4½″ *belt*, 10″ *teak*
*backing. Engines and speed MINOTAUR*
*trunk;* 6,700 *h.p. AGINCOURT return*
*connecting-rod;* 6,870 *h.p. NORTHUM-*
*BERLAND horizontal trunk;* 6,560 *h.p.*,
9½ *knots under sail*, 14 *to* 14½ *knots under*
*steam. Remarks The only five-masters in any*
*battle-fleet, and among the worst sailers.*
*Second and fourth masts removed in the*
Northumberland *in* 1875, *and in the*
Minotaur *and* Agincourt *in* 1893.

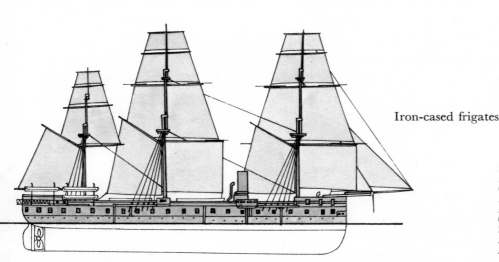

Iron-cased frigates

ZEALOUS and ROYAL ALFRED, both 1864
*ZEALOUS* 6,100 *tons* 252′ × 58½′ × 25′. *ROYAL ALFRED*
6,700 *tons* 273′ × 58½′ × 27′. Guns *ZEALOUS* 20 7″ *M.L.R.*
*ROYAL ALFRED* 10 9″ *M,L.R.*, 8 7″ *M.L.R.* Main armour
*ZEALOUS* 4½″ *to* 2½″ *belt and battery. ROYAL ALFRED belt*
6″ *to* 4″ *Engines and speed ZEALOUS return connecting-rod;*
3,450 *h.p.*; 10 *knots under sail*, 11¾ *knots under steam. ROYAL*
*ALFRED Return connecting rod*; 3,230 *h.p.*; 12½ *knots under sail and*
*steam. Remarks Converted wooden liners.*

We are always regretting the passing of familiar things, so tried and proven, but Their Lordships had more reasons besides nostalgia to regret the demise of the wooden battleship. Saddled with great dockyards geared to wooden building, they had to face up to soaring costs as Victorian technology created the new iron ships. As young Lord Camperdown (who owed his peerage to his great-grandfather's wooden fleet at the Battle of Camperdown) put it in a House of Lords debate in 1869: 'The really comfortable ships were those floating castles, the towering, roomy three-deckers. Hard necessity has forced us to displace such stately structures by floating iron chests, in which the crews are "cribbed, cabined, and confined". We cannot help it. Walking the quarter-deck during a rough sea will soon be a thing of the past; and some day, perhaps, sailors will be as much shut out from the daylight as miners.' This last has come to pass.

## Iron Hulls in the Navy Before 1860

Although the navy did not seriously turn to iron-hulled warships until 1860, for reasons that will follow, some thirty-five iron vessels of various types had been built or bought for it over the previous twenty years. Few of these ever served as warships, or were intended to, and it is fair to ask why it was that the navy dragged so far behind the merchant marine in this field.

There were, in fact, quite cogent reasons for caution. It was peacetime in the 1840s when a large proportion of the fleet was laid up in reserve, so that there was no great need for extensive new building. In the dockyards there were great stocks of timber, and the shipwrights were trained only for wooden building. The expense, too, of building iron ships in private yards was not to be encouraged in time of peace when the Treasury purse-strings were always tightest. Iron hulls for fighting ships were, indeed, positively discredited following firing tests against a lightly-built iron vessel called the *Ruby* in 1840. The results were most disquieting; the *Ruby*'s sides shattered under the blows, sending showers of lethal splinters round the interior, to a much worse degree than was found with an equivalent wooden hull. This brittleness of iron at that time was a perfectly valid objection to its use in warships, and it was not until the improvements of Bessemer and others that it could be used. In the meantime the Admiralty built experimental vessels at the rate of one and a half a year to cover all the cruising types; though as a result of the *Ruby* experiment the four iron frigates then building were converted into transports before going into service.

The earliest iron vessel in the navy was not a warship at all but a cross-Channel postal packet launched in 1840 and called the *Dover*. In the following year three little paddle-vessels were built for service on the west coast of Africa, where it was thought that iron would withstand the climate and the fauna better than wood. After these there was a fairly steady increase in the number of paddle-vessels acquired (see Appendix 2). The first launch of a large iron ship for the navy was the paddle-frigate *Birkenhead* in the town of that name in 1845. She was converted, for reasons already stated, to a trooper, and became the subject of one of the most famous heroic tragedies in maritime history when she foundered on the south coast of Africa in 1852. The other four frigates converted were screw-propelled and launched in 1849; but with these experiences, building major warships in iron languished for ten years.

## Armour

One extraordinary class of vessel emerged in the middle fifties as a result of the Crimean War – the armoured floating-battery. The idea was a French one. They were anxious about the effect of Russian shell-fire on their wooden ships at close range and, in July 1854, conducted a series of firing tests against iron armour. The results were satisfactory and work began immediately on building batteries to go out to the Crimea. As the British were their allies in this war, the plans were passed across to the Admiralty, which immediately ordered the construction of five of them. These wooden-hulled batteries were laid down in October 1854 and two of them were ready in time to sail for the Crimea in 1855, but missed the fighting in which the three French batteries sent out earlier had been so conspicuously successful.

They were very strange-looking craft, being flat-bottomed, flat-sided with a marked tumble-home, and pointed at both ends. Because they were expected to manoeuvre in action they had engines driving a screw and a light sailing rig to help them to their destination. Trials proved them to be abominable sailers and steamers, and almost unmanageable since they would not answer their helms. It was therefore necessary to tow them most of the time, and a long tow it was out to the Crimea and back. Their armour was 4 inches thick and stretched 3 feet below the water-line. It had been intended to have an armoured deck over the gun-deck, but this would have made them draw too much, so an oak one had to suffice. The battery consisted of fourteen or sixteen 68-pounder muzzle-loaders. They were quite large vessels, the bigger type being 186 feet between perpendiculars, or as long as the *Victory*'s gun-deck, and, whereas all the French ones were wooden, the last three British-built vessels were iron-hulled.

These were completed after the war was over and only one of them, the *Terror*, saw any service. On completion she was towed out to Bermuda to be moored in the harbour at Hamilton as the commissioned base and receiving ship, a duty she performed until 1903.

Whatever the shortcomings of the floating-batteries, one lesson was clear: armour could be used successfully to protect a ship's sides, so the next logical step was to armour a conventional sea-going ship. The British thought about it and made no move, since they did not want to make their battle-fleet, then the largest in the world, obsolete. The French, on the other hand, were the world's second navy and perhaps hoped, as they had with their Paixhans shell-firing gun, to become by this means the first. It was an idle thought, since Britain was the world's greatest industrial country, better equipped, by her technical advances and industrial potential, to surpass the French in iron-hulling than she had been before in wood.

In fact all that M. Dupuy de Lome achieved in 1858 was to hang iron plates round a half-built wooden two-decker, to be called the *Gloire*, which he 'razeed', that is, cut down a deck. It was enough, however, to start the furious technical war in the design of iron- and steel-armoured warships which was to continue until the end of the Second World War. The British answer to the *Gloire* was an original conception, entirely made of iron and 130 feet longer than any liner they had ever built. The ship was designed as a great iron-armoured frigate and launched on 29 December 1860 as the *Warrior*.

# THE BATTLE-FLEET

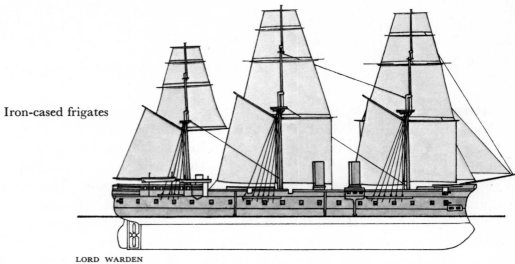

Iron-cased frigates

LORD WARDEN

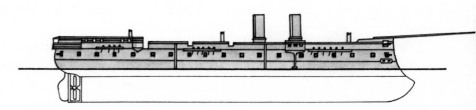

LORD CLYDE

LORD CLYDE 1864 and
LORD WARDEN 1865
*LORD CLYDE 7,750 tons. LORD WARDEN*
*7,940 tons* 280′×59′×27′. Guns *LORD CLYDE*
(1866) 24 7″ *M.L.R.*, (1870) 2 9″ *B.L.*, 14 8″
*M.L.R.*, 2 7″ *M.L.R.*, 2 20-pdrs. B.L. LORD
*WARDEN* (1867) *as LORD CLYDE in* 1870.
Main armour 5½″ to 4½″ belt, oak hull 31½″ thick.
Engines and speed *LORD CLYDE trunk; 6,700 h.p.*
*LORD WARDEN return connecting-rod; 6,700 h.p.,*
*10 knots under sail, 13½ knots under steam.* Remarks
*The heaviest wooden hulls ever built.*

Central-battery armoured ship

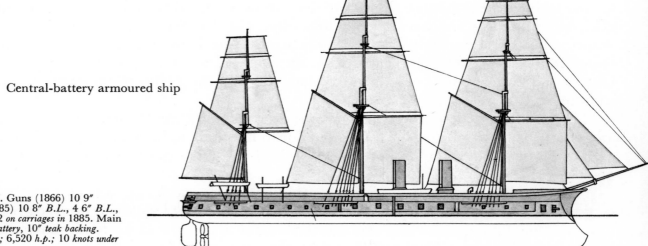

BELLEROPHON 1865
*7,550 tons* 300′×56′×26′. Guns (1866) 10 9″
*M.L.R.*, 5 7″ *M.L.R.* (1885) 10 8″ *B.L.*, 4 6″ *B.L.*,
6 4″ *B.L.* Torpedo tubes 2 *on carriages in* 1885. Main
armour 6″ to 5″ belt and battery, 10″ teak backing.
Engines and speed *Trunk; 6,520 h.p.; 10 knots under*
*sail, 14 knots under steam.*

Iron-cased central-battery ship

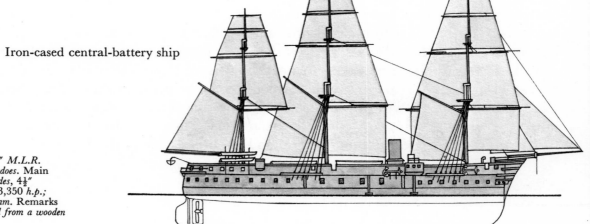

REPULSE 1868
*6,190 tons* 252′×59′×26′. Guns 12 8″ *M.L.R.*
Torpedo tubes 4 *carriages for* 16″ *torpedoes.* Main
armour 6″ to 4½″ belt, box battery 6″ sides, 4½″
*bulkheads.* Engines and speed *Trunk; 3,350 h.p.;*
*10½ knots under sail, 12½ knots under steam.* Remarks
*Last ship in the battle-fleet to be converted from a wooden*
*liner.*

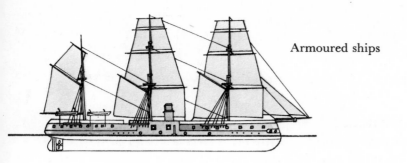

Armoured ships

RESEARCH 1863
1,743 *tons* 195′ × 38′ × 16′. Guns (1864) 4 100-*pdrs.*
*M.L.* (1870) 4 7″ *M.L.R.* Main armour 4½″ *belt and box
battery, 19½″ teak backing. Engines and speed Horizontal
direct-acting*; 1,040 *h.p.*; *about 6 knots under sail and 10
knots under steam. Remarks First small ironclad.*

ENTERPRISE 1864
1,350 *tons* 180′ × 36′ × 15′. Guns (1864) 2 100-*pdrs.
M.L.*, 2 110-*pdrs. B.L.* (1868) 4 7″ *M.L.R.* Main
armour 4½″ *belt and battery, 19½″ teak backing. Engines
and speed Horizontal direct-acting*; 690 *h.p.*; 9¾ *knots
under sail and steam.*

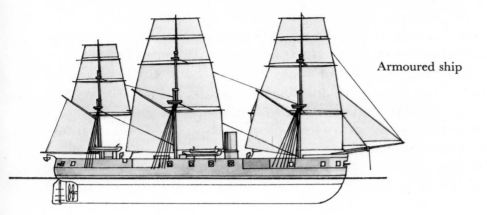

Armoured ship

FAVORITE 1864
3,230 *tons* 225′ × 47′ × 23′. Guns (1866) 8 100-*pdrs.
M.L.* (1869) 8 7″ *M.L.R.*, 2 68-*pdrs. M.L.* Main
armour 4½″ *belt with 26″ teak backing, 4½″ battery with
19″ teak backing. Engines and speed Horizontal direct-
acting*; 1,770 *h.p.*; *under sail about 10 knots, 11¾ knots
under steam.*

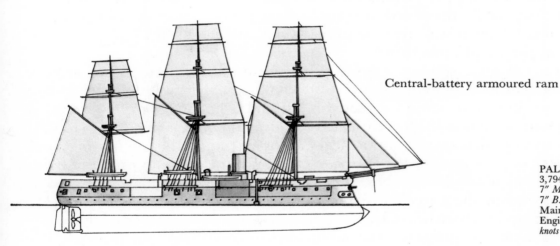

Central-battery armoured ram

PALLAS 1865
3,794 *tons* 225′ × 50′ × 24′. Guns (1866 – *as completed*) 4
7″ *M.L.R.*, 2 7″ *B.L.*, (1866 – *rearmed*) 4 8″ *M.L.R.*, 2
7″ *B.L.*, 2 5″ *B.L.* (1871) 4 8″ *M.L.R.*, 4 6″ *M.L.R.*
Main armour 4½″ *belt and battery, 22″ teak backing.
Engines and speed Compound horizontal*; 3,580 *h.p.*; 9½
*knots under sail, 13 knots under steam.*

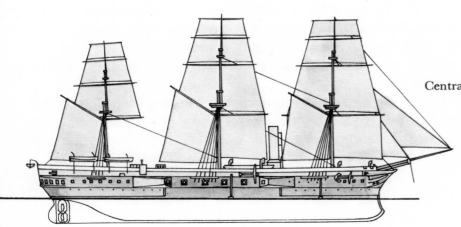

Central-battery iron-cased ship

PENELOPE 1867
4,470 *tons* 265′ × 50′ × 17′. Guns 8 8″ *M.L.R.*, 3 5″
*B.L.R.* Main armour 6″ *to 5″ belt and battery with
10″–11″ teak backing. Engines and speed Return
connecting-rod*; 4,700 *h.p.*; 8½ *knots under sail, 12¾ knots
under steam. Remarks Hoisting twin screws and twin
rudders.*

## The *Warrior* and the Broadside Ironclads

'Is not your Majesty tired of this foolish game?' inquired Lord Palmerston, as he trumped the French Emperor's *Gloire* with his *Warrior*, in a Punch cartoon called 'Beggar my Neighbour', published in March 1861. We are not told what Louis Napoleon replied; but it does not matter, as we know that the men were the prisoners of the cards, and must play on until they could not afford to play any more. The French, who never looked like catching the British, were in fifty years outbid by the Americans, the Germans and the Japanese as well. It was another fifty years before the Royal Navy, though victorious in war to the end, had to throw its hand in; beaten not by any adversary but by the game itself, which is not about war so much as technology and the ever-soaring costs of its advances. Just now it is the Americans and Russians who can afford the world's largest fleets, but the technological costs are beginning to catch up with them, and their navies may wither away by the end of the century for lack of funds to build and maintain the type of equipment that will then be available.

The *Warrior* was the biggest advance on previous warship designs made in the history of naval warfare, and the biggest ever to be made until the building of the first nuclear submarine. It was not so much her general design (basic layout was that of a conventional frigate) but her iron construction that enabled her to be so big that she could carry the heavier guns and the proof armour, and be subdivided into watertight compartments below, a thing not possible in a wooden ship. Of course she did cost £377,292 against £105,000 for the wooden frigate *Undaunted*, launched in the same week; but what of that if the *Warrior* was superior to the *Gloire*, and the British kept the lead over the French in the naval arms race?

The length of the *Warrior*, 380 feet between perpendiculars, had been arrived at by an original requirement for a battery mounting fifteen 68-pounder guns on a tier with 15 feet between each gun, and beyond a good run aft and a fine long bow to give her speed. Her maximum beam was 58½ feet with a 26-foot draught, and she was 9,210 tons. Her frigate form was decided by the impracticability of extending the armour-belt to more than one deck of guns and, in the *Warrior*'s case, not for the whole length of the hull. It took the form of an oblong box 213 feet long, stretching down from her upper-deck to 6 feet below the water-line, 22 feet deep in all. The iron armour was 4½ inches thick, backed up by 18 inches of teak. At each end was an armoured bulkhead, leaving the bow and stern unprotected but subdivided to compensate for the lack of protection. It had been intended that she should mount a uniform armament of 68-pounder smooth-bore muzzle-loaders on slides, but before completion the 110-pounder breech-loading rifled gun firing conical shell had become available and ten of these were installed, eight in the armoured area and two as bow and stern chasers on the upper-deck. In addition four 70-pounder B.L.s on trucks were on the quarter-deck, mainly for saluting purposes. The rest of the armament consisted of twenty-six 68-pounder muzzle-loading smooth bores which were all on the gun-deck, eighteen inside the armour-belt and eight without.

This assembly of heavy guns was far and away superior to anything seen before and made the *Warrior* invincible. A measure of her modernity was her breech-loading rifled guns firing conical shell in 1861, while over twenty years later the best American naval gun was a muzzle-loading smooth bore firing spherical shell. The Armstrong breech-loader was before its time and had its troubles, which resulted in their being removed in 1867 and replaced with rifled muzzle-loaders, which became standard in the navy until the 1880s.

The *Warrior*'s engines, the most powerful then fitted in a warship, were of the horizontal trunk type, designed to give her 14 knots for 5,000 horsepower. The armoured masted fleet did not sail well because of the weight of the armour, but the *Warrior* was one of the best, with a maximum speed under sail of 13 knots. Such then was the forebear of all British armoured ships, and strangely she was to last the longest; for she is still afloat over a hundred years later, many years after the last British battleship has gone to the scrap-yard.

When applied to the *Warrior*, the system of rating men-of-war in 1861 produced a curious anomaly. She was first called an armoured frigate because of her layout; this was unsatisfactory as frigates were cruisers. The number of her guns and hence her complement fell far short of that laid down for a first-rate: six hundred and seventy against over a thousand. She was therefore made a third-rate and her captain's pay adjusted accordingly. The difficulty was not really resolved until the introduction of the word 'battleship' in the 1880s.

Eleven iron-built and nine wooden-hulled ironclads, armed on the broadside principle, followed the *Warrior* in the 1860s. Of the iron-hulled ships, five were of the largest type. The *Black Prince* was sister to the *Warrior*, while the straight-bowed *Achilles* was the only four-masted ship in the black battle-fleet; she was also the first iron ship to be built in a royal dockyard, being floated out at Chatham in 1863. The other three were the famous ram-bowed five-masters *Minotaur*, *Agincourt* and *Northumberland*. The first two were true sisters and differed from the *Warrior* in having an armour-belt the whole length of the hull. This meant that there was no need for armoured bulkheads to interrupt the splendid view of 400 feet of gun-deck. Because of their imposing appearance these ships were natural flagships, and they acted as such continuously in the Channel Squadron for twenty years. The *Northumberland* did not have much share of this glory, but was in the end the last to wear a flag, in 1890, by which time the *Admiral* class was completed, and the old *Minotaurs* rendered antediluvian. The *Northumberland* was a modified *Minotaur* as she had transverse armoured bulkheads and was armed in a different manner within the box. She was the first ship in the navy to have power-assisted steering, the lack of which had become a serious problem in such large ships. During the summer cruise of 1868 the Channel Squadron struck some heavy weather and the *Agincourt*, then new, with fifteen men on her four-tier wheel and seventy on the relieving tackles, still took charge on occasion. All these ships were later fitted with steam steering gear.

The remaining five were smaller, cheaper ships; two of them, the *Resistance* and *Defence*, were laid down in 1859, the same year as the *Warrior* and the *Black Prince*, and they revived the ram bow, instead of *Warrior*'s graceful knee, which though less beautiful was more practical. They were unique also in the armoured fleet in being painted with the broad white frigate strake in their early days, all the other ships from the *Warrior* being painted black, except many years later the *Alexandra* which was white when she was flagship in the Mediterranean. Two rather similar ships, the *Hector* and *Valiant*, followed; the main difference being in the armour-belt which stretched the whole length of the hull instead of being boxed in *Warrior* style, as in *Resistance* and *Defence*. Last of the iron broadside ships was Reed's *Bellerophon*, launched in 1865 and built on the double bracket-frame system. This framing was cellular instead of solid, forming the double bottom and thus saving a lot of weight. The *Bellerophon* was for most of the time between 1873 and 1892 the flagship on the North America station.

The other broadside ironclads were wooden-hulled and were called iron-cased ships. They fell into two categories, those that were converted wooden liners and those that were built as ironclads. The decision to convert the seven two-deckers which were then building arose from the threat of the French navy out-building the British; so that the conversion of these wooden ships to armoured ships was an economical method of keeping ahead, as well as a practical means of doing so since the dockyards were used to building in wood, not iron, and the civilian yards with experience in iron-building were already overtaxed. The two-deckers were lengthened by 21 feet to accommodate their machinery and armour, which in itself stiffened the hulls to a great extent, though it did not entirely eradicate sagging and straining in the wooden hulls.

The first of the converted two-deckers, the *Royal Oak*, was completed in 1863 at a cost of over £250,000, which was a good deal less than the cost of one of the large iron ships, and she was at least the match of the French ironclads. She was followed into the service by the *Prince Consort* (1864), the *Caledonia* (1865), which went out to the Mediterranean as our first armoured flagship, the *Ocean* (1866), the *Zealous* (1866), the *Royal Alfred* (1867) and finally the *Repulse* (1870). All had been laid down in 1859 or 1860 as ninety-gun wooden liners and five of them were lengthened from the original 252 feet to 273 feet, the exceptions being *Zealous* and *Repulse*. They all had a steaming speed of over 12 knots, and the most notable difference between the early ones and the late ones to complete was the change in armament. As gun calibres got bigger so fewer guns could be carried and, whereas the *Royal Oak* in her first commission in 1863 mounted sixteen guns to a tier, the *Repulse* of 1870 mounted only four. It cannot be said that these ships gave very good value, since, with the exception of the *Repulse*, none was in service more than ten years after completion, and some of them less. Because of their small size they tended to spend their commission on foreign stations.

The two most interesting wooden ironclads were the *Lord Clyde* launched in 1864 and the *Lord Warden* in 1865. These two ships were not conversions but new wooden hulls designed from the beginning to be iron-cased, and were slightly larger than the rest of the wooden ironclads. They carried an extra inch of armour, making 5½ inches, as well as engines of twice the power, which in fact gave them only about one extra knot.

The decision to build them was taken mainly in order to use up the great stocks of timber in Pembroke and Chatham dockyards, and certainly plenty of timber went into them. They had a framework of oak ribs 2 feet thick, filled between with oak; outside this was a skin of 1½-inch iron plates, and over them a 6-inch oak layer as backing for the armour; over the armour beneath the water-line was a sheathing of 4 inches of oak, and the whole bottom was sheathed with Muntz metal. Though sisters, the *Lord Clyde*, completing first, was given a battery of twenty-four 7-inch M.L.R. guns whereas the

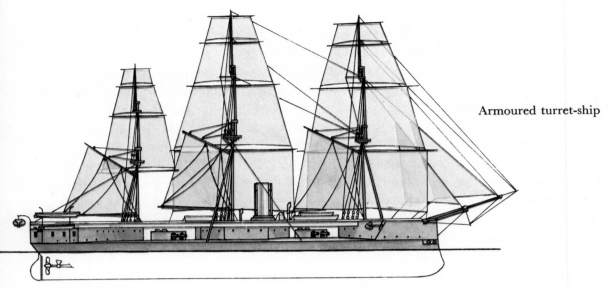

Armoured turret-ship

CAPTAIN 1869
7,767 tons 320′ × 53½′ × 25½′. Guns 4 12″ M.L.R., 2 7″ M.L.R. Main armour 7″ to 4″ belt, 10″ to 8″ turrets. Engines and speed Trunk; 5,400 h.p.; about 13 knots under sail, 14 knots under steam. Remarks Among the early experimental masted ironclads, the Captain proved the one fatal design.

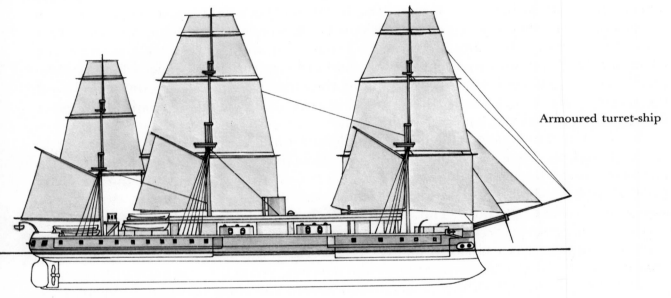

Armoured turret-ship

MONARCH 1868
8,300 tons 330′ × 57½′ × 26′. Guns (1869) 4 12″ M.L.R. (1871) 4 12″ M.L.R., 2 9″ M.L.R. 1 7″ M.L.R. Main armour 7½″ to 4½″ sides, 4½″ bulkheads, 10″ to 8″ turrets. Engines and speed Return connecting-rod; 7,840 h.p.; 13 knots under sail, 15 knots under steam. Remarks First turret-ship in the battle-fleet.

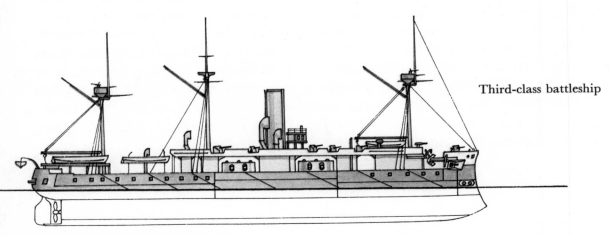

Third-class battleship

MONARCH 1868 (as modernized 1897)
As before. Guns As before. Main armour As before. Engines and speed Triple expansion; 8,216 h.p., 15¾ knots, range 6,000 miles. Remarks Her 45 years on the effective list constituted the longest service of any ship in the armoured battle-fleet. Her modernization refit took seven years.

*Lord Warden* completed with mixed calibre M.L.R. guns; also there was a difference in their bows, the *Lord Clyde* having a pronounced and elegant ram.

Their histories are interesting, too. While the *Lord Warden* completed eighteen years of honourable active service, including six as flagship of the Mediterranean Fleet, the poor *Lord Clyde* had a short and deeply troubled career. Her engines, unlike her sister's which were of the return connecting-rod type, were trunk engines, the largest fitted up to that time, and their torque was too much for even her wooden hull, so that their oscillations wore them out in two years. Worse than this was the amount of green timber that had gone into her construction, the stocks of seasoned timber at Pembroke having been insufficient. In 1868, she was sent home from Malta in the middle of her first commission to be re-engined and the opportunity was taken at the same time to re-arm her like her sister. Back in the Mediterranean in 1871 she ran ashore at Pantellaria six months after her arrival and was badly damaged. Sent home to Plymouth for repairs, it was found that a virulent form of fungus had attacked her damaged bottom. For three years the dockyard shipwrights wrestled with her disease, but every palliative failed, and she was sold in 1875 for a meagre £3,730.

Living conditions aboard all the frigate-type ironclads were uncomfortable for the officers, but not too bad for the men. The latter had been brought up from below the gun-deck, where they had messed and slept in the wooden frigates, to mess and sleep between the guns. The officers, however, if they were to have their cabins and ward-room bulkheads made permanent fixtures, had to be on the deck below, which is where they were housed. This was two decks below the natural light and air source and, with the scuttles, if any, so close to the water that they could be opened only in harbour, the atmosphere was gloomy and malodorous.

Under sail the wooden-hulled and smaller iron-hulled ships could make 10 or 11 knots, though the *Royal Oak* once logged 13½ knots in a gale, but were not steady gun-platforms, since they rolled so heavily. The *Lord Clyde* and her sister were the worst, the *Repulse* the best. The worst performers under sail were the five-masters which never logged more than 9½ knots. The *Achilles*, which started life with a four-masted rig, carried the biggest spread of canvas ever seen in a warship, 44,000 square feet, and even when reduced to three masts still had the largest rig in the fleet. She was a splendid sea boat and a steady gun-platform, though she never equalled the *Warrior*'s 13 knots.

Although by the 1870s the earlier broadside ironclads had become obsolete, their armour too thin and their guns too light, the Admiralty continued to hold them in high regard, especially the six longest; that is the three five-masters, the *Minotaur*, the *Agincourt*, the *Northumberland*, the *Warrior*, the *Black Prince* and the *Achilles*. By 1879 it was agreed that they should be regarded as cruisers for commerce protection, but they still continued in the battle-fleet. One of the reasons was that there was plenty of accommodation space, which was especially valuable to a flagship which had to accommodate the admiral's staff. As late as 1888 the Director of Naval Construction, the constructor's title since 1875, submitted that all iron-armoured ships should be kept fit for possible service, as in the event of a war the poorest of them would prove useful when better ones on either side had been put out of action. It was this attitude that led to the *Minotaur* being re-boilered as late as 1893.

# 12

## Turret Versus Broadside

'If of your antipathy I am the Narcissus, then you are free to pine into a sound with hating me.' That an eminent public servant should write this line in a letter to be published in a national newspaper is an indication of the contentious nature of the debate on the design of our ironclads in the 1860s. The writer was Edward Reed, Chief Constructor of the Royal Navy, who ever afterwards was known as 'Narcissus' Reed, and the words were part of a reply to a letter of wholesale condemnation of his policies, which appeared in the *Standard* in April 1868, signed 'A Flag Officer'.

Before pursuing the reasons for the conflict, let us regard for a moment the men responsible for the design and construction of Britain's warships, the Chief Surveyors of the navy. Captain Sir William Symonds retired in 1847, having introduced the first steam-assisted line of battleship the previous year. A change in the organization then occurred, as his successor, Captain Sir Baldwin Wake-Walker, for the first time was not a naval architect. He administered the department while the design work was carried out by the assistant surveyors. A few months before his retirement in 1860 a further reorganization involved changing the title of Chief Surveyor to Chief Constructor.

They created the latest and largest of the steam-assisted wooden liners in a heavy building programme until 1859 when they were faced with the challenge of the French ironclad *Gloire*, and a demand for an ironclad battle-fleet. On Sir Baldwin's retirement Isaac Watts was promoted in his place, which office he kept for three years. He was responsible for all the frigate-type broadside-armed ironclads, both the long-hulled iron-built ones and the wooden-built ships, including the converted ninety-gun liners. In addition he was the designer of the navy's first iron turret-ship, the coast-defence monitor *Prince Albert*, which will be described later.

When Isaac Watts retired in 1863, the choice of his successor was an unusual one, firstly because he was brought in from outside the service and secondly because he was only thirty-three years old. Edward James Reed did in fact start his career in the surveying department, but soon left for private work as a naval architect. He had submitted plans to the Admiralty from time to time; an ironclad frigate in 1854, a central-battery ship in 1861, and plans to convert wooden ships into ironclads in 1862. It was this last project that found favour with the Board and he was taken on to construct two ships which later appeared as the *Pallas* and *Bellerophon*. During his office as Chief Constructor he favoured the central-battery type of ironclad, short-hulled for manoeuvrability and with a good ram. He opposed the centre-line turret system in rigged ships

### AUDACIOUS Class
### central-battery armoured ships

AUDACIOUS 1869, INVINCIBLE 1869,
IRON DUKE 1870, VANGUARD 1870
6,010 *tons* 280′ × 54′ × 23′. Guns 10 9″ *M.L.R.*,
4 6″ *M.L.R.* Main armour 8″ *to* 6″ *belt*, 6″ *to* 4″
*battery*, 5″ *to* 4″ *bulkheads*, 10″ *teak backing.* Engines
and speed *2 horizontal return connecting-rod; 4,830 h.p.;
about 10 knots under sail, 13 knots under steam.* Remarks
*Steady ships, but their twin screws and light draught
make them poor sailers.*

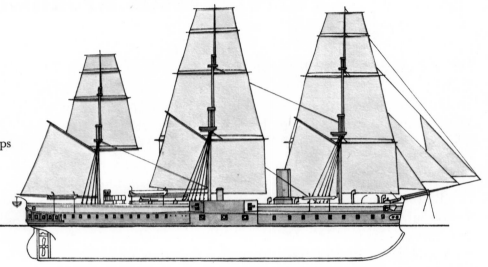

### Central-battery armoured ships

SWIFTSURE and TRIUMPH, both 1870
*SWIFTSURE* 6,910 *tons*, *TRIUMPH* 6,640 *tons*
280′ × 55′ × 26′. Guns 10 9″ *M.L.R.*, 4 6″ *M.L.R.* Main
armour 8″ *to* 6″ *belt*, 6″ *to* 4″ *battery*, 5″ *to* 4″ *bulkheads*, 10″
*teak backing.* Engines and speed *One return connecting-rod;
SWIFTSURE 4,910 h.p., TRIUMPH 4,890 h.p.; about 12½
knots under sail, 13¾ knots under steam.* Remarks *Last ships in
the battle-fleet to have hoisting screws.*

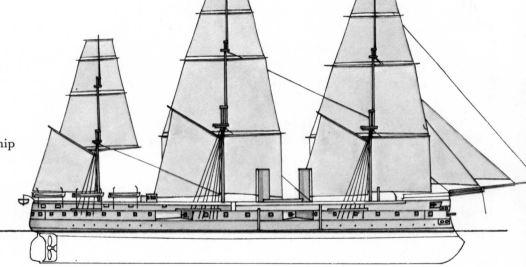

### Central-battery armoured ship

HERCULES 1868
8,680 *tons* 325′ × 59′ × 26′. Guns 8 10″
*M.L.R.*, 2 9″ *M.L.R.*, 4 7″ *M.L.R.* (1892)
6·4·7″ *Q.F.*; later replaced by 2 6″ *Q.F.*
Main armour 9″ *to* 5″ *belt and bulkheads.*
Engines and speed *Trunk; 6,750 h.p.;
11 knots under sail, 14¼ knots under steam,
range 1,600 miles at 8 knots.*

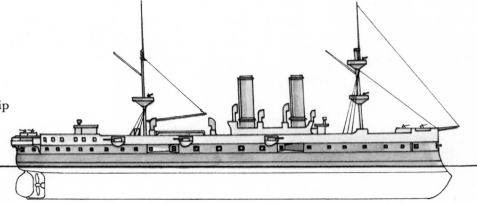

### Third-class battleship

HERCULES 1868 (as modernized in 1893)
*As before.* Guns 8 10″ *M.L.R.*, 2 9″ *M.L.R.*, 2 7″ *M.L.R.*, 2
6″ *Q.F.*, 6 4.7″ *Q.F.* Main armour *As before.* Engines and
speed *Triple expansion; 8,500 h.p.; 14½ knots.*

because its field of fire was so limited, though he had to build one, the *Monarch*, in 1869. The following year he resigned his post to return to the commercial world, and in 1871 set up in private practice as a naval architect again, later entering Parliament, where he became a gad-fly on naval matters, attacking the Admiralty's every constructional project. In spite of this Reed had not built his last ship to serve in the Royal Navy. In 1903 two battleships being privately built for the Chilean Government to the designs of Sir Edward, as he was by then, were purchased by the British Government. Like two of his central-battery ships of thirty years before, they were added as the *Swiftsure* and *Triumph*. Earlier, in 1878, the British Government had purchased his masted turret-ship *Neptune* and his central-battery ship *Superb*.

The controversy in the 1860s over the best type of ironclad to build arose mainly from the introduction of heavier guns in the main battery; and from the problem of how best to distribute the ever-thickening armour. In combination this meant a sharp decrease in the number of guns carried, which made it possible also to shorten the armour-belt protecting the gun-deck, so that the later broadside ironclads housed a main battery of a dozen guns or less in a relatively small armoured box amidships. This shrinkage decreased the battery's field of fire, when it was essential to increase the field of fire of individual guns as the number carried decreased. One answer was to put them into revolving turrets, and this would have been agreeable to all if it had not been for the continued requirement for masts and sails, and the mass of rigging that was necessary to hold them up. It was most difficult to fire a large gun from the centre-line of the upper-deck of a masted ship without bringing a lot of gear down around one's ears.

All sorts of devices were used to keep the field of fire as clear as possible: notably the tripod mast instead of shrouds, and a flying-deck over the turret to which the running rigging was brought. Further limitations to the turrets' fields of fire resulted from their position in the ship. Because of their weight they tended to be carried, at any rate in the smaller ships, on the same decks as the main armament of a broadside ship, but ideally the turret-ships' sides would stop at gun-deck height to give the guns an all-round field of fire. The limitations imposed by a full rig have already been mentioned, but such a ship would have a very low freeboard which would make working the head-sails, or indeed being on deck at all, very hazardous in anything but the calmest weather. Add to this the crew accommodation problem and the lack of stability of such a low-freeboard ship when she heeled to the wind, then the arguments for the provision of a considerable poop and fo'c'sle are irresistible. Once hemmed in by these structures the turrets' guns lose any sort of capability for end-on fire, which would be a serious disability in a chase action.

In the case of the *Captain*, her fatal weakness was that, with her turrets at gun-deck level and despite poop and fo'c'sle, there was not enough stability in the hull when her sails heeled the ship over against the water, so that one day she turned over and sank, taking with her all but seventeen seamen and the gunner who got ashore in the pinnace. Among those drowned were the designer, Captain Cowper Coles, and the midshipman son of Mr Hugh Childers, the First Lord, who had been sent to her by his father to show his confidence in Coles's ship against the views of his Chief Constructor, Edward Reed.

Armoured turret-ships

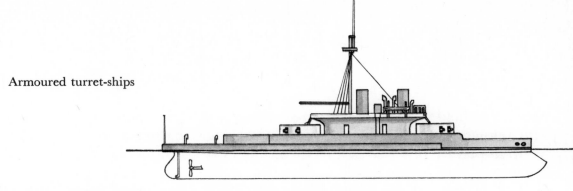

**DEVASTATION 1871 and THUNDERER 1872**
9,330 *tons* 285' × 62¼' × 27½'. Guns *DEVASTATION* 4 35-*ton* 12" *M.L.R. THUNDERER* 2 35-*ton* 12" *M.L.R.*, 2 38-*ton* 12" *M.L.R.*
(1891) *both converted to* 10" *B.L.R.* Main armour 12" to 8½" sides and breastwork, 14" to 10" turrets, 9" to 6" conning tower, 3" to 2" deck,
18" teak backing. Engines and speed *DEVASTATION trunk*; 6,650 *h.p.*; 13¾ knots, range 4,700 miles at 10 knots. *THUNDERER*
*horizontal direct-acting*; 6,270 *h.p.*; 13 knots, range 4,700 miles at 10 knots. (1891) *both ships triple expansion*; 7,000 *h.p.*; 14 knots. Remarks *The first*
*mastless turret-ships in the battle-fleet.*

Armoured turret-ship

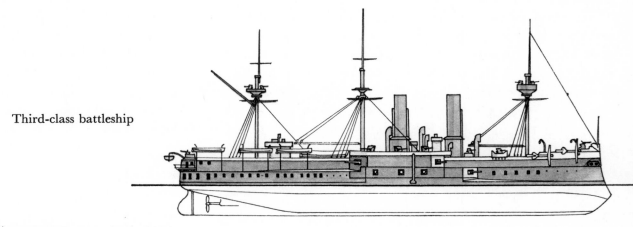

**DREADNOUGHT 1875**
10,886 *tons* 320' × 63¾' × 26¾'. Guns 4 38-*ton* 12½" *M.L.R.*, 6 6-*pdrs.* Main armour 14" to 8" sides, 14" turrets, 13" bulkheads, 14" to 6" conning
*tower*, 3" to 2½" deck, 18" teak backing. Engines and speed *Compound vertical triple expansion*; 8,210 *h.p.*; 14 knots, range 5,700 miles at 10 knots.
Remarks *The first naval ship to have forced ventilation.*

Central-battery armoured ship

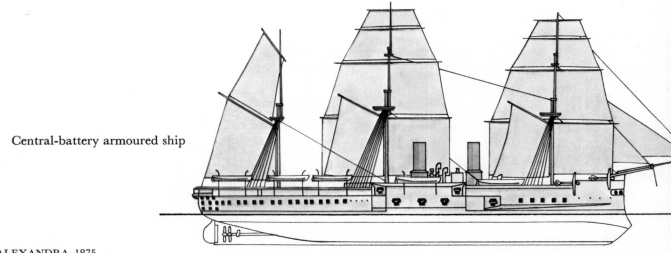

**ALEXANDRA 1875**
9,490 *tons* 325' × 63¾' × 26½'. Guns 2 11" *M.L.R.*, 10 10" *M.L.R.*, 6 13-*cwt B.L.* Torpedo tubes 4 *torpedo carriages*. Main armour 12" to
6" sides, 8" to 5" bulkheads, 1½" deck, 12" teak backing. Engines and speed *Vertical inverted compound*; 8,610 *h.p.*; 15 knots, 6 knots under sail.

Third-class battleship

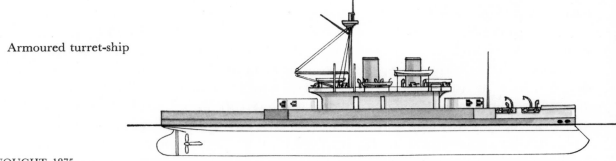

**ALEXANDRA 1875 (as modernized 1891)**
Guns 4 9·2" *B.L.*, 8 10" *M.L.R.*, 6 4" *B.L. Q.F.* (1898) 4" *exchanged for* 4·7". Torpedo tubes *As before*. Main armour *As before*.
Engines and speed *As before*.

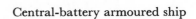

Central-battery armoured ship

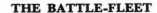

SULTAN 1870
9,290 *tons* 325′ × 59′ × 28′. Guns 8 10″ *M.L.R.*, 4 9″
*M.L.R.*, 7 20-*pdrs. B.L.R.* Main armour 9″ to 6″
belt, 9″ main-deck battery, 8″ upper-deck battery, 12″ teak
backing. Engines and speed *Trunk;* 7,720 h.p.; about
12½ knots under sail, 14 knots under steam. Remarks 7 4″ B.L.
guns and 4 14″ torpedo carriages added in 1879.

Third-class battleship

SULTAN 1870 (as modernized 1896)
*Beam increased by* 18″. Guns 4 4·7″ added to the upper-
deck amidships in place of the 4″ B.L., 32 light Q.F. added.
Main armour *As before.* Engines and speed *Triple
expansion;* 6,531 h.p.; 14½ knots.

Armoured turret-ship

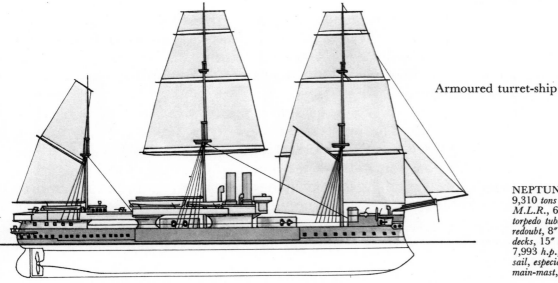

NEPTUNE 1878
9,310 *tons* 300′ × 63′ × 25′. Guns 4 12″ *M.L.R.*, 2 9″
*M.L.R.*, 6 20-*pdrs. B.L.* Torpedo tubes 2 14″
torpedo tubes. Main armour 12″ to 9″ belt, 10″ to 8″
redoubt, 8″ to 6″ bulkheads, and conning tower, 3″ to 2″
decks, 15″ teak backing. Engines and speed *Trunk;*
7,993 h.p.; 14 knots. Remarks *A poor performer under
sail, especially after the yards were taken off the
main-mast, because the funnel smoke rotted the rigging.*

Third-class battleship

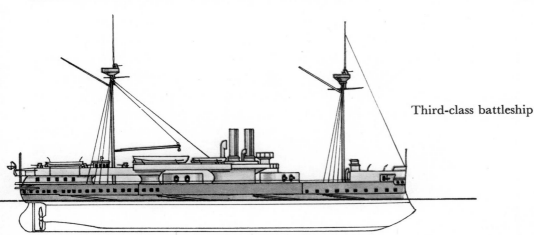

NEPTUNE 1878 (as refitted 1886)
Remarks *In 1886 her sailing rig was removed and
replaced by two masts with military tops.*

The *Captain* disaster in September 1870 was the culmination of nearly ten years of controversy in which the chief protagonists had been Reed and Coles, and two months before the latter drowned for his principles, Reed had resigned his office, largely because he was at odds with Childers. Certainly, on the issue of freeboard, Reed was cruelly justified. His own sea-going turret-armed ironclad, the *Monarch*, which had been in commission for a year before the *Captain* appeared and which was built against his inclinations at the behest of the Board, had her turrets a deck higher than those of the *Captain*. This her size made her able to bear, and with a freeboard of 14 feet against the *Captain*'s 9 feet she was safe in any weather.

Cowper Coles was a naval captain who had brought his ideas home from the Crimean War where he had had some success with guns mounted on rafts. He was a gifted amateur who believed in the low-freeboard turret-ship without fully appreciating its perils. It has been popularly put about that the *Captain* was lost because the Admiralty insisted on a full sail-plan on top of Coles's design: but this is nonsense; the poor fuel economy of marine steam-engines of the middle 1860s, not to mention the poor coaling facilities, made a sailing rig an essential item for any ocean-going ship's make-up. The collier with her steam derricks for coaling at sea had not been evolved. Coles never doubted that the *Captain* must have a sailing rig, and grandly chose a number one; indeed she had the tallest and heaviest masts in the fleet. However, if Coles's services ended in disaster for himself and his big ironclad, his achievements on a smaller scale were most valuable both as an example and for the experience that was gained from them.

## The Coast-Defence Ship

From the very beginning of the introduction of armour, there had crept in the belt-and-braces theory of defence that a fleet to keep the seas was not enough, and that smaller, heavily armoured ships with a small steaming radius should be employed for harbour defence. Along with these were built a rash of static fortifications and sea towers: the French did the same.

The coast-defence ships were all armoured ships, mostly with a minimal rig. The first one was Coles's brain-child. The new three-decker *Royal Sovereign* was cut down to her gun-deck upon which were placed four turrets, three mounting one, and one mounting two 300-pounder guns, on slides. The whole of her exposed hull to a depth of 3 feet below the water-line was covered in 5½ inches of armour, and the turrets in 10 inches. On her appearance in 1864 she was certainly a formidable fighting ship, and she was less restricted in her sphere of action than some later ones, being quite able to operate throughout the Channel, where she would have been much more than a match for any French ironclad.

The other early coast-defence ship, and the first British iron-built turret-ship, was an original design by Isaac Watts, though not completed until four years after his retirement, in 1867. She had four turrets, or 'cupolas' as they were then often called, spaced on the centre-line, two forward and two aft. She had a very light fore and aft rig on two masts, no poop or fo'c'sle, but 5-foot iron bulwarks that hinged outwards when she cleared for action, and otherwise gave her that much more freeboard. She was a trim-looking craft – not antique-looking even now – and somewhat before her time. For all that, she would not have lasted in service for thirty-three years had not Queen Victoria requested that she should be spared redundancy because of her name: the *Prince Albert*.

The two other little early turret-ships acquired by the navy at this time were the famous Mersey rams. These were laid down at Laird's of Birkenhead for the Confederate Navy under cover of being built for the Turks to comply with the requirement of the British Government. The Government, however, were not to be circumvented in their determination to keep the ships out of Confederate hands and, in a tense political drama in 1865, seized them, subsequently paying Laird for them. They were naturally intended to be sea-going and had barque rigs, fo'c'sles and poops and high, hinged bulwarks. They had been acquired for the wrong reasons, and there was no really useful role for them to play. Their names were *Scorpion* and *Wivern*.

Reed was responsible for four small armoured ships, three of them conversions from wooden hulls then building, and one a new construction. Reduction in size and increased design hazards from loss of buoyancy could not be compensated for by a proportionate weight reduction, since the armour must remain as thick as in the larger ships. Weight-saving, then, had to be achieved by a reduction in the number of guns, which also permitted a smaller armoured box for the battery. The two smallest were the *Research* and *Enterprise* and were conversions of sloop hulls. The box-battery amidships contained only four guns, and had, as well as the broadside gun-ports, ports cut at the corners fore and aft, and the upper part of the hull embrasured to improve the arc of fire. They were the first ships to have such a refinement. They had barque rigs, but were poor performers under sail or steam and of dubious war potential.

The third conversion was of a corvette, the *Favorite*, and at 225 feet between perpendiculars, 40 feet longer than the sloops, she proved altogether more successful. The battery contained eight guns instead of four, which gave her a reasonable broadside. In spite of a fixed screw (doubled on the shaft) she was a fair sailer, though her steaming powers were inferior to the larger ships. The fourth ship, the same length as the *Favorite*, was one of the two designs that recommended Edward Reed to the Admiralty before he joined the team, and was the first ship to be designed for the navy by someone outside the organization. She was called the *Pallas* and differed from the *Favorite* in having her armament split between the box-battery and the bow and stern. The stern gun was unprotected but the bow gun was housed behind an armoured shield. Her original armament consisted of six 7-inch guns, four muzzle-loaders and two breech-loaders. Much had been hoped of this ship as a cheap, fast, small type of ironclad whose other weapon was a vicious ram. In service, however, she never made the promised 14 knots and performed poorly under sail.

## The Masted Central-battery Ironclad Battleships

When the main battery had shrunk into a small armoured box amidships the term for this refinement of the broadside principle was called 'central-battery'. It was this system that Reed championed against the turret principle. The pros and cons of the latter have already been discussed; what then were the merits and demerits of the central-battery? The overriding advantage in masted ships was that the guns protruded from the ship's side, so that they had an unrestricted field of fire for the angle allowed by

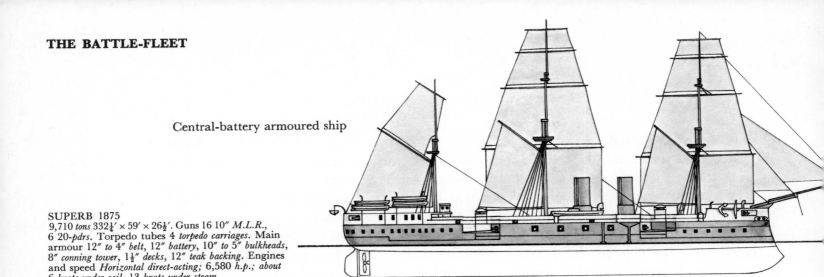

Central-battery armoured ship

SUPERB 1875
9,710 *tons* 332¼′ × 59′ × 26½′. Guns 16 10″ *M.L.R.*,
6 20-*pdrs.* Torpedo tubes 4 *torpedo carriages.* Main
armour 12″ *to* 4″ *belt,* 12″ *battery,* 10″ *to* 5″ *bulkheads,*
8″ *conning tower,* 1½″ *decks,* 12″ *teak backing.* Engines
and speed *Horizontal direct-acting;* 6,580 *h.p.; about*
6 *knots under sail,* 13 *knots under steam.*

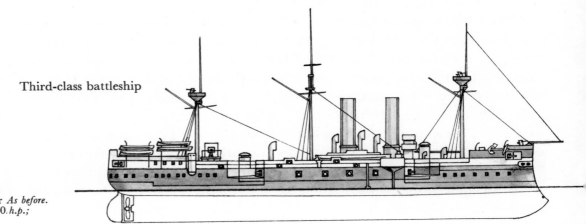

Third-class battleship

SUPERB 1875 (as modernized 1891)
*As before.* Guns 4 *of the* 10″ *M.L.R. and the* 6
20-*pdrs. replaced by* 6″ *B.L.* Main armour *As before.*
Engines and speed *Triple expansion;* 8,500 *h.p.;*
14½ *knots.*

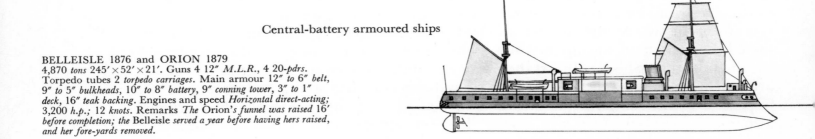

Central-battery armoured ships

BELLEISLE 1876 and ORION 1879
4,870 *tons* 245′ × 52′ × 21′. Guns 4 12″ *M.L.R.,* 4 20-*pdrs.*
Torpedo tubes 2 *torpedo carriages.* Main armour 12″ *to* 6″ *belt,*
9″ *to* 5″ *bulkheads,* 10″ *to* 8″ *battery,* 9″ *conning tower,* 3″ *to* 1″
*deck,* 16″ *teak backing.* Engines and speed *Horizontal direct-acting;*
3,200 *h.p.;* 12 *knots.* Remarks *The Orion's funnel was raised* 16′
*before completion; the* Belleisle *served a year before having hers raised,
and her fore-yards removed.*

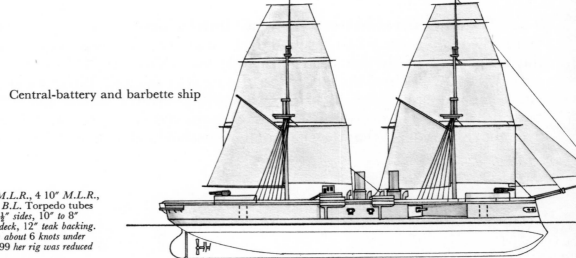

Central-battery and barbette ship

TEMERAIRE 1876
8,540 *tons* 285′ × 62′ × 27¼′. Guns 4 11″ *M.L.R.,* 4 10″ *M.L.R.,*
6 20-*pdrs.* (1884) 20-*pdrs. exchanged for* 4″ *B.L.* Torpedo tubes
2 *torpedo carriages.* Main armour 11″ *to* 5½″ *sides,* 10″ *to* 8″
*barbettes,* 8″ *to* 5″ *bulkheads,* 8″ *battery,* 1″ *deck,* 12″ *teak backing.*
Engines and speed *Compound,* 7,520 *h.p.; about* 6 *knots under
sail,* 14⅗ *knots under steam.* Remarks *In* 1899 *her rig was reduced
to signal yards, and her funnels were raised.*

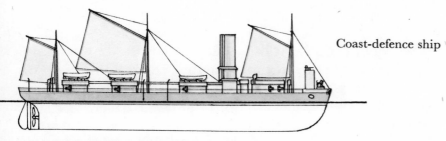

Coast-defence ship

ROYAL SOVEREIGN 1857 (converted 1862–4)
5,080 *tons* 240½′×62′×25′. Guns 5 300-*pdrs. M.L.* Main armour 5½″ *of iron, sides and conning tower, 10″ to 5½″ turrets.* Engines and speed
*Return connecting-rod; 2,400 h.p.; 11 knots under steam.* Remarks *The only wooden-hulled turret-ship built for the Royal Navy.*

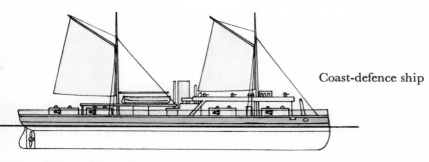

Coast-defence ship

PRINCE ALBERT (1864)
3,880 *tons* 240′ × 48′ × 19′. Guns 4 9″ *M.L.R.* Main armour 4½″ *iron belt, turrets 10″ to 5″, deck 1⅛″.* Engines and speed *Horizontal direct-acting; 2,130 h.p.; under steam 11 knots.* Remarks *First iron-built turret-ship in the Royal Navy.*

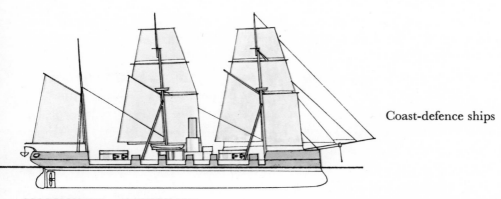

Coast-defence ships

SCORPION 1863 and WIVERN 1863
2,750 *tons* 224½′ × 42½′ × 17′. Guns 4 9″ *M.L.R.* Main armour 4″ *to 3″ belt, 10″ teak backing turrets, 10″ to 5″.* Engines and speed *Horizontal direct-acting; 1,450 h.p.; about 12 knots under sail, 11½ knots under steam.* Remarks *Originally intended for the Confederate Navy, they were purchased for the Royal Navy to prevent their being used against the Federals.*

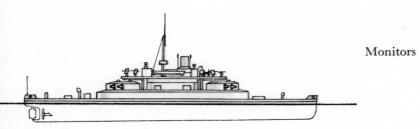

Monitors

CERBERUS 1868 and MAGDALA 1870
3,340 *tons* 225′×45′×15′ 3″. Guns 4 10″ *M.L.R.* (1892) *MAGDALA* 4 8″ *B.L.R.* Main armour 8″ *to 6″ sides, 9″ to 8″ breastwork, 10″ to 9″ turrets, 11″ teak backing.* Engines and speed *CERBERUS return connecting-rod; 1,370 h.p.; 9¾ knots. MAGDALA return connecting-rod; 1,436 h.p.; 10½ knots.*

the port. Secondly, as there had to be guns on both broadsides, a central-battery ship could fight with her maximum force on both sides at once. Against the system, the bow and stern fire from within the battery was poor, even with embrasured hulls. The guns were restricted in size because they had to be duplicated, and the box-battery itself was a larger area to armour than were turrets. A dangerous flaw in the system was the large size and number of the gun-ports in the armoured box; there might be a dozen, and they had to be large if the big guns were to have any useful fire-arc. One large shell inside the battery would have been disastrous. Taken all round, however, though the turret system was best for training and protecting guns, it was not really practicable in masted ships, where the central-battery system proved the best compromise.

There is a fine distinction between the latest of what may be regarded as true broadside ships, and the earliest central-battery ships. The term here includes only broadside ships with angled gun-ports for bow and quarter fire. If the *Research, Enterprise, Favorite* and *Pallas*, already mentioned, are included, there were sixteen of them and a seventeenth which combined a central-battery with open barbettes. The first ship to qualify for the battle-fleet, though she had also been called an 'armoured corvette', was the *Penelope* of 1867. She was the first twin-screw ironclad, which made her hopeless under sail, and she mounted eight 8-inch M.L.R. guns, in the box-battery, the corner ones having two gun-ports. She was one of the few ironclads to see action, forming part of the inshore bombarding force at Alexandria in 1882, which her shallow draught permitted. Similarly laid out but with a much better armour protection outside the battery was the *Hercules* of 1868, which at 325 feet long was 60 feet longer than the *Penelope*. The *Hercules* also had, in addition to the 10-inch M.L.R. guns in the battery, two 9-inch guns on the same deck behind armour as bow and stern chasers. On the deck above were embrasured 7-inch guns for further bow and stern fire.

The following year, 1869, came the *Audacious, Invincible, Iron Duke* and *Vanguard*, a class of four, which was the largest number of true sisters in the black battle-fleet. At 280 feet long they were on the small side and were in fact intended to be second-class ironclads for service abroad, where French or other foreign armoured ships might be met with. They were the first to have the central-battery on two decks, though on the upper-deck the armour was confined to a three-sided shield. The battery consisted of six 9-inch M.L.R. guns without embrasured ports on the main-deck, and above them four 9-inch M.L.R. guns bearing only through embrasured ports and without broadside ports, the whole structure jutting out over the main-deck battery. These were for bow and quarter fire. Two further ships, *Triumph* and *Swiftsure*, almost sisters to the *Audacious* class, were built at the same time, but whereas the latter were twin-engined and twin-screwed, these two were given single hoisting screws, which made them better sailers, if poorer steamers. The system of building out the upper-deck armoured battery from the ships' sides was taken a step further in the *Sultan* (1870) in which it formed the widest part of the ship; it also, for the first time, had transverse armour, so that she had complete box-batteries on two decks. This upper battery of two 9-inch guns had ports for side and stern fire; the rest of the broadside ports and an embrasured port for forward firing were on the main-deck below.

A long pause now elapsed, during which the navy concentrated on mastless turret-battleships, starting with the *Devastation*, followed by the *Thunderer* and *Dreadnought*. The abandoning of masts and yards had been made possible by the improved economy of marine steam-engines. It is astonishing therefore that just as the first of these was completing, a further masted central-battery ship should have been laid down; but in March 1873 such a ship was laid down which did not complete until 1877. On her gun-deck she had six 10-inch M.L.R. guns in a broadside box-battery with a further two em-brasured guns firing forward in a separate enclosed armoured battery. On the deck above was another complete armoured battery, with two 11-inch guns and two 10-inch firing through embrasures so deep and long that the guns could fire directly fore and aft. Although by the late seventies the *Alexandra*, as she was called, was obsolescent even when new, she yet had a golden career. From the moment of her grand launching by the Princess of Wales in the presence of other Royalty, the Archbishop of Canterbury, the Board of Admiralty and a large section of the Cabinet and Parliament, she continued grandly on to be a flagship all her active career, and became especially famous in the Mediterranean, painted white on the orders of one of her flag officers, H.R.H. The Duke of Edinburgh. She set a new standard in smartness, as the *Marlborough* on the same station had done in the fifties. The standards the *Alexandra* set made appearances a fetish and gave rise to stories of powder-dumping captains, who would not fire the guns in case the paint was spoilt. Stories that were perhaps apocryphal.

The *Alexandra* had been built to the designs of Nathaniel Barnaby, who followed Reed as Chief Constructor in 1872, and who also designed the last and the strangest of all the masted ironclads built for the Royal Navy, the *Temeraire* (1876). In two respects the latter was unique in that she was given a brig rig and fixed open barbettes for bow and stern fire. Amidships on the main-deck was a central-battery arranged on the lines of the *Alexandra*'s on the main-deck; but, instead of an upper-deck midship battery, she had two pear-shaped armoured barbettes situated in the bow and stern with armoured trunks down to the magazine. Each contained one 11-inch M.L.R. gun mounted on an ingenious turntable designed by Captain Scott, which also had hydraulic arms to the trunnions of the gun which raised and lowered it. Lowered and reversed, it could be loaded without exposing the crew; it was then raised and trained above the armoured barbette. Its chief advantage was that the bow barbette was placed forward of the fore-mast and the stern one aft of the main-mast, so that the system gave the most unrestricted field of fire with centre-line revolving guns ever achieved in a masted ship. This success was marred only by a weight-for-space penalty which prevented its being used again.

While the *Temeraire* was the last masted ironclad to be built for the navy, two more were acquired by purchase during the Russian war scare of 1878, both designed by Edward Reed for foreign powers. The better of the two was a single-deck central-battery ship intended for the Turkish Navy as the *Hamidieh* and renamed the *Superb*. She was similar to the *Hercules* but with an enlarged battery of six 10-inch M.L.R. guns to each tier, though the two end guns could fire only through the embrasured ports and she lacked a broadside port, unlike the *Hercules*. Being designed for the Mediterranean, the absence of an upper-deck battery, which could work in rough seas when the lower could not, was a small handicap. The second Reed ship, the *Neptune*, was building for the Brazilians to be called the *Independencia*. The Brazilians had ordered a masted

*Devastation*; what they nearly got was a modified *Monarch* with such superstructures that the turrets' fields of fire were even more restricted. Sticking out of the central pile before the main-mast and close together were two non-retractable funnels, which made her the ugliest of all the masted battle-fleet: she proved an expensive misfit. Two other ships purchased at this time may be mentioned here though they could not be described as masted, being designed with a token rig in their early days, and were really only coast-defence ships, designed for the Egyptians. These were the *Belleisle* (ex-*Peik-i-Sheref*) and the *Orion* (ex-*Bourdjou-Zaffer*). Each had an upper-deck octagonal casement battery housing four 12-inch M.L.R. guns all angled to fire through ports giving on to the bows and quarters. They had neither the speed nor the stamina to join the battle-fleet, and the *Belleisle* spent her active years as coastguard ship at Kingstown; but the *Orion* had a more active career of general duties in the Mediterranean and as guardship at Singapore.

# 13

## The Early Mastless Battleships

By 1869 the increase in gun size had tilted the balance of opinion in the broadside and turret controversy in favour of turrets, especially in the mind of the First Lord, Hugh Childers. The belt-and-braces brigade still regarded the shedding of the great sailing rigs as indecent; nevertheless, the time had come to be brave. The objections to continuing them in turret-ships have been partly dealt with in the previous chapter, but in addition at least a foot of iron armour was required to stop a shell from one of the new 12-inch guns. Loaded down with such a belt, even if the hull size was greatly increased, such a ship must be a poor performer under sail, as the *Alexandra* and *Temeraire* proved to be, and before this Mr Childers asked Reed for a design for a smaller ocean-going turret-ship.

A light sailing rig was suggested, and this must have proved worse than useless. What emerged from the drawing office was a twin-screw, low-freeboard, mastless steamer closely modelled on his breastwork monitor *Cerberus* (see page 113), but larger. One important feature was the improvement in steaming radius made possible by new and improved engine designs, particularly the compound engines which really made the discarding of a sailing rig possible, though in fact the first pair just missed them. Whereas the *Warrior* had a steaming radius of 1,400 miles, the first mastless battleship could cover 4,700 miles.

This vessel, the *Devastation*, was launched in 1871, but in the meantime the low-freeboard ironclad *Captain* had met with disaster, so that the newly built ship and her sister the *Thunderer* caused general alarm since it was thought they would follow the *Captain* to the bottom. A committee on designs was therefore set up to look into the matter and found that, subject to Nathaniel Barnaby's modifications, the design was sound. Barnaby had been made Chief Constructor in 1872 after Reed's resignation in 1870. The most important alteration extended the breastwork out to the side of the ship so that her freeboard for a considerable part of her length was raised a deck, thus improving both stability and accommodation. Basically the layout of the *Devastation* was ideal, and the one returned to eventually after excursions into other plans. Her superstructure, mast and funnels were just forward of amidships and the two turrets on the centre-line fore and aft gave the best possible all-round field of fire.

The *Devastation* was completed in April 1873 and her trials were watched with interest, but she proved seaworthy and a good gun-platform, and her sister used to be held up as a model of steadiness in the Victorian navy. A third ship of this type was laid

## DEVASTATION 1871

*Armoured hulls soon reached a weight where a sailing rig was useless, and it was the Devastation which first acknowledged this in the battle-fleet. Her layout had a classic simplicity which, after many experiments with other combinations, later warships were bound to follow. Up to the 1870s several factors had discouraged the abandonment of sailing rigs for units of the battle-fleet. The scarcity of coaling stations combined with the poor fuel economy of the early marine steam-engines made it essential that the old form of propulsion be retained, however badly the ships might sail – and as thicknesses of armour increased this was badly indeed. The new compound engines and the rapidly growing fleets of steamers on world routes led to more facilities for them; so by 1869 it was feasible to lay down the world's first sea-going mastless turret-battleship, the Devastation.*

**A** Recoil exhaust water tank
**B** Recoil cylinder
**C** Hydraulic loading rams
**D** Reversing gear
**E** Captain's cabin
**F** Officers' cabins
**G** Conning tower
**H** Steering position
**I** 12-inch (charge) magazine
**J** 12-inch shell room
**K** Engineers
**L** Starboard engine
**M** Starboard stokehold

Scale in Feet

0   10   20   30   40   50

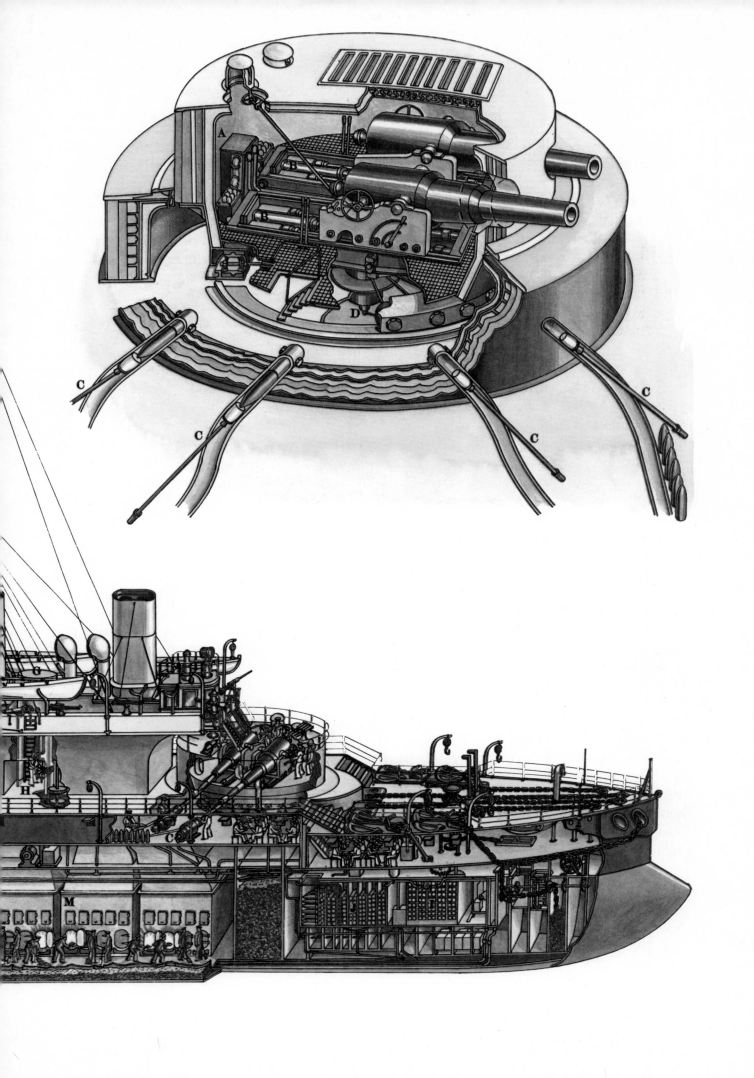

down in 1872, but was larger and with compound engines. She was called the *Dreadnought* and for many years was one of the most admired warships in the world.

## The *Inflexible* and the Central-Citadel Battleships

The policy of the Admiralty towards the introduction of new and deadly types of warship had not changed. Just as it had waited for the French to build the *Gloire* before building the *Warrior*, so it waited for the Italians to build the *Duilio* before building the *Inflexible*. It was up to the foreign navies to try and outdate our designs and, when they did, Britain could rely on her superior experience and industrial potential swiftly to overtake them.

It was unfortunate, therefore, that it was a British firm which initiated one of the most expensive upheavals in naval architecture of the century. The Italians had decided in the early 1870s on a naval policy of owning a very small number of battleships, but nevertheless the most powerful in the world. It was a policy aimed against the French, who they feared might attack them, rather than the British, who were not expected to be belligerent, and against whose navy they would in any event have been powerless. The *Duilio* and her sister, the *Dandolo*, were therefore to be rather like the *Dreadnought* and similarly armed. Armstrong, who was supplying the guns, offered Benedetto Brin, the Italian constructor, 15-inch guns of 50 tons. The Italians were delighted by the thought, but were obliged to make radical changes in their design. On the principle that a ship should be able to receive the fire that she could give, the *Duilio*'s armour-belt had to thicken from about 12 inches to 20 inches. Such a weight could not be spread the length of the hull, or even the distance required if the plan remained like the *Dreadnought*. The turrets had to be brought closer together in the middle of the ship and in fact were placed one on each side of the ship in echelon. The extremities were unprotected and continued buoyancy under fire was aimed at by subdivisions – some of the compartments had to be filled with cork. She further had an armoured deck below the water-line, and it was intended that the buoyancy of the central citadel and the area below the armoured deck would prove sufficient; but before she was launched in 1876, the guns further increased in size to 17·7-inch of 100 tons each, and this probably made it impossible. The Italians began to speak of giving her great speed so that she could keep the range open, a theory that was to find later echoes in the arguments on the merits of the battle-cruisers. The last uprating had been at the request of the Italians; having heard that the British answer to the *Duilio* was to mount 80-ton 16-inch guns, they were determined by this time that their ships would be the most powerful in the world. In fact the huge size of the guns was against them, since each would get a round off only about once every five minutes, and if at the same time the range was to be kept long the chances of success were not hopeful against a more rapidly firing opponent with say 12-inch guns. She was, nevertheless, a most powerful influence on world design. Her guns, steel armour and engines were made in England.

The British answer to the *Duilio* was a battleship built on a similar plan with 16-inch guns, the largest muzzle-loaders to be carried in a British ship, and the citadel had at the water-line 24 inches of compound armour, steel on iron, with 17 inches of teak backing, the thickest armour ever carried in any ship. Her name was the *Inflexible*, and in her

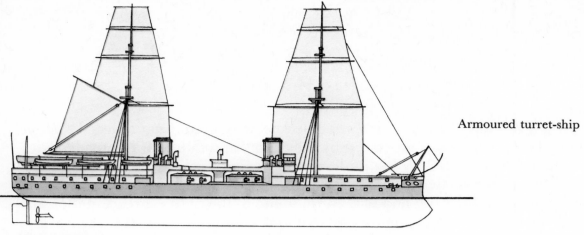

Armoured turret-ship

INFLEXIBLE 1876
11,880 *tons* 320′ × 75′ × 24½′. 4 16″ *M.L.R.* 6 20-*pdrs.* Torpedo tubes 2 *carriages,* 2 *submerged tubes.* Main armour 24″ *to* 16″ *citadel,*
22″ *to* 14″ *bulkheads,* 17″ *to* 16″ (*compound*) *turrets,* 12″ *conning tower,* 17″ *teak backing.* Engines and speed *Compound;* 8,407 *h.p.;* 14¾ *knots.*

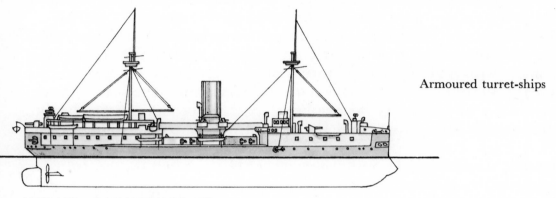

Armoured turret-ships

AJAX 1880 and AGAMEMNON 1879
8,510 *tons* 280′ × 66′ × 23′. Guns 4 12½″ *M.L.R.,* 2 6″ *B.L.* Main armour 18″ *to* 15″ *citadel,* 16½″ *to* 13½″ *bulkheads,* 16″ *to* 14″ *turrets,*
12″ *conning tower,* 3″ *deck,* 18″ *teak backing.* Engines and speed *Compound;* 6,000 *h.p.;* 13 *knots.*

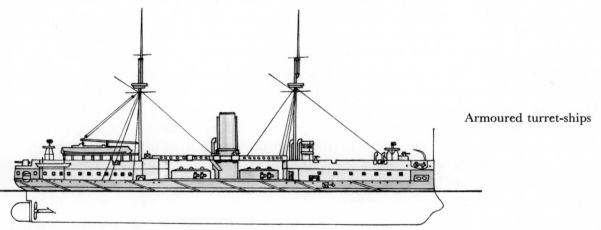

Armoured turret-ships

COLOSSUS and EDINBURGH, both 1882
9,150 *tons* 325′ × 68′ × 25′. Guns 4 12″ *B.L.,* 5 6″ *B.L.* Torpedo tubes 2 14″. Main armour *Compound,* 18″ *to* 14″ *citadel,* 16″ *to* 14″ *turrets,* 14″ *conning*
*tower,* 3″ *to* 2½″ *deck and* 22″ *teak backing.* Engines and speed *Compound; COLOSSUS* 7,488 *h.p.;* 16½ *knots, EDINBURGH* 6,808 *h.p.;* 16 *knots.*
Remarks *The first British capital ships to mount a main armament of breech-loaders.*

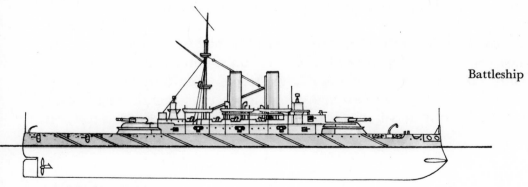

Battleship

COLLINGWOOD 1882
9,500 *tons* 325′ × 68′ × 26′. Guns 4 12″ *B.L.,* 6 6″ *B.L.,* 12 6-*pdrs.* Torpedo tubes 4 *above water.* Main armour 18″ *to* 8″ *belt,* 16″ *to* 7″
*end bulkheads,* 11½″ *to* 10″ *barbettes,* 12″ *to* 2″ *conning tower,* 20″ *teak backing.* Engines and speed *Compound;* 7,000 *h.p.;* 15½ *knots.* Forced
*draught;* 9,600 *h.p.;* 16¾ *knots.*

case the unarmoured ends above the armoured deck were definitely not necessary to her buoyancy or stability, which was supported by the citadel and raft, as was intended with the *Duilio*. Her turrets revolved by hydraulic power, which also loaded the huge guns. A ram punched home the shell at a shallow angle through a hole in the deck. This meant that, as after each firing the turret had to traverse round to the right degree and the guns be depressed to receive the next charge and shell, it took about two minutes to reload.

Although *Inflexible* was originally given a brig sailing rig, it would not be reasonable to include her with the sailing ironclads; the rig was useless as a means of propulsion, since, apart from anything else, she had no staysails or headsails. It was merely meant to keep the men's hands in aloft, as their next ship would almost certainly be a real sailer, and thus, in a peacetime navy, the *Inflexible* could join in sailing drill with the fleet. This mistake was soon recognized and in 1885 after four years' service her rig was changed to pole masts with military fighting tops. As late as 1900 there were plans to modernize this great Victorian battleship, which were however misguided, as both her speed and the rate of fire of her muzzle-loaders were by then too slow for fleet work. But they showed that the prestige of her youth had not entirely ebbed away after nearly twenty years.

Nathaniel Barnaby designed two more classes of battleship based on the *Inflexible* plan. The first pair were the *Ajax* and *Agamemnon*, much-reduced versions of their model, reverting to the 12·5-inch gun, and the last class of British battleship to mount muzzle-loading guns. Whereas the *Inflexible* was a handsome, powerful-looking ship, these two, with their great centrally mounted single funnels, have strong claims as the ugliest battleships ever to serve in the Royal Navy. They were smaller even than the first mastless ironclad the *Devastation*, and, though completed ten years later, were inferior in several important respects. Their armour was thicker where it existed, but, unlike the *Inflexible*, they could not have survived the flooding of the unarmoured ends without capsizing, which was their worst feature. Marginally heavier in fire-power, their turrets' fields of fire were comparatively restricted, and they were nearly a knot slower. They were also poor sea boats, and steered so badly at near full speed that they could hardly be said to be under control, which made them dangerous company. The *Ajax* served for only six years, then went into reserve for ever, and her sister served only ten.

The second pair, similar in layout and appearance, but larger and with 12-inch breech-loaders, were the *Colossus* and *Edinburgh*. The increase in size enabled some of the worst features of the *Ajax* to be mitigated, notably in buoyancy under fire and sea-going qualities. The rate of fire of the breech-loaders was an improvement, being under two minutes a round. Yet still the guns could be loaded only in one position so that the turret had to traverse to the point where the hole at the back of the turret came opposite the ram. The guns were then elevated to the correct angle for loading.

## The *Collingwood* and the *Admiral* Class Barbette Ships

No sooner were the last central-citadel ships laid down than a demand arose for a new class of faster battleship. It was a time of interesting foreign building, notably of a remarkable Italian vessel, like a high-freeboard *Duilio* and with 15-inch breech-loaders in open barbettes, no side armour at all, and a speed of 17 knots. The French too were building ships on the high-freeboard system with multiple open barbettes and 15 knots. Barnaby offered several suggestions including an improved *Dreadnought*, still considered by many as the ideal type. In the end the design for the *Collingwood*, though the armour plan was radically different, brought back the *Dreadnought*'s basic layout, but was influenced also by the French *Caiman* class coast-defence ships. The armour was still a short belt with unarmoured ends, but instead of levelling with the base of the turrets, as when they were placed close together, it rose only 3 feet above the water-line which was two decks below the main battery. This was placed in two open barbettes, one above and beyond each end of the belt, the ammunition hoists armoured down to it. The large unarmoured area between the barbettes was isolated as far as possible by an armoured deck and transverse armoured bulkheads, and within this was mounted a powerful secondary armament, on two decks. The crew of the four 12-inch guns in open barbettes were vulnerable to quick-firers now coming into use, from shell flash and direct hits, but the weight of a full turret would have been more than the design could stand. The *Collingwood* was launched in 1882 and preceded her half-sisters by two to four years. There were really five of these: four true sisters, *Anson*, *Camperdown*, *Howe* and *Rodney*, which mounted 13·5-inch guns instead of *Collingwood*'s 12-inch, and a fifth, the *Benbow*, which was given two huge 16·25-inch guns. These greatly impressed the public but could get a round off only every four or five minutes, and as there were only two of them this reduced the rate to two rounds per gun in about ten minutes, which, with hitting averages at about one in twelve, was not to be recommended. All these ships were low freeboard and steamed at more than 17 knots through a swell like half-tide rocks, and were said to be an impressive sight, throwing great cascades of white foam from their fo'c'sles.

## The Last of the Low-Freeboard Battleships

With the building of the *Admirals* Their Lordships were back on the right track, but it was difficult for them always to know it. Following the neglectful building policy of the seventies, which had resulted in panic buying of such Queen's bad bargains as the *Neptune* and the *Orions* in the war scare of 1878, there was some improvement in the eighties, but economic limitations beset construction, which in the face of rapid technological advances still expected competitive designs for similar or less money.

One of the troubles was the increased efficiency of the torpedo and of the means of delivering it, which caused a school of thought to dismiss the expensive armoured battleships as out of date. This opinion was strengthened by the appearance of huge guns which could penetrate all but the thickest armour. Armour still won against these arguments, for in an action between two similarly armed ships that with the armour had all the advantage. She could use common shell, with its comparatively high explosive potential, whereas the unarmoured ship had to use armour-piercing shell with its relatively small powder content.

The logical continuation to the *Admiral* class was for larger, high-freeboard *Admirals*, but these were to be delayed while the Board played with other ideas. A return to the turret seemed desirable because of the development of light quick-firers, which could seriously annoy an open barbette ship, or so it was thought. In the turret were to be two

**THE BATTLE-FLEET**

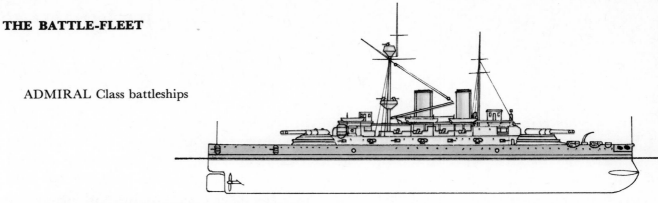

ADMIRAL Class battleships

ANSON 1886, CAMPERDOWN, HOWE, RODNEY all 1885
*ANSON and CAMPERDOWN* 10,600 *tons* 330′ × 68½′ × 28½′. *HOWE and RODNEY* 10,300 *tons* 325′ × 68′ × 28⅓′. Guns 4 13·5″ *B.L.*, 6 6″ *B.L.* 12
6-*pdrs.* Torpedo tubes 5 *above water. RODNEY* 4, *no bow tube.* Main armour (*Compound*) 18″ *to* 8″ *belt,* 16″ *to* 7″ *bulkheads.* 14″ *to* 12″ *barbettes in*
*ANSON and CAMPERDOWN.* 11½″ *to* 10″ *barbettes in HOWE and RODNEY.* 12″ *to* 2″ *conning tower,* 3″ *to* 2½″ *decks.* Engines and speed *Compound;*
7,500 *h.p.*; 15½ *knots.* Forced draught; 11,500 *h.p.*; 17⅓ *knots.*

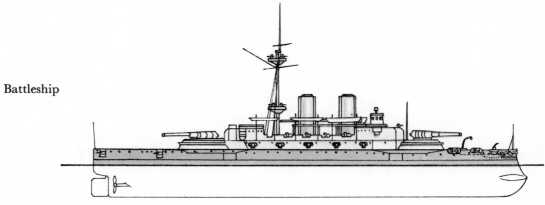

Battleship

BENBOW 1885
*Same as ANSON.* Guns 2 16·25″ *B.L.*, 10 6″ *B.L.*, 12 6-*pdrs.* Torpedo tubes 5 *above water.* Main armour *Same as ANSON.* Engines and
speed *Same as ANSON.*

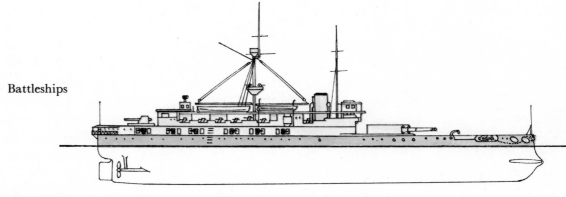

Battleships

SANS PAREIL and VICTORIA, both 1887
10,470 *tons* 340′ × 70′ × 29′. Guns 2 16·25″ *B.L.*, 1 10″ *B.L.*, 12 6″ *B.L.*, 12 6-*pdrs.* Torpedo tubes 1 *bow,* 1 *stern,* 2 *submerged, and* 2 *on*
*carriages.* Main armour 18″ *belt to* 16″ *bulkheads, a* 17″ *turret on an* 18″ *redoubt,* 14″ *to* 2″ *conning tower,* 3″ *submerged deck,* 6″ *bulkheads*
*to battery.* Engines and speed *Triple expansion;* 7,500 *h.p.*; 15¼ *knots.* Forced draught; 14,000 *h.p.*; 17 *knots.* Remarks *Drawing shows the*
Victoria *as delivered with short funnels, raised* 1890; *Sans Pareil completed with tall funnels.*

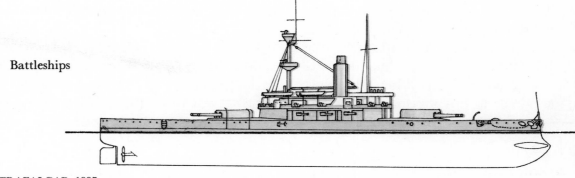

Battleships

NILE 1888 and TRAFALGAR 1887
12,589 *tons* 345′ × 73′ × 28′. Guns 4 13·5″ *B.L.*, 6 4·7″ *Q.F.* (*later* 6″), 8 6-*pdrs,* 9 3-*pdrs.* Torpedo tubes 1 *bow,* 1 *stern,* 2 *submerged and*
2 *above water.* Main armour (*Compound*) 20″ *to* 14″ *belt,* 16″ *forward bulkhead,* 14″ *after bulkhead,* 18″ *to* 16″ *citadel,* 18″ *turrets,* 14″ *conning tower,*
3″ *deck.* Engines and speed *Triple expansion;* 7,500 *h.p.*; 15 *knots.* Forced draught; 12,000 *h.p.*; 16¾ *knots.*

ROYAL SOVEREIGN Class battleships

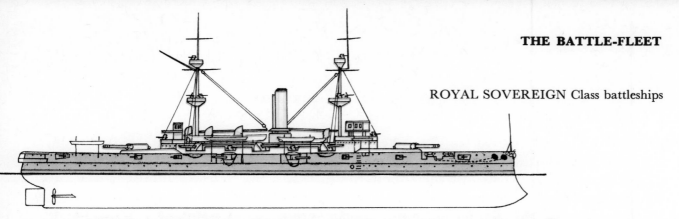

EMPRESS OF INDIA 1891, RAMILLIES 1892, REPULSE 1892, RESOLUTION 1892, REVENGE 1892, ROYAL OAK 1892, ROYAL SOVEREIGN 1891
15,585 (*max.*) *tons* 380′ × 75′ × 27′. Guns 4 13·5″, 10 6″ *Q.F.* 16 6-*pdrs. Q.F.*, 12 3-*pdrs. Q.F.* Torpedo tubes 7 – 4 *above water abeam*, 1 *above water astern and* 2 *submerged forward*. Main armour (*Compound and steel*) 18″ *to* 14″ *belt, to* 16″ *to* 14″ *bulkheads*, 17″ *to* 11″ *barbettes*, 14″ *forward conning tower*, 6″ *main-deck casemates*. Engines and speed *Triple expansion*; 9,000 *h.p.*; 15½ *knots. Forced draught*; 11,000 *h.p.*; 16½ *knots. ROYAL SOVEREIGN only* 13,360 *h.p.*; 18 *knots*.

Battleship

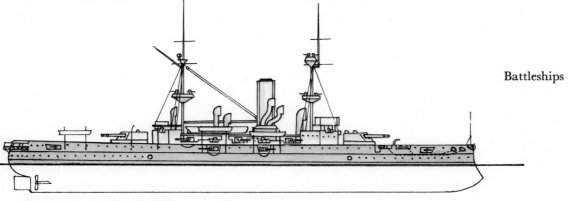

HOOD 1891
*Similar to the ROYAL SOVEREIGN but with turrets instead of barbettes, cut down fore and aft to compensate for their weight. The last low-freeboard British battleship.*

Battleships

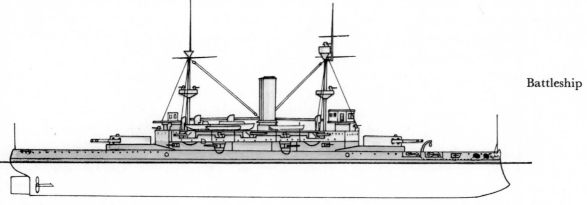

BARFLEUR and CENTURION, both 1892
10,500 *tons* 360′ × 70′ × 26′. Guns 4 10″, 10 4·7″ *Q.F.*, 8 6-*pdrs. and* 12 3-*pdrs.* Torpedo tubes 4 *beam and* 1 *astern above water*, 2 *submerged forward*. Main armour (*Compound and steel*) 12″ *belt to* 8″ *bulkheads*, 9″ *barbettes with* 6″ *shields*, 12″ *forward conning tower*, 2½″ *deck*. Engines and speed *Triple expansion*; 9,000 *h.p.*; 17 *knots. Forced draught*; 13,000 *h.p.*; 18½ *knots.* Remarks *The drawing shows ventilating cowls as in the* Centurion. *Both ships reconstructed 1901–4; their 4·7″ replaced by 6″ Q.F. in casements, as in* Renown.

Battleship

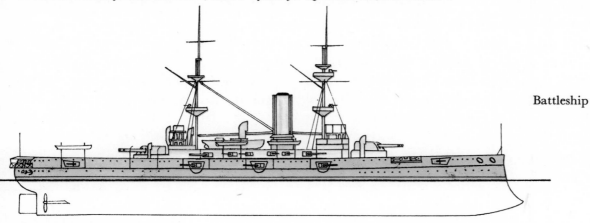

RENOWN 1895
12,350 *tons* 380′ × 72′ × 26¾′. Guns 4 10″, 10 6″ *Q.F.*, 12 12-*pdrs.*, 12 3-*pdrs.* Torpedo tubes 4 *submerged*, 1 *astern above water*. Main armour (*Steel*) 8″ *to* 6″ *belt*, 10″ *barbettes with* 6″ *shields*, 9″ *conning tower*, 6″ *to* 4″ *casemates*. Engines and speed *Triple expansion*; 12,000 *h.p.*; 18 *knots*.

110-ton B.L. guns, which in a 10,500-ton hull meant just one turret. Thus the navy acquired that strange pair of sisters, the *Sans Pareil* and the ill-fated *Victoria*. The huge turret was placed forward of the superstructure, which extended almost to the stern. The monster guns were slow to reload and, having only two, the ships suffered from the same disability as the *Benbow*, without the benefit of her field of fire. One of the *Victoria*'s guns bent on trials and the other also had to be returned to Armstrong, and, though they were modified and said to be satisfactory, they were never fully trusted or repeated. These ships carried a powerful secondary armament, a 10-inch gun aft as well as 6-inch and 6-pounders, but all without any protection. They had only six mountings for launching torpedoes. Although capable of over 17 knots from their triple expansion engines, their low freeboard would have prevented the turret being worked at that speed in anything but the calmest weather.

As was the fashion they were given lethal-looking rams with flanges. These weapons generally proved more dangerous to friends than enemies, with whom one is too seldom in contact, and the *Victoria* provided dramatic proof of this. The details are too well known to need repeating, but briefly, during manœuvres in the Mediterranean on 22 June 1893, the fleet was steaming in two lines, which the Admiral ordered to turn inwards. The result was a collision of the two flagships, which were the leaders, and the *Victoria* with the Commander-in-Chief went to the bottom, as did most of her crew. The great weight of her guns and turret contributed to the rapid capsizing. Her antagonist, the *Camperdown*, suffered severe flooding forward and was also very close to capsizing. This mishap is generally forgotten in the light of later, greater disasters, but at the time the shock to the public can be rated with the loss of the *Titanic*. It seemed unbelievable that the senior flagship of the premier naval power in the world could be lost in such a way.

There were to be three more low-freeboard battleships built, the *Nile* and *Trafalgar*, and the razeed member of the *Royal Sovereign* class, the *Hood*, which is dealt with elsewhere. The *Nile* and *Trafalgar* were in effect enlarged and more powerful *Dreadnoughts*, though their compound armour, which was 20 inches at its thickest, did not cover their extremities. Now that side-by-side funnels have come back, the fashion for them in the late eighties and nineties does not seem quite so strange, but the *Nile*, after her funnels were lengthened, had funnel casings that stopped short of the caps to give her a most bizarre appearance. They were completed in 1890 and 1891 and their compound armour was 33·5 per cent of their total weight, the highest proportion of any British armoured ships.

They were designed by William White who had taken over as Chief Constructor from Nathaniel Barnaby in rather peculiar circumstances. White had been in the Constructor's office under Barnaby but had left for Armstrongs. When Barnaby decided the strain was too much and left, the First Lord, on the advice of Captain Sir Arthur Hood, offered to take White back as Chief Constructor, but without consulting the Controller who ran that Department and who was naturally most incensed. This was in July 1885. White was to prove one of the great constructors, evolving a type of capital ship of which we built no less than forty-six for ourselves, and many more for other navies, which also built their own versions.

## Further Victorian Coast-Defence Ships

On the vexed question of what to build and for what purpose, nothing was so misguided as the adoption of the coast-defence monitor. This had to be small and of light draught yet carry heavy guns behind thick armour. To achieve this, sacrifices had to be made somewhere; thus they emerged with a very low freeboard, poor bunkerage and weak engines.

Although two of them were built for harbour defence in Bombay and a third for Melbourne, and all managed to arrive, these ships were not thought fit to go out in all weathers. They therefore lay around in the home ports wasting money that could have been used to improve the sea-going fleet. Their employment was based on the false premises that if the battle-fleet were defeated or unavailable, these ships and the new coast defences on which so much money was lavished would save Britain's bacon. They would not have, of course; if the battle-fleet had been defeated all would have been lost. The answer was that if the money had been spent to make the battle-fleet invincible, then the enemy would have been bottled up in his harbours, never getting sight of Britain's shores. Lord St Vincent and Lord Exmouth (Sir Edward Pellew) understood this in the Napoleonic Wars when William Pitt did not, and their counsel prevailed. In the 1860s it was Sir Charles Napier who understood it and Lord Palmerston and the army that did not, and unfortunately this time their view prevailed. They may have had in mind that the last invasion of England, that of William of Orange, succeeded because Lord Dartmouth and the British Fleet were trapped in the Thames Estuary by strong easterly winds and could not intercept the Dutch Fleet; but if Lord Dartmouth had been sitting outside Briel, then it is doubtful if William would have sailed at all.

As regards the ships themselves, the building of the first three was reasonably excusable since they were not built for British waters but for harbour defence in Bombay and Melbourne, where their powerful guns and thick armour would have acted as a powerful deterrent to an enemy raider. The first was the *Cerberus*, laid down in 1867, and she is interesting in that her novel design clearly foreshadowed the *Devastation* and the classic battleship layout that eventually emerged. As there was no question of a sailing rig or deep-water operations Reed could ignore those limitations and design a low-freeboard armoured breastwork amidships, at each end of which was an armoured turret containing two 10-inch M.L.R. guns. Between the turrets was an unarmoured superstructure and the funnel. A sister ship, the *Magdala*, was built for Bombay and a third, similarly laid out, armed and armoured, but slightly smaller, was also destined for Bombay and was called *Abyssinia*. The *Cerberus* was sent to Melbourne, and for the long journey out she had a temporary fo'c'sle and poop added to give stability for the three-masted sailing rig. The *Magdala* went out to India also under sail for much of the time, but without the extra freeboard added. The *Abyssinia* steamed out without a sailing rig, accompanied by hired steamers for bunkering and to keep an eye on her.

The first to be built for home service was the *Glatton*, laid down in 1868. She was similar to the three just described except that she had only one turret and thicker armour, which increased the draught to 19½ feet, thus defeating half the purpose of this type of vessel: her ability to fight in shallow waters. A further four ships, the *Cyclops* class, were laid down in 1870, and these closely followed the design of the *Cerberus*. In

# RAMS and MONITORS

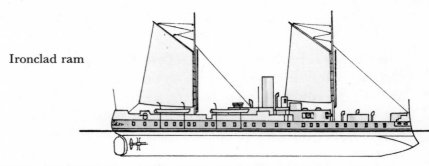

Ironclad ram

### HOTSPUR 1870
4,010 *tons* 235′ × 50′ × 20′. Guns 1 12″ *M.L.R.*, 2 64-*pdrs. M.L.R.* Main armour 11″ *to* 8″ *belt*, 8″ *breastwork*, 10″ *to* 8½″ *turret*, 10″ *to* 6″ *conning tower*, 2¾″ *to* 1″ *decks*. Engines and speed 3,500 *h.p.*; 12½ *knots*. Remarks *The single* 12″ *gun fired from embrasures in a fixed turret.*

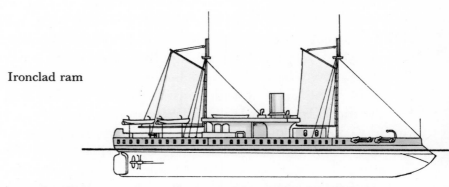

Ironclad ram

### RUPERT 1872
5,440 *tons* 250′ × 53′ × 23′. Guns (1874) 2 10″ *M.L.R.*, 2 64-*pdrs. M.L.R.* (1887) 2 10″ *M.L.R.*, 2 6″ *B.L.R.* (1892) 2 9·2″ *B.L.R.*, 2 6″ *B.L.R.* Main armour 11″ *to* 9″ *sides*, 12″ *breastwork*, 14″ *to* 12″ *turret*, 12″ *conning tower*, 3″ *to* 2″ *decks*, 14″ *teak backing*. Engines and speed 4,630 *h.p.*; 13½ *knots*.

### GLATTON 1871 (Monitor)
4,910 *tons* 245′ × 54′ × 19½′. Guns 2 12″ *M.L.R.* Main armour 12″ *to* 10″ *sides*, 12″ *breastwork*, 14″ *to* 12″ *turret*, 9″ *to* 6″ *conning tower*, 3″ *deck*, 21″ *teak backing*. Engines and speed *Horizontal two-cylinder;* 2,870 *h.p.;* 12 *knots. Similar in appearance to the* Rupert *but not a sister.*

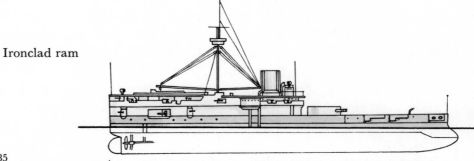

Ironclad ram

### CONQUEROR 1881 and HERO 1885
6,200 *tons* 270′ × 58′ × 22′. Guns 2 12″ *B.L.*, 4 6″ *B.L.*, 7 6-*pdrs.* Torpedo tubes 6 14″ *above water.* Main armour 12″ *to* 8″ *belt*, 12″ *to* 10½″ *citadel*, 12″ *to* 14″ *turret*, 12″ *to* 6″ *conning tower*, 11″ *to* 10½″ *bulkheads*, 2½″ *to* 1¼″ *decks*. Engines and speed *Compound;* 4,500 *h.p.;* 14 *knots.*

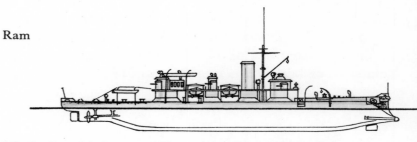

Ram

### POLYPHEMUS 1881
2,640 *tons* 240′ × 40′ × 21½′. 6 6-*pdrs.* Torpedo tubes 6 14″ − 5 *submerged*, 1 *above water.* Main armour 3″ *sides and deck*, 6″ *conning tower.* Engines and speed *Compound;* 3,000 *h.p.;* 7,000 *h.p. forced draught;* 18 *knots.*

this class the sea-going qualities were improved in the 1880s by building up the sides the length of the breastwork and decking over, which gave them more freeboard for much of their length. This was a feature of the *Devastation* from her beginning. However, even with this improvement it was thought unwise to send them to sea. They had been designed purely for harbour defence, so it is perhaps unfair to criticize them for being dangerous sea boats, except that the Admiralty chose to regard them as coast-defence ships, and therefore theoretically fit to go to any part of the coast at any time, which clearly was out of the question. This type of vessel was popular with smaller navies that lacked a strong battle-fleet.

## The Rams

The success of the Confederate rams during the American Civil War, and more especially the ramming and sinking of the Italian flagship at the Battle of Lissa in 1866, brought the idea of the ram as an offensive weapon into high favour. The first British ram was the *Hotspur*, launched in 1870, followed by the larger *Rupert* in 1872. These little ships were supposed to operate with the fleet, but their poor speed and short radius of action made it impossible for them to work far from a base, and the lack of speed especially meant it would have been very difficult to place them for an attack that could have been anything less than suicidal. They had a single turret forward, fixed, in the *Hotspur*'s case, with a single 12-inch M.L.R., but this was later changed to two guns, as in the *Rupert*. At first their guns were regarded as secondary to their rams, but in a few years it was realized that they could never get their rams near an enemy bottom, so that their role declined to that of harbour-defence monitors.

**COAST-DEFENCE SHIPS**

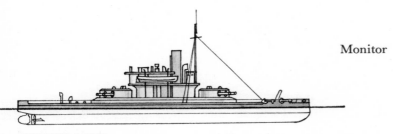

Monitor

ABYSSINIA 1870
2,900 *tons* 225′ × 42′ × 14′ 6″. Guns 4 10″ *M.L.R. Rearmed* (1892) 4 8″ *B.L.R. Main armour 7″ to 6″ sides, 8″ to 7″ breastwork, 10″ to 8″ turrets, 11″ teak backing.* Engines and speed 1,200 *h.p.*; 9½ *knots.*

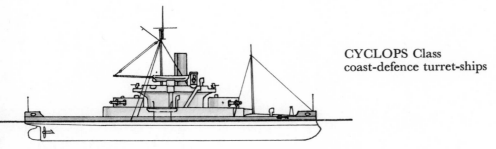

CYCLOPS Class
coast-defence turret-ships

CYCLOPS, GORGON, HECATE, HYDRA, all 1871
3,480 *tons* 225′ × 45′ × 16¼′. Guns 4 10″ 18-*ton M.L.R. Main armour 9″ to 6″ sides and breastwork, 10″ to 9″ turrets, 9″ to 8″ conning tower, 1½″ deck, 11″ teak backing.* Engines and speed *CYCLOPS compound tilt hammer*; 1,660 *h.p.*; 11 *knots. HYDRA compound tilt hammer*; 1,472 *h.p.*; 11¼ *knots. HECATE horizontal direct-acting*; 1,670 *h.p.*; 11 *knots. GORGON horizontal direct-acting*; 1,755 *h.p.*; 10½ *knots.*

Before finally abandoning the fleet ram, two more were built in which the short-comings of the first two were supposed to be overcome. This temptation to persevere was partly inspired by the rams' relative cheapness to build, compared to the fleet ironclads. The *Conqueror* and *Hero* looked like little *Victorias*, and they were indeed their progenitors, so far as layout was concerned – that is, a long low-freeboard fo'c'sle, a single turret and aft of it a superstructure extending to the stern. A good deal bigger than the *Rupert*, the very low-freeboard bow made them bad sea boats and wet gun-platforms. Much water entered the fo'c'sle, which made them very uncomfortable. Also in the vital matter of speed, they had 14 knots which was about the same as the best French ironclads when the *Conqueror* was laid down in 1879; but, as she took seven years to complete, she appeared when the new battleships were doing 2 or 3 knots more. If they were ever to succeed, then by the late 1880s it was too late, and, though they did go to sea for fleet exercises, it only showed up their weaknesses.

One pure ram, the *Polyphemus*, was projected as an experiment in the late 1870s. She was to have been without any armament but her wicked ram, and she presented as inconspicuous a profile as possible, so that she proved very wet with a most unusual rolling movement. In the event, they could not resist adding Whitehead torpedoes and a light armament. Intended to accompany the fleet, her sea-keeping qualities would not permit it, so an improved version, designed for more comfortable living was projected, but not carried out. The *Polyphemus* therefore remained an interesting oddity whose use in wartime against an enemy battle-fleet must be the nearest the British got to a *kamikaze* weapon.

# 14

## Iron- and Steel-built Masted Cruisers

While the 1860s had brought a revolution in the appearance of the battle-fleet, no similar transformation took place in the cruising fleet, which continued to be entirely made of wood until 1868. The restriction this put on the size of the engines resulted in the curious anomaly that these vessels which before were the fast eyes of the fleet were now inferior in steaming powers to the iron-armoured ships, which put them at their mercy, and even inferior to many steam merchant liners, whose movements they might have on occasion been called upon to aid or impede.

The American Civil War had shown the destructive powers of the large, comparatively fast commerce-raiding wooden cruisers, and so it was with this in mind that when a change was made it was an iron frigate that was built, of very large, indeed over-large, dimensions. This fine ship was the *Inconstant*, launched in 1868, and with a length between perpendiculars of 337 feet she was longer than all but six of the battle-fleet. In order to overcome the still-present danger from splintering iron plates in an action, her sides were sheathed with a thick double layer of wood. She carried a powerful armament of ten 9-inch M.L.R. guns on the lower-deck and six 7-inch on the upper-deck. She was one of the fastest ships under sail or steam in the world, being capable of 13½ knots under sail and 16 under steam.

Two other large iron frigates were later built, the *Shah* which was very slightly larger and the *Raleigh* which was 298 feet between perpendiculars. In the event the *Inconstant* and *Shah* proved too expensive to run in peacetime, though the *Shah* on her one sea-going commission fought the only big-ship action of the Victorian navy. It was with an English-built armoured turret-ship, the *Huascar*, belonging to the Peruvian Navy, which managed to escape, though the *Shah* had the best of it. The *Raleigh* being smaller made a good flagship for foreign parts, and from 1875 she was almost continuously employed, being the last sailing ship in the navy to wear an admiral's flag and the last to round Cape Horn under canvas.

The next down in size were three sisters, *Bacchante*, *Boadicea* and *Euryalus*, which completed in the late 1870s. Of the three the *Boadicea* was distinguished from her sisters by a handsome knee bow, and proving somewhat accident-prone, was known in the service as the '*Bumper*', from her frequent contact with passing vessels. These ships were 280 feet long, 45 feet in the beam and could steam at 14 to 15 knots. Under canvas they were rather poor performers. Because of their smaller complement they were classed as corvettes, though they carried their main armament on the main-deck as with

131

## MASTED CRUISERS

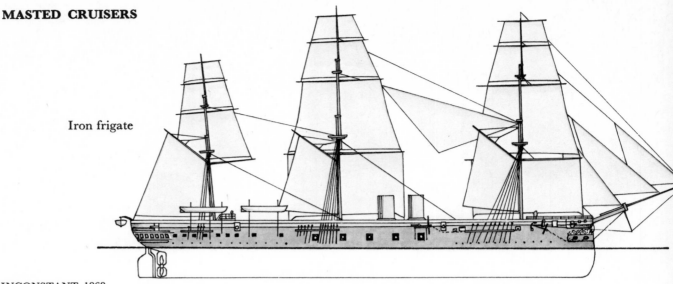

Iron frigate

**INCONSTANT 1868**
5,780 *tons* 337′ × 50¼′ × 25½′. Guns 10 9″ *M.L.R.*, 6 7″ *M.L.R.* Torpedo tubes 2 *carriages for* 16″ *added about* 1877. Engines and speed *Trunk*; 7,360 *h.p.*; 13½ *knots under sail*, 16 *knots under steam.*

Iron frigate

**SHAH 1873**
6,250 *tons* 334′ × 52′ × 25½′. Guns 2 9″ *M.L.R.*, 16 7″ *M.L.R.*, 8 64-*pdrs. M.L.R.* (*on trucks*). Torpedo tubes 2 16″ *torpedo carriages*. Engines and speed *Trunk*; 7,480 *h.p.*; 13 *knots under sail*, 16 *knots under steam.*

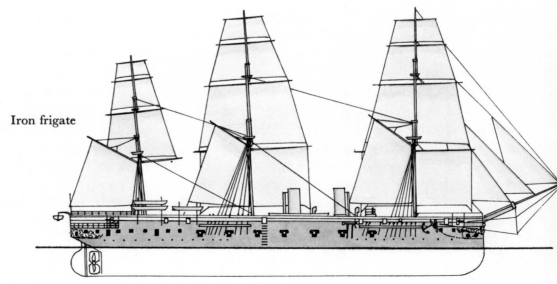

Iron frigate

**RALEIGH 1873**
5,200 *tons* 298′ × 49′ × 24½′. Guns (1874) 2 9″ (*chase*), 14 7″ (*on trucks*), 6 64-*pdrs. M.L.R.* (*on trucks*). (1884) 9″, 64-*pdrs.*, *and* 6 7″ *removed, replaced by* 8 6″ *B.L.R.*, 8 5″ *B.L.R.* Torpedo tubes 2 *carriages for* 16″ *in* 1884. Engines and speed *Return connecting-rod*; 5,640 *h.p.*; 13 *knots under sail*, 15½ *knots under steam.*

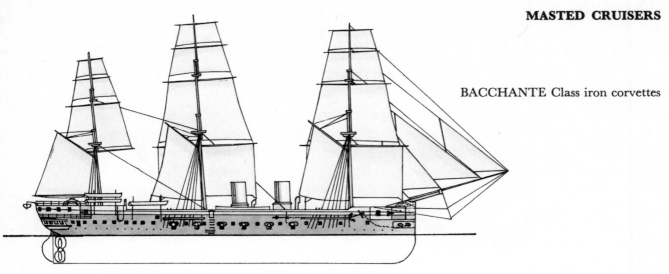

BACCHANTE Class iron corvettes

BACCHANTE 1876, BOADICEA 1875, EURYALUS 1877
*BACCHANTE 4,070 tons 280′ × 45½′ × 23¾′. BOADICEA 3,913 tons 280′ × 45′ × 23⅔′. EURYALUS 3,932 tons 280′ × 45½′ × 23¼′. Guns 14 7″*
*M.L.R. (slides). 2 6″ M.L.R. (on trucks, BOADICEA and EURYALUS only). Later 2 or 4 7″ replaced by 6″ B.L.R. Torpedo tubes 2 carriages for 14″ added.*
*Engines and speed Compound return connecting-rod; about 5,100 h.p.; about 11 knots under sail, about 15 knots under steam. Remarks The last main-deck,*
*broadside armed warships built for the navy. The BOADICEA had a knee bow, the other two were straight stemmed.*

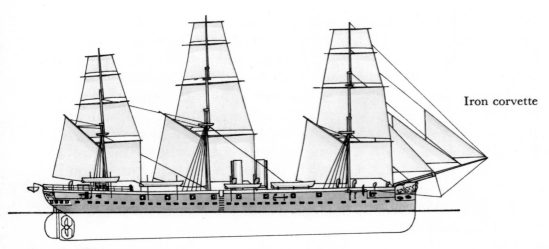

Iron corvette

ROVER 1874
*3,460 tons 280′ × 43½′ × 23′. Guns (1875) 2 7″ M.L.R., 16 64-pdrs. M.L.R. (1879) 14 6″ B.L.R. Torpedo tubes 2 carriages for 14″ in 1879. Engines*
*and speed Compound; 4,960 h.p.; 11 knots under sail, 14½ knots under steam.*

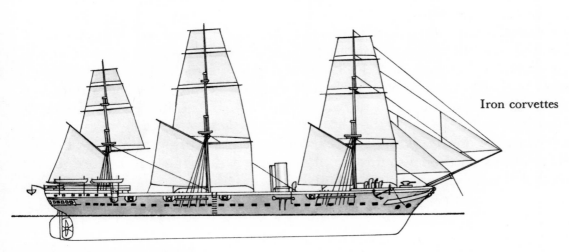

Iron corvettes

ACTIVE and VOLAGE, both 1869
*3,080 tons 270′ × 42′ × 22′. Guns (1870) 6 7″ M.L.R. (on slides), 4 64-pdrs. M.L.R. (2 on slides, 2 on trucks). VOLAGE (1872) 18 64-pdrs. M.L.R. (16 on*
*trucks, 2 on slides). Both (1879) 10 6″ B.L.R., 2 6″ M.L.R. (on slides). Torpedo tubes 2 carriages for 14″ torpedoes. Engines and speed ACTIVE return*
*connecting-rod; 4,130 h.p.; 12½ knots under sail, 15 knots under steam. VOLAGE trunk; 4,530 h.p.; 12½ knots under sail, 15¼ knots under steam.*

frigates, and were as large as their wooden contemporaries. The term 'corvette' as a type applies better to three more iron cruisers which were about the same size as the *Bacchantes*, but carried their main armament on their upper-deck. These were the straight-bowed twin-funnelled *Rover* (1874), and the knee-bowed sisters *Active* and *Volage*, both launched in 1869. These three, with the *Calypso* and finally the *Raleigh*, eventually formed the sail training squadron, the last refuge of the sailing navy, except for the brigs and one or two steel sloops, which continued into the twentieth century.

## The Protected Cruisers

The late seventies produced three curiosities dear to the heart of the Chief Constructor Nathaniel Barnaby. These were the *Shannon* and the sisters *Nelson* and *Northampton*. In these three the armour was not so much, as in the battleships, to protect the battery which was left almost entirely unprotected, but a water-line belt with an armoured deck above it, intended to protect the ship's vitals, her engine- and boiler-rooms, steering gear and magazines.

At 260 feet long, the *Shannon* was smaller than any of the other masted cruisers, and yet she had to bear this extra weight. Her battery of six broadside-mounted 9-inch M.L.R. guns, and the stern-mounted one, stood unprotected on the open upper-deck, but two 10-inch guns forward were trained through embrasured ports behind an armoured shield, which also embraced the conning tower. Theoretically, the ship would present her bow to an enemy and the crews of the guns could shelter behind the armour shield. When she turned her broadside, her guns could be fired electrically by remote control. In fact, the ship was not fit to stand in the line with the battle-fleet ironclads, and, though powerful as a cruiser, she lacked the speed both under sail and steam to compete with unarmoured ships.

In the *Nelson* and *Northampton* efforts were made to improve on the *Shannon* by building them larger so that the steaming speed increased from 12 to 14 knots. They also had an extra deck covering the battery. The armoured shield round the forward guns was augmented by another round the embrasured stern guns. Like the *Shannon* the *Nelson* and *Northampton* were meant to operate as foreign flagships, almost as battleships. The *Nelson* did one commission as such on the Australia station (1881–9) and the *Northampton* did one on the North America and West Indies station (1879–86). The *Shannon* also visited the Pacific and China stations, though not as flagship. Steel was used in the framing of the two later ships.

In 1881 two more large protected cruisers were laid down, the sisters *Warspite* and *Imperieuse*. These had, as well as an armoured deck, a short and shallow armour-belt. The gun arrangement was novel and Frenchified: four 9·2-inch B.L. guns singly mounted in round barbettes with shields, their hoists armoured down to the armoured deck, and distributed two fore and aft and two on the beams. Another French feature was a marked tumble-home. Initially they had their troubles: alterations to increase the specifications of their guns, bunkerage and accommodation during building, added to serious miscalculations on their weights, resulted in their drawing 2 feet more than was designed, so that the armour-belt peeped only 14 inches above the water. Also their brig rig, designed for them and fitted in the *Imperieuse*, for they were the last armoured ships built with sail, refused to budge them at all. Accordingly this was replaced by a single military mast between the two funnels. Thus lightened by 100 tons they proved good steamers and with their powerful armament and large size (313 feet long), these odd-looking ships did good service as flagships in the Pacific.

## The River Class Gunboats

The Victorian gunboats normally were of wooden and composite construction, and classes of the latter continued to be built until 1889. The exceptions were a class of twelve iron-hulled gunboats of which the first was the *Medina*, launched in 1876. She was one of the strangest-looking vessels ever built for the navy, and was specially designed for the great rivers of China where navigation was sufficiently hazardous to make watertight subdivisions in a hull desirable, hence the comparatively expensive use of iron. She had a topsail schooner rig and a very tall funnel: but the strangest feature of all was her bow. Owing to a weight-distribution problem, the two 64-pounders housed forward behind the protection of an oval gunwale and decked over, could not be placed right forward in the hull, which continued forward at deck-level to a ram bow. The bowsprit protruded from the top of the gunwale over the bow in a most ludicrous manner. As well as China, two of these gunboats, the *Dee* and the *Don*, served in Egypt in 1882.

## Steel and the Last Masted Cruisers

The first two steel ships to be built for the navy were the *Iris* (1877) and *Mercury* (1878), the first fast mastless cruisers, or more correctly dismasted cruisers, for they began with a light barquentine rig (see pages 136–7); also in the same year as the *Mercury* were launched six of a class of nine steel-framed, iron-plated corvettes of the *Comus* class; these were followed by three more in 1880 and 1881, and finally two sisters very close to the *Comuses*, the *Calliope* (1884) and *Calypso* (1883). Almost the last sailing corvettes to be built for the navy, they were first of the smaller cruisers to be given all-metal hulls, though cased with timber and coppered below the water-line.

These were built as replacements for the wooden and composite hulls that were wearing out, and did not greatly differ in layout. A refinement was a $1\frac{1}{2}$-inch steel deck about 3 feet under the lower-deck to protect the engines and boilers. Also, although the first ships of the class completed with muzzle-loaders, by the time of later launching the new 6-inch breech-loader had made its appearance, and some of these were mounted behind shields in sponsons which bulged out over the ships' sides and gave a much-improved field of fire compared to the embrasured ports of the earliest ships. After their first commissions the latter were to various extents modified to conform. At the same time that the *C* class corvettes were building, a curious class of four sisters, rated as second-class cruisers, was also on the stocks. These ships were the *Leander* class and were close to the *Mercurys* in that their lengths were over six times their beams and they had powerful engines. They were initially given barque rigs, necessarily on a rather light scale, but these were quickly reduced to barquentine and finally to schooner rigs. In their last days, those that saw any service were stripped of their spars. With these ships

## MERCURY 1878

*This vessel, with her sister ship the IRIS, were the prototypes of all modern cruisers. They were essentially fast steamers with an unprecedented amount of space taken up with machinery, and so narrow in the beam for their length that they could only bear a very light sailing rig. This was still thought to be necessary as a means of saving coal stocks, but was later discarded. Their design was so good that they were thought worthy of three changes of armament during their service.*

**A** Captain's cabins
**B** Officers' cabins
**C** Torpedo tube
**D** Magazine
**E** Starboard engine
**F** After stokehold
**G** Fore stokehold
**H** Torpedo magazine

0    10    20    30    40    50 Scale in Feet

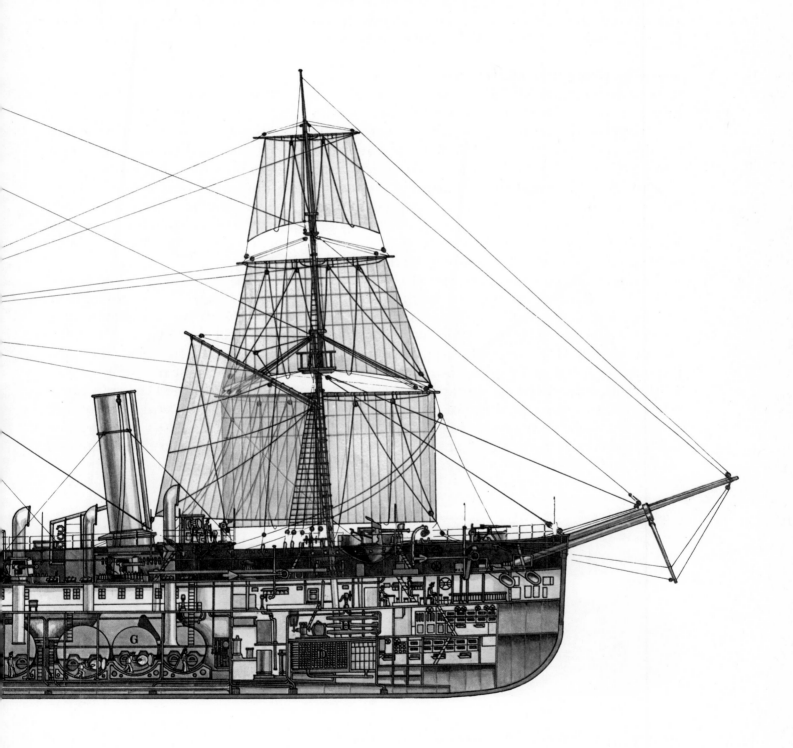

and the *Mercurys* came the return of a type of cruiser which had a faster performance than a battleship.

The last sailing class of all were the steel sloops of the *Alert* type, sixteen of which were built between 1894 and 1903, so that the last masted warship did not leave the slipway until after the death of Queen Victoria. They began with barque rigs, but ended up as topsail schooners, except for three, *Fantome*, *Merlin* and *Mutine*, which finished up without any rig in the surveying service and served on into the 1920s. The last masted cruiser to return from a commission was not any of these but a composite cruiser called the *Pylades* which docked at Sheerness on Wednesday, 24 May 1905.

## The Re-emergence of the Fast Cruiser

In the late seventies Mr White built two all-steel dispatch vessels whose chief characteristic was speed. They were, as already mentioned, the first steel ships in the navy, the *Iris* (1877) and *Mercury* (1878). They were sisters, but the *Iris* had a knee bow and the *Mercury* a straight one. The *Iris* also had slightly more powerful engines, which for 7,514 horsepower gave her the remarkable speed of 18·6 knots from her twin screws. The weight of her machinery naturally reduced the proportion of weight available for her guns, which consisted of ten 64-pounder rifled muzzle-loaders. Their slim lines, 300 feet long and 46 feet in the beam, restricted the size of their sparring to a light barquentine rig, a feature still deemed essential, but which only marred their steaming performance, and which was subsequently discarded.

It is interesting to compare them to one of the large iron corvettes of the same period such as the *Boadicea* (1875). She was iron-built and wooden-sheathed with a length of 280 feet and a beam of 45 feet, displacement 3,913 tons. With her proportionately greater beam she carried a full ship rig and an armament of fourteen 7-inch rifled muzzle-loaders. Her single hoisting screw and 5,130 horsepower gave her the then respectable speed of 14·3 knots, but this was only as fast as the best of the ironclads. With their great speed the *Iris* and *Mercury* might again have performed the traditional role of cruiser, to scout ahead of the lumbering battle-fleet. In fact, having been called dispatch vessels, their proper role tended to be overlooked, and the *Mercury* in any case lay in reserve for years after her trials. It was nearly ten years before cruisers were laid down which could boast a similar superiority in speed over the battle-fleet.

# 15

## The Torpedo

Some means by which a lethal quantity of explosive could be placed against the side of a ship and detonated had long exercised the minds of those interested in the development of naval weapons, but as in so many fields their ideas were baulked by their inability to harness the necessary artificial power or to procure the right materials for the packaging of the motive power and the explosive.

On 12 July 1776 an attempt was made by an American rebel to blow up Lord Howe's flagship, the *Eagle* 60, as she lay at anchor off New York. The man, whose name was Lee, approached in some kind of submersible rowing-boat and successfully reached the ship's side. However he was unable to fasten the charge to her side. Having failed, he escaped, leaving his boat and the charge to drift away and explode harmlessly.

This early attempt was not repeated in that war or even in the French Revolutionary Wars, though attempts to create submarine boats for the purpose are associated with another American, Robert Fulton; they came to nothing.

The Russians dabbled with mines in the war of 1854–5, but for the first effective results from torpedo warfare we must turn again to the Americans and the Civil War of the 1860s. The device used was called the 'spar torpedo'. This consisted of a charge on the end of a pole rigged out on the bow or the beam of a small steamboat and set to travel a foot or two beneath the water surface. The idea was that the intrepid crew would take the steamboat at full speed within a few feet of the enemy so that the torpedo could explode on impact. This desperate adventure was first successfully attempted by a Union officer called Cushing who sank the Confederate ship *Albemarle* and, though his boat was also blown up, he escaped to report his success.

Like many breakthroughs in weaponry, the torpedo was regarded in the service as unsporting, and by the public as diabolical. It was a major issue in Rear-Admiral de Horsey's fall from grace in 1876 that he sent torpedoes after the Peruvian ironclad *Huascar* into Iquique Harbour at night, where he thought, erroneously, that she was lying. This force from the *Shah* included spar torpedoes, but mainly relied on a Whitehead torpedo.

With the arrival of Whitehead's invention the potential of torpedo warfare assumed entirely new dimensions and became a menace to the mighty capital ships which was never overcome. Invented by an Englishman, it turned out to be a weapon that was more useful to Britain's enemies than to herself, for, as always, large numbers of her ships, both naval and merchant, were to be at sea in wartime while the German and

## MASTED CRUISERS

Armoured cruiser

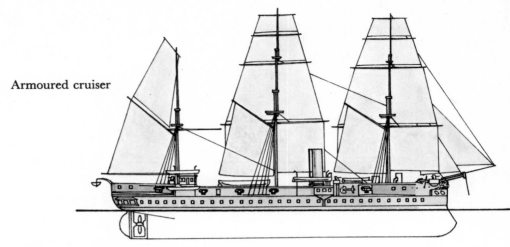

SHANNON 1875
5,670 *tons* 260′ × 54′ × 23½′. Guns 2 10″ *M.L.R.*, 7 9″ *M.L.R.*, 6 20-*pdrs*. Torpedo tubes (1881) 4, *plus* 2 *carriages*. Main armour 9″ *to* 6″ *belt*, 9″ *to* 8″ *bulkheads*, 9″ *to* 4″ *conning tower*, 3″ *to* 1″ *decks*, 12″ *teak backing*. Engines and speed *Compound*; 3,370 *h.p.; about* 9 *knots under sail*, 12¼ *knots under steam*. Remarks *The navy's first armoured cruiser.*

Armoured cruisers

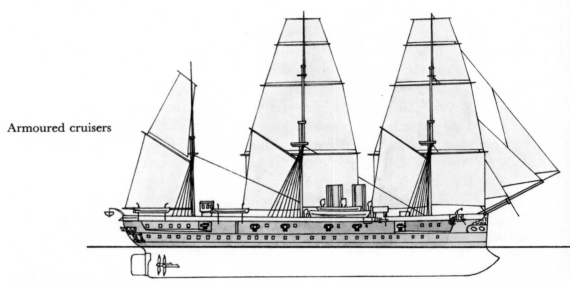

NELSON 1876 and NORTHAMPTON 1876
7,630 *tons* 280′ × 60′ × 25¾′. Guns 4 10″ *M.L.R.*, 8 9″ *M.L.R.*, 6 20-*pdrs*. Torpedo tubes 2 60′ *torpedo-boats*. Main armour 9″ *to* 6″ *belt and bulkheads*, 9″ *conning tower*, 3″ *to* 2″ *decks*, 12″ *teak backing*. Engines and speed *NELSON compound*; 6,624 *h.p.; about* 10 *knots under sail*, 14 *knots under steam. NORTHAMPTON compound*; 6,073 *h.p.; about* 10 *knots under sail*, 14 *knots under steam.*

Armoured cruisers

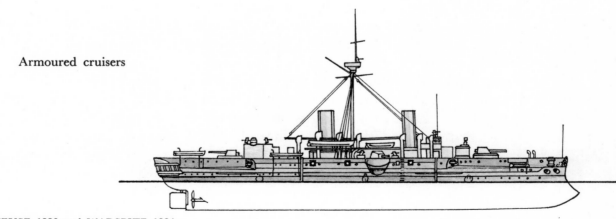

IMPERIEUSE 1883 and WARSPITE 1884
8,500 *tons* 315′ × 62′ × 27¼′. Guns 4 9·2″ *B.L.*, 10 6″ *B.L.*, 4 6-*pdrs*. Torpedo tubes 6 18″ (*above water*). Main armour (*Compound*) 10″ *belt to* 9″ *bulkheads*, 8″ *barbettes with* 2″ *shields and* 3″ *hoists*, 9″ *conning tower*, 2″ *deck over belt*, 4″ *deck fore and aft of it.* Engines and speed *Compound*; 8,000 *h.p.*; 16 *knots. Forced draught*; 10,000 *h.p.*; 16½ *knots*. Remarks Imperieuse *ran trials with a brig sailing rig, but it was found to be worse than useless and discarded.*

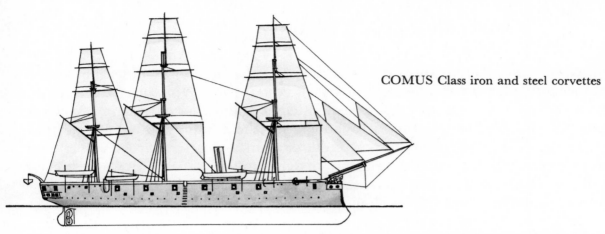

COMUS Class iron and steel corvettes

CANADA 1881, CARYSFORT 1878, CHAMPION 1878, CLEOPATRA 1878, COMUS 1878, CONQUEST 1878, CONSTANCE 1880, CORDELIA 1881, CURACOA 1878
2,380 *tons* 225′ × 44½′ × 19¼′. Guns *First armament* 2 7″ *M.L.R.*, 12 64-*pdrs. except CANADA and CORDELIA* (10 6″ *B.L. and* 2 *torpedo carriages*) *and COMUS* (4 6″ *B.L.*, 8 64-*pdrs. and* 2 *torpedo carriages*). *Some rearmed from* 1885: *CHAMPION, CLEOPATRA and CURACOA had* 4 6″ *B.L.*, 8 5″ *B.L. and* 2 *torpedo carriages; CONQUEST had* 9 6″ *B.L. and* 2 *torpedo carriages.* Main armour 1½″ *steel deck over engines.* Engines and speed *Compound;* 2,310 to 2,670 *h.p.;* 12¾ *to* 13¾ *knots.*

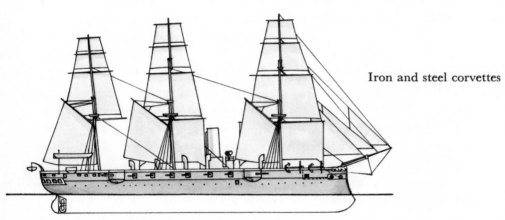

Iron and steel corvettes

CALLIOPE 1884 and CALYPSO 1883
2,770 *tons* 235′ × 44½′ × 20′. Guns 4 6″ *B.L.*, 12 5″ *B.L.* Torpedo tubes 2 *torpedo carriages.* Main armour 1½″ *deck over engines.* Engines and speed *Compound;* 4,023 *h.p.;* 14¾ *knots.*

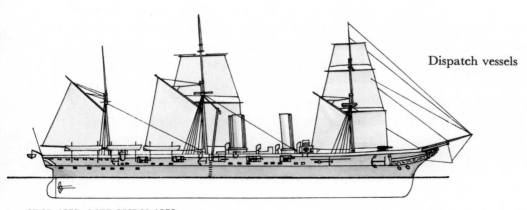

Dispatch vessels

IRIS 1877, MERCURY 1878
3,730 *tons IRIS* 333′ (o/a), *MERCURY* 315′ (o/a) × 46′ × 22′. Guns *First* 10 64-*pdrs. M.L.R. Second* 2 64-*pdrs. M.L.R.*, 4 6″ *B.L.*, 4 5″ *B.L. Third* 13 5″ *B.L.* Torpedo tubes 4 *torpedo carriages.* Engines and speed *Compound; IRIS* 7,330 *h.p., MERCURY* 7,735 *h.p.; IRIS* 17¾ *knots, MERCURY* 18½ *knots.* Remarks Mercury *had a straight bow (see pages* 136–7).

Italian ships were not, so that this made the British Navy the more vulnerable to the torpedo, especially when carried by a submarine. To return to Whitehead's invention, his first torpedo in 1866 was a steel cylinder, pointed at both ends; in the front of it was the gunpowder and behind this the air cylinders for the compressed-air engine that drove a propeller. The most ingenious part, and for years a closely guarded secret, was the means of keeping the torpedo running at a set depth under water. This was achieved by using the water pressure, which increases with the depth, to control a set of fins just in front of the propeller. Initially, its slow speed of 8 knots made it ineffective against moving targets, and difficult to aim at stationary ones except at short range. After 1872 Whitehead devoted himself exclusively to the development of his invention. Guncotton replaced gunpowder, which gave three times the explosive power, and the adoption of Brotherhood's three-cylinder air engine increased the speed to a useful 18 knots. A further change was to a snub nose instead of a pointed one which not only improved the running but allowed an increase in the size of the charge. Whitehead also invented the servo engine which controlled the angle of the run. By the end of the century 18-inch torpedoes were carrying 200 pounds of guncotton at 30 knots. An indication of the effectiveness of this weapon can be read from the losses to the British battle-fleets in the two world wars. No British battleship was sunk by gunfire in either war, but nine were sunk by torpedoes.

## Torpedo-Boats and Torpedo-Cruisers

The limitations of the torpedo were speed and range; before the days of submarines it had to be transported on the surface close enough to the enemy to give a reasonable chance of a hit, and this would have to be well within the range of the target's guns. To meet this challenge the torpedo-boat was evolved, a small vessel capable of the highest speed then obtainable, which would at the same time present the smallest target for the shortest time. Even so, unless surprise could be achieved under cover of darkness or in bad visibility, an attack must always have been extremely hazardous.

The first torpedo-boat was an 87-foot vessel constructed by Thornycroft in 1876 called *Lightning*, capable of 19 knots. The early boats carried their torpedoes in a swivel mounting on the bow or stern, or two hanging from frames each side of the boat. With the latter type, and with later boats which had two torpedoes firing through fixed tubes in the bows, the boats had to be aimed at the enemy, instead of just the mounting, which was an additional hazard since it meant that they must steam towards the enemy up to the moment of firing. In their early role the function of the torpedo-boats was essentially defensive since they were not fit to keep the seas for long and were therefore tied to their home ports. The anomaly of an essentially offensive weapon tied to a defensive role was realized, and various attempts were made to overcome the difficulty. An obvious answer was bigger boats which could operate with the fleet. The desperately slim, narrow-gutted lines were kept but lengths were increased to 110 feet, then 125 feet. At this, the boats were found capable of standing up to ocean conditions, but it was the men who gave up. They could not stand the exhaustion and lack of sleep which resulted from any lengthy stay aboard a drenched and wildly plunging torpedo-boat, and they were a constant anxiety to the admiral when exercising with the Channel Fleet.

In the middle 1880s two other solutions were tried. Two little torpedo-cruisers were built, the *Scout* and *Fearless*. These were proper ships which could go anywhere, but in an attack were slower than the T.B.s and a larger target. It is difficult to believe that they would not have been massacred. A more hopeful solution seemed to be the *Vulcan*, launched in 1889. She looked like a large cruiser, except for the two big cranes on either side just aft of her funnels. These were for launching and stowing the six torpedo-boats she carried. Her role was to take them within striking distance and drop them. Difficulties might arise, once the hunt was up, in getting them on board again, but she was so promising that many people thought the whole idea unsporting and rather bad form. Promising or not, she had no consorts and remained a lone experiment. She had a particularly long life afloat, forming with the *Inconstant* and *Andromeda*, part of the composite H.M.S. *Defiance*, the last existing large Victorian cruisers, until broken up in the middle 1950s.

The T.B.s were seen as powerful deterrents to a blockading squadron, so torpedo-boat-destroyers, or T.B.D.s, were designed to work with the blockading fleet. These were like huge torpedo-boats, upwards of 200 feet long and armed with guns as well as torpedoes. They were faster than the smaller T.B.s and soon usurped their role and replaced them. They developed into the destroyer, the smallest type of cruising and escort vessel to be employed with the battle-fleet, and the pure torpedo-boat disappeared for a time, until the increasing size of the destroyers reopened a niche which was filled by the small very fast motor torpedo-boats of the First World War and later.

In the 1870s the adoption of the Whitehead torpedo became general for all new ships down to cruisers, and in the eighties some older ones were given them. It was at this time too that the submerged tube was perfected. By 1890 many people thought that the development of the torpedo and the torpedo-boat had rendered the battleship obsolete. To combat the effects of a torpedo explosion, extended subdividing of the hulls was proposed, and in the long run this has been the best solution for survival, though it does not prevent a ship being crippled. For total immunity the steel net apron was devised; one of the least popular appendages to the late Victorian and Edwardian battle-fleet, it consisted of a skirt of steel mesh boomed out round the ship's side. When not in use, it was secured to a shelf, on the ship's side, with the booms laid diagonally above it. The business of getting it in and out was awkward and dangerous, and everyone was relieved when the improvements in torpedo design so far anticipated the resisting powers of the net that it was abandoned. This happened just before the First World War, although it had a brief, ill-considered re-adoption at the outbreak of hostilities. The last British battleships to use nets while under way were the *Majestic* and *Triumph* at the Dardanelles in 1915, and both were sunk within three days of each other by *U21* with torpedoes which pierced their nets. The *Triumph* went down in twenty minutes, the *Majestic* turned over in seven.

## MASTED and TORPEDO-CRUISERS

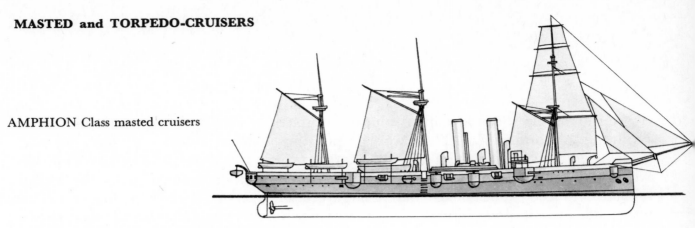

### AMPHION Class masted cruisers

AMPHION, ARETHUSA, LEANDER, PHAETON, all 1882–3
4,300 *tons* 300′×46′×22¾′. Guns 10 6″, 4 3-*pdrs*. Torpedo tubes 4 *above water*. Main armour 1½″ *deck over engines*. Engines and speed *Compound*; 5,500 *h.p.*; 16½ *knots*.

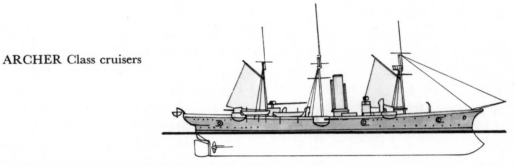

### ARCHER Class cruisers

ARCHER, BRISK, COSSACK, MOHAWK, PORPOISE, RACOON, SERPENT, TARTAR, all 1885–7
1,770 *tons* 240′ (*o/a*) × 36′ × 16′. Guns 6 6″, 8 3-*pdrs*. Torpedo tubes 3 14″ *above water*. Main armour ⅜″ *deck*, 3″ *conning tower*. Engines and speed *Compound*; 2,500 *h.p.*; 15 knots. *Forced draught*; 3,500 *h.p.*; 16½ *knots except RACOON and SERPENT* 4,500 *h.p.*; 17½ *knots*.

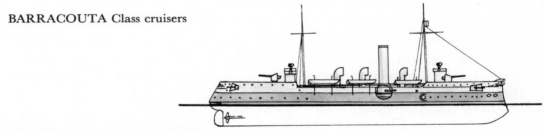

### BARRACOUTA Class cruisers

BARRACOUTA, BARROSA, BLANCHE, BLONDE, all 1889
1,580 *tons* 233′ (*o/a*)×35′×16′. Guns 6 4·7″, 4 3-*pdrs*. Torpedo tubes 2 14″ *above water*. Main armour 2″ *deck*. Engines and speed *Triple expansion*; 1,750 *h.p.*; 15 *knots. Forced draught*; 3,000 *h.p.*; 16½ *knots*.

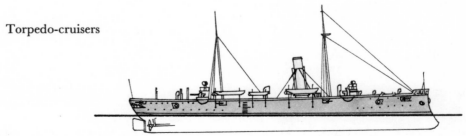

### Torpedo-cruisers

FEARLESS 1886 and SCOUT 1885
1,580 *tons* 220′ × 34′ × 14½′. Guns 4 5″. Torpedo tubes 1 *above water* and 2 *torpedo carriages*. Engines and speed *Compound*; 2,000 *h.p.*; 16 *knots. Forced draught*; 3,200 *h.p.*; 17 *knots*.

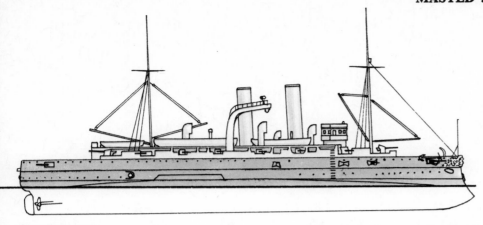

Torpedo-boat carrier

VULCAN 1889
6,629 *tons* 350′ × 58′ × 24¾′. Guns 8 4·7″, 12 3-*pdrs*. Torpedo tubes 2 *submerged, 4 above water; 6 second-class torpedo-boats*. Main armour
5″ *deck and engine hatches, 6″ conning tower*. Engines and speed *Triple expansion; 8,167 h.p.; 18 knots. Forced draught 12,000 h.p.; 20 knots.*

## CONDOR and CADMUS Class small masted cruisers

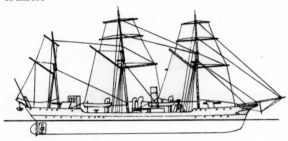

ALERT, TORCH, both 1894
960 *tons* 180′ × 32½′ × 11½′. Guns 6 4″ *Q.F.*, 4 3-*pdrs*. Engines and
speed *Triple expansion; 1,400 h.p.; 13¼ knots.*
ALGERINE, PHOENIX, both 1895
1,050 *tons* 185′ × 32½′ × 13′. Guns 6 4″ *Q.F.*, 4 3-*pdrs*. Engines and
speed *Triple expansion; 1,400 h.p.; 13 knots.*
CONDOR, MUTINE, RINALDO, ROSARIO,
SHEARWATER, VESTAL, all 1898–1900
980 *tons* 180′ × 32½′ × 11½′. Guns 6 4″ *Q.F.*, 4 3-*pdrs*. Engines and
speed *Triple expansion; 1,400 h.p.; 13½ knots.*
CADMUS, CLIO, ESPIEGLE, FANTOME, MERLIN,
ODIN, all 1900–3
1,070 *tons* 185′ × 33′ × 11¼′. Guns 6 4″ *Q.F.*, 4 3-*pdrs*. Engines and
speed *Triple expansion; 1,400 h.p.; 13¼ knots.*

## VIXEN Class armoured gunboats

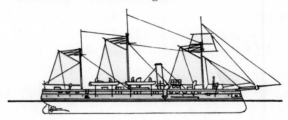

VIPER 1865, VIXEN 1865, WATERWITCH 1866
1,230 *tons* 160′ × 32′ × 11½′. *VIXEN beam* 32½′; *WATERWITCH*
1,280 *tons* 162′ × 32′ × 12′. Guns 2 7″ *M.L.R.*, 2 20-*pdrs. B.L.*
Main armour 4½″ *iron belt*, 10″ *teak backing*. Engines and speed
*VIPER Horizontal reciprocating; 700 h.p.; 9½ knots: VIXEN
Horizontal reciprocating; 740 h.p.; 8¾ knots: WATERWITCH
Ruthven hydraulic turbine; 780 h.p.; 8¾ knots.* Remarks Viper *and*
Vixen *were first twin-screwed vessels in the navy; Vixen composite built,
other two iron.*

## MEDINA Class iron gunboats

DEE, DON, ESK, MEDINA, MEDWAY, SABRINA,
SLANEY, SPEY, TAY, TEES, TRENT, TWEED, all
1876–7
386 *tons* 110′ × 34′ × 5½′. Guns 3 64-*pdrs. M.L.R.* Engines and
speed *Reciprocating; 310 h.p.; 9½ knots.*

## CURLEW Class steel gun vessels

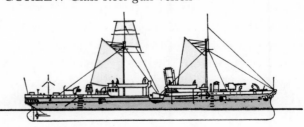

CURLEW 1885 and LANDRAIL 1886
950 *tons* 195′ × 28′ × 10½′. Guns 1 6″ *B.L.*, 3 5″ *B.L.* Torpedo
tubes 3 (1 *bow tube*, 2 *on carriages*). Engines and speed *Compound;*
1,500 *h.p.; 14½ knots.*

# 16

## The Naval Defence Act of 1889 and the Navies of Foreign Powers

In 1876 Disraeli, by the Royal Titles Act, made Queen Victoria Empress of India, and the new Queen Empress gave him an earldom in return. He was not equally generous to the navy, but then his parsimony was politically motivated by what he thought the market would bear, that is to say, the taxpayer with the vote. In the eighties, however, the temper of the people shifted as they began to realize the vastness of their ever-growing possessions, and there grew a willingness to assume the responsibilities and accept the cost of the necessary trappings. An all-powerful navy was an attraction, and the taxpayer is understandably more willing to pay out for a navy that must win against all comers than one that may lose.

The state of the battle-fleet relative to France, the second naval power in 1889, was as follows. Britain had sixteen battleships of the first class and seventeen of the second class, while France had twelve of the first class and eighteen of the second class. So there was already a superiority in numbers, and that superiority extended in other respects. The French cruisers were less than half as strong, and at a time when the navies of some other foreign powers, particularly the United States of America, were undergoing expansion and modernization, a combination with France would have proved difficult to resist.

The outcome of these pressures was the Naval Defence Act of 1889 which ordered the immediate building of eight first-class battleships (the *Royal Sovereigns* and the *Hood*), and two second-class battleships (the *Centurion* and *Barfleur*). Sixty new cruisers were also to be laid down. Thus by 1894, the battle-fleet would be raised including the *Nile* and *Trafalgar* already building, to twenty-six of the first class whereas France would have only fifteen, and in modern cruisers of 17 knots and over Britain would have ninety-two against France's nineteen, a formidable lead.

### The Qualities of Foreign Armoured Ships in 1894

When the French abandoned the broadside ironclad, they yet wished to retain the high freeboard in whatever type they adopted. This was admirable in theory but difficult to apply when tonnage was strictly limited by policy as in England. For the *Amiral Duperré* they chose a complete water-line belt, necessarily shallow up to an armoured deck. Above this was a considerable area of unarmoured hull, topped by four 13·4-inch

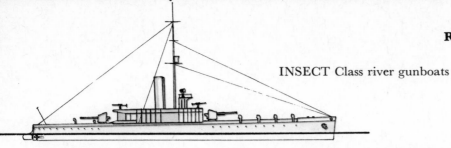

INSECT Class river gunboats

APHIS, BEE, CICALA, COCKCHAFER, CRICKET, GLOWWORM, GNAT, LADYBIRD, MANTIS, MOTH, SCARAB, TARANTULA, all 1915–6
625 *tons* 237½' (*o*/*a*) × 36' × 4'. Guns 2 6", 2 12-*pdrs.* (*later replaced by* 1 3" *A.A. and smaller*). Engines and speed *Triple expansion; 2,000 h.p.; 14 knots.*

River gunboats

DRAGONFLY, GRASSHOPPER, LOCUST, MOSQUITO, SCORPION, all 1937–9
585 *tons* 197' (*o*/*a*) × 33' × 5'; *SCORPION* 670 *tons* 208¾' (*o*/*a*) × 34½' × 5'. Guns 2 4" *L.A.*, 1 3·7" *howitzer.* Engines and speed *Turbines; 3,800 h.p.; SCORPION 4,500 h.p.; 17 knots.*

ANT Class coastal gunboats

ANT, ARROW, BADGER, BLAZER, BLOODHOUND, BONETTA, BOUNCER, BULLDOG, BUSTARD, COMET, CUCKOO, FIDGET, GADFLY, GRIPER, HYAENA, INSOLENT, KITE, MASTIFF, PICKLE, PIKE, PINCHER, PLUCKY, SCOURGE, SNAKE, SNAP, STAUNCH, TICKLER, WEAZEL, all 1867-81.
*ANT Class* 254 *tons* 85' × 26' × 6'. Guns 1 10" *M.L.R.* Engines and speed *Reciprocating; 260 h.p.; 8½ knots.* Remarks Plucky *and* Staunch *were prototypes for the ANT Class and slightly smaller with a 9" gun.* Bouncer *and* Insolent *built of steel and slightly larger.*

TEAL Class China river gunboats

MOORHEN 1901, TEAL 1901, WIDGEON 1904
180 *tons* 160' × 24½' × 2¼'. Guns 2 6-*pdrs. Bullet-proof hull.* Engines and speed *Compound; 550 h.p.; 13 knots.* Remarks *Smaller and single-funnelled but similarly armed were* Woodcock 1897 *and* Woodlark 1897 (145'), *and* Nightingale, Robin, Sandpiper, Snipe, *all* 1897 (100').

breech-loaders in four armoured, but open, barbettes, which were fed by armoured hoists. She was able to carry her guns dry when the *Devastations* might have had trouble working their turrets, but otherwise seemed a vulnerable target. The difficulties of this type were steadily relieved by the adoption of compound and steel armour which radically reduced the thickness required and so permitted a widening of the belt and the addition of shields for the barbettes. Indeed, the pattern of French battleship development follows a more consistent and steady line than that of the British.

The US Navy had pioneered the turreted monitor in the Civil War; after it the people looked to the opening up of the West, and the navy was neglected. There were no manufacturing facilities to make the thick armour that was necessary to a modern battle-fleet. As late as 1883 the best gun in the fleet was a 15-inch smooth-bore firing ball. In that year a board was set up to look into the means of manufacturing modern ordnance, and the whole of the defence structure was reassessed. One of its recommendations was for the building of armoured coast-defence ships of 4,000 to 7,000 tons as soon as it was possible to do so. By 1887 it was, and the four monitors launched in 1883 could be completed. The first ocean-going armoured ship of their navy was the *Texas* of 1891, built to an English design, of 6,300 tons. So that she could have a high freeboard and two 12-inch guns in separate turrets the armour-belt had to be very short with the guns mounted on each side in echelon, like the *Inflexible*. She was followed by the three *Indianas*, inspired by the *Dreadnought* but with the chief part of their powerful secondary armament also in turrets, as were the four 13-inch guns. One big advance was that the turret guns had all-round loading positions. These ships, launched in 1893, represented America's first class of ocean-going battleship.

In Germany Kaiser Wilhelm II had succeeded to the throne in 1888, and he was all his life a keen battleship man who made drawings of ideal ships. His enthusiasm made him envious of his grandmother's navy and eager to build one of his own that would emulate it, and perhaps one day beat it. He found his own navy very much a coast-defence affair and immediately started a heavy programme. Eight high-freeboard coast-defence battleships were put in hand and a class of five 10,000-ton high-freeboard ocean-going battleships were launched by 1892. These favoured the French system of armour coverage, with a fairly shallow belt the full length of the hull and armoured barbettes.

# 17

## Screw-Steam Propulsion in the Second Half of the Nineteenth Century

The earliest screw-driven iron ship in the navy was the royal yacht *Fairy* of 1845 which had a geared vertical oscillating engine, with the shaft driven through gear-wheels from the crank-shaft, so that the screw made five revolutions for every one of the crank-shaft. This system was continued into the early 1850s for some steam liners, up to the *Duke of Wellington*. Thereafter, in order to keep the machinery as low in the hull as possible, and therefore out of the firing line, engines were coupled directly to the shaft and the problems of the increased speed of the crank-shaft were overcome.

Two firms had a near monopoly of engine-building for the Royal Navy in the early years: Penn and Son with their trunk engines and Maudsley and Field with their horizontal double piston-rod return connecting-rod engines. This latter type was used in *Victoria*, the three-decker of 1859 and the last and finest example of a wooden first-rate that the world would ever know. Her engines were of 3,054 horsepower. In 1860 the *Warrior's* were to be of over 5,000 horsepower and the contract was given to Penn. So important a responsibility was it thought to be that two Chief Engineers were appointed to her.

The next improvement, apart from engine size, was the introduction of the compound engine. This was first fitted to the frigate *Constance*, which had been built as a sailing frigate in 1846, but was altered for steam in 1862. Her engine was constructed by the Scottish firm of Randolph and Elder and consisted of six cylinders in triplets, a high-pressure one between two low-pressure ones. The initial steam pressure in the central cylinders was 60 pounds, which was cut off at half stroke and exhausted into the side cylinders. By this means the steam was used twice instead of being lost and a much better economy was procured. The compound engine of the *Constance* in fact gave trouble, but that put into the ironclad *Pallas* in 1865 by Humphreys and Tennant was a success. It had only two cylinders, one four times the size of the other. The high-pressure steam first went into the small one and then on to the big one. This type of engine superseded the trunk and reciprocating engines eventually, but was not repeated in the battle-fleet until 1875 when it was used in the masted *Alexandra* and mastless *Dreadnought*.

The year 1867 saw the first introduction of twin screws into a ship of the battle-fleet, the *Penelope*, and from 1870 onwards only the *Swiftsure* and *Triumph* were built without them. With the *Iris* and *Mercury*, their compound engines consisted of four cylinders for each 3,500 horsepower engine, and they had two each. Owing to the narrowness of their hulls they had to be placed one ahead of the other, so that the ships were full of machinery to an extent that had been hitherto quite unacceptable, but it did make them the fastest ships in the world, steaming in the case of the *Iris* at over 18 knots.

## Boilers

In the 1850s and 1860s the simple rectangular shell-boiler was in general use, with low pressures of 20 to 30 pounds per square inch. In the 1870s the cylindrical Scotch fire-tube boiler was introduced, a type that became widely favoured for marine use. In this boiler tubes about 3 feet wide passed from the furnace through the shell-boiler heating the water round them. The cylindrical shape plus thicker skins permitted high steam pressures so that the fire-tubes were often corrugated in section to withstand them, and pressures of as much as 250 pounds per square inch were eventually developed in steel boilers of this type. The disadvantages of the Scotch boiler were, one, the great weight of the shell needed in a high-pressure boiler and two, the waste of fuel, some of which, especially with forced draught, would blow half burnt through the tubes and continue burning uselessly and smokily at the base of the funnel.

Meanwhile, in the 1880s, a new type of boiler was being evolved with qualities especially applicable to warships, the water-tube boiler. In this the process was reversed; the water was contained in tubes which passed through the furnace. The pressure being inside instead of outside the tube, there was no danger of them collapsing and with small-bore tubes the thickness of metal required to resist bursting at high pressures was comparatively light, though the bigger the tube the thicker the metal. Apart from the overall saving of weight, the small quantity of water required meant that steam pressure could be increased much more quickly than with the cylindrical boiler, a vital consideration in a naval vessel, which, in the nature of her service, is given to sudden departures from cold boilers, or needs instant speed on the sighting of an enemy.

In Britain Babcock and Wilcox, and Yarrow, were experimenting with them, but the French led the field with a small-tube boiler called the 'Belleville' which they started installing in battleships in the early 1890s. It was the middle nineties before the Royal Navy experimented with water-tube boilers, installing a variety of types in torpedo-gunboats. Between 1895 and 1898 the following were tried: in *Sharpshooter* Belleville's; in *Sheldrake* Babcock and Wilcox's; in *Seagull* Niclausse's (à German make); in *Spanker* Du Temple's; in *Salamander* Mumford's; and in *Speedy* Thornycroft's. In the event the French experience in large ships persuaded Their Lordships to order Bellevilles in the *Canopus* class battleships, the first of which was launched in 1897, and in the two huge cruisers *Powerful* and *Terrible*, both launched in 1895.

The water-tube boiler was much more complex than the fire-tube, and its adoption was strongly resisted in some quarters, through fear of troubles and breakdowns. Troubles and breakdowns were unfortunately all too frequent initially, for the British did not have engineers with the experience and knowledge to look after the boilers. Those who could showed marvellous results. Eventually, after a Committee of Inquiry had recommended the dropping of the water-tube boiler, and the Admiralty had compromised by ordering ships with both types – a bad arrangement – the larger-tubed Yarrow-type water-tube boiler was adopted. By this time the difficulties with the Belleville boilers had been overcome and they worked perfectly. The last ship in the navy to steam with them was the royal yacht *Victoria and Albert* which was broken up in 1954.

# 18

## William White's Battleships

Although White had put his name to the design for the *Nile* and *Trafalgar*, already described, these had been built to the dictate of the First Sea Lord, Sir Arthur Hood, who wanted improved *Dreadnoughts*, and got them. In 1888, on the eve of the Naval Defence Act, White was asked to produce a further design for a class of battleship which became the *Royal Sovereign* class, and which Hood hoped would be improved *Niles*. White's ideas prevailed in one very important respect in that the ships were to be high-freeboard, raised by one deck. This improvement on the *Admirals* was made possible by an increase of 60 feet in the length, 7 feet in the beam, and an improvement in compound armour which made a 2-inch reduction in thickness possible over the *Niles*, with the subsequent saving in weight. These benefits, however, did not permit the main armament to be housed in turrets at the new elevation, so the 13·5s were put in open barbettes.

At last a formula had been evolved which could be repeated with confidence and the battle-fleet was about to assume a relatively uniform appearance, after the strange assortment of misfits that had been the legacy of fifteen years of trial and error. For the first time there was a class of mastless battleship that looked right, and with their ability to fight their guns dry at 17 knots, they were a great advance on any other capital ship.

The *Royal Sovereign*, name ship of the class, was the first to be built, and she was built in a hurry in Portsmouth dockyard, completing in two years eight months (1889–92). Considering that the royal dockyards had always been notoriously slow compared with commercial firms, taking six or seven years over each of the *Admirals*, this sudden spurt says much for the persuasive powers of the Admiral Superintendent, Rear-Admiral John Fisher. (It must still be noted that the *Revenge* of this class of seven was built at Palmer's yard in three years and a month.) Fisher was soon to become the overpowering influence on warship design for the Royal Navy, but not just yet. Sir Arthur Hood's more cautious approach, which had been so influential on design since the early 1860s, was still important in 1889, and what would have been the eighth *Royal Sovereign* was modified to carry two turrets, which involved lowering the main armament a deck fore and aft, so that she was a low-freeboard ship and indeed an improved *Nile*. He called her the *Hood*, presumably after one of his more illustrious ancestors. She naturally did not perform so well as her half-sisters, and so proved the superiority of the high-freeboard type. In 1914 she was sunk in the south entrance to Portland Harbour to prevent torpedoes being fired through it, and she is still there.

Only one of the *Royal Sovereigns* saw any service in the First World War, the rest having been sold, or, in the case of the *Empress of India*, sunk as a target ship, just before it. The *Revenge*, however, survived as the gunnery training ship and, at the beginning of the war, fitted with blisters that could be trimmed to list her to starboard so as to increase the elevation of her guns, she did service as a monitor off the Belgian coast and was renamed *Redoubtable* in 1915.

Even more successful was the class that followed, the nine *Majestics* which completed in the middle and late 1890s. The particular advance in these ships was the adoption of Harvey's steel armour which allowed a reduction of half the thickness of armour on the belt from 18 inches compound in the *Royal Sovereigns* to 9 inches of steel for the same protection. Naturally, the saving in weight on the belt allowed for additional weight elsewhere. Armoured shields were fitted over the barbettes which encased the guns and moved round with them. Although there was a difference in principle between the functioning of the old round turrets and the shielded barbette, people soon started calling the latter 'turrets' again, as it was easier. The *Majestics* were not the first to get them but the *Centurions*, which will be described with the smaller battleships. The *Majestic* and *Magnificent* became well known as the first and second flagships of the Channel Fleet from 1895 to 1904. All saw some service in the First World War, though obsolescent by then. The *Majestic* was the only war casualty, sunk by a *U*-boat while a flagship with the Dardanelles Fleet. *Jupiter*, *Hannibal* and *Caesar* were at sea for the war, but the rest were confined to harbour duties before the Armistice.

The *Majestics* were followed three years later by the six ships of the *Canopus* class, which were essentially the same as the *Majestics*, the main improvements being armour protection to their bows and boilers. They differed in appearance, as the two side-by-side funnels gave way to two in line. Like the *Majestics*, they were employed as second-class battleships in the war in distant parts of the Empire, far from the German High Seas Fleet. Two of them, *Goliath* and *Ocean*, were sunk by the Turks during the Dardanelles operations in 1915. Altogether the British lost five old battleships during this campaign, which was the greatest loss in terms of capital ships since the Dutch came up the Medway in 1667.

Hard on the heels of the *Canopus* class came the *Formidables* and *Londons*, slightly bigger, with improved 12-inch guns of higher velocity. There were three *Formidables* and only one survived the war. The *Formidable* herself was torpedoed in the Channel with the Fifth Battle Squadron in 1915 and the *Irresistible* was the victim of a mine in the Dardanelles in the same year. Of the five *Londons*, four served the war in the Mediterranean, but the fifth, the *Bulwark*, was destroyed at Sheerness in November 1914, by an accidental explosion. The last class of the second generation of White's battleships was the *Duncans*. These were to be 19- instead of 18-knot battleships, and were built 5 feet longer and some hundreds of tons lighter than the *Formidables*. Of the six of them, the *Montagu* suffered the rare indignity to a battleship of being wrecked, in fog on Lundy Island in 1906. Two more were lost during the war in the Mediterranean, the *Cornwallis* by torpedoes from a *U*-boat and the *Russell* by a mine. They were the first class to cost more than £1,000,000 per ship.

The last class and final expression of White battleships were the eight *King Edward*

# THE BATTLE-FLEET

CAESAR 1896, HANNIBAL 1896, ILLUSTRIOUS 1896, JUPITER 1895, MAGNIFICENT 1894, MAJESTIC 1895, MARS 1896, PRINCE GEORGE 1895, VICTORIOUS 1895
14,900 *tons* 390′ × 75′ × 26½′. Guns 4 12″, 12 6″, 16 12-*pdrs.*, 12 3-*pdrs.* Torpedo tubes 18″, 1 *stern mounted, 4 submerged.* Main armour (*Harvey steel*) 9″ *belt to* 14″ *forward bulkhead and* 12″ *aft bulkhead,* 14″ *barbettes and* 10″ *shields,* 6″ *casemates,* 4″ *to* 2½″ *decks,* 14″ *conning towers.* Engines and speed *Triple expansion; 10,000 h.p.; 16 knots. Forced draught; 12,000 h.p.; 17 knots.*

MAJESTIC Class battleships

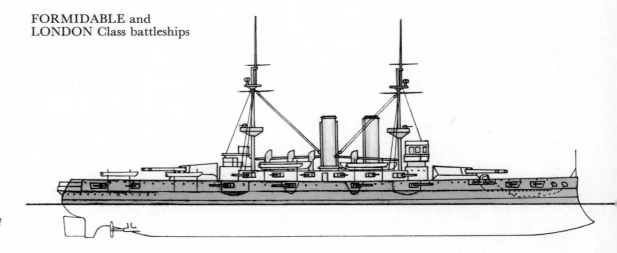

ALBION 1898, CANOPUS 1897, GLORY 1899, GOLIATH 1898, OCEAN 1898, VENGEANCE 1899
12,950 *tons* 390′ × 74′ × 25¾′. Guns 4 12″, 12 6″, 10 12-*pdrs.*, 6 3-*pdrs.* Torpedo tubes 4 18″ (*submerged*). Main armour (*Steel, belt and barbette Krupp*) 6″ *belt,* 10″ *to* 6″ *forward bulkhead,* 12″ *to* 6″ *aft bulkhead,* 12″ *to* 6″ *barbettes with* 8″ *shields,* 2″ *to* 1″ *decks,* 12″ *conning towers.* Engines and speed *Triple expansion; 13,500 h.p.; 18¼ knots.* Remarks *Built shallow draught to go through the Suez Canal.*

CANOPUS Class battleships

FORMIDABLE 1898, IMPLACABLE 1899, IRRESISTIBLE 1898, BULWARK 1899, LONDON 1899, PRINCE OF WALES 1902, QUEEN 1902, VENERABLE 1899
15,000 *tons* 431¾′ (*o/a*) × 75′ × 25′. Guns 4 12″, 12 6″, 16 12-*pdrs.*, 6 3-*pdrs.* 4 18″ (*submerged*). Main armour (*Steel*) 9″ *to* 3″ *belt to* 12″ *to* 9″ *aft bulkhead,* 3″ *bow and* 1½″ *stern plating,* 12″ *to* 6″ *barbettes with* 10″ *to* 8″ *shields, casemates* 6″, 2½″ *to* 1″ *decks,* 14″ *conning towers.* Engines and speed *Triple expansion; 15,000 h.p.; 18 knots.* Remarks *There were differences in the distribution of the deck armour between the two classes, and in the London's the heavy forward armoured bulkhead was suppressed.*

FORMIDABLE and LONDON Class battleships

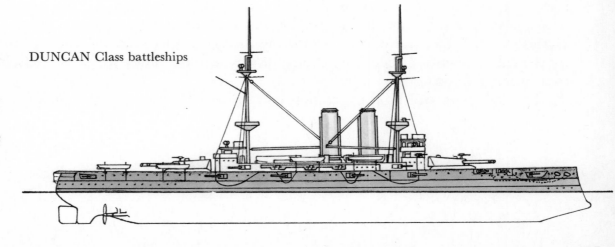

ALBEMARLE, CORNWALLIS, DUNCAN, EXMOUTH, MONTAGU, RUSSELL, all 1901
14,000 *tons* 432′ (*o/a*) × 75½′ × 25¼′. Guns 4 12″, 12 6″, 10 12-*pdrs.*, 6 3-*pdrs.* Torpedo tubes 4 18″ (*submerged*). Main armour 7″ *to* 3″ *belt,* 3″ *bows,* 1½″ *stern,* 11″ *to* 7″ *aft bulkhead,* 11″ *to* 4″ *barbettes with* 10″ *to* 8″ *shields,* 6″ *casemates,* 2″ *to* 1″ *decks,* 12″ *conning towers.* Engines and speed *Triple expansion; 18,000 h.p.; 19 knots.* Remarks *Last battleships to be painted in the old black, white and buff before the navy went grey.*

DUNCAN Class battleships

*VIIs*. They were bigger by over 20 feet in the length and 3 feet in the beam, and had a very powerful secondary armament which included four 9·2-inch guns as well as the 6-inch. Owing to a quirk in the design of their underwater lines, they moved slightly crabwise through the water, their bows pointing a little to port or to starboard of the course they were steering. When seen steaming together as a squadron they appeared to make a crooked line and were known as a class as the 'Wobbly Eight'. In the war, though powerful ships, their 19 knots were no good to a battle-fleet of dreadnoughts which manœuvred at 21 knots. So they remained round the home ports or in the Mediterranean. The name ship of the class, when launched by King Edward VII, was by his order always to be a flagship. At the beginning of 1916, while playing her part as flagship of the Third Battle Squadron, she had temporarily to leave it for Devonport to change her guns. On the return trip to reclaim her admiral, as a private ship, she was mined off Cape Wrath and sank. The only other casualty in the class was the *Britannia*, which was sunk by *UB50* off Cape Trafalgar in November 1918, two days before the Armistice.

Altogether forty-seven of White's high-freeboard battleships were built for the Royal Navy over ten years, and their general uniformity speaks for the excellence of their conception. They never saw action against a foreign battle-fleet, but White-type battleships, built in private yards for the Japanese Navy, utterly defeated a Russian fleet at the Battle of Tsushima in 1905.

## White's Three Smaller Battleships

A requirement for smaller, lighter-draught battleships for service abroad, especially on the China station, produced two sisters that were between the *Royal Sovereigns* and the *Majestics*. These were the *Barfleur* and *Centurion*, which, while they retained a belt of compound armour, had steel shields over the barbettes of their 10-inch guns. The *Centurion* did plenty of China time as flagship, 1894–1901 and 1903–5. Her crew under Captain Jellicoe played a prominent part in settling the Boxer Rebellion in 1900. The *Barfleur* also did a commission as second flagship in China over the period of the Boxer Rising and her commander, David Beatty, was in the thick of it.

The third, the *Renown*, was three years younger and a reduced *Majestic*. Because she impressed Vice-Admiral Sir John Fisher as a fast ship, he thrice hoisted his flag in her in spite of her 10-inch guns, the second time for the supreme honour as flagship of the Mediterranean Fleet. She was also the principal flagship at Queen Victoria's Diamond Jubilee Review in 1897, and in 1905 took the Prince and Princess of Wales to India and back. None of the trio survived quite to the war.

Sir William White's splendid services as Constructor came to an end when he resigned from ill-health in 1902, said to have been largely brought about by his mortification over the accident to the *Victoria and Albert III*. This was the new steel-built screw yacht which White designed to replace the old wooden paddle-wheel yacht, and which was launched in May 1899. After being engined she was dry-docked for fitting out. It was now that little changes and additions were made, often at the insistence of the Queen's courtiers and family, who had suggestions on what the Queen might like. It was not easy for White's subordinates, who were executing his plan, to resist requests

*H.M.S.* Royal Sovereign (1891) *was the name ship of a class of high-freeboard battleship of a powerful balanced design, which could fight their guns in nearly all weathers, and which could keep up their knots steaming in heavy seas far better than the low-freeboard ships. Over forty battleships based on the* Royal Sovereign *design were subsequently built for the Royal Navy, and many more were either purchased by foreign navies from British yards or built abroad.*

| | | | |
|---|---|---|---|
| **A** | Captain's cabin | **H** 6-pdr. guns | **P** Torpedo magazine |
| **B** | Wardroom | **I** Torpedo tubes | **Q** 13·5-inch shell room |
| **C** | Officers' cabins | **J** Conning tower | **R** 13·5-inch (charge) magazine |
| **D** | 13·5-inch guns in barbettes | **K** Midshipmen | **S** Engineers |
| **E** | Secretaries', Clerks' and Writers' offices | **L** Ablutions | **T** Engines |
| **F** | 3-pdr. guns | **M** Sick bay | **U** Stokehold |
| **G** | 6-inch guns | **N** Diving equipment | **V** 6-inch ammunition |
| | | **O** O.Rs' bar | |

0    10    20    30    40    50  Scale in Feet

from the Court, though in the end they clearly were negligent in assessing the extent and possible effect of the increasing top weight the vessel was taking on. One item not in Sir William's plans was a heavy hand capstan, in case the Queen might like to see the anchor weighed in the traditional manner to the accompaniment of sea-shanties and a fiddler standing on top of it.

The enrichments completed, it was planned to float the yacht out on 3 July 1900. Early that morning the water was let in, but so much top-hamper was on her by this time that when the water rose high enough, the biggest, newest yacht in the world, and the Queen of England's too, fell over in the dock. 'Oh won't there be a row about this,' said the Lords of the Admiralty, and so there was. There was nothing wrong with the original design, but the accident was ultimately Sir William's responsibility, and he is said to have been furious with the Queen's Marine Painter, the Chevalier de Martino, for suggesting to him before the accident that the yacht might be becoming unstable. It was a great shame that his career in the Admiralty should have closed on such a note, but it cannot dim his achievement in forging for his country an unbeatable naval instrument.

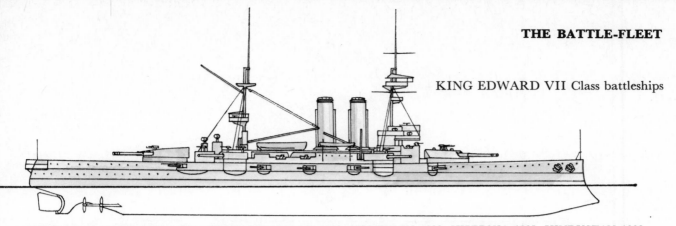

KING EDWARD VII Class battleships

AFRICA 1905, BRITANNIA 1904, COMMONWEALTH 1903, DOMINION 1903, HIBERNIA 1905, HINDUSTAN 1903, KING EDWARD VII 1903, NEW ZEALAND 1904
16,350 *tons* 453¾′ (o/a) ×78′×25′. Guns 4 12″, 4 9·2″, 10 6″, 14 12-*pdrs.*, 14 3-*pdrs.* Torpedo tubes 4 18″ (*submerged*). Main armour 9″-*to* 4″ *belt,* 12″ *to* 8″ *aft bulkhead,* 12″ *to* 6″ *barbettes with* 12″ *to* 8″ *shields,* 9·2″ *barbettes with* 9″ *to* 5″ *shields,* 7″ *battery,* 2½″ *to* 1″ *decks,* 12″ *conning tower.* Engines and speed *Triple expansion;* 18,000 *h.p.;* 18½ *knots.*

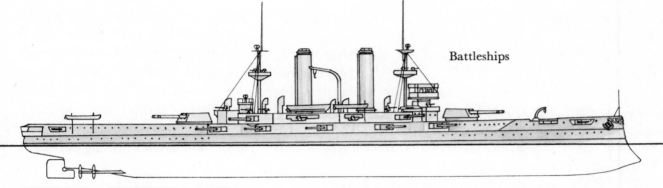

Battleships

SWIFTSURE and TRIUMPH, both 1903
11,800 *tons* 479¾′ (o/a) ×71′×25⅓′. Guns 4 10″, 14 7·5″, 14 14-*pdrs.*, 2 12-*pdrs.*, 4 6-*pdrs.* Torpedo tubes 2 18″ (*submerged*). Main armour 7″ *to* 3″ *belt,* 3″ *aft bulkhead,* 7″ *battery with* 6″ *bulkheads,* 10″ *barbettes with* 10″ *shields,* 7″ *to* 3″ *casemates,* 3″ *to* 1″ *decks,* 11″ *conning tower.* Engines and speed *Triple expansion;* 12,500 *h.p.;* 19 *knots.* Remarks *Intended for Chile as the* Constitucion *and* Libertad, *purchased* 1903.

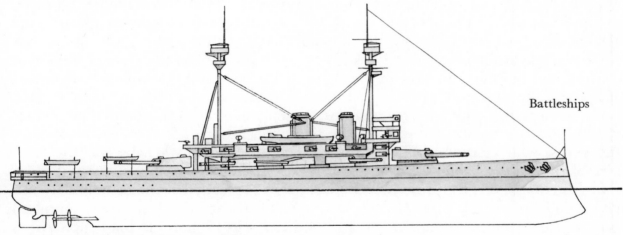

Battleships

AGAMEMNON and LORD NELSON, both 1906
16,500 *tons* 443½′ (o/a) ×79½′×25½′. Guns 4 12″, 10 9·2″, 24 12-*pdrs.*, 2-3 *pdrs.* Torpedo tubes 5 18″ (*submerged*). Main armour 12″ *to* 4″ *belt,* 8″ *aft bulkhead,* 6″ *to* 4″ *bow plating,* 12″ *barbettes and turrets,* 9·2″ *turrets* 7″, 12″ *conning tower,* 4″ *to* 1″ *decks.* Engines and speed *Triple expansion;* 16,750 *h.p.;* 18 *knots.*

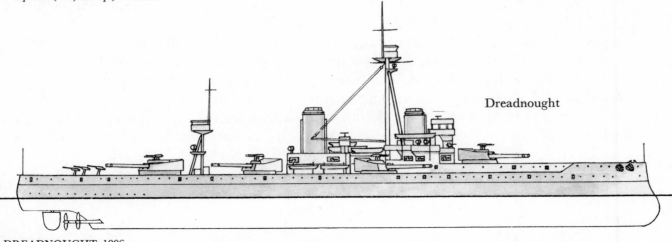

Dreadnought

DREADNOUGHT 1906
17,900 *tons* 527′ (o/a) ×82′×26½′. Guns 10 12″, 27 12-*pdrs.* Torpedo tubes 5 18″ *submerged.* Main armour 11″ *to* 4″ *belt,* 8″ *bulkheads,* 11″ *barbettes and turrets,* 4″ *to* ¾″ *decks,* 11″ *to* 8″ *conning tower.* Engines and speed *Turbines;* 23,000 *h.p.;* 21 *knots.*

# 19

# Watts and the Dreadnoughts

The most stimulating time in the history of British warship construction must surely have been the ten years following the appointment of Sir John Fisher as First Sea Lord in 1904, when there was created the mightiest fleet of battleships and battle-cruisers the world was ever to see. It was during this period that the designs were presided over by Sir Philip Watts, who succeeded Sir William White in 1902 and continued as Constructor until 1912. All but nine of the battle-fleet that fought at Jutland were Watts's ships. Born in 1846, the son of an Admiralty Constructor, Watts spent the first fifteen years of his professional life in royal dockyards. He then went to Elswick as Chief Naval Architect, succeeding William White, as seventeen years later he was again to succeed him as Chief Constructor of the Royal Navy.

Initially it was other people's battleships that were joining the service. The whole class of White's *King Edward VIIs* was building or to be built; the *Hibernia* did not complete until January 1907, a month after the *Dreadnought* which had made her obsolete. Then there were the *Triumph* and *Swiftsure*. These were two light-weight 10-inch battleships, designed for Chile by Sir Edward Reed, and bought while fitting out by the Government for political reasons. They were very unlike the style of ships that Sir Edward had built for the navy in the 1860s, being lean and fast and heavily armed for their size. Like most purchases they had some indigestible qualities, like their 10-inch main armament, and 7·5-inch secondary armament, unique in the battle-fleet. Their outstanding feature in appearance was the two great goose-necked cranes amidships, up and across which Edmund Carver used to send defaulters when he was the commander of the *Swiftsure*. She went out to the East Indies as flagship in 1913 and her sister was in Hong Kong the same year. Both ships were recalled to the Middle East and served at the Dardanelles. *Triumph*, because she had come straight from China and had not had an opportunity to land them, still had her nets rigged. German submarines appeared in the area, and the Admiral ordered her to get them out. When the attack came the torpedo went through them like butter and she shortly afterwards sank.

Watts felt that the time had come for a substantially faster and more heavily-armed type of battleship than the White battleships, but he received little support from his employers, who were not in a hurry to make their battle-fleet obsolete prematurely, with some of it not built. He did get permission to carry on with a pair of battleships to be called *Lord Nelson* and *Agamemnon*. These two were the last of the pre-*Dreadnought* battleships, and their most interesting feature was a mixed main armament. This comprised the four 12-inch as usual, but with an additional ten 9·2-inch in turrets amidships. This gun was a favourite with Watts in his early days as Constructor and had already been designed in strength into the new heavy armoured cruiser classes, *Duke of Edinburgh*, *Warrior* and *Minotaur*.

## H.M.S. *Dreadnought*

Events abroad were soon to realize Watts's dream of creating a new British battle-fleet of multi-turreted big-gun ships, much larger and faster than those of the White generation. In May 1905 the Japanese laid down two battleships with armaments of four 12-inch and twelve 10-inch guns, the second of them, the *Aki*, to have 20 knots. The Americans too were preparing to lay down in 1906 two fine battleships, the *South Carolina* and *Michigan*, which were to have eight 12-inch guns in four turrets borne on the centre-line, two forward and two aft.

With the prospect of foreign competition of this calibre it was time for the Admiralty to make its move and, as in similar circumstances in 1860, the new battleship that Watts produced radically broke with the past, being superior in armament, speed and protection to any battleship in the world, so much so that the word 'battleship' was dropped for ships of her type, and her name, the *Dreadnought*, was used instead; so that until after the Kaiser's war the world spoke of dreadnoughts and super-dreadnoughts and the battleships became the antediluvian pre-dreadnoughts. H.M.S. *Dreadnought* was 80 feet longer than the *King Edward VII*, carried ten 12-inch guns instead of four, eight of which could bear at once on a broadside, but had no secondary armament. She was the first large warship to have turbine propulsion, giving her 3 knots more than the old battle-fleet. In this she was in line with the two great Cunarders *Lusitania* and *Mauretania*, which started their careers in 1906 and 1907 respectively. The *Dreadnought* not only outmatched her rivals, she also outpaced them for, having been laid down in Portsmouth in October 1905, she was completed by December 1906, nearly two years before any of her rivals; indeed the Japanese ships took five and six years to build. The *Michigan* and *South Carolina*, laid down at the same time as the *Dreadnought*, completed in 1909. As with all revolutionary designs, not everything could be surely foreseen and she was heavily scantled to withstand the shock of the recoil of so great a broadside. Only after her trials had proved all was well could Watts relax. The *Dreadnought* was the first of several classes of capital ship to have her accommodation reversed, the men aft and the officers forward, the idea being to have the officers nearer to their duties on such a long ship. During the war she had the unique experience for a capital ship of running down a *U*-boat, but she did not join her fellow dreadnoughts at Jutland. Ironically, just before this battle, she was transferred as flagship of the Third Battle Squadron in home waters, formed from the *King Edward VII* class.

## The Dreadnoughts and Super-Dreadnoughts

The abandonment for practical reasons of a mixed main battery became necessary with the introduction of a central fire-control, but the abandonment of all secondary armament was open to criticism. In actions between big ships events were to prove that they would be fought at a distance at which the secondary armament would be superfluous, but in a fleet action where destroyers and light cruisers might get into torpedo-firing range, then they might strike before the slow-firing great guns could make a hit. In these

## THE BATTLE-FLEET

### BELLEROPHON Class dreadnoughts

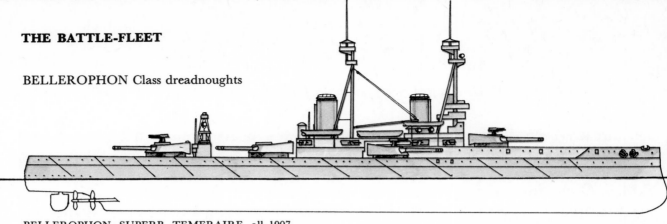

BELLEROPHON, SUPERB, TEMERAIRE, all 1907
18,600 *tons* 526′ (*o/a*) ×82½′ ×27′. Guns 10 12″, 16 4″, 4 3-*pdrs.* (*saluting*). Torpedo tubes 3 18″ (*submerged*). Main armour 10″ *to* 5″ *belt,*
9″ *to* 5″ *barbettes,* 11″ *turrets,* 11″ *conning tower,* 4″ *to* ½″ *decks.* Engines and speed 23,000 *h.p.;* 20¾ *knots.*

### ST VINCENT
### Class dreadnoughts

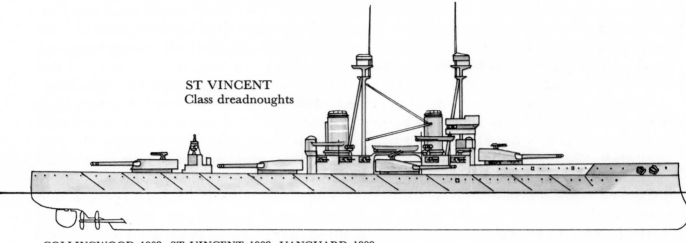

COLLINGWOOD 1908, ST VINCENT 1908, VANGUARD 1909
19,250 *tons* 536′ (*o/a*) ×84′ ×25½′. Guns 10 12″, 20 4″, 4 3-*pdrs.* (*saluting*). Torpedo tubes 3 18″. Main armour 10″ *to* 7″ *belt to* 8″ *to* 4″
*bulkheads,* 9″ *to* 5″ *barbettes with* 11″ *turrets,* 11″ *to* 8″ *conning tower,* 3″ *signal tower,* 3″ *to* 1½″ *decks.* Engines and speed *Turbines;* 24,000 *h.p.;*
21 *knots.* Remarks 12″ *guns,* 50-*calibre.*

### Dreadnought

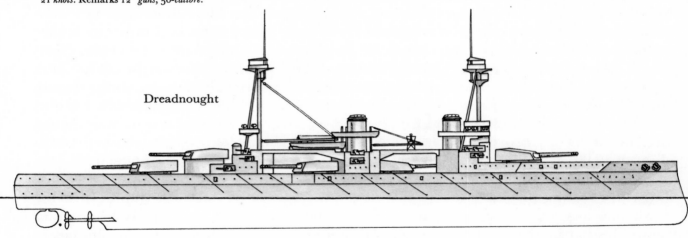

NEPTUNE 1909
19,900 *tons* 546′ (*o/a*) ×85′ ×24′. Guns 10 12″, 16 4″, 4 3-*pdrs.* (*saluting*). Torpedo tubes 3 18″. Main armour 10″ *to* 2½″ *belt to* 8″ *to* 4″
*bulkheads,* 9″ *to* 5″ *barbettes with* 11″ *turrets,* 11″ *conning tower,* 3″ *signal tower,* 3″ *to* 1½″ *decks.* Engines and speed *Turbines;* 25,000 *h.p.;*
21 *knots.*

### Dreadnoughts

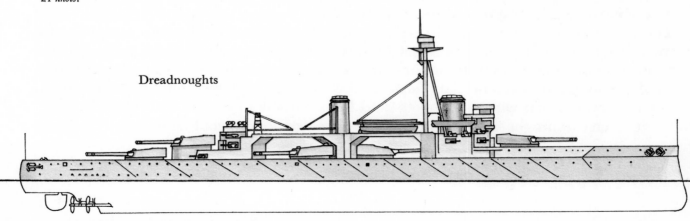

COLOSSUS and HERCULES, both 1910
20,000 *tons* 546′ (*o/a*) ×85′ ×25½′. Guns 10 12″, 16 4″, 4 3-*pdrs.* (*saluting*). Torpedo tubes 3 21″. Main armour 11″ *to* 7″ *belt to* 10″ *to* 4″
*bulkheads,* 11″ *to* 4″ *barbettes with* 11″ *turrets,* 11″ *conning tower,* 3″ *signal tower,* 4″ *to* 1½″ *decks.* Engines and speed *Turbines;* 25,000 *h.p.;*
21 *knots.*

circumstances a battery of quick-firing lighter guns would be most helpful. *Dreadnought* did not have this advantage; only a sprinkling of 12-pounders, some on top of the turrets. It is difficult to imagine that many could have been manned if the main battery was in action. In the three dreadnoughts that quickly followed, this deficiency was in some measure remedied by placing sixteen 4-inch guns in the superstructure. These were the *Bellerophon*, *Temeraire* and *Superb*, and were almost repeats of the *Dreadnought*, but distinguished from her by being given two tripod masts instead of one.

In the following year, 1908, emerged a further class, *St Vincent, Collingwood* and *Vanguard*. These again were almost repeats but slightly enlarged to offset the weight of their 50-calibre guns. All six fought at Jutland without a casualty between them. *Vanguard*, however, blew up at anchor in Scapa Flow on 9 July 1917 with a loss of eight hundred and four of her people. The explosion is supposed to have been due to faulty ammunition.

There had been criticism of the turret layout of the early dreadnoughts on the grounds that only four out of five turrets could ever bear at once. With the *Neptune* and her near sisters *Colossus* and *Hercules* an attempt was made to achieve a measure of broadside fire on all turrets. The two side turrets were therefore staggered and one turret had to fire across the ship under a flying catwalk. The blast problem was considerable; the guns firing across the deck had only a 5-degree tolerance either way. In order to give the mid-ship turrets as much space as possible the fourth turret was raised so that it could traverse over the fifth, but again blast effects made it impossible to fire over the aftermost turret.

The *Colossus* class was the last of the 12-inch dreadnoughts and the first of the 1909 'We want eight and we won't wait' programme; the other six were four super-dreadnoughts, and the battle-cruisers *Lion* and *Princess Royal*. The super-dreadnought was so called because the size of guns was raised to 13·5-inch. This was done because the higher velocity 50-calibre 12-inch guns caused the shells to wobble in the air, with a consequent loss of accuracy. By reducing the calibre to 45 and increasing the weight of the shell, both penetration and steadiness were achieved. The second feature of the super-dreadnought was that the main armament was placed on the centre-line, which fell in with American practice in multi-turreted ships. One of the side turrets was moved behind the forward turret and raised to traverse it, while the second remained amidships. This layout gave a better field of fire from all points except dead ahead.

The dreadnoughts were now approaching their classic silhouette with the modified *Orions*, the *King George V* class. The most obvious differences were the removal of the tripod mast from between the funnels to forward of them and the much heavier platform; the forward part of the superstructure bristled with 4-inch guns and there were four in main-deck casements. All the *Orions* except the *Monarch* fought at Jutland, as did the *King George Vs*, except for the *Audacious* which was sunk by a mine off Lough Swilly in Donegal at the beginning of the war. The *Centurion*, by virtue of being converted into a radio-controlled target ship between the wars, survived the longest. In the Second World War she played a number of roles. Fitted with wooden turrets and guns, she went to Bombay as a mock-up of the *Anson* to fool the enemy. Later she was a flak ship in the Suez Canal, and her final service and resting-place was as a blockship on the Normandy beaches in 1944.

The last improved *Orions* were the *Iron Duke* class, like the *King George Vs*, of four ships. They were over 40 feet longer than the *Orions*, nearly 100 feet longer than their progenitor, the *Dreadnought*, and 1 foot 6 inches wider in the beam. This was necessary for carrying the heavier armour and the 6-inch battery which replaced the 4-inch of the previous classes. Unlike the latter which was mainly housed in the superstructure, the 6-inch battery was mainly in the casements in the fo'c'sle on the upper-deck; being well forward and fairly low they proved extremely wet and so much water entered the seamen's quarters that they became very uncomfortable and unhealthy. Steps had to be taken to fit new bulkheads behind the guns to contain this water, and rubber joints between the shields also helped. The two 6-inch placed aft and one deck lower were found to be quite impracticable and were removed to the after superstructure. The *Iron Duke* herself, being the first of the class to complete in March 1914, was the first warship to mount an anti-aircraft armament, of two 3-pounders.

All four ships fought at Jutland, the *Iron Duke* famous as the Grand Fleet flagship. She was also the longest lived, for when the Treaty of Washington in 1930 swept her sisters away, she was merely demilitarized and turned into a gunnery and boys' training ship. When the Second World War began, though without her belt armour and two of her turrets, she still mounted six 13·5-inch guns, went to Scapa Flow as a coast-defence and depot ship, and was not towed away to the breakers until 1946. The *Marlborough* was hit amidships by a torpedo at Jutland, but managed to continue in the line for some time, though with a list to starboard.

## The *Queen Elizabeth*

Just occasionally a ship is designed and built which, taken overall, is of such an essential rightness that she must be forever remembered as the classic of her type. Such a one was the battleship *Queen Elizabeth*, the name ship of a class of five. It does not matter that ships were to be built later which surpassed her in fire-power, protection and speed. What matters is that in the context of her time, the First World War, she represented the ultimate expression of the *Dreadnought* type, with beautifully balanced graceful profile, superior speed, superior armament and protection. It was fitting that the *Queen Elizabeths* should be Watts's last class of battleship.

In the *Queen Elizabeths*, the ten 13·5-inch guns gave place to eight 15-inch, Q turret being abolished; the horsepower was raised to 75,000 from the 29,000 of the *Iron Dukes*, to give them 24 knots, which was 3 knots more than the rest of the battle-fleet. It is interesting to note that these 3 knots required over double the horsepower to achieve. They were the first class to be oil-fired.

The *Queen Elizabeth* was the first to complete, in January 1915, and, being a slight misfit until her sisters joined her to form the fast battle-squadron, she was sent out to the Dardanelles to act as flagship of the East Mediterranean Squadron, and supported the Gallipoli landing in the Dardanelles. Her stay was brief, however, for at the first sniff of a German submarine in the area she was ordered to sail smartly for home. She missed Jutland, but shortly afterwards was chosen by the new Commander-in-Chief of the Grand Fleet, Sir David Beatty, to be the fleet flagship, which she remained until after the war. She then became one of the navy's best-remembered and enduring peacetime flagships. In times of many national domestic difficulties and privations, the

*A bow view of H.M.S.* Warspite *as she appeared at the time of the Battle of Jutland; she and her sisters of the Queen Elizabeth Class represented the apogee in super-dreadnought design, and were the finest and handsomest capital ships of their day. The Warspite's services in the First and Second World Wars were so exceptional that she must surely have been the most successful battleship ever built (see page 166). The flag hoist spells out 'Rule Britannia'.*

people took some comfort in the prestige of their fleet – and this ship achieved immense prestige. During a big refit in 1926–7, she had her two funnels trunked into one, to take the smoke further aft, and anti-torpedo bulges fitted. In 1937–40 she had a much more extensive refit, amounting to a partial rebuilding. This came about through the Washington Treaty terms which restricted the building of new battleships, and the best of the old capital ships were therefore reconstructed to attempt to repel attacks from the ever-increasing potential of the aeroplane. Her trunked funnel and superstructure, engines, boilers and 6-inch battery were all taken out and replaced with lighter small-tube boilers, geared turbines, a new profile of a single and smaller funnel, a tower bridge and a secondary armament of high-angle 4·5-inch guns in twin turrets. The saving in weight permitted increased deck armour and her 15-inch main battery was modified to give a maximum elevation of 30 degrees, which increased the range from 23,400 yards to 32,000 yards. In this guise, the *Queen Elizabeth* went out again as flagship of the Mediterranean Fleet, but had the indignity of being badly damaged by a limpet mine placed on her bottom by intrepid Italian frogmen in December 1941, as was her sister the *Valiant* at the same time. After being repaired, the *Queen Elizabeth* went to the Far East early in 1944, and fought the Japanese, still as a flagship.

All her sisters served at Jutland as the Fifth Battle Squadron, the *Barham* as flagship. They were ahead of the battle-fleet in support of the battle-cruisers. This brought them into close action with the High Seas Fleet and they were the most heavily engaged ships in the battle-fleet. The *Barham* achieved notoriety in the Second World War when she was sunk by a salvo of torpedoes in November 1941 off Crete and blew up with the loss of fifty-six officers and eight hundred and six men.

Of the three remaining sisters, *Valiant* underwent a refit similar to the *Queen Elizabeth* and spent an active war in the Mediterranean until joining the Far East Fleet in 1944. *Malaya*, the extra ship and the gift of the Federated Malay States, was not fully rebuilt, but remained, like the *Barham*, in her peacetime appearance. The *Barham* herself was still in her second trunked-funnel state when war broke out, and apart from some emergency deck armour, which could not be extensive because of the weight distribution, and some additional anti-aircraft guns, nothing further could be done to fit her for a war role.

Finally, the most famous of them all, the *Warspite*. Battleships did not often have a chance to fire their guns in anger, and mostly lay around in peacetime looking grand and menacing – the threat in being. So, as the *Queen Elizabeth* became famous in peace, the *Warspite* was to be in war; carving out a reputation with her 15-inch guns that is unique in naval history. At Jutland she was the most heavily engaged British battleship and withstood thirteen hits with heavy shells. In 1934 she was the first of the *Queen Elizabeths* to be taken in hand for the big rebuilding similar to that described for the *Queen Elizabeth* and *Valiant*. In *Warspite*'s case, the 6-inch battery was reduced to eight guns, but not suppressed altogether, and decked over, so that dual-purpose guns, capable of being used against aircraft, could have been mounted on deck, as they should have been.

It was in the Second World War that *Warspite* came into her own, known throughout the service as the 'Old Lady'. In the Norwegian debacle in 1940, she sailed up a fjord near Narvik, accompanied by destroyers, and sank eight German destroyers. As flagship in the Mediterranean in 1941, she hit the cruisers *Fiume* and *Zara* at the Battle of Matapan,

ORION Class super-dreadnoughts

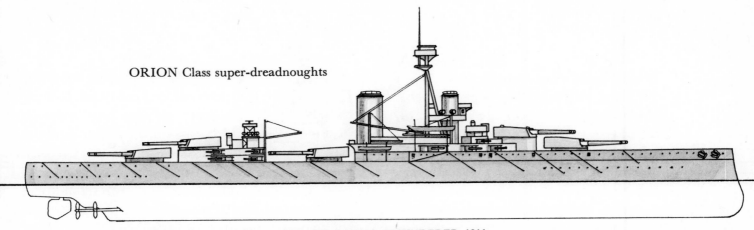

CONQUEROR 1911, MONARCH 1911, ORION 1910, THUNDERER 1911
22,500 *tons* 581' (*o/a*) ×88½' ×25'. Guns 10 13·5", 16 4", 4 3-*pdrs.* (*saluting*). Torpedo tubes 3 21". Main armour 12" to 9" *belt to* 10" *to* 3" *bulkheads*, 10" *to* 3" *barbettes with* 11" *turrets*, 11" *conning tower*, 6" *spotting tower*, 3" *director tower*, 4" *to* 1" *decks*, 1¾" *magazines.* Engines and speed *Turbines;* 27,000 *h.p.;* 21 *knots.*

KING GEORGE V Class
super-dreadnoughts

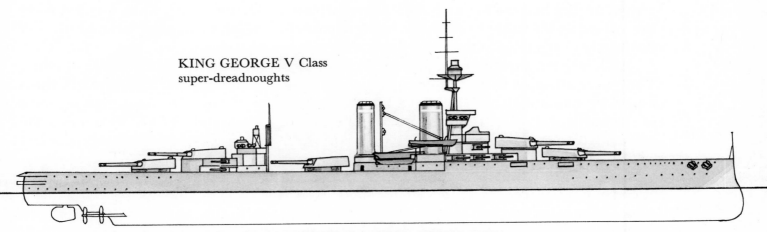

AJAX 1912, AUDACIOUS 1912, CENTURION 1911, KING GEORGE V 1911
23,000 *tons* 597½' (*o/a*) × 89' × 26¾'. Guns 10 13·5", 16 4", 4 3-*pdrs.* (*saluting*). Torpedo tubes 3 21". Main armour 12" *to* 8" *belt to* 10" *to* 4" *bulkheads*, 10" *to* 3" *barbettes with* 11" *turrets*, 3" *forward battery*, 11" *conning tower*, 6" *director tower*, 4" *to* 1" *decks.* Engines and speed *Turbines;* 31,000 *h.p.;* 21$\frac{7}{10}$ *knots.*

IRON DUKE Class super-dreadnoughts

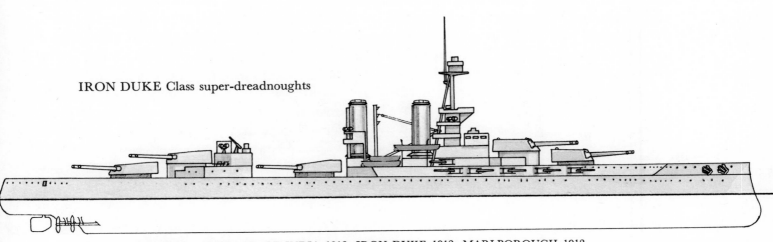

BENBOW 1913, EMPEROR OF INDIA 1913, IRON DUKE 1912, MARLBOROUGH 1912
25,000 *tons* 622¾' (*o/a*) ×90' ×27½'. Guns 10 13·5", 12 6", 2 3" A.A., 4 3-*pdrs.* (*saluting*). Torpedo tubes 4 21". Main armour 12" *to* 4" *belt to* 8" *to* 1½" *bulkheads*, 10" *to* 3" *barbettes with* 11" *to* 3" *turrets*, 11" *conning tower*, 2½" *to* 1" *decks and magazines.* Engines and speed *Turbines;* 29,000 *h.p.;* 21¼ *knots.*

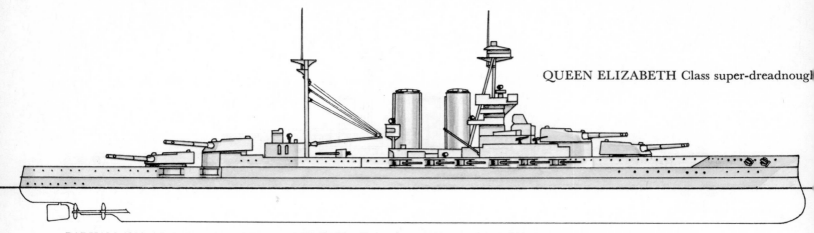

QUEEN ELIZABETH Class super-dreadnough[

**BARHAM 1914, MALAYA 1915, QUEEN ELIZABETH 1913, VALIANT 1914, WARSPITE 1913**
27,500 *tons* 645¾′ (*o/a*) × 90½′ × 29½′. Guns 8 15″, 14 6″, 2 3″ A.A., 4 3-*pdrs.* (*saluting*). Torpedo tubes 4 21″. Main armour 13″ *to* 6″ *belt
to* 6″ *to* 4″ *bulkheads,* 10″ *to* 4″ *barbettes with* 13″ *to* 11″ *turrets,* 11″ *conning tower,* 6″ *director tower,* 6″ *to* 4″ *tubes,* 3″ *to* 1″ *decks.* Engines and
speeds *Turbines;* 75,000 *h.p.;* 24 *knots.*

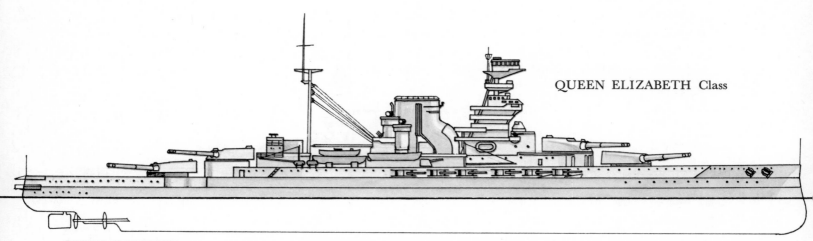

QUEEN ELIZABETH Class

QUEEN ELIZABETH
**Remarks** *As refitted in* 1926–7 *with anti-torpedo bulges, trunked funnels, rebuilt bridge platforms and control-top and light A.A. guns. Similarly refitted,* 1924–6
Warspite, 1927–9 Malaya, 1929–30 Valiant, 1930–3 Barham *which also was given an aircraft catapult on X turret and a tripod mast.*

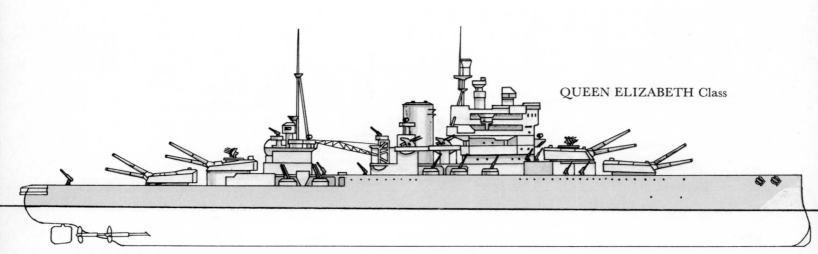

QUEEN ELIZABETH Class

QUEEN ELIZABETH and VALIANT reconstructed
**Remarks** *These two ships had the most complete reconstruction of the class – the former* 1937–40, *the latter* 1937–9. *The 6″ battery was suppressed
and the upper-deck built out to the full width of the hull. Ten twin 4·5″ dual purpose turrets replaced it. The maximum elevation of the 15″ guns was
raised to* 30°. *A new funnel and tower bridge was built with room abaft it for an aircraft catapult athwartships. Deck armour was increased, the
middle deck to 4″. The extra weight was mainly compensated for by fitting new high-pressure boilers.*

and bombarded Capuzzo, Valona, Bardia and Tripoli. She was badly hit by a bomb off Crete, and went to America for repairs and then to the Far East. She came back to the Mediterranean in 1943 for the Italian landings and had the honour of leading the surrendered Italian Fleet into Malta. At the landings, her shots were outstandingly accurate until she had her bottom blown out by one of the Germans' new glider bombs, which nearly sank her. After temporary repairs at Malta and Gibraltar, which included a good deal of concrete, she sailed home for a more thorough refit. 'Overlord', the invasion of Europe, was imminent and the services of such a well-worked-up ship could not be missed, so she made the D-Day bombardments and those that followed in a damaged state. Returning to Rosyth for new gun-barrels, she was hit by a mine aft which jammed Y turret. Patched up again, she supported the Walcheren landings, her last service. In all, from the time of the landings at D-Day, she had fired 1,500 shells from her main armament.

## The *Revenge* Class

Although these five ships do not properly belong to the Watts era, for he resigned in 1912, they closely relate to Watts's later ships, which the next pair of battleships, *Nelson* and *Rodney*, do not at all. Regarded by many as cut-price *Queen Elizabeths*, they were more accurately 15-inch *Iron Dukes*. Reverting to the latter's dimensions meant there was no room for the *Queen Elizabeths*' more powerful machinery. It is natural, though unfair, to regard them as the *Queen Elizabeths*' poor relations, since, though built specifically to operate with the Grand Fleet at 21 knots, they survived into the Second World War by virtue of their 15-inch guns and the tardiness of the Government to replace them.

As with the *Queen Elizabeths*, the adoption of 15-inch guns impelled the abandonment of Q turret, and with only three boiler-rooms they were the only dreadnoughts to have only one funnel. They were the last class to have the 6-inch secondary armament on the main-deck, and, this being placed much further aft than in the *Iron Dukes* and *Queen Elizabeths*, were much less incommoded by the sea. Two of them, the class-name ship *Revenge* and the *Royal Oak*, were present at Jutland and from November 1916 *Revenge* was the second flagship of the Grand Fleet. Between the wars, the *Revenges* and the *Queen Elizabeths* formed the backbone of the battle-fleet, but while the *Queen Elizabeths* went through extensive refits and rebuilds to keep up with developments, lack of knots made the *Revenges* increasingly obsolescent, and so nothing much was done to them and they were kept on in the hope that the politicians would permit their replacement before the next conflagration.

Unfortunately, this did not come to pass and these fine ships, major units of the fleet, found themselves in September 1939 plunged into another war for which they had not been designed and for which they were ill prepared. The best that could be done was to add light anti-aircraft guns wherever space permitted, and to give them a coat of camouflage paint and hope that the enemy would not see them.

In the event they gave reassuring presence to many a convoy, and only one was lost. As a class they had been the first to adopt the anti-torpedo bulges, and none so bulging as in the *Royal Oak*. This did not, however, prevent her being sunk by *U47* in Scapa Flow in October 1939, with a loss of seven hundred and eighty-six officers and men. In September 1940 the *Resolution* formed part of the force that was to land De Gaulle to a hero's welcome at Dakar. However, information on the temper of his compatriots there proved to be faulty, and in a debacle, not without its humorous side, the Allied force retreated, licking its wounds, one of which was in the *Resolution*, torpedoed by the French submarine *Beveziers*. Another victim was the *Ramillies*, which was damaged by a torpedo from a Japanese midget submarine while supporting the Allied landings in Madagascar. The *Royal Sovereign* had the unique experience of being lent to the Russians in 1944 for use in the Archangel area; they called her the *Archangelsk*.

## Three Purchased Dreadnoughts

To conclude the battleships of the Grand Fleet, mention must be made of four ships bought while building or completing for foreign powers at the beginning of the Kaiser's war. One of these eventually completed as a carrier, so will be mentioned elsewhere, but the other three proved first-class dreadnoughts and not at all the misfits this type of addition had tended to be. Two, indeed, were building for the Turks who were shortly to be at war with Britain, so that their presence in the Mediterranean in a hostile role, with, as it turned out, the German battle-cruiser *Goeben*, would have inevitably meant a serious drain on the Grand Fleet to right the balance of power there.

The third dreadnought was building for Chile to be called the *Almirante Latorre*, and was added as the *Canada*. She closely resembled the *Iron Duke* class, but was bigger and mounted 14-inch guns. She fought in the Fourth Battle Squadron at Jutland, and after the war was sold to the Chileans. For this reason she became by far the longest-lived of the dreadnoughts that fought at Jutland, a decorative sight at Valparaiso until 1958. Of the two building for Turkey, the *Reshadieh* was one of the two ships ordered from Britain in 1910. The Balkan War held them up and one was cancelled, the other was resumed in time to complete in August 1914. She also was very similar to the *Iron Dukes* in layout and armament, but shorter and beamier. As the *Erin* she fought at Jutland in the Second Battle Squadron, and was scrapped after the war. The other ship building for Turkey was the most interesting of the trio – indeed, the most interesting dreadnought in the Grand Fleet. She had originally been ordered by Brazil at a time when that country and Chile and the Argentine were having one of their remarkable naval building races. She was to be the most powerful of all dreadnoughts, and certainly her fourteen 12-inch in seven turrets along the centre-line were the most impressive-looking battery ever seen. She was laid down at Elswick's in 1911, and launched in 1913 as the *Rio de Janeiro*, but by this time Brazil no longer wanted her and she was put on the market. The Turks bought her and renamed her the *Sultan Osman I*. As she completed before war broke out, there was considerable danger of her being delivered, but her departure was delayed on one pretext or another until war came and she was taken over and renamed the *Agincourt*. Apart from her huge main armament, twenty 6-inch bristled from the main- and upper-deck batteries, and to bear the seven turrets, named after the days of the week, she had to be the largest dreadnought. Thirty-five dreadnoughts had been built or bought for the Royal Navy from 1907 and fought in the war, of which thirty-three survived it.

QUEEN ELIZABETH Class battleship

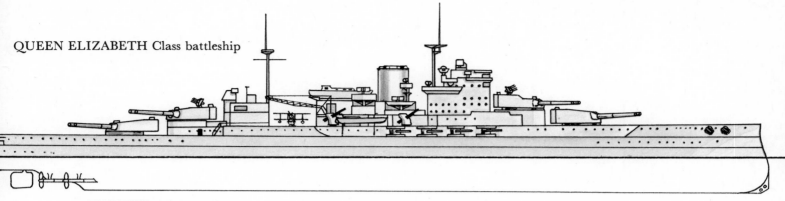

WARSPITE reconstructed

Remarks *Just as she had been the first to be taken in hand for the first big refit, so she was the first to be reconstructed, in 1934–7. This took much the same form as the Queen Elizabeth and Valiant, the main difference being that the 6″ battery was only partially suppressed, eight guns remaining; eight 4″ A.A. were added. The Malaya, though not rebuilt, was given a big refit in 1934–6 whereby she acquired two hangars and cranes for seaplanes, four twin 4″ mountings amidships, and an eight-barrel 20-mm. pom-pom each side of the trunked funnels. The war came before the Barham could be altered from her 1933 state.*

REVENGE Class super-dreadnoughts

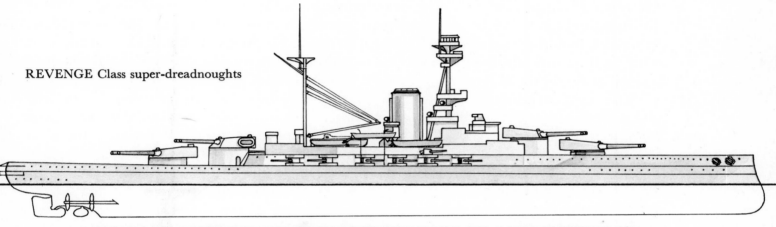

RAMILLIES 1916, RESOLUTION 1915, REVENGE 1915, ROYAL OAK 1914, ROYAL SOVEREIGN 1915

27,500 *tons* 624¼′ (*o/a*) × 88½′ × 28¾′. Guns 8 15″, 14 6″, 2 3″ *A.A.*, 4 3-*pdrs.* (*saluting*). Torpedo tubes 4 21″. Main armour 13″ *to* 1″ *belt to* 6″ *to* 4″ *bulkheads,* 10″ *to* 4″ *barbettes with* 13″ *to* 4½″ *turrets,* 11″ *conning tower,* 4″ *to* 1″ *decks. Engines and speed Turbines;* 40,000 *h.p.;* 21 *knots.*

REVENGE Class super-dreadnought

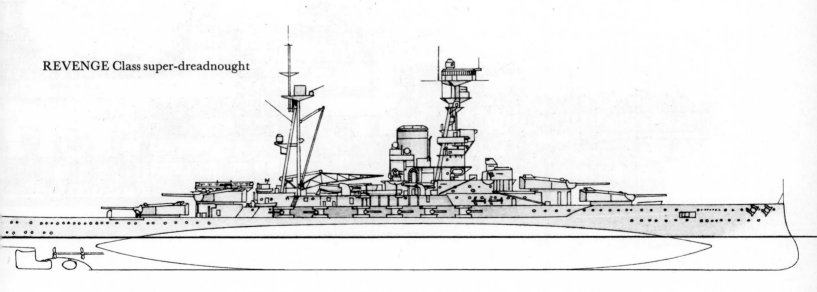

ROYAL OAK in 1939

Remarks *The main additions – an anti-torpedo bulge, an aircraft catapult on X turret and an improved control top.*

Scale in Feet

0   10   20   30   40   50

*H.M.S.* Barham, *as she appeared after her 1933–4 refit, when an aircraft catapult was placed on X turret. Like the rest of the* Queen Elizabeth *class, she had already had her bridge modified and her funnels trunked 1928–9, and at the end of the 1930s she was supposed to undergo the extensive reconstruction that was accorded the* Queen Elizabeth *and* Valiant, *but the war prevented this. She fought the battle of Jutland as flagship of the Fifth Battle squadron, which that day comprised the* Warspite, Valiant, Malaya *and herself. In World War 2 she fought at the Battle of Matapan and helped to sink the Italian cruiser* Zara. *On 25 November 1941, while on patrol between Crete and Cyrenaica, she was hit by a salvo of three torpedoes from a German U-boat, rolled over and blew up, with the loss of 56 officers and 806 men.*

A  Admiral's day cabin
B  Admiral's dining cabin
C  Pantry
D  Secretary
E  Flag Commander's cabin
F  Captain's day cabin
G  Band instruments
H  Admiral's steward
I  W/T office
J  Admiral's galley
K  Electric boat-lowering machine
L  Remote control office
M  Torpedo control
N  H.A. director
O  Spotting top
P  Gun director tower

Q  Admiral's chart house
R  Range finder
S  Flour and biscuit store
T  Boy seamen
U  Station plotting table
V  Dispensary
W  Sick bay
X  Petty Officers' pantry
Y  Carpenters' working space
Z  Petty Officers' mess
a  Clothing store
b  Clothing issue room
c  Lamp room
d  No. 5 prison
e  Boatswain's stores
f  Paint room

g  Seamen's heads
h  Paint store
i  Petrol tank compartment
j  Awning room
k  Canvas and cordage room
l  Capstan engine room
m  Fresh-water tank
n  Refrigerating and icemaking compartment
o  Meat room
p  Torpedo head magazine
q  Submerged torpedo room
r  Telephone exchange
s  15-inch shell room
t  15-inch magazine
u  Switchboard room

v  Hydraulic machinery
w  6-inch shell room
x  6-inch magazine
y  Lower conning tower
z  Boiler rooms
1  Printing office
2  Secretaries', Clerks' and Writers' offices
3  Captain's stores
4  Berths and cabins
5  Engineers
6  Mid. engine room
7  Oil tank
8  Engineers' racks
9  Electric lift
10 Telephone cabinet

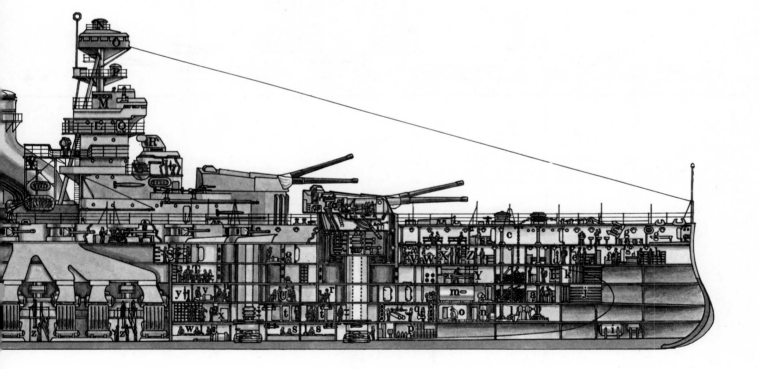

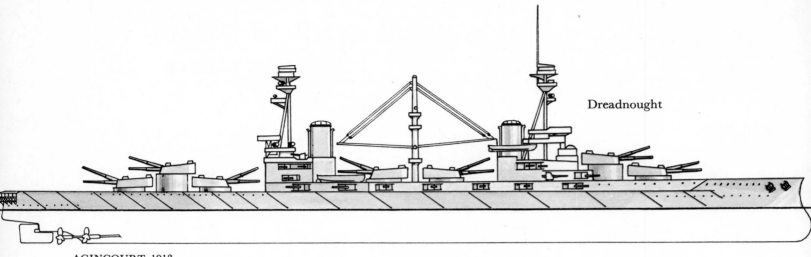

Dreadnought

**AGINCOURT 1913**
27,500 *tons* 671½ (*o/a*) ×89′ ×27′. Guns 14 12″, 20 6″, 10 3″, 2 3″ *A.A.* Torpedo tubes 3 21″. Main armour 9″ *to* 4″ *belt to* 6″ *to* 3″ *bulkheads,* 9″ *to* 3″ *barbettes with* 12″ *to* 8″ *turrets,* 6″ *battery,* 12″ *conning tower,* 2½″ *to* 1″ *decks.* Engines and speed *Turbines;* 34,000 *h.p.;* 22 *knots.* Remarks *Privately built for Brazil, purchased while fitting out by Turkey, forced purchase in 1914.*

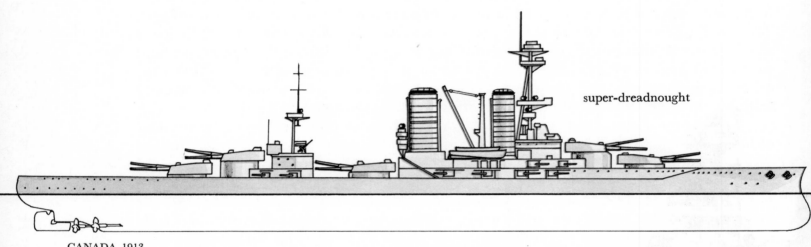

super-dreadnought

**CANADA 1913**
28,000 *tons* 661′ (*o/a*) ×92′ ×29′. Guns 10 14″, 16 6″, 2 3″ *A.A.,* 4 3-*pdrs.* (*saluting*). Torpedo tubes 4 21″. Main armour 9″ *to* 4″ *belt to* 4½″ *to* 3″ *bulkheads,* 10″ *to* 4″ *turrets and barbettes,* 11″ *conning tower,* 6″ *director tower,* 4″ *to* 1″ *decks,* 2″ *to* 1½″ *magazines.* Engines and speed *Turbines;* 37,000 *h.p.;* 22¾ *knots.* Remarks *Laid down for the Chileans as the* Almirante Latorre, *she was purchased in 1914, but sold to Chile after the war.*

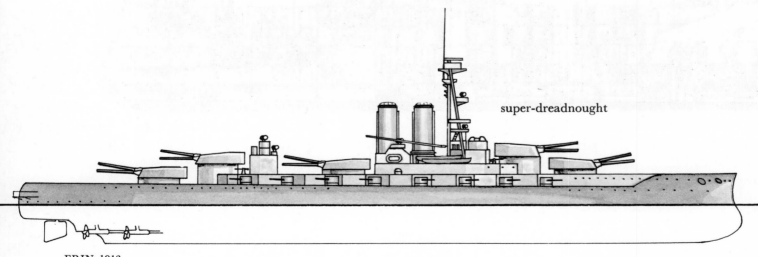

super-dreadnought

**ERIN 1913**
23,000 *tons* 559½′ (*o/a*) ×91½′ ×28⅜′. Guns 10 13·5″, 16 6″, 6 6-*pdrs.,* 2 3″ *A.A.* Torpedo tubes 4 21″. Main armour 12″ *to* 4″ *belt to* 8″ *to* 4″ *bulkheads,* 5″ *battery,* 10″ *to* 3″ *barbettes with* 11″ *to* 3″ *turrets,* 12″ *conning tower,* 3″ *to* 1″ *decks.* Engines and speed *Turbines;* 26,500 *h.p.;* 21 *knots.* Remarks *Privately built for the Turks, purchased 1914.*

# 20

## The Post-Dreadnought Battleships

Disarmament conferences, as we know, are the merest sophistry, but when there is a mutual desire to reduce the bills for the armed services, then some measures of agreement may be reached. So it was at the Washington Conference in 1921, at which Britain, America, France, Japan and Italy agreed on a formula by which their battle-fleets were reduced to a set tonnage, and the tonnage of ships to be built was restricted. The chief sufferer was the Royal Navy, which had its battle-fleet reduced to little more than the size of that of the Americans, and the long-term effect of this conference and subsequent ones was that old equipment had to be kept on beyond its useful life. One outcome was that the evil ambitions of the Germans and Japanese were more nearly fulfilled, they themselves abandoning their own undertakings when it suited them.

An outcome of the conference was that while Britain would be scrapping twenty-two of her dreadnoughts, she was to be allowed to build two battleships, the only two for ten years, which might have 16-inch guns, but must not exceed 35,000 tons. Construction could begin at once, so the restrictions forced Sir Tennyson d'Eyncourt completely to rethink their conception, as against the relative freedom of design that characterized the dreadnoughts. Every effort was to be made to get the maximum out of every ton. Triple mountings saved weight, two would be too few, so there were three, making a forceful main battery of nine 16-inch, one more than the American *Maryland* class, then building, and up to that time the most powerful ever to have been mounted, and only exceeded by the Japanese *Yamato* class with its nine 18-inch guns which appeared in the Second World War. As a further saving, the three turrets were mounted close together on the biggest fo'c'sle ever seen. Aft of this was the first of the tower bridges, an impressive structure, known in the service as 'Queen Anne's Mansions' after that part of the Admiralty. Further aft was a large single funnel, a great tripod mast and six twin 6-inch high-angle turrets, three each side. Armour was thick where it occurred but was restricted to protect her propulsion, guns and conning tower; all the rest was free of it. Her anti-torpedo bulge was also built in rather than extending over the outer plates as with the *Royal Sovereigns*. The use of aluminium and light fire-proofed woods helped to keep weights down and permit a large high-freeboard hull. The *Nelson* and *Rodney*, as they were named, were ingeniously designed ships of very high potential. By the time it came to fighting they were slow at only 23 knots, otherwise more powerful than anything they might meet in European waters, and it was mainly the guns of the *Rodney* that pulverized the *Bismarck*. Both fought distinguished wars, but the *Nelson* was unlucky in being hit on various occasions by two mines and a torpedo. The *Rodney* was hit by a bomb in 1940, but otherwise was untouched.

## The *King George V* Class and the *Vanguard*

It was not until 1 January 1937 that Britain was partially freed of the terms of the 1930 agreements, which by this time her potential enemies had renounced or were not a party to. There could now be no question of further delay in laying down new construction, even though the designs prepared were still based on restricted tonnage and calibre. There was, however, no time to change them, and a class of five battleships mounting ten 14-inch guns was immediately put in hand. They were to be Britain's last class, and the last class to see action. Compared with the *Nelsons* they presented a balanced and most handsome appearance. The two impressive quadruple turrets were placed fore and aft, and a twin turret abaft and above the fore turret. Protection showed a return to a more comprehensive belt, which rose to main-deck level and to beyond the turrets, and to lower-deck level almost to the bow and stern. As with the rebuilt *Queen Elizabeths* and the *Renown*, space was left for a fixed catapult athwartships to carry a Walrus spotting plane. When these were discarded, the boats were taken down from the superstructure and stowed on deck, thus making space for light anti-aircraft guns, for which there was pressing and increasing need. By raising the horsepower to over 100,000 it was hoped to reach 30 knots, but 27 or 28 were the most achieved in service.

None of the class was ready by the war, but the name ship was ready by December 1940; the last was the *Howe*, completed in August 1942. By the time the *Bismarck* made her first and last sortie in May 1941, the *King George V* was the Home Fleet flagship, and to her and the *Rodney* went the honour of sinking the German. The *Prince of Wales* had just completed, but went into action with dockyard 'maties' still aboard. The new 14-inch mounting gave trouble in both ships and the *Prince of Wales* was badly mauled. Her career was to be short and eventful. She took Churchill to meet Roosevelt that July for the momentous Atlantic Charter Conference, and in November went with the *Repulse* to the Far East to daunt the bellicose Japanese. They, however, were not to be put off, and by the time the two ships reached Singapore, war had begun. The Japanese at that time had an extremely well-trained fleet air arm which effectively exposed the vulnerability of the unescorted battleship and battle-cruiser by finding and sinking them both.

The *Duke of York*, as Home Fleet flagship in December 1943, fought the last British gun duel between capital ships when she engaged the *Scharnhorst*. Again the flagship of Sir Bruce Fraser in the Far East in 1945, she was in Tokyo Bay for the surrender of the Japanese. The *Anson*, as flagship of the First Battle Squadron in the Pacific, was the command ship at the retaking of Rangoon, and the *Howe* took part in the bombardment in support of the invasion of Italy, and later of islands in the Pacific. After the war the carrier overtook the battleship in prestige and when the flag was struck aboard the *Duke of York* in May 1949, to make way for a carrier, the role of the battleship in naval history virtually ended.

There is a touching story told about the *Anson* when she was guardship at Hong Kong after the war. A good number of Allied naval vessels were also present in the harbour when news of an imminent hurricane caused the order to be given for all ships

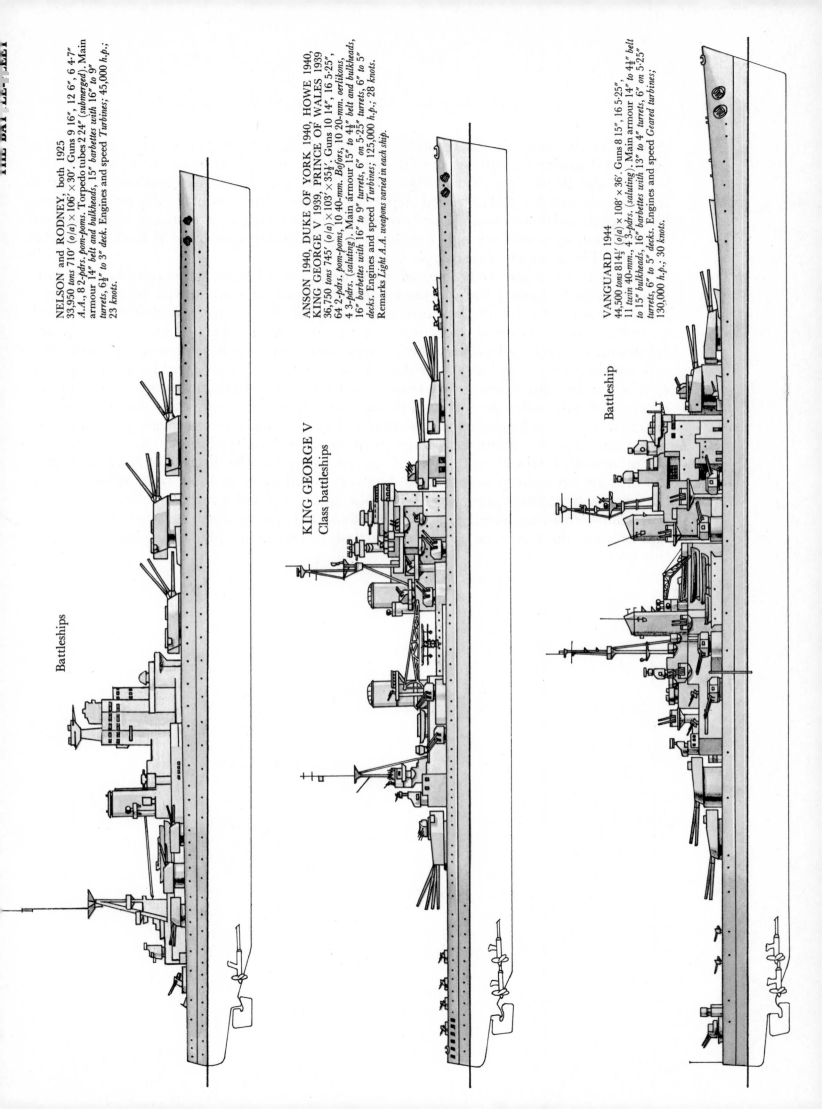

Battleships

NELSON and RODNEY, both 1925
33,950 tons 710' (o/a) × 106' × 30'. Guns 9 16", 12 6", 6 4·7"
A.A., 8 2-pdrs. pom-poms. Torpedo tubes 2 24" (submerged). Main
armour 14" belt and bulkheads, 15" barbettes with 16" to 9"
turrets, 6½" to 3" deck. Engines and speed Turbines; 45,000 h.p.;
23 knots.

KING GEORGE V
Class battleships

ANSON 1940, DUKE OF YORK 1940, HOWE 1940,
KING GEORGE V 1939, PRINCE OF WALES 1939
36,750 tons 745' (o/a) × 103' × 35½'. Guns 10 14", 16 5·25",
64 2-pdrs, pom-poms, 10 40-mm. Bofors, 10 20-mm. oerlikons,
4 3-pdrs. (saluting). Main armour 15" to 4½" belt and bulkheads,
16" barbettes with 16" to 9" turrets, 6" on 5·25" turrets, 6" to 5"
decks. Engines and speed Turbines; 125,000 h.p.; 28 knots.
Remarks Light A.A. weapons varied in each ship.

Battleship

VANGUARD 1944
44,500 tons 814⅓' (o/a) × 108' × 36'. Guns 8 15", 16 5·25",
11 twin 40-mm., 4 3-pdrs. (saluting). Main armour 14" to 4½" belt
to 15" bulkheads, 16" barbettes with 13" to 4" turrets, 6" on 5·25"
turrets, 6" to 5" decks. Engines and speed Geared turbines;
130,000 h.p.; 30 knots.

to leave for the open sea immediately. The Allied ships jostled their way out as best they could, and as the clamour of the crashes and the curses died away there was left the units of the Royal Navy's Far East Fleet. Then the signal flags fluttered from the *Anson*'s halliards for a disciplined departure in the proper order at the proper speed. As the great battleship swung slowly out into the lowering sky, the strains of the marine band on her quarter-deck and the thuds of the saluting guns floated back across the harbour. The grandeur had not yet departed.

There remains now only one sad afterthought of a battleship to consider. She was inappropriately named the *Vanguard* – *Rearguard* would have served better. In 1941 there still survived the obsolete turrets and guns of the *Courageous* and *Glorious*, landed when they were converted to carriers after the First World War. A new war emergency battleship was designed to carry them, a new battleship with her great-aunts' teeth. The hull was impressive, 55 feet longer than the *King George V*'s and 4 feet beamier than the *Hood*'s, and her displacement was over 1,000 tons more than that great ship. She did not commission until after the war and, though already an anachronism, it seemed a shame to throw her away, having spent the money. The *Vanguard* served as a sea-going training ship, with occasional moments as flagship on exercises. Finally, she could be seen at a buoy in Portsmouth Harbour, as flagship of the reserve fleet at the disposal of NATO, so that the bills for her upkeep were shared. She was towed away in 1960, sadly missed as the dockyard's most useful luncheon club. She had proved the finest sea boat of all the battleships, steaming swiftly on in conditions that during Exercise Mariner in 1953, had brought the largest of her Allies' battleships to a near halt, wallowing like a half-tide rock.

# 21

## The Battle-Cruiser

The great commerce raider or commerce protector, larger, faster and more powerfully armed than the normal run of cruising vessel, was a type of fighting ship which had appeared over the years. The American monster frigates were a successful type in the 1812 war, and it was the further successes of the large fast cruiser in the American Civil War that prompted the Admiralty to lay down *Inconstant*, *Shah* and *Raleigh* (see pages 131, 132) in the late 1860s and early 1870s, ships with the size and armament of a battleship, but with protection sacrificed to superior speed. The word 'battle-cruiser' was never applied to these ships, which were found too expensive to run on a peacetime budget, especially after the *Shah*'s experience in having to take on an armoured turret-ship, the *Huascar*, which could in theory have sunk her.

The word 'battle-cruiser' applies to a small group of dreadnought-type vessels built between 1906 and 1920 which combined the hitting power of a unit of the battle-fleet with much greater speed. Originally, the intention was that these ships should only have to be able to outrun and outgun any contemporary cruiser, and a mixed armament of 10-inch and 7·5-inch was considered; later a single calibre, like the projected *Dreadnought*, was favoured, and the 9·2-inch gun seemed suitable. And so it would have been if the original requirement had remained the same, but two considerations raised the calibre to the current primary battleship armament, the 12-inch gun. The Japanese were building large ships with a high speed and a mixed armament of 12-inch and 8-inch guns; secondly, a role was seen for squadrons of battle-cruisers in support of the battle-fleet. As the original intention had only been to protect them against 8-inch shells, this new demand held sinister implications. The battle-cruisers were just not built to tangle with the battle-fleet, but what guarantee was there that in the event of a fleet action the Commander-in-Chief would not at some stage feel compelled to throw in so powerful a force, even if it meant throwing it away? In the event it was not the dreadnoughts that troubled the battle-cruisers, but the battle-cruisers themselves, for battle-cruisers were not built to fight battle-cruisers, or at least the early ones were not. Such a clash, however, once both sides had them, was inevitable.

The Battle of the Falkland Islands at the beginning of the First World War was the classic instance of the correct use of battle-cruisers, when *Invincible* and *Inflexible* were sent far from home to intercept and destroy Graf Spee's successful cruiser squadron, so dangerous to our trade routes, and which had proved so fatal to Admiral Cradock at Coronel. The battle-cruiser achieved the apogee of its prestige at the Falklands, destroying

179

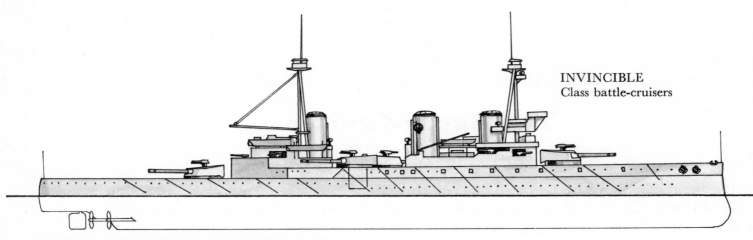

INVINCIBLE
Class battle-cruisers

INDOMITABLE, INFLEXIBLE, INVINCIBLE, all 1907
17,250 *tons* 567′ (*o/a*) × 78½′ × 25½′. Guns 8 12″, 16 4″, 1 3″. Torpedo tubes 5 18″. Main armour 6″ *to* 4″ *belt to* 7″ *to* 6″ *bulkheads,*
7″ *to* 2″ *barbettes with* 7″ *turrets,* 10″ *conning tower,* 2½″ *to* 1″ *decks,* 2½″ *magazines.* Engines and speed *Turbines;* 41,000 *h.p.;* 25 *knots.*
Remarks *All had their fore funnels raised by March* 1915.

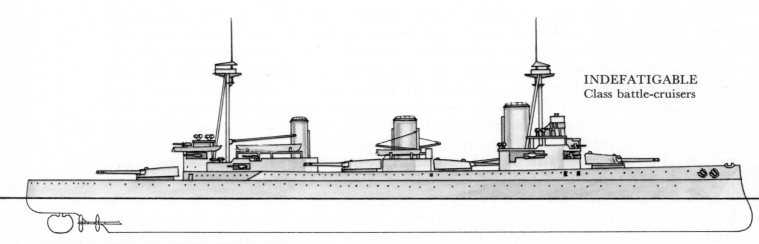

INDEFATIGABLE
Class battle-cruisers

INDEFATIGABLE 1909, NEW ZEALAND 1911
18,800 *tons* 590′ (*o/a*) × 80′ × 24¾′. Guns 8 12″ (50-*calibre*), 16 4″ (50-*calibre*), 4 3-*pdrs.* (*saluting*). Torpedo tubes 2 18″. Main armour 6″
*to* 4″ *belt to* 4″ *bulkheads,* 7″ *to* 3″ *barbettes with* 7″ *turrets,* 10″ *conning tower,* 6″ *spotting tower,* 2½″ *to* 1″ *decks,* 2½″ *magazines.* Engines and
speed *Turbines;* 43,000 *h.p.;* 25 *knots.* Remarks Australia (1911) *of this class was built for the Royal Australian Navy.*

Graf Spee and his squadron more completely and inevitably than he had destroyed Cradock's. At Dogger Bank in January 1915, it was battle-cruiser against battle-cruiser and the weaknesses showed up. The Germans were defeated and the *Blucher*, a heavy cruiser, sunk; also their flagship, the *Seydlitz*, was badly damaged and should not have escaped. On the British side the heavy shells that fell against the *Lion*'s side-armour failed to pierce it, but did push in the frames behind it, so that serious flooding resulted and she had to be towed home with a heavy list by the *Indomitable*.

At Jutland the battle-cruisers met again and this time it was to be disastrous for the British, with *Invincible*, *Indefatigable* and the splendid *Queen Mary* blowing up under fire with huge loss of life. Thereafter, the battle-cruisers were held suspect for the role they had been set, as well they might be. Indeed, had they really been used on the Empire trade routes they would have been an extravagance even in wartime, for the old battleships and cruisers, not required in the Grand Fleet, populated the oceans in large numbers and had the situation well in hand.

The first class of battle-cruiser was the three *Invincibles* in 1907, and they equated in the public estimation very much with the *Dreadnought*. They were bigger and faster though mounting only eight 12-inch instead of the *Dreadnought*'s ten. The public, already used to a heavy, big-calibre armament, was intrigued by their size and speed, and in the arms race with Germany were not over-critical of their possible use. In fact two of the class well paid for themselves at the Falkland Islands, and one paid the price at Jutland with the loss of one thousand and twenty-six men killed, only five of the crew surviving the explosion that tore her in two.

The next class of battle-cruiser, the *Indefatigables*, was laid down in 1909 and were only stretched *Invincibles*, with the same armament, except that the 12-inch guns were the 50-calibre variety and less accurate than the 45-calibre, since the shells tended to turn over in flight. Two of these ships, *Australia* and *New Zealand*, were paid for by those Dominions. New Zealand presented hers to the Royal Navy, but Australia wanted hers for her own protection. In the war they all fought with the Grand Fleet. The name ship of the class blew up at Jutland, with the loss of one thousand and fifteen out of the crew of one thousand and seventeen, while the *New Zealand* survived both Dogger Bank and Jutland without casualties, a deliverance possibly aided by the magical powers of the Maori grass skirt and greenstone tiki, presented to the ship on her visit to New Zealand before the war to ward off evil, and worn by the captain over his uniform throughout both actions. The *Australia* missed all the major actions through being in dock when they occurred.

## The 'Splendid Cat' Class

With the *Lion*, *Queen Mary* and *Princess Royal*, the original conception of the great commerce raider ceased to make any sense. The only criterion now was outbuilding the latest German battle-cruisers, in this case the *Moltke* class, designed for 27 knots. When the *Lion* was launched in 1910, she was 120 feet longer than her contemporary dreadnought the *Orion*, and 6 or 7 knots faster. Whatever may be said about their purpose in or fitness for a war of dreadnoughts, they must be remembered, with the *Tiger*, *Renown*, *Repulse* and *Hood* as a sight of power, grace, grandeur and beauty without equal. In peace they were unbeatable for the prestige they brought when making their breath-catching appearances abroad. Even the jaded palate of the Imperial Russian Court was astonished by Beatty's battle-cruisers when he tied the *Lion* and another battle-cruiser together and gave the Tsar the party of the century off St Petersburg, just before the war in 1914. After the war, the even more striking *Renown* and *Repulse* were the natural choice for the Prince of Wales's immensely successful Empire and foreign tours.

When the *Lion* did her trials in 1912 she exceeded 26 knots and burnt 950 tons of coal in a day. The heat from the fore-funnel made life in the control top, just aft on a tripod mast as with the other dreadnoughts up to that time, so unbearable that her whole forward superstructure had to be redesigned and brought forward. When war came she was Beatty's flagship at Dogger Bank and Jutland, where the battle-cruisers were the most heavily engaged squadrons in either fleet. Both *Lion* and *Princess Royal* were hit many times, *Lion* having Q turret amidships knocked out and *Princess Royal* losing the aftermost X turret. The *Queen Mary* was also hit but was less fortunate than her sisters, blowing up with the loss of twelve hundred and sixty-six lives. The two surviving ships were discarded following the Washington Treaty of 1922.

## The *Tiger*

Another splendid cat, though not of the class, followed two years after the *Lion*. The *Tiger* was slightly larger with a 6-inch secondary battery instead of a 4-inch and a considerably altered appearance since her boilers were brought together to enable the three funnels to be equidistant, whereas in the *Lion* Q turret was forward of the aftermost. This placing of Q turret aft of the funnels naturally gave it a much better field of fire. She joined the First Battle-Cruiser Squadron in time for the Battle of Dogger Bank. At Jutland she was heavily engaged and was hit seventeen times. The *Tiger* was the last British capital ship to burn coal, and a frightful labour it must have been since she required 1,245 tons daily, at speed. She converted to oil fuel after the war and survived until 1932, when she fell victim to one of the curious little clauses in the Washington Treaty which sentenced her to death within ten years.

## The *Renown* and *Repulse*

Jutland had been a shock in some respects, and the chief of these was that of the nine battle-cruisers present, three, a third of the force, had been destroyed. When therefore the two new members of the battle-cruiser fleet appeared it was to pursed lips. A hundred feet longer than the *Lions* and beautiful, their obvious lack of armour made them very suspect weapons. Indeed, they were worse than they looked, for the protection was not even on the scale of the *Lions* but on that of the *Indefatigables*. Also they had only six guns in the main armament instead of eight, though these were 15-inch.

Fortunately, they were never put to the test of action in that war, and after it went through so many major alterations that they became known in the service as *Refit* and *Repair*. Curiously, their first big postwar refits made them very different ships. The *Repulse* got a better armour-belt, *Renown* extra anti-torpedo bulges. In 1934 *Repulse* had another big refit. In this a space was cleared just before the main-mast for an athwart-ships catapult seaplane, or later a Walrus amphibian. Forward of that came a hangar,

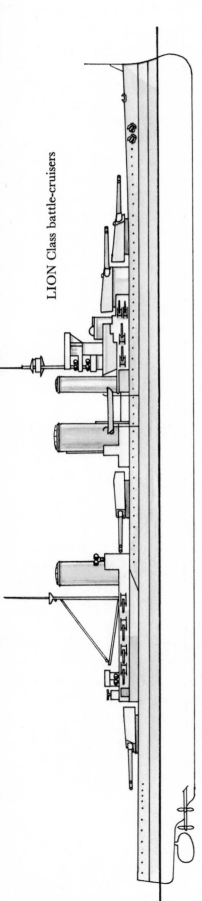

LION Class battle-cruisers

LION 1910, PRINCESS ROYAL 1911, QUEEN MARY 1912
26,350 tons 700′ (o/a) × 88½′ × 26½′. Guns 8 13·5″, 16 4″, 4 3-pdrs. (saluting). Torpedo tubes 2 21″. Main armour 9″ to 4″ belt to 4″ bulkheads, 9″ to 3″ barbettes with 9″ turrets, 10″ conning tower, 6″ spotting tower, 2½″ to 1″ decks and magazines. Engines and speed Turbines; 70,000 h.p.; 27 knots. Remarks Drawn as modified for service.

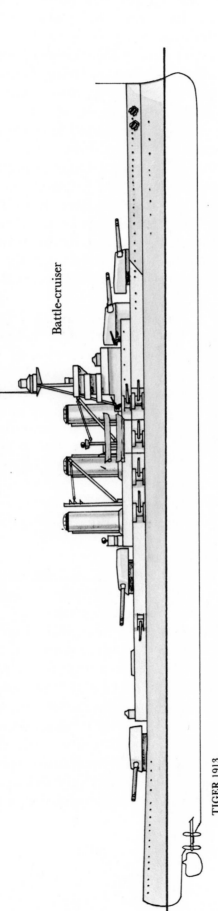

Battle-cruiser

TIGER 1913
28,500 tons 704′ (o/a) × 90¼′ × 28¼′. Guns 8 13·5″, 12 6″, 4 3-pdrs., 2 3″ A.A. Torpedo tubes 4 21″. Main armour 9″ to 3″ belt to 4″ to 2″ bulkheads, 9″ to 1″ barbettes with 9″ to 3½″ turrets, 10″ conning tower, 3″ to 1″ decks, 2½″ to 1″ magazines. Engines and speed Turbines; 108,000 h.p.; 29 knots. Remarks Last coal-burner to join the battle-fleet.

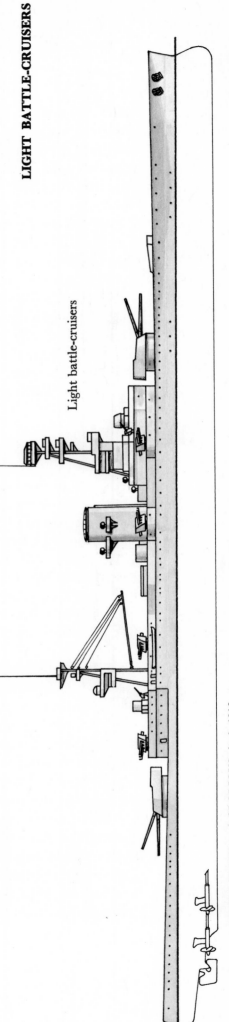

Light battle-cruisers

COURAGEOUS and GLORIOUS, both 1916
18,600 tons 786′ (o/a) × 81′ × 23½′. Guns 4 15″, 18 4″, 2 3″ A.A. Torpedo tubes 2 21″. Main armour 3″ to 2″ belt and bulkheads, 7″ to 3″ barbettes with 13″ to 4½″ turrets, 10″ conning tower, 3″ to 1″ decks. Engines and speed Turbines; 90,000 h.p.; 31½ knots.

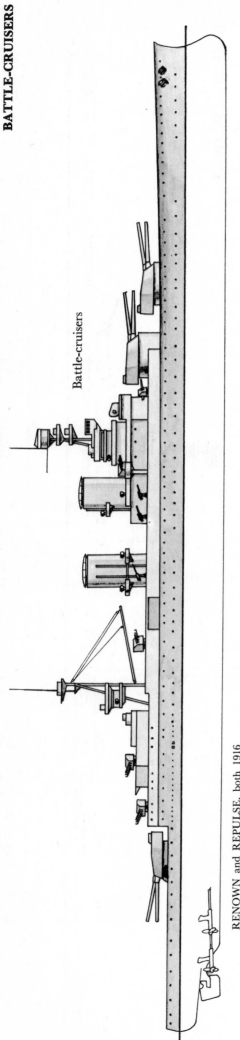

Battle-cruisers

RENOWN and REPULSE, both 1916

26,500 tons 794' (o/a) × 90' × 25¾'. Guns 6 15", 17 4", 2 3" A.A., 4 3-pdrs. (saluting). Torpedo tubes 2 21" (submerged). Main armour 6" to 1½" belt to 4" to 3" bulkheads, 7" to 4" barbettes with 11" to 7" turrets, 10" conning tower, 3" to ½" decks. Engines and speed Turbines; 112,000 h.p.; 31½ knots. Forced draught; 126,000 h.p.; 32½ knots.

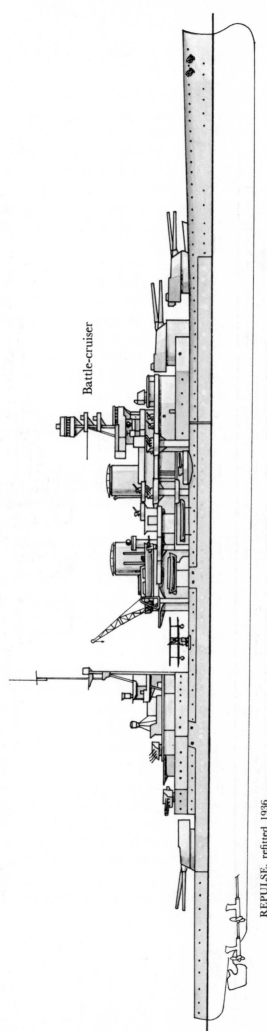

Battle-cruiser

REPULSE, refitted 1936

Remarks In 1919–20 she was given more side armour. The 6" belt was replaced by a 9" one, and above, a 6" belt rose the height of the main-deck, blocking out two-thirds of the scuttles. Eight 21" torpedo tubes were added in pairs on the forecastle deck. Beam increased 102', draught to 27'. In 1934 she was taken in hand again, a hangar for four seaplanes and a cross-deck catapult replacing the flying-off platform on X turret. New platforms were added round the funnels to take additional anti-aircraft guns and boats. The cross-deck catapult replaced one triple 4" mounting, and one twin 4" A.A. mounting was added to each side of the after superstructure.

and beside the funnels were platforms for extra anti-aircraft guns. Both these ships had borne a system of triple-mounted 4-inch guns as secondary armament, which was also fitted to *Courageous* and *Glorious*. This had never been satisfactory, but some were retained in *Repulse* to the end. In October 1941 she was sent with the new battleship *Prince of Wales* to the Far East, arriving just before the Japanese attacked Pearl Harbour and Malaya. Both she and her consort were quickly sunk by Japanese naval aircraft while trying to stem the Japanese invading fleet. Just as Jutland had pointed the lesson of weak armour, so this action showed up the vulnerability of the battleship to air attack and the importance of air cover.

The second big refit for the *Renown* amounted to a rebuilding on the lines of the *Queen Elizabeth*'s final treatment. Away went her superstructure, funnels, secondary armament, engines and boilers. New small-tube boilers and geared turbines saved 2,700 tons in weight, and this was transformed into armour, a tower bridge, new funnels, a hangar, a cross-deck catapult and twenty 4·5-inch dual-purpose guns as her principal secondary armament. She emerged a fast modern ship of great hitting power, but still vulnerable to heavy shells. In the war she had a brief brush with the *Scharnhorst* during the Norwegian campaign, but it was indecisive. From 1940 to 1941 she was busy as flagship of Force H at Gibraltar, had a brief action with the Italian Fleet and bombarded Genoa. From 1944 to 1945 she was in the Far East attacking the Japanese and was present at the bombardments of Sebang and Car Nicobar. After a doubtful beginning this ship had vindicated herself with a fine war record.

## The *Courageous, Glorious* and *Furious*

No class of capital ship ever built for the navy emerged from so ephemeral a conception, made so strange an appearance, or suffered so radical a metamorphosis, as the three ships of the *Courageous* class. Ephemeral because they were designed for a campaign that lived only in the First Sea Lord's imagination and died with his resignation, an event which preceded their launching. This had been to attack Germany's northern coast in an amphibious operation, and Fisher wanted support ships that could carry at high speed a few guns of the heaviest calibre into the shallow coastal waters of the Baltic. This in effect meant large shallow-draught hulls, longer than the *Lions*, with very little armour. Ordered for political reasons as large light-cruisers, they were officially classed as battle-cruisers, though quite unfit for the battle-cruiser squadrons, as their armour-belt was only 3 inches at the thickest and the four 15-inch in *Courageous* and *Glorious* were too few to give much chance of adequate hits.

Still less so was the projected main armament of the third of the trio, *Furious*, which was to mount two 18-inch guns in single turrets. She was to the *Courageouses* what *Benbow* had been to the *Admirals*. In the event she was never furnished as intended; only the after gun was mounted, the forward part of the ship being given a flight-deck. No bigger gun was put in a capital ship, and it was equalled only by those in the Japanese *Yamato* class battleships in the Second World War. *Courageous* and *Glorious* joined the cruiser squadrons of the Grand Fleet for the last two years of the Kaiser's war. Although regarded as freaks, the type was to have echoes in the navy of Nazi Germany with what were familiarly called their 'pocket battleships'. These ships were real battle-cruisers in the original commerce-raider context; large cruiser hulls with light armour and a very heavy punch, six 11-inch disposed in two turrets.

After the war *Courageous* and *Glorious* might well have been discarded except that the *Furious* was already in the second of three major alterations that changed her into a fleet aircraft carrier, and it was borne in mind that those huge fast hulls, over 30 knots, could well join their sister in her new vocation. This is in fact what did happen, beginning in 1924, as described on page 262.

## The *Hood*

The ordering of this great ship and her three sisters marks the high point of the battle-cruiser-to-beat-battle-cruiser building race; they were to be Britain's reply to Germany's projected 15-inch battle-cruisers. When the Admiralty were just ready to order them, Jutland overtook them, and as a result the design was amended to give armour protection comparable to the *Queen Elizabeths* so that they would emerge as huge very fast battleships rather than battle-cruisers. In 1917 the Germans abandoned their building programme and three of the four ships were cancelled on the stocks. The fourth was so far advanced that she was finished, and completed as the *Hood* in 1920. All her life she was to be the heaviest warship in the world, thought by many to be the most beautiful, then and ever. By the late 1930s her protection both in guns and armour against aircraft attack made a rebuilding on *Renown* lines desirable. This was planned for 1939; but the war came before it could be put in hand, so she went to fight as she had always been. She first fired her guns in anger against the Vichy French ships in Oran as the flagship of Sir James Somerville in 1940. In May 1941, back home and wearing the flag of Vice-Admiral Holland, she and the *Prince of Wales* intercepted the *Bismarck* in the Denmark Strait, as that vessel was trying to break into the Atlantic and attack British trade routes. After a short action the *Hood* blew up, only three of her people surviving. It has been generally thought that, as with the other battle-cruisers at Jutland, she was a victim of a thin skin. Part of the fault may have been due to the difference between the British and German cordite bags, in that the gunpowder detonators of the former were unprotected, unlike the German ones which were in brass cases. This vulnerability may also have ensured the destruction of the three battle-cruisers at Jutland, which might have received only severe fire damage instead of being blown up.

## The Monitors

The role of the Victorian monitor had been coast defence; the role of the new generation of monitors which fought in the First and Second World Wars was coast offence. At the beginning of the First World War there were three monitors building for Brazil and two coast-defence ships building for Norway, which were taken over. The ex-Brazilian ships were really for river work and carried only 6-inch, but the *Mersey* and the *Severn* sank the German cruiser *Königsberg* which was blockaded in the Rufiji River in German East Africa in July 1915. The ex-Norwegian ships were not completed until 1918, and did not see much service; one of them, the *Glatton*, had to be sunk in Dover Harbour when her cordite started smouldering and it looked as if she would blow up.

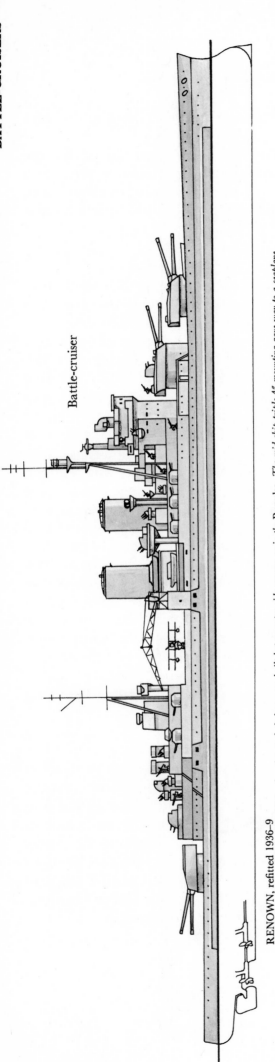

Battle-cruiser

RENOWN, refitted 1936-9
Remarks In her 1923-6 refit additional anti-torpedo bulges were built but no extra side armour as in the Repulse. The mid-ship triple 4" mounting gave way to a seaplane catapult, and an enlarged control-top towered above the bridge structures. In 1936 she underwent a major rebuild on the lines of the Queen Elizabeth, with a new tower bridge, funnels, cross-deck catapult, secondary armament and small-tube high-pressure boilers. Though nothing could be done about her side armour, 3" to 4" was added to parts of her deck armour. The new secondary armament consisted of 20 4·5" dual-purpose guns, plus 3 8-barrel 2-pdr. pom-poms. The torpedo tubes were suppressed.

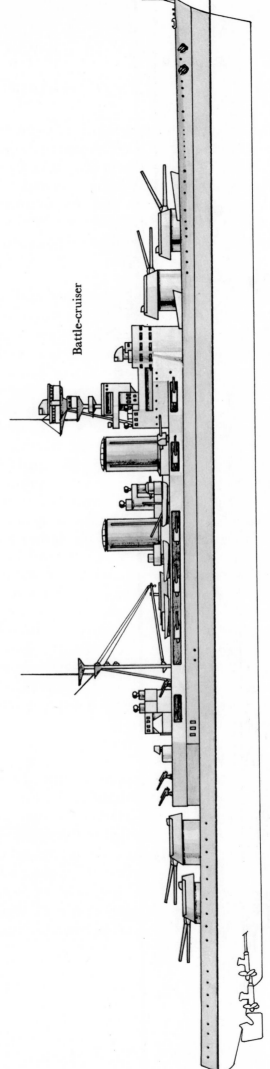

Battle-cruiser

HOOD 1918
41,200 tons 860' (o/a) ×104' (o/a) ×28½'. Guns 8 15", 12 5·5", 4 4" A.A., 4 3-pdrs. Torpedo tubes 6 21" (2 submerged). Main armour 12" to 5" belt to 5" to 4" bulkheads, 12" to 5" barbettes with 15" to 5" turrets, 11" conning tower, 6" director tower, 3" to 1" decks. Engines and speed Turbines; 144,000 h.p.; 31 knots.

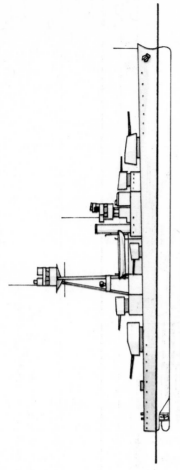

GLATTON and GORGON, both 1914
5,700 *tons* 310′ × 73⅔′ × 16⅓′. Guns 2 9·2″, 4 6″, 2 3″ *A.A.* Main armour 2″ *deck*. Engines and speed *Triple expansion*; 4,000 *h.p.*; 13 *knots*. Remarks *Building for the Norwegians, taken over.*

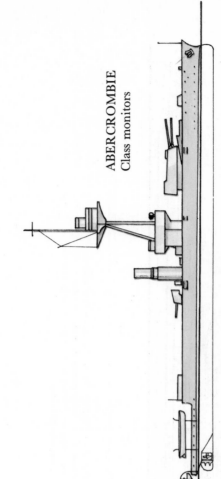

ABERCROMBIE
Class monitors

ABERCROMBIE, HAVELOCK, RAGLAN, ROBERTS, all 1915
6,150 *tons* 334¼′ × 90′ × 10′. Guns (*as completed*) 2 14″, 2 12-*pdrs.*, 1 3-*pdr. A.A.*; 1 6″ *added later.* Main armour 2″ *deck*, 4″ *sloping belt*. Engines and speed *ABERCROMBIE and HAVELOCK, Quadruple expansion*; 2,000 *h.p.*; 7 *knots*; *RAGLAN Triple expansion*; 2,310 *h.p.*; 7½ *knots*; *ROBERTS Triple expansion*; 1,800 *h.p.*; 5¾ *knots*.

Monitors

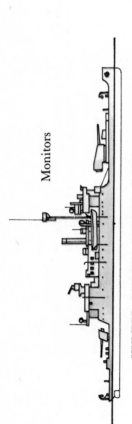

HUMBER, MERSEY, SEVERN, all 1913
1,260 *tons* 266¾′ × 49′ × 5½′. Guns (*as accepted into R.N. service*) 2 6″, 2 4·7″ *howitzers.* Main armour 3″ *belt.* Engines and speed *Triple expansion*; 1,450 *h.p.*; 11 *knots*. Remarks *Built for the Brazilians, purchased August 1914.*

LORD CLIVE Class monitors

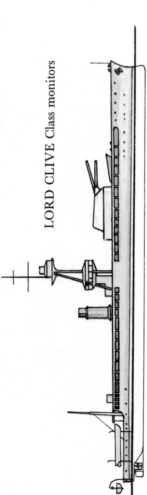

EARL OF PETERBOROUGH

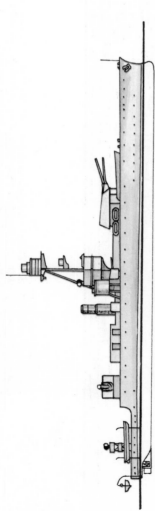

LORD CLIVE

EARL OF PETERBOROUGH, GENERAL CRAUFURD, GENERAL WOLFE, LORD CLIVE, PRINCE EUGENE, PRINCE RUPERT, SIR JOHN MOORE, SIR THOMAS PICTON, all 1915
5,900 *tons* 335¼′ × 87½′ × 9½′. Guns 2 12″, 2 3″ *A.A.*; 1–4 6″ *added later.* Main armour 2″ *deck*, 6″ *sloping belt*. Engines and speed *Triple expansion*; 1,600–2,500 *h.p.*; 7 *knots*. Remarks *General Wolfe and Lord Clive had a single 18″ gun mounted aft in 1918, later the Lord Clive mounted an experimental triple 15″ turret.*

MARSHAL NEY Class monitors

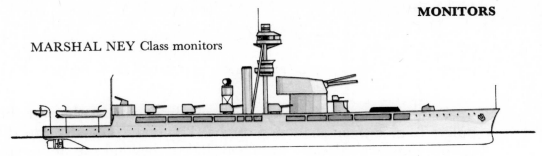

**MARSHAL NEY, MARSHAL SOULT, both 1915**
6,670 *tons* 355⅔' (*o/a*) × 90¼' × 10½'. Guns 2 15", 2 12-*pdrs.*; *MARSHAL NEY* (1918) 6 6", 2 3" *A.A.*; *MARSHAL SOULT* (1918) 2 15", 8 4", 2 3"
*A.A.*; 2 12-*pdr. A.A.* Main armour 4" *belt*, 13" *to* 4½" *turret*, 6" *conning tower*, 4" *to* 1" *deck*. Engines and speed *Diesel*; 1,500 *h.p.*; 6½ *knots*.

EREBUS Class monitors

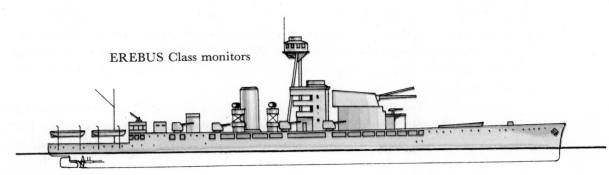

**EREBUS and TERROR, both 1916**
8,000 *tons* 405' (*o/a*) × 88' × 11⅔'. Guns 2 15", 2 6", 2 12-*pdr.*, 2 3" *A.A.*; (1918) 2 15", 8 4", 2 12-*pdr. A.A.*, 2 3" *A.A.* Main armour 4" *to* 1" *deck*.
Engines and speed *Triple expansion*; 6,000 *h.p.*; 14 *knots*.

M15 Class monitors

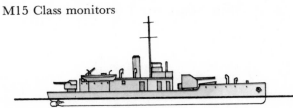

**M15 to M28 and M29 to M33**
*M15–M28* 540 tons 177¼' × 31' × 6½', *M29–M33* 535 tons 177¼' × 31' × 6'. Guns *M15–M28* 1 9·2", 1 12-*pdr*; *M29–M33* 2 6"; *M21, M23–M26 later
had* 1 7·5" *in place of* 9·2"; *M27 later* 3 4" *in place of* 9·2". Engines and speed *Triple expansion*; 400 to 800 *h.p.*; *M18–M20, M23, M25–M28 Diesel*, 480 to
640 *h.p.*; *M24 Paraffin engine*, 640 *h.p.*; 11 *knots*; *M29–M33* 9 *knots*.

ROBERTS Class monitors

**ABERCROMBIE 1942 and ROBERTS 1941**
7,850 *tons* 373¼' (*o/a*) × 89¾' × 11'. Guns 2 15", 8 4" *A.A.*, 16 2-*pdrs., A.A.*, 16 20 *mm. A.A.* Main armour 6" *to* 4" *belt*, 13" *to* 4¼" *turret*,
6" *control tower*, 4" *to* 1" *deck*. Engines and speed *Turbines*; 4,800 *h.p.*; 12 *knots*.

Four classes of large monitors were built during the war, beamy ships with great bulges to give them shallow draught. The main difficulty was that the supply of large-calibre guns was already stretched slightly beyond the limit supplying the battle-fleet, so that the monitors had to put up with what could be scratched together. The four *Abercrombie* class were given the American-built guns intended for a battle-cruiser being built in Germany for the Greeks, and, when the war began, going spare. The *Lord Clive* class was given twin 12-inch gun turrets removed from four of the old *Majestic* class battleships. In addition two of the *Lord Clive* class were given the *Furious*'s 18-inch guns in fixed turrets. These were mounted aft pointing out to starboard and were used in coastal bombardment towards the end of the war. The *Erebus* class, completed in 1916, were able to have a modern British armament of two 15-inch guns. These two ships, the *Erebus* and *Terror*, survived to fight in the Second World War, and the *Terror* was sunk by aircraft off the Libyan coast after giving yeoman service. The *Marshal Ney* and the *Marshal Soult* also carried 15-inch guns.

Two new monitors were built in the Second World War, both mounting 15-inch in a twin turret, the *Roberts* and *Abercrombie*. The military names given to these ships reflect their role as army support units, but to call one class the *Marshal Soult* and *Marshal Ney* was rather singular. It is even understood that the First Lord, Mr Churchill, wanted to call one after the Confederate soldier, General Lee, but was dissuaded. The *Roberts* was to carry the last British 15-inch turret. She was sold for scrapping a few years after the war, but hired back by the navy as an accommodation ship at Devonport and retained on a rental until 1965. It is believed that the ship-breakers who had bought her recovered their purchase price in rent and then had her for scrap at the end. One of her guns (No. 102) has been preserved and is now mounted, with a second, in the grounds of the Imperial War Museum, London.

## 22

# The Mastless Steel Cruiser

## The First-class Belted and Protected Cruisers

In the late 1880s, the *Imperieuse* and *Warspite*, already mentioned (page 134), once stripped of their sailing rig (only fitted in *Imperieuse* for her trials) became the navy's first armoured mastless cruisers. They were a strange-looking pair with their wide-set funnels, central military masts and frigate sterns. In 1886, the first of the seven *Orlando* class cruisers was launched, and with them emerged the silhouette of the modern cruiser that was to be familiar for many years to come: two funnels slightly forward of centre, two masts with a single cross yard on each; main armament fore and aft, secondary in sponsons on the broadside. These cruisers were only slightly smaller than the *Warspites*, though through lighter scantling only two-thirds the tonnage; they also had a belt of 10-inch compound armour. When the first of them made their appearance at Queen Victoria's Golden Jubilee Review, some not quite finished and temporarily fitted with wooden guns, it was seen that they were only 25 feet shorter than the contemporary battleships and considerably higher in the freeboard. Although a successful type of cruiser, the *Orlandos* lacked the necessary balance of speed between the battleship and the cruiser, an essential attribute if the cruiser was to escape destruction.

The *Iris* and *Mercury* had shown the way, but the *Orlandos* were only good for about 16 knots in service, and this was no more or even less than the speed the contemporary *Admiral* class battleships could make. The result was a reversion to the protected type of cruiser; no belt but an armoured deck to protect the engines and magazines. This saving in weight was accompanied by a considerable increase in size and engine-power in the next class of large cruiser. These were the *Blenheim* and *Blake*, similarly armed but 75 feet longer and with more than twice the horsepower to give them 21 knots. Two similar classes were built on the *Blake* model in the early 1890s; the *Edgar* class of seven ships and the *Crescent* and *Royal Arthur*. These were the oldest type of large cruiser to survive to serve in the Kaiser's war. Some, like *Blake*, *Blenheim* and *Royal Arthur*, acted only as submarine or destroyer depot ships, but of the rest, *Crescent* was the flagship of the Commander-in-Chief west of Scotland and the *Edgars* served as cruisers in the Mediterranean, except for the *Hawke*, which was torpedoed by a U-boat in the North Sea in October 1914.

There were three more classes of first-class protected cruisers built; two were almost identical, the four *Diadems* and the four slightly faster *Ariadnes* (1896–8). Again the size was increased and they were 60 feet longer than the *Blakes* with four funnels and sixteen of the new 40-calibre 6-inch guns, instead of two 9·2-inch and ten or twelve of the old 26-calibre 6-inch. The third class retained the old mixed 9.2-inch and 6-inch armament,

191

## PROTECTED CRUISERS

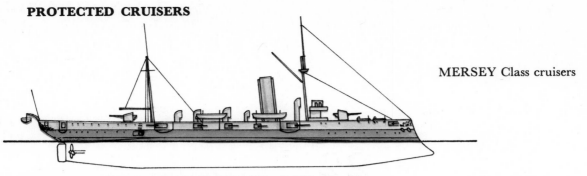

MERSEY Class cruisers

FORTH 1886, MERSEY, SEVERN, THAMES, all 1885
4,050 *tons* 300′ × 46′ × 19½′. Guns 2 8″, 10 6″. Torpedo tubes *SEVERN* (1 *submerged*, 2 *above water*). *MERSEY* (2 *submerged*, 2 *above water*).
*FORTH, THAMES, (none submerged, 2 above water).* Main armour 3″ *deck.* Engines and speed *Compound;* 4,500 *h.p.;* 17 *knots. Forced*
*draught;* 6,000 *h.p.;* 18 *knots. Shown with funnel raised.*

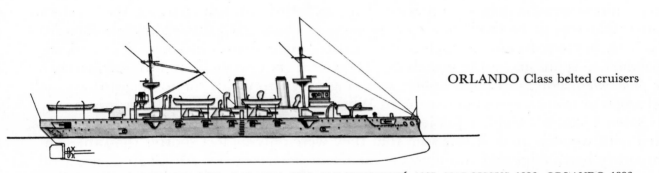

ORLANDO Class belted cruisers

AURORA 1887, AUSTRALIA 1886, GALATEA 1887, IMMORTALITÉ 1887, NARCISSUS 1886, ORLANDO 1886,
UNDAUNTED 1886
5,600 *tons* 300′ × 56′ × 22½′. Guns 2 9·2″, 10 6″, 10 3-*pdrs.* Torpedo tubes 4 *above water*, 2 *submerged.* Main armour (*Compound*) 10″ *belt*, 16″ *bulkheads*,
12″ *conning tower*, 3″ *steel deck.* Engines and speed *Triple expansion;* 5,500 *h.p.;* 17 *knots. Forced draught;* 8,500 *h.p.;* 18 *knots.*

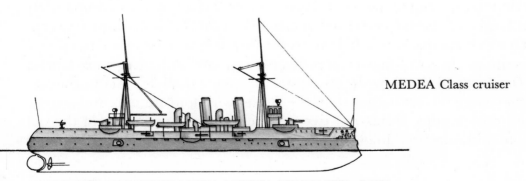

MEDEA Class cruiser

MAGICIENNE, MARATHON, MEDEA, MEDUSA, MELPOMENE, all 1888
*MEDEA and MEDUSA* 2,800 *tons* 265′ × 41′ × 16½′; *rest* 2,950 *tons* 265′ × 42′ × 16½′. Guns 6 6″, 9 6-*pdrs.* Torpedo tubes 4 *above water.* Main
armour *MEDEA and MEDUSA* 2″; *rest* 1½″ *deck*, 5″ *engine hatches.* Engines and speed *Compound;* 5,000 *h.p.;* 16 *knots. Forced draught;* 9,000 *h.p.;*
20 *knots.* Remarks Melpomene, Magicienne *and* Marathon *were sheathed and coppered.*

Cruisers

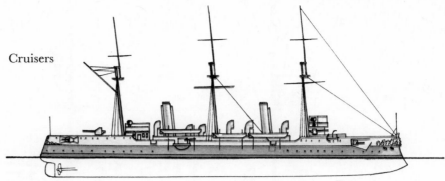

**BARHAM** 1889 and **BELLONA** 1890
1,830 *tons* 280′ × 35′ × 13¼′. Guns 6 4·7″, 4 3-*pdrs.* Torpedo tubes 2 (*above water*). Main armour 2″ *deck*. Engines and speed *Triple expansion*; 3,600
*h.p.*; 16 *knots. Forced draught*, 6,000 *h.p.*; 19 *knots.*

PALLAS Class cruisers

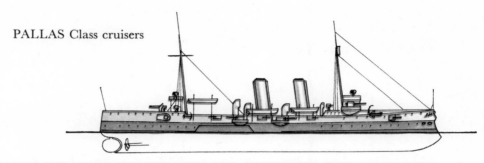

**KATOOMBA** 1889, **MILDURA** 1889, **PALLAS** 1890, **PEARL** 1890, **PHILOMEL** 1890, **PHOEBE** 1890, **RINGAROOMA** 1889,
**TAURANGA** 1889, **WALLAROO** 1889
2,575 *tons* 265′ × 41′ × 15½′. Guns 8 4·7″, 8 3-*pdrs.*, 4 *Nordenfelts.* Torpedo tubes 4 14″ (*above water*). Main armour 2″ *deck.* Engines and speed *Triple
expansion*; 4,000 *h.p.*; 17 *knots. Forced draught*; 7,500 *h.p.*; 19 *knots.*

APOLLO Class cruisers

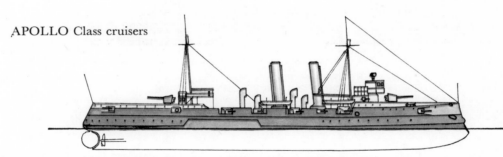

**AEOLUS** 1891, **ANDROMACHE** 1890, **APOLLO** 1891, **BRILLIANT** 1891, **INDEFATIGABLE** 1891, **INTREPID** 1891,
**IPHIGENIA** 1891, **LATONA** 1890, **MELAMPUS** 1890, **NAIAD** 1890, **PIQUE** 1890, **RAINBOW** 1891, **RETRIBUTION** 1891,
**SAPPHO** 1891, **SCYLLA** 1891, **SIRIUS** 1890, **SPARTAN** 1891, **SYBILLE** 1890, **TERPSICHORE** 1890, **THETIS** 1890,
**TRIBUNE** 1891
3,400 *tons* 300′ × 43′ × 17½′ (*sheathed vessels* 3,600 *tons*, 300′ × 43⅔′ × 18½′). Guns 2 6″, 6 4·7″, 8 6-*pdrs.*, 1 3-*pdr.* Torpedo tubes 4 14″ *above water.*
Main armour 5″ *engine hatches*, 4½″ *gun shields*, 3″ *conning tower*, 2″ *deck.* Engines and speed *Triple expansion*; 7,000 *h.p.*; 18½ *knots. Forced draught*;
9,000 *h.p.*; 20 *knots.*

HERMIONE Class cruisers

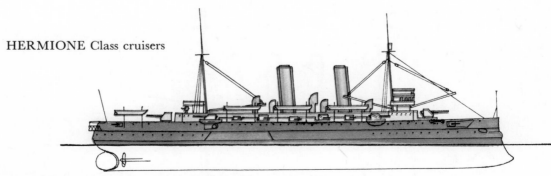

**ASTREA, BONAVENTURE, CAMBRIAN, CHARYBDIS, FLORA, FORTE, FOX, HERMIONE,** all 1892–3
4,360 *tons* 320′ × 49½′ × 19′. Guns 2 6″, 8 4·7″, 10 6-*pdrs.*, 1 3-*pdr.* Torpedo tubes 4 18″ *above water.* Main armour 5″ *engine hatches*, 4½″ *gun shields*, 3″
*conning tower*, 2″ *deck.* Engines and speed *Triple expansion*; 7,500 *h.p.*; 18 *knots. Forced draught*; 9,500 *h.p.*; 19½ *knots.*

# PROTECTED CRUISERS

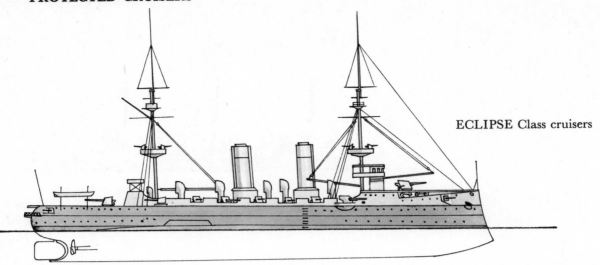

ECLIPSE Class cruisers

DIANA 1895, DIDO 1896, DORIS 1896, ECLIPSE 1894, JUNO 1895, ISIS 1896, MINERVA 1895, TALBOT 1895, and VENUS 1895

5,600 *tons* 364′ (*waterline*) × 53½′ × 20½′. Guns 5 6″, 6 4·7″, 8 12-*pdrs.*, 6 3-*pdrs.* (*later* 11 6″ *mounted in all except ECLIPSE*). Torpedo tubes 3 18″ (2 *submerged*, 1 *above water*). Main armour 6″ *engine hatches and conning tower,* 3″–1½″ *deck.* Engines and speed *Triple expansion;* 8,000 *h.p.;* 18½ *knots. Forced draught;* 9,600 *h.p.;* 19½ *knots.*

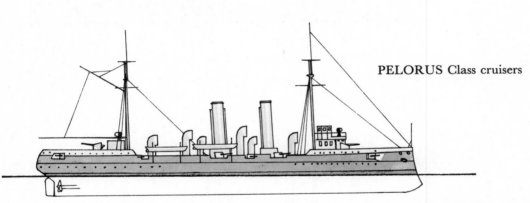

PELORUS Class cruisers

PACTOLUS 1896, PANDORA 1900, PEGASUS 1897, PELORUS 1896, PERSEUS 1897, PIONEER 1899, POMONE 1897, PROMETHEUS 1898, PROSERPINE 1896, PSYCHE 1898, PYRAMUS 1897

2,135 *tons* 300′ × 36½′ × 16′. Guns 8 4″, 8 3-*pdrs.* Torpedo tubes 2 14″ (*above water*). Main armour 2″–1½″ *deck.* Engines and speed *Triple expansion;* 5,000 *h.p.;* 18½ *knots. Forced draught;* 7,000 *h.p.;* 20 *knots.*

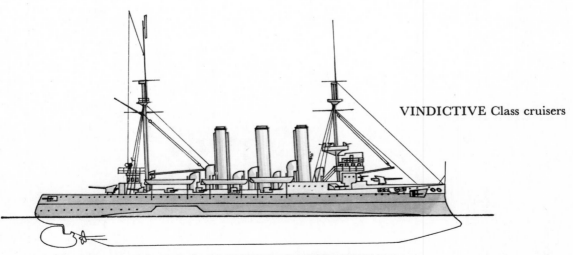

VINDICTIVE Class cruisers

ARROGANT 1896, FURIOUS 1896, GLADIATOR 1896, VINDICTIVE 1897

5,750 *tons* 320′ × 57½′ × 20′. Guns 4 6″, 6 4·7″ (*later* 10 6″), 8 12-*pdrs.*, 3 3-*pdrs.* Torpedo tubes 3 18″ (2 *submerged*, 1 *above water*). Main armour 4″ *engine hatches,* 9″ *conning tower,* 3″–1½″ *deck.* Engines and speed *Triple expansion, Forced draught;* 10,000 *h.p.;* 19 *knots.*

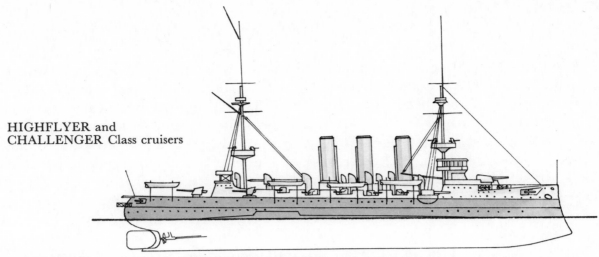

HIGHFLYER and
CHALLENGER Class cruisers

CHALLENGER and ENCOUNTER, both 1902, HERMES, HIGHFLYER, HYACINTH, all 1898
5,600 *tons* 350′ × 54′ × 22′, *CHALLENGER* 5,880 *tons* 355′ × 56′ × 21½′. Guns 11 6″, 9 12-*pdrs.*, 6 3-*pdrs.* Torpedo tubes 2 18″ (*submerged*).
Main armour 5″ *engine hatches,* 6″ *conning tower,* 3″ *to* 2″ *deck.* Engines and speed *Triple expansion;* 10,000 *h.p.;* 20 *knots. CHALLENGER*
12,500 *h.p.;* 21 *knots.*

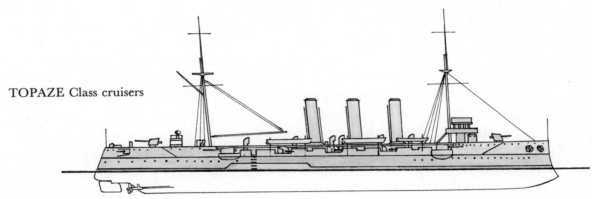

TOPAZE Class cruisers

AMETHYST 1903, DIAMOND 1904, SAPPHIRE 1904, TOPAZE 1903
3,000 *tons* 360′ × 40′ × 14½′. Guns 12 4″, 8 3-*pdrs.* Torpedo tubes 2 18″ (*above water*). Main armour 2″ *deck.* Engines and speed *Triple
expansion; Forced draught;* 9,800 *h.p.;* 21¾ *knots. AMETHYST Turbines;* 12,000 *h.p.;* 22½ *knots.* Remarks Amethyst *was the first cruiser to be given turbine
engines.*

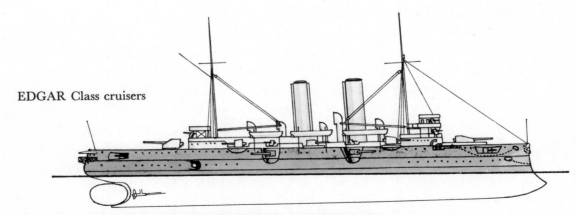

EDGAR Class cruisers

EDGAR 1890, ENDYMION 1891, GIBRALTAR 1892, HAWKE 1891, ST GEORGE 1892, THESEUS 1892
7,350 *tons* (*GIBRALTAR and ST GEORGE copper sheathed* 7,700 *tons*) 360′ × 60′ × 23¾′. Guns 2 9·2″, 10 6″, 12 6-*pdrs.*, 5 3-*pdrs.* Torpedo tubes 4 18″
(*submerged*). Main armour 6″ *casemates,* 7″ *hoists to* 9·2″ *guns,* 12″ *conning tower,* 5″ *deck.* Engines and speed *Triple expansion;* 10,000 *h.p.;* 18½ *knots.*
*Forced draught;* 12,000 *h.p.;* 20 *knots.*

but the two ships *Powerful* and *Terrible* were so colossal that they must be set aside from the main stream of cruiser development. At 14,000 tons and a length of 500 feet they were almost 100 feet longer than the latest battleships and nearly the same tonnage. Although lightly armed and armoured for their size, they were real commerce-protectors with an abnormal range. They were, however, expensive to run, as had been the *Inconstant* and *Shah*, and both were off the effective list before war broke out in 1914. The smaller *Diadems*, except *Andromeda*, did serve, *Amphitrite* beginning the war as flagship of the Ninth Cruiser Squadron and ending it as a minelayer. Her sister *Ariadne*, similarly converted, was torpedoed off Beachy Head in July 1917. Curiously enough *Andromeda*, which had been taken off the effective list to be a boys' training ship before the war, served thereby the longest, into the middle 1950s.

## Second-class Protected Cruisers

Of these fifty-one were launched between 1885 and 1902. The earliest class, the four single-funnelled *Merseys*, looked as if they had been designed for a sailing rig but the *Apollos*, *Piques*, *Hermiones* and *Eclipses* were reduced *Edgars* and looked very similar. So were the *Arrogants*, *Highflyers* and *Challengers*, which had three funnels. The early ships were about 3,500 tons and 300 feet long, while the later ones were around 350 feet and 5,700 tons. They chiefly relied on a 6-inch armament.

Most of these ships survived into the war, *Thames* and *Forth* of the oldest class as submarine depot ships. Of the *Apollos*, ten served, seven as minelayers. *Intrepid, Iphigenia* and *Thetis* were sunk as blockships at Zeebrugge in April 1918 and *Brilliant* and *Sirius* were scuttled at Ostend. The *Vindictive* won immortality in this raid and less than a month later she was sunk as a blockship at Ostend. Less well known was the *Vindictive*'s role in the destruction of Graf Spee's squadron off the Falkland Islands. She was at that time the navy's wireless experimental ship, and at a time of very tall wireless masts in ships, hers were tremendous. She was the only ship that could keep in wireless touch with a squadron on very distant duty, so when Sturdee took the battle-cruisers to the Falkland Islands to look for Graf Spee, the *Vindictive* was sent half-way, to wallow in mid-Atlantic and relay wireless signals to the Admiralty. Hermes of the *Highflyer* class was converted into a seaplane carrier just before the war, the navy's first, but was sunk by a torpedo a few weeks after war began.

## Third-class Protected Cruisers

Forty-seven of these small cruisers were built between 1885 and 1904. The first, the *Archer* class, had a protective deck only three-eighths of an inch thick and so only just qualified, but of the remainder most had 2-inch decks. Displacement rose over the years from just under 2,000 tons to 3,000 tons and at 360 feet the *Gem* class of 1904 were longer than the *Highflyers*. Some of these ships, such as the *Archer*, the *Barracouta* and *Medea* classes were poor steamers, with only about 15 knots in them. Five of the *Pallas* class were transferred to the Royal Australian Navy as well as two of the *Peloruses*. *Amethyst,* one of the *Gems* of 1903–4, was the Royal Navy's first cruiser to be turbine-engined. The *Pegasus* of this class was disabled and beached at Zanzibar in September 1914, after being in action with the German cruiser *Königsberg*.

# 23

# The Return of the Armoured Cruiser

In the late 1890s opinion was swinging back to the idea that it was better to keep enemy shells out of British ships than contain the damage once they were inside. The size of the hulls and engines also made a return to belt-armour possible, without disastrous restrictions in speed and armament. Two years after the first *Diadems* were laid down in 1895 the belted *Cressy* class was begun. Almost identical in size and profile, they mounted two 9·2-inch in turrets fore and aft, instead of the *Diadems'* homogeneous main armament of 6-inch. The *Cressy's* armoured-belt was 11 feet deep and ran from just before the conning tower under the bridge to aft of the 6-inch sponsons. It was 6 inches of Krupp steel armour, which was much lighter than the old compound armour for the same strength. The armour thinned out to 2 inches at the bow, and a 3-inch deck. In the war this class suffered a particularly heavy blow early on. The *Aboukir*, *Hogue* and *Cressy* were units of the Seventh Cruiser Squadron, patrolling off the Dutch coast in September 1914. Their flagship, the *Euryalus* of the same class, and their light-cruiser and destroyer screen had been temporarily forced to return to base, leaving these three on their own. Early in the morning of the 22nd the *Aboukir* was torpedoed by *U9*. At first it was thought she had been mined and the *Hogue* went to the assistance of the survivors of the sinking ship. She too was torpedoed, and this time the *U*-boat surfaced and was fired on. As the *Hogue* sank, the *Cressy's* captain now knowing the danger, should have left the field in a hurry, as would have happened a year or two later. But at that time they did not yet think in such an ignoble and heartless, though right and necessary, way. The *Cressy* now came to a stop among the survivors from her sisters, and she too was torpedoed and sunk. About half the crews were lost and this loss would have been very much greater but for the brave intervention of two Dutch coasters and an English trawler. A whole term of Dartmouth naval cadets was aboard these ships, and many were lost. Of the other three ships of the class, *Euryalus*, after the decimation of the Seventh Cruiser Squadron, went to serve in the Mediterranean where also could be found the *Bacchante*, which was at the Dardanelles operations in 1915. *Sutlej* was in the Tenth Cruiser Squadron at the beginning of the war, and after serving as a guardship at Scapa, she ended the war a depot ship at Rosyth.

Similar to the *Cressys*, but 60 feet longer with more powerful engines and a heavier 6-inch battery, was the *Drake* class of 1901. These ships were back to the dimensions of the *Powerfuls*, but far superior in protection and with speeds of around 23 knots. Of the four ships in this class, only two survived the war. The *Good Hope* was Rear-Admiral

# PROTECTED CRUISERS

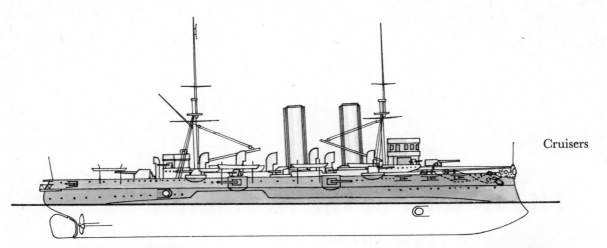

Cruisers

**BLAKE** 1889 and **BLENHEIM** 1890
9,150 *tons* 375′ × 65′ × 24′. Guns 2 9·2″, 10 6″, 16 3-*pdrs*. Torpedo tubes 4 14″ (2 *submerged, 2 above water*). Main armour 6″ *casemates,*
7″ *for* 9·2″ *gun hoists,* 12″ *conning tower,* 6″ *to* 3″ *deck.* Engines and speed *Triple expansion;* 13,000 *h.p.;* 20 *knots. Forced draught;* 20,000 *h.p.;*
22 *knots.*

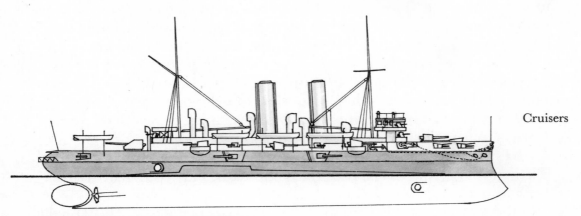

Cruisers

**CRESCENT** 1892 and **ROYAL ARTHUR** 1891
7,700 *tons* 360′ × 60¾′ × 24′. Guns 1 9·2″, 12 6″, 12 6-*pdrs*. Torpedo tubes 4 18″ (*submerged*). Main armour 6″ *casemates,* 12″ *conning tower,*
5″ *deck.* Engines and speed *Triple expansion;* 10,000 *h.p.;* 18 *knots. Forced draught;* 12,000 *h.p.;* 20 *knots.*

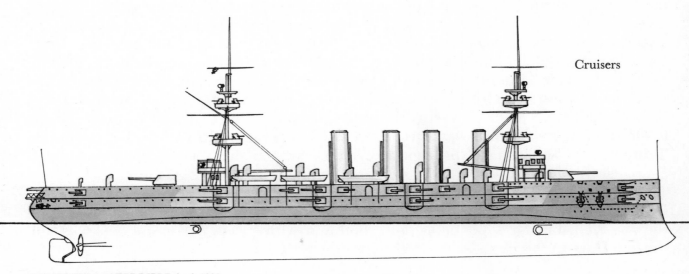

Cruisers

**POWERFUL** and **TERRIBLE**, both 1895
14,200 *tons* 520′ (*waterline*) × 71′ × 27′. Guns 2 9·2″, 12 (*later* 16) 6″, 16 12-*pdrs.,* 12 3-*pdrs*. Torpedo tubes 4 18″ (*submerged*). Main armour 6″
*barbettes, turrets and casemates,* 12″ *conning tower,* 6″ *deck.* Engines and speed *Triple expansion;* 25,000 *h.p.;* 22 *knots.*

DIADEM Class cruisers

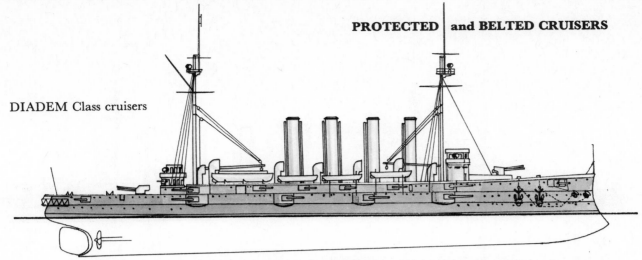

AMPHITRITE 1898, ANDROMEDA 1897, ARGONAUT 1898, ARIADNE 1898, DIADEM 1896, EUROPA 1897, NIOBE 1897, SPARTIATE 1898
11,000 *tons* 462½′ (o/a) × 69′ × 25½′. Guns 16 6″, 14 12-*pdrs.*, 3 3-*pdrs.* Torpedo tubes 3 18″ (2 *submerged*, 1 *above water*). Main armour 4½″ *casemates,* 12″ *conning tower,* 4″ *deck.* Engines and speed *Triple expansion*; 16,500 *h.p.*; 20¼ *knots (first four).* 18,000 *h.p.*; 20¾ *knots (rest).*

CRESSY Class cruisers

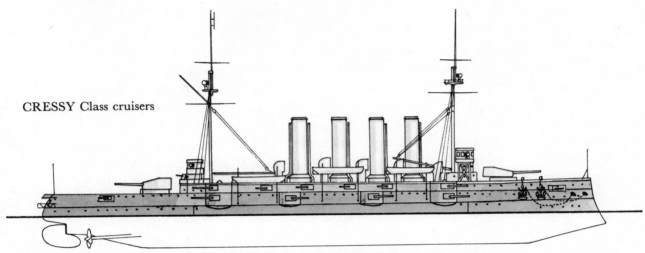

ABOUKIR 1900, BACCHANTE 1901, CRESSY 1899, EURYALUS 1901, HOGUE 1900, SUTLEJ 1899
12,000 *tons* 472′ (o/a) × 69½′ × 26′. Guns 2 9·2″, 12 6″, 12 12-*pdrs.*, 3 3-*pdrs.* Torpedo tubes 2 18″ (*submerged*). Main armour 6″ *to* 2″ *belt,* 5″ *bulkheads,* 6″ *barbettes and turrets,* 5″ *casemates,* 12″ *conning tower,* 3″ *deck.* Engines and speed *Triple expansion*; 21,000 *h.p.*; 21 *knots.*

MONMOUTH Class cruisers

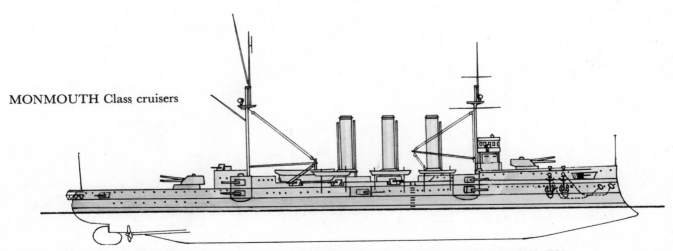

BEDFORD 1901, BERWICK 1902, CORNWALL 1902, CUMBERLAND 1902, DONEGAL 1902, ESSEX 1901, KENT 1901, LANCASTER 1902, MONMOUTH 1901, SUFFOLK 1903
9,800 *tons* 463½′ (o/a) × 66′ × 25′. Guns 14 6″, 10 12-*pdrs.*, 3 3-*pdrs.* Torpedo tubes 2 18″ (*submerged*). Main armour 4″ *to* 2″ *belt,* 5″ *bulkheads,* 5″ *barbettes and turrets,* 4″ *casemates,* 10″ *conning tower,* 2″ *deck.* Engines and speed *Triple expansion*; 22,000 *h.p.*; 23 *knots.*

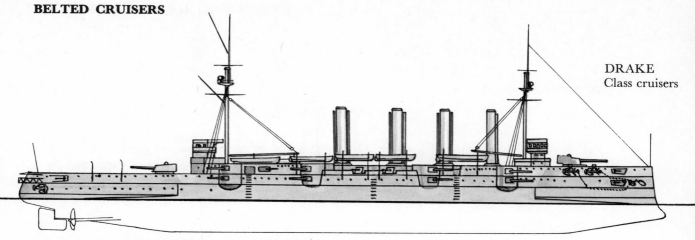

DRAKE
Class cruisers

DRAKE, GOOD HOPE, KING ALFRED, LEVIATHAN, all 1901
14,150 *tons* 533½′ (*o/a*) × 71⅓′ × 26′. Guns 2 9·2″, 16 6″, 14 12-*pdrs.*, 3 3-*pdrs.* Torpedo tubes 2 18″ (*submerged*). Main armour 6″ *to* 2″ *belt,* 5″ *bulkheads,* 6″ *barbettes and turrets,* 5″ *casemates,* 12″ *conning tower,* 2½″ *to* 1″ *deck.* Engines and speed *Triple expansion;* 30,000 *h.p.;* 23 *knots.* Remarks *There was no after bridge on* Drake.

Cradock's flagship when she was sunk with all hands by Graf Spee's squadron at Coronel on 1 November 1914, and the *Drake* was torpedoed off Church Bay, Rathlin Island in October 1917. The survivors were *Leviathan* and *King Alfred*.

The last two classes of cruiser designed by Sir William White were the *Monmouths* and the *Devonshires*, both second-class *Drakes*. The three-funnelled *Monmouths* were shorter by 60 feet, with an all-round armament of 6-inch and a 4-inch belt; they provided a less effective but more economical vessel for guarding the Empire trade routes. They mounted a twin 6-inch turret fore and aft, the first cruiser class to do so. Unfortunately, the mountings gave trouble and it was to be some time before the experiment was repeated. Indeed, the *Devonshires* went back to a single turret on the fo'c'sle and quarter-deck, with two similar wing turrets just abaft and below the fo'c'sle on the upper-deck. The sides of the fo'c'sle were cut back to allow all three guns head-on fire. This was the first class to carry the forward armament in this manner, and was to be copied in Watts's early Dreadnoughts and cruisers.

There were originally ten *Monmouths*, but the *Bedford* was wrecked on the China station in 1910. When war came, the name ship of the class was an early casualty, being sunk by Graf Spee's squadron with all hands at Coronel; but when the opportunity for revenge came it was with the aid of two of her sisters that Graf Spee and his squadron were destroyed. The *Kent*, burning the wardroom furniture to get the last knot, caught up with and sank the *Nürnberg*, while the *Leipzig* was sunk by the *Cornwall* and *Glasgow*, the latter not of the class. The rest of the class survived the war, as did four out of the six

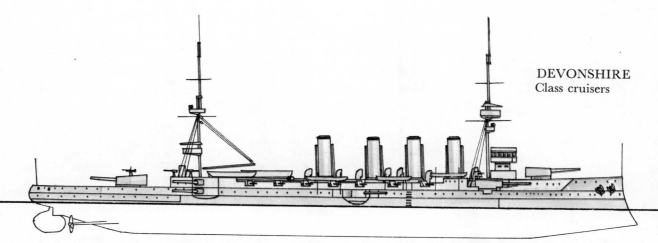

DEVONSHIRE
Class cruisers

ANTRIM 1903, ARGYLL 1904, CARNARVON 1903, DEVONSHIRE 1904, HAMPSHIRE 1903, ROXBURGH 1904
10,850 *tons* 450′ × 68′ × 24′. Guns 4 7·5″, 6 6″, 2 12-*pdrs.*, 18 3-*pdrs.* Torpedo tubes 2 18″ (*submerged*). Main armour 6″ *to* 2″ *belt,* 5″ *bulkheads,* 6″ *barbettes with* 5″ *turrets,* 12″ *conning tower,* 2″ *deck.* Engines and speed *Triple expansion;* 21,000 *h.p.;* 22¼ *knots.*

*Devonshires*. The unlucky two were the *Argyll* which was wrecked on Bell Rock in October 1915 and, much more dramatically, the *Hampshire*. She had been detailed off to take Lord Kitchener to Russia in June 1916. Sir John Jellicoe saw the great war lord off at Scapa and a few hours later he was drowned when the *Hampshire* was mined off the Orkneys.

## Watts's Armoured Cruisers

Watts came to the Admiralty with a reputation from Elswicks of aggressively arming his ships. Certainly there was an immediate jump in the gun-power of his first large cruisers. Shorter and beamier than the *Drakes*, the *Duke of Edinburgh* and *Black Prince* had six 9·2-inch guns in single turrets, four on the corners of the upper-deck, one on the fo'c'sle and one on the quarter-deck. Below this were ten 6-inch guns in casemates on the main-deck, too low to be valuable in a seaway. This placing of guns on the main-deck had been criticized in White's ships, and the failure of the batteries in these ships brought a change in the *Duke of Edinburgh* in 1917, when they were plated over and some guns moved on to the upper-deck. The armour was similar in thickness to the *Drakes* but covered a greater area. Both the *Duke of Edinburgh* and the *Black Prince* were part of the four ships of Arbuthnot's First Cruiser Squadron at the Battle of Jutland, where the *Black Prince* was sunk by gunfire in the night action that followed the main encounter; indeed the *Duke of Edinburgh* was the only ship of the squadron to survive the battle.

In the following year, 1904, a further four cruisers were laid down; they were originally to have been sister ships to the *Duke of Edinburgh*, but the failure of their secondary armament resulted in a rethink about guns. The six 9·2-inch turrets were deployed as before, but instead of the 6-inch battery on the main-deck, four turrets each containing a 7·5-inch gun were placed on the upper-deck, two each side. This was a gun cribbed from the *Triumph* and *Swiftsure* (see page 160), and the system proved highly satisfactory and the ships a great success. They were, however, an unlucky class in the war. The *Natal* blew up in Cromarty Firth on 30 December 1915 during a children's party; faulty cordite was suspected. The *Warrior*, one of Arbuthnot's cruisers, was so badly damaged at Jutland that she had to be sunk the following day, and the *Cochrane* was wrecked in the Mersey in November 1918. Only the *Achilles* came through the war, to which she contributed by sinking the raider *Leopard* off the Shetlands in March 1917.

The third class of Watts's armoured cruisers was bigger and armed in a manner that presented one of the most ferocious sights in the fleet. The twin turret was revived, and there were two of them for the four 9·2-inch, one fore, one aft. Along each side were no less than five turrets of 7·5-inch guns, single mounted. Although powerful ships outside the battle-fleet, by their use at Jutland as wing support they showed up their weakness and that of the *Warriors*. The *Defence* was Rear-Admiral Arbuthnot's flagship when that incautious officer managed to bring his squadron into too close contact with the enemy battle-fleet and was sunk with all hands. The *Minotaur* and *Shannon*, part of the Second Cruiser Squadron at Jutland, came through unscathed. Apart from the battle-cruisers, these were the last large cruisers to be built until the late 1920s.

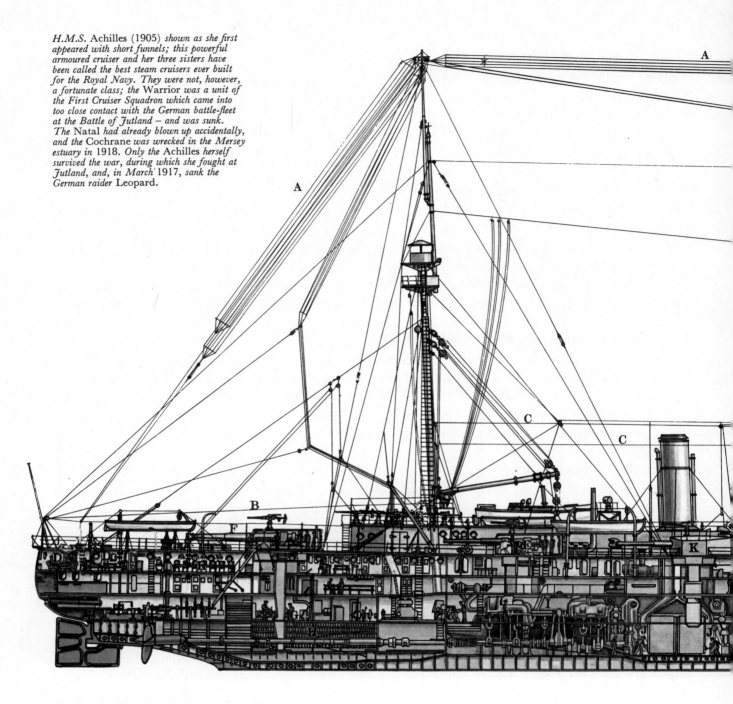

*H.M.S.* Achilles (1905) *shown as she first appeared with short funnels; this powerful armoured cruiser and her three sisters have been called the best steam cruisers ever built for the Royal Navy. They were not, however, a fortunate class; the* Warrior *was a unit of the First Cruiser Squadron which came into too close contact with the German battle-fleet at the Battle of Jutland – and was sunk. The* Natal *had already blown up accidentally, and the* Cochrane *was wrecked in the Mersey estuary in 1918. Only the* Achilles *herself survived the war, during which she fought at Jutland, and, in March 1917, sank the German raider* Leopard.

0    10    20    30    40    50    **Scale in Feet**

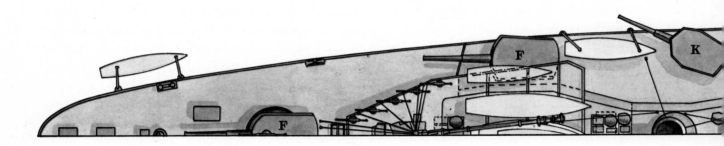

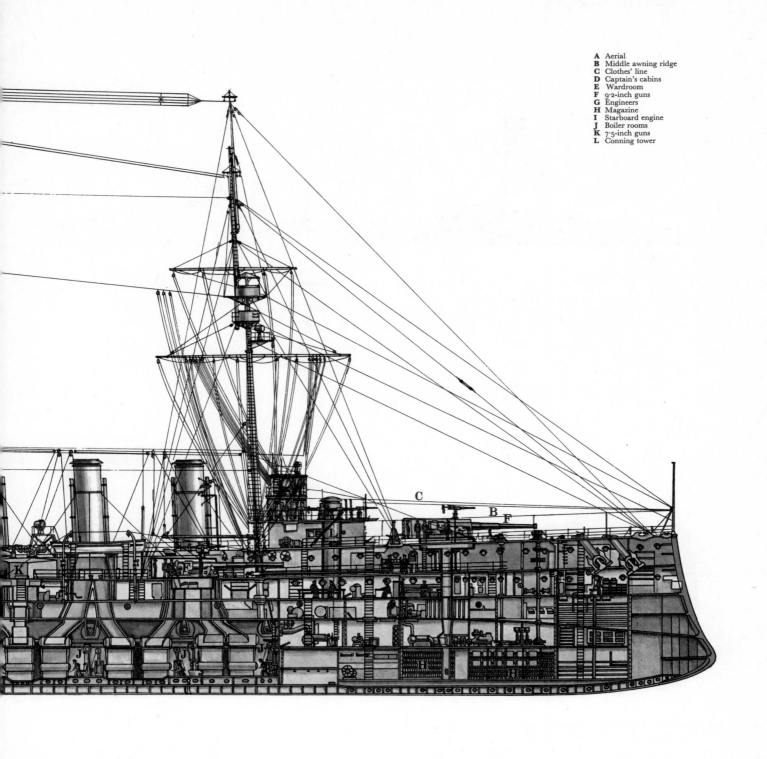

## BELTED CRUISERS

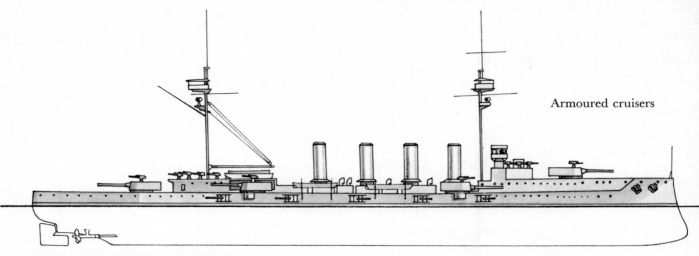

Armoured cruisers

**BLACK PRINCE, DUKE OF EDINBURGH, both 1904**
13,550 *tons* 505½′ (*o/a*) × 73½′ × 26′. Guns 6 9·2″, 10 6″, 22 3-*pdrs*. Torpedo tubes 3 18″ (*submerged*). Main armour 6″ *to* 3″ belt, 6″ *to* 3″ barbettes with 7½″ *to* 4½″ turrets, 10″ conning tower, 6″ battery, 1½″ *to* ¾″ decks. Engines and speed *Triple expansion*; 23,000 *h.p.*; 23 knots. *Forced draught*; 23,500 *h.p.*; 23⅔ knots. Remarks *Funnels subsequently raised.*

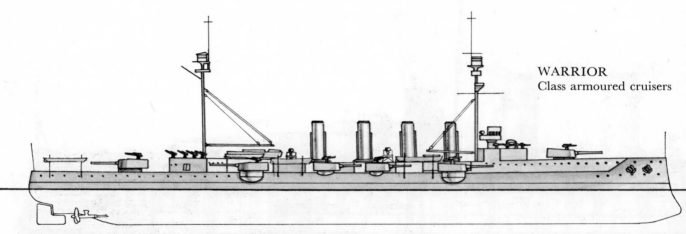

WARRIOR
Class armoured cruisers

**ACHILLES, COCHRANE, NATAL, WARRIOR, all 1905**
13,550 *tons* 505½′ (*o/a*) × 73½′ × 25′. Guns 6 9·2″, 4 7·5″, 26 3-*pdrs*. Torpedo tubes 3 18″ (*submerged*). Main armour 6″ *to* 3″ belt, 6″ *to* 3″ barbettes with 7½″ *to* 4½″ turrets, 1½″ *to* ¾″ decks. Engines and speed *Triple expansion*; 23,000 *h.p.*; 23 knots. Remarks *Funnels subsequently raised.*

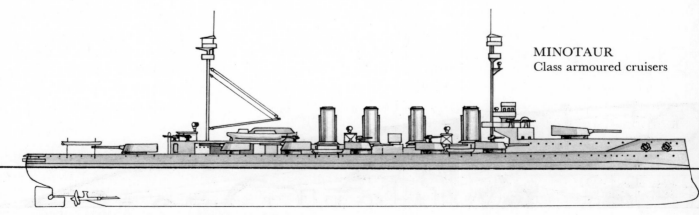

MINOTAUR
Class armoured cruisers

**DEFENCE 1907, MINOTAUR 1906, SHANNON 1906**
14,600 *tons* 519′ (*o/a*) × 74½′ × 26′. Guns 4 9·2″, 10 7·5″, 16 12-*pdrs*. Torpedo tubes 5 18″ (*submerged*). Main armour 6″ *to* 3″ belt, barbettes, 9·2″ turrets 8″ *to* 7″, 7·5″ turrets 8″ *to* 4½″, 10″ conning tower, 1½″ *to* ¾″ decks. Engines and speed *Triple expansion*; 27,000 *h.p.*; 23 knots. Remarks *Funnels subsequently raised.*

# 24

# The Light-Cruisers

Contemporary with the *Gem* class of small protected cruiser, a new type called the light-cruiser evolved in which the emphasis was put on speed to the cost of protection and armament. The first four classes of this type were ordered in 1903 from four commercial firms, Vickers-Maxim, Laird, Fairfield and Armstrong, to be under 3,000 tons, carry an armament of 10 12-pounders and achieve 25 knots. The gun layout was also standardized. Each firm produced two ships, Armstrong's *Adventure* and *Attentive* had four funnels and a 2-inch deck. Fairfield's *Forward* and *Foresight* had a 2-inch belt amidships and a weaker deck. Laird's *Pathfinder* and *Patrol* had only a 1½-inch deck, and Vickers-Maxim's *Sentinel* and *Skirmisher* a 1½-inch deck. The last six ships had three funnels. They were called 'scouts' at that time, the eyes of the fleet. All survived the war except the *Pathfinder* which was sunk by a torpedo in September 1914.

After the building of these four classes, there was a lull until seven very similar ships were built at Pembroke dockyard between 1907 and 1913. The first two, *Bellona* and *Boadicea*, were wretchedly armed, with only six 4-inch guns and two torpedo tubes, one each side. At Jutland they attended the First and Second Battle Squadrons respectively. The next pair, the *Blanche* and *Blonde*, had the number of guns raised to ten, while the *Active*, *Amphion* and *Fearless* were similar to the *Blanche* except for the line of the bow. These three also had a double skin amidships, but the rest had no armour at all. All could steam in excess of 25 knots. They were suitable to act as destroyer leaders but not very effective on their own. The *Fearless* led the First Flotilla at Jutland, though she did sink a British submarine, *K17*, at the 'Battle of May Island' (see p. 271). The *Amphion* was lost to a mine at the very beginning of the war on 6 August 1914.

Following the laying down of these ships, a further three classes of four-funnelled cruisers were built, all completing by 1912. They were larger and faster and introduced the 6-inch gun to their type. The first was the *Bristol* class of five ships where single 6-inch fore and aft reinforced ten 4-inch guns. In the war, *Glasgow* of this class escaped the fate of the *Good Hope* and *Monmouth* at Coronel and lived to fight the same enemy off the Falklands. In the three ships of the *Chatham* class and the four *Weymouths* the 4-inch armament was dropped and replaced by eight 6-inch. These two classes were very similar although the *Chathams* had a double skin on their waterline. At Jutland the *Southampton* was the leader of Commodore Goodenough's light-cruiser squadron, which was generally thought to have done better than any other that day by their splendid job in keeping in touch with the German High Seas Fleet and by keeping the Commander-in-Chief informed. The *Dublin*

# SCOUTS

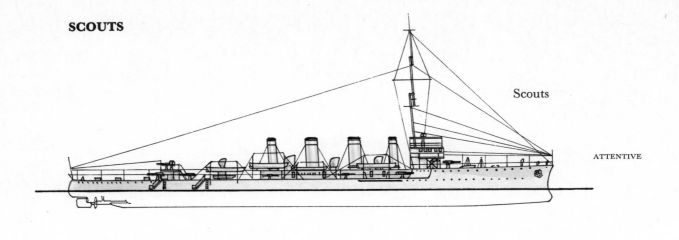

Scouts

ATTENTIVE

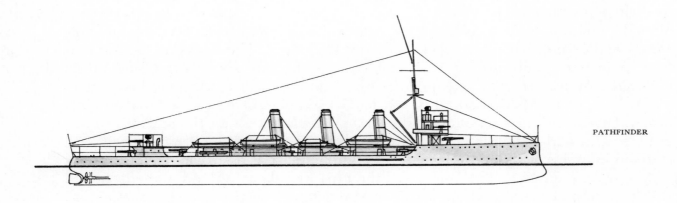

FORESIGHT

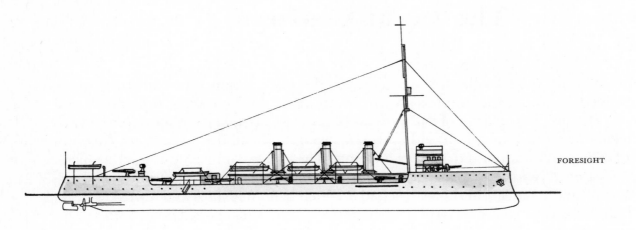

PATHFINDER

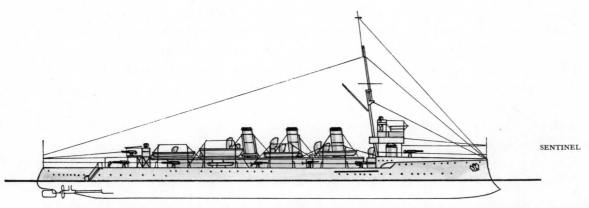

SENTINEL

ADVENTURE, ATTENTIVE, FORESIGHT, FORWARD, PATHFINDER, PATROL, SENTINEL, SKIRMISHER, all 1904
2,640 *to* 2,900 *tons*, *ADVENTURE*/*ATTENTIVE* 374' × 38¼' × 13'. *FORESIGHT*/*FORWARD* 365' × 39' × 14', *PATHFINDER*/*PATROL*
370' × 38¼' × 13', *SENTINEL*/*SKIRMISHER* 360' × 40' × 13'. Guns 10 12-pdrs. (*later replaced by* 9 4"), 8 pom-poms. Torpedo tubes 2(*above water*).
Main armour 2" *to* ⅝" *deck*. Engines and speed *Triple expansion;* 16,000–17,000 *h.p.;* 25 *knots*. Remarks Foresight *and* Forward *had poops*.

BOADICEA light-cruisers

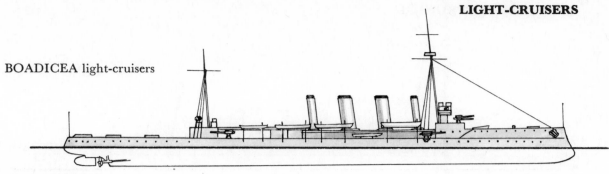

**BELLONA 1909, BOADICEA 1908**
3,300 *tons* 385′ × 41′ × 13½′. Guns 6 4″, 4 3-*pdrs.* (*saluting*). Torpedo tubes 2 18″ (*above water*). Main armour 4″ *conning tower*, 2½″ *torpedo tubes, 1″ deck.* Engines and speed *Turbines;* 18,000 *h.p.;* 25½ *knots.* Remarks Bellona *did not have her bow guns on a platform.*

ACTIVE Class light-cruisers

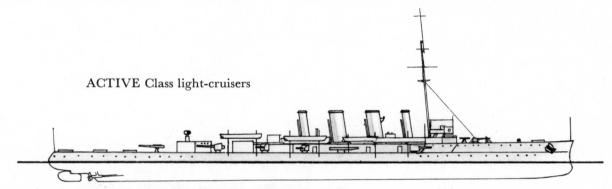

**ACTIVE 1911, AMPHION 1911, BLANCHE 1909, BLONDE 1910, FEARLESS 1912**
3,440 *tons* (*BLANCHE, BLONDE* 3,350 *tons*) 385′ × 41½′ × 14′. Guns 10 4″, 4 3-*pdrs.* (*saluting*). Torpedo tubes 2 21″ (*above water*). Main armour *ACTIVE, AMPHION, FEARLESS double skin amidships, otherwise as BOADICEA class.* Engines and speed *Turbines;* 18,000 *h.p.;* 25 *knots.* Remarks *The bows of* Active, Amphion, Fearless *curved forward to fo'c'sle level.*

BRISTOL Class light-cruisers

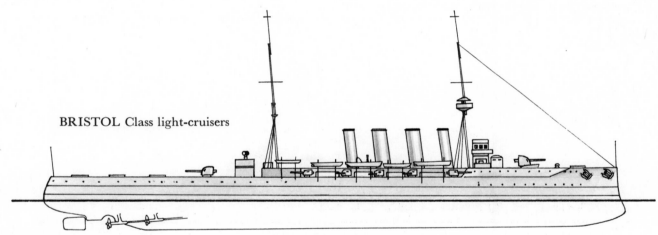

**BRISTOL 1910, GLASGOW, GLOUCESTER, LIVERPOOL, NEWCASTLE, all 1909**
4,800 *tons* 453′ (*o/a*) × 47′ × 15¼′. Guns 2 6″, 10 4″, 4 3-*pdrs.* (*saluting*). Torpedo tubes 2 18″ (*submerged*). Main armour 6″ *conning tower,* 4″ *torpedo tubes,* 3″ *to* ¾″ *deck.* Engines and speed *Turbines;* 22,000 *h.p.;* 25 *knots.* Remarks Bristol *had twin screws, the others four.*

WEYMOUTH Class light-cruisers

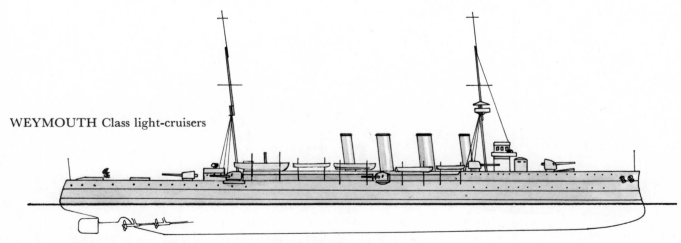

**DARTMOUTH 1910, FALMOUTH 1910, WEYMOUTH 1910, YARMOUTH 1911**
5,250 *tons* 453′ (*o/a*) × 48½′ × 15¼′. Guns 8 6″, 4 3-*pdrs.* (*saluting*). Torpedo tubes 2 21″ (*submerged*). Main armour 2″ *deck.* Engines and speed *Turbines;* 22,000 *h.p.;* 25 *knots.* Remarks Yarmouth *had twin screws, the rest four.*

# BELTED LIGHT-CRUISERS

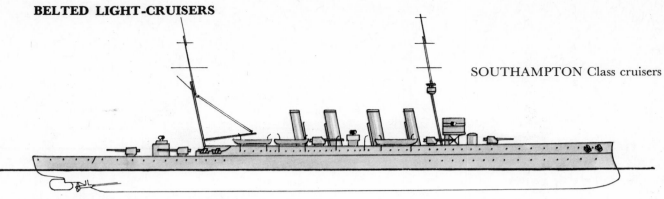

SOUTHAMPTON Class cruisers

CHATHAM 1911, DUBLIN 1912, SOUTHAMPTON 1912
5,400 *tons* 458' (*o/a*) × 49' × 16'. Guns 8 6", 4 3-*pdrs*. Torpedo tubes 2 21" (*submerged*). Main armour *Double skin at water-line, 2" deck*. Engines and speed *Turbines;* 25,000 *h.p.;* 25½ *knots.*

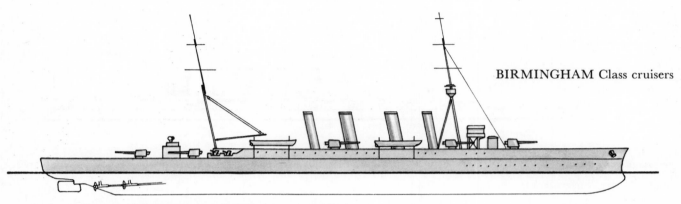

BIRMINGHAM Class cruisers

BIRMINGHAM, LOWESTOFT, NOTTINGHAM, all 1913
5,440 *tons* 457' × 50' × 16'. Guns 9 6", 1 3" A.A. Torpedo tubes 2 21". Main armour *3" belt*. Engines and speed *Turbines;* 25,000 *h.p.;* 25 *knots.*

ARETHUSA Class cruisers

ARETHUSA 1913, AURORA 1913, GALATEA 1914, INCONSTANT 1914, PENELOPE 1914, PHAETON 1914, ROYALIST 1915, UNDAUNTED 1914
3,520 *tons* 436' × 39' × 13½'. Guns 2 6", 6 4", (*later* 3 6", 4 4", 2 3" A.A. in all except *AURORA* and *UNDAUNTED* which only had 1 4" A.A. added). Torpedo tubes 4 (*later* 8) 21". Main armour *3" belt, 1" deck*. Engines and speed *Turbines;* 40,000 *h.p.;* 29 *knots.*

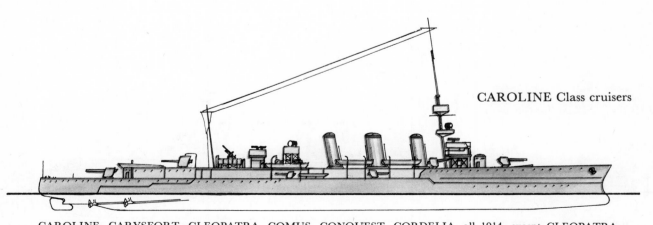

CAROLINE Class cruisers

CAROLINE, CARYSFORT, CLEOPATRA, COMUS, CONQUEST, CORDELIA, all 1914, except CLEOPATRA, CONQUEST 1915
3,750 *tons* 446' × 41½' × 14½'. Guns 2 6", 8 4" (*later* 4 6", 2 3" *or* 4" A.A.). Torpedo tubes 4 (*later* 8) 21". Main armour *3" belt, 1" deck*. Engines and speed *Turbines;* 40,000 *h.p.;* 29 *knots.*

was also in the squadron. The *Falmouth* was sunk by a German U-boat in the North Sea in 1916. A fourth class of the same dimensions, but having an extra gun forward and an armour-belt, the *Nottingham*, *Birmingham* and *Lowestoft*, completes the list of the larger prewar light-cruisers. The *Nottingham* and *Birmingham* were the other two ships in Goodenough's squadron at Jutland, but the *Nottingham* was sunk by a submarine in the North Sea a few weeks later, in August 1916.

None of the foregoing classes carried torpedoes, but a smaller, more balanced class of cruiser emerged with a thicker belt and torpedo tubes as well as guns. These were the *Arethusa* and *Caroline* classes. They were fine ships, though the *Arethusas* particularly were cramped so far as accommodation went. In wartime, when a rapid expansion of the fleet is required, a standard must be accepted to which a large number of ships will be built. In the First World War it was the *Caroline* class that set the pattern for the famous C class cruisers and the larger D class. The *Calliope* and *Champion*, in which the mixed armament of 4-inch and 6-inch later gave way to four 6-inch and two 3-inch anti-aircraft guns, had a thicker belt and introduced two funnels to the type. Twenty-two of these little ships were built, the first completing in 1915, and the last in 1922 and they, with the slightly larger Ds, became the navy's standard light-cruisers and destroyer leaders until the Second World War. Of their progenitors, the *Arethusas* and the *Carolines*, only the *Arethusa* was lost in the war, mined off Felixstowe in 1916. During this time the mixed armament was modified to varying degrees in both classes, the 4-inch guns being taken out and the 6-inch and 3-inch anti-aircraft guns increased or substituted. All these ships were out of the service by the early 1930s, except the *Caroline*, which became the RNVR ship at Belfast, without guns or boilers. She is still there, the last ship afloat that fought at Jutland.

By the Second World War, the Cs and Ds were old-fashioned with their single gun mountings, and soon began to show their age when sent on North Atlantic patrol. They had always been wet ships forward, though the modification of a trawler bow to some of them had helped. Nevertheless, in spite of some prewar scrappings, there were still twenty-one of them, and every ship was needed. The most effective way of using them was to rearm them as anti-aircraft flak ships, a process that began just before the war.

Only one of them had been lost in the First World War era, the *Cassandra*, mined in the Baltic a few weeks after the Armistice, but in the Second World War the casualty rate rose sharply. Four were sunk in the Mediterranean, the *Cairo*, *Calcutta*, *Calypso* and *Coventry*; the *Curlew* was bombed and sunk at Narvik in 1940 and the *Dunedin* torpedoed in the South Atlantic in 1941. The most spectacular exit was made by the *Curaçoa* which was run down by the *Queen Mary* in 1942, and the most humiliating end was the *Durban*'s, expended as a breakwater in the Normandy landings.

Other light-cruiser classes begun during the First World War were the *Emerald* and *Enterprise*, and the *Frobisher* class of five ships. The E class were stretched Ds and three-funnelled to give them a speed of over 30 knots; also they carried one more 6-inch. The *Enterprise* was given a twin turret forward as an experiment, and no class was subsequently built with single mountings.

The *Frobisher* class were large for light-cruisers, nearly 10,000 tons, and curiously armed with single-mounted 7·5-inch guns. The first to complete was the *Vindictive*, as an aircraft carrier, but she was subsequently refitted as a cruiser between the wars. Loss by accident is not common with large expensive ships, but the *Raleigh* cast away on the coast of Labrador in 1922 and the *Effingham* hit a rock during the Norwegian campaign in 1940 and sank. The *Vindictive* was converted to a cadet training ship before the war and was scrapped by the end of it. The *Frobisher* became the cadet training ship after the war.

Finally, mention should be made of two First World War cruisers which were bought into the service in 1914. These were the *Birkenhead* and the *Chester*, both being built for the Greek Navy by Cammell Laird. They were the same dimensions as the *Birminghams*, but armed with ten 5·5-inch guns, unique in the service at that time.

CAMBRIAN Class cruisers

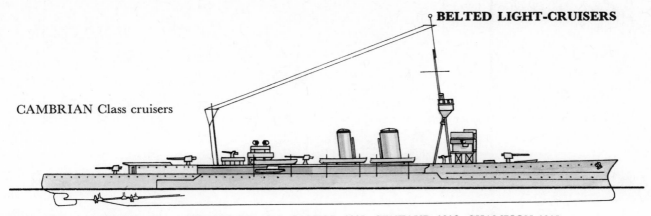

CALLIOPE 1914, CAMBRIAN 1916, CANTERBURY 1915, CASTOR 1915, CENTAUR 1916, CHAMPION 1915, CONCORD 1916, CONSTANCE 1915
3,750 *tons* 446′ × 41½′ × 14½′. Guns 2 6″, 8 4″, 1 or 2 3″ or 4″ A.A. (*CENTAUR and CONCORD* 5 6″, 2 3″ A.A.), (*later all except CENTAUR and CONCORD had 4 6″, 2 3″ or 4″ A.A.*). Torpedo tubes 4 *to* 8 21″ (*CENTAUR and CONCORD* 2 21″). Main armour 3″ *belt*, 1″ *deck*. Engines and speed *Turbines*; 40,000 h.p.; 29 knots. Remarks *CALCUTTA, CALEDON, CAIRO, CARLISLE, COLOMBO, COVENTRY, CURACOA and CURLEW refitted as anti-aircraft cruisers in the late 1930s and early 40s, with 4″ A.A. guns and multiple pom-poms.*

CALEDON Class cruisers

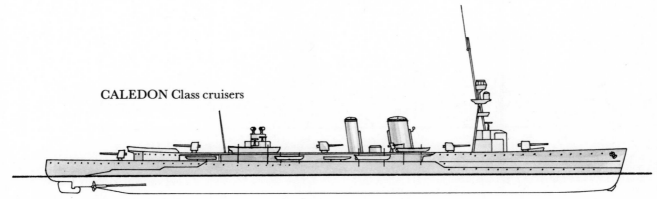

CALEDON, CALYPSO, CARADOC, CASSANDRA, all 1916, except CALYPSO 1917
4,120 *tons* 450′ × 42¾′ × 14½′. Guns 5 6″, 2 3″ A.A. Torpedo tubes 8 21″. Main armour 3″ *belt*, 1″ *deck*. Engines and speed 40,000 h.p.; 29 knots.

CERES Class cruisers

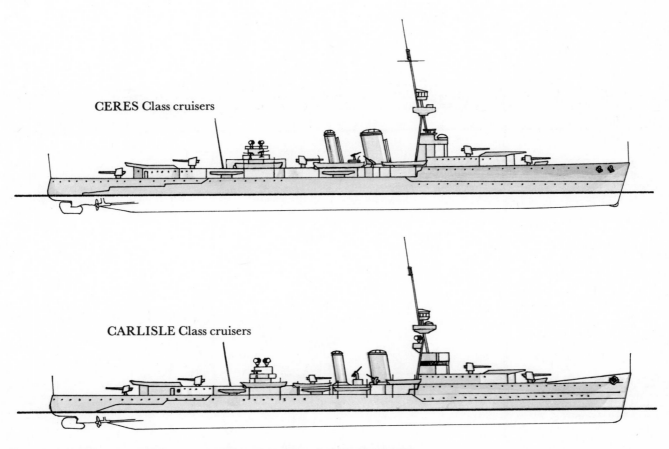

CARLISLE Class cruisers

CERES Class CARDIFF, CERES, COVENTRY, CURAÇOA, CURLEW, all 1917
CARLISLE Class CALCUTTA 1918, CAIRO 1918, CAPETOWN 1919, CARLISLE 1918, COLOMBO 1918
4,190 *tons* 450′ (*CERES Class* 4,290 *tons* 451½′) × 43½′ × 14½′. Guns 5 6″, 2 3″ A.A. Torpedo tubes 8 21″. Main armour 3″ *belt*, 1″ *deck*. Engines and speed *Turbines*; 40,000 h.p.; 29 knots. Remarks Carlisle *Class had trawler bows, and* Carlisle *completed with a combined aircraft hangar and bridge.*

# BELTED LIGHT-CRUISERS

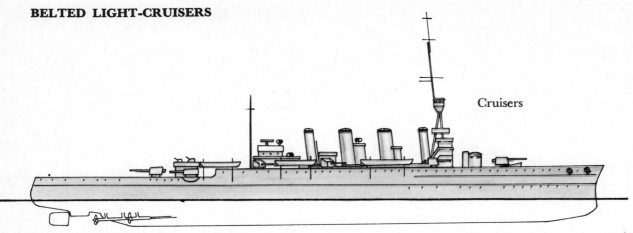

Cruisers

**BIRKENHEAD, CHESTER, both 1915**
5,200 *tons* BIRKENHEAD 446', CHESTER 456' × 50' × 15½'. Guns 10 5·5", 1 3" *A.A.* Torpedo tubes 2 21". Main armour 3" *belt.*
Engines and speed *Turbines.* BIRKENHEAD 25,000 *h.p.*; 25 *knots*; CHESTER 31,000 *h.p.*; 26½ *knots*. Remarks *Building for the Greeks,*
*taken over.*

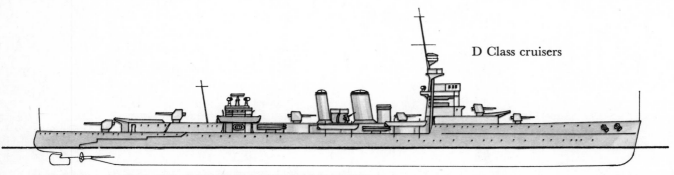

D Class cruisers

**DANAE Class DANAE 1918, DAUNTLESS 1918, DRAGON 1917**
**DELHI Class DELHI 1918, DESPATCH 1919, DIOMEDE 1919, DUNEDIN 1918, DURBAN 1919**
4,650 *tons* 471' × 46' × 15'. Guns 6 6", 2 3" *A.A.* Torpedo tubes 12 21". Main armour 3" to 1½" *belt, 1" deck.* Engines and speed *Turbines;* 40,000
*h.p.;* 29 *knots*. Remarks *The* Delhi *Class had trawler bows.* Dauntless *and* Dragon *completed as* Carlisle.

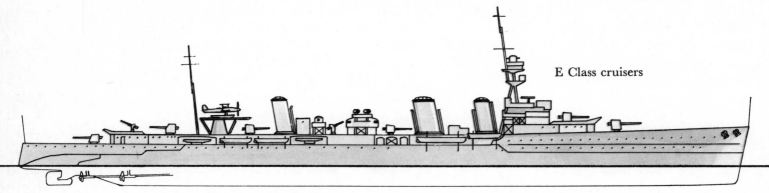

E Class cruisers

**EMERALD 1920, ENTERPRISE 1919**
*EMERALD* 7,550 *tons,* ENTERPRISE 7,580 *tons* 570' (*o/a*) × 54½' × 18½'. Guns 7 6", 3 4" *A.A.* Torpedo tubes 12 (*later* 16) 21". Main armour 3" *to*
1½" *belt, 1" deck.* Engines and speed *Turbines;* 80,000 *h.p.;* 33 *knots*. Remarks *Twin* 6" *mounting forward in* Enterprise.

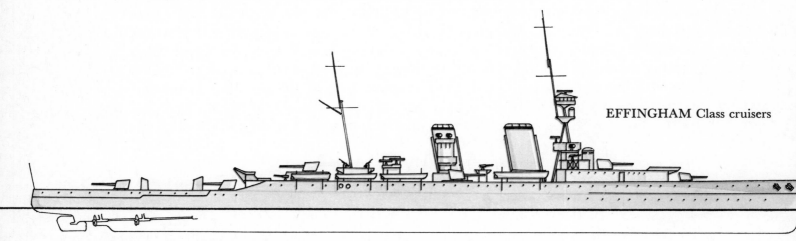

EFFINGHAM Class cruisers

**EFFINGHAM 1921, FROBISHER 1920, HAWKINS 1917, RALEIGH 1919, VINDICTIVE 1918**
9,550 *to* 9,860 *tons* 605' (*o/a*) × 65' × 17½'. Guns 7 7·5", 4 3" *A.A.* or 3 4" *A.A.,* 4 3-*pdrs.* (*FROBISHER later* 5 7·5"; *EFFINGHAM later rearmed with* 9
6", 8 4" *A.A.*; *VINDICTIVE completed with* 5 7·5" *later increased to* 6). Torpedo tubes 6 21". Main armour 3" to 1½" *belt,* 2½" *to* 1" *gun shields,* 3"
*conning tower,* 1½" *deck.* Engines and speed *Turbines;* 65,000 *h.p.;* 30½ *knots*. Remarks Vindictive *completed as an experimental aircraft carrier, converted*
*back to a cruiser 1923–5, became a cadet training ship 1937 and a repair ship in 1940.*

# 25

# The Washington Treaty Cruisers

The Treaty limits for cruisers depended, as with the battleships, on the largest class of new ships that any one of the negotiating powers possessed, and which it did not want to lose. In the case of the battleships, it was the 16-inch ships that the USA and Japan had, or were building, that settled that point; with cruisers it was Britain's big new *Frobisher* class (page 208) with their 7·5-inch guns. The limit was set at 10,000 tons and 8-inch guns. Immediately, all the signatories felt that they must build to the limit, so that the late 1920s saw a new generation of large 8-inch cruisers. Japan and the USA built belted cruisers; the Japanese, favouring twin mountings, managed to pack five turrets into their *Atago* class, while the Americans went in for a triple mounting and carried nine guns in their ships. The Italians combined a belt with light scantling for speed, while the French abandoned armour altogether. The British ships carried eight 8-inch in huge, almost unarmoured, hulls. The first were designed by Sir Eustace Tennyson-d'Eyncourt and the commodious high-freeboard hulls were reminiscent of the *Nelson* and *Rodney*. They were also reminiscent of the last class of large protected cruiser, the *Diadems* of the late 1890s, which also depended on a light protective deck at the water-line, and a very large hull which could absorb a good many hits and flooding without being stopped. For this reason these *County* class cruisers were given a low centre of gravity so that they could withstand flooding without risk of capsizing, a factor that made them heavy rollers and poor gun-platforms in bad weather. Speculations also arose as to the effect of firing torpedoes from so great a height. However, apart from their expense to maintain and operate, they were splendid ships for a world empire at peace. Their fine presence, wonderful accommodation, with their 8-foot deck-heads, and their ability to steam great distances at a high average speed, regardless of the weather, made them able guardians of the Pax Britannica. It was, in fact, their steaming qualities that in wartime amply made up for their deficiencies in armour and gun-power. For the Royal Navy war has always meant great movements of troops and equipment to protect, with little contact with the enemy's surface ships. The great hulls could also take a considerable additional anti-aircraft protection in the way of guns without straining their sea-going qualities; there was also a large hangar aft in some ships. Just before the war, the *Cumberland* and *Suffolk* were taken in hand for their quarter-deck to be lowered a deck. This was not, as might be thought, a practical move to cut down the top weight but a political one, since the class was somewhat in excess of the Treaty limits and this lighten-

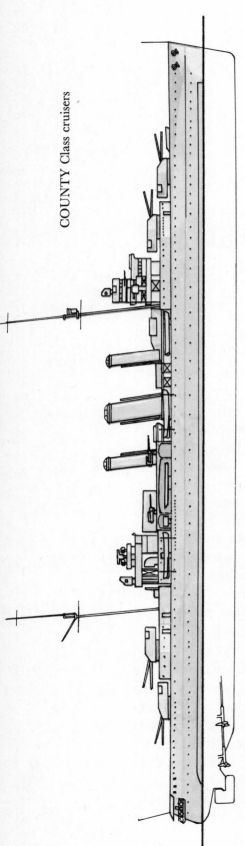

COUNTY Class cruisers

**BERWICK, CORNWALL, CUMBERLAND, KENT, SUFFOLK,** all 1926
9,750 to 9,850 tons 630′ (o/a) × 68¼′ × 16¼′. Guns 8 8″, 4 (later 8) 4″ A.A., 4 2-pdrs. A.A. Torpedo tubes 8 21″. Aircraft 1 to 4 later carried. Main armour 5″ to 3″ belt; 2″ to 1½″ turrets, 3″ conning tower, 1½″ deck. Engines and speed Turbines; 80,000 h.p.; 31½ knots.

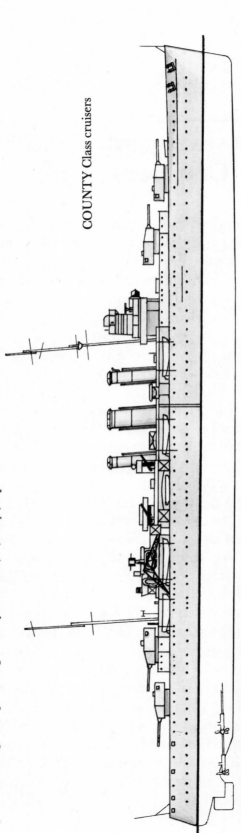

COUNTY Class cruisers

**DEVONSHIRE** 1927, **LONDON** 1927, **SHROPSHIRE** 1928, **SUSSEX** 1928.
9,830 to 9,850 tons 633′ (o/a) × 66′ × 17′. Guns 8 8″, 4 (later 8) 4″ A.A., 4 2-pdrs. A.A. Torpedo tubes 8 21″. Aircraft 1 to 3 later carried. Main armour 2″ to 1¼″ turrets, 3″ conning tower, 4″ to 1½″ deck. Engines and speed Turbines; 80,000 h.p.; 32¼ knots.

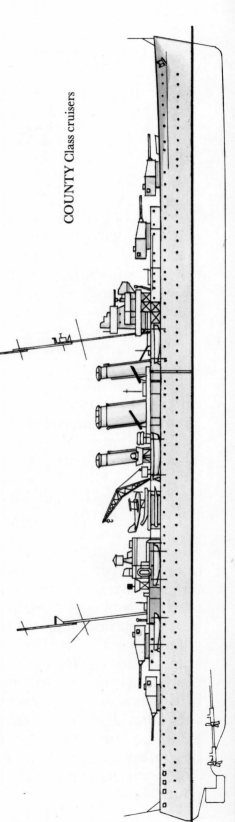

COUNTY Class cruisers

DORSETSHIRE 1929, NORFOLK 1928

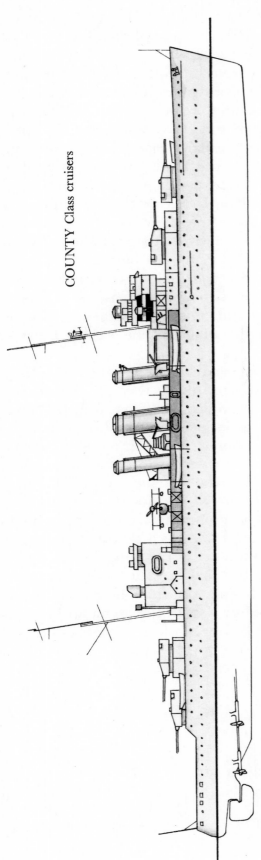

COUNTY Class cruisers

CUMBERLAND *and* SUFFOLK *as reconstructed* 1935-6.

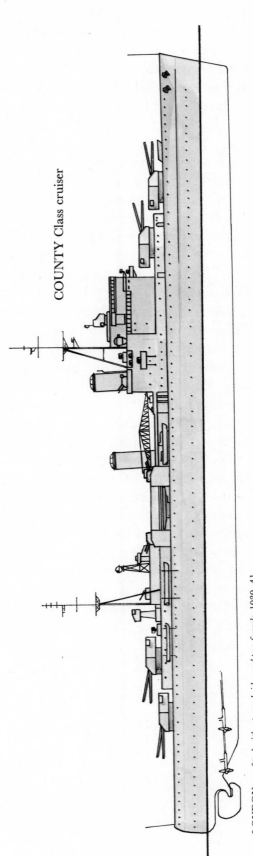

COUNTY Class cruiser

LONDON *as refitted with a tower bridge and two funnels,* 1939–41.

ing was a gesture. The war came before any of the others could be taken in hand. They were the last class on which the stern-walk might be seen, though not on all.

There were five ships in the first batch, four in the second, Sir W. Berry's first cruisers, and two in the third. The later six differed very little from the *Kents*, except in having internal instead of external anti-torpedo bulges, and their bridges were brought 15 feet aft to give A and B turrets a better quarter fire. Two more *Kents* were built for the Australians.

In the war the Royal Navy lost two of them, *Cornwall* and *Dorsetshire*, both on 5 April 1942 to Japanese aircraft in the Indian Ocean. The Australian *Canberra* was also lost in action with the Japanese, torpedoed by surface craft at the battle off Savo Island in August 1942. The *Cornwall* was part of the 1940 Dakar expedition and was hit by a French heavy shell, probably from the battleship *Richelieu*. In the *Scharnhorst* action the *Norfolk* was twice hit by 11-inch shells. The *London*, class name of the second batch, was taken in hand for modifications during 1939 and re-emerged with two upright funnels and a tower bridge, very much like a *Colony* class cruiser in appearance (see page 218).

The *Devonshire*, which sank the famous German raider *Atlantis*, followed the *Frobisher* as the cadet training ship until 1953, but the longest survivor was the *Cumberland* which became the navy's floating test-bed for new equipment and guns, most notably a spectacular pre-wetting system of water-jets to clear off atomic pollution. She was not broken up until 1959.

Before a reversion to the 6-inch gun in cruisers, two smaller versions of the *Counties* appeared, the *York* and *Exeter*. In these ships one of the after turrets was suppressed and the foremost of the three funnels was trunked into the middle one so that they had one thick and one thin. Also the high hull broke down a deck from amidships. Though cheaper and of more sensible proportions, these ships suffered from their reduced endurance. They were both lost in the war, but not before the *Exeter* at least had had more than her share of action with surface ships. Very early in the war she was one of Harwood's three cruisers that chased the *Admiral Graf Spee* into Montevideo and, being the heaviest of them, was engaged by the German ship. Quite unprotected against 11-inch shells, she received some deep wounds, but fought on until she was a shambles and was lucky not to have been sunk. Repaired, she went to the Far East in time for the early surface actions with Japanese cruisers and was sunk in the Java Sea in March 1942 when part of an Anglo-Dutch–US squadron under a Dutch admiral. The *York*'s career was less glorious. In May 1941 she was heavily damaged by a small Italian motor boat in Suda Bay, Crete, was beached and later hit by German bombers before being abandoned as a total loss.

# 26

## The Return of the 6-inch Cruiser

In the early 1930s, three new classes of 6-inch cruisers were built to replace the *C* and *D* class. The two larger of these were the *Orion* class of five ships, and the three *Amphions*, modifications of the former. In the *Orions* the twin turret, tried out experimentally in the *Enterprise*, was used throughout, two forward and two aft. They were particularly beautiful cruisers, with their two funnels trunked into one large one. The side armour-belt also returned with a light 3-inch belt.

At the very beginning of the war, *Ajax* and *Achilles* of this class became the focus of world news when they, with the *Exeter*, chased the *Admiral Graf Spee* into Montevideo. *Neptune* of this class was lost in 1941 and both *Achilles* and *Leander*, which had been lent to the Royal New Zealand Navy, were badly damaged in action with the Japanese.

The *Amphion*, *Apollo* and *Phaeton* were modified in that their boilers were more widely separated to prevent total flooding of the boiler-rooms, a possibility in the *Orions*. They therefore had two funnels, fairly widely spaced. All three ships were transferred to the Royal Australian Navy before the war as the *Perth*, *Hobart* and *Sydney*, but subsequently they were unlucky enough to lose two of them. The *Perth* was torpedoed by the Japanese at the end of the disastrous action in the Java Sea, when an allied force of ships under the Dutch Admiral Doorman were destroyed by superior Japanese forces. The *Sydney*'s fate was an unlikely one. In November 1941 she fell in with a merchantman purporting to be Dutch off the coast of Western Australia. In spite of strict Admiralty injunctions, she placed herself on the ship's broadside at 2,000 yards. The 'Dutchman' then opened her concealed batteries and revealed herself as the German armed mer-chant-cruiser *Kormoran*. This surprise so told against the *Sydney* that, although she disabled the *Kormoran*, which as a result had to end her cruise and scuttle herself, she herself was forced to break off the action in flames and was lost without trace or survivors.

A smaller class of four ships, the *Arethusas* had only six guns in three turrets and were considered badly under-gunned. Two of them, *Galatea* and *Penelope*, were torpedoed in the Mediterranean, though previously the *Penelope* had earned herself the nickname of H.M.S. *Pepperpot* after the severe strafing she received in the Malta convoys.

## The *Southampton*, *Belfast*, *Colony* and *Superb* Classes

The Americans and Japanese by the late 1930s were bringing into service large 6-inch cruisers carrying fifteen guns in five triple turrets. Britain's initial reply was the eight ships of the *Southampton* class, carrying twelve 6-inch in triple turrets. Armour protection was greatly increased with a 3- to 4-inch belt. These were very fine ships and were followed by the larger *Belfast* and *Edinburgh* which had a heavier belt. All these were completed before the war, while eleven ships of the *Colony* class were building, slightly smaller than the *Southamptons*, but with the *Belfast*'s armour; they could be distinguished from the former by their upright funnels. Of the *Southamptons* three were lost; the *Manchester*, which had been the last cruiser to appear in the Far East in white and buff before the war, was torpedoed by an Italian motor-torpedo-boat in 1942. The *Southampton* had previously been lost to German aircraft during the most ferociously attacked of the Malta convoys in January 1941, while the *Gloucester* succumbed to the same enemy during the expensive operations resulting in the loss of Crete.

Of the rest, the *Sheffield* had a distinguished war record which included taking part in the sinkings of the *Bismark* and *Scharnhorst* and she was at the Barents Sea action on 31 December 1942, when she arrived in time to save Sherbrooke's heroic destroyers and drive off, with the *Jamaica*, the German cruisers *Hipper* and *Lutzow*; an action that sickened Hitler of his surface forces. The *Sheffield* continued after the war to be the last of her class and was scrapped in 1967. The *Glasgow*, with the *Enterprise*, engaged German destroyers in a running action in bad weather in late December 1943 and sank three of them. The two cruisers were under air attack at the same time. The *Liverpool*, which had her bows blown off by an aerial torpedo in 1940, was repaired but torpedoed again in June 1942 and remained out of service until October 1945. The *Birmingham* distinguished herself in the bombardments of the Korean War of 1950 to 1952.

The *Belfast* and *Edinburgh* with their wide-spaced funnels separated by the mainmast differed very much in appearance from the *Southamptons* and *Colonies*. The *Belfast* was mined and broke her back early in the war but was repaired in time to take a distinguished part in the sinking of the *Scharnhorst*. She will be Britain's last conventional cruiser afloat, since she has been preserved as a museum ship on the River Thames. The *Edinburgh* was sunk during an Arctic convoy action in May 1942.

The *Colonies* numbered eleven ships which completed between 1940 and 1943. The growing preoccupation with anti-aircraft defence caused the suppression of turrets in the later ships, so as to save space and weight for more anti-aircraft guns. Two were lost in the war, both to German aircraft: the *Fiji* off Crete in 1941 and the *Trinidad* in the Barents Sea in 1942. The *Gambia* was lent to the Royal New Zealand Navy and the *Uganda* to the Royal Canadian Navy. The *Kenya* and the *Nigeria* were damaged by torpedoes during the Malta convoy called 'Pedestal' in August 1942. The *Jamaica*, as already mentioned, fought the *Lutzow* and *Hipper* in the Barents Sea and she was also in action, steaming with the *Duke of York*, when they sank the *Scharnhorst*. After the war these cruisers continued to serve into the 1960s, the last survivor being the *Gambia*. The *Nigeria*, which was the only one to retain her X turret, has been part of the Indian Navy since 1957 and the *Newfoundland* and *Ceylon* have been with the Peruvian Navy since 1960.

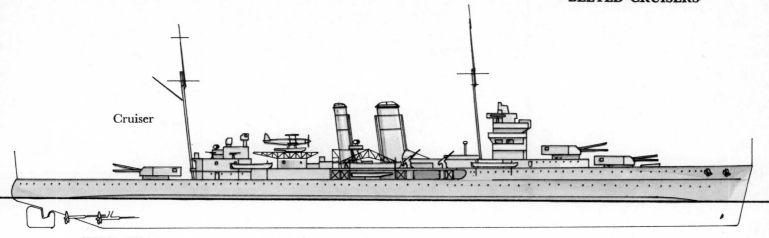

Cruiser

**YORK 1928**
8,250 *tons* 575' (o/a) × 57' × 17'. Guns 6 8", 4 4" *A.A*, 2 2-pdrs. *A.A.* Torpedo tubes 6 21". Aircraft 1. Main armour 3" *to* 2" *belt*, 2" *to* 1½" *turrets*, 3" *conning tower*, 2" *deck*. Engines and speed *Turbines*; 80,000 *h.p.*; 32 knots.

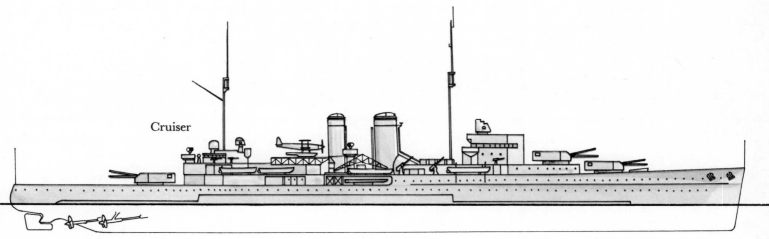

Cruiser

**EXETER 1929**
8,390 *tons* 575' (o/a) × 58' × 17'. Guns 6 8", 4 (*later* 8) 4" *A.A.*, 2 2-pdrs. *A.A.* Torpedo tubes 6 21". Aircraft 2. Main armour 3" *to* 2" *belt*, 2" *to* 1½" *turrets*, 3" *conning tower*, 2" *deck*. Engines and speed *Turbines*; 80,000 *h.p.*; 32 knots.

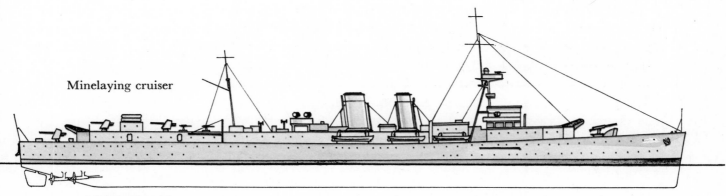

Minelaying cruiser

**ADVENTURE 1924**
6,740 *tons* 520' (o/a) × 59' × 14½'. Guns 4 4·7" *A.A.*, 8 2-pdrs. *A.A.* Mines 280 *large or* 340 *small*. Engines and speed *Turbines*; 40,000 *h.p.*; 27¾ knots; *Diesel-electric for cruising*. Remarks *Drawing shows vessel as first completed*.

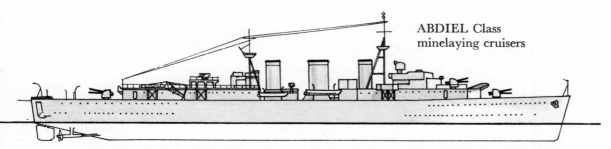

**ABDIEL Class minelaying cruisers**

**ABDIEL 1940, APOLLO 1943, ARIADNE 1943, LATONA 1940, MANXMAN 1940, WELSHMAN 1940**
2,650 *tons* 418' (o/a) × 40' × 11¼'. Guns 6 4" *A.A.*, 4 2-pdrs. *A.A.*, 8 0·5" *A.A. APOLLO and ARIADNE* 4 4" *A.A.*, 4 40-mm. *A.A.*, 12 20-mm. *A.A.* Mines 156. Engines and speed *Turbines*; 72,000 *h.p.*; 40 knots. Remarks *Fastest steamers ever built for the Royal Navy*.

## BELTED CRUISERS

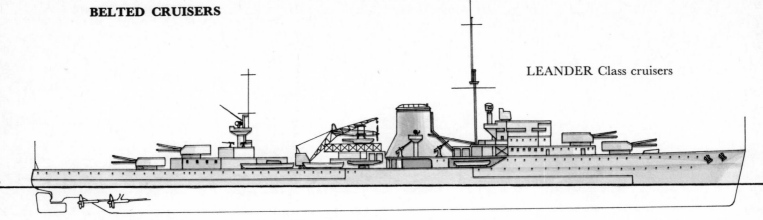

LEANDER Class cruisers

ACHILLES 1932, AJAX 1934, LEANDER 1931, NEPTUNE 1933, ORION 1932
6,985 *to* 7,270 *tons* 554½′ (*o/a*) × 55¼′ × 16′. Guns 8 6″, 4 (*later* 8) 4″ *A.A.*, Torpedo tubes 8 21″. Aircraft 1. Main armour 4″ *to* 2″ *belt*, 1″ *turrets*, 1″ *conning tower*, 2″ *deck. Engines and speed Turbines; 72,000 h.p.; 32½ knots.*

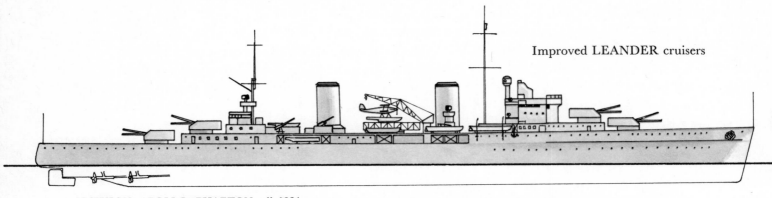

Improved LEANDER cruisers

AMPHION, APOLLO, PHAETON, all 1934
6,830 *to* 7,105 *tons* 555′ (*o/a*) × 56¾′ × 15¾′. Guns 8 6″, 4 (*later* 8) 4″ *A.A.* Torpedo tubes 8 21″. Aircraft 1. Main armour 4″ *to* 2″ *belt, 1″ turrets, 1″ control tower, 2″ deck. Engines and speed Turbines; 72,000 h.p.; 32½ knots. Remarks All transferred to the Royal Australian Navy as* Perth, Hobart *and* Sydney *respectively.*

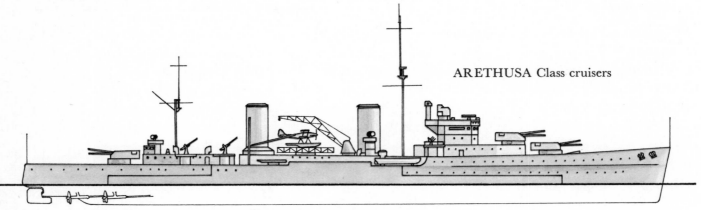

ARETHUSA Class cruisers

ARETHUSA 1934, AURORA 1936, GALATEA 1934, PENELOPE 1935
5,220 *to* 5,270 *tons* 506′ (*o/a*) × 51′ × 13¾′. Guns 6 6″, 8 4″ *A.A.* Torpedo tubes 6 21″. Aircraft 1 (*not AURORA*). Main armour 2″ *belt, 1″ turrets, 1″ control tower, 2″ deck. Engines and speed Turbines; 64,000 h.p.; 32 knots.*

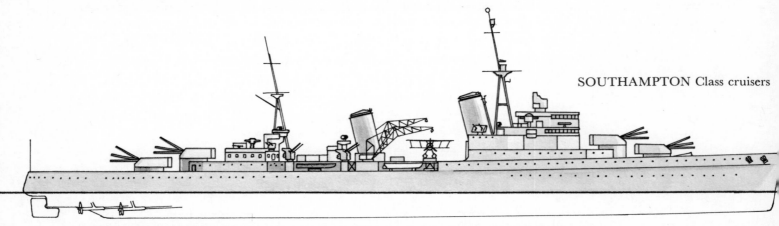

SOUTHAMPTON Class cruisers

BIRMINGHAM 1936, GLASGOW 1936, GLOUCESTER 1937, LIVERPOOL 1937, MANCHESTER 1937, NEWCASTLE 1936, SHEFFIELD 1936, SOUTHAMPTON 1936
9,100 *to* 9,400 *tons* 591½′ (*o/a*) × 62′ × 17′. Guns 12 6″, 8 4″ *A.A.*, 8 2-*pdrs. A.A.* Torpedo tubes 6 21″. Aircraft 3. Main armour 4″ *to* 3″ *belt, 2″ to 1″ turrets, 4″ control tower, 2″ deck. Engines and speed Turbines; 75,000 h.p.; 32 knots (GLOUCESTER, LIVERPOOL and MANCHESTER 82,500 h.p.; 32½ knots).*

A third batch of almost identical cruisers, the *Superb*, *Swiftsure* and *Minotaur*, followed. The *Minotaur* was transferred new to Canada as the *Ontario*, and the *Swiftsure* was involved in a dramatic collision with the destroyer *Diamond* in 1953. The paint-store in the *Diamond*'s bows caused a fierce fire to rage under the cruiser's bridge, which dropped 2 feet. Much time and money was spent on refitting her in Chatham dockyard but this was not completed and she never served again. The *Superb*, although the latest of the *Southampton* and *Colonies* type, was one of the first to be broken up. Prewar ships lasted longer – the difference between wartime and peacetime building.

## The *Tiger* Class

When the war ended in 1945 three more cruisers similar to the *Superbs* were launched but not fitted out. They were moth-balled and two even later ships were cancelled on the stocks. For nine years their fate was undecided, then in 1954 it was announced that they would be completed, but with a very much modified armament. The number of 6-inch guns was cut to four, in two turrets. These were completely automatic and gave the guns a firing rate of one in every three seconds instead of one in ten seconds in the older ships. Two turrets instead of four made a great saving in space and weight for other sophisticated equipment. Unfortunately, the complicated hydraulics of the *Lions* turrets would not stand the shaking up they took when firing for spells of more than about thirty seconds. When this limitation became evident, boffins of the utmost fame were called at once, but they found the patients incurable. The *Lion* even killed one of them.

Another difficulty when running ships of this size and complexity was that the supply of non-commissioned technicians in service fell short of the demand, with the result that when the last of them, *Blake*, commissioned in 1961, she had to be taken out of service before completing a commission, to implement the priority requirements of one of the commando carriers. The *Blake* did not commission again until 1969, by which time she had been transformed. The after turret was removed and a great hangar and flight-deck put there for helicopters. She still had one turret forward, rather like the early days of the *Furious* in reverse. The *Tiger* was similarly treated but not the *Lion*, which was scrapped in 1975. *Blake* commenced breaking up late in 1982 with *Tiger* awaiting disposal.

## The *Dido* Class

The 5·25-inch gun in a twin turret which was used in the *King George V* class battleships as their secondary armament appeared as main armament in a large class of improved *Arethusas*, laid down in 1937–9. Because the guns could be trained to a very high angle, these ships appeared as anti-aircraft cruisers, and fine ships they were, if a trifle cramped for their role. There were eleven in the first batch. Three of them, the *Bonaventure*, *Hermione* and *Naiad* were sunk by submarines in the Mediterranean and the *Charybdis* was torpedoed in fog in the Channel by German light surface forces. The *Argonaut* had her bow and stern blown off by torpedoes at the same time in 1942, but got to Algiers and Gibralter where, after very temporary repairs, she managed to steam to Philadelphia for what amounted to a one-third rebuild.

It was three of this class that fought the best cruiser action of the war, when *Cleopatra*,

*Euryalus* and *Dido* with the *Penelope* and sixteen destroyers beat off an Italian force which included the battleship *Littorio*, two heavy cruisers and a light-cruiser, and which had been sent to intercept their convoy to Malta. This was Admiral Vian's finest hour, in the *Cleopatra*. He had another flagship of the same class, the *Scylla*, when he directed D-Day bombardments for the Normandy landings.

A second batch of *Didos* with C turret suppressed and shorter, straight funnels followed. There were five ships, one of which, the *Spartan*, was sunk off Anzio in 1944, an early victim of the German glider bomb. After the war the *Black Prince* and *Bellona* were lent to the Royal New Zealand Navy. In 1956 they returned *Bellona* in exchange for another of the class, the modernized *Royalist*. The fourth ship, the *Diadem*, was sold to Pakistan in 1956 and is called the *Babur*. She is the last as the *Royalist* was scrapped in 1968.

## Minelaying Cruisers

In the Kaiser's War a variety of types of vessel had been modified for minelaying; merchant passenger liners, the battleship *London*, the 15-inch gunned cruisers *Courageous* and *Glorious*, and big old cruisers like the *Euryalus*. The Royal Navy's first custom-built minelaying cruiser was the *Adventure*, launched in 1924 but not completed until 1927. At the beginning of the war in 1939 she and the *Plover* laid the mine barrage across the Straits of Dover, though shortly afterwards she herself was damaged by a German magnetic mine. She was later used to take supplies to Gibraltar for Malta, and on one return trip in 1943 she intercepted the German blockade runner *Irene* which was scuttled.

In the 1938 naval estimates there was provision for the building of three fast minelaying cruisers with an additional one in the 1939 estimates and two in the 1941 War Programme. These were called the *Abdiel* class and with a top speed of around 40 knots were the fastest oceangoing vessels in the Royal Navy. With such a speed they could rush in at night, lay their mines and be far from the scene of operations by dawn. On one occasion the *Manxman* crossed the Gulf of Lyons in daylight disguised as a French cruiser, dashed in to lay her mines off Leghorn after dark and then streaked back to the Gulf, again appearing as a French cruiser once daylight came.

When Malta and Tobruk were under seige in 1941, the *Abdiels* with their roomy mine decks and great speed were the chief means of supporting them with supplies and troops. It was hazardous work and *Latona* was lost off Tobruk. *Welshman* was torpedoed off Tobruk in 1943 and *Abdiel* was mined at Taranto in the same year.

*Apollo*, *Ariadne* and *Manxman* survived the war, although the latter was badly damaged by torpedo in 1942. As later as 1960 the *Apollo* was the seagoing flagship of the C. in C. Home Fleet, on his rare moments afloat, while the *Manxman* was converted to a minesweeper support ship, losing some of her boilers and thus her famous speed. She served east of Suez 1963 to 1968 and was the engineers' seagoing training ship from 1968 until being broken up in 1971. *Apollo* and *Ariadne* were broken up in 1962 and 1965 respectively.

Cruisers

BELFAST and EDINBURGH, both 1938
10,000 *tons* 613½′ (o/a) ×63¼′×17¼′. Guns 12 6″, 12 4″ *A.A.*, 16 2-*pdrs. A.A.* Torpedo tubes 6 21″. Aircraft 3. Main armour 4½″ *belt*,
2½″ to 1″ *turrets*, 4″ *control tower*. Engines and speed *Turbines*; 80,000 *h.p.*; 32 *knots*.

COLONY Class

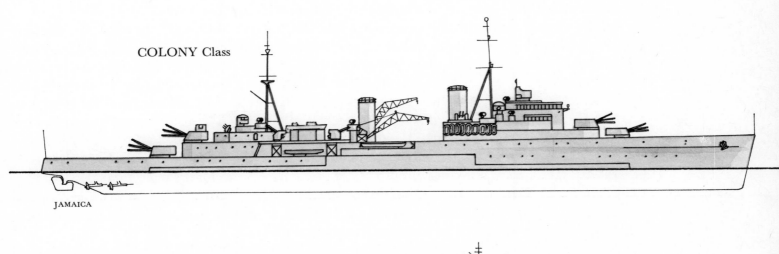

JAMAICA

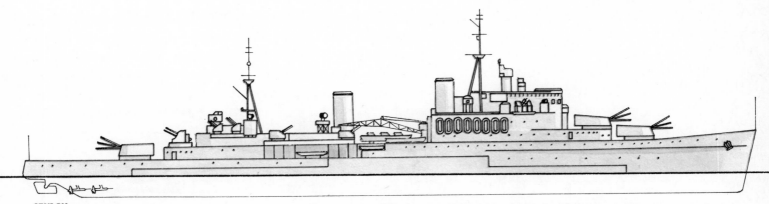

CEYLON

BERMUDA 1941, CEYLON 1942, FIJI 1939, GAMBIA 1940, JAMAICA 1940, KENYA 1939, MAURITIUS 1939,
NEWFOUNDLAND 1941, NIGERIA 1939, TRINIDAD 1940, UGANDA 1941
8,000 *tons* (*CEYLON, NEWFOUNDLAND, UGANDA* 8,800 *tons*) 555½′ (o/a) ×62′×16½′. Guns 12 6″ (*CEYLON, NEWFOUND-
LAND, UGANDA* 9 6″), 8 4″ *A.A.*, *various light A.A. guns.* Torpedo tubes 6 21″. Aircraft 3 (*none in the 8,800-tonners*). Main armour 3½″ *belt*, 2″
*turrets*, 4″ *control tower*, 2″ *deck*. Engines and speed *Turbines*; 72,500 *h.p.*; 33 *knots*. Remarks Ceylon, Newfoundland *and* Uganda *were completed with*
X *turret suppressed and extra A.A. guns mounted. The other surviving ships, except* Nigeria, *were similarly modified.*

# BELTED CRUISERS

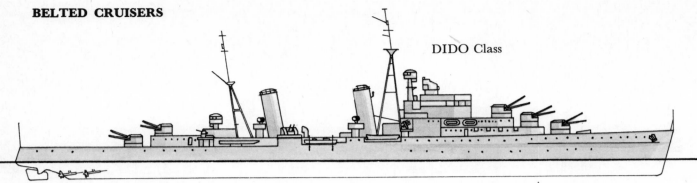

## DIDO Class

ARGONAUT 1941, BONAVENTURE 1939, CHARYBDIS 1940, CLEOPATRA 1940, DIDO 1939, EURYALUS 1939, HERMIONE 1939, NAIAD 1939, PHOEBE 1939, SCYLLA 1940, SIRIUS 1940
5,450 *tons* 512′ (*o*/*a*) × 50½′ × 14′. Guns (*as designed*) 10 5·25″ D.P., 8 2-*pdrs.* A.A. (*BONAVENTURE, DIDO and PHOEBE completed with* 8 5·25″ *D.P. and* 1 4″; *CHARYBDIS had* 8 4·5″ *D.P. and* 1 4″ *whilst SCYLLA only had* 8 4·5″ *D.P.*). Torpedo tubes 6 21″. Main armour 3″ *to* 2″ *belt*, 2″ *to* 1″ *turrets*, 1″ *control tower*, 2″ *to* ½″ *deck*. Engines and speed *Turbines*; 62,000 *h.p.*; 33 *knots*.

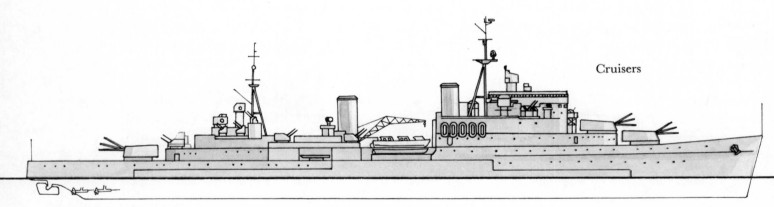

## Improved DIDOS

BELLONA, BLACK PRINCE, DIADEM, ROYALIST, SPARTAN, all 1942
5,770 *tons* 512′ (*o*/*a*) × 50½′ × 14¾′. Guns 8 5·25″ D.P., 12 2-*pdrs.* A.A. Torpedo tubes 6 21″. Main armour 3″ *to* 2″ *belt*, 2″ *to* 1″ *turrets*, 1″ *control tower*, 2″ *to* ½″ *deck*. Engines and speed *Turbines*; 62,000 *h.p.*; 33 *knots*.

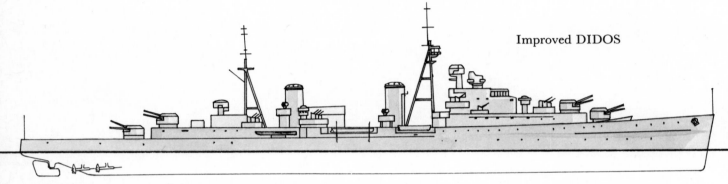

## Cruisers

SUPERB and SWIFTSURE, both 1943
8,800 *tons* 555½′ (*o*/*a*) × 63′ (*SUPERB* 64′) × 17′. Guns 9 6″, 10 4″ A.A., 16 2-*pdrs.* A.A., 8 40-*mm.* A.A. Torpedo tubes 6 21″. Main armour 3¼″ *belt*, 2″ *turrets*, 4″ *control tower*, 2″ *deck*. Engines and speed *Turbines*; 72,500 *h.p.*; 32½ *knots*. Remarks *Similar to the modified Colony Class.*

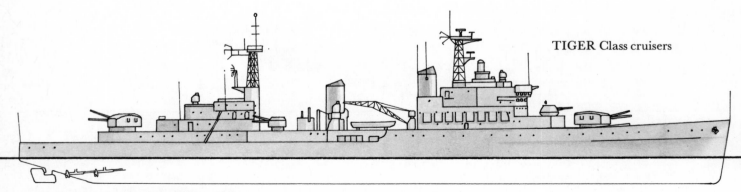

## TIGER Class cruisers

BLAKE 1945, LION 1944, TIGER 1945
9,550 *tons* 555½′ (*o*/*a*) × 64′ × 21′. Guns 4 6″ D.P. *fully automatic*, 6 3″ A.A. *fully automatic*. Main armour 3¼″ *belt*, 2″ *turrets*, 4″ *control tower*, 2″ *deck*. Engines and speed *Turbines*; 80,000 *h.p.*; 31½ *knots*.

# 27

## Torpedo-Gunboats and Destroyers

The development of the small fast steam torpedo-boat naturally resulted in the development of an antidote. Initially, some torpedo-boats were stripped of their torpedoes and had guns mounted instead; but these vessels were too small to keep the seas as an outer guard for the battle-fleet, and something larger was required. The result was the torpedo-gunboat; like small elegant cruisers, thirty-three of them were built, following the *Rattlesnake* of 1886. In general they had a lean, low profile with two or three tall, wide-spaced funnels and a high fo'c'sle. In one class, the *Dryads*, they were given a long poop as well as a fo'c'sle. They were armed with two 4·7-inch, one fore and one aft, and 3-pounders, a fixed 18-inch torpedo tube in the bows and paired tubes on each side amidships. Their role as guardians of the fleet was not long-lived as their 18 or 19 knots was soon inadequate; however, they proved suitable for employment as fishery protection vessels and later as minesweepers. The real torpedo-boat destroyer, herein after called the destroyer, evolved not from the torpedo-gunboat, but from the torpedo-boat (see page 142).

As so often with the smaller type of vessel, a tradition of centuries, destroyers were built under contract to general specifications. So though they might conform in size and armament, they differed in appearance. The main builders were Thornycroft, Yarrow, White, Hawthorn, Denny, Laird and Palmer. Speed was the first criterion and it did not take long for their Parsons turbines to give them the tremendous speed of 34 knots with the *Viper* of 1899, which was hardly to be exceeded as a service requirement. The early Class *As* of 1893–5 needed only 4,000 horsepower to achieve 27 knots, and the Class *Bs* 5,700 horsepower to make 30 knots. As they extended in size and became more seaworthy, so the horsepower increased until the *Swift* of 1907 needed 30,000 horsepower to give her 36 knots. The armament of the early boats was slight compared with the torpedo-gunboats, one 12-pounder and two torpedo tubes. They were mainly boilers and engines and very uncomfortable.

While sizes had been rising steadily through the Classes *C*, *D* and *E* to 225 feet, a jump in size and tonnage came with Class *F* in 1907, 270 feet and 856 tons, and these were the first destroyers to be officially described as ocean-going. The classes had reached *L* before the Kaiser's war broke out and these were 30-knot destroyers armed with three 4-inch and four torpedo tubes in pairs. At the beginning of the war there were two hundred and twenty-five on the active list. With the war, a furious building programme ensued. The larger *M* class set the pattern for most of the war emergency

*H.M.S.* Hornet *was one of six privately designed and built vessels originally to be called Torpedo-boat Catchers, but subsequently known as Torpedo-boat Destroyers. These six, the Twenty-six Knotters, formed the first generation of the true destroyer. The* Hornet *was one of a pair delivered by Yarrow. The other two pairs were built by Thornycroft and Laird Brothers. Designed as a counter-measure against the swarms of French torpedo-boats, they brought a new dimension to naval warfare. Their cramped discomfort discouraged the starchy formality of the late Victorian navy's large ships, and strongly influenced a new generation of naval officers, more interested in ships as fighting units, than as a pleasant way of life.*

| | | | | | |
|---|---|---|---|---|---|
| **A** | Engineers' store | **M** | After stokehold | **Z** | Torpedo tube |
| **B** | Bread room | **N** | Petty Officers' W.C. | **a** | Pantry stores |
| **C** | Officers' W.C. | **O** | Pump | **b** | Spirit room |
| **D** | Wardroom pantry | **P** | Torpedo trolley | **c** | Wardroom stores and Electrical stores |
| **E** | 6-pdr. guns | **Q** | Fore stokehold | **d** | 6-pdr. magazine |
| **F** | Wardroom | **R** | Galley | **e** | Engineers' store |
| **G** | Commander's cabin | **S** | Air-compressing engine | **f** | 12-pdr. shell room and Engineers' store |
| **H** | Torpedo tubes | **T** | Fresh water | **g** | 12-pdr. magazine |
| **I** | Artificers' and Chief Stokers' berths | **U** | 12-pdr. guns | **h** | Torpedo head magazine |
| **J** | Main engines | **V** | Seamen's heads | **i** | Naval stores |
| **K** | Hawser reel | **W** | Conning tower | | |
| **L** | Chart table | **X** | Crew space | | |
| | | **Y** | Cable locker | | |

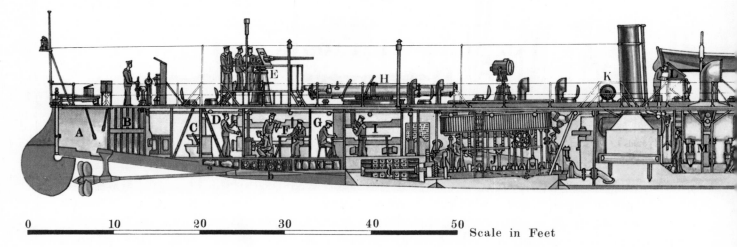

0    10    20    30    40    50    Scale in Feet

# TORPEDO-BOATS and TORPEDO-GUNBOATS

## GRASSHOPPER Class torpedo-gunboats

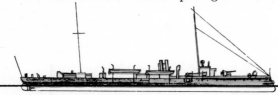

GRASSHOPPER, SANDFLY, SPIDER, all 1887,
RATTLESNAKE 1886
525 *tons* 200′ × 23′ × 9′. Guns 1 4″, 6 3-*pdrs.* Torpedo tubes 4 14″
*above water.* Main armour ¾″ *over machinery.* Engines and speed
*Triple expansion;* 1,600 *h.p.;* 16¾ *knots.* Forced draught; 2,700 *h.p.;*
19 *knots.* Remarks Rattlesnake *differed in appearance.*

## SHARPSHOOTER Class torpedo-gunboats

ASSAYE 1890, BOOMERANG 1889, GLEANER 1890,
GOSSAMER 1890, KARAKATTA 1889, PLASSEY 1890,
SALAMANDER 1889, SEAGULL 1889, SHARPSHOOTER
1888, SHELDRAKE 1889, SKIPJACK 1889, SPANKER 1889,
SPEEDWELL 1889
735 *tons* 230′ × 27′ × 10½′. Guns 2 4·7″, 4 3-*pdrs.* Torpedo tubes 5
14″ (*ASSAYE and PLASSEY* 3) *all above water.* Engines and speed
*Triple expansion;* 2,500 *h.p.;* 16½ *knots.* Forced draught; 3,500 *h.p.;*
19 *knots.* Remarks *Individual ships varied in detail.*

## SPEEDY torpedo-gunboat

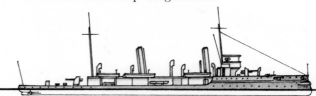

Remarks Alarm *Class, but with three funnels, the only one of the
class to make her designed speeds.*

## ALARM Class torpedo-gunboats

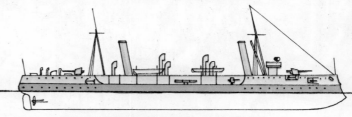

ALARM 1892, ANTELOPE 1893, CIRCE 1892, HEBE
1892, JASEUR 1892, JASON 1892, LEDA 1892, NIGER
1892, ONYX 1892, RENARD 1892, SPEEDY 1893
810 *tons* 230′ × 27′ × 12½′. Guns 2 4·7″, 4 3-*pdrs.* Torpedo
tubes 5 14″ or 3 18″ *above water.* Engines and speed *Triple
expansion;* 2,500 to 4,500 *h.p.;* 17½ to 20 *knots.* Remarks *Individual
ships varied in detail.*

## Torpedo-boats

TB1 (LIGHTNING)

TB80
Nos. 1 *to* 117, *all* 1876–1904
220 *to* 28 *tons,* 116′ *to* 86′. Torpedo tubes 2 *to* 5. Engines and speed
*Triple expansion;* 3,050 *to* 360 *h.p.;* 25 *to* 17 *knots.*

TB15
Nos. 1 *to* 36, *all* 1906–9
305 *to* 225 *tons,* 185′ *to* 175′. Guns 2 12-*pdrs.* Torpedo tubes 3 18″.
Engines and speed *Turbines;* 4,000 *h.p.* to 3,700 *h.p.;* 26 *knots.*

## DRYAD Class torpedo-gunboats

DRYAD 1893, HALCYON, HARRIER, HAZARD,
HUZZAR, all 1894
1,070 *tons,* 250′ × 30½′ × 11½′. Guns 2 4·7″, 4 6-*pdrs.* Torpedo
tubes 5 18″ (*above water*). Engines and speed *Triple expansion;*
2,500 *h.p.;* 17 *knots.* Forced draught; 3,500 *h.p.;* 18½ *knots.*

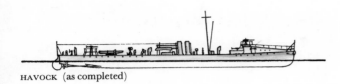

HAVOCK (as completed)

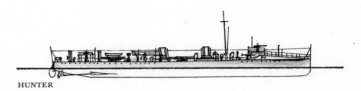

HUNTER

HAVOCK (after reboilering)

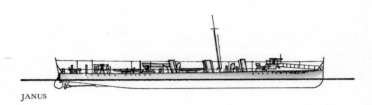

JANUS

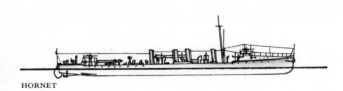

HORNET

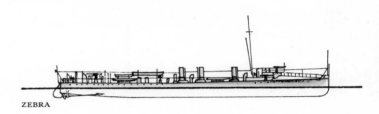

ZEBRA

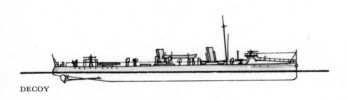

DECOY

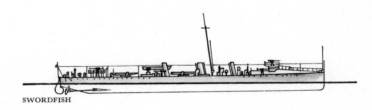

SWORDFISH

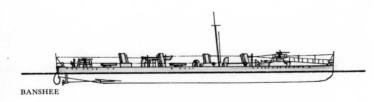

BANSHEE

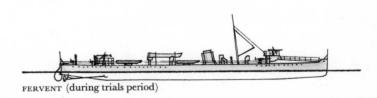

FERVENT (during trials period)

Torpedo-boat destroyers

A Class torpedo-boat destroyers

DARING, DECOY, HAVOCK, HORNET, FERRET,
LYNX, all 1893–4
*DARING, DECOY* 260 tons 185½′ × 19′ × 13′. *HAVOCK,
HORNET* 240 tons 180′ × 18½′ × 11′. *FERRET, LYNX*
280 tons 195′ × 19¼′ × 11½′. Guns 1 12-pdr., 3 6-pdrs. Torpedo
tubes 1 18″ bow, 2 single tubes on deck. Engines and
speed *DARING, DECOY* compound, others triple expansion;
3,500 to 4,500 h.p.; 27 knots. Remarks *As usual with the smaller
experimental type of vessel, general specifications were given to
private firms which drew up their own designs, so that though the
results were similar they differed in their funnel layout, etc.*

ARDENT, BANSHEE, BOXER, BRUISER, CHARGER,
CONFLICT, CONTEST, DASHER, DRAGON,
FERVENT, HANDY, HARDY, HART, HASTY,
HAUGHTY, HUNTER, JANUS, LIGHTNING,
OPOSSUM, PORCUPINE, RANGER, ROCKET,
SALMON, SHARK, SKATE, SNAPPER, SPITFIRE,
STARFISH, STURGEON, SUNFISH, SURLY,
SWORDFISH, TEAZER, WIZARD, ZEBRA,
ZEPHYR, all 1894–5
250 to 310 tons 190′ to 208½′ × 18½′ to 20′ × 11¼′ to 13′. Guns
1 12-pdr., 5 6-pdrs. Torpedo tubes 2 single tubes on deck.
Engines and speed *ARDENT, BOXER, BRUISER*
compound, others triple expansion; 2,960 to 4,844 h.p.; 27 knots.
Remarks *Performance varied from* Charger's 26 knots to
Boxer's 29 knots.
TAKU 1898, *German built, captured from the Chinese during the
Boxer Rebellion in 1900.*

# TORPEDO-BOAT DESTROYERS

## B Class torpedo-boat destroyers

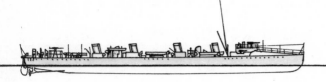

## C Class torpedo-boat destroyers

## D Class torpedo-boat destroyers

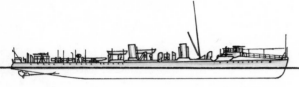

*B Class* ALBACORE, BONETTA, EARNEST, GRIFFON, KANGAROO, LIVELY, LOCUST, MYRMIDON, ORWELL, PANTHER, PETEREL, QUAIL, SEAL, SPARROWHAWK, SPITEFUL, SPRIGHTLY, SUCCESS, SYREN, THRASHER, VIRAGO, WOLF, all 1895–1901
*C Class* AVON, BAT, BITTERN, BRAZEN, BULLFINCH, CHAMOIS, CHEERFUL, CRANE, DOVE, ELECTRA, FAIRY, FALCON, FAWN, FLIRT, FLYING FISH, GIPSY, GREYHOUND, KESTREL, LEE, LEOPARD, LEVEN, MERMAID, OTTER, OSPREY, OSTRICH, RACEHORSE, RECRUIT, ROEBUCK, STAR, SYLVIA, THORN, TIGER, VIGILANT, VIOLET, VIXEN, VULTURE, WHITING, all 1896–1901
*D Class* ANGLER, ARIEL, COQUETTE, CYGNET, CYNTHIA, DESPERATE, FAME, FOAM, MALLARD, STAG, all 1896–9
310 *to* 440 *tons* 209′ *to* 218½′ × 19½′ *to* 21½′ × 12′ *to* 13½′. Guns 1 12-*pdr.* 5 6-*pdrs.* (*ALBACORE and BONETTA* 3 12-*pdrs*). Torpedo tubes 2 18″ *single tubes. Engines and speed D Class were compound, ALBACORE and BONETTA had turbines, others were triple expansion; 5,800 to 7,000 h.p.; 30 knots.* Remarks *Also three slightly larger vessels,* Albatross, Arab *and* Express, *were built for 31 knots.*

## Torpedo-boat destroyers (turbine)

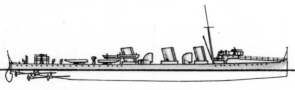

COBRA 1899, VELOX 1902, VIPER 1899
*COBRA* 375 *tons* 223½′ × 20½′ × 13½′; *VELOX* 400 *tons* 210′ × 21′ × 13′; *VIPER* 344 *tons* 210½′ × 21′ × 12½′. Guns 1 12-pdr., 5 6-pdrs. Torpedo tubes 2 18″. *Engines and speed Turbines; 4 shafts, 8 screws (COBRA 12 screws); 8,000 to 11,500 h.p.; 30 knots (VIPER 33·8 knots).* Remarks Cobra *had four funnels.*

## RIVER Class torpedo-boat destroyers

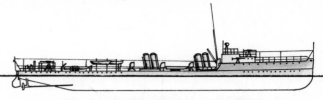

ARUN, BLACKWATER, BOYNE, CHELMER, CHERWELL, COLNE, DEE, DERWENT, DOON, EDEN, ERNE, ETTRICK, EXE, FOYLE, GALA, GARRY, ITCHEN, JED, KALE, KENNET, LIFFEY, MOY, NESS, NITH, OUSE, RIBBLE, ROTHER, STOUR, SWALE, TEST, TEVIOT, URE, USK, WAVENEY, WEAR, WELLAND, all 1903–5
540 *to* 570 *tons* 220′ *to* 230′ × 13½′ × 15′. Guns 1 (*later* 4) 12-*pdrs.*, 5 6-*pdrs.* (*later removed*). Torpedo tubes 2 18″. *Engines and speed Triple expansion (EDEN, turbines); 7,000 to 8,000 h.p.; 25 knots.* Remarks *Funnel arrangement and gun positions varied.*

## TRIBAL Class torpedo-boat destroyers

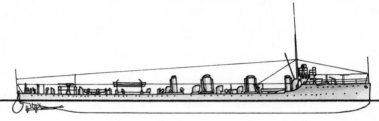

AFRIDI, AMAZON, COSSACK, CRUSADER, GHURKA, MAORI, MOHAWK, NUBIAN, SARACEN, TARTAR, VIKING, ZULU, all 1907–9
850 *to* 1,090 *tons* 250′ *to* 280′ × 24½′ *to* 27½′ × 15½′ *to* 17½′. Guns 3 12-*pdrs* (*later* 5) *in early boats,* 2 4″ *in later boats.* Torpedo tubes 2 18″. *Engines and speed Turbines; 14,000 to 15,500 h.p.; 33 knots. Differed in appearance.* Remarks *After* Nubian *torpedoed and* Zulu *mined, the stern of the* Nubian *was joined to the bow section of* Zulu; *resulting ship named* Zubian, 1917.

## Torpedo-boat destroyer (leader)

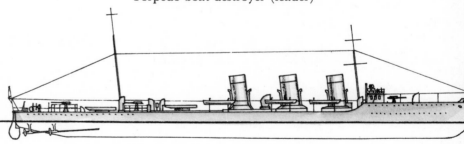

SWIFT 1907
2,390 *tons* 345′ × 34′ × 21¾′. Guns 4 4″. Torpedo tubes 2 18″. *Engines and speed Turbines; 30,000 h.p.; 36 knots.*

## BEAGLE Class torpedo-boat destroyers

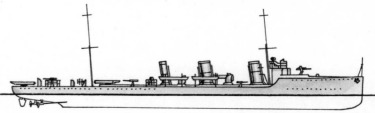

BASILISK, BEAGLE, BULLDOG, FOXHOUND, GRAMPUS, GRASSHOPPER, HARPY, MOSQUITO, PINCHER, RACOON, RATTLESNAKE, RENARD, SAVAGE, SCORPION, SCOURGE, WOLVERINE, all 1909–10
900 *to* 975 *tons* 264′ *to* 275′ × 27′ *to* 28½′ × 16½′ *to* 17½′. Guns 1 4″, 3 12-*pdrs.* Torpedo tubes 2 21″. *Engines and speed Turbines; 14,300 h.p.; 27 knots.* Remarks Grampus *named* Nautilus *until* 1913.

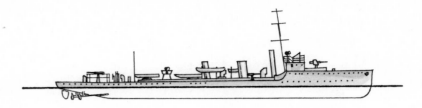

### H and I Class torpedo-boat destroyers

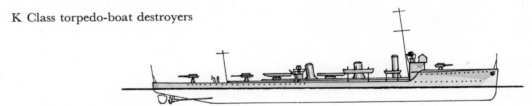

*H Class* ACORN, ALARM, BRISK, CAMELEON, COMET, FURY, GOLDFINCH, HOPE, LARNE, LYRA, MARTIN, MINSTREL, NEMESIS, NEREIDE, NYMPHE, REDPOLE, RIFLEMAN, RUBY, SHELDRAKE, STAUNCH, all 1910–11
*I Class* ACHERON, ARCHER, ARIEL, ATTACK, BADGER, BEAVER, DEFENDER, DRUID, FERRET, FIREDRAKE, FORESTER, GOSHAWK, HIND, HORNET, HYDRA, JACKAL, LAPWING, LIZARD, LURCHER, OAK, PHOENIX, SANDFLY, TIGRESS, all 1911, except FIREDRAKE, HYDRA, LURCHER and OAK, all 1912.
745 *to* 810 *tons* 246′ (o/a) × 25¼′ *to* 25⅔′ × 15½′. Guns 2 4″, 2 12-*pdrs*. Torpedo tubes 2 21″. Engines and speed *Turbines*; 13,500 *to* 16,000 *h.p.*; 27 *knots. Remarks Firedrake, Lurcher and Oak were 15′ longer, 20,000 h.p. and over 32 knots.*

### K Class torpedo-boat destroyers

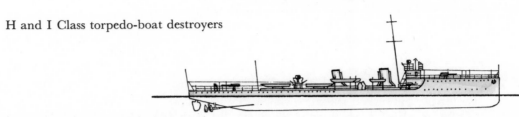

ACASTA, ACHATES, AMBUSCADE, ARDENT, CHRISTOPHER, COCKATRICE, CONTEST, FORTUNE, GARLAND, HARDY, LYNX, MIDGE, OWL, PARAGON, PORPOISE, SHARK, SPARROWHAWK, SPITFIRE, UNITY, VICTOR, all 1912–13
1,072 *tons* 267½′ (o/a) × 27′ × 16½′. Guns 3 4″. Torpedo tubes 2 21″ *single*. Engines and speed *Turbines*; 24,500 *h.p.*; 30 *knots. Remarks Ardent two funnels, Fortune had curved bow.*

### L Class torpedo-boat destroyers

LAERTES, LAFOREY, LANCE, LANDRAIL, LARK, LASSOO, LAUREL, LAVEROCK, LAWFORD, LEGION, LENNOX, LEONIDAS, LIBERTY, LINNET, LLEWELLYN, LOCHINVAR, LOOKOUT, LOUIS, LOYAL, LUCIFER, LYDIARD, LYSANDER, all 1913–14, except LASSOO and LOCHINVAR (wartime additions, 1915)
1,112½ *tons* 269′ (o/a) × 27⅔′ × 16½′. Guns 3 4″. Torpedo tubes 4 21″ *paired*. Engines and speed *Turbines*; 24,500 *h.p.*; 29 *knots. Six had two funnels.*

## DESTROYERS

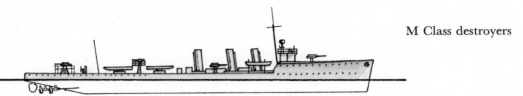

M Class destroyers

MAENAD, MAGIC, MAMELUKE, MANDATE, MANLY,* MANNERS, MANSFIELD, MARMION, MARNE, MARTIAL,
MARVEL, MARY ROSE, MASTIFF,† MATCHLESS, MEDINA, MEDWAY, MENACE, MENTOR, METEOR,† MICHAEL,
MILBROOK, MILNE, MINDFUL, MINION, MINOS,* MIRANDA,* MISCHIEF, MONS, MOON,* MOORSOM,
MORESBY, MORNING STAR,* MORRIS, MOUNSEY,* MUNSTER, MURRAY, MUSKETEER,* MYNGS, MYSTIC,
NAPIER, NARBOROUGH, NARWHAL, NEGRO, NEPEAN, NEREUS, NERISSA,* NESSUS, NESTOR, NICATOR,
NIZAM, NOBLE, NOMAD, NONPAREIL, NONSUCH, NORMAN, NORSEMAN, NORTHESK, NORTH STAR, NUGENT,
OBDURATE, OBEDIENT, OBERON, OBSERVER, OCTAVIA, OFFA, ONSLAUGHT, ONSLOW, OPAL, OPHELIA,
OPPORTUNE, ORACLE, ORCADIA, ORESTES, ORFORD, ORIANA, ORIOLE, ORPHEUS, OSIRIS, OSSORY, PALADIN,
PARTHIAN, PARTRIDGE, PASLEY, PATRICIAN,† PATRIOT,† PELICAN, PELLEW, PENN, PEREGRINE, PETARD,
PEYTON, PHEASANT, PHOEBE, PIGEON, PLOVER, PLUCKY, PORTIA, PRINCE, PYLADES, RAPID,† READY,†
RELENTLESS,* RIVAL,* all 1914–17
883 *to* 1,154 *tons* 269½′ *to* 274½′ × 25½′ *to* 27¼′ × 16¼′ *to* 16¾′. Guns 3 4″. Torpedo tubes 4 21″ *paired.* Engines and speed *Turbines;* 23,000 *to* 27,000
*h.p.; 35 knots.* Remarks *Some Ms and all Ns, Os, Ps and Rs were reorders. In addition to those destroyers built for the Royal Navy, a few were taken over from
private yards building for foreign navies. They were four Turkish, added as the* Talisman, Termagant, Trident *and* Turbulent, *and four Greek,* Medea,
Medusa, Melampus, Melpomene, *all 1914–15 and all similar in size and performance to the M Class. A ninth and smaller destroyer building in Genoa for the
Portuguese was also acquired, the* Arno; *she never left the Mediterranean.* * Two-funnelled. † Centre funnel thick. Mansfield *and* Mentor *two screws, four
funnels.*

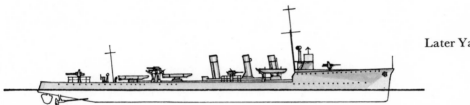

Later Yarrow M and R Class destroyers

RADIANT,† RADSTOCK, RAIDER, RECRUIT, REDGAUNTLET, REDOUBT, RESTLESS, RETRIEVER,† RIGOROUS,
ROB ROY, ROCKET, ROMOLA, ROSALIND,† ROWENA, SABLE, SABRINA,* SALMON, SARPEDON, SATYR, SCEPTRE,
SETTER, SHARPSHOOTER, SIMOON, SKATE, SKILFUL, SORCERESS, SPRINGBOK, STARFISH, STORK,
STRONGBOW,* STURGEON, SURPRISE,* SYBILLE,* SYLPH, TANCRED, TARPON, TAURUS,† TEAZER,†
TELEMACHUS, TEMPEST, TENACIOUS, TETRARCH, THISBE, THRUSTER, TORMENTOR, TORNADO, TORRENT,
TORRID, TRUCULENT,* TYRANT,* ULLESWATER,* all 1916–17
1,173 *tons* 273½′ *to* 276′ × 25½′ *to* 27¼′ × 16¼′ *to* 16¾′. Guns 3 4″. Torpedo tubes 4 21″ *paired.* Engines and speed *Turbines;* 27,000 *h.p.; 36 knots.*
* *Later Yarrow Ms had two funnels.* † *Centre funnel thick.*

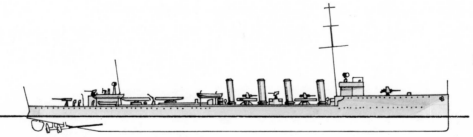

MARKSMAN Class destroyers

ABDIEL, GABRIEL, ITHURIEL, KEMPENFELT, LIGHTFOOT, MARKSMAN, NIMROD, all 1915-16.
1,604 *to* 1,655 *tons* 325′ × 31¾′ × 19½′. Guns 4 4″, 1 3″ *A.A.,* 2 2-pdrs. *A.A.* Torpedo tubes 4 21″. Engines and speed *Turbines;* 36,000 *h.p.; 34 knots.*
Remarks Abdiel *completed as a minelayer, fore funnels raised on all but* Abdiel.

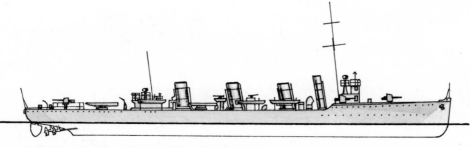

BROKE Class destroyer leaders

BOTHA, BROKE, FAULKNOR, TIPPERARY, purchased 1914
*c.* 1,700 *tons* 331′ × 32½′ × 11′. Guns 6 4″, 2 2-pdrs. *A.A. Later* 2 4·7″, 2 4″. Torpedo tubes 4 21″. Engines and speed *Turbines* 30,000 *h.p.; 32 knots.*
Remarks *Originally laid down at White's for the Chileans.* Tipperary *not rearmed.*

Modified R Class destroyers

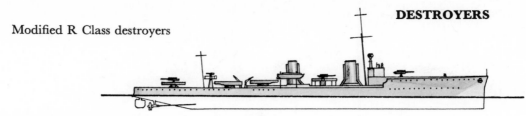

TIRADE, TOWER, TRENCHANT, TRISTRAM, ULSTER, ULYSSES, UMPIRE, UNDINE, URCHIN, URSA, URSULA, all 1917, except TRENCHANT 1916

1,080 *tons* 276′ × 26⅔′ × 16⅔′. Guns 3 4″, 1 2-*pdr*. Torpedo tubes 4 21″ *paired*. Engines and speed *Turbines; 27,500 to 29,000 h.p.; 35 knots.*

SCOTT Class flotilla leaders

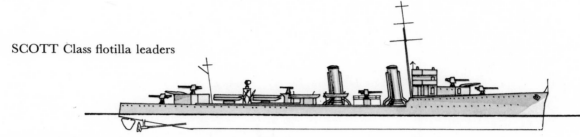

BRUCE, CAMPBELL, DOUGLAS, MACKAY, MALCOLM, MONTROSE, SCOTT, STUART, all 1918, except SCOTT 1917 and MALCOLM 1919

1,580 *tons* 332½′ (*o/a*) × 31¾′ × 19¾′. Guns 5 4·7″, 1 3″ *A.A.* Torpedo tubes 6 21″ *triple-mounted.* Engines and speed *Turbines; 40,000 h.p.; 35 knots. MONTROSE and STUART 43,000 h.p.; 36 knots.*

S Class destroyers

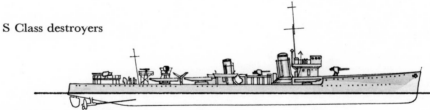

SABRE, SALADIN, SARDONYX, SCIMITAR, SCOTSMAN, SCOUT, SCYTHE, SEABEAR, SEAFIRE, SEARCHER, SEAWOLF, SENATOR, SEPOY, SERAPH, SERAPIS, SERENE, SESAME, SHAMROCK, SHARK, SHIKARI, SIKH, SIMOOM, SIRDAR, SOMME, SPARROWHAWK, SPEAR, SPEEDY, SPINDRIFT, SPLENDID, SPORTIVE, STALWART, STEADFAST, STERLING, STONEHENGE, STORMCLOUD, STRENUOUS, STRONGHOLD, STURDY, SUCCESS, SWALLOW, SWORDSMAN, TACTICIAN, TARA, TASMANIA, TATTOO, TENEDOS, THANET, THRACIAN, TILBURY, TINTAGEL, TOBAGO, TOMAHAWK, TORBAY, TORCH, TOREADOR, TOURMALINE, TRIBUNE, TRINIDAD, TROJAN, TRUANT, TRUSTY, TRYPHON, TUMULT, TURBULENT, TURQUOISE, TUSCAN, TYRIAN, all 1918–19, except THRACIAN 1920

1,075 *tons* 276′ (*o/a*) × 25½′ to 27½′ × 16½′. Guns 3 4″, 1 2-*pdr*. Torpedo tubes 4 21″ *paired*, 2 18″ *single*. Engines and speed *Turbines; 27,000 to 29,000 h.p.; 36 knots.*

V Class destroyers

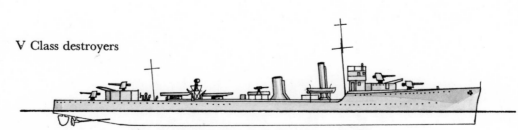

VALENTINE, VALHALLA, VALKYRIE, VALOROUS, VAMPIRE, VANCOUVER, VANESSA, VANITY, VANOC, VANQUISHER, VECTIS, VEGA, VEHEMENT, VELOX, VENDETTA, VENETIA, VENTUROUS, VERDUN, VERSATILE, VERULAM, VESPER, VICEROY, VIDETTE, VIMIERA, VIOLENT, VISCOUNT, VITTORIA, VIVACIOUS, VIVIEN, VORTIGERN, all 1917, except VANESSA, VANITY and VIDETTE 1918

1,457 *tons* 312′ (*o/a*) × 29½′ (*VICEROY, VISCOUNT* 30¾′) × 18½′. Guns 4 4″, 1 3″ *A.A.* Torpedo tubes 4 21″ *paired* (*VAMPIRE* 6 *triple-mounted*). Engines and speed *Turbines; 27,000 h.p.; 34 knots.* Remarks *First five listed were leaders.*

# DESTROYERS

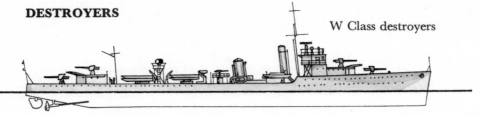

W Class destroyers

VOYAGER, WAKEFUL, WALKER, WALPOLE, WALRUS, WARWICK, WATCHMAN, WATERHEN, WESSEX, WESTCOTT, WESTMINSTER, WHIRLWIND, WHITLEY, WINCHELSEA, WINCHESTER, WINDSOR, WOLFHOUND, WOLSEY, WOOLSTON, WRESTLER, WRYNECK, all 1917–18.
*Dimensions and performance similar to the V Class, but completed with 6 tubes.*
*Modified V and W Classes* VANSITTART, VENOMOUS, VERITY, VETERAN, VOLUNTEER, WANDERER, WHITEHALL, WHITSHED, WILD SWAN, WISHART, WITCH, WITHERINGTON, WIVERN, WOLVERINE, WORCESTER, WREN, all 1918–19.
*Dimensions the same as Vs and Ws, but armament different. Guns 4 4·7″, 1 3″ A.A. Torpedo tubes 6 21″ triple-mounted. Remarks funnel styles varied.*

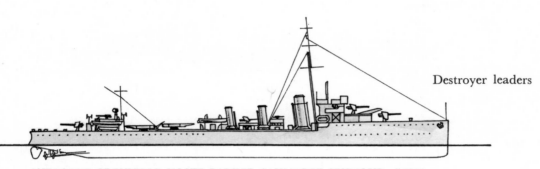

Destroyer leaders

ANZAC 1917, GRENVILLE, HOSTE, PARKER, SAUMAREZ, SEYMOUR, all 1916.
1,665 *tons* 325′ (o/a) × 31¾′ × 19½′. Guns 4 4″, 2 2-*pdrs. pom-poms*. Torpedo tubes 4 21″. Engines and speed *Turbines*; 36,000 *h.p.*; 34 *knots*.

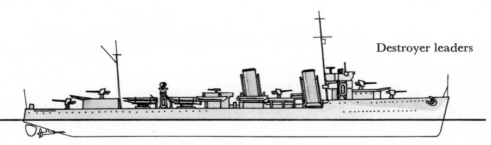

Destroyer leaders

BROKE, KEPPEL, SHAKESPEARE, SPENSER, WALLACE, all 1917–20.
1,554 *tons* 329′ (o/a) × 31½′ × 19¾′. Guns 5 4·7″, 1 3″ A.A. Torpedo tubes 6 21″ triple-mounted. Engines and speed *Turbines*; 40,000 *h.p.*; 36 *knots*.

Destroyers

AMAZON and AMBUSCADE, both 1926
*AMAZON* 1,352 *tons* 323′ (o/a) × 31½′ × 19¼′. *AMBUSCADE* 1,173 *tons* 322′ (o/a) × 31′ × 18¾′. Guns 4 4·7″, 2 2-*pdrs. pom-poms.* Torpedo tubes 6 21″ triple-mounted. Engines and speed *Turbines; AMAZON* 42,000 *h.p.; AMBUSCADE* 35,500 *h.p.*; 37 *knots*.

programme, being over 1,000 tons and capable of 35 knots, so that with the *Ms* must be included all ships built to the modified *R* class, one hundred and sixty-three in all.

The following *V* and *W* classes appeared first in 1917 and were designed to counter the new generation of German destroyers. The first *Vs* were large and called 'leaders', though the general run were not so much larger than the *Ms* but with better accommodation. Of the fifty-one built, over half survived to fight in the Second World War as well as the First, some in the Royal Australian Navy. A few of the smaller *S* class also served in the Second World War. There were sixty-seven *S* class built in 1918 and 1919. The last wartime class were the modified *Vs* and *Ws* with 4.7-inch guns, of which sixteen were built.

After such a flood of destroyers, and with the cutting back of the service following the war, it was some years before the next generation appeared. This was in the year 1926 with a fresh start back to the beginning of the alphabet, all the class having names beginning with *A*. The first two ships were *Amazon* and *Ambuscade*, and attention was concentrated on improved accommodation and sea-keeping. The eight ships that followed in 1929 were designed from experience with the first two. They were followed by the slightly larger but similar *Bs*, *Cs*, *Ds*, *Es*, *Fs*, *Gs*, *Hs* and *Is*. In addition, a small number of slightly larger ships called 'destroyer leaders' were built for the use of Captains D, a term used for the senior officer in the flotilla.

In 1937 the first of a new large class of heavily armed destroyer was launched, the *Tribal* class. These ships were 40 feet longer and 500 tons heavier than the previous destroyers and mounted eight 4.7-inch guns in twin mountings. Of these beautiful ships sixteen were built and they fought such a furious war that only four survived. The night action of the *Cossack*, *Maori*, *Sikh* and *Zulu* against the *Bismarck* was notably gallant. The *Punjabi* had a curious fate, sunk in collision with the battleship *King George V* in 1942; she went down before her depth-charges could be set at safe. The resulting underwater explosions badly damaged the battleship.

While the *Tribals* had stood out as a break from the prewar trend in design, the last two flotillas that followed them, and which were completed before or at the beginning of the war, were smaller but maintained the trend of twin mountings in shields. These were the *J* and *K* classes which were distinguished by being the first single-funnelled destroyers built since 1894, a feature of all the wartime-built destroyers that followed. There were sixteen *Js* and *Ks* of which ten were lost, the usual heavy toll for fleet destroyer classes that served throughout the war. One that survived, the *Javelin*, had her bow and stern blown off by torpedoes from German destroyers in a Channel action in 1940. She was painted Mountbatten pink at the time, which was supposed to make her invisible, and she certainly nearly dropped out of sight; it is remarkable that she managed to stay afloat to reach dry-dock in Devonport. The *Kelly* was the famous ship of the *Ks*. For a desperate ninety-one hours in May 1940 she was towed into the Tyne very much awash after being torpedoed in the engine-room. She was finally sunk by German bombers with her sister, the *Kashmir*, off Crete in 1941. A repeat class of *Ks*, the *Ns*, were built early in the war. Of the eight of them, three were transferred to the Royal Australian Navy and two to the Royal Netherlands Navy.

## DESTROYERS

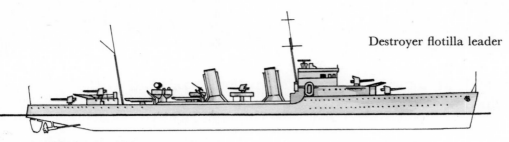

Destroyer flotilla leader

CODRINGTON 1929
*1,540 tons* 343′ (o/a) × 33¾′ × 19¾′. Guns 5 4·7″, 2 2-*pdrs*. Torpedo tubes 8 21″. Depth charges. Engines and speed *Geared turbines;* 40,000 *h.p.;* 35 *knots*.

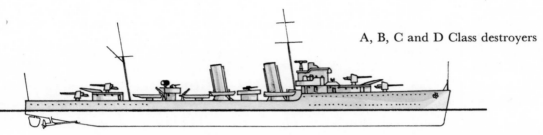

A, B, C and D Class destroyers

*A Class* ACASTA, ACHATES, ACHERON, ACTIVE, ANTELOPE, ANTHONY, ARDENT, ARROW, all 1929, except ACHERON 1930
*B Class* KEITH BASILISK, BEAGLE, BLANCHE, BOADICEA, BOREAS, BRAZEN, BRILLIANT, BULLDOG, all 1930; KEITH was leader but the same size
*C Class* COMET, CRESCENT, CRUSADER, CYGNET, KEMPENFELT, all 1931; KEMPENFELT was leader.
*D Class* DAINTY, DARING, DECOY, DEFENDER, DELIGHT, DIAMOND, DIANA, DUCHESS, DUNCAN, all 1932.
*1,350 tons* 323′ (o/a) × 32½′ × 19′. Guns 4 4·7″. Torpedo tubes 8 21″. Depth charges. Engines and speed *Geared turbines;* 34,000 *h.p.;* 36 *knots*. Remarks *The Cs were acquired by the Royal Canadian Navy in 1937 and 1938.*

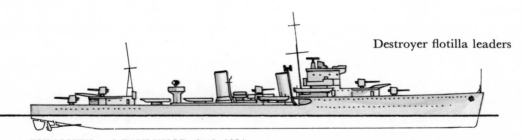

Destroyer flotilla leaders

EXMOUTH and FAULKNOR, both 1934
*1,475 tons* 343′ (o/a) × 33¾′ × 20′. Guns 5 4·7″, 8 0·5″ *A.A.* Torpedo tubes 8 21″. Depth charges. Engines and speed *Geared turbines;* 38,000 *h.p.;* 36 *knots*.

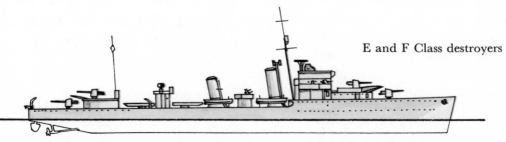

E and F Class destroyers

*E Class* ECHO, ECLIPSE, ELECTRA, ENCOUNTER, ESCAPADE, ESCORT, ESK, EXPRESS (all 1934)
*F Class* FAME, FEARLESS, FIREDRAKE, FORESIGHT, FORESTER, FORTUNE, FOXHOUND, FURY (all 1934)
*1,350 tons* 329′ (o/a) × 33¼′ × 19¼′. Guns 4 4·7″. Torpedo tubes 8 21″. Engines and speed *Geared turbines;* 36,000 *h.p.;* 36 *knots*.

Destroyer flotilla leaders

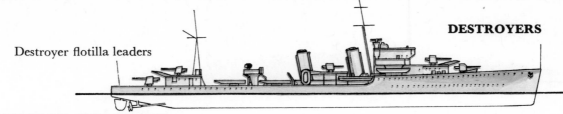

GRENVILLE 1935, HARDY 1936, INGLEFIELD 1936
1,505 *tons* (*GRENVILLE* 330′ (o/a) × 34½′ × 19½′, *HARDY* 337′ (o/a) × 34′19½′), *INGLEFIELD* 1,530 *tons* 337′ (o/a) × 34′ × 19¾′. Guns 5 4·7″,
8 0·5″ *A.A.* Torpedo tubes 8 or 10 21″. Depth charges. Engines and speed *Geared turbines*; 38,000 *h.p.*; 36 *knots*.

G, H and I Class destroyers

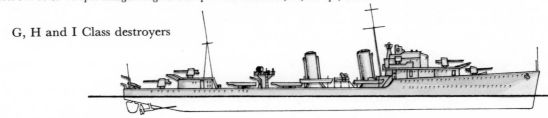

*G Class* GALLANT, GARLAND, GIPSY, GLOWWORM, GRAFTON, GRENADE, GREYHOUND, GRIFFIN, all 1935
*H Class* HASTY, HAVOCK, HEREWARD, HERO, HOSTILE, HOTSPUR, HUNTER, HYPERION, all 1936
1,335 *tons* 323′ (o/a) × 33′ × 19¼′. Guns 4 4·7″. Torpedo tubes 8 21″. Depth charges. Engines and speed *Geared turbines*; 34,000 *h.p.*; 36 *knots*.
Remarks Gloworm *had 10 21″ torpedo tubes*.
*I Class* ICARUS 1936, ILEX 1937, IMOGEN 1936, IMPERIAL 1936, IMPULSIVE 1937, INTREPID 1936, ISIS 1936, IVANHOE 1937
1,370 *tons* 323′ (o/a) × 33′ × 19¼′. Guns 4 4·7″. Torpedo tubes 10 21″. Depth charges. Engines and speed *Geared turbines*; 34,000 *h.p.*; 36 *knots*.

The following destroyers were building for foreign powers at the outbreak of war and were acquired: Ex-Brazilian HARVESTER, HAVANT,
HAVELOCK, HESPERUS, HIGHLANDER, HURRICANE, all 1939. Ex-Turkish INCONSTANT 1941, ITHURIEL 1940. They were
similar to the Royal Navy's *I* Class.

TOWN Class destroyers

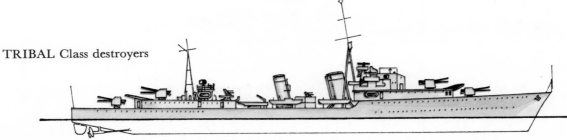

BATH, BELMONT, BEVERLEY, BRADFORD, BRIGHTON, BROADWATER, BROADWAY, BURNHAM, BURWELL,
BUXTON, CALDWELL, CAMPBELTOWN, CAMERON, CASTLETON, CHARLESTOWN, CHELSEA, CHESTERFIELD,
CHURCHILL, CLARE, GEORGETOWN, LANCASTER, LEAMINGTON, LEEDS, LEWES, LINCOLN, LUDLOW,
MANSFIELD, MONTGOMERY, NEWARK, NEWMARKET, NEWPORT, RAMSEY, READING, RICHMOND, RIPLEY,
ROCKINGHAM, ROXBURGH, SALISBURY, SHERWOOD, STANLEY, ST ALBANS, ST MARY'S, WELLS, all 1917–20
1,020 *to* 1,190 *tons* 314½′ (o/a) × 30½′ × 18′. Guns 3 4″, 1 3″ *A.A.*, 3 0·5″ *A.A. The 2 beam 4″ replaced by lighter A.A. guns in most ships. Hedgehog A/S
weapon in some ships.* Torpedo tubes 3 to 6 21″. Engines and speed *Geared turbines*; 18,500 to 27,000 *h.p.*; 30 to 35 *knots*. Remarks Leeds *and* Ludlow
*3 funnels; these 42 ships, plus 6 to the R.C.N., were borrowed from the U.S.A. under the Lend-Lease agreement of 1941.*

TRIBAL Class destroyers

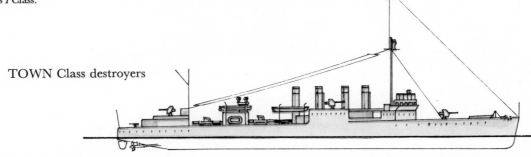

AFRIDI, ASHANTI, BEDOUIN, COSSACK, ESKIMO, GURKHA, MAORI, MASHONA, MATABELE, MOHAWK,
NUBIAN, PUNJABI, SIKH, SOMALI, TARTAR, ZULU, all 1937
1,870 *tons* 377½′ (o/a) × 36½′ × 21½′. Guns 8 4·7″. Torpedo tubes 4 21″. Engines and speed *Geared turbines*; 44,000 *h.p.*; 36·5 *knots*.

J, K and N Class destroyers

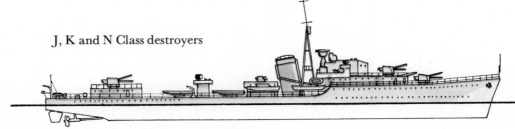

*J Class* JACKAL, JAGUAR, JANUS, JAVELIN, JERSEY, JERVIS, JUNO, JUPITER, all 1938
*K Class* KANDAHAR, KASHMIR, KELLY, KELVIN, KHARTOUM, KIMBERLEY, KINGSTON, KIPLING, all 1939,
except KELLY 1938
*N Class* NAPIER 1940, NERISSA 1940, NESTOR 1940, NIZAM 1940, NOBLE 1941, NONPAREIL 1941, NORMAN 1940,
NORSEMAN 1941
1,690 *tons* 356½′ (o/a) × 35¾′ × 20½′. Guns 6 4·7″, 4 2-pdrs. *A.A. and smaller.* Torpedo tubes 10 21″. Engines and speed *Geared turbines*; 40,000 *h.p.*;
36 *knots*. Remarks Noble *and* Nonpareil *were transferred to the Netherlands Navy on completion.*

# DESTROYERS

HUNT Class escort destroyers

*First Group* ATHERSTONE, BERKELEY, CATTISTOCK, CLEVELAND, COTSWOLD, COTTESMORE, EGLINTON, EXMOOR, FERNIE, GARTH, HAMBLEDON, HOLDERNESS, MENDIP, MEYNELL, PYTCHLEY, QUANTOCK, QUORN, SOUTHDOWN, TYNEDALE, WHADDON, all 1940, except ATHERSTONE, EGLINTON and HAMBLEDON 1939
907 *tons* 280' (o/a) × 29' × 17'. Guns 4 4" *D.P.*; Engines and speed *Geared turbines*; 19,000 *h.p.*; 26 *knots*.
*Second Group* AVON VALE, BADSWORTH, BEAUFORT, BEDALE, BICESTER, BLACKMORE, BLANKNEY, BLENCATHRA, BRAMHAM, BURTON (renamed EXMOOR), BROCKLESBY, CALPE, CHIDDINGFOLD, COWDRAY, CROOME, DULVERTON, ERIDGE, FARNDALE, GROVE, HEYTHROP, HURSLEY, HURWORTH, LAMERTON, LAUDERDALE, LEDBURY, LIDDESDALE, MIDDLETON, OAKLEY, PUCKERIDGE, SILVERTON, SOUTHWOLD, TETCOTT, TICKHAM (renamed OAKLEY), WHEATLAND, WILTON, ZETLAND, all 1940–2
1,050 *tons* 282½' (o/a) × 31½' × 17'. Guns 6 4" *D.P. BLENCATHRA, BROCKLESBY and LIDDESDALE* 4 4" *D.P.*; Engines and speed *Geared turbines*; 19,000 *h.p.*; 25 *knots*.
*Third Group* AIREDALE, ALBRIGHTON, ALDENHAM, BELVOIR, BLEAN, BLEASDALE, BOLEBROKE, BORDER, CATTERICK, DERWENT, EASTON, EGGESFORD, ESKDALE, GLAISDALE, GOATHLAND, HALDON, HATHERLEIGH, HAYDON, HOLCOMBE, LIMBOURNE, MELBREAK, MODBURY, PENYLAN, ROCKWOOD, STEVENSTONE, TALYBONT, TANATSIDE, WENSLEYDALE, all 1941–3
1,087 *tons* 282½' (o/a) × 31½' × 17'. Guns 4 4" *D.P.* Torpedo tubes 2 21". Engines and speed *Geared turbines*; 19,000 *h.p.*; 25 *knots*.
*Fourth Group* BRECON, BRISSENDEN, both 1942
1,175 *tons* 296' (o/a) × 33⅓' × 23⅓'. Guns 6 4" *D.P.* Torpedo tubes 3 21". Engines and speed *Geared turbines*; 19,000 *h.p.*; 25 *knots*.

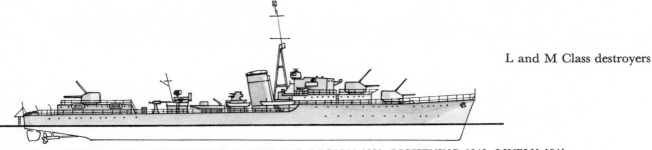

L and M Class destroyers

*L Class* GURKHA 1940, LAFOREY 1941, LANCE 1940, LEGION 1939, LIGHTNING 1940, LIVELY 1941, LOOKOUT 1940, LOYAL 1941
*M Class* MAHRATTA 1942, MARNE 1940, MARTIN 1940, MATCHLESS 1941, METEOR 1941, MILNE 1941 MUSKETEER 1941, MYRMIDON 1942
1,920 *tons* 362½' (o/a) × 37' × 20½'. Guns 6 4·7" *D.P. GURKHA, LANCE, LEGION and LIVELY* 8 4" *A.A.*, 4 2-pdrs. *A.A.* Torpedo tubes 8 21".
Engines and speed *Geared turbines*; 48,000 *h.p.*; 36 *knots*.

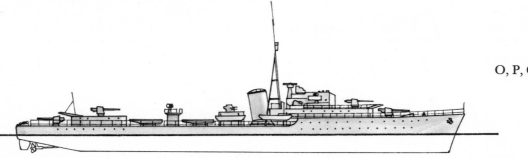

O, P, Q and R Class destroyers

*O and P Classes* OBEDIENT 1942, OBDURATE 1942, OFFA 1941, ONSLAUGHT 1941, ONSLOW 1941, OPPORTUNE 1942, ORIBI 1941, ORWELL 1942, PAKENHAM, PALADIN, PANTHER, PARTRIDGE, PATHFINDER, PENN, PETARD, PORCUPINE, all 1941
1,540 *tons* 345' (o/a) × 35' × 20½'. Guns 4 4" (*OFFA, ONSLAUGHT, ONSLOW and ORIBI* 4 4·7"). 4 2-pdrs. *A.A.* Torpedo tubes 8 21". Engines and speed *Geared turbines*; 40,000 *h.p.*; 36¾ *knots*. Remarks Obedient, Obdurate, Opportune *and* Orwell *fitted for minelaying*.
*Q and R Classes* QUADRANT 1942, QUAIL 1942, QUALITY 1941, QUEENBOROUGH 1942, QUENTIN 1941, QUIBERON 1942, QUICKMATCH 1942, QUILLIAM 1941, RACEHORSE, RAIDER, RAPID, REDOUBT, RELENTLESS, ROCKET, ROEBUCK, ROTHERHAM, all 1942
1,705 *tons* (*QUILLIAM* 1,725 *tons*. *ROTHERHAM* 1,750 *tons*) 358¾' (o/a) × 35¾' × 20½'. Guns 4 4·7", 4 2-pdrs. *A.A.* Torpedo tubes 8 21". Engines and speed *Geared turbines*; 40,000 *h.p.*; 36 *knots*.

S, T, U, V, W and Z Class destroyers

*S and T Classes* SAUMAREZ 1942, SAVAGE 1942, SCORPION 1942, SCOURGE 1942, SERAPIS 1943, SHARK 1943, SUCCESS 1943, SWIFT 1943, TEAZER 1943, TENACIOUS 1943, TERMAGANT 1943, TERPSICHORE 1943, TROUBRIDGE 1942, TUMULT 1942, TUSCAN 1942, TYRIAN 1942
*U and V Classes* GRENVILLE, HARDY, ULSTER, ULYSSES, UNDAUNTED, UNDINE, URANIA, URCHIN, URSA, VALENTINE, VENUS, VERULAM, VIGILANT, VIRAGO, VIXEN, VOLAGE, all 1943, except GRENVILLE, ULSTER and VIGILANT 1942
*W and Z Classes* KEMPENFELT, WAGER, WAKEFUL, WESSEX, WHELP, WHIRLWIND, WIZARD, WRANGLER, all 1943, MYNGS 1943, ZAMBESI 1943, ZEALOUS 1944, ZEBRA 1944, ZENITH 1944, ZEPHYR 1943, ZEST 1943, ZODIAC 1944
1,730 *tons* 362¾' (o/a) × 35¾' × 20½'. Guns 4 4·7" *SAVAGE, MYNGS and all Zs* 4 4·5", *light A.A. guns varied.* Torpedo tubes 8 21". Engines and speed *Geared turbines*; 40,000 *h.p.*; 36 *knots*.

C Class destroyers

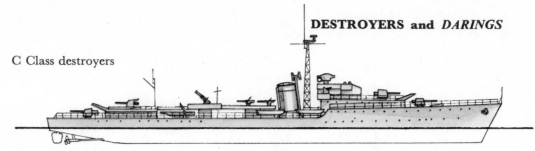

CAESAR, CAMBRIAN, CAPRICE, CARRON, CARYSFORT, CASSANDRA, CAVALIER, CAVENDISH, CHAPLET,
CHARITY, CHEQUERS, CHEVIOT, CHEVRON, CHIEFTAIN, CHILDERS, CHIVALROUS, COCKADE, COMET,
COMUS, CONCORD, CONSORT, CONSTANCE, CONTEST, COSSACK, CRISPIN, CREOLE, CRESCENT,
CROMWELL, CROWN, CROZIERS, CRUSADER, CRYSTAL, all 1943–5
1,710 *tons* 362¾′ (o/a) × 35¾′ × 20½′. Guns 4 4·5″ *D.P.* Torpedo tubes 4 21″ (CAs 8). Engines and speed *Geared turbines;* 40,000 *h.p.;* 36 *knots.*

C Class destroyers (modified as frigates)

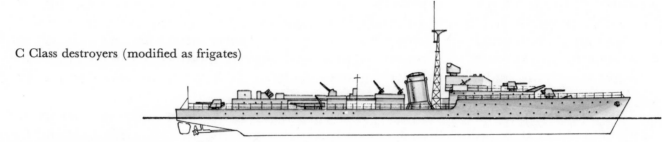

CAESAR, CAMBRIAN, CAPRICE, CARRON, CARYSFORT, CASSANDRA, CAVALIER, CAVENDISH, in 1966
*As before.* Guns 3 4·5″ (*X mounting suppressed*), 4 40-mm. A.A., 2 *Squid anti-submarine mortars, triple-barrelled,* 1 *Seacat missile launcher in CAPRICE and*
*CAVALIER* (1960). Torpedo tubes 4 21″, *later removed from most.* Engines and speed *Geared turbines;* 40,000 *h.p.;* 35 *knots.* Remarks *The remaining*
*ships of this class underwent a variety of modifications of a less drastic nature.*

BATTLE Class destroyers

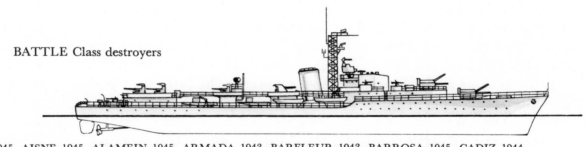

AGINCOURT 1945, AISNE 1945, ALAMEIN 1945, ARMADA 1943, BARFLEUR 1943, BARROSA 1945, CADIZ 1944,
CAMPERDOWN 1944, CORUNNA 1945, DUNKIRK 1945, FINISTERRE 1944, GABBARD 1945, GRAVELINES 1944,
HOGUE 1944, JUTLAND 1946, LAGOS 1945, MATAPAN 1945, ST JAMES 1945, ST KITTS 1944, SAINTES 1944,
SOLEBAY 1944, SLUYS 1944, TRAFALGAR 1944, VIGO 1945
2,315 *tons* to 2,400 *tons* 379′ (o/a) × 40¼′ × 22′. Guns 4 4·5″ *D.P.,* 14 40-mm. A.A. or 1 4″ and 12 40-mm. A.A. Torpedo tubes 8 21″. *AGINCOURT,*
*AISNE, ALAMEIN, BARROSA, CORUNNA, DUNKIRK, JUTLAND, MATAPAN* 5 4·5″ *D.P.,* 8 40-mm. A.A. Torpedo tubes 10 21″. Engines
and speed *Geared turbines;* 50,000 *h.p.;* 36 *knots.*

WEAPON Class destroyers

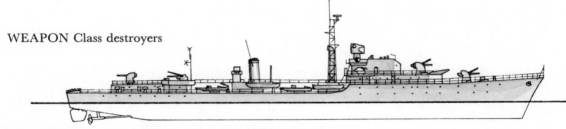

BATTLEAXE 1945, BROADSWORD 1946, CROSSBOW 1945, SCORPION 1946
1,980 *tons* 365′ (o/a) × 38′ × 20¾′. Guns (*as designed*) 6 4″ *D.P.,* 6 40-mm. A.A., 4 20-mm. A.A. (*as completed*) 4 4″ *D.P.,* 6 40-mm. A.A. Torpedo tubes 10
21″. Engines and speed *Turbines;* 40,000 *h.p.;* 35 *knots.*

DARING Class destroyers

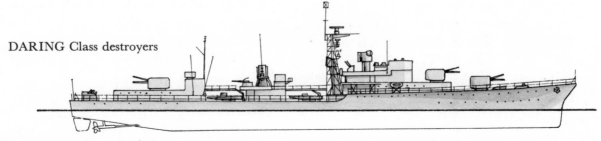

DAINTY 1950, DARING 1949, DECOY 1949, DEFENDER 1950, DELIGHT 1950, DIAMOND 1950, DIANA 1952,
DUCHESS 1951
2,610 *tons* 390′ (o/a) × 43′ × 22½′. Guns 6 4·5″ *D.P.,* 6 40-mm. A.A., 1 *Squid anti-submarine mortar.* Torpedo tubes 10 21″. Engines and speed *Turbines;*
54,000 *h.p.;* 34 *knots.*

At the same time a slightly larger type, the *Ls*, were under construction. These eight ships and the eight *Ms* that followed were the first destroyers constructed during the war. Four, serving as anti-aircraft escorts, had eight twin 4-inch guns behind shields, but the remainder had power-operated twin 4·7-inch guns in enclosed turrets, which gave them an impressive appearance. These ships were to be the last peacetime-inspired destroyers, with their high standard of finish; the wartime classes that followed had to sacrifice finish for speed of delivery. These were the *O, P, Q* and *R* classes, thirty-two of them altogether. A severe gun-barrel shortage arose during their building, and the *Ps* and four *Os* had 4-inch instead of 4·7-inch. The *S* to *Z* classes that followed were officially known as 'utility ships', but otherwise were only slightly modified *Ks*. Altogether forty-eight were built, and after the war the survivors from the *Rs* onwards were taken in hand for conversion into anti-submarine frigates (see page 252).

Having exhausted the alphabet, there was still a requirement for more destroyers, so the next class were called the *Cs*, divided into four groups, the *CAs, CHs, COs* and *CRs*. These were close to the *Zs* but with 4·5-inch guns in dual-purpose mountings. There were thirty-two of them, the later ships being of an all-welded construction. After the war some of them were in commission well into the late sixties, converted to an anti-submarine role, though not turned into full frigates of the *Type 15* class.

The last class to see active service in the war, though not all of them, were the big handsome *Battle* class, twenty-four of which were built. The early ships carried four 4·5-inch guns in two turrets forward, but the later ones were given a fifth gun amidships on the insistence of Lord Cunningham, the First Sea Lord. A few were converted into radar pickets in the 1960s, the rest scrapped. The last large destroyers built for the war, but too late to participate, were four survivors of what was intended to be a much larger class. They were the *Weapon* class, and were completed as anti-submarine escorts and given a curious appearance by reverting to two funnels, one in the lattice-mast and one aft resembling a cigarette, which was not handsome. They were all converted into radar pickets in the 1950s.

The second wartime type, the *Hunt* class, was an escort. Almost like frigates, they were designed for merchant convoy work and did not need the speed of a destroyer, built to screen the battle-fleet. They still could raise 27 knots and, although 70 feet or so shorter than the fleet destroyers, mounted a gun armament of four or six 4-inch. It was in the provision of torpedo tubes that their role as defensive rather than offensive ships was shown; the first ships had none at all, but the *Type IIIs* were given two in place of two 4-inch. There were eighty-six of them built, of which all but twenty survived the war, and many subsequently found their way into foreign navies as good, cheap-to-run destroyers, having done fine service in convoy protection. The decision to name them after hunts was an attractive one, and had been used before, but in fact resulted in many sleepy rural names, like the *Chiddingfold* and *Wensleydale*.

The last class of gun destroyer built for the navy were the eight *Darings*, but so much larger than any before that they were initially classed not as destroyers, but as darings. Nearly 400 feet long and 2,600 tons, they were like young cruisers, but without a cruiser's armament. Their six 4·5-inch guns were housed in the first fully automatic, radar-controlled twin turrets. These were the model subsequently fitted to the new frigates, and like the automatic 6-inch and 3-inch mountings, their hydraulics, and to some extent electrics, gave a great deal of trouble over a long period. With their size they could carry ten torpedo tubes, plus anti-submarine mortars and good anti-aircraft defence. Their postwar role was almost that of the general-purpose small cruiser, but they have now been scrapped or sold.

## American-built Destroyers

In 1940, a deal was made with the Americans, who were still at peace with the world, that, in exchange for a lease of some bases in colonial territories, fifty old US destroyers would be transferred to the Royal Navy. There was a great need for more escort vessels at that time, and they served a useful purpose. Some of them had been laid up for many years, and all dated from the First World War or just after, so that the hard conditions of Atlantic convoy work took their toll, and these ships required much dockyard time which could ill be spared. Nearly all of them were four-funnelled with their upper-deck running flush at a slight angle from stem to stern, as with so many American naval ships then and now. One of them, the *Campbeltown*, went on the Saint-Nazaire raid, her bows full of explosives, and blew up, with herself, the gates of the great dry-dock in which the *Normandie* had been built.

# 28

# Sloops, Corvettes and Frigates

**Minesweeping Sloops of the First World War**

By 1914 the once-plentiful sloops had dwindled away to fewer than a dozen of the late steel masted ones, though by then without their yards (see page 138). The war brought a need for many new types of vessel, typically for a class of minesweeper to work with the fleet at sea and augment the torpedo-gunboats converted to this work. So, early in the war, the *Flower* class was ordered and built very quickly in private yards. There were seventy-two built of one type and forty of another, all to Lloyd's specifications, since few of the yards that built them had experience in building to naval practice.

The first type were twin-funnelled with a light armament of two 3-, 4- or 4·7-inch guns. When submarine attacks on British merchant ships became a serious menace, many of them were put on escort duty and carried depth-charges. These ships were good sea boats but so lively in rough weather that staysails were often rigged to steady them. The second type of *Flower* class sloop is the more interesting. These ships not only were built to civilian specifications, they were built to look like merchantmen. This was because the *U*-boats always dived at the sight of a naval-type ship, and because of the success of the *Q* ships, converted merchantmen, in which hidden guns were placed. Unfortunately, as the war progressed, the Germans became wary of using their guns on small merchantmen and preferred to use a torpedo and be safe. In an effort to counter this difficulty a number of fast patrol boats were converted to look like tramps. The idea was that the *U*-boat's torpedo would pass under the vessel's shallow-draught hull, which would then turn in along the track with an unexpected burst of speed and attack with depth-charges. Two *Flower* class sloops, the *Chrysanthemum* and *Saxifrage*, survive today as the headquarter ships of London's RNR in the Thames. A second class of slightly bigger ships, which looked like naval ships, called the *Twenty-four* class because there were to have been twenty-four of them, were built towards the end of the war. Not all were completed, and since they proved poor sea boats they saw little service, and many were converted to surveying ships after hostilities. All were named after famous racehorses.

**Minesweepers**

During the war three other types of minesweeper emerged and these were not classed as sloops. By far the largest class was the *Hunt*, of which over a hundred were built. They

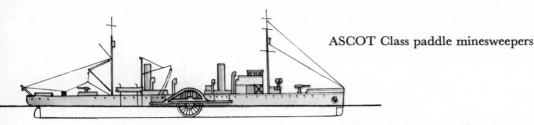

ASCOT Class paddle minesweepers

ASCOT, ATHERSTONE, CHELMSFORD, CHELTENHAM, CHEPSTOW, CROXTON, DONCASTER, EGLINTON, EPSOM, ERIDGE, GATWICK, GOODWOOD, HALDON, HURST, KEMPTON, LINGFIELD, LUDLOW, MELTON, NEWBURY, PONTEFRACT, PLUMPTON, REDCAR, SANDOWN, TOTNES, all 1916
810 *tons* 246′ × 29′ (58′ *at paddle-boxes*) × 7′. Guns 2 12-*pdrs.* Engines and speed *Compound; 1,400 h.p.; 15 knots.* Remarks *Popularly known as the Racecourse Class.*

The 'Improved Racecourse' type, all 1917–18
BANBURY, HARPENDEN, HEXHAM, LANARK, LEWES, SHINCLIFFE, SHIRLEY, WETHERBY
820 *tons* 250′ (*o/a*) × 29′ (58′ *at paddle-boxes*) × 7′. Guns 1 12-*pdr.*, 1 3″ A.A. Engines and speed *Same as the first group. A further group was cancelled.*

HUNT Class fleet minesweepers

BELVOIR, BICESTER, BLACKMOREVALE, CATTISTOCK, COTSWOLD, COTTESMORE, CROOME, DARTMOOR, GARTH, HAMBLEDON, HEYTHROP, HOLDERNESS, MEYNELL, MUSKERRY, OAKLEY, PYTCHLEY, QUORN, SOUTHDOWN, TEDWORTH, ZETLAND, all 1916–17
750 *tons* 231′ (*o/a*) × 28′ × 7′. Guns 2 12-*pdrs.*, 2 2-*pdrs.* Some 1 12-*pdr.*, 1 6-*pdr.* Engines and speed *Three-cylinder triple expansion; 1,800 h.p.; 16 knots.* Remarks *No drawing.*

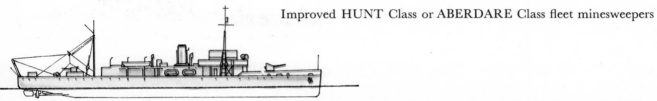

Improved HUNT Class or ABERDARE Class fleet minesweepers

ABERDARE, ABINGDON, ALBURY, ALRESFORD, APPLEDORE, BADMINTON, BAGSHOT, BANCHORY, BARNSTAPLE, BATTLE, BLACKBURN, BLOXHAM, BOOTLE, BRADFIELD, BURSLEM, BURY, CAERLEON, CAMBERLEY, CARSTAIRS, CATERHAM, CHEAM, CLONMEL, CRAIGIE, CUPAR, DERBY, DORKING, DUNDALK, DUNOON, ELGIN, FAIRFIELD, FAREHAM, FAVERSHAM, FERMOY, FORD, FORFAR, FORRES, GADDESDEN, GAINSBOROUGH, GOOLE, GRETNA, HARROW, HAVANT, HUNTLEY, INSTOW, IRVINE, KENDAL, KINROSS, LEAMINGTON, LONGFORD, LYDD, MALLAIG, MALVERN, MARAZION, MARLOW, MISTLEY, MONOGHAN, MUNLOCHY, NAILSEA, NEWARK, NORTHOLT, PANGBOURNE, PENARTH, PETERSFIELD, PONTYPOOL, PRESTATYN, REPTON, ROSS, RUGBY, SALFORD, SALTASH, SALTBURN, SELKIRK, SHERBORNE, SHREWSBURY, SLIGO, STAFFORD, STOKE, SUTTON, SWINDON, TIVERTON, TONBRIDGE, TRALEE, TRING, TRURO, WEM, WEXFORD, WEYBOURNE, WIDNES, YEOVIL, all 1918–19
800 *tons* 231′ (*o/a*) × 28½′ × 7½′. Guns 1 4″, 1 12-*pdr.* Engines and speed *Triple expansion; 2,200 h.p.; 16 knots.* Remarks *Like the earlier Hunts, but no break in the hull line aft, and a searchlight was mounted on a forward extension of the bridge.*

DANCE Class tunnel minesweepers, all 1917–18

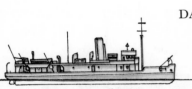

COTILLION, COVERLEY, FANDANGO, GAVOTTE, HORNPIPE, MAZURKA, MINUET, MORRIS DANCE, PIROUETTE, QUADRILLE, SARABANDE, STEP DANCE, SWORD DANCE and TARANTELLA
265 to 290 *tons* 130′ (*o/a*) × 27′ × 3½′. Guns 1 12-*pdr.* or 1 6-*pdr.* or 1 3-*pdr.* Engines and speed *Compound; 450 h.p.; 9½ to 10 knots.* Remarks *Called tunnel minesweepers because their screws worked in tunnels.*

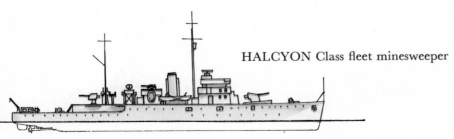

HALCYON Class fleet minesweeper

BRAMBLE 1938, BRITOMART 1938, FRANKLIN 1937, GLEANER 1937, GOSSAMER 1937, HALCYON 1933, HARRIER 1934, HAZARD 1937, HEBE 1936, HUSSAR 1934, JASON 1937, LEDA 1937, NIGER 1936, SALAMANDER 1936, SCOTT 1938, SEAGULL 1937, SHARPSHOOTER 1936, SKIPJACK 1934, SPEEDWELL 1935, SPEEDY 1938, SPHINX 1939
*First 7* 815 *tons*, *next 9* 835 *tons*, *rest* 875 *tons* 245′ (*o/a*) × 33½′ × 6¾′ *to* 8′. Guns *First 7* 1 4″, 1 4″ A.A. *Others* 2 4″ A.A. Engines and speed *First 5 Compound, next 2 Triple expansion, rest Geared turbines; First 5* 1,770 *h.p.*, *next 2* 2,000 *h.p.*, *rest* 1,750 *h.p.*; 17 *knots.* Remarks *The Seagull was the first all-welded ship in the navy. The* Franklin, Gleaner, Gossamer, Jason *and* Scott *completed as surveying vessels.*

# MINESWEEPERS

BANGOR Class fleet minesweepers

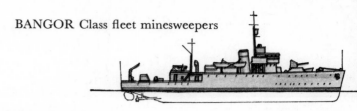

*Diesel engined* BANGOR, BLACKPOOL, BRIDLINGTON, BRIDPORT, all 1940
*Reciprocating engined* BAYFIELD, BLYTH, BUDE, CANSO, CARAQUET, CLYDEBANK, CROMER, EASTBOURNE, FELIXSTOWE, FORT YORK, FRASERBURGH, GUYSBOROUGH, INGONISH, LOCKEPORT, LYME REGIS (i), PARRSBOROUGH, PETERHEAD, QUALICUM, RHYL, ROMNEY, SEAHAM, SHIPPIGAN, SIDMOUTH, STORNOWAY, TADOUSSAC, TILBURY, WEDGEPORT, all 1940–2
*Turbine engined* ARDROSSAN, BEAUMARIS, BOOTLE, BOSTON, BRIXHAM, CLACTON, CROMARTY, DORNOCH, DUNBAR, GREENOCK, HARTLEPOOL, HARWICH, HYTHE, ILFRACOMBE, LLANDUDNO, MIDDLESBROUGH, NEWHAVEN, PADSTOW, POLRUAN, POOLE, ROTHESAY, RYE, TENBY, WHITEHAVEN, WORTHING, LYME REGIS (ii), all 1940–2
*Diesel engined* 590 *tons* 162′ (o/a) × 28′ × 8½′. *Reciprocating engined* 672 *tons* 180′ (o/a) × 28½′ × 8½′. *Turbine engined* 656 *tons* 174′ (o/a) × 28½′ × 8½′. Guns 1 3″ A.A., 1 2-pdr. A.A. Engines and speed *Diesel:* 2,000 h.p.; 16 knots. *Reciprocating:* 2,400 h.p.; 16 knots. *Turbine:* 2,400 h.p.; 16 knots. Remarks *The Canadians built 48 for themselves and the Indians built 4. 56 rather similar minesweepers called the* Bathurst *Class were built in Australia, 20 of which served in the Royal Navy, plus 4 built for the Royal Indian Navy.*

ALGERINE Class of fleet minesweeper

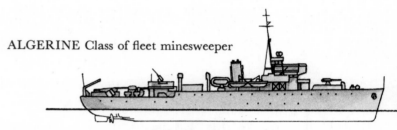

*Turbine engined* ALARM, ALBACORE, ALERT, ALGERINE, BRAVE, CADMUS, CHAMELEON, CHEERFUL, CIRCE, ESPIÈGLE, FANCY, FANTOME, HARE, JEWEL, LIBERTY, MUTINE, ONYX, PICKLE, PINCHER, PLUCKY, RATTLER, READY, RECRUIT, RIFLEMAN, RINALDO, ROSARIO, SPANKER, SQUIRREL, VESTAL, all 1942–44
*Reciprocating engined* ANTARES, ARCTURUS, ARIES, BRAMBLE, CLINTON, COCKATRICE, COQUETTE, COURIER, FELICITY, FIERCE, FLY, FLYING FISH, FRIENDSHIP, GOLDEN FLEECE, GOZO, HOUND, HYDRA, JASEUR, LAERTES, LARNE, LENNOX, LIGHTFOOT, LIONESS, LYSANDER, MAENAD, MAGICIENNE, MAMELUKE, MANDATE, MARINER, MARMION, MARVEL, MARY ROSE, MELITA, MICHAEL, MINSTREL, MOON, MYRMIDON, MYSTIC, NERISSA, NIGER, OCTAVIA, ORCADIA, ORESTES, OSSORY, PELORUS, PERSIAN, PLUTO, POLARIS, POSTILLION, PROMPT, PROVIDENCE, PYRRHUS, RATTLESNAKE, REGULUS, ROMOLA, ROSAMUND, ROWENA, SEABEAR, SERENE, SKIPJACK, STORMCLOUD, SYLVIA, TANGANYIKA, THISBE, TRUELOVE, WATERWITCH, WAVE, WELCOME, WELFARE, all 1942–5
850 *tons* 225′ (o/a) × 35½′ × 8½′. Guns 1 4″ D.P., 8 20-mm. A.A. Engines and speed *Turbine:* 2,000 h.p.; 16½ knots. *Reciprocating: similar.* Remarks *Like the* Bangors *the majority of the reciprocating-engined vessels were built in Canada.*

CATHERINE Class minesweeping sloops

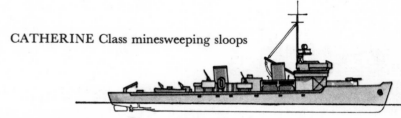

CATHERINE, CATO, CHAMOIS, CHANCE, COMBATANT, CYNTHIA, ELFREDA, FAIRY, FLORIZEL, FOAM, FROLIC, GAZELLE, GORGON, GRECIAN, JASPER, MAGIC, PIQUE, PYLADES, STEADFAST, STRENUOUS, TATTOO, TOURMALINE, all 1942–3
890 *tons* 220½′ (o/a) × 32′ × 9½′. Guns 1 3″ A.A., 6 20-mm. A.A. Engines and speed *Diesel, electric;* 3,500 h.p.; 18 knots. Remarks *Lend-Lease from the U.S.A.*

Motor minesweepers
1940–4 (smaller type)
1943–5 (larger type)

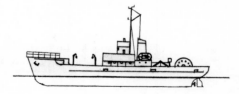

165 *tons* 119′ (o/a) × 23′ × 9½′, 255 *tons* 140′ (o/a) × 26′ × 10½′. Guns *Varied, but mainly M.G.s.* Engines and speed *Diesel;* 500 h.p.; 11 knots *(both types).* Remarks *Wooden-hulled and built in large numbers to combat magnetic and acoustic mines sown in the shallow waters of estuaries and harbour entrances.*

### Motor minesweepers (BYMSs)

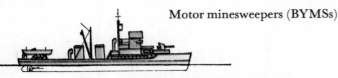

About 150 vessels, numbered, all 1942–4
207 *tons* 135½′ (*o*/*a*) × 24½′ × 6′. Guns 1 3″ *A.A.*, 2 20-*mm*. Engines and speed *Twin diesels; 1,000 h.p.; 14 knots.* Remarks *Lend-lease from the U.S.A., the first eighty had twin funnels.*

### TON Class coastal minesweepers

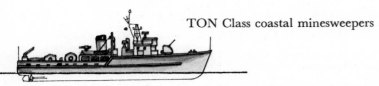

ALCASTON, ALDINGTON, ALFRISTON, ALVERTON, AMERTON, APPLETON, ASHTON, BADMINTON, BEACHAMPTON, BELTON, BEVINGTON, BICKINGTON, BILDESTON, BLAXTON, BOSSINGTON, BOULSTON. BRERETON, BRINTON, BRONINGTON, BURNASTON, BUTTINGTON, CALTON, CARHAMPTON, CASTLETON, CAUNTON, CHAWTON, CHEDISTON, CHILCOMPTON, CHILTON, CLARBESTON, CONISTON, CRICHTON, CROFTON, CUXTON, DALSWINTON, DARLASTON, DARTINGTON, DERRITON, DILSTON, DUFTON, DUMBLETON, DUNKERTON, DURWESTON, EDDERTON, ESSINGTON, FENTON, FISKERTON, FITTLETON, FLOCKTON, FLORISTON, GAVINTON, GLASSERTON, HAZELTON, HEXTON, HICKLETON, HIGHBURTON, HODGESTON, HOUGHTON, HUBBERSTON, ILMINGTON, INVERMORISTON, IVESTON, JACKTON, KEDLESTON, KELLINGTON, KEMERTON, KILDARTON, KIRKLISTON, LALESTON, LANTON, LETTERSTON, LEVERTON, LEWISTON, LULLINGTON, MADDISTON, MARYTON, MAXTON, MONKTON NURTON, OAKINGTON, OVERTON, OULSTON, PACKINGTON, PENSTON, PICTON, POLLINGTON, PUNCHESTON, QUAINTON, RENNINGTON, REPTON, RODINGTON, SANTON, SEFTON, SHAVINGTON, SHERATON, SHOULTON, SINGLETON, SOBERTON, SOMERLEYTON, STRATTON, STUBBINGTON, SULLINGTON, SWANSTON, TARLTON, THANKERTON, UPTON, WALKERTON, WASPERTON, WENNINGTON, WHITTON, WISTON, WILKIESTON, WOLVERTON, WOOLASTON, WOTTON, YARNTON, all in 1952–9
360 *tons* to 425 *tons full load* 152′ (*o*/*a*) × 28¾′ × 8¼′. Guns 1 40-*mm Bofors A.A.*, 2 20-*mm. A.A.* Engines and speed *Twin diesels; 1,250 h.p.; 15 knots.* Remarks *Transfers abroad: six to Australia, one to Ghana, four to India, seven to Malaysia, eight to South Africa, six to Argentina and three to Eire. Some have covered bridges and most were given stabilizers after 1958.*
WILTON 1972. Similar to TON Class but constructed of glass reinforced plastic – the world's first G.R.P. warship.

### HAM and LEY Class inshore minesweepers

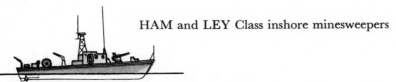

ABBOTSHAM, ARLINGHAM, BASSINGHAM, BIRDHAM, BISHAM, BITTERSHAM, BLUNHAM, BODENHAM, BOREHAM, BOTTISHAM, BRIGHAM, BUCKLESHAM, CARDINGHAM, CHELSHAM, CHILLINGHAM, COBHAM, CRANHAM, DAMERHAM, DARSHAM, DAVENHAM, DITTISHAM, DOWNHAM, EDLINGHAM, ELSENHAM, ETCHINGHAM, EVERINGHAM, FELMERSHAM, FLINTHAM, FORDHAM, FRITHAM, GEORGEHAM, GLENTHAM, GREETHAM, HALSHAM, HARPHAM, HAVERSHAM, HOVINGHAM, INGLESHAM, LASHAM, LEDSHAM, LUDHAM, MALHAM, MICKLEHAM, NEASHAM, NETTLEHAM, OCKHAM, ODIHAM, OTTRINGHAM, PAGHAM, POLSHAM, POPHAM, PORTISHAM, POWDERHAM, PULHAM, PUTTENHAM, RACKHAM, RAMPISHAM, REEDHAM, SANDRINGHAM, SAXLINGHAM, SHIPHAM, SHRIVENHAM, SIDLESHAM, THAKEHAM, THATCHAM, THORNHAM, TONGHAM, TRESHAM, WARMINGHAM, WINTRINGHAM, WOLDINGHAM, WRENTHAM, YAXHAM, all 1952–8
AVELEY, BREARLEY, BRENCHLEY, BRINKLEY, BROADLEY, BROOMLEY, BURLEY, CHAILEY, CRADLEY, DINGLEY
120 *tons* to 159 *tons full load* 106½′ (*o*/*a*) × 21¼′ × 5½′. Guns 1 40-*mm Bofors A.A.*, 1 20-*mm. Oerlikon A.A.* Engines and speed *Twin diesels; 550 h.p.; 14 knots.* Remarks *The Leys are composite built, using non-ferrous metals; the Hams are wooden-hulled. Superstructures vary. Fifteen vessels were built for France in 1954–5. Transfers abroad: two to India, two to Royal East African Navy, six to Malaysia, two to Hong Kong, two to Libya, three to South Arabia (later Yemen) and three to Australia.*

### Admiralty trawler

570 *tons* 150′ × 25′ × 12′. Guns 1 4″. Depth charges. Engines and speed *Reciprocating; 700 h.p.; 12 knots.* Remarks *Over a thousand trawlers and the smaller drifters were built or purchased between 1914 and 1945. The statistics given above are an average for the trawlers. The drawing represents the* Isles *Class of trawler of which 145 were built between 1940 and 1945.*

### KIL Class patrol sloops
KILBIRNIE, KILBRIDE, KILCHATTAN, KILCHRENAN, KILDARY, KILDWICK, KILHAM, KILHAMPTON, KILKENZIE, KILMALCOLM, KILMARNOCK, KILMARTIN, KILMELFORD, KILMINGTON, KILMORE, all 1943
795 *tons* 184¼′ (*o*/*a*) × 33′ × 9½′. Guns 1 3″ *A.A.*, 3 40-*mm. A.A.*, 4 20-*mm. A.A.* Engines and speed *Diesel; 1,500 to 1,800 h.p.; 18 knots.* Remarks *Lease-Lend from the U.S.A., no drawing.*

# SLOOPS

### FLOWER Class sloops

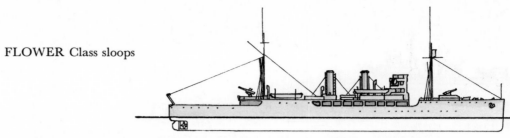

*ACACIA type* ACACIA, ANEMONE, ASTER, BLUEBELL, DAFFODIL, DAHLIA, DAPHNE, FOXGLOVE, HOLLYHOCK, HONEYSUCKLE, IRIS, JONQUIL, LABURNUM, LARKSPUR, LAVENDER, LILAC, LILY, MAGNOLIA, MALLOW, MARIGOLD, MIMOSA, PRIMROSE, SUNFLOWER, VERONICA, all 1915
*AZALEA type* AZALEA, BEGONIA, CAMELLIA, CARNATION, CLEMATIS, HELIOTROPE, JESSAMINE, MYRTLE, NARCISSUS, PEONY, SNOWDROP, ZINNIA, all 1915
*ARABIS type* ALYSSUM, AMARYLLIS, ARABIS, ASPHODEL, BERBERIS, BUTTERCUP, CAMPANULA, CELANDINE, CORNFLOWER, CROCUS, CYCLAMEN, DELPHINIUM, GENISTA, GENTIAN, GERANIUM, GLADIOLUS, GODETIA HYDRANGEA, LOBELIA, LUPIN, MARGUERITE, MIGNONETTE, MYOSOTIS, NASTURTIUM, NIGELLA, PANSY, PENTSTEMON, PETUNIA, POPPY, PRIMULA, ROSEMARY, SNAPDRAGON, VALERIAN, VERBENA, WALLFLOWER, WISTERIA, all 1915–16
1,200 *to* 1,250 *tons* 262½' *to* 267¾' × 33½' × 11'. Guns 2 4·7" *or* 12-*pdrs., depth charges.* Engines and speed *Triple expansion; 1,800 to 2,000 h.p.; 17 knots.* Remarks *All similar.*

### FLOWER Class Q ships

*AUBRIETIA type* ANDROMEDA, AUBRIETIA, GAILLARDIA, HEATHER, HIBISCUS, LYCHNIS, MONTBRETIA, POLYANTHUS, SALVIA, TAMARISK, TULIP, VIOLA, all 1916–7
*ANCHUSA type* ANCHUSA, ARBUTUS, AURICULA, BERGAMOT, BRYONY, CANDYTUFT, CEANOTHUS, CHRYSANTHEMUM, CONVOLVULUS, COREOPSIS, COWSLIP, DIANTHUS, EGLANTINE, GARDENIA, GILIA, HAREBELL, IVY, MARJORAM, MISTLETOE, PELARGONIUM, RHODODENDRON, SAXIFRAGE, SILENE, SPIRAEA, SWEETBRIAR, SYRINGA, TUBEROSE, WINDFLOWER, all 1917–18
*AUBRIETIA type* 1,250 *tons* 267¼' × 33½', *ANCHUSA type* 1,290 *tons* 262½' × 35' × 11'. Guns 2 4", 2 12-*pdrs., depth-charge throwers.* Engines and speed *Triple expansion; 2,500 h.p.; 16–17½ knots.* Remarks *Built to resemble merchant coasters and lure the U-boats. They were similar in appearance to (but slightly larger than) the P-boat Q ships (see p. 250).*

### 24 Class sloops

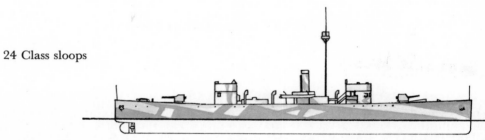

ARD PATRICK, BEND OR, CICERO, DONOVAN, FLYING FOX, HARVESTER, IROQUOIS, ISINGLASS, LADAS, MERRY HAMPTON, MINORU, ORBY, ORMONDE, PERSIMMON, ROCK SAND, SANFOIN, SEFTON, SILVIO, SIR BEVIS, SIR HUGO, SIR VISTO, SPEARMINT, all 1918-19
1,320 *tons* 267¼' × 35' × 10½'. Guns 2 4" *but varied.* Engines and speed *Triple expansion; 2,500 h.p.; 17 knots.* Remarks *Two further ships to make up the 24 were cancelled.*

### BRIDGEWATER Type sloops

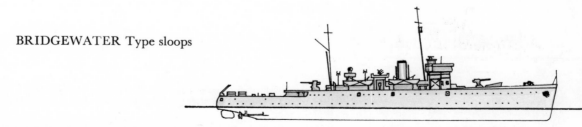

BIDEFORD 1931, BRIDGEWATER 1928, DUNDEE 1932, FALMOUTH 1932, FOLKESTONE 1930, FOWEY 1930, HASTINGS 1930, MILFORD 1932, PENZANCE 1930, ROCHESTER 1931, SANDWICH 1928, SCARBOROUGH 1930, SHOREHAM 1930, WESTON 1932
1,045 *to* 1,105 *tons* 266' (o/a) × 34' × 8¼' *to* 9'. Guns 2 4" A.A., 4 0·5" A.A. Engines and speed *Turbines; 2,000 h.p.; 16 knots.*

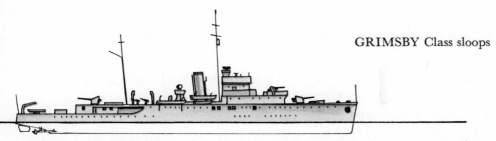

GRIMSBY Class sloops

ABERDEEN 1936, DEPTFORD 1935, FLEETWOOD 1936, GRIMSBY 1933, LEITH 1933, LONDONDERRY 1935, LOWESTOFT 1934, WELLINGTON 1934
990 *tons* 266′ (*o*/*a*) × 36′ × 7½′. Guns 2 4·7″, 1 3″ *A.A.* (*ABERDEEN and FLEETWOOD* 4 4″ *A.A.*). Engines and speed *Turbines;* 2,000 *h.p.;* 16½ *knots.*

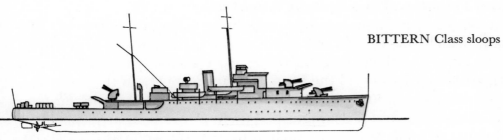

BITTERN Class sloops

BITTERN 1937, ENCHANTRESS 1934, STORK 1936
1,190 *tons* 282′ (*o*/*a*) × 37′ × 8½′. Guns 4 4·7″ (*BITTERN* 6 4″ *A.A.*), 4 0·5″ *A.A.* Engines and speed *Turbines;* 3,300 *h.p.;* 18¾ *knots.*
Remarks *Drawing represents* Bittern.

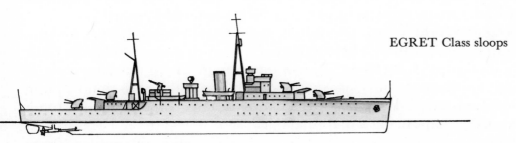

EGRET Class sloops

AUCKLAND, EGRET, PELICAN, all 1938
1,200 *tons* 292½′ (*o*/*a*) × 37½′ × 8½′. Guns 8 4″ *A.A.*, 4 0·5″ *A.A.* Engines and speed *Turbines;* 3,600 *h.p.;* 19 *knots.*

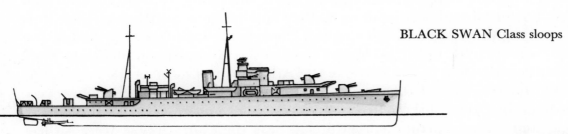

BLACK SWAN Class sloops

BLACK SWAN 1939, ERNE 1940, FLAMINGO 1939, IBIS 1940, WHIMBREL 1942, WILD GOOSE 1942, WOODCOCK 1942, WOODPECKER 1942, WREN 1942
*Modified BLACK SWAN Class* ACTAEON, ALACRITY, AMETHYST, CHANTICLEER, CRANE, CYGNET, HART, HIND, KITE, LAPWING, LARK, MAGPIE, MERMAID, MODESTE, NEREIDE, OPOSSUM, PEACOCK, PHEASANT, REDPOLE, SNIPE, SPARROW, STARLING, all 1942–5, except SPARROW 1946
*BLACK SWAN* 1,250 *tons* 299½′ (*o*/*a*) × 37½′ × 8½′. *Modified BLACK SWAN* 1,350 *tons* 299½′ (*o*/*a*) × 38½′ × 8¾′. Guns 6 4″ *A.A.*, 4 2-*pdrs.* *A.A.*, 4 0·5″ *A.A. Modified BLACK SWANS* 12 20-mm. *A.A.* instead of 2-*pdrs.* and 0·5″. Engines and speed *Turbines;* 3,600 *h.p.;* 19 *knots. Modified BLACK SWANS* 4,300 *h.p.;* 20 *knots.*

were 20 feet shorter than the *Flowers* and exchanged twin funnels and a single screw for a single funnel and twin screws, which gave them a better turning circle.

There were two other classes built during the war; a small number of little sweepers for river and estuary work, all named after dances, and, strangely, a class of no less than thirty-two paddle-sweepers. These were built because in the early days of the war, when all sorts of merchant vessels were pressed into service, a number of paddle-packets and ferries were converted into minesweepers. They proved so successful that two classes of new ones were built. After the war a few were converted into pleasure-steamers, so completing the cycle.

## Sloops, Corvettes and Frigates of the Second World War

Only three of the First World War sloops survived as fighting ships in the Second. The new generation of sloop, which was to bear the brunt of the convoy work, began with the *Grimsby* and *Sandwich* classes, replacements for the *Flower* class, which had been used after the war for policing the four corners of the Empire. They were about the same size, with a single funnel and featuring a long fo'c'sle deck without the well of the *Flowers*; this was to be common to them all and it distinguished them from the destroyers. Their speed and main armament, 16 knots and two 4-inch guns, was the same as the *Flowers*. In spite of spending the whole war at sea, only three were lost out of over twenty. This was partly accounted for by the *U*-boat policy of attacking the merchant ships in a convoy and not the escorts. There were two other classes of escort vessel, called 'patrol vessels' and later 'corvettes', which consisted of nine little ships of the *Guillemot* and *Kingfisher* class, and they looked like tiny destroyers. These were faster than the sloops, 20 knots, and had a main armament of one 4-inch mounted forward.

Just before the Second World War a few faster, more heavily armed type of ships, named after birds began to join the fleet. These mounted six 4-inch guns (*Black Swan* Class and *Bittern*) or eight 4-inch guns (*Egret* Class) in twin mountings. There were thirty-six of them, the last ships built for the navy and classed as sloops. It was of this class that Captain Walker's famous *U*-boat hunting pack was formed. Some of the later ships had names other than of birds, the *Mermaid* perhaps being a marginal one.

The 1939 Supplementary Estimates provided for a large class of smaller escort vessels and for these the flower names were revived. Initially, fifty-six of them were ordered. They were based on a civilian whaler design by Smith's Dock Company of South Shields and were quick and easy to build. Tough, very seaworthy ships, they floated like corks, which for North Atlantic convoying was very exhausting for the crews. Well over a hundred appeared in 1940 to 1941, and many were later transferred to other navies. Essentially submarine chasers, they had only one 4-inch gun, plus anti-aircraft guns and depth-charges. To distinguish these little ships from the sloops, the word 'corvette' was revived, but it no longer bore any relation to complement. They made a valuable contribution to the Battle of the Atlantic until more of the larger type could complete and nineteen of them were lost. After the war the British ones were quickly disposed of, but some of those in foreign navies continue in service to this day.

The second and larger wartime corvette class was the *Castle*. These were 50 feet longer than the *Flowers* and, though similar in armament and speed, had a much greater endurance. The first of them did not appear until late 1943 and many were transferred to foreign navies. At the end of the war, the Royal Navy had twenty-four of them and had lost two. Their duties were as anti-submarine escorts and they were armed with Hedgehog and later Squid. The Hedgehog was a device that fired a group of explosive projectiles. These armed themselves by a propeller screw on entering the water and exploded on contact with the submarine. In service they occasionally armed themselves and exploded on board, damaging the ship. Squid is a mortar, firing depth-charges set with a hydrostatically armed time-fuse.

A third type of escort built during the war was the frigate, another name revived. These ships were very like the *Black Swan* class sloops in appearance, but larger, though less heavily armed. In the first class were sixty-five *Rivers* (some of which were at first called corvettes), twelve of which were transferred to foreign or Empire navies and five of which were sunk. They began to join the fleet in the spring of 1942. Then came the thirty-one *Loch* class and the twenty-four *Bay* class ships. There were no losses from these two classes, which went into service fairly late in the war. After the war many of these, as well as the *Castles* and *Black Swans* continued to serve in the peacetime navy at home and abroad throughout the 1950s.

In addition the Americans lent a large number of escorts, mostly new, the crews being shipped out to take them from the builders. The British had twenty-one of their *Asheville* class which were in fact American-built *Rivers*: all these were given the names of colonies. Of their *Evarts* class the British took thirty-two. These were American-designed and diesel-engined; while the forty-six ships we had of the *Buckley* class had turbo-electric engines, giving them 24 knots, 4 knots more than the otherwise almost identical *Evarts*. All were given the names of past naval officers and lumped together as *Captain* class frigates.

In 1941 ten American coastguard cutters, the *Lulworths* were lent to Britain and classed as sloops. This completes the wartime fleet of the escort type of ship, an astonishing total of more than four hundred, and to these should really be added the one hundred and twenty-six fleet minesweepers of the *Halcyon* and *Algerine* classes which were larger than, and as well armed as, the *Flower* class corvettes, and were frequently used as escorts, with a comparable speed of 16½ knots. Of the *Algerines*, five were lost, including the name ship. After the war a few were used for fishing protection, and their high deck-heads and good accommodation made them comfortable for their size. Slightly smaller and slightly earlier, but similar in appearance and performance were the thirty-nine *Bangor* class. There were also twenty-one American-built sweepers of the *Raven* class which were renamed the *Gazelles*. Finally there was a class of twenty-five *Hunts* built in the First World War which survived to fight through the Second, eight of these being lost. Altogether the Royal Navy employed in commission at sea more than one thousand destroyers and escorts, two thousand including trawlers, during the Second World War.

## PATROL BOATS, SLOOPS and CORVETTES

### P-boats

P11, 12, 14 to 41, 45 to 50, 52 to 54, 57 to 59, 64, 75, all 1915–17
613 *tons* 244½' × 23¼' × 8'. Guns 1 4" *and smaller*. Torpedo tubes 2 14". Engines and speed *Turbines;* 3,500 *to* 4,000 *h.p.;* 20 *knots*.

### PC boats

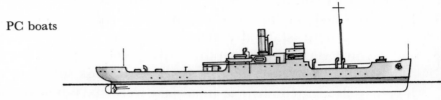

Twenty P-boats were built as Q ships to resemble merchantmen; their numbers were PC42 to 44, 51, 55, 56, 60 to 63, 65 to 74

### KIL Class patrol gunboats

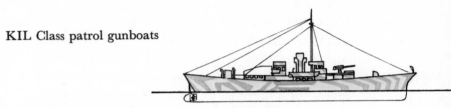

KILBEGGAN, KILBERRY, KILBIRNIE, KILBRIDE, KILBURN, KILCHATTAN, KILCHREEST, KILCHRENAN, KILCHVAN, KILCLARE, KILCLIEF, KILCLOGHER, KILCOCK, KILDALKEY, KILDANGAN, KILDARE, KILDARY, KILDAVIN, KILDIMO, KILDONAN, KILDOROUGH, KILDORREY, KILDRESS, KILDWICK, KILDYSART, KILFENORA, KILFINNY, KILFREE, KILFULLERT, KILGARVAN, KILGOBNET, KILHAM, KILKEEL, KILLENA, KILLERIG, KILLINEY, KILLOUR, KILLOWEN, KILLYBEGS, KILLYGORDON, KILMACRENNAN, KILMAINE, KILMALCOLM, KILMALLOCK, KILMANAHAN, KILMARNOCK, KILMARTIN, KILMEAD, KILMELFORD, KILMERSDON, KILMINGTON, KILMORE, KILMUCKRIDGE, KILMUN, all 1917–19
890 *tons* 182' × 30' × 10½'. Guns 1 4". Engines and speed *Triple expansion;* 1,400 *h.p.;* 13 *knots*. Remarks *Some adapted for minesweeping*

### KINGFISHER Type corvettes

GUILLEMOT 1939, KINGFISHER 1935, KITTIWAKE 1936, MALLARD 1936, PINTAIL 1939, PUFFIN 1936, SHEARWATER 1939, SHELDRAKE 1937, WIDGEON 1938
510 *to* 580 *tons* 233¼' *to* 243¼' × 25½' *to* 26½' × 6' *to* 7¼'. Guns 1 4" *A.A. and smaller*. Engines and speed *Turbines;* 3,600 *h.p.;* 20 *knots*.

### LULWORTH Class sloops

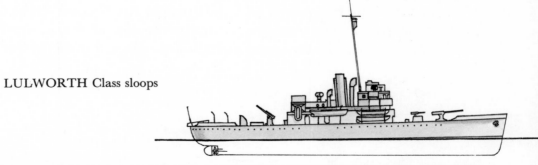

BANFF, CULVER, FISHGUARD, GORLESTON, HARTLAND, LANDGUARD, LULWORTH, SENNEN, TOTLAND, WALNEY, all 1927–31
1,546 *tons* 256' (*o/a*) × 42' × 16'. Guns 1 5", 2 3" *A.A.* (*TOTLAND, WALNEY* 3). Engines and speed *Turbo-electric;* 3,200 *h.p.;* 16 *knots*.
Remarks *Ex U.S. Coastguard cutters*.

FLOWER Class corvettes

ABELIA, ACANTHUS, ACONITE, ALISMA, ALYSSUM, AMARANTHUS, ANCHUSA, ANEMONE, ARABIS, ARBUTUS,
ARMERIA, ARROWHEAD, ASPHODEL. ASTER, AUBRIETIA, AURICULA, AZALEA, BALSAM, BEGONIA, BELLWORT,
BERGAMOT, BITTERSWEET, BLUEBELL, BORAGE, BRYONY, BURDOCK, BUTTERCUP, CALENDULA, CAMELLIA,
CAMPANULA, CAMPION, CANDYTUFT, CARNATION, CELANDINE, CHRYSANTHEMUM, CLARKIA, CLEMATIS, CLOVER,
COLTSFOOT, COLUMBINE, CONVOLVULUS, COREOPSIS, CORIANDER, COWSLIP, CROCUS, CYCLAMEN, DAHLIA,
DELPHINIUM, DIANELLA, DIANTHUS, EGLANTINE, ERICA, EYEBRIGHT, FENNEL, FLEUR DE LYS, FREESIA,
FRITILLARY, GARDENIA, GENISTA, GENTIAN, GERANIUM, GLADIOLUS, GLOXINIA, GODETIA (i), GODETIA (ii),
HEATHER, HELIOTROPE, HEARTSEASE, HEPATICA, HIBISCUS, HOLLYHOCK, HONEYSUCKLE, HYACINTH,
HYDRANGEA, JASMINE, JONQUIL, KINGCUP, LARKSPUR, LAMALOUINE, LAVENDER, LOBELIA, LOOSESTRIFE, LOTUS
(i), LOTUS (ii), MALLOW, MARGUERITE, MARIGOLD, MAYFLOWER, MEADOWSWEET, MIGNONETTE, MIMOSA,
MONKSHOOD, MYOSOTIS, NARCISSUS, NETTLE, NASTURTIUM, NIGELLA, ORCHIS, OXLIP, PENNYWORT, PEONY,
PENTSTEMON, PERIWINKLE, PETUNIA, PICOTEE, PIMPERNEL, PINK, POLYANTHUS, POPPY, POTENTILLA, PRIMROSE,
PRIMULA, RANUNCULUS, RHODODENDRON, ROCKROSE, ROSE, SALVIA, SAMPHIRE, SAXIFRAGE, SNAPDRAGON,
SNOWDROP, SNOWBERRY, SNOWFLAKE, SPIKENARD, SPIRAEA, STARWORT, STONECROP, SUNDEW, SUNFLOWER,
SWEETBRIAR, TAMARISK, THYME, TRILLIUM, TULIP, VERBENA, VERONICA, VERVAIN, VETCH, VIOLET,
WALLFLOWER, WINDFLOWER, WOODRUFF, ZINNIA, all built 1940–42
*Modified Flower Class* ARABIS (ii), ARBUTUS (ii), BETONY, BUDDLEIA, BUGLOSS, BULRUSH, BURNET, CANDYTUFT,
CEANOTHUS, CHARLOCK, COMFREY, CORNEL, DITTANY, FLAX, HONESTY, LINARIA, LOUISBURG, MANDRAKE,
MILFOIL, MUSK, NEPETA, PRIVET, ROSEBAY, SMILAX, STATICE, WILLOWHERB, all built 1942–4
925 *tons* 205′ (*o/a*) × 33′ × 11½′. Guns 1 4″, 1 2-*pdr.* A.A. or 4 0·5″ A.A., 4 0·303″ A.A. Depth charges. *Modified* Flowers *hedgehog.*
Engines and speed *Single-screw, reciprocating;* 2,750 *h.p.;* 16 knots. Remarks *The Modified* Flowers *were* 3½′ *longer with a slightly more powerful
engine. The Royal Canadian Navy principally, but also other Empire and foreign navies, took delivery of over 130 more.*

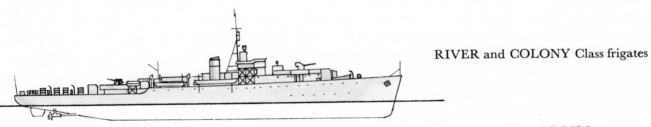

RIVER and COLONY Class frigates

AIRE, ANNAN, AVON, AWE, BALLINDERRY, BANN, BARLE, BRAID, CAM, CHELMER, CUCKMERE, DART, DERG,
DEVERON, ETTRICK, EVENLODE, EXE, FAL, FINDHORN, FROME, HALLADALE, HELFORD, HELMSDALE, INVER,
ITCHEN, JED, KALE, LAGAN, LAMBOURNE, LOCHY, LOSSIE, MEON, MONNOW, MOURNE, MOYOLA, NADDER, NENE,
NESS, NITH, ODZANI, PARRET, PLYM, RIBBLE, ROTHER, SHIEL, SPEY, STRULE, SWALE, TAFF, TAVY, TAY, TEES, TEME,
TEST, TEVIOT, TORRIDGE, TOWY, TRENT, TWEED, USK, WAVENEY, WEAR, WINDRUSH, WYE, all built 1941–3, except
HALLADALE 1944
1,370 *tons* 301¼′ (*o/a*) × 36½′ × 9′. Guns 2 4″, 10 20-*mm.* A.A. *Hedgehog anti-submarine weapon.* Engines and speed *Reciprocating;* 5,500 *h.p.;*
20 knots. Remarks *Over 80 in the Royal Canadian Navy, a few in the U.S. Navy.*

COLONY Class frigates
ANGUILLA, ANTIGUA, ASCENSION, BAHAMAS, BARBADOS, CAICOS, CAYMAN, DOMINICA, LABUAN,
MONTSERRAT, NYASALAND, PAPUA, PERIM, PITCAIRN, ST HELENA, SARAWAK, SEYCHELLES, SOMALILAND,
TOBAGO, TORTOLA, ZANZIBAR, all 1943, built in the U.S.A.
1,318 *tons* 304′ (*o/a*) × 37½′ × 12′. Guns 3 3″ A.A., 4 40-*mm.* A.A., 4 20-*mm.* A.A. Engines and speed *Reciprocating;* 5,500 *h.p.;* 18 knots.

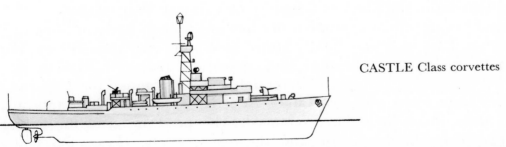

CASTLE Class corvettes

ALLINGTON CASTLE, ALNWICK CASTLE, AMBERLEY CASTLE, BAMBOROUGH CASTLE, BARNARD CASTLE, BERKELEY
CASTLE, CAISTOR CASTLE, CARISBROOKE CASTLE, DENBIGH CASTLE, DUMBARTON CASTLE, FARNHAM CASTLE,
FLINT CASTLE, GUILDFORD CASTLE, HADLEIGH CASTLE, HEDINGHAM CASTLE, HEVER CASTLE, HURST CASTLE,
KENILWORTH CASTLE, KNARESBOROUGH CASTLE, LANCASTER CASTLE, LAUNCESTON CASTLE, LEEDS CASTLE,
MORPETH CASTLE, NORHAM CASTLE, NUNNERY CASTLE, OAKHAM CASTLE, OXFORD CASTLE, PEMBROKE CASTLE,
PEVENSEY CASTLE, PORTCHESTER CASTLE, RISING CASTLE, RUSHEN CASTLE, SANDGATE CASTLE, SHERBORNE
CASTLE, SHREWSBURY CASTLE, TAMWORTH CASTLE, TINTAGEL CASTLE, WALMER CASTLE, WOLVESEY CASTLE, all
built 1943 and 1944
1,010 *tons* 252′ (*o/a*) × 36¾′ × 10′. Guns 1 4″, 10 20-*mm.* A.A. *Squid anti-submarine weapon.* Engines and speed *Single-screw, reciprocating;* 2,880 *h.p.;*
16½ knots.

# 29

## Post-Second World War
## Frigates and Destroyers

In 1950 all escort classes were gathered together under the name 'frigate'; these consisted of fifty *Hunt* class destroyers, twenty-two *Black Swan* class sloops, twenty-four *Castle* class and two *Flower* class corvettes, as well as the sixty-six ships that had always been frigates. The remaining *T* and *C* class destroyers also joined the frigates after a limited conversion two or three years later.

A more ambitious conversion was made of the destroyers of the *R* to *Z* classes. Starting with the *Relentless* and *Rocket* in 1949–51, the *Type 15s* had their fo'c'sle deck extended almost to the stern. The forward guns were removed and a large low bridge structure built, stretching the width of the ship and forward of the mast to where the guns had been. A twin 4-inch mounting was placed three-quarters of the way aft on the upper-deck. In order to reduce the excess top weight, a large percentage of aluminium was used. These conversions and most of those that followed had enclosed bridges. The position of the gun mountings also varied, some in front of the bridge, some behind it, some well aft. Two A.A. Bofors were also mounted. Squid and Limbo depth-charge mortars were carried, and later, in some, homing torpedoes for a time. These were large, very fast, roomy frigates and a successful conversion. They continued in service until the end of the 1960s.

The first of new postwar all-welded ships were the twelve *Type 14 Blackwood* class, named after former naval officers. The story of who chooses the names is an interesting one over the years, but on this occasion it is believed to have been Their Lordships, with the curious result that the *Pellew* and *Exmouth* were named after the same man, as Sir Edward Pellew became Lord Exmouth, and the *Dundas* was named after two men, since it has never been established whether she is named after Richard Dundas in the Baltic or Sir James Dundas in the Black Sea during the Crimean War in 1855.

They had a flared fo'c'sle which kept them dry forward though lively in a seaway, and an enclosed bridge. They were very lightly armed as to guns, only three Bofors, and could steam at about 25 knots. At the time they appeared, the larger Russian submarines often carried two 4-inch, and so could certainly have outgunned the *Blackwoods* on the surface. They were fitted with two Limbo three-barrel depth-charge mortars, and four torpedo tubes which were later removed. The postwar trend for lighter scantling was taken too far in these ships and the first one, the *Hardy*, was badly strained soon after her acceptance in 1955, which resulted in the first of several

## CAPTAIN Class frigates

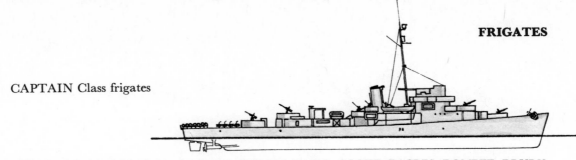

*Diesel-electric type* BAYNTUN, BAZELY, BERRY, BLACKWOOD, BURGES, CAPEL, COOKE, DACRES, DOMETT, DRURY, FOLEY, GARDINER, GARLIES, GOODALL, GOODSON, GORE, GOULD, GRINDALL, HOSTE, INGLIS, INMAN, KEATS, KEMPTHORNE, KINGSMILL, LAWFORD, LAWSON, LORING, LOUIS, MANNERS, MOORSOM, MOUNSEY, PASLEY
*Turbo-electric type* AFFLECK, AYLMER, BALFOUR, BENTINCK, BENTLEY, BICKERTON, BLIGH, BRAITHWAITE, BULLEN, BYARD, BYRON, CALDER, CONN, COSBY, COTTON, CRANSTOUN, CUBITT, CURZON, DAKINS, DEANE, DUCKWORTH, DUFF, EKINS, ESSINGTON, FITZROY, HALSTED, HARGOOD, HOLMES, HOTHAM, NARBROUGH, REDMILL, RETALICK, RIOU, ROWLEY, RUPERT, RUTHERFORD, SEYMOUR, SPRAGGE, STAYNER, STOCKHAM, THORNBROUGH, TORRINGTON, TROLLOPE, TYLER, WALDEGRAVE, WHITTAKER, all 1942-3
*Diesel-electric type* 1,085 *tons* 289½' (*o/a*) × 35' × 9'. *Turbo-electric type* 1,300 *tons* 306' (*o/a*) × 36¾' × 9'. *Guns Diesel-electric type* 3 3" *A.A.*, 2 40-*mm. A.A.*, 10 20-*mm. A.A. Turbo-electric type* 3 3" *A.A.*, 1 2-*pdr. A.A.*, 2 40-*mm. A.A.*, 8 20-*mm. A.A.*, or 10 20-*mm. A.A. Engines and speed Diesel-electric*; 6,000 *h.p.*; 20 *knots. Turbo-electric*; 12,000 *h.p.*; 26 *knots. Remarks Lend-lease ships from the U.S.A. Drawing represents the Turbo-electric type.*

## BAY Class frigates

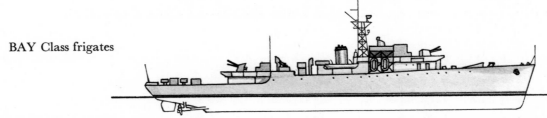

BIGBURY BAY, BURGHEAD BAY, CARDIGAN BAY, CARNARVON BAY, CAWSAND BAY, DUNDRUM BAY (ALERT yacht), ENARD BAY, GERRANS BAY (SURPRISE yacht), HERNE BAY, LARG BAY, LUCE BAY, MORECAMBE BAY, MOUNTS BAY, PADSTOW BAY, PEGWELL BAY, PORLOCK BAY, ST AUSTELL BAY, ST BRIDE'S BAY, START BAY, THURSO BAY, TREMADOC BAY, VERYAN BAY, WHITESAND BAY, WIDEMOUTH BAY, WIGTOWN BAY, all 1944-5
1,580 *tons* 307¼' (*o/a*) × 38¼' × 9½'. *Guns* 4 4" *A.A.*, 4 40-*mm. A.A.*, 4 20-*mm. A.A. Hedgehog or Squid anti-submarine mortars. Engines and speed Reciprocating*; 5,500 *h.p.*; 20 *knots. Remarks* Herne Bay, Luce Bay, Pegwell Bay *and* Thurso Bay *completed as surveying vessels* Dampier, Dalrymple, Cook *and* Owen *respectively.*

## LOCH Class frigates

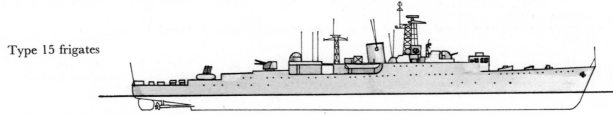

LOCH ACHANALT, LOCH ACHRAY, LOCH ALVIE, LOCH ARKAIG, LOCH CRAGGIE, LOCH DUNVEGAN, LOCH ECK, LOCH FADA, LOCH FYNE, LOCH GLENDHU, LOCH GORM, LOCH INSH, LOCH KATRINE, LOCH KILLIN, LOCH KILLISPORT, LOCH LOMOND, LOCH MORE, LOCH MORLICH, LOCH QUOICH, LOCH RUTHVEN, LOCH SCAVAIG, LOCH SHIN, LOCH TARBERT, LOCH TRALAIG, LOCH VEYATIE, all 1943-5
1,435 *tons* 307' (*o/a*) × 38½' × 8¾'. *Guns* 1 4" *A.A.*, 4 2-*pdrs. A.A.*, 6 20-*mm. A.A. Hedgehog or Squid anti-submarine mortars. Engines and speed Triple expansion (except LOCH ARKAIG and LOCH TRALAIG turbines)*; 5,500 *h.p.*; 20 *knots.*

## Type 15 frigates

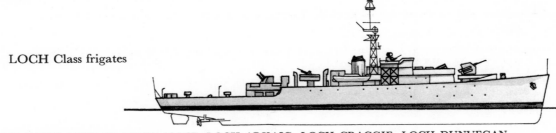

GRENVILLE, RAPID, RELENTLESS, ROCKET, ROEBUCK, TROUBRIDGE, ULSTER, ULYSSES, UNDAUNTED, UNDINE, URANIA, URCHIN, URSA, VENUS, VERULAM, VIGILANT, VIRAGO, VOLAGE, WAKEFUL, WHIRLWIND, WIZARD, ZEST, all 1942-3
2,030 to 2,300 *tons* 362½' (*o/a*) × 35½' × 16', *except R Class* 358¼' (*o/a*). *Guns* 2 4" *A.A.*, 2 40-*mm. A.A.*, 2 Limbo or Squid anti-submarine mortars. Torpedo tubes *Some temporarily fitted with 8 tubes for homing torpedoes. Engines and speed Turbines*; 40,000 *h.p.*; 36 *knots. Remarks Converted fleet destroyers.*

## BLACKWOOD Class frigates (Type 14)

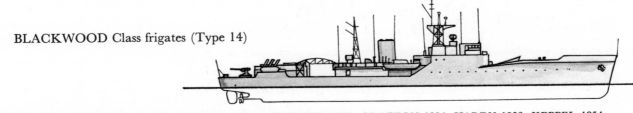

BLACKWOOD 1955, DUNCAN 1957, DUNDAS 1953, EXMOUTH 1955, GRAFTON 1954, HARDY 1953, KEPPEL 1954, MALCOLM 1955, MURRAY 1955, PALLISER 1956, PELLEW 1954, RUSSELL 1954
1,100 *tons* 310' (*o/a*) × 33' × 10'. *Guns* 3 40-*mm. A.A.*, 2 *triple-barrelled Limbo anti-submarine mortars. Engines and speed Turbines*; 15,000 *h.p.*; 24 *knots. Remarks* Exmouth *converted to gas turbine engines as a floating test-bed. Some temporarily carried* 4 21" *torpedo tubes.*

# FRIGATES

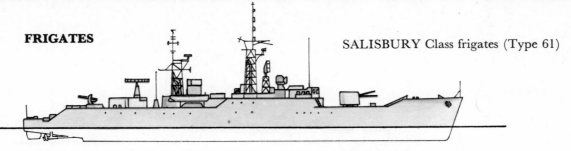

## SALISBURY Class frigates (Type 61)

CHICHESTER 1955, LINCOLN 1959, LLANDAFF 1955, SALISBURY 1953
1,738 *tons* 340′ (*o/a*) × 40′ × 11½′. Guns 2 4·5″ *D.P.*, 2 40-mm. *A.A.*, 1 *Squid triple-barrelled anti-submarine mortar.* Engines and speed *Diesels, 8 engines; 16,000 h.p.; 25 knots (gas turbine alternator in LLANDAFF).* Remarks *Designed as aircraft direction frigates to work with the carriers.*

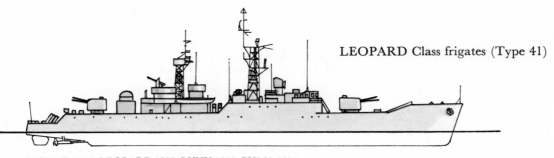

## LEOPARD Class frigates (Type 41)

JAGUAR 1957, LEOPARD 1955, LYNX 1955, PUMA 1954
1,800 *tons* 340′ (*o/a*) × 40′ × 12′. Guns 4 4·5″ *D.P.*, 2 40-mm. *A.A.*, 1 *Squid triple-barrelled anti-submarine mortar.* Engines and speed *Diesels, 8 engines; 16,000 h.p.; 25 knots.* Remarks *Designed to give convoy protection against aircraft.*

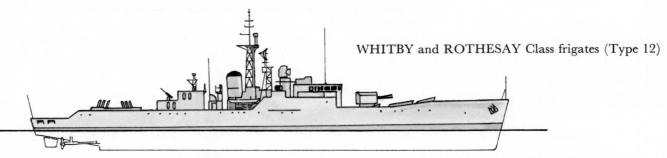

## WHITBY and ROTHESAY Class frigates (Type 12)

BERWICK 1959, BLACKPOOL 1957, BRIGHTON 1959, EASTBOURNE 1955, FALMOUTH 1959, LONDONDERRY 1958, LOWESTOFT 1960, PLYMOUTH 1959, RHYL 1959, ROTHESAY 1957, SCARBOROUGH 1955, TENBY 1955, TORQUAY 1954, WHITBY 1954, YARMOUTH 1959
2,380 *tons* 370′ (*o/a*) × 41′ × 12′. Guns 2 4·5″ *D.P. automatic,* 1 *or* 2 40-mm. *A.A.*, 2 *triple-barrelled anti-submarine mortars.* Engines and speed *Turbines; 30,000 h.p.; 30 knots.* Remarks *Rothesay class reconstructed 1966–72.*

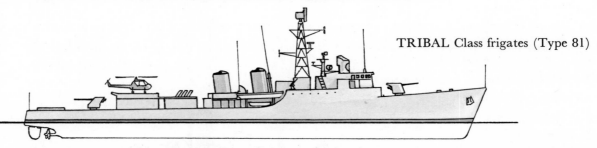

## TRIBAL Class frigates (Type 81)

ASHANTI 1959, ESKIMO 1960, GURKHA 1960, MOHAWK 1962, NUBIAN 1960, TARTAR 1960, ZULU 1962
2,300 *tons* 360′ (*o/a*) × 42¼′ × 12½′. Guns 2 4·5″ *single mounted,* 2 40-mm. *A.A. later replaced by 2 quadruple Seacat missile launchers.* 1 *anti-submarine helicopter.* Engines and speed *Steam turbine: 12,500 h.p.; gas turbine: 7,500 h.p.; 28 knots.*

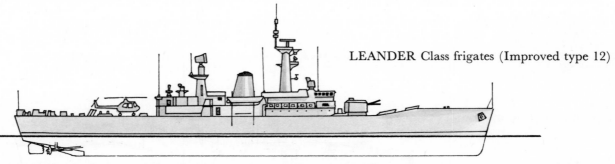

## LEANDER Class frigates (Improved type 12)

ACHILLES 1968, AJAX 1962, ANDROMEDA 1967, APOLLO 1970, ARETHUSA 1963, ARGONAUT 1966, ARIADNE 1971, AURORA 1962, BACCHANTE 1968, CHARYBDIS 1968, CLEOPATRA 1964, DANAE 1965, DIDO 1961, DIOMEDE 1969, EURYALUS 1963, GALATEA 1963, HERMIONE 1967, JUNO 1965, JUPITER 1967, LEANDER 1961, MINERVA 1964, NAIAD 1963, PENELOPE 1962, PHOEBE 1964, SCYLLA 1968, SIRIUS 1964
2,450 *tons* 372′ (*o/a*) × 41′ *or* 43′ × 14′. Guns 2 4·5″ *D.P.*, 2 40-mm. *A.A.*, 1 *or* 2 20-mm. *A.A. The NAIAD and following ships given a quadruple Seacat missile launcher instead of the 40-mm.;* 1 *anti-submarine helicopter.* Engines and speed *Turbines; 30,000 h.p.; 30 knots.*

strengthenings, and a general strengthening of the class. They were conceived from the first as second-class utility anti-submarine frigates. In 1966 the *Exmouth* was taken in hand for conversion to gas turbine propulsion, with two Proteus engines for cruising and an Olympus for emergency speeds. This did away with the weighty, bulky boilers which took up so much room in the older ships, and gas turbine engines are now standard in all new frigates and carriers. None are now operational.

In the late 1950s came the four ships of the *Leopard* class (*Type 41*), anti-aircraft frigates which were diesel engined and not very fast, but powerfully gunned, with two twin 4·5-inch fully automatic turrets as fitted in the *Darings*. Though primarily designed for anti-aircraft protection they had a single 3-barrelled Squid depth-charge mortar.

A variation on the *Leopards* were the four Type 61 *Salisburys*. These mounted two huge tower masts for radar scanners for their role as aircraft direction ships to work with the aircraft carriers. With the phasing out of the carriers they too were scrapped.

Also in the late 1950s and the beginning of the 1960s came the Type 12 anti-submarine general purpose frigates, as large and nearly as fast as the Type 15 converted destroyers, which they resemble. The six ships of the *Whitby* class had hulls radically different from the fine bowed destroyers which cut through the waves rather than over them. The *Whitbys* were given a fine entry up to a flared and raised fo'c'sle and a full, beamy midship section, which, combined with low propeller revolutions, resulted in fine sea keeping qualities and the ability to keep up a high average speed in heavy weather. The fo'c'sle deck was extended well aft.

The main armament was one twin 4·5-inch fully automatic turret as in the *Darings* and Limbo 3-barrelled depth charge mortars. Only *Torquay* remains in service, as the navigation/direction and trials ship at Portsmouth.

The *Whitbys* were followed by the nine *Rothesays*, apparently identical except for their funnels, but in fact with an internally improved layout. They all commissioned in 1960 and 1961, and between 1966 and 1972 the whole class was modernized and given a flight deck and hangar aft to carry a Westland Wasp helicopter equipped with anti-submarine homing torpedoes, and a Seacat anti-aircraft missile launcher replaced the 40-mm Bofors gun. Like the *Whitbys*, the *Rothesays* are currently being phased out, though the *Rothesay* herself and the *Yarmouth* have had recent big refits and may stay in service for some time. During the Falklands War the *Plymouth*, serving as picket in Port San Carlos was hit by four bombs which failed to go off, but set off a depth charge which caused a fire and damage.

In the middle 1960s into the early 1970s the twenty-six ships of the *Leander* class completed. They were the ultimate development of the *Whitby* type, and can be easily recognized from the modernized *Rothesays* by their lack of scuttles in the main hull, a feature now general in subsequent classes, which may be operationally desirable, but is sad from the habitability point of view. The *Leanders* fall into two sub-classes as the last ten to be built are 2 feet broader in the beam and are known as the Broad-beamed *Leanders*. This class is generally considered to be the most successful frigate design of the post-war era, and is in service with a number of Commonwealth and foreign navies. They are Australia, which built its own, New Zealand, India, Chile, and the Netherlands, which also built their own.

They carry a Wasp or Lynx helicopter, and in the 1970s the first 8 ships of the class had their turrets removed and replaced by an Ikara anti-submarine homing torpedo launcher, while still retaining their anti-submarine helicopter and Limbo depth-charge mortar. Their only guns are two 40-millimetre Bofors, so they have ceased to have a role as general purpose frigates and can only operate their anti-submarine role in a hostile environment with the aid of an anti-aircraft, anti-ship escort. The Australian *Leanders* have a lighter weight Ikara launcher on each quarter, so retaining their turret and general purpose capability. The next eight *Leanders* also lost their gun turrets, this time to the French surface skimming anti-ship missile, the dreaded Exocet, and so they too lost their general purpose capability, for Exocet is a totally specialized weapon. The gun, on the other hand, can warn, illuminate, or strike at ship or shore. It was the guns of H.M.S. Plymouth and Antrim that persuaded the Argentine soldiers on South Georgia to put out white flags in remarkably quick time. The Broad-beamed *Leanders* retain their gun turrets.

Just before the *Leanders*, another class of general purpose frigate was built, the Type 81 *Tribals*. There were seven of these, designed to replace *Loch* and *Bay* class frigates for service in the Persian Gulf and foreign stations. For that reason they were fully air conditioned. They were two-funnelled and looked rather like destroyers. They had two 4·5-inch dual purpose guns fore and aft, normally operated behind shields. They were originally designed to have Seacat anti-aircraft missiles, but these were not ready in time so they served for years with two 40-millimetre Bofors guns. Most were fitted with Seacat in the end. They carried a helicopter in a hangar aft and, like the *Blackwoods*, were single screw. Their machinery was the most advanced thing about them. In the old destroyers a lot of the huge space taken up by the boilers was to get the last few knots out of the engines. The *Tribals* had only enough boiler space to give them 12,000 horsepower and a reasonable cruising speed, while the *Leanders* had 30,000 horsepower. Emergency speed was achieved by a gas turbine engine which boosted the system on demand and also made it possible to go to sea from cold boilers in a few minutes. When *Ashanti*, the first to complete, appeared in 1961, she sailed for the U.S.A. to show herself to the U.S. Navy. She never got there. A big wave knocked her bottom in one and a half feet; like the *Blackwoods*, the *Tribals* were initially too lightly scantled. They were being phased out when the losses of the Falklands War put most of them back in commission.

A one-off frigate, the *Mermaid*, deserves a mention since she briefly served. She was originally ordered by President Nkrumah of Ghana as the country's flagship and yacht. She was diesel powered and carried two 4-inch guns in a twin mount forward, four 40-millimetre Bofors and a Squid anti-submarine mortar. After Nkrumah was deposed the order was cancelled when the ship was nearly completed, and Yarrow put her on the market. In 1972 the Royal Navy bought her and she commissioned in 1973. In 1977 she was resold to the Malaysian Navy.

The latest class of frigate, the eight Type 21 *Amazons*, completed in the 1970s. They are not an Admiralty design, as at the time they were projected the design staff at the Admiralty were over stretched on the Polaris programme. So Vosper Thornycroft and Yarrow designed and built them. They are very handsome ships and the long sloping funnel gives them a deceptively small appearance in comparison with the *Leanders*, which are in fact similar in size and tonnage. Their upperworks are of aluminium, which saves 60 tons and enables them to carry a powerful armament. But there was a penalty which the designers must have known, and which showed up with a vengeance in the Falklands War. Aluminium burns with, once going, a ferocious heat that cannot be extinguished.

As designed the ships had one 4·5-inch automatic quick firing gun forward, two 20-millimetre Oerlikons, and one quadruple Seacat surface-air missile launcher. The later ships of the class were to have had the Seawolf surface-air system, but it was not ready in time. Since completion a four-missile Exocet launcher has been added before the bridge. They have a hanger for an anti-submarine Wasp or Lynx helicopter that carries homing torpedoes. Their machinery comprises four gas turbines driving twin screws. During the Falklands War in 1982 the *Ardent* was hit by fifteen missiles and sunk on 22 May, and the *Antelope* was hit in Port San Carlos by a bomb which initially did not go off, but exploded while being defused. Both ships burned fiercely, fueled not only by the aluminium but also by the plastic lagging of their wiring, which gave off clouds of black, toxic smoke. Sadly this class was also too lightly scantled and the whip of the hull caused cracks in the aluminium deck and superstructure; all are to be strengthened.

## Guided Missile Light Cruisers

These were the eight *County* class ships built in the 1960s. All originally had four 4·5-inch guns in two automatic turrets forward, but B turret in some was later replaced by an Exocet mounting. They also had a Seaslug mounting aft and two quadruple Seacat mountings in each side of the helicopter hangar. The machinery follows the same principle as the *Tribals*, combined turbines and boilers with four booster gas turbines to twin screws, COSAG. The first to complete, the *Devonshire*, exceeded expectations. These are fine ships with handsome, purposeful lines, and the Exocet armed ones are the most powerful surface ships in the fleet. It is therefore a great pity that there are only three of the original eight left in the service, the rest being sold or broken up long before the end of their useful life. The *Norfolk* was sold to Chile in 1982 after only twelve years in the fleet. The reason was that the government, forever seeking economies, found them expensive to run with their complements of 470 compared with the 260 of the later *Leanders*. During the Falklands War the *Glamorgan*, which had undergone a £63 million refit from 1977–80, was hit by a land-based Exocet missile which failed to go off, and she survived.

The other light cruiser is the Type 82 *Bristol*. Slightly shorter than the *County* class, she is 1 foot broader in the beam and has a unique three funnel layout, with one midships and two side by side aft of the mast. There were originally to have been four *Bristols*, which were designed to be close escorts for the projected new strike carrier CVA 01, and to carry the Sea Dart anti-aircraft missile system. When the strike carrier was cancelled so were three of the *Bristols*. The *Bristol*, a very expensive ship, was completed to be an experimental weapon ship and partly to fulfil our commitment to be a vehicle for a new Anglo-Dutch radar system, subsequently cancelled. As well as Sea Dart she has a fully automatic 4·5-inch gun forward, an Ikara homing torpedo launcher, two 20-millimetre Oerlikons guns and originally a Limbo depth charge mortar, now removed. Built to work with carriers she has no helicopter hanger, but can land one aft. She was the last ship to have the COSAG combined steam and gas turbine propulsion. In 1979–80 she was fitted as a flagship, a role she fulfilled in the South Atlantic after the Falklands War. At least as expensive to run as the remaining *County* class and comparatively poorly armed, her future has been in doubt.

## Guided Missile Destroyers

There are two classes described as destroyers, the fourteen Type 42 *Sheffields* and the Type 22 *Broadswords*. The *Sheffields* and the *Amazons* were the first classes to be wholly gas turbine powered. They have two Rolls Royce Tynes of 8,500 shaft horsepower for cruising and two Olympuses of 56,000 shaft horsepower for emergencies. They are a little bigger than the frigates, but in performance and armament are very similar, and it was in recognition of this that the last four of the class were stretched 42 feet, with an increase in beam of 2 feet. This was to enable them to carry an additional arms system. At present they have a quick firing 4·5-inch gun forward, two 20-millimetre Oerlikons, a Sea Dart missile launcher and a Lynx helicopter to carry anti-submarine torpedoes. In the Falklands War the *Sheffield* demonstrated how vulnerable the use of aluminium for their topsides has made these ships. The Exocet missile that hit her on 4 May 1982 did not even go off on impact, but the rocket's heat ignited the aluminium and the plastic lagging causing a lethal fire that gutted her and led to her foundering six days later.

The other class, the eight *Broadswords*, only half of which have completed at the time of writing, are the first British destroyers to have no major gun armament. Instead they carry Exocet forward. Like the *Sheffields* the last four ships have been stretched 41 feet but without any addition to their beam. They were the first class to be armed with the Seawolf anti-aircraft missile launcher, which *Broadsword* herself used with the Task Force off the Falklands. They also carry two Lynx helicopters armed with homing torpedoes. Their weaponry is monitored by the sophisticated Ferranti CAA IS system. They are large roomy ships, with a capacity to carry a contingent of Royal Marines.

Helicopter cruisers

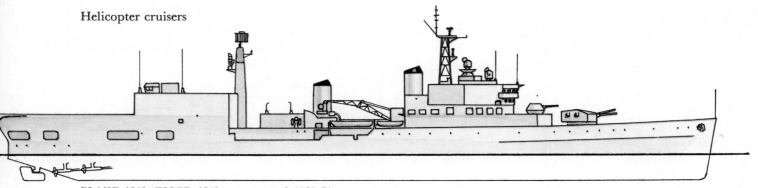

BLAKE 1945, TIGER 1945, as converted 1969–71
9,500 *tons* 566½' (*o*/*a*) ×64'×23'. Guns 2 6" *D.P.*, 2 3" *D.P.*, 2 *quadruple Seacat missile launchers*, 4 *Sea King anti-submarine helicopters*. Main
armour 3" *belt*, 3" *to* 1" *turret*, 2" *deck*. Engines and speed *Turbines*; 80,000 *h.p.*; 31½ *knots*.

Type 42 SHEFFIELD guided missile destroyers

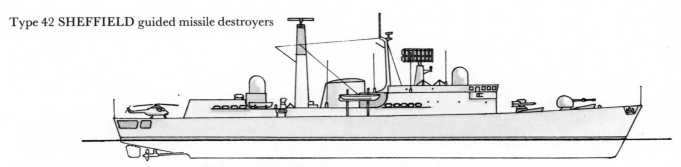

BIRMINGHAM 1973, CARDIFF 1974, COVENTRY 1974, EXETER 1978, GLASGOW 1976, LIVERPOOL 1980, NEWCASTLE 1975,
NOTTINGHAM 1980, SHEFFIELD 1971, SOUTHAMPTON 1979
3,500 *tons* 412' (*o*/*a*) × 47' × 19'. Guns 1 4·5" *rapid firing*, 2 20-mm *Oerlikons*, 1 *twin Sea Dart missile launcher*. 1 *anti-submarine Lynx helicopter*. Engines
and speed 2 *Rolls Royce Olympus gas turbines* 56,000 *h.p.*; 2 *Rolls Royce Tyne gas turbines* 8,500 *h.p.*; 29 *knots* (*Olympus*), 18 *knots* (*Tyne*). Remarks
Sheffield *lost off the Falklands* 10 *May* 1982, *and* Coventry *on May* 25. *Replacements ordered*.

Stretched Type 42 SHEFFIELDS
EDINBURGH 1982, GLOUCESTER 1982, MANCHESTER 1980, YORK 1982
463' (*o*/*a*) × 49' × 19·9'. *All lengthened* 42' *with* 2' *extra to the beam*.

Type 22 BROADSWORD Class missile destroyers

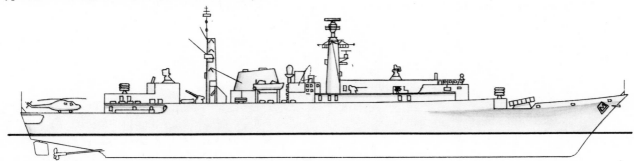

BATTLEAXE 1977, BRAZEN 1980, BRILLIANT 1978, BROADSWORD 1976
4,000 *tons full load* 430' (*o*/*a*) × 48·5' × 19·9'. Guns 2 40-mm *Bofors*, 4 *Exocet single cell ship to ship missile launcher*. 2 *Sea Wolf anti-aircraft missile launchers*.
2 *anti-submarine Lynx helicopters*. Engines and speed 2 *Rolls Royce Olympus gas turbines* 56,000 *h.p.*, 2 *Rolls Royce gas turbines* 8,500 *h.p.*; 30 *knots*.
(*Olympus*), 18 *knots* (*Tyne*). Remarks Brilliant *carries Mark* 32 *torpedoes*. Broadsword *and* Brilliant *served with the Falklands Task Force*.

Stretched Type 22 BROADSWORDS
BEAVER 1982, BOXER 1981, BRAVE, LONDON.
471' (*o*/*a*) × 48·5' × 19·9'. *The last four ships of the class lengthened* 41', *as shown above*.

# GUIDED MISSILE DESTROYERS and FRIGATES

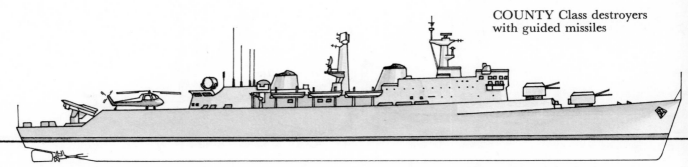

COUNTY Class destroyers
with guided missiles

ANTRIM 1967, DEVONSHIRE 1960, FIFE 1964, GLAMORGAN 1964, HAMPSHIRE 1961, KENT 1961, LONDON 1961,
NORFOLK 1967
5,440 *tons* 520½' (*o/a*) × 54' × 20'. Guns 4 4·5" *D.P.*, 2 20-*mm. A.A.*, 1 *twin Seaslug missile launcher*, 2 *quadruple Seacat missile launchers*,
2 *sextuple* 3" *Mk 4 launchers*, 1 *anti-submarine helicopter*. Engines and speed *Steam turbines:* 30,000 *h.p.; gas turbines:* 30,000 *h.p.;* 32½ *knots.*
Remarks *In* 1983 *only* Antrim, Glamorgan *and* Fife *were still in service. All have B turret replaced by 4 Exocet single cell ship to ship missile launchers.*
Glamorgan *damaged by an unexploded Exocet missile during the Falklands War.*

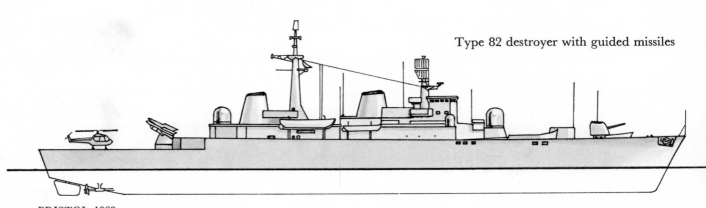

Type 82 destroyer with guided missiles

BRISTOL 1969
5,650 *tons* 507' (*o/a*) × 55' × 22½'. Guns 1 4·5" *D.P.*, 2 40-*mm. A.A.*, 1 *Sea Dart twin missile launcher*, 1 *Ikara single missile launcher*,
1 *Limbo depth charge mortar*. Engines and speed *Steam turbines:* 30,000 *h.p.; gas turbines:* 30,000 *h.p.;* 30 *knots.*

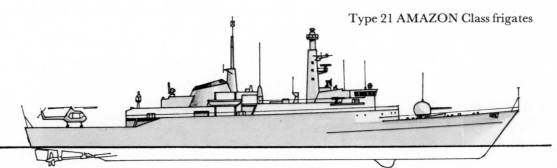

Type 21 AMAZON Class frigates

ACTIVE 1972, ALACRITY 1974, AMAZON 1971, AMBUSCADE 1973, ANTELOPE 1972, ARDENT 1975, ARROW 1974, AVENGER
1975
3,250 *tons full load* 384' (*o/a*) × 41.7' × 19·5'. Guns 1 4·5" *quick firing*, 2 20-*mm Oerlikons*, 4 *Exocet single cell ship to ship missile launchers*, 1 *quadruple Seacat anti-aircraft missile launcher*. 1 *Lynx anti-submarine helicopter*. Engines and speed 2 *Rolls Royce Olympus gas turbines* 56,000 *h.p.*, 2 *Rolls Royce Tyne gas turbines* 8,500 *h.p.;* 30 *knots* (*Olympus*), 18 *knots* (*Tyne*). Remarks Ardent *sunk by Argentine aircraft* 21 *May* 1982, Antelope *sunk by aircraft* 24 *May* 1982.

# 30

# The Air Arm of the Navy

Having for centuries moved about on the waters, the navy of the first decade of the twentieth century was forced to consider craft which moved under them and over them. Both pressures initially came from America where the Holland-type submarine and the Wright brothers' aeroplane were the first practical machines in their respective fields. The Admiralty was not over-eager to rush into the air, and politely declined the Wright brothers' offer in 1907 to sell the Royal Navy all their patents. They would not have been much of a bargain anyway, as by this time the French were the leaders in the technique of heavier-than-air machines, and Count Zeppelin in the lighter-than-air rigid-framed dirigible balloon.

The possibilities of such airships fitted with radio as spotters for the fleet was attractive, and in 1909 an order for one was placed. The result was a fine craft over 500 feet long, which unfortunately never actually flew. It broke its back when caught in a cross wind while being taken out of its shed after some modifications and was a write-off. The Admiralty lost interest in airships after this until the war, when there was a revival concentrated on the blimp type. These were gas envelopes without any rigid structure, from which hung a gondola with an engine or engines. These were, of course, much smaller than the rigid type, and during the war were operated by naval crews with safety and success. Another use for the balloon was the captive type attached to the sterns of the larger units of the fleet. These were winched up with an observer aboard with a telephone, who could see much further than the captain on the bridge. By late 1916 a few rigid airships were projected, and after the German Zeppelin L33 was forced down, almost undamaged, there was a brief return of interest in the rigid type of airship, and R33 and R34 built on her lines for the Admiralty resulted. R34 achieved immortality by flying the Atlantic both ways in 1919, the first machine to do so. This was the end of the Royal Navy's interest in airships. In the Second World War the balloon was used again from ships in convoy, but as a barrage of cables against low-flying enemy aircraft. The most enduring naval interest in the airship was exhibited by the US Navy – which continued to fly them for reconnaissance and anti-submarine patrol purposes up to the 1960s.

Before further pursuing this subject, a word about the flying boats that shared with the blimp the ability to cruise aloft with a fair range. They had beautifully built wooden hulls created by the men who before the war built yachts. Like all aircraft of that day they had low wing loadings and it was not unknown on stormy days for them to fly at their moorings like kites. Once in a storm in the Isles of Scilly, the leading boat snapped its mooring while flying in this fashion and fell back on the next, and the next, so that shortly there were five of them wrecked on Tresco's beaches.

Like these the operating of airships was exclusively from fixed bases, and so does not greatly concern this book, though blimps did operate from the *Furious*. It is the development of the heavier-than-air machine that does concern us, for almost from the first it was looking for a place to rest its foot aboard ship. The earliest flights were made in the spirit of pure experiment, as when Lieutenant Samson took off in a Short S27 from a ramp on the fore-deck of the battleship *Africa* in January 1912. The *Africa* had been at anchor, but in the same year the same feat was performed on the *Hibernia* while that vessel was doing 10 knots.

The war brought a pause to this type of launching, but in 1911 a plane with floats, this time an Avro, successfully took off from the water. Early experience with sea-going aircraft carriers was therefore concentrated on seaplane carriers such as the *Pegasus*. These vessels were conversions of merchant ships or cruisers and their essential fittings were a hangar and a crane to lift the seaplanes out and in. The cruiser *Hermes* was fitted with a flying-off deck forward, but was torpedoed too early in the war to be evaluated. More interesting was the converted Cunarder *Campania*. She was fitted with a flight-deck 200 feet long for launching seaplanes from trolleys. She operated with the fleet, and should have been at Jutland, but failed to read the order to sail in time. She was sunk in collision in 1918.

Experiments had been made with land aircraft on ships and it was found that scouts could successfully take off from platforms on the turrets of the battle-cruisers. The first trial was from B turret of the *Repulse*, and later in 1917–18 all the battle-cruisers and some of the battleships carried aircraft in this manner. As the planes could not land again, they had to ditch in the sea, which meant ships being stopped to pick them up, a dangerous proceeding in wartime.

The appearance of the first torpedo aircraft in 1915, the Short Type 184, encouraged the construction of a real carrier with a flight-deck and hangar below. A half-completed liner building for an Italian firm was taken over and the result was the *Argus*. She did not complete until September 1918, just before the Armistice, but she was the first true carrier ever built. Contemporary with her were the partially converted battle-cruiser *Furious* and the cruiser *Vindictive*. Initially the former was fitted only with a flight-deck over the fore-deck. The original bridge and funnel remained, making an approach to land hazardous, yet in August 1917 a Sopwith Pup was sideslipped past this obstruction and the first deck landing was made. In a second attempt the machine went over the side and the pilot was killed. The *Furious* was then fitted with a flying deck aft of the funnel, but the eddies caused by the central superstructure made landing there risky also, so in 1921 she was taken in hand for a complete conversion into a fleet aircraft carrier. When she was nearing completion her sisters *Courageous* and *Glorious* were docked for similar treatment and by 1930 all three were in service. They were very similar really, but the fact that the *Furious* had no side island, venting her smoke through her side of deck, made her look very different. In the Second World War she was given a small side island. These were three big, very fast carriers.

*Courageous* was sunk by torpedoes from a *U*-boat a fortnight after the beginning of the

Light battle-cruiser and aircraft carrier

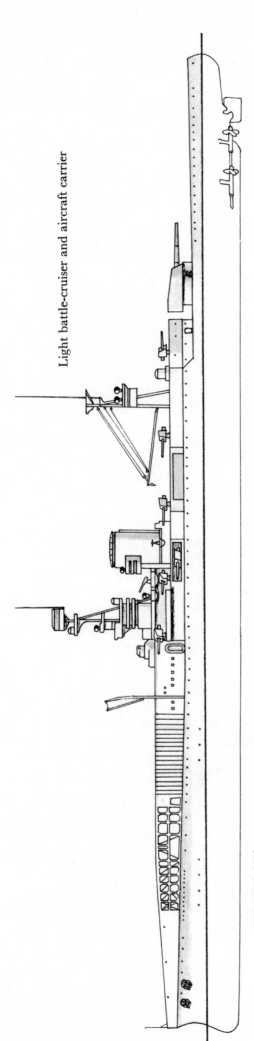

FURIOUS 1916
19,513 tons 786½' (o/a) ×88'×19¾'. Guns 1 18", 11 5·5", 2 3" A.A., 4 3-pdrs. (saluting). Torpedo tubes 6 21" (2 submerged). Main armour 3" to 1" belt to 3" to 2" bulkheads, 7" to 4" barbette with a 13" to 4½" turret, 10" conning tower, 3" to 1" decks. Engines and speed Turbines; 94,000 h.p.; 31½ knots. Remarks Originally designed as a third Glorious, but to mount two 18" guns instead of four 15". Her aircraft-carrying role was purely experimental. Drawing represents appearance in 1917.

Fleet aircraft carrier

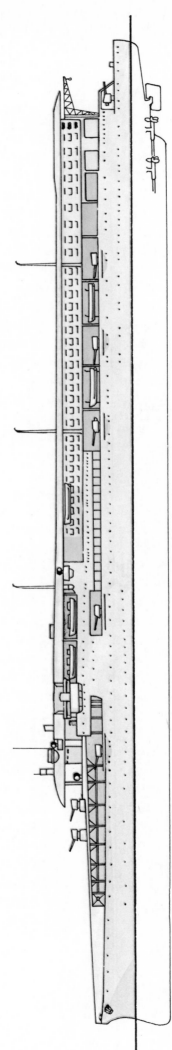

FURIOUS 1916, ex-light battle-cruiser
22,450 tons 786¼' (o/a) ×100' (flight deck) ×21¾'. Guns 10 5·5", 6 4" A.A. (in 1925); 12 4" A.A. (in 1939). Aircraft 35. Engines and speed Turbines; 90,000 h.p.; 31 knots. Remarks Drawing represents appearance in 1925.

## Aircraft carrier

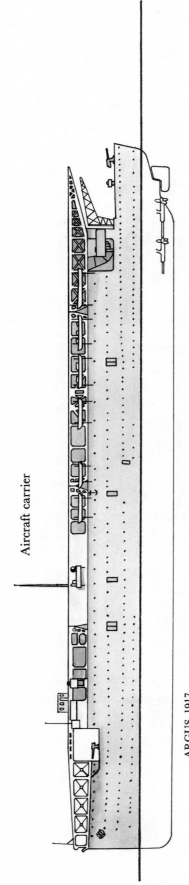

ARGUS 1917
14,000 *tons* 560' (*o/a*) × 68' × 21'. Guns 6 4" (*removed* 1937; *four* 4" *D.P. installed during the Second World War, plus lighter A.A. guns*). Aircraft 20 *in her early days.* Engines and speed *Turbines*; 20,000 *h.p.*; 20 *knots.* Remarks *Originally converted from a half-built liner in the First World War. Bulges added* 1925–6, *converted to the handling and maintenance of radio-controlled target aircraft in* 1937. *In wartime mainly used as a ferrying carrier.*

## Fleet aircraft carrier

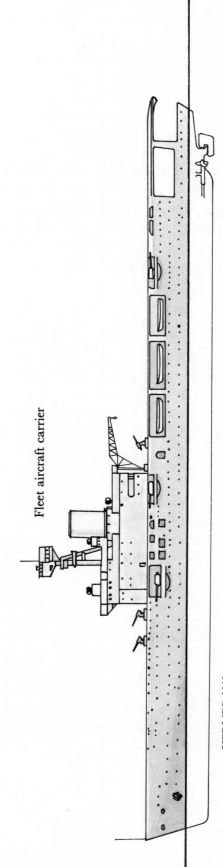

HERMES 1919
10,850 *tons* 598' (*o/a*) × 90' (*flight-deck*) × 18¾'. Guns 6 5·5", 3 4" *A.A.* Aircraft *Initially* 20, *later* 15. Engines and speed *Turbines*; 40,000 *h.p.*; 25 *knots.* Remarks *First vessel designed as an aircraft carrier.*

war in September 1939. She had been on anti-submarine patrol when it happened and her loss ended this type of operation, until later in the war when it was revived with 'Woolworth' carriers and frigates. *Glorious* also was lost early on, caught by the German battle-cruisers *Scharnhorst* and *Gneisenau* while returning home from evacuation of Norway in June 1940. The *Furious* survived the war, the only prewar fleet carrier to do so. The *Argus*, which was used for ferrying aircraft and as an escort carrier, also came through. The fifth conversion was a half-built battleship, the sister of the *Canada*, which had also been building for the Chileans. Not as big and not as fast as the *Furious*, she was nevertheless satisfactory for operating the prewar aircraft. In 1942 the *Eagle* was one of three carriers which formed part of a convoy to get supplies through to besieged Malta. They met furious opposition from the German air force and *Eagle* was lost to a U-boat. The sixth and last of the first generation of carriers was the little *Hermes*. Under 11,000 tons, she was designed from the start as a carrier, the first such ship in the world. She was launched in 1919 and completed in 1923. During the Second World War, while operating with the Eastern Fleet she was sunk by Japanese naval aircraft off Ceylon.

These six ships were the first generation of carriers, a field in which Britain led. By 1930 the Americans had only two fleet carriers, *Lexington* and *Saratoga*, though very large ones, nearly 900 feet long. Again these were conversions from projected battle-cruisers. They were unique for carriers, in that they mounted eight 8-inch guns in four turrets fore and aft of the island.

## Ark Royal

The navy's first aircraft carrier to be launched as such was a cargo vessel taken over on the stocks and converted into a seaplane carrier called the *Ark Royal* in 1914. In 1935, a new *Ark Royal* was to be built, the harbinger of a new generation of carriers to fight the Second World War.

Like the *Hermes*, *Ark Royal* was built as a carrier and looked all of a piece. She established the carrier look, with her long flight-deck jutting squarely over bow and stern, and she was a good deal more commodious than older carriers of the same tonnage, with aircraft hangars on two decks with three lifts. Her sixteen 4·5-inch dual-purpose guns were carried in twin turrets high up beside the flight-deck, which gave them a better field of fire than in the older carriers which carried theirs lower down their sides.

When war was declared the *Ark Royal* was the only one of the new generation in service and soon became famous for being sunk by German propaganda, and then bobbing up again. In the first weeks of the war she and the battle-cruiser *Renown* were hunting for the *Admiral Graf Spee* when the news came that she had been found by Harwood's cruisers and driven into Montevideo. It was the threat of this powerful reinforcement, the imminence of which was cleverly exaggerated by the British Ambassador Sir Eugene Millington-Drake, through the German-owned telephone system, that prompted the German cruiser to be scuttled. The *Ark Royal*'s great service was her contribution to the sinking of the *Bismarck* in May 1941. This battleship, which had just inflicted a grievous hurt to the Royal Navy by sinking the *Hood* and badly damaging the *Prince of Wales*, was fleeing towards Brest with no hope of being caught by the *King George V* and the *Rodney* unless she could be slowed down. Swordfish from *Ark Royal*, launched in appalling weather, did better. One of their torpedoes jammed the *Bismarck*'s steering gear, so that the British battleships caught her up with ease and destroyed her. The famous *Ark*'s triumph was short-lived. On 13 November she was torpedoed off Gibraltar and sank fourteen hours later. That she was not saved has been an often-quoted case of bad damage control.

### *Illustrious* and *Indefatigable* classes

The first of the *Illustrious* class began to join the fleet in 1940. They were very similar to the *Ark Royal* but with one deck less, which made them better looking. The *Illustrious* herself was the first to join, and in November 1940 took part in the famous Taranto raid, steaming into the Ionian Sea and sending her aircraft to torpedo the Italian ships in their base. Three battleships and a cruiser were badly damaged. *Illustrious* is best remembered for her service in the Mediterranean, especially the desperate Malta convoys, but later in the war she played a major role against the Japanese in the far East, as did her sisters, *Victorious* and *Formidable*. The *Indomitable*, though very similar, had a two-deck hangar like *Ark Royal*. *Victorious* had joined in time to take part in sinking the *Bismarck*, slowing her with a torpedo hit from one of her Swordfish. It is interesting to reflect that had not the *Indomitable* gone aground while working up off Jamaica in 1941 and been held up by repairs she would have joined the *Prince of Wales* and *Repulse* on their fatal mission in the defence of Malaya. The two ships (see pages 176, 185) were sunk for lack of air cover, but whether the *Indomitable*'s aircraft could have been enough to thwart the Japanese aircraft at that time of the war, when the quality of their crews was at its peak, seems doubtful, and it is more likely that she too would have been destroyed.

The two ships that followed, *Indefatigable* and *Implacable*, were similar but with four screws instead of three. *Indefatigable* was one of the carriers involved in the attacks on the battleship *Tirpitz* with Barracuda dive bombers. She later served in the Far East.

Although the toll on the prewar carriers almost amounted to annihilation, the war spared all the later carriers, though some experienced furious attacks. By 1949, when the battleships had more or less retired from the scene, the big fleet carrier was king, but was built only for aircraft weights of wartime vintage, and some of these, such as the American Corsairs, were heavy enough. For them to have flown the new generation of jet planes would have involved costly rebuilding. It was not thought worth while to enter into a general rebuilding of these hard-worked ships, and the navy was to rely on its two new large carriers and light-fleet carriers whose completion had been held up when they were half built or launched, and which were now lying around the ports awaiting some decision or other. Only one of the old fleet carriers, the *Victorious*, was given the treatment. Dismantled in Portsmouth dockyard almost to her keel, with only her engines remaining, she was rebuilt from there to emerge in 1958 with a fully angled deck, steam catapults and the finest radar in the world. The work of conversion took eight years and cost triple the estimate. She served successfully until finally paid off in 1968.

### The Light-Fleet Carriers

The pressing wartime need for more carriers resulted in a crash building programme of what came to be known as 'light-fleet carriers'. These ships fall into two main classes:

Fleet aircraft carrier

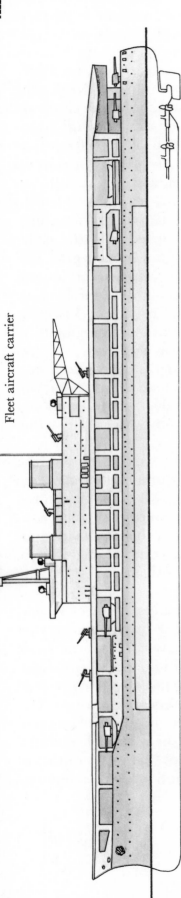

**EAGLE 1918**
22,600 tons 667' (o/a) × 100' (flight-deck) × 24'. Guns 9 6", 5 4" A.A. Aircraft 21. Engines and speed Turbines; 50,000 h.p.; 24 knots. Remarks Laid down as a Chilean battleship, sister to the Canada, purchased 1917. Trial partial conversion in 1920, completed 1924.

Fleet aircraft carriers

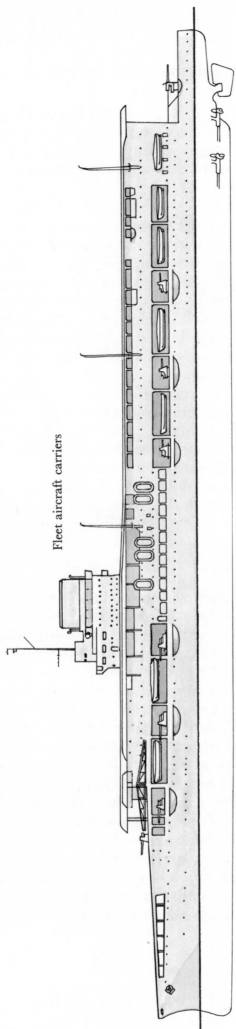

**COURAGEOUS and GLORIOUS**, both 1916, ex-light battle-cruisers
22,000 tons 786¼' (o/a) × 100' (flight-deck) × 22'. Guns 16 4·7" D.P., 4 3-pdrs. (saluting). Aircraft 48. Engines and speed Turbines; 90,000 h.p.; 30½ knots.

Fleet aircraft carrier

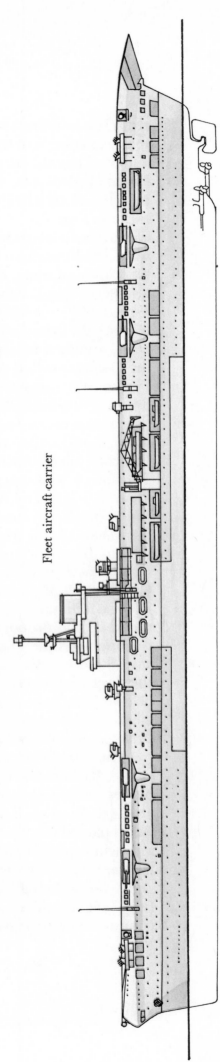

**ARK ROYAL 1937**
22,000 tons 800' (o/a) × 94' × 23'. Guns 16 4·5" D.P., 4 3-pdrs. (saluting), 6 multiple pom-poms. Aircraft 72. Main armour 4½" belt, 3" to 2½" decks. Engines and speed Turbines; 102,000 h.p.; 30 knots.

the 14,000-tonners begun in 1942–3 and the larger 18,000-tonners, begun in 1944. As many as sixteen of the smaller class were launched, but only two of them before the war ended. That this might happen was appreciated by their designers, as their hulls up to the main-deck were built to Lloyd's specifications in case they might be converted into merchantmen after the war. This never happened to any of them, perhaps because there was an abundance of merchant shipping and the cost of conversion was too much. Certainly there were many more of them than the navy needed, and their service life was to be limited by the growth in the size and weight of aircraft which their decks could take, though some, the *Glory*, *Ocean* and *Theseus*, were strengthened to withstand 8 tons and served in the Korean War. They were broken up at the end of the fifties. The *Perseus* and *Pioneer* completed as aircraft maintenance ships. The *Pioneer* was broken up in 1954, but the *Perseus*, which had been used for trials with the new steam catapult in 1951, and as a transport to the Far East, lasted until 1958. The *Magnificent* was lent to the Canadians and returned when they took delivery of the *Powerful* which they called *Bonaventure*; she was broken up in 1965. The *Triumph* was converted into the cadet training ship and relieved the cruiser *Devonshire* in 1953. She was again transformed, this time into a heavy-repair ship, commissioning in 1965. The *Venerable* was sold to Holland in 1948 and called the *Karel Doorman*. This was an ironic choice for the Dutch, since Duncan's flagship when he defeated the Dutch at Camperdown was called the *Venerable*. The *Colossus* was lent to the French after the war as the *Arromanches* and finally bought by them in 1951. The *Hercules*, completed for India as the *Vikrant*, was delivered in 1961. The *Terrible* was handed over to the Royal Australian Navy in 1948 as the *Sydney*, and the *Majestic* as the *Melbourne* in 1955. The *Vengeance*, having been on loan to Australia, was sold to Brazil in 1956 as the *Minas Gerais*, and the *Warrior* to the Argentine as the *Independencia* in 1958 (scrapped 1971). The *Karel Doorman* is also now Argentine as the *Veinticinco De Mayo*.

It is difficult to understand what any nation wants with a one-carrier navy. Ships spend a good proportion of their time in refit, so that it would be quite likely that when the enemy came knocking, the navy's largest unit would be uselessly in dock. In any case three was the minimum operational force to give constant collective air cover, in the days when it mattered. Perhaps strangest of all was the career of the *Leviathan*. Built on the Tyne, she was towed round to Portsmouth dockyard for completion in 1946. There she lay with a maintenance crew for twenty-two years until towed off to the breakers in 1968, a Queen's bad bargain if ever there was one.

The second larger class of light-fleet carrier consisted of four ships, three of which, *Albion*, *Bulwark* and *Centaur*, completed in the early 1950s, were strong enough to carry jet planes such as Venoms and Sea Vixens. They and the two big new carriers, the *Eagle* and *Ark Royal* took over from the old fleet carriers during the middle fifties; *Ark Royal* had a partially angled deck. Between 1959 and 1962, *Albion* and *Bulwark* were converted into what were called 'commando carriers', that is, full of helicopters and marines. The *Centaur* was further refitted for continued work as a fleet carrier, until she was broken up in 1972. The fourth ship, the *Hermes*, was not launched until 1953 and she was finished with a fully angled deck and strengthened for jet aircraft. Even so, within months of commissioning, she was back in dockyard hands for strengthening, and further strengthen-

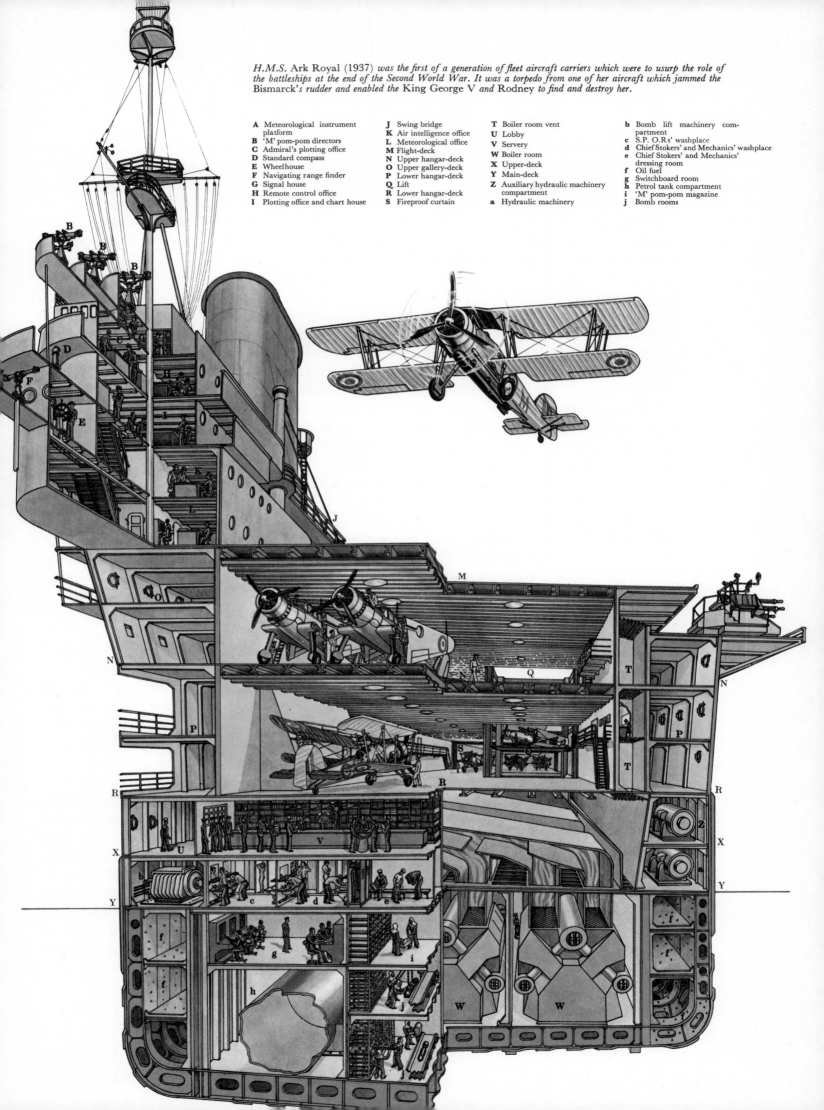

*H.M.S.* Ark Royal (1937) *was the first of a generation of fleet aircraft carriers which were to usurp the role of the battleships at the end of the Second World War. It was a torpedo from one of her aircraft which jammed the* Bismarck*'s rudder and enabled the* King George V *and* Rodney *to find and destroy her.*

A Meteorological instrument platform
B 'M' pom-pom directors
C Admiral's plotting office
D Standard compass
E Wheelhouse
F Navigating range finder
G Signal house
H Remote control office
I Plotting office and chart house

J Swing bridge
K Air intelligence office
L Meteorological office
M Flight-deck
N Upper hangar-deck
O Upper gallery-deck
P Lower hangar-deck
Q Lift
R Lower hangar-deck
S Fireproof curtain

T Boiler room vent
U Lobby
V Servery
W Boiler room
X Upper-deck
Y Main-deck
Z Auxiliary hydraulic machinery compartment
a Hydraulic machinery

b Bomb lift machinery compartment
c S.P. O.Rs' washplace
d Chief Stokers' and Mechanics' washplace
e Chief Stokers' and Mechanics' dressing room
f Oil fuel
g Switchboard room
h Petrol tank compartment
i 'M' pom-pom magazine
j Bomb rooms

ing has had to take place since.

In 1971 she was taken in hand for conversion to a commando carrier like the *Albion* and *Bulwark*, both of which have by now been scrapped. Then in 1977 she was further modified to carry Sea Harrier jump jet aircraft and given the bulbous ski jump on her bow. She continued to carry Sea King helicopters as well, and it was in this role that she became flagship of the Task Force sent to the Falkland Islands in 1982. With the completion of the third *Invincible* it seems likely that she will be scrapped.

## War Emergency Escort Carriers

Although the idea of a submarine hunter group centred on a carrier had to be dropped very early in the war following the torpedoing of *Courageous*, it was revived with great success for convoy protection by including a small 'Woolworth' carrier in the escort. She only carried about half a dozen aircraft: Swordfish for anti-submarine work, and fighters such as Sea Hurricanes to fend off the German long-range Condors, or other aircraft. Air cover for a convoy made life particularly difficult for the *U*-boats which had to spend half their time on the surface recharging their batteries. Without air cover they had been able to follow the convoy's smoke by day and close in for the kill at night. With aircraft overhead guiding in destroyers and sloops, this was no longer possible, not to mention the *U*-boats the Swordfish sank with their own bombs and depth-charges.

All these ships had merchant-type hulls of about 12,000 tons and were either built or converted into carriers. Although the first British ones appeared in 1941, they did not join the fleet in any numbers until 1942–3 and then they were mostly American lend-lease ships. The navy acquired forty-three of them and lost five in action. In addition to these there were also ships that traded under the red ensign with a flight-deck and hangar which were also used for escort purposes; these were known as MAC ships.

## The *Eagle* and *Ark Royal*

In addition to the light-fleet carriers building during the war, seven large fleet carriers were also ordered. The war ending, the three of the larger type and two of the other four were cancelled. The two remaining, *Eagle* and *Ark Royal*, were completed in 1951 and 1955 respectively. They were the last and biggest carriers to be built for the navy, and at 53,000 tons full load they were the heaviest ships ever to serve. They were basically sisters but because of the differences in their dates of completion, the *Ark Royal* incorporated a number of postwar British inventions, being the first to have the new steam catapults, improved arrester gear and deck landing aids based on light beams. She was one of the first British carriers to have an angled flight-deck, though only partially angled, and a side lift. This angled deck was a British idea already fully exploited by the Americans. In 1959, the *Eagle* was docked for modernization which included a fully angled deck, new deck armour, and a new and larger island and radar system. She completed in 1964. The main virtue of the angled deck was that if a returning aircraft failed to catch an arrester wire when landing, it could rev up and fly off the angle to go round again without risk. Before the introduction of the angled deck, an aircraft missing the wires was obliged to crash into a barrier erected across the deck, behind which were parked aircraft which had landed earlier. A lot of aircraft were damaged this way. Another advantage was that the

ILLUSTRIOUS Class fleet aircraft carrier

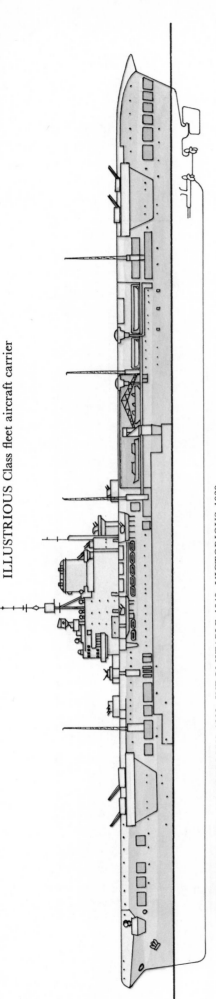

FORMIDABLE 1939, ILLUSTRIOUS 1939, INDOMITABLE 1940, VICTORIOUS 1939
23,000 *tons* 753′ (*o/a approx.*) × 95′×24′. Guns 16 4·5″ *D.P. Aircraft About* 54. Main armour 4½″ *sides and hangar sides*, 3″ *flight-deck*, 2½″ *hangar-deck.*
*Engines and speed Turbines; triple screw;* 110,000 *h.p.*; 31 *knots.* Remarks *Victorious was almost entirely rebuilt in the* 1950s, *see page* 266. Indomitable *had an additional half hangar.*

Fleet aircraft carriers

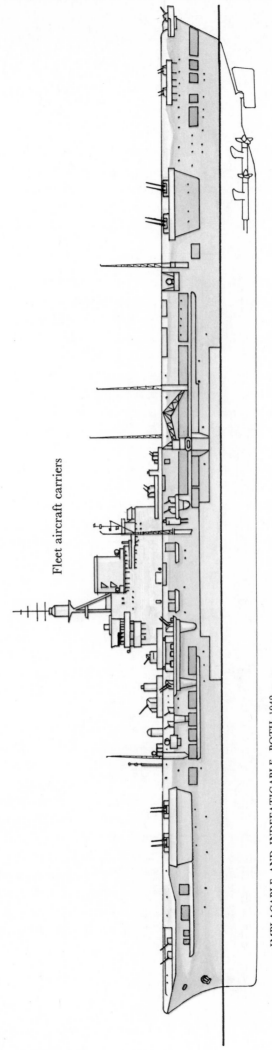

IMPLACABLE AND INDEFATIGABLE, BOTH 1942
26,000 *tons* 766′ (*o/a*) × 95¾′ × 26′. Guns 16 4.5″ *D.P. Aircraft About* 72. Main armour *As ILLUSTRIOUS Class except* 1½″ *hangar sides. Engines and speed Turbines;*
*four screws;* 148,000 *h.p.*; 32 *knots.*

## COLOSSUS and MAJESTIC Classes light-fleet aircraft carriers

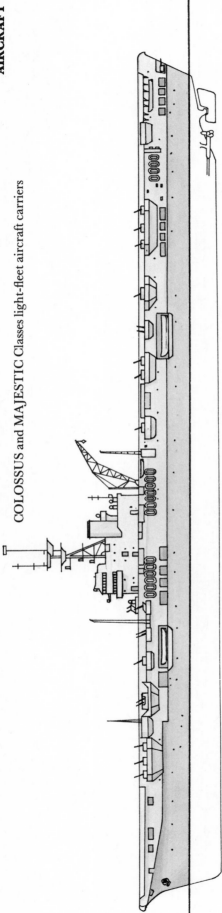

COLOSSUS 1943, GLORY 1943, LEVIATHAN 1945, MAGNIFICENT 1944, OCEAN 1944, PERSEUS 1944, PIONEER 1944, THESEUS 1944, TRIUMPH 1944, VENERABLE 1943, VENGEANCE 1944, WARRIOR 1944
13,190 *to* 14,000 *tons* 695′ (*o*/*a*) × 80¼′ × 18¼′ *to* 23′. Guns 24 2-*pdrs. pom-poms and lighter A.A. Aircraft About* 40. Engines and speed *Geared turbines;* 42,000 *h.p.;* 25 *knots.* Remarks *Several of this class lent, sold or completed for other navies.* Perseus *and* Pioneer *completed as maintenance and transport ships,* Leviathan *never served, see page 268.* Majestic *completed as* H.M.A.S. Melbourne, Powerful *as* H.M.C.S. Bonaventure, Terrible *as* H.M.A.S. Sydney, *and* Hercules *as* I.N.S. Vikrant.

Escort aircraft carriers

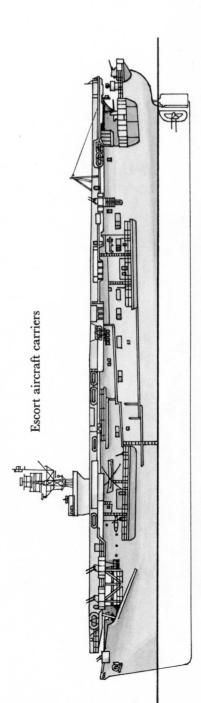

British built ACTIVITY 1942, CAMPANIA 1943, VINDEX 1943, NAIRANA 1943
ACTIVITY 11,800 *tons;* CAMPANIA 12,450 *tons;* VINDEX 13,455 *tons;* NAIRANA 14,050 *tons.* Guns 2 4″ *A.A., and numerous lighter A.A. guns.* Aircraft 15. Engines and speed *Diesel, twin screwed;* 17 *knots.*

American built ARCHER *Class* (8,200 *tons*) ARCHER, AVENGER, BITER, DASHER, all 1939–41
ATTACKER *Class* (11,450 *tons*) ATTACKER, BATTLER, CHASER, FENCER, PURSUER, STALKER, STRIKER, TRAILER, all 1941-2
RULER *Class* (11,420 *tons*) ARBITER, AMEER, ATHELING, BEGUM, EMPEROR, EMPRESS, KHEDIVE, NABOB, PATROLLER, PREMIER, PUNCHER, QUEEN, RAJAH, RANEE, RAVAGER, REAPER, RULER, SEARCHER, SHAH, SLINGER, SMITER, SPEAKER, THANE, TRACKER, TROUNCER, TRUMPETER, all 1942-3, built in the U.S.A.
Guns 2 4″ *A.A. and numerous lighter A.A. guns.* Aircraft ARCHER *and* ATTACKER *Classes* 15, RULER *Class* 24. Engines and speed ARCHER *Class diesel, single screw;* 17 *knots.* ATTACKER *and* RULER *Classes turbines;* 17 *knots.* Remarks *The* Archers *were merchant ship conversions and only had a half-deck hangar.*

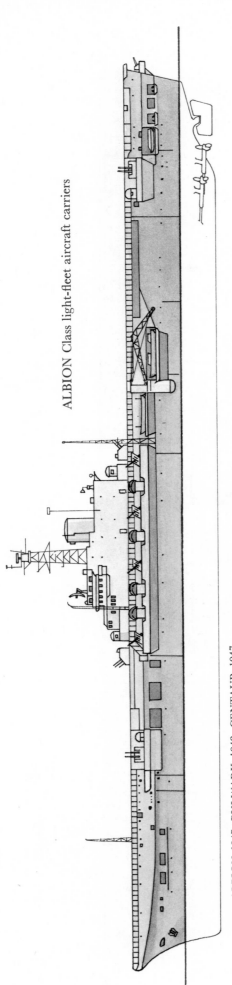

ALBION Class light-fleet aircraft carriers

ALBION 1947, BULWARK 1948, CENTAUR 1947
22,000 *tons* 736½′ (o/a) × 123′ (*flight-deck*) × 27′. Guns 32 40-mm A.A. Aircraft 50. Main armour 1″ *flight-deck*. Engines and speed Turbines; 2 *screws*; 80,000 *h.p.*; 29½ *knots*. Remarks *These ships completed with a modified angled deck. Not large enough or strong enough to operate the bigger, heavier aircraft due in service in the 1960s, Albion 1961–2 and Bulwark 1959–60 were converted into commando carriers with helicopters. Catapults, angled deck and arrester gear were suppressed.*

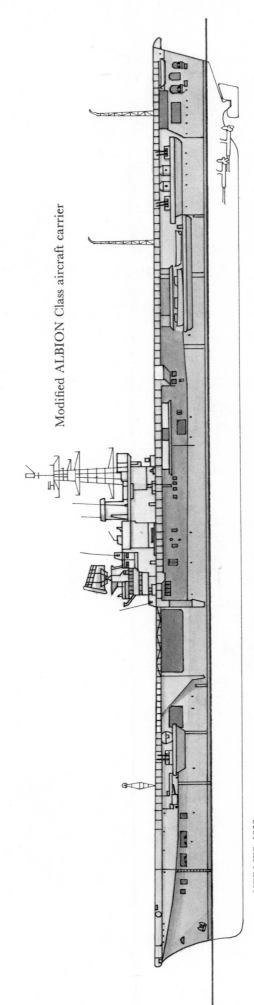

Modified ALBION Class aircraft carrier

HERMES 1953
23,000 *tons* 744½′ (o/a) × 144½′ (*flight-deck*) × 24′. Armament 16 *Seacat missile launchers. Aircraft 20 and 8 helicopters. Main armour 1″ flight-deck.* Engines and speed Turbines; 80,000 *h.p.*; 27½ *knots.* Remarks *Was given a fully angled deck and strengthened to operate Scimitars and Buccaneers. 1971–3 converted to a commando carrier with helicopters. 1980–1 adapted for operating Sea Harriers as well, and given a ski jump forward.*

Fleet aircraft carrier

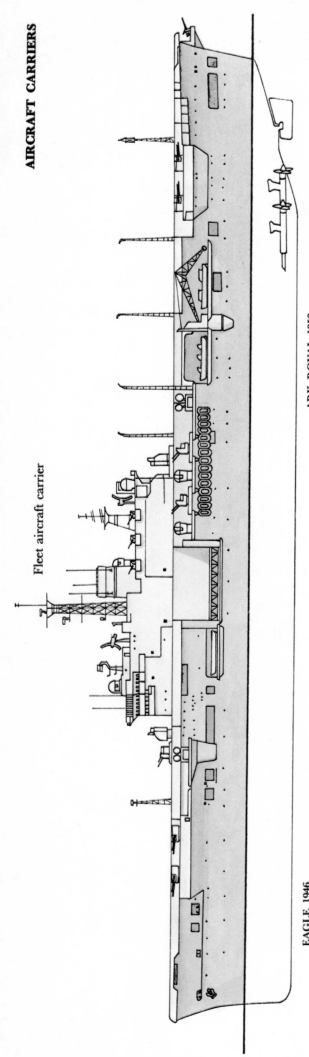

**EAGLE 1946**

36,800 tons 803' (o/a) × 113' × 33¼'. Guns 16 4·5", 58 40-mm.
Bofors A.A., 4 3-pdrs. (saluting). Aircraft Over 80. Main armour
4·5" belt, 4" flight-deck, 2½" hangar-deck, 1½" hangar sides.
Engines and speed Turbines; 152,000 h.p.; 31¼ knots. Remarks
She had a big refit from 1959 to 1964, when she was given a fully
angled flight-deck, a new island and steam catapults.

**ARK ROYAL 1950**

36,800 tons 808' (o/a) × 158' (flight-deck) × 33¼'. Guns 16 4·5"
D.P., 34 40-mm. Bofors A.A., 4 3-pdrs. (saluting). Aircraft
Over 80. Main armour 4½" belt and flight-deck, 2½" hangar-
deck, 1½" hangar sides. Engines and speed Turbines; 152,000 h.p.;
31¼ knots. Remarks Laid down as a sister to the Eagle, but
completed with a partially angled deck and a side lift to port, also
steam catapults and a new type of arrester gear. In 1967 she was
taken in hand for a fully angled flight-deck, and strengthened to
operate Phantom aircraft; completed in 1970, the overall dimensions
increased to 845' × 166' × 36', and 43,000 tons.

Fleet aircraft carrier

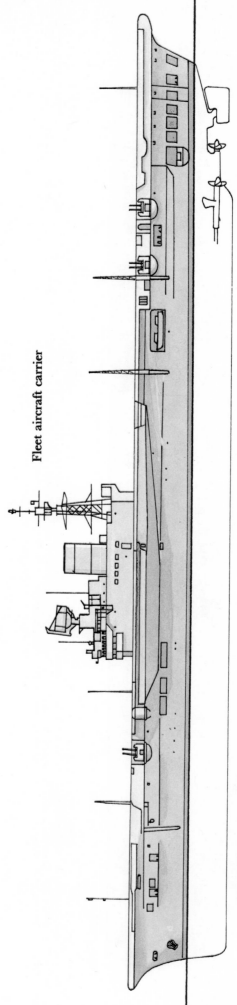

**VICTORIOUS, rebuilt 1950-8**

Remarks The only one of the wartime fleet carriers to be modernized, she was given a fully angled deck and was lengthened by 30'. New boilers and
a new armament of twelve 3" D.P. guns; when she was first commissioned her direction-control radar was the most modern in the world.

INVINCIBLE Class light aircraft carrier

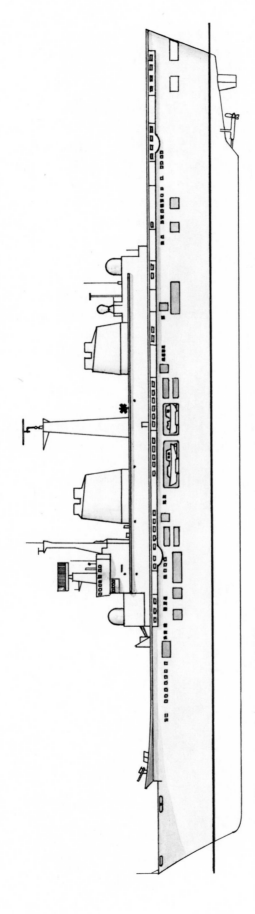

**ARK ROYAL, 1981, ILLUSTRIOUS 1978, INVINCIBLE 1977**
19,500 tons full load 677´ (o/a) × 90´ × 24´. Missiles Twin Sea Dart, plus two Vulcan Phalanx guns in Illustrious and Ark Royal. Aircraft 5 Sea Harrier jump jets, 10 Sea King helicopters. Engines and speed 4 Rolls Royce Olympus gas turbines; 112,000 h.p.; 28 knots. Remarks Invincible commissioned in July 1980 and was on offer to Australia when the Argentines invaded the Falklands; served with the Task Force, and the sale to Australia was rescinded. Illustrious completed in time to relieve the Invincible after the war.

angle provided extra parking space forward which did not impede the continued operation of aircraft. In 1967 the *Ark Royal* also docked for a rebuild and was strengthened to operate Phantom aircraft. She was scrapped in 1982.

## The *Invincible* Class of Light Aircraft Carrier

Originally called through-deck cruisers, these three ships were projected as back up ships for the projected strike carrier CVA OI, along with the four *Bristols*. When the carrier was cancelled three of the four *Bristols* were cancelled also, but the *Invincibles*, seen as replacements for the *Albion*, *Bulwark* and *Hermes*, were not.

Originally in their cruiser role, the *Invincibles* were to have carried Exocet ship to ship missile launchers, but this was changed to Sea Dart anti-aircraft missile launchers. Their role was then seen as being the centre of an anti-submarine squadron, with fifteen Sea King helicopters armed with homing torpedoes. Then in a further change of plan she was adapted to carry five Harrier jump jets and given a ski jump forward.

As the Harriers cut down the number of helicopters that could be carried to the detriment of their anti-submarine role, the wisdom of including them came into question. In fact, when the *Invincible* sailed with the task force to the Falklands, the role of the Harriers equipped with Sidewinder air to air missiles was of critical importance to the defeat of the Argentine air force.

As three aircraft carriers is the minimal number that can expect to give a continuous service, it was astonishing that less than two years after the *Invincible* commissioned the government wanted to sell her to the Australians. Fortunately the lessons of the Falklands War brought reality and sanity on a number of fronts and rescued her from this foolish sale.

They are handsome ships and *Ark Royal*, when she completes, will be able to be identified by her 15 degree ski jump against *Invincible*'s and *Illustrious*'s 7 degrees.

# 31

## Submarines

In spite of the enormous advances in technology in surface ships in the second half of the nineteenth century, the practice of naval warfare was still regarded among the majority of naval officers as subject to honourable rules on a fairly rigid basis. New weapons that demanded a major rethink were naturally unwelcome. The torpedo had had a cool reception in the 1870s, but in the 1890s the idea that this weapon should be launched from a submarine boat without any sort of warning could only be regarded as un-British. Thus it was that, when it was first mooted, the Controller of the Navy, Rear-Admiral 'Tug' Wilson, a future Admiral of the Fleet and First Sea Lord in the Edwardian navy, voiced the general opinion by suggesting that submarine crews should be outlawed, and face possible hanging if captured.

It was the adoption of the submarine by the French that nudged the Admiralty into a similar experiment in 1900, and since there were no British plans for such craft, they had to be purchased from abroad. In the event it was a design of Mr J. P. Holland of America which was chosen and from 1902 to 1903 five boats were constructed.

The irony of the choice of Holland's design was that he was a militant Irish-American Fenian, who developed the submarine with a view to damaging the British. Like so many of his kind he ended by working for them.

These little boats had a crew of two officers and five men, a petrol engine for surface work and a battery-powered one for diving. These gave them 8 knots on the surface and 5 submerged. They had about 4 feet or so of freeboard on the surface and only a little hump of a conning tower. In the original American-built boats, the conning-tower scuttles were the only way the commander could see out without going on deck. In the British boats, a 12-foot periscope was introduced. This did not retract but was either rigged or hinged down along the deck. Any idea of using these boats beyond sheltered waters was out of the question, but they provided useful experience and none was ever lost operationally.

Next came the first British-designed boats, the *A* class, of which thirteen were built. These boats were 100 feet long, with an increased speed of 11 knots on the surface and 7 under water. The last to be built had a heavy-oil engine instead of a petrol one, and all had two torpedo tubes instead of one, as in the American design. A notable feature was the conning tower, enlarged during service.

Holland submarines

No. 1 to No. 5, all 1901–3
No. 1 104 to 122 tons (rest 150 tons submerged)
63½ × 11¾'. Torpedo tubes 1 14" bow. Engines and
speed Petrol, electric; No. 1 160/74 h.p., rest 250/74
h.p.; 8/5 knots.

A Class submarines

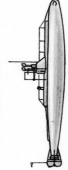

A1 to A13, all 1903–5
A1 to A4 165 to 180 tons 100' × 11½'. Rest
180 to 207 tons 99' × 12¾'. Torpedo tubes
2 18". Engines and speed Petrol, electric; A1 to A4
450/80 h.p.; rest 450/150 h.p.; 11½/7 knots (A13 had
a heavy-oil engine).

B Class submarines

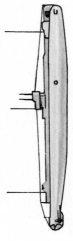

B1 to B11, all 1904–6
280 to 314 tons 135' × 13½'. Torpedo tubes 2 18"
bow. Engines and speed Petrol, electric; 600/190
h.p.; 12–13/7–9 knots.

C Class submarines

C1 to C38, all 1906–10
290 to 320 tons (C19 to C38 321 tons submerged)
143' × 13½'. Torpedo tubes 2 18" bow.
Engines and speed Petrol, electric; 600/300 h.p.;
13–14/8–10 knots.

D Class submarines

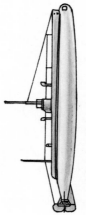

D1 to D8, all 1908–11
D1 550 to 595 tons (rest 604 to 620 tons submerged)
162' × 20½'. Guns 1 to 2 12-pdrs. Torpedo tubes 3 18" 2
bow, 1 stern. Engines and speed Diesel, electric; 1,200/550
h.p.; 16/9 knots (D2 to D8, 1,750/550 h.p.; 16/10 knots).

E Class submarines

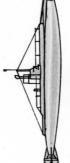

E1 to E56 (no E28), all 1913–17
660 to 800 tons 181' × 22½'. Gun 1 12-pdr.
Torpedo tubes 5 18" 2 bow, 2 beam, 1 stern. Engines
and speed Diesel, electric; 1,600/840 h.p.; 16/10
knots. Remarks E24, 34, 41, 45, 46, 51, adapted for
mine-laying, beam torpedo tubes suppressed.

In 1904, we had our first 'subsmash', a type of disaster that has always caught the public imagination as being particularly horrific and poignant. *A1* was run down in the Solent and all in her lost. She was raised a month later. One or two later accidents to these *A* boats have left behind a reputation of their being a dangerous class, which was not really justified.

The *B* and *C* classes were 35 feet longer than the *As* and generally more seaworthy with a 1,500-mile range. The *D* class were the first, apart from *A13*, to have diesel engines, a type that came into general use for almost all classes of submarine built until the end of the Second World War. With this class the submarine assumed its classic form, and on *D4* a small gun was introduced for the first time; wireless was also fitted for the first time. By the eve of the First World War the Royal Navy had nearly eighty submarines, whereas the Germans, who were to profit most by this arm, had thirty-three. By this time the first of the *E* class were completing, four times the size of the Holland boats of ten years before.

When war came the *As* were relegated to harbour defence, the *Bs* and *Cs* mostly did surface patrols from the principal ports, while the *Ds* and *Es* had the range for overseas patrol. Some *Es* and *Cs* went to the Baltic and operated under a Russian admiral, other *Es* went to the Dardanelles and attacked the Turks in the Sea of Marmora, sinking two battleships, a destroyer and many other vessels. Three of the commanders won the Victoria Cross.

As the war progressed, ideas broadened. A requirement went out for a class of submarine to work with the battle-fleet, which meant 21 knots plus on the surface. The fast *J* class boats with a speed of 19 knots were building, but that was not enough, and no diesel engine available could give the extra knots. The only form of marine propulsion which could give such a speed was steam, so the steam-turbine-engined *K* class came into being. Big powerful boats with a surface speed of 24 knots, but dangerous as first built since their longitudinal stability was poor. On the surface, they looked more like patrol boats with their two funnels and big conning tower. Working with the fleet blacked out at night was always hazardous, and in January 1918 there occurred what is known as the 'Battle of May Island', when, after a collision between two of the *Ks*, the flotilla were sufficiently held up to be overtaken by the battle-cruisers and cruisers. Two of the *Ks* were sunk. In 1923 the only enlarged *K* completed, *K26*.

The last three vessels of this class were completed with diesel engines as the monitor *M* class. These vessels (and only *M1* was completed in the war), were to have a 12-inch gun and to bob up off the enemy coast and bombard. Though it looked dangerous the big gun in fact helped them to behave very well, diving quickly and steadying the submarine once under. *M2* had her gun exchanged for a small seaplane in 1927, but both submarines came to a disastrous end, *M1* being rammed and sunk, and *M2* foundering when her aircraft hangar hatch was open when it should have been shut.

Other submarines of the war were the *N1* or *Nautilus*, an experiment in large submarine-building by Vickers. The *Swordfish* was the first British steam submarine. Both these submarines were outside the main stream of submarine development, which was represented by the *Fs*, *Gs* and *Hs*, some of the latter being built abroad, and the first to have a bow salvo of four torpedo tubes. This was increased to a salvo of six in the

*L* class, which were in general layout improved *Es* but 50 feet longer. Not all of this class of thirty-four was completed by the end of the war and three survived to patrol in the early part of the Second World War. The last wartime class were the *Rs*. These were very specialized boats which were designed to be the submarine's answer to the *U*-boat. They were small with very powerful electric engines and streamlined conning towers to give them an underwater speed of 15 knots, faster than their surface speed. They were *U*-boat hunters, but only one of them ever had the opportunity to attack one, and that failed. The whole class was scrapped after the war. The three little *S* class boats of 1914–15 were sold to Italy in 1915.

## The Submarine between the Wars

Though begun in wartime, the *M* class and the enlarged *K* boat *K26* served only in peace. The first peacetime-designed submarine was a huge cruiser type called the *X1*. Launched in 1923, she was 3,600 tons with four 5·2-inch guns carried in two turrets. She also had a good surface speed of $18\frac{1}{2}$ knots and great range. She was dogged by engine trouble, and the restrictions on submarine tonnage imposed by the Washington Treaty inhibited the building of any more. It was mainly for this reason that she was scrapped in 1937 and her tonnage used to build three smaller boats.

The first peacetime class to follow the *Ls* was the *Os* or *Oberons*. They were a little larger than the *Ls* and had a greater range. They also had a stronger pressure hull for deeper diving, two stern tubes and a 40-foot periscope. The *Oberon*, which was launched in 1926, was the first submarine to carry the new anti-submarine weapon, ASDIC. This took over from the hydrophone which could not measure the speed, course or distance of an enemy vessel with any accuracy. The ASDIC sent out a directional signal or 'ping' which, when it struck the enemy's hull, bounded back to give an echo to the operator. It was the time elapsed between the 'pings' and the returning echo which showed the range and echo pitch gave an indication of target movement. The *Os*, however, suffered from incurable oil leaks from their fuel tanks which were outside the pressure hull, and this trouble also dogged the improved *Os* and their derivatives, the *Ps* and *Rs*. Also affected in this way were the three large cruising-type boats and the six minelayers. The cruisers were the *River* class, only slightly smaller than *X1*, which had been the largest submarine in the world until the French built the *Surcouf* in 1929.

The *Poseidon* was lost in a collision in 1931, but the rest of the *Os*, *Ps* and *Rs*, eighteen boats, served in the war with heavy losses, which was to be the fate of submarines generally, both British and enemy. Of the eighteen, twelve were lost, but the *Pandora*, which was sunk by enemy aircraft at Malta, was raised and scrapped.

Of the three *Rivers* one was lost and so too were five out of the six minelaying *Porpoise* class. The *Seal*, one of these, had the unique experience for a British submarine of being captured in the Baltic in 1940 and spending the rest of the war as a German *U*-boat.

The problem of leaking fuel tanks was solved by putting them inside the pressure hull, which was done in the three new classes developed in the 1930s. These boats, the large *T* class, the smaller *Ss* and the little *Us*, were to bear the brunt of the fighting due to the large numbers involved. The dimensions of the *Ts* was similar to the *Oberons*, and between the *Triton* of 1937 and the *Tabard*, launched in November 1945, fifty-three were built. The second boat, the *Thetis*, provided one of the great prewar dramas and tragedies by sinking in the Mersey on trials in 1939; all the world watched while the losing battle was fought to get her people out. She was later raised and renamed *Thunderbolt*, and was lost again in 1943. Also lost were fourteen of her sisters. Many of the remainder continued to serve after the war, and the last eight underwent a drastic rebuilding during 1951–6 when an extra section was built into the pressure hull to make room for a second set of electric engines and thus increase their underwater speed to 18 knots. Their guns were removed and an enlarged conning tower built. In this form they served on into the 1960s; the last to strike her pendant was the *Tabard*, in 1969.

It says a good deal for the design of the smaller *S* class that the first of them, the *Swordfish*, was launched in 1931, while the last, the *Sentinel*, not so greatly modified, went down the slip in July 1945. Out of sixty-two built eighteen were lost during the war. A number were sold after the war to foreign navies. The little *U* and *V* classes were really developed as training boats and suffered somewhat from lack of range. They were ideal, however, for the Mediterranean, where distances are short and detection is frequent in the clear water. It was found that their small hulls would withstand more severe depth-charging than their larger sisters. The very large number of seventy-one boats were built, of which only twenty were lost in the war.

An enlarged version of the *T* class, the *As*, with a longer range for action in the Pacific against the Japanese, was building towards the end of the war. None completed in time to fight. One of them, the *Affray*, was lost in 1951 when her schnorkel broke off under water and flooded her. This was a device developed by the Dutch before the war, by which an air intake was raised, so that the submarine could continue to use her diesels just submerged. She could therefore cruise under water by day as well as night at a much greater speed and better endurance than by using her electric engines, for which batteries had to be recharged periodically. The great advantage was that her chance of being found by day was greatly reduced. On the other hand these submarines were not designed to be lived in submerged for long periods, which made them very damp from condensation, so that mould grew everywhere. Experiments in long voyages under water with a schnorkel (or 'snort', as we call it) were conducted by the *Andrew* in 1953, which initially made a voyage to Bermuda and back. Of the sixteen built, all except the *Affray* and *Aurochs* were modified in the late 1950s. The rest were given a great fin conning tower 26½ feet high and a radar dome on their bows.

## Postwar Submarines

With the end of the war there were more than enough new submarines for a peacetime service, so that ten years elapsed before any new submarine appeared. When it did, it was one of two unarmed experimental boats called *Explorer* and *Excalibur*, whose main interest was in their propulsion. This was a development of a German invention of what was called a hydrogen peroxide engine. This was a steam turbine with the steam being supplied not from a boiler but from the decompression of high-test hydrogen peroxide with burning diesel oil. This type of engine needed no outside air supply and so would work under water on its own resources giving the submarine a very high speed, 27 knots in the case of these two boats, which was 21 knots faster than their diesel engines

## SUBMARINES

### G Class submarines

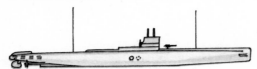

G1 to G14, all 1915–16 except G14 (1917)
700 *to* 975 *tons* 187′ × 22½′. Gun 1 3″ *A.A.* Torpedo tubes
1 21″ *stern*, 2 18″ *bow*, 2 18″ *beam*. Engines and speed *Diesel, electric*; 1,600/840 *h.p.*; 14½/10 *knots*.

### H Class submarines

H1 to H12, all 1915
364 *to* 434 *tons* 150′ × 15½′. Torpedo tubes 4 18″ *bow*. Engines and speed *Diesel, electric*; 480/320 *h.p.*; 13/11 *knots*. Remarks *Others of this type went to Chile and Canada.*
H21 to H34, H41 to H44, H47 to H52, all 1917–19
440 *to* 500 *tons* 171′ × 16′. Gun 1 3″ *A.A.* Torpedo tubes 4 21″ *bow*. Engines and speed *Diesel, electric*; 480/320 *h.p.*; 13/10½ *knots*. Remarks *The missing numbers in this series were cancelled.*

### L Class submarines

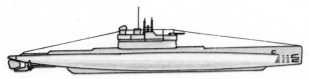

L1 to L12, L14 to L27, L32 and L33, L52 to L56, 69, 70, 71 all 1917–19
890 *to* 1,070 *tons* 231′ × 23½′, L52 *on* 960 *to* 1,150 *tons* 235′ × 23½′. Guns 1 3″ *or* 4″, L52 *on* 2 4″. Torpedo tubes 4 18″ *bow*, 2 18″ *beam*, L9 to L33 4 21″ *bow*, 2 18″ *beam*, L52 *on* 6 21″ *bow*. Engines and speed *Diesel, electric*; 2,400/1,600 *h.p.*; 17½/10 *knots*. Remarks *The later Ls had a longer superstructure.*

### O Class submarines

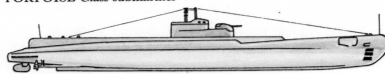

*First group* OBERON, OTWAY, OXLEY, all 1926
*Second group* ODIN, OLYMPUS, ORPHEUS, OSIRIS, OSWALD, OTUS, all 1928 except ORPHEUS (1929)
*First group* 1,350 *to* 1,870 *tons* 283½′ (*o/a*) × 27¾′. *Second group* 1,475 *to* 2,030 *tons* 283½′ (*o/a*) × 29¾′. Gun 1 4″
Torpedo tubes 8 21″ (*6 in bow, 2 in stern*). Engines and speed *Diesel, electric*; first group 3,000/1,350 *h.p.*; 15½/9 *knots*. Second group 4,400/1,320 *h.p.*; 17½/9 *knots*.

### P and R Class submarines

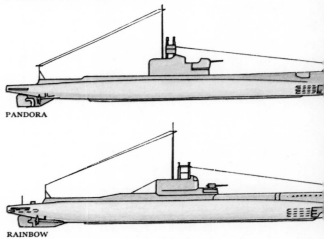

PANDORA

RAINBOW

PANDORA, PARTHIAN, PERSEUS, PHOENIX, POSEIDON, PROTEUS, all 1929, RAINBOW, REGENT, REGULUS, ROVER, all 1930
1,475 *to* 2,040 *tons*, Rs 2,030 *tons* 290′ (*o/a*) × 29¾′. Guns 1 4″. Torpedo tubes 8 21″ (*6 bow, 2 in stern*). Engines and speed *Diesel, electric*; 4,400/1,320 *h.p.*; 17½/9 *knots*.

### PORPOISE Class submarines

CACHALOT 1937, GRAMPUS 1936, NARWHAL 1935, PORPOISE 1932, RORQUAL 1936, SEAL 1938
1,520 *to* 2,157 *tons* 289′ (*o/a*) × 25½′ (*PORPOISE* 1,500 *to* 2,053 *tons* 288′ (*o/a*) × 29¾′. Gun 1 4″. Torpedo tubes 6 21″ *bow*. Engines and speed *Diesel, electric*; 3,300/1,630 *h.p.*; 15/8¾ *knots*.

Submarine

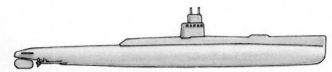

NAUTILUS (later N1) 1914
1,270 to 1,694 tons 242½′ × 26′. Gun 1 12-pdr. Torpedo tubes 2 21″
bow and stern, 4 18″ beam. Engines and speed Diesel, electric;
3,700/1,000 h.p.; 17/10 knots.

S Class submarines

S1, S2, S3, all 1914–15
265 to 386 tons 148′ × 14′. Torpedo tubes 2 18″ bow. Engines and
speed Diesel, electric; 650/400 h.p.; 13¼/8½ knots. Remarks All sold
to Italy in 1917.

F Class submarines

F1, F2, F3, all 1915–17
353 to 525 tons 151½′ × 16′. Gun 1 small. Torpedo tubes 3 18″,
2 bow, 1 stern. Engines and speed Diesel, electric; 900/400 h.p.;
14½/9 knots.

J Class submarines

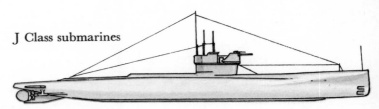

J1 to J7, all 1915–17
1,210 to 1,820 tons (J7 1,760 tons) 275½′ × 23½′. Guns 1 or 2 3″ or
4″. Torpedo tubes 6 18″, 4 bow, 2 beam. Engines and speed
Diesel, electric; 3,600/1,400 h.p.; 19½/9½ knots. Remarks J7
modified with a long superstructure; all but J6 (lost 1918) transferred
to the Royal Australian Navy.

Submarine

SWORDFISH (later S1) 1916
932 to 1,475 tons 231¼′ × 23′. Guns 2 12-pdrs. Torpedo tubes
2 21″ bow, 4 18″ beam. Engines and speed Turbines, electric;
3,750/1,500 h.p.; 18/10 knots. Remarks Converted to a surface
patrol boat.

W Class submarines

W1 to W4, all 1914–15
W1 340 to 508 tons 171½′ × 15½′ (W2 to W4 149¾′ × 17′).
Gun 1 12-pdr. Torpedo tubes 2 18″ bow. Engines and speed
Diesel, electric; 710/480 h.p.; 13/8½ knots. Remarks The Ws
were one of three classes sold off to Italy during the war; the Ws by
Armstrong based on a Laubeuf design, the S Class by Scott on a
Laurenti, and the Vs a special Vickers Class, all of similar size.

*H.M. Submarine A1 (1902). It was ironical that the first designs for a submarine for the Royal Navy should have been bought from a militant Irish Fenian called Holland, who had created his boats specifically as a weapon which he hoped might bring about the destruction of the British fleet. The A boat was an enlarged and improved version of the* Holland *boats and proved successful coastal submarines.*

| | | | | | |
|---|---|---|---|---|---|
| A | Thrust bearing | I | Main ballast tanks | P | Air flasks |
| B | After trimming tank | J | Hydroplane control | Q | Torpedo |
| C | Electric motor | K | Steering positions | R | Compensating tanks for torpedo |
| D | Engine exhaust | L | Buoyancy tanks | | |
| E | Water ballast tanks | M | Electric storage batteries, and space for storage batteries | S | Torpedo tube |
| F | 16-cylinder petrol engine | | | T | Bow cap |
| G | Main bilge pump | N | Conning tower | U | Fore trimming tank |
| H | Stores | O | Auxiliary bilge pump | V | Petrol tank |

*H.M.S.* Swordfish *was the first of a class of sixty-two small attack submarines built over a period of fifteen years. From the S Class there developed the larger Ts and As, and the smaller Us and Vs. Of these it was the Ss and Ts which were the submarine service's main weapon in the Second World War. The* Swordfish *herself was lost on patrol in November 1940.*

| | | | | | |
|---|---|---|---|---|---|
| A | Disappearing bollards | R | Engine exhaust tank | i | 3-inch quick-firing guns |
| B | W/T masts | S | Oil fuel tank | j | No. 1 battery tank |
| C | Steering shaft | T | Compressors | k | Folding boat |
| D | Auxiliary tank | U | Engine room hatch | l | Compression tanks |
| E | Engine exhaust | V | Elm blocks | m | Gangplank stowed |
| F | Hydroplane unit | W | Bilge pump | n | Seamen's mess |
| G | Store | X | W/T silent cabinet | o | Wardroom |
| H | Steering unit | Y | W/T office | p | Oil fuel |
| I | Compression tank | Z | Control room | q | Hydroplanes |
| J | Davis escapes | a | Indicator buoy | r | Elm |
| K | Main motor | b | Conning tower | s | No. 1 main tank |
| L | Elm with 10 lbs centre plate | c | E.R.Rs' mess | t | Bow buoyancy tank |
| M | Main motor cooler | d | No. 2 battery tank | u | Torpedo embarking |
| N | Cast-iron blocks | e | Petty Officers' mess | v | 21-inch torpedoes (stowed) |
| O | Lead filled | f | Water tight hatch | w | Torpedo tubes |
| P | Lubricating oil drain tank | g | Gun ammunition tank | x | Firing platform |
| Q | Engine | h | Gun trough | y | Air bottles |

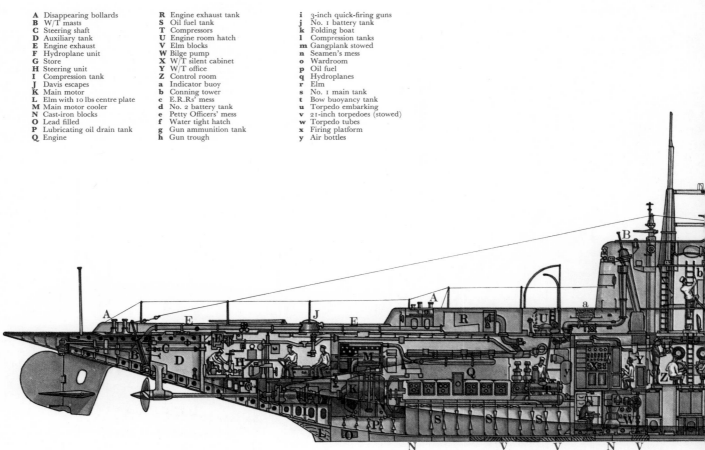

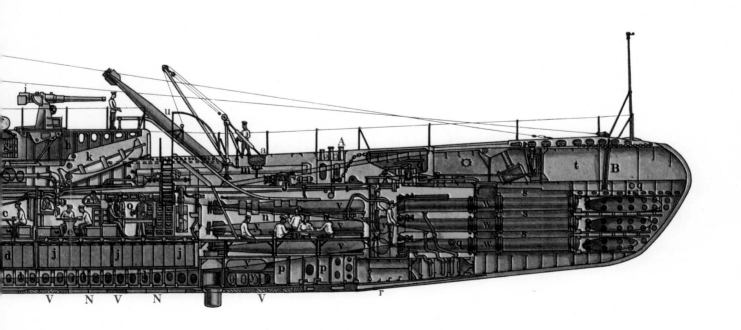

**SUBMARINES**

K Class submarines

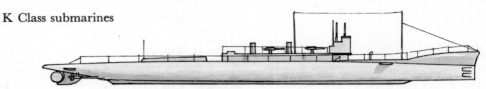

K1 to K17, K22, all 1916–17
1,883 *to* 2,565 *tons* 338′×26¾′. Guns 1 *or* 2 4″, 1 3″ *A.A.* K17 *had* 2 5·5″. Torpedo tubes 8 18″ 4 *bow*, 4 *beam*. Engines and speed *Turbines, electric;* 10,500/1,400 *h.p.;* 24/9 *knots. Remarks Later the bows were altered to a bulbous shape, as shown, to increase stability. K22 was originally K13, renumbered after she had been sunk and raised in the Gareloch.*

R Class submarines

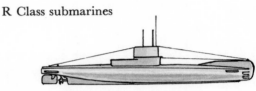

R1 to R4, and R7 to R12, all 1918
420 *to* 500 *tons* 163′ × 15¾′. Torpedo tubes 6 18″ *bow*. Engines and speed *Diesel, electric;* 240/1,200 *h.p.;* 9½/15 *knots.*
Remarks *Designed as U-boat hunters.*

Submarine

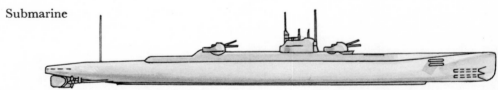

X1 1923
2,780 *to* 3,600 *tons* 363½′ (*o/a*)×29¾′. Guns 4 5·2″. Torpedo tubes 6 21″ *bow*. Engines and speed *Diesel, electric;* 6,000/2,600 *h.p.;* 19½/9 *knots.*

THAMES Class submarine

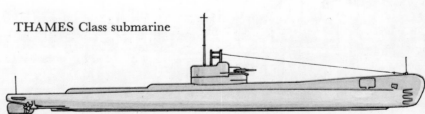

CLYDE 1934, SEVERN 1934, THAMES 1932
1,850 *to* 2,723 *tons* (*THAMES* 1,805 *to* 2,680 *tons*) 345′ (*o/a*)×28′. Guns 1 4″. Torpedo tubes 8 21″ (6 *bow*, 2 *stern*). Engines and speed *Diesel, electric;* 10,000/2,500 *h.p.;* 22/10 *knots.*

M Class submarines

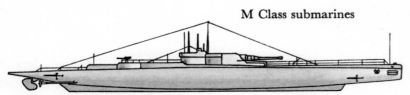

M1 1917, M2 1918, M3 1918
1,600 *to* 1,950 *tons* 296′ to 305′ × 24½′. Gun 1 12″. Torpedo tubes 4 21″ *bows*. Engines and speed *Diesel, electric;* 2,400/1,600 *h.p.;* 15½/9½ *knots*.

M2 as altered to carry a seaplane

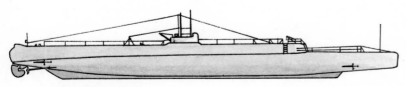

M3 as altered to a minelayer

Improved K Class

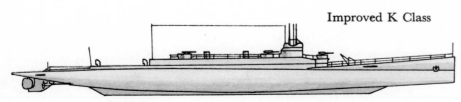

K26 1919
2,140 *to* 2,770 *tons* 351½′ × 28′. Guns 3 4″. Torpedo tubes 6 21″ (*bow*), 4 18″ (*beam*). Engines and speed *Turbines, electric,*
10,000/1,400 *h.p.;* 23½/9 *knots*.

gave them on the surface.

These boats represented the Royal Navy's choice for the development of a true type of submarine, and was adopted instead of the nuclear type of engine, which the Americans had, at the same time, decided to install in their future submarines. The decision to go for H.T.P. instead of nuclear was taken on the grounds of the initial cost of development, which would have been much more for the nuclear engine. In the event, it turned out to have been just one more of the lamentable miscalculations that have dogged British defence planning since the war, and cost the nation and taxpayer so dear.

Experiments with the British H.T.P. submarines compared with the USS *Nautilus* showed that whereas the nuclear submarine could steam submerged at 30 knots for sixty days, the H.T.P.s had a submerged endurance of only ten hours, and only two of these at the maximum speed of 27 knots. In addition, the H.T.P. gas proved volatile and dangerous. This was underlined in 1955 when H.M. Submarine *Sidon*, doing trials with an H.T.P.-engined torpedo, was sunk with loss of life in Portland Harbour, when the gas in a torpedo's engine blew up. Following this accident, the whole programme was abandoned as too dangerous, and the navy belatedly turned to nuclear power. Britain launched her first nuclear submarine the *Dreadnought* with an American engine in 1960, seven years after the *Nautilus*.

Before turning to the nuclear submarines, mention must be made of the two classes of conventional submarines built from wartime experience and completed in the late 1950s and early 1960s, the *Porpoises* and *Oberons*. These have diesel-electric and battery engines to give them a speed of 19 knots snorting and 15 knots fully submerged. Their tall conning tower, now called a 'sail', encloses the periscopes, etc., and enables high speed to be maintained while snorting. The outer casings of the late *Os* are made of glass reinforced plastic laminate, except for the *Orpheus* which is of aluminium. These submarines, incorporating as they do the lessons of the *Ts* and *As* and the later German *U*-boats, which we captured at the end of the war, are the finest of their type in the world. However, with the development of nuclear submarines, which are true submarines rather than submersibles, it seemed to many that the *Oberons* would be the last conventional submarine class.

In fact, it has recently been confirmed that a new class of conventional submarine is to be added, the reasons being that a conventional submarine can get into places where the bulky nuclear submarine can not. They are also more silent. During the Falklands War H.M.S. *Onyx* was sent out to work with the S.A.S., landing parties of them around the Falklands and on the Argentine mainland itself. Somewhere she hit a rock jamming one of her torpedoes in the tube, and it had to be removed in dock on her return home. It appears that the new class of submarine will have a similar shape to the nuclear fleet submarines.

## Nuclear-Powered Submarines

The nuclear-powered submarine is a steam-turbine-driven boat, the nuclear fuel providing the heat to boil the water in the boilers. Unlike the old *K* boats, however, this fuel does not require oxygen to make it burn, so that the engine can work enclosed under water, or on the surface, for many months without refuelling.

By the time Britain's first nuclear submarine was launched the U.S. Navy had twenty and Russia a few. Now the Royal Navy has fifteen fleet submarines and four building, plus four ballistic missile submarines. The U.S. Navy now has one hundred hunter killers and thirty-seven ballistics, and the Russians have over one hundred hunter killers and eighty ballistics.

The original fleet submarine, the *Dreadnought*, paid off in the early 1980s, and like the rest her role was as a hunter-killer. She was equipped with powerful sonar to track an enemy ship or submarine, Tigerfish homing torpedoes and a surface anti-ship missile called Sub Harpoon. The *Dreadnought* was followed by the all-British *Valiant* and *Churchill* classes, five in all, then the six *Swiftsures* with a deeper diving capacity, and now the improved *Swiftsures*, the *Trafalgar* class.

Each patrol lasts about three months, so to keep them at sea each boat has two crews, called port and starboard. While one is at sea the other is on leave or working in the base. During the Falklands War when the *Conqueror* sank the Argentine cruiser *Belgrano*, she used two of the old WW2-designed aimed torpedoes which are much less expensive to expend than Tigerfish.

By the 1960s the end of the role of the nuclear bomber seemed to be in sight, so that at the Bermuda Conference of 1963 Mr Macmillan persuaded President Kennedy to let Britain buy the American Polaris nuclear missile system, which would be fitted into British built submarines. There are four of these called the *R* class, of which the first was the *Resolution* which became operational in 1967. They are 5 knots slower than the 30-knot fleet submarines, and at 7,500 tons, bigger than any of the surface warships except the *Invincibles*. They carry sixteen Polaris missiles aft of the conning tower, and they have six torpedo tubes. As in all the nuclear submarines, great emphasis has been put on their habitability, since the crews are incarcerated in them for three months at a time.

With the purchase of the Trident missile system a new class of ballistic missile submarine will have to be built. As with the *R*s there will be four of them, but they will be twice the size of their predecessors.

# SUBMARINES

## S Class submarines

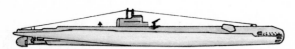

*Pre-war group* SALMON 1934, SEAHORSE 1932, SEALION 1934, SEAWOLF 1935, SHARK 1934, SNAPPER 1934, SPEARFISH 1936, STARFISH 1933, STERLET 1937, STURGEON 1932, SUNFISH 1936, SWORDFISH 1931

*Wartime group* P222, SAFARI, SAGA, SAHIB, SANGUINE, SARACEN, SATYR, SCEPTRE, SCORCHER, SCOTSMAN, SCYTHIAN, SEA DEVIL, SEADOG, SEA NYMPH, SEA ROVER, SEA SCOUT, SELENE, SENESCHAL, SENTINEL, SERAPH, SHAKESPEARE, SHALIMAR, SIBYL, SICKLE, SIDON, SIMOOM, SIRDAR, SLEUTH, SOLENT, SPARK, SPEARHEAD, SPIRIT, SPITEFUL, SPLENDID, SPORTSMAN, SPRINGER, SPUR, STATESMAN, STOIC, STONEHENGE, STORM, STRATAGEM, STRONGBOW, STUBBORN, STURDY, STYGIAN, SUBTLE, SUPREME, SURF, SYRTIS all 1941–5

*First group* 670 to 960 tons 208¾' (o/a) × 24' (*first four 640 to 927 tons and 6' shorter*). *Second group* 715 to 990 tons 217' (o/a) × 23½'. Gun 1 3" (1 4" in later boats of second group). Torpedo tubes *First group* 6 21" (bow). *Second group* 7 21" (*extra tube external at stern, suppressed in later boats*). Engines and speed *Diesel, electric. First group* 1,550/1,300 h.p.; 13¾/10 knots (*SUNFISH* 1,900/1,300 h.p.; 15/10 knots). *Second group* 1,900/1,300 h.p.; 14¾/9knots.

## U and V Class submarines

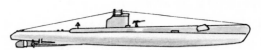

*First group* UMPIRE,* UNA,* UNBEATEN,* UNDAUNTED,* UNDINE, UNION, UNIQUE, UNITY, UPHOLDER, UPRIGHT, URCHIN,* URGE,* URSULA, USK,* UTMOST, all 1937–41

*Second group* P32, P33, P36, P38, P39, P48, ULTIMATUM, ULTOR, UMBRA, UNBENDING, UNBROKEN, UNISON, UNITED, UNIVERSAL, UNRIVALLED, UNRUFFLED, UNRULY, UNSEEN, UNSHAKEN, UNSPARING, UNSWERVING, UNTAMED, UNTIRING, UPROAR, UPSTART, USURPER, UTHER, VANDAL, VARANGIAN, all 1940–3

*Third group* UPSHOT, URTICA, VAGABOND, VAMPIRE, VARIANCE, VARNE, VELDT, VENGEFUL, VENTURER, VIGOROUS, VIKING, VINEYARD, VIRTUE, VIRULENT, VISIGOTH, VIVID, VOLATILE, VORACIOUS, VORTEX, VOTARY, VOX, VULPINE, all 1943–4

*First group* 630 to 730 tons 191½' (o/a) × 16' (*starred names* 196¾' (o/a)). *Second group* 648 to 735 tons 196¾' (o/a) × 16'. *Third group* 670 to 740 tons 206' (o/a) × 16'. Gun 1 3" (*not UNDINE or UNITY*). Torpedo tubes 4 21" (*non-starred names in first group had six*). Engines and speed *Diesel, electric. First and second groups* 615/825 h.p.; 11½/9 knots. *Third group* 800/760 h.p.; 13/9 knots.

## T Class submarines

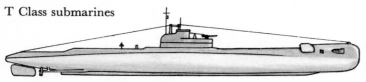

P311 TABARD, TACITURN, TACTITIAN, TAKU, TALENT, TALISMAN, TALLY-HO, TANTALUS, TANTIVY, TAPIR, TARN, TARPON, TASMAN, TAURUS, TELEMACHUS, TEMPEST,* TEMPLAR, TEREDO, TERRAPIN, TETRARCH, THERMOPYLAE, THETIS, THISTLE, THORN,* THOROUGH, THRASHER,* THULE, THUNDERBOLT, TIGRIS, TIPTOE, TIRELESS, TOKEN, TORBAY, TOTEM, TRADEWIND, TRAVELLER,* TRENCHANT, TRESPASSER, TRIAD, TRIBUNE, TRIDENT, TRITON, TRIUMPH, TROOPER,* TRUANT, TRUCULENT, TRUMP, TRUNCHEON, TRUSTY,* TUDOR, TUNA, TURBULENT, TURPIN, all 1937–45
1,090 to 1,575 tons 275' (o/a) × 26½'. Gun 1 4". Torpedo tubes 10 21" (8 bow, 2 external, 3 stern (all external), *starred names had 11 tubes*). Engines and speed *Diesel, electric;* 2,500/1,450 h.p.; 15½/9 knots.

## A Class submarines

ACHERON, AENEAS, AFFRAY, ALARIC, ALCIDE, ALDERNEY, ALLIANCE, AMBUSH, ANCHORITE, AMPHION, ANDREW, ARTEMIS, ARTFUL, ASTUTE, AURIGA, AUROCHS, all 1944–7
1,120 to 1,630 tons 281¾' (o/a) × 22¼'. Guns 1 4", 1 20-mm. A.A. (*both later removed*). Torpedo tubes 10 21" (6 at bow, 4 at stern, 2 of the bow tubes and 2 of the stern tubes are external). Engines and speed *Diesel, electric;* 4,300/1,250 h.p.; 18/8 knots.

## T Class modernized

TALENT, TAPIR, TEREDO, TIRELESS, TOKEN *were streamlined, their guns and external torpedo tubes removed 1955–60. Their periscopes and snorkels were encased in a tall sail fin, riveted-hulled boats.* TABARD, TIPTOE, TRUMP, TRUNCHEON *lengthened 20',* TACITURN 14', THERMOPYLAE, TOTEM, TURPIN 12'. *These welded boats had sections inserted 1951–6, extra batteries raised the electric h.p. to 2,900, giving 15 knots under water.*

## A Class modernized

*From 1955 to 1960 all the A class except* AFFRAY, *which had been lost, and* AUROCHS, *were modernized. All external torpedo tubes were removed and a sail conning tower built. Guns could be refitted in some.*

PORPOISE and
OBERON Class submarines

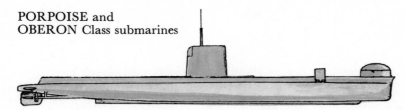

CACHALOT 1957, FINWHALE 1959, GRAMPUS 1957, NARWHAL 1957, OBERON 1959, OCELOT 1962, ODIN 1960, OLYMPUS 1961, ONSLAUGHT 1960, ONYX 1966, OPOSSUM 1963, OPPORTUNE 1964, ORACLE 1961, ORPHEUS 1959, OSIRIS 1962, OTTER 1961, OTUS 1962, PORPOISE 1956, RORQUAL 1956, SEALION 1959, WALRUS 1959
2,030 *to* 2,405 *tons* 295′ (*o/a*) × 26½′. Torpedo tubes 8 21″ 6 *bow*, 2 *stern*. Engines and speed *Diesel, electric;* 3,680/6,000 *h.p.;* 15/19 *knots.*

Submarines

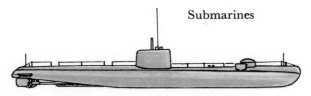

EXCALIBUR 1955 and EXPLORER 1954
780 *to* 1,000 *tons* 225½′ (*o/a*) × 15⅔′. Engines and speed *Experimental high-test peroxide and diesel engines,* 6/27 *knots.*

Nuclear-powered submarine

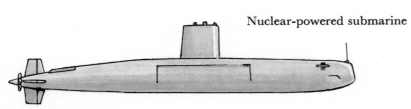

DREADNOUGHT 1960
3,500 *to* 4,000 *tons* 265⅔′ × 32′. Torpedo tubes 6 21″. Engines and speed *Nuclear-powered turbines;* 15,000 *h.p.;* 28 *knots submerged.*

VALIANT Class fleet submarines

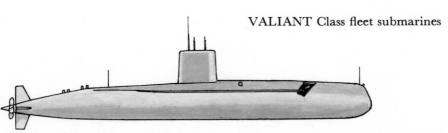

CHURCHILL 1968, CONQUEROR 1969, COURAGEOUS 1970, VALIANT 1963, WARSPITE 1965
4,400 *to* 4,900 *tons* 285′ × 33′. Torpedo tubes 6 21″. Engines and speed *Nuclear-powered turbines;* 15,000 *h.p.;* about 30 *knots submerged.*

# POST-WAR SUBMARINES

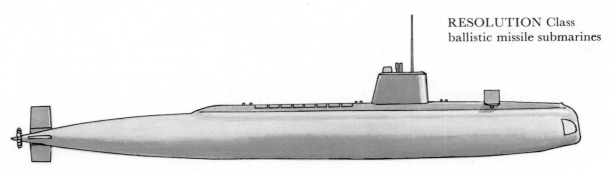

RESOLUTION Class
ballistic missile submarines

RENOWN 1967, REPULSE 1967, RESOLUTION 1966, REVENGE 1968
7,500 *to* 8,400 *tons* 425′ (*o/a*) × 33′. Armament 16 *Polaris rocket missiles*. Torpedo tubes 6 21″ *bow*. Engines and speed *Nuclear-powered turbines; 20 knots surface, 25 knots submerged.*

SWIFTSURE Class fleet submarines

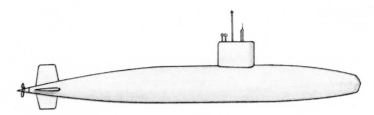

SCEPTRE 1976, SOVEREIGN 1973, SPARTAN 1978, SPLENDID 1979, SUPERB 1974, SWIFTSURE 1971
4,200 *tons standard* 4,500 *tons dived* 272′ × 32.3′ × 27′. Torpedo tubes 5 21″ *and Tigerfish homing torpedoes*. Engines and speed *Nuclear-powered turbines; 30 knots dived*. Remarks *These submarines are improved* Valiants.

TRAFALGAR Class fleet submarines
TACTICIAN, TALENT, TIRELESS, TORBAY, TRAFALGAR all 1981, TURBULENT 1982
Remarks *These submarines are improved* Swiftsures.

# 32

## Coastal Craft

### The Coastal Motor Boat

By the First World War the little steam torpedo-boat of the Victorian navy had grown into the big destroyer, and although a good many of the early torpedo-boats still survived, they were already obsolete, and a new generation of small, fast coastal craft was required. The development of the internal combustion engine offered a motive power that needed much less room to house, and also weighed much less than steam boilers and machinery, so that quite small vessels could be given a compact and powerful engine. The speed-boat had already made its appearance by 1914. The first coastal motor boats were developed by Thornycrofts in 1916 in great secrecy, doing their trials by night. They were handsome whale-backed craft, 45 feet long and could exceed 30 knots with their 250 horsepower petrol engine. They carried two torpedoes in troughs on their sterns; these they launched by dropping them behind at speed and then swerving out of their path. Called the 40-foot C.M.B.s, they were followed by the 55-foot and 70-foot C.M.B.s, the latter intended as minelayers. Both the larger types had twin engines and screws, giving the 55-foot boats speeds up to 40 knots.

Slightly larger but slower were the motor launches which carried a small gun and were equipped for anti-submarine work. They were mostly built in America. Also evolved were the steam patrol boats. These were much larger and specially designed as *U*-boat hunters. Later *P* boats were disguised as merchantmen and called *P.C.* boats (see page 250).

By the middle 1930s, most of the First World War coastal craft had disappeared and a new generation was developing, designed by Vosper, Thornycroft and the British Power Boat Company. Vosper provided the first standard motor-torpedo-boats, which had hard chine hulls and a torpedo tube mounted on each side amidships, firing forwards. These boats had a speed of about 40 knots. Later, during the war, many were adapted as motor gunboats to deal with the German *E*-boats, and still later the M.T.B.s and M.G.B.s merged, being given both guns and torpedoes. They were initially very noisy and so Denny produced a round-bilged, steel, steam-turbine boat which moved more silently but proved vulnerable to gunfire. The motor-powered boats were later largely silenced.

Other, slower types of wooden motor launches, on the whole larger than the M.T.B.s, were used for various purposes: for harbour defence, H.D.M.L.s; for sea rescue, R.M.L.s; for anti-submarine work, MA/s Bs; and magnetic-mine weapons, M.M.S.s.

Altogether more than thirteen hundred of these craft were built in Britain and another three hundred in America and Canada. More than two hundred and fifty were lost during the war.

After the war there was a wholesale disposal of the coastal forces and only a nucleus was kept. In the early 1950s, the seaward defence boats began to be replaced by a new class, the *Ford* class. These have diesel engines and are distinguished by their two funnels aft, placed side by side. They are not fast at 18 knots but are specially equipped to detect submarines in approaches to harbours and in shallow coastal waters. At the same time, a final class of petrol-driven M.T.B.s was built, the *Gay* class, mounting a special 4·5-inch gun. These disappeared in the 1960s, when the new *Dark* class of diesel-engined boat was built. The construction of these is interesting as they mark a return to composite construction, with aluminium framing and wooden sheathing.

In the early and late 1950s, two classes of two boats each were built by Vosper powered by gas-turbine engines, the *Bolds* and the *Braves*, giving the latter 50 knots. On the whole, coastal craft have fallen to a very low ebb in the navy, and their parent establishment, H.M.S. *Hornet*, is shut down. The navy has always been good at naming its ships, in sharp contrast to the Americans, and the naming of the postwar M.T.B.s was particularly happy. The words *Gay*, *Dark*, *Bold* and *Brave* were used as prefixes to give names like *Gay Bruiser*, *Dark Intruder*, *Bold Pathfinder* and *Brave Borderer*. In 1970 a class of three training boats was added, the *Cutlass*, *Sabre* and *Scimitar*, which have both diesel and gas-turbine engines.

Fishery protection in home waters has, for many years, largely been performed by *Ton* Class wooden minesweepers. In the mid 1970s four *Bird* Class large patrol craft were built, but proved unsuitable. More recently two classes have been built, the *Island* class of about 1,000 tons and the larger *Castle* Class at about 1,400 tons. The latter has a landing pad aft for a helicopter. They are both lightly armed with one 40-millimetre Bofors. A further class, called the *Peacock* Class, is to be built to replace the *Tons* in Hong Kong.

## Wooden Minesweepers

Up to 1940 mines were moored in deep water and swept with cable and paravane; then a new type of mine appeared, the magnetic mine. This was laid in shallow waters without cables and was magnetically attracted to the ships' steel hulls. This triggered off a new generation of wooden warship, the wooden minesweeper, in which ferrous metals were kept to a minimum so as not to attract the mines.

Initially, converted motor launches were used and a number were built based on the commercial motor fishing-vessel type. Later in the war a larger, more habitable type of wooden minesweeper was produced by the Americans which was 135 feet long with a high fo'c'sle and a proper bridge. The Royal Navy took more than one hundred and eighty-four of these craft, known as British Yard Minesweepers, or B.Y.M.S.s.

Following the magnetic mine came the acoustic mine, and a combination of the two, so these little ships were fitted with acoustic hammers to set them off at a distance.

In the early 1950s, since the trend in mine design seemed to dwell on free-sown mines planted in shallow waters, two new types of wooden sweeper emerged, the *Coastals* and the *Inshores*. The *Coastals* are known as the *Ton* class since the names of all one hundred and sixteen of those in the Royal Navy ended in -*ton*. Quite a few have now been disposed of, and many are in NATO and the Commonwealth navies. They are not unlike the wartime American ships; only 5 feet longer and with the high fo'c'sle and large bridge and funnel. With their shallow draught and tall slab sides they are tremendously buoyant and bob about like ping-pong balls, which can be very uncomfortable for the crew. Some were later fitted with stabilizers. Going aboard a Dutch one and a British one tied together, it was interesting to compare the approach to living accommodation. The Dutch officers' wardroom was very plain with metal and plastic furniture, the British was carpeted, with wooden furniture and chintz-covered cushions, in the tradition of *le confort anglais*. Those in service are mainly doing fishery protection.

The *Inshores*, or *Hams*, are smaller, in the M.L. tradition, with a flush upper-deck and deck-houses. All their names end in -*ham*, and there were originally seventy-one of them, but the majority are now gone.

## River Gunboats

Patrolling the great waterways of the Empire called for a special type of craft designed for smooth and shallow waters. The smaller river gunboats, which did not change greatly in form from the late Victorian navy until the Second World War, had a hull like a raft, which contained the machinery, bunkers and stores. All accommodation was in the superstructures above, which had two, or even three, decks. Some later, larger gunboats did have accommodation in the main hull as well. It was a strange service, particularly on the Chinese rivers, like the Yangtze, which left an indelible impression on those who worked them. The river gunboats suffered heavily in the Second World War, twelve out of twenty-two being lost, either to the Japanese or in the Mediterranean and one at Dunkirk (see page 147).

## Trawlers and Drifters

There can be few more demanding occupations for a ship than fishing the North Atlantic waters, so that the design of the steam trawlers was a well-tried one by the First World War, when the navy took over many of them and also built many. They continued to be built between the wars and during the Second World War, so that by its end more than two hundred and fifty of them were in the service, not to mention no less than three hundred and forty-seven lost during hostilities. A large proportion of these fell victims to mines and enemy aircraft. They were maids of all work, often retaining their ex-civilian crew and skipper, but with a junior naval officer in nominal control. They were the last coal-burning warships to serve in the navy, and some continued in commission into the late 1950s.

## Assault Ships and Craft

In the First World War, apart from the Dardanelles expedition, for which small landing craft called *Beetles* were built, there was no requirement for specialized craft to carry an army to the open beaches of Europe, since the British were already there. In the Second World War, however, having been forced out of Europe in 1940, the only way back was by sea to the beaches, in specially designed craft, until ports were captured and the men and supplies transported by conventional freighters.

Initially, the small L.C.A.s (landing craft assault) and L.C.V.s (landing craft vehicles) were transported on landing ships, usually converted merchantmen. Soon large L.S.T.s (landing ships tanks), with shallow draught and bow doors made their appearance, and with them a variety of other types that could operate right on to the beach.

As the Allies had started from scratch in this field, and as the potential requirement was enormous, it is no wonder that any early plans for a return to Europe were delayed by lack of transport. Not only were there the landings in Italy from North Africa and Normandy from England to be considered; the Americans, who were building most of these vessels, could fight their way back through the Pacific Islands to Japan only by means of landing ships and craft.

After the war there was a mass scrapping of landing ships and craft and only a few were kept for training purposes, and to keep the idea of amphibious warfare in being. One L.C.T., the *Rampart*, was actually guardship at Cowes Week in the middle 1950s.

Interest in more powerful units, for dealing with 'bush fire' warfare was coming into vogue, mainly because of the development of the military helicopter which could not be carried by the landing craft. First the light fleet carriers *Albion* and *Bulwark* were taken in hand in 1959 for conversion to commando carriers to embark troops and vehicles of the Royal Marines which could be put ashore by their helicopters. In 1971–3 the carrier *Hermes* was similarly treated and replaced the *Albion* when completed. During the 1970s experiments were made with operating Harrier jump jets, and these now form part of the equipment of the *Hermes*, the only one of the three still operational.

In the meantime two further replacements for the Amphibious Warfare Squadron were completed in the middle 1960s, the two assault ships *Fearless* and *Intrepid*. These are large ships based on the wartime American L.S.D., which had a great well deck from the bridge aft carrying landing craft. The landing craft were launched through the rear door by flooding ballast tanks in the ship, enabling them to float out. The assault ships can carry a battalion with its vehicles in comfort, and considerably more on short hauls. They can carry five Wessex or Gazelle helicopters or four Sea Kings. Harrier jump jets can operate from them if desired. They have a very powerful communications system and are fitted as command headquarters ships, a role that *Fearless* played during the landings at Port San Carlos during the Falklands War.

They are supported by the six logistic landing ships of the *Sir Lancelot* class. These ships wear the blue ensign of the Royal Fleet Auxiliaries, though they were originally built for the army. They are multipurpose troop and vehicle carriers and can operate helicopters from their well-decks and from the helicopter deck aft. All six were employed in the landings on the Falklands, and two of them, *Sir Galahad* and *Sir Tristram* were severely damaged, the former being scuttled.

## Coastal motor boats (C.M.B.s)

40' single-screw type
Nos. 1 to 13, 40 to 61, 112, 121 to 123,
all 1916–20
5 *tons* 45' (*o*/*a*) × 8½'. Guns 2 *to* 4 *Lewis
guns*. Torpedo tubes 1 *torpedo*. Engines
and speed *Petrol*, 250 to 275 *hp.*; 34 *to*
37 *knots.*

## Motor gunboats

British Power Boat Company type
No. 77, 1942
47 *tons* 71¾' (*o*/*a*) × 20¾' × 5'. Guns
1 2-*pdr.*, 2 20-*mm.*, 4 0·303 *machine-guns*.
Engines and speed *Petrol*; 4,050 *h.p.*;
40 *knots*. Remarks *Over 250 built in various
sizes and forms, the largest being the 165-ton
Denny type, powered by steam turbines.*

## 20 FORD Class
### seaward defence boats

20 '-ford' Class seaward defence boats
120 to 160 *tons* 117¼' (*o*/*a*) × 20' × 5'.
Guns 1 40-*mm.* A.A. Engines and speed
*Diesel*; 1,100 *h.p.*; 18 *knots*. Remarks
*All names ended in '-ford'.*

## Coastal motor boats (C.M.B.s)

Twin-screw type
55' C.M.B.s Nos. 14A to 20A, 21B to
23B, 24A, 25BD, 26B, 27A to 29A, 30B,
31BD, 32A to 37A, 38B, 39B, 62BD to
64BD, 65A, 66BD, 67A, 68B, 69A to
72A, 73BD, 74BD, 75B, 76A, 77A, 78E,
79A, 80CE, 81CE, 82C, 83CE, 84CE,
85CE, 86BD, 87B, 88BD, 89BD, 90BD,
91B, 92BD, 93E to 97E, 98ED, 99ED,
113CK, 114D, 115DE, 116D to 119D,
120F, all 1917–20, 70' C.M.B.s
Nos. 100M, 101M, 102MT 1919,
103MT, 104MT 1920
11 *tons* 60' (*o*/*a*) × 11', *and* 24 *tons*
72½' (*o*/*a*) × 14'. 55' boats 4 *Lewis guns*,
70' *boats* 6 *Lewis guns*. Torpedo tubes
55' boats 1 *or* 2 18" *torpedoes*, 70' *boats*
5 18" *torpedoes or* 4 *mines*. Engines and
speed 55' boats – *petrol*; 750–900 *h.p.*;
34–42 *knots*. 70' boats – *petrol*; 900–
1,500 *h.p.*; 28½ *knots.*

## 2 BOLD Class
### motor gun- or torpedo-boats

2 BOLD Class motor gun- or torpedo-
boats 1951
130 *tons* 121' (*o*/*a*) × 25' × 6'. Guns 2 4·5"
1 40-*mm.* A.A.; *or* 1 40-*mm.* A.A., 4 21"
*torpedoes*. Engines and speed *Gas turbines*;
9,000/5,000 *h.p.*; 40 *knots.*

## 18 DARK Class
### motor gun- or torpedo-boats

18 DARK Class motor gun- or torpedo-
boats 1954–7
50 *tons* 71¼' (*o*/*a*) × 19½' × 5'. Guns 1 4·5"
*D.P.*, 1 40-*mm.* A.A.; *or* 1 40-*mm.* A.A.,
4 21" *torpedoes or* 6 *mines*. Engines
and speed *Diesel*; 5,000 *h.p.*; 40 *knots*.
Remarks *First diesel-engined type.*

## Motor-torpedo-boats

Vosper type 1939
35¾ *tons* 70' × 14¾' × 3¼' to 5'. Guns 4 0·5"
*automatic*. Torpedo tubes 2 21". Engines
and speed *Petrol*; 3,600 *h.p.*; 42 *knots*.
Remarks *Over 600 M.T.B.s to this and
similar designs, notably by Thornycroft and
the British Power Boat Company.*

## 12 GAY Class
### motor gun- or torpedo-boats

12 GAY Class motor gun- or torpedo-
boats all 1952–4
50 *tons* 75' (*o*/*a*) × 20' × 4'. Guns 1 4·5"
*D.P.*, 1 40-*mm.* A.A.; *or* 2 40-*mm.* A.A.,
2 21" *torpedoes*. Engines and speed *Petrol*;
5,000 *h.p.*; 40 *knots.*

## 2 BRAVE Class
### motor gun- or torpedo-boats

2 BRAVE Class motor gun- or
torpedo-boats 1958
75 *tons* 99' (*o*/*a*) × 25½' × 6'. Guns 2 40-*mm.*
*power-operated Bofors*, 2 21" *torpedoes; or*
1 40-*mm.*, 4 21" *torpedoes*. Engines and
speed *Gas turbines*; 10,500 *h.p.*; 50 *knots.*

## COASTAL CRAFT

### BIRD Class large patrol boats

**CYGNET 1975, KINGFISHER 1974, PETEREL 1976, SANDPIPER 1977**
190 *tons* 120′ × 21·7′ × 6·5′. Gun 1 40-*mm Bofors*. Engines and speed 2 *Paxman diesels;* 4,200 *h.p.;* 18 *knots*. Remarks *Designed for fishery protection but sea keeping qualities unsuitable.*

### CASTLE Class
large patrol boats

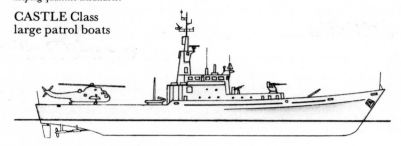

**DUMBARTON CASTLE 1981, LEEDS CASTLE 1980**
1,450 *tons* 265′ × 37·7′ × 14′. Gun 1 40-*mm Bofors*. Engines and speed 2 *Ruston diesels;* 5,640 *h.p.;* 20 *knots*.

### ISLAND Class
offshore patrol craft

**ALDERNEY 1979, ANGLESEY 1978, GUERNSEY 1977, JERSEY 1976, LINDISFARNE 1977, ORKNEY 1976, SHETLAND 1976**
925 *tons* 195·3′ (*o/a*) × 36′ × 14′. Gun 1 40-*mm Bofors*. Engines and speed *Ruston diesels;* 4,380 *h.p.;* 17 *knots*.

HUNT Class
minesweepers

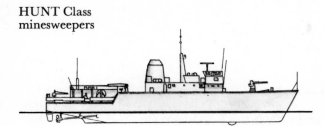

BRECON 1978, BROCKLESBY 1982, CATTISTOCK 1981, CHIDDINGFOLD 1983, COTTESMORE 1982, HURWORTH 1983,
DULVERTON 1983, LEDBURY 1979, MIDDLETON 1982
725 tons full load 197′ (o/a) × 32·8′ × 8·2′. Gun 1 40-*mm Bofors*). Engines and speed 2 *Ruston diesels*; 3,800 *h.p.*; 16 *knots*.

Assault ships

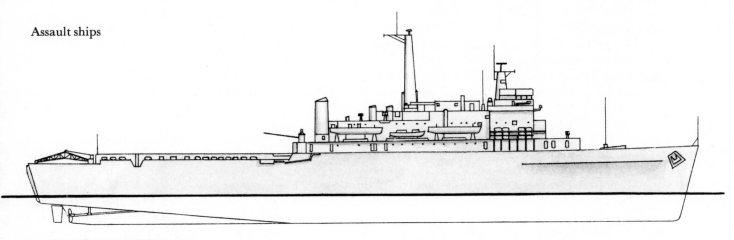

FEARLESS 1963, INTREPID 1964
12,000 *tons full load* 520′ × 80′ × 20′. Guns 2 40-*mm Bofors*. 4 *quadruple Seacat anti-aircraft missile launchers*. Helicopters 5 *Wessex or Gazelles or* 4 *Sea Kings*.
4 *landing craft in dock and* 4 *in davits*. Engines and speed 2 *steam turbines*; 22,000 *h.p.*; 21 *knots*.

# Appendix 1
## A Summary of British Naval Events
## from A.D. 897—1983

**897** King Alfred built his new type of fighting ships (see p. 1) and defeated the Danes.

**973** King Edgar was rowed in a barge on the River Dee by seven English kings as a token of their subjection to him.

**991** Olaf Tryggvason took a fleet of four hundred and fifty ships to sack Sandwich and Ipswich, and going on to Maldon, defeated King Ethelred's army.

**994** The same Olaf, allied to Swegen of Norway made an abortive attempt to reach London, then ravaged Kent, Sussex and Hampshire. Ethelred created a disastrous precedent by buying him off with £16,000, the first of the Danegeld.

**997** A Danish fleet descended on the West Country, going up the Tamar, and carried away immense booty.

**999** Another invasion ravaged Kent from Rochester, the English fleet being inferior.

**1001** The Danes again descended on the West Country, bought off with £24,000.

**1013** Danes under Swegen drove Ethelred into exile after a series of successful invasions following Ethelred's partially successful attempt to murder all Danes resident in England on St Brice's day, 13 November 1002.

**1052** After a confusion of pretenders and loyalties, the great Saxon Earl Godwin, with his son Harold, reasserted the English influence in the government, when he brought a fleet up to London and forced King Edward to modify his Norman leanings.

**1066** William of Normandy successfully evaded a large English fleet and landed his army at Pevensey, which he led to triumph over Harold at the Battle of Hastings.

**1100** The Conqueror's eldest son, Duke Robert, invaded with an army to depose his youngest brother Henry, who had seized the crown after his brother William Rufus's death. He failed to dislodge him.

**1120** The loss of the *White Ship* which set out from Barfleur. King Henry I's only legitimate son, Prince William, was drowned.

**1137** King Stephen invaded Normandy and restored it to the English crown, but shortly afterwards the Empress Matilda invaded England which remained in a state of virtual anarchy until 1153, when the opposing sides signed the Treaty of Wallingford.

**1189** **11 December** King Richard I embarked at Dover for the Third Crusade to the Holy Land.

**1213** The Battle of Damme. King John had been at war with Philip of France since 1202, except for a two-year truce. In this battle an English fleet arrived on the coast of Flanders to help the Count of Flanders against the French. They took vessels and burnt about a hundred more, most of the French being ashore.

**1214** King John led an army in an unsuccessful expedition against the French.

**1216** Prince Louis of France, with the sea mercenary called Eustace the Monk, who had previously fought for King John, invaded England. Defeated at Lincoln in 1217.

**1217** **24 August** An English fleet defeated a French fleet under Eustace the Monk off Dover, which was bringing across another army to reinforce Prince Louis (see p. 5).

**1230** **30 April** Henry III embarked on an abortive expedition to force the French to restore the English duchies in France.

**1293** Norman attacks on English ships caused a fleet from the Cinque Ports to retaliate and attack the Normans in the Seine, taking six vessels.

**14 April** A battle between English and Normans was arranged to take place in mid-Channel, at a spot marked by an anchored hulk; the English won it, capturing about two hundred and forty sail.

**1295** A French army landed at Dover and burnt part of the town before being driven off.

**1336** **August** A French success off the Isle of Wight, when a squadron of their galleys captured some of the king's ships.

**1337** A French force landed at Portsmouth and

burnt and plundered most of the town; also St Peter's Port in Guernsey.

**10 November** An English squadron under the Earl of Derby landed on Gadzand in the mouth of the Scheldt, which was the home of some very damaging Flemish corsairs, and destroyed them, sacking the place.

**1338** Two of King Edward III's finest ships, the *Christopher* and the *Edward*, were captured by the French fleet.

**1339** A fleet under Sir Robert Morley, which included the Cinque Port's fleet, burnt five towns in Normandy and eighty ships.

**1340** **22 June** Edward III sailed to invade France to claim the crown.

**24 June** The Battle of Sluys (see p. 5).

**1350** **29 August** The Battle of Winchelsea. Don Carlos de la Cerda, the Spanish freebooter, with a fleet of forty ships was attacked and defeated by the English fleet commanded by the king himself. Both the king's ship and the Black Prince's ship sank during the action, but not before the English had taken the opposing Spanish ships and transferred themselves to them. Prisoners were nearly always thrown overboard.

**1372** **22 and 23 June** The Earl of Pembroke with a squadron sent to relieve La Rochelle, besieged by the French, was intercepted off the town by a more powerful fleet from Castille. The first day's fighting was inconclusive, but in the second Pembroke was captured with his ship and the entire English squadron taken or destroyed. The Spanish admiral was Ambrosio Bocanegra.

**1377** **29 June** A force under Jean de Vienne landed near Rye and sacked the town.

**1379** **15 December** Sir John Arundel's fleet with reinforcements for Brittany was scattered by a storm and twenty-six ships were wrecked on the Irish Coast including the flagship, with great loss of life.

**1403** **July** An English force raiding the coast of Brittany was defeated by a Breton fleet under Sire de Penhert, Admiral of Brittany, losing about forty ships.

**1405** **30 March** The young Prince James of Scotland captured by the English freebooter Prendergast off Flamborough Head. The prince was kept in England by King Henry, for about 18 years.

The same year an English fleet under Prince Thomas captured three carracks in the Channel, then burnt the town of La Hogue,

Harfleur and thirty-eight others, pillaging the Normandy coast for a depth of thirty miles.

**1415** **11 August** Henry sailed for France to renew the English claim on the French crown, and his success at Agincourt ended serious French resistance on the sea for many years.

**1511** Andrew Barton, the Scottish pirate, brought to action by two King's ships under Lord Thomas and Lord Edward Howard, was killed and his ships taken.

War with France. Lord Edward Howard made lord admiral.

**1512** **12 August** The Battle of Brest, when the French fleet under Jean de Thénouënel fought an indecisive action with the English. One of the finest English ships, the *Regent*, was burnt when the magazine of the 'Great Carrack of Brest' the *Marie la Cordelière* went up while they were grappled together.

**1513** **25 April** Lord Edward Howard attacked some galleys at Le Conquêt, near Brest, and with seventeen followers entered the flagship of the French admiral, Prégent de Bidoux. Unfortunately the lord admiral's galley failed to grapple and drifted away, leaving the lord admiral and his companions to be overwhelmed and hurled over the side, where they drowned. A desultory action followed but nothing was effected.

**1514** Peace with France.

**1522** War with France and Scotland.

**1523** Sir William Fitz-William's fleet defeated a Franco-Scottish fleet and burnt Le Tréport.

**1525** Peace with France and Scotland.

**1544** War with France and Scotland.

**17 July** Henry VIII landed with an army at Calais and laid siege to Boulogne, which fell.

**1545** **19 July** The loss of the *Mary Rose* which foundered through keeling over her open lower ports, as she and the fleet came out of Portsmouth to meet the French fleet in the Solent. The French, under Claude D'Annebaut, were driven off.

**15 August** A fleet engagement in the Channel which was indecisive, though the French galleys under Polain did sufficiently well to persuade King Henry to increase his own galley fleet.

**1546** **18 May** An engagement in the Channel between eight English and a like number of French ships. One French galley taken.

**7 June** Peace with France.

**1547** War with France and Scotland; Edinburgh plundered by Lord Clinton's fleet.

**1550** Peace with France.

**1554** Philip of Spain on his way to England to marry Queen Mary I was met by the Lord Admiral, who took a fleet to greet him but fired a loaded cannon when the prince's ship did not dip her flag or lower her topsails to him, which she then did.

**1556** War with France.

**1557** **7 January** Calais lost.

**1559** Peace with France.

**1562/3** John Hawkins took his first cargo of slaves from Sierra Leone to the West Indies, a highly profitable venture. He therefore made a second and equally successful voyage in 1564/5, and a third in 1567, when his cousin Francis Drake joined his fleet with a little ship he had inherited, called the *Judith*.

**1572** **22 July** Drake took Nombre de Dios on the Isthmus of Panama where the Peruvian treasures were collected, and found a great heap of silver bars. In February the following year he crossed the Isthmus and intercepted a caravan of mules loaded with gold, returning to England a rich man.

**1577** **13 December** Drake sailed from Plymouth on his voyage round the world, the second one to be made, returning to Plymouth Sound on 26 September 1580.

**1587** **19 April** 'The Singeing of the King of Spain's Beard.' A squadron under Sir Francis Drake entered Cadiz harbour and took or destroyed about one hundred vessels, mostly full of stores for the Armada preparing against England. The object of the expedition was to embarrass and delay this venture. Continuing to the Tagus Drake took and plundered about a hundred more.

**1588** **19 July** The Spanish Armada was sighted in the mouth of the channel.

**27 July** After a week's fighting the Duke of Medina Sidonia brought his fleet to an anchor off Calais with the loss of only three ships (flagships) preparatory to embarking the Duke of Parma's army for England.

**28 July** Drake sent in fireships against the Spanish who cut their cables and were driven eastwards.

**29 July** The Battle of Gravelines. The Anglo-Dutch fleet defeated and scattered the Spaniards, who drove into the North Sea.

**1589** **May** A squadron under Drake and Sir John Norreys, assisted by some Dutch, took Corunna at the beginning of an attempt to put Don Antonio on to the throne of Portugal. Arriving at Lisbon, however, they found no support for the Don, and lacking the means to make a siege of it, returned to England.

**1591** **31 August** The last fight of the *Revenge*.

**1594** **October–November** Sir Martin Frobisher retook the peninsula of Camaret near Brest from the Spanish, to help the French King. He died of a wound shortly after returning to England.

**1595** **28 August** Drake and Hawkins set out on an expedition to seize the treasure of Panama. The commanders died before they could carry out their plans, Hawkins on 13 November and Drake on 28 January 1596.

**1596** **1 June** There sailed a strong squadron, including the Dutch, under Lord Howard of Effingham, the lord admiral, against Cadiz, which was taken on 21 June. Howard refused an offer of two million ducats to spare the shipping. The Spanish loss has been estimated at 20,000,000 ducats, or £9,300,000.

**1597** The Islands Voyage under Lord Essex, aimed against Corunna and Ferrol; and then the Azores, where they intended to capture bases and await the Spanish treasure ships. The plan to attack the mainland towns was dropped in the event, but in the Azores Essex and Raleigh took Fayal. No rich prize was taken and the expedition returned home disappointed.

**1602** **3 June** Sir William Monson and Sir Richard Leveson took a great carrack at Cezimbra, worth a million ducats; two galleys were also taken.

Nine galleys that had escaped destruction at Cezimbra left to cruise on the coast of Flanders under the command of Federigo Spinola. They were intercepted by an English squadron under Sir Robert Mansell in the Straits of Dover on 23 September. The handy English ships not only outgunned them, but rammed them and sailed over them. Only one, Spinola's own galley, managed to get safely into Dunkirk. This was the last considerable action between galleys and galleons in Northern Waters.

**1603** **24 March** Death of Queen Elizabeth I.

**1604** **August** James I made peace with Spain.

**1623 27 February** The Dutch at Amboyna in the East Indies seized the English residents, tortured them, murdered ten and drove the rest from the Island. This act long rankled with the English at home and was one of the more conscious causes of the First Dutch War in 1652.

**1625** In spite of Amboyna Anglo-Dutch squadrons of East Indiamen fought several fierce actions against the Portuguese to gain a footing in India. The principal English captain involved was John Weddell.

**1625** Viscount Wimbledon's expedition against Spain. He briefly took and held Fort Puntal, near Cadiz; then abandoned it and tried to intercept the Plate fleet, but failed and returned home empty handed.

**1626** War with France.

**1627 June to November** The Duke of Buckingham's first expedition to assist La Rochelle against King Louis XIII, which turned out a failure.

**1628 23 August** The Duke of Buckingham, the lord high admiral, was murdered at Portsmouth by John Felton, just before the second expedition to relieve La Rochelle sailed. The expedition went without him but their desultory efforts were soon brought to an end when La Rochelle surrendered to the French king's army. In the Mediterranean Sir Kenelm Digby, with a privateer squadron, defeated a Franco-Venetian squadron at Scanderoon, taking three French ships and sinking one.

**1636** Loss of the *Anne Royal*, which bilged on her own anchor in the Medway.

**1637** Building of the *Sovereign of the Seas*, the first ship to carry one hundred guns (see page 22).

**1638** H.R.H. James, Duke of York, was made lord high admiral at the age of five.

**1639** The Battle of the Downs, when the Dutch fleet under Marten Tromp defeated the Spanish in English waters. The English fleet, which was neutral, looked on.

**1642** The Civil War, the fleet sided with Parliament under the Earl of Warwick. In August he helped to take Portsmouth from the Royalists.

**1643 August** Warwick failed to take Exeter and lost three ships.

**1644 May** Warwick relieved Blake who was besieged at Lyme in Dorset.

**1648** Revolt of part of the fleet to the Royalists, Prince Rupert took command.

**1649** Prince Rupert operated against Parliamentary shipping in home waters and later in the Mediterranean.

**1650** A Parliamentary fleet under Robert Blake left England in February to seek out Prince Rupert, and appeared in the Tagus, where it blockaded the Royalist squadron until October, when Rupert escaped to the Mediterranean. Blake chased him and finally engaged and defeated him in Cartagena Bay on 5 November, though Rupert escaped.

**1652/4** The First Dutch War.

**1652 19 May** The Battle off Dover, the first fleet engagement of the Dutch Wars, was fought when Britain was nominally still at peace. Marten Tromp led the Dutch fleet down on to Blake's fleet, who fired several warning shots for Tromp to dip his flag, which was finally answered with a broadside, and general action was joined and lasted all day. The Dutch lost two ships, but one the *St Maria*, 37, which was abandoned by the English as sinking, was later reboarded by the Dutch and taken to Holland. The English lost no ships.

**27 August** Van Galen defeated a squadron under Captain Richard Badiley off Elba.

**28 September** The Battle of the Kentish Knock saw the Dutch under De With beaten by the English under Blake.

**1653 18 February** Tromp had two hundred merchant ships that he was convoying home from the Mediterranean, when he was attacked by the English fleet under Blake off Portland. The action continued for a further two days, but the results were indecisive.

**4 March** Captain Badiley and his squadron had left Elba and appeared off Leghorn where Appleton's squadron of six ships lay. These were supposed to come out and join him, but were intercepted and defeated by Van Galen before Badiley could beat up to Appleton's assistance. Only one ship fought her way through, and as a result the English temporarily abandoned the Mediterranean.

**2-3 June** The Battle of the Gabbard. Blake had been wounded at Portland and was ashore, so the command was shared by the two Generals at Sea, George Monck and Richard Deane. Deane was killed at the start of the action, which went well for the English and even better on the following day when the Dutch fell into confusion and defeat. Eleven prizes were then brought in.

**3 July** The Battle of Scheveningen, the final defeat of the Dutch fleet and with it the death of their great admiral, Marten Tromp. Through Blake's illness the honours were shared by Monck and William Penn.

**1656 8 September** Captain Stayner and his squadron captured a ship of the Plate fleet off Cadiz and destroyed three more.

**1657 20 April** Blake destroyed the Spanish fleet at Santa Cruz, Teneriffe.

**7 August** Blake died at sea as his squadron was entering Plymouth Sound.

**1660** The Restoration of King Charles II.

**1665/7** The Second Dutch War.

**1665 3 June** The Battle of Lowestoft, when the Dutch under Obdam were heavily defeated by the English, commanded by the King's brother and lord high admiral, H.R.H. the Duke of York. The Dutch flagship, the *Eendracht*, blew up in action with the Duke, and Obdam with most of his crew were killed. The Dutch lost about thirty ships, and their fleet was unable to appear again that year.

**3 August** Repulse at Bergen. One of the results of Lowestoft was that the returning Dutch East India fleet had to put into Bergen to avoid capture. The English bribed the Danish king into waiving his neutrality and allow them to enter Bergen harbour to take the fleet. The Danish governor, however, either because he had not received his orders, or because he chose to ignore them, supported the Dutch ships with his shore batteries, so that the English squadron was forced to withdraw and abandon this discreditable venture.

**1666 1–4 June** The Four Days Fight. The English fleet had been foolishly split, with Monck, now the Duke of Albemarle, to the east awaiting De Ruyter, and Prince Rupert to the west watching for the French, who never came. Thus Albemarle had to fight alone for two days, greatly outnumbered, before retreating to join Rupert on the third. In spite of their better order and discipline the English suffered heavily that day, since disabled ships that fell behind were taken, and one of our finest ships, the *Royal Prince* 90, (the rebuilt *Prince Royal* of 1610, see p. 20) went aground on the Galloper Sand and had to surrender. On the fourth day Monck and Rupert fought united,

but the fleets parted exhausted, without a decision. It was the great Dutch victory in a fleet action of the wars, but not one that gave unqualified satisfaction to those of them in the know. 'If we cannot destroy the English divided,' they asked, 'how can we defeat them united?'.

**25 and 26 July** The answer came seven weeks later off the North Foreland on St James's Day and the day following, when Rupert and Albermarle decisively defeated De Ruyter. The Dutch fleet was driven off the seas for the second year running.

**8 August** Sir Robert Holmes His Bonfire. An outcome of the defeat of the Dutch fleet was that Sir Robert, with a small squadron, could sail into the Vlie and destroy about one hundred and seventy Dutch merchantmen.

**1667 9–28 June** The English made the mistake of demanding unacceptable terms at the peace-table at Breda in May, on the strength of the previous year's victories, but at the same time did not mobilise the fleet. De Ruyter prepared swiftly and secretly and descended on the English fleet lying in ordinary in the Medway, taking Sheerness. The best English ship, the *Royal Charles* 80, was taken and three others burnt, and a few smaller ones taken or burnt; not to mention those sunk by the English to prevent the Dutch getting to Chatham. It was the greatest defeat in English naval history and enabled the Dutch to get better terms in the peace treaty that followed.

**1672/3** The Third Dutch War.

**1672 12 and 13 March** Sir Robert Holmes attacked a Dutch convoy of their Smyrna fleet off the Isle of Wight, though King Charles did not declare war until the 19th; and the French followed on the 27th

**28 May** The Battle of Solebay. The Duke of York allowed himself to be caught at anchor in the bay with the result that the Allied fleet went into battle in some disorder. Partly for this reason the *Royal James* 100, the flagship of Lord Sandwich, was burnt by a fireship and the admiral drowned. The Dutch lost two ships, and the French, who were to play a feeble part in the engagements, did not get into action at all.

**1673** The three actions fought this year were all aimed at neutralising the Dutch fleet so that an army could be landed on the coast of

Holland. It was De Ruyter's skill in the use of the greatly improved Dutch fleet (though smaller than the Allied one) which prevented the Allies from gaining a decisive victory, and obliged them to quit the Dutch coast for repairs. The first two battles, called the First and Second Battles of Schoonveld, 28 May and 4 June, with Prince Rupert in command of the Allies, were tactically indecisive. In the first the French lost two ships and the Dutch one, in the second neither lost any. The last action of the war, the Battle of Texel on August 11th, was very fiercely fought, and the English came near to losing the *Royal Prince* 100, which made a classic defence; but at the end only one vessel, an English yacht, was lost on either side.

**1681 22 May** The *Kingfisher* Action. This was one of the many actions fought by ships of the 'Streights Fleet', kept in the Mediterranean to protect our merchant shipping against the Barbary corsairs. On this occasion the *Kingfisher* 46, Captain Sir John Kempthorne, fought alone with seven of them from 1.0 p.m. to 1.0 a.m. and beat them off. Kempthorne was killed.

**1689 1 May** The Battle of Bantry Bay. The first fleet action of the long French Wars, the English fleet was under Admiral Arthur Herbert (afterwards the Earl of Torrington). The French were found in Bantry Bay delivering stores for King James's army. Herbert had to work to windward to meet the French, who bore down on him in good order, and in superior numbers. The French had the best of it though they took no ships. As a result of the action war was formally declared, known as the War of the English Succession 1689–97.

**1690 30 June** The Battle of Beachy Head. On this occasion the English fleet was joined by the Dutch who formed the van squadron, the whole commanded by Torrington. Even so the French could put into the contest sixty-eight ships against fifty-six, due to two squadrons of English ships being away from the main fleet. Again the battle was indecisive, only one small Dutch ship being taken, though the loss in men was heavier on the Anglo/Dutch side. The French admiral was the Comte de Tourville.

**1692 19–24 May** The Battle of Barfleur and the subsequent destruction of the French

ships at La Hogue. The Allied admiral was Edward Russell (afterwards the Earl of Orford), and this time he came in overwhelming force against Tourville, with ninety-six ships of the line to the French forty-four. In the fleet action on the 19th the French lost no ships, though they were fortunate that a fog enabled them to escape. They were chased to the French coast and a large part took shelter in the Bay of La Hogue where the allies burnt twelve of them on the 23rd and 24th. Tourville's flagship, the *Soleil Royal* 106, and two others were similarly treated near Cherbourg. James II, who was at La Hogue, thus saw his hopes of regaining the British crown literally go up in smoke.

**1697 11 September** The Treaty of Rijswijk ended the war.

**1702** War with France and Spain, the War of the Spanish Succession.

**1702 20–24 August** Benbow and Ducasse. This four-day action in the West Indies is remembered best for the gallantry of Admiral John Benbow, who died afterwards of his wounds, and the drama attending the infamous conduct of most of his captains.

**12 October** After an abortive attack on Cadiz, the Allied fleet was returning home when news came of the Spanish treasure fleet and its French escort of fifteen ships in Vigo Bay. All the French ships and the Spanish treasure ships were taken or burnt, and the spoils included £3,000,000 in specie. The Allied commander-in-chief was Sir George Rooke.

**1703 16 November** The Great Storm, in which thirteen English men of war were lost.

**1704 24 July** Rooke and the Allied fleet captured Gibralter.

**13 August** The Battle of Malaga. The Anglo-Dutch fleet evenly matched the Franco-Spanish one; the former under Rooke and the latter under a natural son of Louis XIV, the Comte de Toulouse. Neither side had a ship taken.

**1703 23 September** Barcelona was taken, the English naval commander being Sir Clowdisley Shovell.

**1707 22 October** Sir Clowdisley's flagship, returning home, was wrecked off The Isles of Scilly with the loss of all hands. With the *Association* 96, was lost the *Eagle* 70, *Romney* 50 and the *Firebrand*, a fireship.

**1708 28 May** Commodore Wager's action. Wager met the Spanish treasure fleet off Carthagena in the West Indies. He himself engaged the flagship which unfortunately blew up. He captured the third largest, but the second largest managed to beach herself and was burnt by her crew.

**1713** The Treaty of Utrecht and peace.

**1718** War with Spain.

**11 August** Sir George Byng defeated the Spanish fleet off Cape Passaro, taking or burning twenty-two of their fleet. On the whole the Spanish ships were wretchedly officered and manned throughout the century, so that there came to be a French saying, 'to chase a Spaniard is to capture one'.

**1720** Peace with Spain.

**1739** War with Spain, called the War of Jenkins' Ear.

**21 November** With six ships, Edward Vernon took Porto Bello, a town in what is now called Venezuela.

**1740/4** Anson made his voyage round the world.

**1741 March to May** Vernon's unsuccessful attempt to capture Carthagena.

**1743 20 June** Anson captured the Manila treasure ship *Nuestra Signora de Covadonga* in the Pacific. The booty from her filled thirty wagons on his return.

**1744 11 February** After watching for the French fleet to leave Toulon for two years, Mathews was rewarded at last, though England was not formally at war with France. The action proved disappointing (see p. 40) and Mathews and the French admiral, Monsieur de Court, were court-martialled and disgraced by their respective governments.

**1744 5 October** The loss of the *Victory* 100 (see p. 35).

**1747 3 May** The first Battle of Finisterre. A French fleet destined partly for operations in North America and partly for India was intercepted by Anson's fleet, which was the stronger. In the chase both French commanders, the Marquis de la Jonquière and Monsieur Saint George, were captured, also six other warships, three indiamen and numerous other vessels. Anson was given a baronetcy.

**14 October** The Second Battle of Finisterre. A superior English fleet, this time under Sir Edward Hawke, including twelve ships of the line and two fifties, defeated a French squadron of eight ships of the line, six of which were captured, though the French commodore, Monsieur de L'Etenduere, escaped.

**1748 1 October** Knowles's action off Havana. In this not very well conducted action between six Spanish and six English ships of the line, the Spanish lost only one ship captured but a second subsequently had to be burnt by her crew. Knowles was court-martialled and sentenced to be reprimanded for not bringing his squadron into action in better order.

**1749** Peace with France and Spain.

**1755 14 February** The taking of Geriah. This port with its fortress was the seat of the notorious Mahrattan pirate Tulagee Angria, whose outrages on Indian and European traders finally brought down on him a strong force of naval and Company ships and a small detachment of Mahrattan grabs, under Rear-Admiral Charles Watson, with Clive in charge of the troops. After a bombardment on the 12th the port surrendered, but refused to let in Clive the following morning, so was bombarded again, and Clive and his troops finally marched in on the 14th. They found a great quantity of cannon and stores, and £100,000 in rupees; the shipping in the harbour was destroyed.

**1756/63** War with France, the Seven Years War.

**1756 May–June** Byng's action off Minorca and the subsequent loss of the island with its valuable base at Port Mahon.

Although the British government knew from October 1755 that the French were preparing an expedition at Toulon to take the island, yet it was March the following year before Vice-Admiral the Hon. John Byng and a scraped together fleet were dispatched to strengthen the defences. Nothing was done to relieve the octogenarian military governor. The French military commander was the able playboy duke, De Richelieu. On 20 May the fleets of Byng and the French naval commander, Monsieur de la Galissonnière, met at Minorca, both with twelve ships in the line. In the action that followed neither side took a ship, but the British suffered the heavier damage and casualties. At a council of war aboard Byng's flagship it was decided that further attacks on the French fleet were unlikely to drive them off and it was better to return to protect Gibraltar, which was done. Port Mahon fell on 29 June, and Byng was subsequently court martialled and shot. The only benefit the English derived from this sad affair came from Richelieu's chef, who devised a new dressing which he named in honour of the occasion, mahonaise, or as we know it, mayonnaise.

**1757** **2 January** Calcutta captured from the French by Rear-Admiral Watson, and on the 23rd, Chandernagore.

**21 October** Forest's action off Cape Francois (North America). Two sixties and a sixty-four had been sent to intercept a French convoy, but when they met it, Captain Forest made out the escort to be five two-deckers and two frigates; two of them were seventy-fours. Nevertheless, after consulting Captains Suckling and Laughton he decided to accept battle, and a two-and-a-half hours action ensued. It ended with the French commodore, Monsieur de Kersaint, having his ship towed out of the line and the whole lot made off, to their discredit.

**1758** **28 February** The *Monmouth* 64 took the *Foudroyant* 84 (see page 42).

**29 April** Vice-Admiral George Pocock fought an action with Comte d'Aché's squadron off Cuddalore, and had the best of it, though no ship was taken.

**5 to 12 June** The Hon. Richard Howe commanded a fleet that landed near St Malo but failed to take it.

**26 July** Admiral Boscawen took Louisbourg.

**3 August** Pocock and D'Aché fought a second action which ended with the French in flight, though no ships were taken.

**17 August to 10 September** Howe again took the Duke of Marlborough's army to Brittany, but again it failed to take St Malo. This time, however, the adventure ended in disaster, as the French army attacked while the English were being taken to the ships in the Bay of St Cas. Over eight hundred soldiers were captured, as well as four post-captains superintending the embarkation.

**20 December** The capture of Goree. This is the island off Dakar, which was the French base in West Africa and which menaced English trade with the East. The English were obliged to take it several times during the French wars, but always gave it back.

This time Commodore the Hon. Augustus Keppel and a small squadron took it.

**1759** The year of victories.

**1 May** The capture of Guadeloupe.

**18 August** The Battle of Lagos. In light winds Boscawen, with an advantage in numbers, fifteen, to twelve in the French line, brought De la Clue to action and badly beat him, taking three ships and burning two. M. de la Clue, who had run his flagship ashore, died in Lagos of his wounds.

**2 September** The third and fiercest action between Pocock and D'Ache which followed the same pattern as before, but this time the French casualties reached the high figure of fifteen hundred; the British figure was five hundred and sixty-nine. As a result D'Ache who had been wounded, abandoned Indian waters.

**June to September** Vice-Admiral Charles Saunders was in charge of the naval side of the defeat of the French in Canada, bringing a great fleet, which included twenty ships of the line, up to Quebec for the final assault.

**20 November** The Battle of Quiberon Bay. This dramatic action was fought in a gale, when Sir Edward Hawke chased the French fleet in a running fight into Quiberon Bay where, because of the rocks, the French thought they would not be followed. The *Soleil Royal* 80, the flagship of Monsieur de Conflans, was beached and burnt by her crew before we could get to her; another flagship, the *Formidable* 80 was captured; the *Thesée* 74 was one of the rare ships to founder in action, another was taken and burnt and another wrecked. Several of those ships that sought shelter in the mouth of the River Vilaine and had got out their guns and stores to escape the British reach by going up the river, never could be got down again. It was the end of any serious French naval effort in the war.

**1761** **15 January** The capture of Pondicherry. On New Year's Day that year a great storm nearly destroyed Rear-Admiral Stevens's blockading squadron; as it was, a fifty, a twenty and a fireship drove ashore and were wrecked; a sixty and a sixty-four foundered with nearly all hands, and four more were dismasted. The blockade was resumed on 3 February and Pondicherry was reduced by famine to surrender.

**8 June** The capture of Belle Isle. A force

was dispatched in April under Commodore Keppel and Major General Hodgson, who took the island which was held for the rest of the war.

**8 June** On the same day Commodore Sir James Douglas captured Dominica.

**5 October** The capture of Manila. On the information of Colonel Draper that the Spanish defences were weak in the Philippines, he was sent in charge of the troops and took Manila, Luzon and all the Spanish islands in the group. Rear-Admiral Cornish was in charge of the naval side.

**1762 16 February** The capture of Martinique. Rear-Admiral Rodney landed the troops in Port Royal Bay on 16 January, but Major-General Monckton found the going hard, and it took a month to reduce the island.

**13 August** The capture of Havana. This was the last and most ambitious of the amphibious operations of the Seven Years War. Admiral Sir George Pocock commanded a fleet of over fifty warships, besides storeships and hospital ships etc., and the troops were commanded by the Earl of Albemarle. The rewards from this success were considerable; stores and species to the value of £3,000,000, and twelve Spanish ships of the line that were in the harbour.

**1763 10 February** The peace treaty signed which ended the Seven Years War.

**1764 21 June** Captain the Hon. John Byron set out on his voyage round the world, with two ships, returning on 9 May 1766.

**1766 22 August** A further expedition under Captain Samuel Wallis set sail for the Straits of Magellan and the Pacific, where he discovered Tahiti. He returned home on 20 May 1768. The other ship under Captain Carteret, which discovered Pitcairn Island, did not get home until March 1769.

**1768 26 July** James Cook sailed on his first voyage to the Pacific in the *Endeavour*. This was a Royal Society expedition to observe the transit of Venus, the navy providing the transport for Mr Joseph Banks and his scientists. The observation was successfully made from Tahiti on 4 June 1769. The expedition also explored on the coasts of New Zealand and Australia, and returned home on 12 June 1771.

**1772 13 July** Cook's second voyage, this time to find out whether there really was a great

sub-continent populated by millions of people, as was widely held. The expedition went in two ships, the *Resolution* and *Adventure*, and Cook returned with his findings on 30 July 1775, having penetrated deep into the Antarctic icefields.

**1775** Rebellion in the American colonies.

**1776 14 July** Cook's third voyage. The *Resolution* went again, this time with the *Discovery*, and the purpose was to see if there was a navigable passage from the Pacific to the Atlantic over Canada. Cook tried to find it in the summers of 1777 and 1778, but was killed in January 1779. With great persistence, his people tried again that year, without success. They finally reached the Nore in the Thames on 4 October 1780.

**1778** War with France.

**27 July** The Battle of Ushant. The British fleet in the Channel under Admiral Keppel met the French fleet under the Comte d'Orvilliers off Ushant; the result was inconclusive and on the British side failure to beat the enemy was generally blamed on the poor manner in which Keppel was supported by his second-in-command, Sir Hugh Palliser. The result was two very ugly courts martial, and feelings ran so high that, at a time of great national peril, several of the best officers would not serve.

**21 August** Sir Edward Vernon captured Pondicherry.

**30 December** The capture of St Lucia. A well-conducted operation by Rear-Admiral the Hon. Samuel Barrington and Major-General James Grant, in the face of a superior French fleet under Comte d'Estaing, which failed to shift Barrington, who fought him at anchor. The French relief forces landed ashore were bloodily repulsed and D'Estaing had to leave the island to its fate.

**1779** Spain declared war against England.

**6 July** Byron's action off Grenada. Vice-Admiral the Hon. John Byron was in command of a fleet of twenty-one ships of the line, which he took into action against D'Estaing's fleet, precipitantly and in bad order, and was lucky not to lose at least one.

**1780 16 January** The Moonlight Battle of St Vincent. Rodney was taking a convoy of reinforcements to Gibraltar on his way to assume command of the Leeward Islands station, when he came upon a Spanish squadron of eleven ships of the line and two frigates, commanded by Admiral Langara. The Spaniards, outnumbered two to one, fled and in a night action six were taken and one blew up.

**17 April, 15 May and 19 May** The dates of the three actions fought by Rodney in the West Indies with the new French commander there, the Comte de Guichen. All were inconclusive, but the strain of the stalking and manœuvring broke the health of the Frenchman, who asked to be recalled.

**1781 3 February** Rodney at Saint Eustatius where, when he had taken it, he found merchandise to the value of £3,000,000.

**16 April** The action at Porto Praya. Commodore Johnstone had been sent with a squadron and troops in an attempt to take Capetown from the Dutch, who had shortly before entered the war against us. The French, hearing of it, sent a squadron of their own after Johnstone to frustrate him. This was commanded by the famous De Suffren, who found Johnstone's ships anchored in a negligent manner at Porto Praya. Had he been properly supported by all his squadron, he might have given us a serious reverse, as it was the British beat off the attack at anchor. Johnstone, who was a most unpleasant fellow and an M.P., managed to waste sufficient time to let De Suffren reach Capetown before him, and could do nothing on his arrival there but turn round and come home.

**16 March** Arbuthnot and De Touches. An action off Chesapeake Bay in which neither side lost a ship.

**29 March** Hood and De Grasse. De Grasse, the new French commander in the West Indies, was bringing a convoy from France when he met Hood, who was the British commander during Rodney's absence in England, with a fleet inferior to the French. Hood was to lee and could not close, so a long-range action took place without effect.

**5 August** The Battle of the Dogger Bank. Vice-Admiral Hyde Parker was convoying home a merchant fleet from the Baltic when he encountered Admiral Zoutmann, with a Dutch squadron, also convoying merchantmen. Both sides had seven ships in the line, though the British were the heavier gunned, and the engagement naturally enough, proved one of the most fiercely fought of the war. No ship was lost in the action, but one Dutchman sank the following day.

**5 September** The Battle of Chesapeake. Rear-Admiral Thomas Graves with nineteen sail of the line was in action with De Grasse who had twenty-four. The two fleets never really got to grips, but the fact that the British were unable to establish naval ascendancy in North American waters at that time was the chief cause of the success of the American colonial rebellion.

**12 December** De Guichen, convoying a supply fleet on its way to De Grasse through the Bay of Biscay, unfortunately found himself ahead and to lee of his charges when Rear-Admiral Richard Kempenfelt was sighted with a squadron of the Channel fleet, and took fifteen of them.

**1782 25 January** De Grasse had invested St Kitts when Hood appeared. The French came out and Hood by smart manœuvring took over the French anchorage. The next day De Grasse tried to shift Hood in a close action, but failed. St Kitts was saved.

**17 February** The first of the five fleet actions between Sir Edward Hughes and De Suffren of the east coast of India. The others were on 12 April, 5 July, 3 September 1782, and 20 June 1783. Neither side lost a ship in these hard-fought actions, but on the whole the French had the strategic advantage, their high point being the taking of Trincomalee. De Suffren was the abler officer, but Hughes, 'Old Hot and Hot', had the advantage of the better discipline and organisation of his service.

**12 April** The Battle of the Saints. De Grasse's fleet was finally brought to book with a shattering defeat that included the capture of the French flagship the *Ville de Paris* 104.

**October** Lord Howe relieved Gibraltar for the last time. Since the Spanish entered the war their most protracted and determined attempt to regain the Rock for Spain had resulted in a classic siege. In spite of strong opposition the British had twice before managed to relieve the place with a convoy of stores. Lord Howe's success in the face of a powerful Franco-Spanish fleet finally made the Spanish despair of success, their only reason for fighting the war, and they sued for peace.

**29 August** The loss of the *Royal George* 100.

**1783** Peace with France, Holland, Spain and the United States of America.

**1791** Commander George Vancouver's expedition to Nootka Sound to re-establish the British flag there, and survey the north-west coast of America. He returned October 1794.

**1793** War with France, the Revolutionary Wars.
**27 August** Lord Hood occupied Toulon with the connivance of the French royalists, and stayed until the middle of December, when the advance of the Republican army forced him to leave. He took with him nineteen French warships, including the *Commerce de Marseilles* 120 (see p. 64), and fourteen more had been burnt. This still left twenty-five in Republican hands. The Anglo-Spanish fleet carried away as many of the royalist population as it could, nearly 15,000, but many thousands left behind, were brutally butchered by the Republicans.

**1794 20 March** Martinique was captured by Vice-Admiral Sir John Jervis and Lieutenant-General Sir Charles Grey. This success was followed by the capture of St Lucia on 4 April.
**1 June** The battle called the Glorious First of June. This was the first fleet action of the long Revolutionary Wars. A French fleet of twenty-six of the line commanded by Rear-Admiral Villaret-Joyeuse, left Brest to convoy an expected merchant fleet from America. Lord Howe with twenty-five of the line brought him to action, captured six of the French ships and sank one. There was no ship lost on the British side.

**1795 14 March** The Hotham's Action off Genoa. Vice-Admiral William Hotham had succeeded Lord Hood who had gone home. He managed to bring the French Mediterranean fleet to a partial action during which the French lost an eighty and a seventy-four out of a fleet of fifteen of the line. Hotham had fourteen.
**17 June** Cornwallis's retreat. A British squadron of four seventy-fours, the *Royal Sovereign* 100 and two frigates encountered the French fleet off Belle Isle and was obliged to retire as the French had twelve of the line two fifties and nine frigates. At one time it looked as if one of the British seventy-fours, the *Mars*, would be captured, having fallen to lee with damage aloft, but Cornwallis himself bore up to her aid in the *Royal Sovereign* and saved her. It was a bold and

gallant gesture, and the French shortly after gave up the pursuit. The French had been purposely misled by Captain Robert Stopford of the *Phaeton* 38, who was making signals to what he pretended was Bridport's fleet; when a fleet of merchantmen were sighted the French thought it was the British fleet.
**23 June** Bridport's Action off the Isle de Groix. Lord Bridport was in command of the channel fleet in the absence of Lord Howe. The action was a general chase, and the first French ship to strike was the *Alexandre* 74, which, as the *Alexander*, had been captured from the British the year before. Two other French ships of the line also captured, but a disappointing action.
**12 July** Hotham's Action off Hyeres. The Mediterranean fleets engaged a second time, the French doing their best to get away. The British engaged in general chase as they came up. One seventy-four struck and then burnt and blew up, but the opportunities of the situation were not exploited by Hotham to advantage.
**26 July** Rear-Admiral Peter Rainier captured Trincomalee. All the Dutch possessions in Ceylon fell by February 1796, as did all the Dutch settlements in India.
**16 August** Cape Colony was taken from the Dutch by Vice-Admiral Sir George Keith Elphinstone.

**1796 April–June** Operations commanded by Rear-Admiral Sir Hugh Cloberry Christian and Lieutenant-General Sir Ralph Abercromby from Barbados led to the capture of St Lucia, St Vincent and Grenada in the West Indies.
**3 August** A Dutch squadron of nine men-of-war commanded by Rear-Admiral Lucas arrived at the Cape and anchored in Saldanha Bay, about 60 miles from Simon's Bay where Elphinstone was moored. The British moved in on Lucas, anchored by him and invited him to surrender, which, as he was much the weaker, he did.
**8 October** War with Spain.

**1797 14 January** The destruction of the *Droits de l'Homme*. This French seventy-four had been on the abortive expedition to Ireland and was returning home with General Humbert and troops, when she was attacked by the British frigates *Indefatigible* 44 and *Amazon* 36. In snowstorms the two frigates hung on to her and so damaged her aloft that when they reached the French coast she drove ashore, as also did the *Amazon*. But whereas the *Amazon*'s crew got ashore with the loss of only six men, the *Droits de l'Homme* was wrecked on a sandbank off shore in a gale in the Bay of Audierne, and is supposed to have lost about a thousand of her people by drowning and exposure.

**14 February** The Battle of St Vincent. The poor quality of the Spanish fleet was highlighted by this action in which their Grand Fleet of twenty-seven ships of the line, which included the great *Santissima Trinidad* 136, the biggest ship in the world, and six three-deckers of 112 guns, was engaged by Sir John Jervis with fifteen of the line, and was lucky to lose only two of their hundred and twelves, an eighty and a seventy-four. Sir John's flagship was the *Victory* 100, and the day was especially memorable for the part played by Commodore Nelson in the *Captain* 74, when he took the *San Nicholas* 80 and the *San Joseph* 112.

**18 February** Trinidad captured from Spain by Rear-Admiral Henry Harvey and Lieutenant-General Sir Ralph Abercromby.

**3 and 5 July** The bombardments of Cadiz which were directed by Rear-Admiral Nelson.

**22 and 24 July** Nelson's abortive attack on Santa Cruz, Teneriffe, where he lost his right arm.

**11 October** The Battle of Camperdown. The last fleet action between the British and Dutch. Both sides had sixteen of the line, the British commanded by Admiral Adam Duncan, the Dutch by Vice-Admiral De Winter. In a bloody action eleven Dutchmen were taken including the two flagships, but none of the prizes was afterwards fit for sea.

**1798 1 August** The Battle of the Nile. Since May, Rear-Admiral Sir Horatio Nelson had been looking for Napoleon's fleet, which however, eluded him and transported Napoleon and his army safely to Egypt. Nelson finally found it at anchor in Aboukir Bay. Of the French fleet of thirteen of the line and four frigates only two frigates and two ships of the line escaped. All the rest were captured except a frigate which was sunk, and the principal flagship the great *L'Orient* 120, which caught fire and blew up

about 10 p.m., three-and-a-half hours after the beginning of the action. The French commander-in-chief, Vice-Admiral Brueys, had been killed by a round shot about 8 p.m. This action doomed the French army in Egypt.

**12 October** Warren's action with Bompart. A French expedition to land troops in Ireland had sailed on 16 September from Brest, and consisted of nine frigates and a seventy-four, commanded by Commodore Bompart. It was intercepted by Commodore Sir John Borlase-Warren off Tory Island before it could reach Lough Swilly. Warren had three ships of the line and five frigates. The main action, when Bompart's flagship and three of the frigates struck, took place on the 12th, but three more of the frigates were taken on the 13th, 18th and 20th.

**15 November** Commodore Sir John Duckworth and General the Hon. Charles Stuart captured Minorca.

**1799 27 August** The British landed at Den Helder and captured thirteen Dutch men-of-war there. They were in ordinary and mostly old, but on the 30th Vice-Admiral Andrew Mitchell's squadron stood into the Vlieter where the Dutch fleet in commission surrendered, twelve ships altogether of which eight were of the line.

**1800 18 February** One of the two French ships of the line which had escaped from Aboukir Bay, the *Genereux* 74, was captured while trying to get a relief convoy into Malta. This island has been captured from the Knights of Malta in 1798 by Napoleon and was now blockaded by the British, augmented for a time by a Russian squadron.

**31 March** The capture of the *Guillaume Tell* 80, the other French liner to escape from the Battle of the Nile, when trying to escape from Malta.

**4 September** Malta surrendered to the British.

**1801 2 April** The Battle of Copenhagen. Britain's answer to the hostile 'armed neutrality' of Russia, Sweden and Denmark was to send a fleet under Admiral Sir Hyde Parker to the Baltic. A detachment of ten ships of the line, two fifties and seven frigates, with bombs and sloops, went into Copenhagen harbour under the second-in-command, Lord Nelson. After a furious engagement the Danes surrendered, and with their fleet gone the Swedes and Russians settled their differences with us amicably.

**6 July** The action off Algeciras. Rear-Admiral Sir James de Saumarez with six of the line attacked a squadron of three French ships of the line and a frigate anchored in Algeciras Bay. Admiral Linois ran his ships ashore, but unfortunately during the action the *Hannibal* 74 went aground near the Spanish batteries and was forced to surrender. De Saumarez retired to Gibraltar and by tremendous efforts repaired his five ships by the 12th, on which day the French admiral, now afloat again, had been joined by five Spanish ships of the line under Vice-Admiral Moreno, two of them of 112 guns, and also a French seventy-four. Although De Saumarez had only four seventy-fours and an eighty, he immediately attacked the combined squadron, took one French seventy-four and burnt and sank both the huge Spanish one-hundred-and-twelves; a small Spanish warship was sunk.

**1802** The peace of Amiens.

**1803** War with France.

**1804 8 March** Goree had been taken by the French in January, but was recaptured by Captain Edward Dickson.

**5 May** The capture of Surinam by Commodore Samuel Hood.

**12 December** War with Spain.

**1805 22 July** Calder's Action. In this, a curtain-raiser to the Battle of Trafalgar, Vice-Admiral Robert Calder with fifteen sail of the line met Villeneuve and the Franco-Spanish fleet off Finisterre with twenty. Because of the misty weather a confused and partial action ensued during which a Spanish eighty and a seventy-four were captured. At home Calder's performance was considered inadequate, and he was recalled and severely reprimanded at a court martial, somewhat unfairly.

**21 October** The Battle of Trafalgar. After much weary searching, which had taken Nelson's fleet to the West Indies and back, he had his reward when he brought the Franco-Spanish fleet under Vice-Admiral Villeneuve to action and utter defeat off Cape Trafalgar. Of the thirty-three Franco-Spanish ships of the line engaged fifteen were lost, and two more taken on the 24th. The British who went into action with twenty-seven of the line lost

none. Lord Nelson was mortally wounded early in the action but lived to hear that he had won the greatest victory in the history of naval warfare. It was the end of any serious naval challenge from Napoleon's Empire for the rest of the war.

**4 November** Captain Sir John Strachan with four of the line and two frigates engaged a squadron of four French ships of the line off Cape Ortegal and captured them.

**1806 12 January** Commodore Sir Home-Popham took Cape Colony again. It had been restored to the Dutch by the Peace of Amiens.

**6 February** Duckworth's action off San Domingo. In a highly successful action, Vice-Admiral Sir John Duckworth, with six of the line and two frigates engaged a force of five French ships of the line, one of them the great *Imperial* 120, two frigates and another vessel. The *Imperial* was driven ashore and wrecked as was another. The other three liners were captured.

**1807 19 February** Sir John Duckworth unfortunately proved less effective against the Turks; for having taken his squadron past the batteries on the Dardanelles on the 19th, he then dithered off Constantinople until retiring back to the Mediterranean.

**2 to 5 September** The bombardment of Copenhagen by Lord Gambier's fleet.

**7 September** The surrender of the Danish fleet. This consisted of seventy vessels, eighteen of them being ships of the line. Only four of these, however, were thought worth refitting for service in the Royal Navy.

**1808 11 April** Lord Cochrane's fireships attack Basque and Aix Roads, when the French shipping there was run aground. This attack was followed up by further action by Lord Gambier's fleet, which he did not direct to the best advantage, though he was acquitted of misconduct at the court martial.

**1809 14 January** Captain James Yeo captured Cayenne from the French.

**24 February** Martinique was captured by Rear-Admiral Sir Alexander Cochrane and Lieutenant-General Beckwith.

**28 July to September** The British Expedition to Walcheren. The fleet which transported Lord Chatham's army to the Schelde was commanded by Rear-Admiral Sir John Strachan.

**1810** **16 February** Rear-Admiral William Drury captured Amboyna from the Dutch.

**9 August** The capture of Banda Neira by Captain Christopher Cole with one hundred and eighty seamen and marines. The surrendered Dutch garrison numbered fifteen hundred.

**1811** **13 March** Hoste's action off Lissa. In this remarkable action, Captain William Hoste with a small squadron of four frigates, consisting of two thirty-twos, a thirty-eight and a twenty-two, engaged and utterly defeated a Franco-Venetian squadron of six frigates, four of them forty-fours, two sloops and two gunboats, commanded by Commodore Dubourdieu. The action ended with two of the frigates taken and one destroyed. A fourth which had struck could not be taken possession of because Hoste had not a boat to send to her.

**27 August** The surrender of Java by the Dutch. The plans for this enterprise had been made by Rear-Admiral William Drury who, however, died before he could fulfil them. Commodore Robert Broughton and Lieutenant-General Samuel Auchmuty carried the plans through.

**1812** War with the United States of America.

**1813** **10 September** Commander Robert Barclay and his squadron on Lake Erie was defeated by an American squadron commanded by Commodore Oliver Perry, U.S.N. This gave the Americans control of the Upper Lakes.

**1814** **24 August** The capture of Washington by Rear-Admiral George Cockburn and Major-General Ross.

**11 September** The Battle of Lake Champlain. In this bloody encounter an American squadron commanded by Captain Thomas Macdonough defeated a British squadron under Commander George Downie, who was killed.

**14 December** The Americans were defeated in a gunboat action on Lake Borgne. The British were led by Commander Nicholas Lockyer.

**1815** The end of the French revolutionary and Napoleonic Wars. Peace with the United States of America.

**1816** **27 August** The Bombardment of Algiers. Admiral Sir Edward Pellew with five ships of the line and some Dutch frigates, which had joined him at Gibraltar, destroyed the Dey's fleet and much of the town and fortifications of Algiers in order to obtain the release of three thousand Christian slaves. He was created Viscount Exmouth.

**1824** **11 May** The capture of Rangoon; the naval forces were commanded by Commodore Grant.

**1827** **20 October** The Battle of Navarino. The last fleet action we fought under sail, in which the Turko-Egyptian fleet was destroyed by an Anglo-Franco-Russian fleet commanded by Vice-Admiral Sir Edward Codrington, as part of the measures to implement the terms of the Treaty of London and end the Greco-Turkish war.

**1839** **19 January** The capture of Aden by Captain Henry Smith.

**1839-42** The first Chinese war.

**23 August** The capture of Hong Kong. After the abandonment of the factory at Canton, Captain Charles Elliot took over Hong Kong. It was formally ceded to Britain in 1841.

**1840** **3 November** The Bombardment of St Jean d'Acre on the coast of Syria and the subsequent occupation of the town. This was the chief action of the operations of the British fleet, augmented by Turkish and Austrian squadrons and commanded by Admiral Sir Robert Stopford, which brought the Turkish port's rebellious vassal, Mahamet Ali, to submission.

**1842** **18 June** The capture of Shanghai.

**1854** War with Russia. An Anglo-French fleet commanded by Admiral Sir Charles Napier was sent to the Baltic. Another Anglo-French fleet, commanded by Vice-Admiral James Dundas, was sent to the Black Sea to support the Anglo-French army in its operations in the Crimea. Odessa was bombarded on 22 April. The army landed on 14 September and Sebastopol was bombarded from 17 to 24 October. In the Baltic the Russian fleet was not brought to action, so that the blockade of the Russian ports and the bombardment of their shore defences were all that could be achieved. The principal success was the destruction of the fortress of Bomarsund.

**1855** The Allied fleet returned to the Baltic, this time commanded by Vice-Admiral the Hon. Richard Dundas. The pattern of operations was similar to the year before, the highlight being the bombardment of Sweaborg from

9 to 11 August, where tremendous damage was done. In the Crimea further bombardments of Sebastopol were undertaken on 9 to 28 April, 6 to 10, 16 and 17 June, 16 to 19 July, 6 to 9 August and 5 to 7 September. The southern part of the fortress and the docks were evacuated by the Russians on 9 to 10 September. Before they left they destroyed their fleet, one hundred and seventeen vessels, including five 120-gun, eight 84-gun and one 80-gun sailing ships of the line and four 60-gun frigates.

**1856** Peace with Russia.

**1856–60** The second China war.

**25 October** Canton was captured by the British commander-in-chief on the China station Rear-Admiral Sir Michael Seymour.

**1857 1 June** The Battle of Fatshan Creek. The Chinese had assembled between seventy and eighty armed junks near a fort in the creek, which was close to Canton. Sir Michael Seymour with two paddle tenders, seven gunboats, and oared boats from the fleet, attacked, captured and burnt all but a very few that escaped to Fatshan.

**1858 20 May** The bombardment by an Anglo-French force of the Taku forts.

**27 June** The Treaty of Tientsin. This should normally have ended the war, but the state of near-anarchy in parts of China prevented the terms of peace being properly implemented. War was formally renewed on 8 April 1859.

**1859 25 June** A force of ten gunboats and a sloop, under the new British commander-in-chief, Rear-Admiral James Hope, was repulsed in its attempt against the Peiho forts. The admiral was severely wounded.

**1860 21 August** Rear-Admiral James Hope captured the Taku forts, and then proceeded up to Tientsin which he occupied. It required the capture of Peking by an Anglo-French army and the destruction of the Summer Palace to persuade the Chinese to ratify the peace of Tientsin permanently.
**29 December** The launch of the *Warrior* (see p. 100).

**1861 29 December** The *Conqueror*, 101 guns, wrecked on Rum Keye in the Bahamas.

**1862 10 May** Capture of Ning Po.

**24 October** Capture of Kahding and the end of the Ti-Ping rebellion.

**1863 15 August** Action against the Japanese in Kagosima Harbour.

**1864 September** Action against the Japanese Prince Choshiu; the Strait of Simonoseki forced.
**14 December** The *Bombay*, 67 guns, burnt at Montevideo; 94 were lost with her.

**1867 17 July** Review at Spithead; with the Queen, the Sultan of Turkey and the Viceroy of Egypt. The wooden 3-decker *Victoria* was the flagship, the last occasion on which a wooden ship of the line performed this office at a review.

**1868 10 April** The Naval Brigade take part in the defeat of the slavers at Arrogie Pass in Abyssinia.
**13 April** Capture of Mogdala during the same campaign.

**1869** The great floating dock towed to Bermuda by ironclads *Black Prince*, *Warrior*, *Agincourt* and *Northumberland*.

**1870 7 September** The ironclad *Captain* capsized and foundered off Finisterre (see page 110).

**1873** The Ashanti War; actions at Elmira, 13 June; Essaman, 14 October; Dunquah, 3 November; Bootoy, 28 October.

**1874 13 February** Peace with the Ashantis.

**1875** Nares' Polar Expedition.

**1875 1 September** H.M.S. *Vanguard* sunk in collision with H.M.S. *Iron Duke*.

**1877 29 May** Action between the *Shah* and the *Huascar* (see p. 131).

**1878 24 March** The training frigate *Eurydice* capsized off the Isle of Wight; about 300 perished.
**July** Occupation of Cyprus.

**1880 1 February** The training frigate *Atalanta* sailed from Bermuda with 280 on board; she was never heard of again.

**1882 11 July** Bombardment of the forts at Alexandria by the Mediterranean Fleet.
**20 August** Occupation of the Suez Canal.
**September** Defeat of the Egyptians at Tell-el-Kebir.

**1887 23 July** Queen Victoria's Golden Jubilee Review at Spithead. Amongst the one hundred and thirty-five vessels present were fourteen battleships, four coast-defence ships and twelve large cruisers.

**1889** **15 March** Hurricane at Apia on Samoa, when the American cruiser *Trenton* and a corvette and sloop, and a German corvette and two gun vessels were lost. Only the British cruiser *Calliope* escaped.

**1893** **22 June** Loss of the *Victoria*, flagship of the Mediterranean Fleet, when in collision with the *Camperdown* during manœuvres, with the loss of 22 officers and 336 men.

**1897** **26 June** Queen Victoria's Diamond Jubilee Review at Spithead. Although not one ship was brought home from foreign stations, the line of ships assembled was over thirty miles long. There were twenty-one battleships present, fifteen of them of the 1st class, over fifty cruisers and one hundred other vessels.

**1899** Outbreak of the Boer War, naval units engaged ashore in South Africa.

**1900** Boxer Rebellion in China.
**13 July** Capture of Tientsin with the aid of naval and marine units.
**14 August** Relief of Peking.

**1902** **16 August** The Coronation Review of King Edward VII at Spithead. Postponed from 28 June owing to the King's illness.

**1904** **18 March** Submarine *A1* sunk in collision with the S.S. *Berwick Castle*, Portsmouth; raised.
**October** The Russian Baltic Fleet, on its way to reinforce the Pacific Fleet during the Russo-Japanese war, fired on British trawlers in the North Sea in the curiously mistaken belief that they were Japanese torpedo-boats. The Russians were therefore closely escorted by British warships until well on their way down the coast of Africa, to ultimate annihilation by the Japanese fleet at Tsushima in May 1905.

**1905** **August** Anglo-French fleets reviewed by the King at Spithead in the name of the 'Entente Cordiale'.

**1906** **2 February** Launch of H.M.S. *Dreadnought*.
**30 May** The battleship *Montagu* wrecked on Lundy Island.

**1909** **March** 'We want eight and we won't wait' expansion of the dreadnought building programme.
**14 July** Submarine *C11* sunk in collision with the S.S. *Eddystone*.

**1911** **29 March** The Coronation Review of King George V at Spithead. Of the one hundred and sixty-seven units of the Royal Navy present, thirty-two were battleships and dreadnoughts and thirty-eight battle-cruisers and cruisers.
**August** Submarine *A1* finally lost during experiments.

**1912** **2 February** Submarine *A3* lost in collision with H.M.S. *Hazard* off the Isle of Wight; raised.
**8 August** Holland type submarine number 5 lost while in tow.
**4 October** Submarine *B2* lost in collision with S.S. *Amerika*.

**1914** **16 January** Submarine *A7* foundered in Whitesand Bay.
**18–20 July** Inspection by the King of the mobilized fleet. Never had the Solent been so full of ships. Over thirty miles of them, fifty-eight of them battleships and battle-cruisers.
**4 August** Outbreak of the First World War.
**28 August** Action in the Heligoland Bight. British light-cruisers sank the German cruiser *Mainz*. Then Beatty's battle-cruisers arrived in support and the cruisers *Köln* and *Ariadne* joined the *Mainz* at the bottom.
**14 September** The British merchant-cruiser *Carmania* sank the German merchant-cruiser *Cap Trafalgar* in the South Atlantic.
**20 September** The cruiser *Pegasus* was disabled and beached after an action with the German cruiser *Königsberg* off Zanzibar.
**22 September** *Cressy*, *Hogue* and *Aboukir* sunk by *U9* (see page 197).
**28 September** H.M.S. *Triumph* assisted the Japanese at the bombardment of Tsingtau.
**1 November** Rear-Admiral Sir Christopher Cradock's squadron defeated at Coronel by Admiral Graf Spee's squadron; the flagship, the *Good Hope*, and the *Monmouth* lost with all hands.
**26 November** The battleship *Bulwark* blew up at Sheerness.
**8 December** Rear-Admiral Sturdee revenges Cradock's defeat by defeating Graf Spee at the Battle of the Falkland Islands. The *Scharnhorst*, *Gneisenau*, *Nürnberg* and *Leipzig* sunk.
**27 October** The super-dreadnought *Audacious* mined and sunk off Loch Swilly.

**1915** **1 January** The battleship *Formidable* torpedoed in the Channel by *U24*.
**24 January** Battle of the Dogger Bank in which Beatty's battle-cruisers fought a running fight with three of Hipper's battle-cruisers and a heavy cruiser. The latter, the

*Blucher*, was sunk (see page 181).

**14 March** The German cruiser *Dresden*, the only one to escape Sturdee at the Falkland Islands, was found by the *Glasgow*, *Kent* and *Orama* at Juan Fernandez; she surrendered and was destroyed by her crew.

**March** Naval operations in support of the landings at Gallipoli; bombardments of the Turkish forts, particularly on 18 March. On this day the battleships *Irresistible* and *Ocean* were mined. In addition the French battleship *Bouvet* was mined and sank in three minutes.

**6 May** The White Star liner *Lusitania* sunk by a German submarine.

**13 May** The battleship *Goliath* sunk by torpedoes from a German-manned Turkish torpedo-boat.

**25 May** The battleship *Triumph* sunk by *U21* in the Dardanelles.

**27 May** The battleship *Majestic* sunk by the same submarine.

**1916 27 April** The battleship *Russell* was mined and sank off Malta.

**31 May** The Battle of Jutland, the last great fleet action for gunners. Of major units, the British lost three battle-cruisers, the Germans a battleship and a battle-cruiser. The British, however, also lost three armoured cruisers with heavy loss of life. The battle-cruisers had all been lost by internal explosions so that the total loss of life was over 6,700 while for the Germans it was only 3,000. It was, however, the last time the High Seas Fleet risked an action with the Grand Fleet.

**1917 9 January** The battleship *Cornwallis* torpedoed and sunk by *U32*.

**9 July** The dreadnought *Vanguard* blew up in Scapa Flow with the loss of 804 lives (see page 163).

**1918 23 April** H.M.S. *Vindictive* and light forces attacked Zeebrugge and Ostend in an attempt to block the entrances to these harbours, and so their use by German submarines and destroyers. The operation was successful against Zeebrugge but not so successful at Ostend, so the gallant *Vindictive* was sent there on a further raid on 9 and 10 May, this time with success.

**11 November** The Armistice.

**21 November** The surrender of the German High Seas Fleet. This was escorted into Rosyth between lines of British and American battleships, where the instrument of surrender was signed aboard the *Queen Elizabeth*. The German ships were shortly afterwards moved to Scapa Flow.

**22 November** Submarine *G11* lost off Howick.

**1919 9 June** Submarine *L55* lost in the Baltic.

**21 June** German Fleet scuttled at Scapa Flow; only one of the battleships, the *Baden*, was saved, as well as three light-cruisers and twenty destroyers.

**18 August** Two Russian battleships and a depot ship sunk at their moorings by units of Rear-Admiral Cowan's squadron (the aircraft carrier *Vindictive* and torpedo-carrying coastal motor boats). This was the naval part of the war against the Bolsheviks (1918–20), which had also featured the sinking of the Russian cruiser *Oleg* by Lieutenant Agar in a C.M.B.

Units of the Royal Navy were also active in support of the land forces at Archangel, in the Black Sea and in the Caspian Sea, and on the other side of Siberia at Vladivostok.

**1921 20 January** Submarine *K5* foundered off Torquay during manoeuvres.

**1922 6 February** Signing of the Limitation of Armament Treaty arising from the Washington Conference (1921–2) (see page 213).

**1922 23 March** Submarine *H42* sunk in collision with H.M.S. *Versatile* off Gibraltar.

**8 August** H.M.S. *Raleigh* wrecked on the coast of Labrador.

**1924 10 January** Submarine *L24* sunk in collision with H.M.S. *Resolution*.

**1925 12 November** Submarine *M1* sunk in collision with the S.S. *Vidar*.

**1926 9 August** Submarine *H29* sank at Devonport.

**1929 9 July** Submarine *H47* sunk in collision with submarine *L12*.

**1931 9 June** Submarine *Poseidon* sunk in collision with the S.S. *Yuta*.

**1931 12–13 September** The Invergordon Mutiny. The Slump brought pay cuts in the public services. Those in the navy fell heaviest on the lowest paid, so a petty officer was reduced from 8s. 6d. per day to 7s. 6d., while an ordinary seaman was reduced from 2s. 9d. to 2s. 0d., a much higher percentage. Twelve thousand men in twelve ships off Invergordon refused duty, but the following day, on being ordered to their home ports, the ships sailed, and the pay-cuts were amended.

**1932** **26 January** Submarine *M2* foundered in the English Channel through submerging with the hangar doors open.

**1935** **16 July** King George V's Silver Jubilee Review at Spithead.

**1937** **20 May** King George VI's Coronation Review at Spithead.

**1939** **1 June** H.M. submarine *Thetis* lost on trials in the Mersey.

**3 September** War with Germany.

**17 September** The aircraft carrier *Courageous* torpedoed and sunk by *U29*.

**14 October** The battleship *Royal Oak* torpedoed and sunk by *U47* in Scapa Flow.

**23 November** The auxiliary cruiser *Rawalpindi* sunk in the North Atlantic by the *Scharnhorst* and *Gneisenau*.

**13 December** Action between the German pocket battleship *Admiral Graf Spee* and the cruisers *Ajax*, *Achilles* and *Exeter* off the River Plate.

**17 December** The *Graf Spee*, which had taken shelter in Montevideo, steamed out into the channel and scuttled herself (see page 216).

**1940** **April** Operations off Norway aimed at thwarting the German occupation.

**10 April** First Battle of Narvik, when five *H* class destroyers surprised some German destroyers in Narvik and sank two. Five more German ships, however, surprised the British on their way out and sank two of them.

**13 April** The Second Battle of Narvik, when the battleship *Warspite* was sent up in support of the destroyers. The eight German destroyers and a *U*-boat there were sunk.

**26 May–4 June** Evacuation of Dunkirk.

**8 June** The aircraft carrier *Glorious* sunk by the German battle-cruisers *Scharnhorst* and *Gneisenau* while evacuating aircraft from Norway. Two destroyers with the *Glorious* were also sunk defending her, though one of them managed to torpedo the *Scharnhorst*.

**3 July** The French battleships in Oran were bombarded and put out of action; the *Bretagne* blew up.

**8 July** The new French battleship *Richelieu* immobilized at Dakar.

**23 September** Attempt to land De Gaulle and Free French Forces at Dakar. Resistance from the Vichy French and their defences bombarded on the 23 and 24; the *Resolution* damaged by a torpedo from a French submarine.

**5 November** The auxiliary cruiser *Jervis Bay* saved her convoy, but was sunk by the pocket battleship *Admiral Scheer*.

**11 November** Swordfish torpedo-bombers attacked the Italian Fleet at Taranto from the aircraft carrier *Illustrious* and three Italian battleships were sunk at their moorings.

**1941** **January** First of the relief of Malta convoys, the aircraft carrier *Illustrious* badly damaged by bombs on the way, and the cruiser *Southampton* sunk.

**9 February** Force H bombarded the port of Genoa.

**27 March** The night action off Matapan, when units of the Mediterranean Fleet, the battleships *Warspite*, *Valiant* and *Barham*, sank the Italian cruisers *Pola*, *Zara* and *Fiume*.

**18 May** The sortie of the German battleship *Bismarck*.

**24 May** The battle-cruiser *Hood* blown up in action with the *Bismarck* and the battleship *Prince of Wales* badly damaged.

**26 May** A strike from the *Ark Royal* of torpedo-carrying Swordfish, in dreadful weather, disabled the *Bismarck*'s rudder.

**27 May** The battleships *King George V* and the *Rodney* were thereby enabled to catch up with *Bismarck* and destroy her.

**13 November** *U81* torpedoed and sank the aircraft carrier *Ark Royal*.

**25 November** The battleship *Barham*, on patrol with the Mediterranean Fleet, torpedoed by *U331* and blown up.

**7 December** The attack by the Japanese on Pearl Harbour. War with Japan.

**10 December** Japanese bombers sank the battleship *Prince of Wales* and the battle-cruiser *Repulse* off Malaya.

**1942** **15 January** Loss of the naval base of Singapore.

**12 February** The German battle-cruisers *Scharnhorst* and *Gneisenau* and the cruiser *Prinz Eugen* successfully made a dash through the English Channel from Brest to Wilhemshaven and the Elbe, though both the *Scharnhorst* and *Gneisenau* were mined on the way.

**27–8 February** The Battle of the Java Sea. A mixed Dutch, American and British force of cruisers and destroyers was defeated by the Japanese surface forces; the *Exeter* was lost, also the Australian cruiser *Perth*, the USS

*Houston*, and the Dutch cruisers *Java* and *De Ruyter*, plus destroyers.

**22 March** The Battle of Sirte. Admiral Vian with five light-cruisers and seventeen destroyers escorting four merchantmen to Malta was attacked by the Italian battleship *Littorio*, two heavy and one light-cruiser. In a five-hour action, the big Italian ships were held off and finally retired.

**27 March** H.M.S. *Campbeltown*'s raid on Saint-Nazaire. This old American lease-lend destroyer and eighteen coastal craft, under the command of Commander Robert Ryder, went up the Loire to attempt to destroy the lock-gates of the huge dry-dock in which the liner *Normandre* had been built at Saint-Nazaire. The *Campbeltown* was full of explosives and she successfully rammed the dock and later blew up, killing the Germans who were aboard to try and make her 'safe'. The dock was put out of action for the war, but only two of the coastal craft got home. Both Ryder and Stephen Beattie, who commanded the *Campbeltown*, were awarded the Victoria Cross.

**5 April** The cruisers *Dorsetshire* and *Cornwall* sunk by Japanese bombers near Ceylon.

**8 April** Japanese bombers also sank the aircraft carrier *Hermes* in the same area.

**June** In half a year, German *U*-boats sank 585 merchantmen, over three million tons of shipping. Most on the west side of the Atlantic, where the Americans were slow to adopt the convoy system.

**27 June** The ill-fated convoy to Russia, P.Q.17, sailed to destruction. The Admiralty thought at one point that the convoy was about to be attacked by the battleship *Tirpitz* and other heavy units and ordered the escort to withdraw and the convoy to scatter. The fact was that there was no immediate threat of that kind, but the Germans made good use of the new situation and *U*-boats and aircraft accounted for twenty-three of the thirty-six merchantmen that set out.

**August** The German tactic of employing 'wolf packs' of *U*-boats was having successes. Convoy S.C.94, for instance, lost eleven ships out of thirty-three in a five-day battle; only two *U*-boats were destroyed, and four damaged. However, successes of this kind were to wane for the *U*-boats. New short-range radar, which could be used for aircraft, and hunter groups of sloops caused heavy losses. The standard of training of the *U*-boat crews also declined with the high losses, and this caused further losses. The provision of an escort aircraft carrier in the convoy made it difficult, or impossible, for the *U*-boat pack to follow the convoy on the surface by day.

**11–13 August** The convoy 'Pedestal' to relieve Malta. In one of the severest actions of the war, five ships of a convoy of fourteen were got through with a massive escort. Of this, one aircraft carrier, the *Eagle*, was torpedoed and sunk, as were the cruisers *Manchester* and *Cairo*. The aircraft carriers *Indomitable* and *Victorious* were damaged by bombs and the cruisers *Kenya* and *Nigeria* by torpedoes.

**19 August** The Dieppe Raid. In this disastrous amphibious operation, surprise was given precedence over preliminary bombardment. As the former was not achieved, the landings were a costly failure; over sixty per cent of the troops were lost, also thirty-three landing craft and a destroyer.

**November** The great convoy to North Africa for the landings there, called operation Torch. The French resistance at Algiers and Oran was soon overcome.

**31 December** Captain Sherbrooke's action. The close support for the convoy J.W.51B to Russia was six destroyers and five escorts under Captain Sherbrooke, while Rear-Admiral Robert Burnett's two cruisers, *Sheffield* and *Jamaica*, were to give general coverage to this and the other half of the convoy which had gone ahead. Sherbrooke's convoy was attacked in the morning by the pocket battleship *Lutzow*, the heavy cruiser *Hipper* and destroyers. The close escort held off their unequal opponents for three hours until Burnett's cruisers arrived, and after a further three hours the Germans withdrew, leaving one destroyer behind and the *Hipper* damaged. The British loss was the destroyer *Achates* and the minesweeper *Bramble*.

Hitler was so angry he ordered the remaining big ships in his navy to be dismantled, though this was later rescinded. The German head of naval operations, Grand-Admiral Raeder, resigned over the affair. Captain Sherbrooke, who lost an eye early in the action, was awarded the Victoria Cross.

**1943 March** Early in the month, three Atlantic

convoys lost thirty-four ships to the *U*-boat packs.

**May** Forty-one *U*-boats were destroyed during this month, a decisive blow against Germany's efforts to win the naval war.

**July** Operation Husky, the code name for the invasion of Sicily.

**11 September** The surrendered Italian fleet led into Malta by the battleship *Warspite*.

**22 September** The battleship *Tirpitz* attacked by two midget submarines, *X6* and *X7* in Altenfiord. Explosions under her hull threw her main armament out of alignment and put all her main turbines out of action. Both the commanders of the *X*-craft, Lieutenants Godfrey Place and Donald Cameron, were captured, and were awarded the Victoria Cross. The dire nature of the damage to the *Tirpitz* was not apparent in the reconnaissance photographs, so that she continued to tie up forces as a threat in being, until sunk by $5\frac{1}{2}$-ton bombs from Lancaster bombers on 12 November 1944.

**26 December** The battleship *Duke of York*, together with the cruisers *Belfast, Jamaica, Norfolk, Sheffield* and destroyers sank the *Scharnhorst*. Only thirty-three out of nearly two thousand of the crew survived the Arctic waters to be picked up.

**28 December** The cruisers *Glasgow* and *Enterprise* engaged a German convoy in the Bay of Biscay and sank one large destroyer and two fleet torpedo-boats.

**1944 February** Captain Walker's attack group of five sloops sank six *U*-boats during one patrol, and in the same period, other groups and aircraft of Coastal Command sank five more.

**3 April** Barracuda dive-bombers from the aircraft carriers *Victorious* and *Furious* damaged the *Tirpitz*.

**19 April** The return of the Royal Navy to the offensive in the Far East opened with a damaging attack on Japanese installations and shipping at Sabang, near Singapore.

**6 June** Operation Neptune, the naval part of Overlord, or the invasion of Normandy, in which over 1,300 vessels of all types put the Allied armies on to the continent of Europe.

**1945 24 and 29 January** Aircraft from the *Illustrious, Indomitable, Victorious* and *Indefatigable* severely damaged the refineries at Palembang in Sumatra.

**8 May** The surrender of the German Fleet.

156 *U*-boats surrendered and 221 scuttled themselves.

**16 May** The Japanese heavy cruiser *Haguro* sunk north of Sumatra by destroyers.

**August–September** The surrender of the Japanese forces.

**1946 22 October** The Communist government of Albania mined the Corfu Channel which had been swept after the war. They had given no warning, and two destroyers hit mines: the *Volage* lost her bow, and the *Saumarez* was so badly damaged as to be not worth repairing. No compensation was ever extracted from the Albanians for this cowardly and treacherous act.

**1950 12 January** The submarine *Truculent* was sunk in the Thames Estuary after being in collision with the Swedish tanker *Dvina*.

**1950–3** The Korean War, in which Royal Naval cruisers, carriers, destroyers and escort vessels gave support to the U.N. forces ashore by bombardments and air strikes against the North Koreans.

**1951 17 April** The submarine *Affray* foundered in the English Channel through schnorkel failure.

**1953 15 June** Queen Elizabeth II's Coronation Review at Spithead.

**1956 31 October to 7 November** Operation Musketeer, or the war over the control of the Suez Canal. In this ill-starred war, although the Anglo-French and Israeli forces were victorious, the politicians were decisively defeated by a combination of allies and enemies; so the military advantage was thrown away.

So far as the Royal Navy was concerned, their part in the assault and landings was impeccable and was notable as being the first time large-scale use was made of the helicopter in an amphibious landing.

**1960 4 August** The *Vanguard*, Britain's last operational battleship, towed out of Portsmouth to be scrapped.

**21 October** The launch of the nuclear submarine *Dreadnought*.

**1962–7** Naval support for Malaysia in the Indonesian 'confrontation'.

**1977 28 June** The Silver Jubilee Review of the Fleet at Spithead by Her Majesty Queen Elizabeth II.

**1982 2 April** Argentina invaded the Falkland Islands. A British Task Force was ordered to retake them.

**3 April** Argentina invaded South Georgia.

**12 April** 200 mile exclusion zone established around Falkland Islands.

**25 April** South Georgia retaken by *Antrim, Plymouth* and *Endurance*.

**2 May** Argentine cruiser *General Belgrano* sunk by 2 torpedoes from H.M.S. *Conqueror*.

**4 May** *Sheffield* hit by an Exocet missile fired from the air, burned and was abandoned.

**7 May** Exclusion zone extended to 12 miles off the coast of Argentina.

**10 May** *Sheffield* sunk under tow.

**21 May** *Ardent* sunk by missiles, *Argonaut* and *Antrim* damaged by bombs.

**23 May** *Antelope* hit by bomb that did not explode.

**24 May** Bomb in *Antelope* exploded, burning and sinking her.

**25 May** *Coventry* sunk by bomb, *Broadsword* damaged by bombs.

**8 June** *Sir Galahad* and *Sir Tristram* bombed at Fitzroy, the former with heavy casualties. *Plymouth* damaged by bombs.

**12 June** *Glamorgan* damaged by Exocet missile fired from the shore.

**14 June** Argentine forces on the Falklands surrender.

**24 June** *Sir Galahad* scuttled off the Falklands as an official war grave.

# Appendix 2
# British and Enemy Losses (ships of over 50 guns) 1688—1855

| | Taken | Destroyed during operations | Lost by wreck | Burnt by accident |
|---|---|---|---|---|
| 1688–1714<br>Wars of the<br>English and<br>Spanish Successions | British<br>16<br>(3 retaken)<br>French<br>11<br>Spanish<br>6 | British<br>1<br><br>French<br>19<br>Spanish<br>2 | British<br>23<br><br>French<br>not known<br>Spanish<br>not known | British<br>4<br><br>French<br>not known<br>Spanish<br>not known |
| 1718–48<br>Spanish War of 1718,<br>War of Jenkins' Ear,<br>1739–48* | British<br>3<br>(2 retaken)<br>French<br>17<br>Spanish<br>16 | British<br>1<br><br>French<br>none<br>Spanish<br>7 | British<br>10 and<br>1 in 1716<br>1 in 1749<br>1 in 1755<br>French<br>not known<br>Spanish<br>3 | British<br>1<br><br>French<br>3<br>Spanish<br>none |
| 1756–63<br>The Seven Years War<br>1755–63<br><br>1762 | British<br>2<br>French<br>23<br>Spanish<br>9 | British<br>none<br>French<br>9<br>Spanish<br>3 | British<br>6<br>French<br>7<br>Spanish<br>3 | British<br>1<br>French<br>3<br>Spanish<br>none |
| 1775–83<br>War of American<br>Independence<br>1778–83<br><br>1778–83<br><br>1780–82 | British<br>3<br>(1 retaken)<br>French<br>14<br>Spanish<br>11<br>Dutch<br>3 | British<br>none<br><br>French<br>1<br>Spanish<br>2<br>Dutch<br>1 | British<br>14<br><br>French<br>1<br>Spanish<br>5<br>Dutch<br>not known | British<br>1<br><br>French<br>none<br>Spanish<br>none<br>Dutch<br>not known |
| 1793–1801<br>Revolutionary Wars,<br>Part I<br>1793–1801<br><br>1795–1801<br><br>1795–1800<br><br>1801 | British<br>6<br><br>French<br>35<br>Spanish<br>5<br>Dutch<br>25<br>Danish<br>5 | British<br>none<br><br>French<br>12<br>Spanish<br>5<br>Dutch<br>none<br>Danish<br>none | British<br>13<br><br>French<br>9<br>Spanish<br>not known<br>Dutch<br>not known<br>Danish<br>not known | British<br>6<br><br>French<br>none<br>Spanish<br>not known<br>Dutch<br>not known<br>Danish<br>not known |
| 1802–15<br>Revolutionary Wars,<br>Part II<br>1802–15<br><br>1803–08 | British<br>none<br><br>French<br>30<br>Spanish<br>12 | British<br>none<br><br>French<br>7<br>Spanish<br>none | British<br>15<br><br>French<br>1<br>Spanish<br>not known | British<br>1<br><br>French<br>none<br>Spanish<br>not known |

* French did not join in until 1744

| | Taken | Destroyed during operations | Lost by wreck | Burnt by accident |
|---|---|---|---|---|
| 1803–10 | Dutch none | Dutch 4 | Dutch 1 | Dutch not known |
| 1807–13 | Danish 17 | Danish 1 | Danish not known | Danish not known |
| 1808–09 | Russian 1 | Russian none | Russian not known | Russian not known |
| 1807–08 | Turkish 1 | Turkish not known | Turkish not known | Turkish not known |
| Navarino 1827 | Turko-Egyptian none | Turko-Egyptian 4 | Turko-Egyptian not known | Turko-Egyptian not known |
| Crimean War 1855–56 | Russian none | Russian 18 | Russian not known | Russian not known |

| 1688–1855 | British | French | Spanish | Dutch | Danish | Russian | Turkish |
|---|---|---|---|---|---|---|---|
| *Taken* | 30 (6 retaken) | 130 | 59 | 28 | 22 | 1 | 1 |
| Destroyed during operations | 2 | 48 | 19 | 5 | 1 | 18 | 4 |
| | 26 | 178 | 78 | 33 | 23 | 19 | 5 |

| Grand Total | British | Foreign |
|---|---|---|
| | 26 | 336 |

Of the British ships on this list lost in action, all were lost to the French, except for one of the two destroyed, the *Dartmouth* 50, which blew up in action with the Spanish *Glorioso* in 1747.

The figures above are based on the lists of William Laird Clowes.

# 𝕸𝖊𝖒𝖔𝖎𝖗𝖘

### OF THE

# RISE AND PROGRESS

### OF THE

# ROYAL NAVY.

---

## By CHARLES DERRICK, Esq.
### OF THE NAVY-OFFICE.

---

Island of bliss! amid the subject seas
That thunder round thy rocky coasts, set up
At once the wonder, terror and delight
Of distant nations; whose remotest shores
Can soon be shaken by thy naval arm:
Not to be shook thyself; but all assaults
Baffling, as thy hoar cliff the loud sea-wave.

THOMSON.

---

For oh it much imports you, 'tis your all,
To keep your trade entire, entire the force
And honour of your fleets; o'er that to watch
E'en with a hand severe, and jealous eye.

IBID.

---

## London:

PRINTED BY H. TEAPE, TOWER-HILL;

SOLD BY BLACKS AND PARRY, LEADENHALL-STREET; CADELL AND DAVIES, STRAND;
AND G. AND W. NICOL, PALL-MALL.

1806.

323

# Appendix 3

# Some Establishments of the Ships, Guns and Men 1517–1805

In 1806 the then Secretary to the Committee of Stores in the Navy Office published a book called *Memoirs of the Rise and Progress of the Royal Navy*. His name was Charles Derrick and his interest in the development of the fleet probably stemmed from the twenty years he had spent in the Surveyor's office, ten as Chief Clerk, prior to transferring to Stores and Slops. He died in 1831.

In this work are collected the earliest lists of royal ships, and for later periods, abstracts showing the number of ships in the service per rate, and also guns and men for given dates. Interspersed with these are historical observations and notes to explain points in the lists.

Since this admirable work must by now be unavailable except in a very few libraries, it has been thought useful to re-publish it here in an abridged form, which includes most of the lists and those notes relating to them. A certain amount of rearrangement has been done to make them more strictly chronological, but otherwise editing has been kept to a minimum.

Further lists to bring the record forward from Derrick's publication in 1806 have been prepared by the author and follow in appendix 4.

## Henry VIII 1509–1547

The following List of all the King's Ships in the 9th year of his reign, is taken from Mr. Pepys's Miscellanies.*

### 1517

| | Men in Harbour. |
|---|---|
| The Henry Grace de Dieu | 12 |
| Katherine Fortune | 4 |
| Gabriel Royal | 4 |
| Great Barbara | 4 |
| John Baptist | 4 |
| Mary Rose | 4 |
| Great Bark | 4 |
| Peter Pomegranate | 3 |
| Mary George | 4 |
| Mary John | 3 |
| Less Bark | 3 |
| Mary James | 1 |
| Henry Hampton | 3 |
| Lizard | 2 |
| Two Row Barges—(one man each) | 2 |
| The Rose Galley | 1 |
| Katherine Galley | 1 |
| Sovereign | 1 |
| Great Nicholas | 1 |
| Great Galley | 10 |
| In all 21 Ships and Vessels. | |

From the same source from which the foregoing List was obtained, the following is also taken, being an Account of the Names and tonnage of all the King's Ships, according to a general survey, dated 1st June, in the 13th Year of his reign:

*Vol. 8.*

### 1521

| | Tons. |
|---|---|
| The Henry Grace de Dieu | 1500* |
| Sovereign | 800 |
| Gabriel Royal | 650 |
| Katherine Forteless† | 550 |
| Mary Rose | 600 |
| John Baptist | 400 |
| Barbara | 400 |
| Great Nicholas | 400 |
| Mary George | 250 |
| Mary James | 240 |
| Henry Hampton | 120 |
| Great Bark | 250 |
| Less Bark | 180 |
| Two Row Barges (60 tons each) | 120 |
| The Great Galley | 800 |
| In all 16 Ships and Vessels. | 7260 |

### 1523

In the Year 1523, Sir William Fitzwilliams had under his command a fleet of Thirty-six large Ships, to cruize on the coasts of France; and Anthony Points had at the same time the command of a considerable fleet to guard the western seas.—but it is not known how many of the Ships were the King's own.‡

*She is in almost every other account said to have been 1000 tons only, which is certainly the most correct.*

*N.B.—The Sovereign was in dock at Woolwich, at this time, and was recommended, by the Officers who surveyed the Ships, to be rebuilt, "as she is a goodly ship."—It also appears that there was a great Storehouse of the King's at Erith, at this time.*

*† So spelt in the original; but Fortileza, according to Charnock.*

*‡ The Cinque Ports, with their Members, were bound by their tenure to supply the King with 57 Ships, containing 21 men and a boy in each ship, for 15 days once in the year at their own expence, if their service was required: and they were frequently obliged to furnish a great number. (See Archæologia, Vol. 6, page 195.) After the 15 days they were paid by the King.*

**1546**

(*The Anthony Anthony Roll*) A List of the Royal Navy in 1546.

| Quality. | Shyppes Names. | Tunnage. | Soldiers. | Mariners. | Soldiers & Mariners. | Gunners. | Total No of Men. |
|---|---|---|---|---|---|---|---|
| Shyppes .. | Harry Grace a Dieu | 1000 | 349 | 301 | ... | 50 | 700 |
| | Mary Roase ...... | 700 | 185 | 200 | ... | 30 | 415 |
| | Peter ........... | 600 | 185 | 185 | ... | 30 | 400 |
| | Mathew.......... | 600 | 138 | 138 | ... | 24 | 300 |
| | Great Barke ...... | 500 | 136 | 138 | ... | 26 | 300 |
| | Jhesus of Lubeck .. | 700 | 118 | 158 | ... | 24 | 300 |
| | Pawncy .......... | 450 | 136 | 140 | ... | 24 | 300 |
| | Murryan ........ | 500 | 138 | 142 | ... | 20 | 300 |
| | Struce .......... | 450 | 140 | 96 | ... | 14 | 250 |
| | Mary Hamborow.. | 400 | 119 | 111 | ... | 16 | 246 |
| | Xtopher of Bream. | 400 | 119 | 111 | ... | 16 | 246 |
| | Trinity Harry..... | 250 | 100 | 100 | ... | 20 | 220 |
| | Smaell Barke ..... | 400 | 105 | 122 | ... | 23 | 250 |
| | Swypstake........ | 300 | 100 | 109 | ... | 21 | 230 |
| | Mynnion.......... | 300 | 100 | 100 | ... | 20 | 220 |
| | Larticque ........ | 100 | 80 | 52 | ... | 8 | 140 |
| | Mary Thomas .... | 90 | 25 | 47 | ... | 8 | 80 |
| | Hope Barke....... | 80 | 28 | 28 | ... | 4 | 60 |
| | George........... | 60 | 18 | 18 | ... | 4 | 40 |
| | Mary Jaymes ..... | 60 | 18 | 18 | ... | 4 | 40 |
| Galleasses | Graunde Masterys. | 450 | ... | ... | 220 | 30 | 250 |
| | Anne Gallante .... | 450 | ... | ... | 220 | 30 | 250 |
| | Harte........... | 300 | ... | ... | 170 | 30 | 200 |
| | Antelop.......... | 300 | ... | ... | 170 | 30 | 200 |
| | Tegar........... | 200 | ... | 100 | ... | 20 | 120 |
| | Bulle ........... | 200 | ... | 100 | ... | 20 | 120 |
| | Salamander ...... | 300 | ... | 200 | ... | 20 | 220 |
| | Unicorne......... | 240 | ... | 124 | ... | 16 | 140 |
| | Swallowe......... | 240 | ... | 130 | ... | 30 | 160 |
| | Galie Subtile...... | 200 | ... | 242 | ... | 8 | 250 |
| | Newe Barke ...... | 200 | ... | 124 | ... | 16 | 140 |
| | Greyhounde ...... | 200 | ... | 124 | ... | 16 | 140 |
| | Jennet .......... | 180 | ... | 106 | ... | 14 | 120 |
| | Lyon ........... | 140 | ... | 88 | ... | 12 | 100 |
| | Dragon ......... | 140 | ... | 98 | ... | 12 | 110 |
| Pynnasses | Phawcon ......... | 80 | ... | 54 | ... | 6 | 60 |
| | Sacar ........... | 80 | ... | 54 | ... | 6 | 60 |
| | Hynde .......... | 80 | ... | 54 | ... | 6 | 60 |
| | Roo ............ | 80 | ... | 46 | ... | 4 | 50 |
| | Phenyx ......... | 40 | ... | 46 | ... | 4 | 50 |
| | Marlyon ......... | 40 | ... | 46 | ... | 4 | 50 |
| | Lesse Pinnas...... | 40 | ... | 40 | ... | 4 | 44 |
| | Bryggendyn ...... | 40 | ... | 40 | ... | 4 | 44 |
| | Hare ........... | 15 | ... | 28 | ... | 2 | 30 |
| | Trego-Ronnyger .. | 20 | ... | 24 | ... | 1 | 25 |
| Roo-Baergys | Double Rose...... | 20 | ... | 39 | ... | 4 | 43 |
| | Flowre de Luce.... | 20 | ... | 39 | ... | 4 | 43 |
| | Portquillice....... | 20 | ... | 34 | ... | 4 | 38 |
| | Harpe .......... | 20 | ... | 36 | ... | 4 | 40 |
| | Clowde in the Sonne | 20 | ... | 36 | ... | 4 | 40 |
| | Rose in the Sonne.. | 20 | ... | 36 | ... | 4 | 40 |
| | Hawthorne ....... | 20 | ... | 34 | ... | 4 | 38 |
| | Thre Ostrydge Feathers ....... | 20 | ... | 33 | ... | 4 | 37 |
| | Fawcon in the Fetterlock ...... | 20 | ... | 41 | ... | 4 | 45 |
| | Maydenhede...... | 20 | ... | 33 | ... | 4 | 37 |
| | Rose Slype ....... | 20 | ... | 33 | ... | 4 | 37 |
| | Jyllyver Flowre.... | 20 | ... | 34 | ... | 4 | 38 |
| | Sonne ........... | 20 | ... | 36 | ... | 4 | 40 |

| Abstract. | No | Tunnage. | Soldiers. | Mariners. | Soldiers & Mariners. | Gunners. | Total No of Men |
|---|---|---|---|---|---|---|---|
| Shyppes ...... | 20 | 7940 | 2337 | 2314 | ... | 386 | 5037 |
| Galleasses .... | 15 | 3740 | .... | 1436 | 780 | 304 | 2520 |
| Pynnaces ..... | 10 | 515 | .... | 432 | ... | 41 | 473 |
| Roo-Baerges .. | 13 | 260 | .... | 464 | ... | 52 | 516 |
| Total | 58 | 12455 | 2337 | 4646 | 780 | 783 | 8546 |

# Edward VI 1547–1553

The following List of the Navy on the 5th January, 1548, is taken from the 6th vol. of the Archæologia, p. 218.*

**1548**

| Names. | Where at. | Tons. | Soldiers, Mariners, &c. | Pieces of Ordnance. Brass. | Pieces of Ordnance. Iron. |
|---|---|---|---|---|---|
| The Henry Grace de Dieu ............ | Woolwich. | 1000 | 700 | 19 | 103 |
| Peter............ | | 600 | 400 | 12 | 78 |
| Matthew ........ | | 600 | 300 | 10 | 121 |
| Jesus............ | | 700 | 300 | 8 | 66 |
| Pauncy.......... | | 450 | 300 | 13 | 69 |
| Great Bark ...... | | 500 | 300 | 12 | 85 |
| Less Bark........ | Ports-mouth. | 400 | 250 | 11 | 98 |
| Murryan ........ | | 500 | 300 | 10 | 53 |
| Shruce of Dawske. | | 450 | 250 | — | 39 |
| Christopher...... | | 400 | 246 | 2 | 51 |
| Trinity Henry.... | | 250 | 220 | 1 | 63 |
| Sweepstake ...... | | 300 | 230 | 6 | 78 |
| Mary Willoughby | | 140 | 160 | — | 23 |
| Anne Gallant .... | | 450 | 250 | 16 | 46 |
| Salamander...... | Galleys at Ports-mouth. | 300 | 220 | 9 | 40 |
| Hart............ | | 300 | 200 | 4 | 52 |
| Antelope ........ | | 300 | 200 | 4 | 40 |
| Swallow......... | | 240 | 100 | 8 | 45 |

| Name | | Tons | | | Total |
|------|---|------|---|---|-------|
| Unicorn | | 240 | 140 | 6 | 30 |
| Jeannet | | 180 | 120 | 6 | 35 |
| New Bark | | 200 | 140 | 5 | 48 |
| Greyhound | Galleys | 200 | 140 | 8 | 37 |
| Tiger | at | 200 | 120 | 4 | 39 |
| Bull | Ports- | 200 | 120 | 5 | 42 |
| Lion | mouth. | 140 | 140 | 2 | 48 |
| George | | 60 | 40 | 2 | 26 |
| Dragon | | 140 | 120 | 3 | 42 |
| Falcon | | 83 | 55 | 4 | 22 |
| Black Pinnace | Pinnaces | 80 | 44 | 2 | 15 |
| Hind | at | 80 | 55 | 2 | 26 |
| Spanish Shallop | Ports- | 20 | 26 | — | 7 |
| Hare | mouth. | 15 | 30 | — | 10 |
| Sun | | 20 | 40 | 2 | 6 |
| Cloud in the Sun | | 20 | 40 | 2 | 7 |
| Harp | | 20 | 40 | 1 | 6 |
| Maidenhead | | 20 | 37 | 1 | 6 |
| Gilly-flower | Row-Barges | 20 | 38 | — | — |
| Ostridge-feather | at | 20 | 37 | 1 | 6 |
| Rose Slip | Ports- | 20 | 37 | 2 | 6 |
| Flower de Luce | mouth. | 20 | 43 | 2 | 7 |
| Rose in the Sun | | 20 | 40 | 3 | 7 |
| Portcullis | | 20 | 38 | 1 | 6 |
| Falcon in the Featherlock† | | 20 | 45 | 3 | 8 |
| Grand Mrs. | | 450 | 250 | 1 | 22 |
| Marlyon | | 40 | 50 | 4 | 8 |
| Galley Subtil, or Row Galley | Deptford | 200 | 250 | 3 | 28 |
| Brigantine | Strand | 40 | 44 | 3 | 19 |
| Hoy Bark | | 80 | 60 | — | 5 |
| Hawthorn | | 20 | 37 | — | — |
| Mary Hamburgh | | 400 | 246 | 5 | 67 |
| Phœnix | In | 40 | 50 | 4 | 33 |
| Saker | Scotland. | 40 | 50 | 2 | 18 |
| Double Rose | | 20 | 43 | 3 | 6 |

Total 11268‡ 7731 237 1848

In all 53 Ships and Vessels.

* Mr. Topham stated to the Antiquarian Society that soon after the death of Henry the Eighth a Commission issued for an inventory to be taken of all his effects of every kind: and that a List of the Names of the King's Ships then in being, together with an Account of the Tonnage, the Stores, and Ammunition of every particular Ship, and the Number of Men carried by each of them, is preserved in Mr. Brander's valuable MSS. from which he took this account.

† Or Falcon in the Fetterlock.

‡ In the Archæologia, and in Charnock, the tonnage is stated to have been 6255; Tons; but the tonnage inserted against the several ships will be found to amount to 11268 tons. The error in the first-mentioned amount must have originated in a mstake in casting up the aggregate, and has been copied since by others who were not aware of the necessity of revising it.

In the second year of his Majesty's reign, (on the 22d January), the following Ships were "thought meet to keep the Seas,—with their Tonnage, number of Men, Wages and Victuals for the same for every Month of twenty-eight days, as a Summer Guard*:"

**1549**

| Names. | Tons. | Soldiers. | Mariners. | Gunners. | Total Number of Men. |
|--------|-------|-----------|-----------|----------|----------------------|
| The Great Bark | 500 | 136 | 138 | 26 | 300 |
| Less Bark | 400 | 105 | 112 | 23 | 240 |
| Sweepstake | 300 | 100 | 109 | 21 | 230 |
| Hart | 300 | — | 180 | 20 | 200 |
| Antelope | 300 | — | 180 | 20 | 200 |
| Swallow | 240 | — | 142 | 18 | 160 |
| New Bark | 200 | — | 124 | 16 | 140 |
| Grayhound | 200 | — | 124 | 16 | 140 |
| Flower de Luce | 50 | — | 56 | 4 | 60 |
| Double Rose | 50 | — | 56 | 4 | 60 |
| | 2540 | 341 | 1221 | 168 | 1730 |

Wages ....... £640  5  0
Victuals ...... 720 16  8 } For One Month.
                1361  1  8

* Pepy's Miscellanies, vol. 8. p. 149.

"And the following as a Winter Guard."*

**1552**

| Names. | Tons. | Soldiers. | Mariners. | Gunners. | Total Number of Men. |
|--------|-------|-----------|-----------|----------|----------------------|
| The Paunsey | 450 | 136 | 140 | 24 | 300 |
| Murrian | 500 | 138 | 142 | 20 | 300 |
| Mary Hamboro | 400 | 108 | 120 | 18 | 246 |
| Jennet | 180 | — | 104 | 16 | 120 |
| Dragon | 140 | — | 104 | 16 | 120 |
| Lion | 140 | — | 104 | 16 | 120 |
| Faulcon | 80 | — | 62 | 8 | 70 |
| Hinde | 80 | — | 54 | 6 | 60 |
| Phoenix | 40 | — | 44 | 6 | 50 |
| Mª. Willoughby | 140 | 36 | 80 | 14 | 130 |
| | 2150 | 418 | 954 | 144 | 1516 |

Wages ....... £543 14  0
Victuals ...... 631 13  4 } Month.
                1175  7  4

* Pepys's Miscellanies, vol. 8. p. 149.

The following Report of the State of the Royal Navy, on 26th August, 1552, is so valuable as to merit being inserted at full length.

**1552**

"GENERAL STATE OF THE KING's SHIPS."
"The State of the King's Majesty's Ships, 26 August, An. 6. R. R. Edward VI."*

The Edward† ..........
Great Bark .........
Paunsey ...........
Trinity ............
Salamander.........
Bull ..............
Tiger .............
Willoughby ........
Primrose ..........
Antelope ..........
Hart ..............
Greyhound .........
Swallow ...........
Jennet ............
New Bark ..........
Falcon ............
Sacre ............
Phœnix ...........
Jer-Falcon ........
Swift ............
Sun ..............
Moon .............
Seven Stars .......
Flower de Luce .....

All these Ships and Pinnaces are in good case to serve, so that they may be grounded and caulked once a year, to keep them tight.
*To be so ordered,*
*By the King's Command.*

Peter .............
Matthew ..........
Jesus .............
Sweepstakes .......
Mᵃ. Hambrough ....
Ann Gallant ........
Hynde ............

These Ships must be docked and new dubbed, to search their Treenails and Iron-work.
*To be ordered likewise.*

Less Bark..........
Lion ..............
Dragon ...........

These Ships be already dry-docked; to be new made at your Lordship's pleasure.
*To prepare things ready for the same.*

Grand Mrs......... Dry-docked—Not thought worthy of new making.
*To lie still, or to take that which is profitable of her for other Ships.*

Struse ............
Unicorn ...........
George ...........

Thought meet to be sold.
*The George kept, and the other Three to be sold.*

Maidenhead ........
Gilly-flower ........
Port-cullis .........
Rose-Slip ..........
Double-Rose .......
Rose in the Sun .....

Not worth keeping.
*To be preserved, as they may with little charge.*

Bark of Bullen....... In Ireland, whose state we know not.

Item. The two Galleys and Brigantine must be yearly repaired, if your Lordship's pleasure be to have them kept.
*To be repaired and kept.*

"Forty-five to be kept."

* *Pepy's Miscellanies, vol. 8. p. 143.*

† *Supposed to have been the Henry Grace de Dieu; and that her name was changed by Edward, soon after his accession.*

# Mary I 1553–1558

**1557**

"A List of Ships appointed 29th May, 1557, to serve under the Lord Admiral, together with the Number of Soldiers and Gunners in the same.*"

| Names. | Burthen. Tons. | Hacbutters, or Arquebusiers. | Soldiers. | Mariners. | Gunners. |
|---|---|---|---|---|---|
| The Great Bark ....... | 500 | 50 | 80 | 190 | 30 |
| Jesus............. | 700 | 50 | 80 | 190 | 30 |
| Trinity........... | 300 | 20 | 40 | 140 | 20 |
| Swallow.......... | 240 | 20 | 40 | 140 | 20 |
| Salamander....... | 300 | 20 | 40 | 140 | 20 |
| Hart............. | 300 | 20 | 40 | 140 | 20 |
| Antelope ......... | 300 | 20 | 40 | 140 | 20 |
| Ann Gallant ...... | 300 | 20 | 40 | 140 | 20 |
| New Bark ........ | 200 | 10 | 20 | 84 | 16 |
| Mary Willoughby† | 160 | 10 | 20 | 84 | 16 |
| Bull.............. | 180 | 10 | 20 | 84 | 16 |
| Tiger ............ | 180 | 10 | 20 | 84 | 16 |
| Greyhound ....... | 180 | 10 | 20 | 84 | 16 |
| Jer Falcon ........ | 120 | 8 | 20 | 66 | 14 |
| Falcon .......... | 80 | 6 | 16 | 54 | 10 |
| George........... | 100 | 6 | 16 | 54 | 10 |
| Bark of Bullen .... | 60 | 4 | 8 | 44 | 8 |
| Saker ........... | 60 | 4 | 8 | 44 | 8 |
| Sonne........... | 50 | 4 | — | 34 | 6 |
| Double Rose ...... | 40 | — | — | 26 | 4 |
| Flower de Luce .... | 30 | — | — | 26 | 4 |
| | 4380 | 302 | 568 | 1988 | 324 |

In all 21 Ships, &c.

* *Pepys's Miscellanies, vol. 7. p. 13.*
† *The two last letters omitted in the original.*

And mention is made in Mr. Pepys's Collection of the

| Minion, | Trinity Henry, |
| Sacret, | and |
| Paunses, | Willoughby; |

which, (if the two latter are the same as the Trinity and Mary Willoughby in the foregoing List,) make twenty-four in all.

The Queen died on 17th November, 1558, when the tonnage of the Navy is said to have been reduced to 7110 tons, and the number of Ships and Vessels to 26; which number very nearly corresponds with the foregoing accounts of the Ships in 1557; but the number in the following List comes still nearer; the date of which, however, I am sorry I cannot ascertain.

## 1558

"List and Charge of Queen Mary's Ships."
"The Names of Queen Mary's Ships, with their several numbers of Men if "they shall be appointed to serve in fashion of War.*"

| Names. | Men. |
|---|---|
| The Great Bark | 260 |
| Matthew | 240 |
| Paronses, or Paunces | 220 |
| Jesus | 240 |
| Mary of Hambrᵒ | 180 |
| Trinity Henry | 160 |
| Sweepstake | 200 |
| Salamander | 200 |
| Hart | 200 |
| Antelope | 200 |
| Ann Gallant | 200 |
| Swallow | 140 |
| New Bark | 120 |
| Jennet | 140 |
| Greyhound | 100 |
| The Mᵃ Willoughby | 120 |
| Faulcon | 60 |
| Saker | 50 |
| Jer-Falcon | 90 |
| Phœnix | 40 |
| George | 40 |
| Bull | 120 |
| Tiger | 120 |
| Seven Stars ⎫ | 35 |
| Sun ⎪ Pinnaces | 30 |
| Swift ⎪ | 30 |
| Flower de Luce ⎭ | 30 |
| | 3565 |

### In all 27 Ships and Pinnaces

| | | | |
|---|---|---|---|
| "Men to serve in them | | | 3565 |
| "Wages and dead Shares....per Month of 28 Days | £1436 | 0 | 0 |
| "Victuals ............. do. | 1782 | 10 | 0 |
| | 3218 | 10 | 0 |
| "Conduct for 3000 Mariners | £450 | 0 | 0" |

* Pepys's Miscellanies, vol. 8. p. 153.

# Elizabeth I 1558–1603

The Royal Navy, on 4th Dec. 1565, consisted of the following Ships and Vessels.

## 1565

"Anno Regni Reginæ Elizᵃ. Octavo."
"The Names of all her Highnesses Ships and other Vessels, with the several Numbers appointed for their safe keeping in Harbour, as hereafter appeareth.*"

| Names. | Men in Harbour. | Names. | Men in Harbour. |
|---|---|---|---|
| Triumph | 21 | Willoughby | 7 |
| White Bear | 21 | Falcon | 3 |
| Elizᵃ. Jonas | 21 | Phœnix | 3 |
| Victory | 18 | Sacre | 3 |
| Mary Rose | 13 | Bark of Bullen | 3 |
| Hope | 13 | Hare | 3 |
| Philip and Mary | 13 | Sun | 3 |
| Lion | 13 | George | 3 |
| Jesus | 13 | Speedwell ⎫ | 3 |
| Minion | 10 | Tryright ⎬ Galleys | 3 |
| Primrose | 10 | Eleanor ⎭ | 3 |
| Antelope | 10 | Make-shift | 1 |
| Jennet | 10 | Post | 1 |
| Swallow | 10 | | |
| New Bark | 7 | In all 29 Ships and | |
| Aid | 7 | Vessels. | |

* Taken from Pepys's Miscellanies, vol. 8. p. 175.

## 1578

A List of the Royal Navy, in 1578, with the burthen of the Ships, and their Number of Men.

| Ships Names. | Burthen, Tons. | Mariners. | Gunners. | Soldiers. | Total Number of Men. |
|---|---|---|---|---|---|
| Triumph | 1000 | 450 | 50 | 200 | 780 |
| Elizabeth Jones | 900 | 300 | 50 | 200 | 600 |
| White Bear | 900 | 300 | 50 | 200 | 600 |
| Victory | 803 | 330 | 40 | 100 | 500 |
| Primrose | 803 | 330 | 40 | 100 | 500 |
| Mary Rose | 600 | 200 | 50 | 100 | 350 |
| Hope | 600 | 200 | 50 | 100 | 350 |
| Bonaventure | 600 | 160 | 30 | 110 | 300 |
| Philip and Mary | 600 | 160 | 30 | 110 | 300 |
| Lion (or Golden Lion) | 600 | 150 | 30 | 110 | 290 |
| Dreadnought | 400 | 140 | 20 | 80 | 250 |
| Swiftsure | 400 | 140 | 20 | 80 | 250 |
| Swallow | 350 | 120 | 20 | 60 | 200 |
| Antelope | 350 | 120 | 20 | 60 | 200 |
| Jennet | 350 | 120 | 20 | 60 | 200 |
| Foresight | 300 | 120 | 20 | 60 | 200 |
| Aid | 240 | 90 | 20 | 50 | 160 |

| Ships Names. | Burthen. Tons. | Mariners. | Gunners. | Soldiers. | Total No of Men. |
|---|---|---|---|---|---|
| Bull ................. | 160 | 70 | 10 | 40 | 120 |
| Tiger ............... | 160 | 70 | 10 | 40 | 120 |
| Falcon ............... | — | 60 | 10 | 20 | 80 |
| Achates .............. | 80 | 30 | 10 | 10 | 60 |
| Handmaid............ | 80 | 30 | 10 | 10 | 60 |
| Bark of Bullen ........ | 60 | 30 | 10 | — | 50 |
| George............... | under 60 | 40 | 10 | — | 50 |

In all 24 Ships, &c.    10506*   3760   630   1900   6570

\* *Estimating the Falcon at 120, and the George at 50 Tons.*

**1588**

| Names. | Burthen. Tons. | Men. |
|---|---|---|
| Ark Royal ......................... | 800 | 425 |
| Elizabeth Bonadventure .............. | 600 | 250 |
| Rainbow .......................... | 500 | 250 |
| Golden Lion ....................... | 500 | 250 |
| White Bear ........................ | 1000 | 500 |
| Vanguard ......................... | 500 | 250 |
| Revenge........................... | 500 | 250 |
| Elizabeth-Jonas .................... | 900 | 500 |
| Victory ........................... | 800 | 400 |
| Antelope .......................... | 400 | 160 |
| Triumph .......................... | 1100 | 500 |
| Dreadnought....................... | 400 | 200 |
| Mary Rose ........................ | 600 | 250 |
| Nonpareil ......................... | 500 | 250 |
| Hope ............................. | 600 | 250 |
| Galley Bonavolia ................... | 250 | 250 |
| Swiftsure ......................... | 400 | 200 |
| Swallow........................... | 360 | 160 |
| Foresight ......................... | 300 | 160 |
| Aid............................... | 250 | 120 |
| Bull .............................. | 200 | 100 |
| Tiger ............................. | 200 | 100 |
| Tramontana ....................... | 150 | 70 |
| Scout ............................ | 120 | 70 |
| Achates .......................... | 100 | 60 |
| Charles .......................... | 70 | 40 |
| Moon............................. | 60 | 40 |
| Advice............................ | 50 | 40 |
| Spy............................... | 50 | 40 |
| Marline .......................... | 50 | 35 |
| Sun............................... | 40 | 30 |
| Cygnet............................ | 30 | 20 |
| Brigantine ........................ | 90 | 35 |
| George Hoy ....................... | 120 | 24 |

Total 34 Ships, &c.    12590   6279

In an Account, dated 1589, intituled "The Ordinary Number of Shipkeepers appointed for the keeping of the Queen's Majesty's Ships in Harbour, at Chatham, &c.—

Also an Account of Her Majesty's Ships at the Seas,*" the following Ships are inserted.

**1589**

Ships in Harbour.

| | |
|---|---|
| Eliz. Jonas | Swallow |
| Triumph | Foresight |
| White Bear | Aid |
| Ark | Bull |
| Mary Rose | Tiger |
| Hope | Scout |
| Revenge | Achates |
| Nonpareil | Marline (or Martin) |
| Lion | Advice |
| Bonadventure | Spy |
| Dreadnought | Sun |
| Swiftsure | Cygnet (or Signet) |
| Brigandine | Rainbow |
| George Hoy | Spanish Ship |
| Bonaviolia | Popinjay |
| Jennet | |

The great Ship at Woolwich
Two great new Ships at Deptford.
The Four lesser new Ships.
The great new Boats (6 in Number).

\* *Pepys's Miscellanies, vol. 8. p. 280.*

An Account of Her Majesty's Ships at Sea.

| | |
|---|---|
| Victory | Tremontane |
| Vanguard | Charles |
| Antelope | Moon. |

Total of Ships, Pinnaces, and Boats 50.

The disposition shewn by the Queen to encourage all undertakings for discoveries, and planting new-found countries, excited a spirit in the nation for such expeditions; and many noblemen and gentlemen became adventurers in them.

**1599**

In the Archœologia,* there is a complete List of the Navy on the 23d May, 1599, taken from an original and beautiful manuscript in the possession of Dr. Leith,† which was exhibited to the Antiquarian Society, and read on 5th May, 1796; with the number of Brass and cast Iron Ordnance of the different species then appropriated to the respective Ships, viz.

| | |
|---|---|
| Cannon | Falconets |
| Demi-Cannon | Port-pece Halls |
| Culverins | Port-pece Chambers |
| Demi-Culverins | Fowler-Halls |
| Sakers | Fowler Chambers |
| Mynions | and |
| Falcons | Curtalls. |

Taken by the Queen's Commission, dated 3d March, in the 37th year of her reign, and directed to Lord Burleigh, Lord High Treasurer, Lord Howard, Lord High Admiral, Lord Hunsdon, &c. &c. and subsequent orders of the said Commissioners, the last whereof is dated 6th April, 1599.

\* *Vol. 13. p. 27.*
† *Of Greenwich, who has favoured me with the use of it.*

As this is an authentic and curious piece of information, with respect to the Ordnance which the Ships carried, a matter about which historians seem, till of late, to have been almost totally in the dark, and which is now by no means generally known, it will be proper to insert the List in this place.*

**1599**

Column headings (printed vertically): Names. | Cannon. | Demi-Cannon. | Culverins. | Demi-Culverins. | Sakers. | Mynions. | Falcons. | Falconets. | Port-piece Halls. | Port-piece Chambers. | Fowler Halls. | Fowler Chambers. | Curtalls. | Total No of Pieces of Ordnance.

```
Achatis .................... 6     2  5            13
Adventure ............ 4 11  5 .......... 2  4 ..  26
Advantage ............ 6  8  4 .............      18
Amity of Harwich† ..... 4  2 ................      6
St. Andrew ......... 8 21  7  2 ........ 3  7  2   50
Antelope .......... 4 13  8 .: . 1 .. 2 4 2 4 ..   38
Advice ............... 4  2  3 ...............      9
Arke .......... 4 4 12 12  6 ...... 4 7 2 4 ..     55
Answer ................ 5  8  2 ........ 2  4 ..   21
Ayde ............... 8  2  4  4 ...........        18
Bear ........................ 2 ................    2
White Bear ...... 3 11  7 10 ....... 2 .. 7 ....   40
Charles ............... 8 .. 2 ... 2  4 ..         16
Crane ................ 6  7  6 ....... 2  3 ..     24
Cygnet .................... 1  2 ...                3
Due Repulse ..... 2 3 13 14  6 ..... 2 4 2 4 ..    50
Dreadnought .... 2 .. 4 11 10 .. 2 ...... 4 8 ..   41
Defiance ........... 14 14  6 ..... 2 4 2 4 ..     46
Daysey† ........... 4 ..............                 4
Elizabeth-Jonas .. 3 6 8 9 9 1 2 .. 1 2 5 10 ..    56
Eliza Bonaventure 2 2 11 14 4 2 .... 2 4 2 4 ..    47
Foresight .......... 14  8  3  2 ...... 3  6 ..    37
Guardland ......... 16 14  4 .. ‡ .. 2 4 2 3 ..    45
Hope ......... 2 4 9 11 4 ..... 4 8 2 4 ..         48
Lion ............ 4 8 14 9 .. 1 ...... 8 16 ..     60
Mary Rose ....... 4 11 10  4 ...... 3  7 .....     39
Mere Honora ..... 4 15 16  4 ...... 2 ....         41
St. Matthew ..... 4 4 16 14 4 4 2 ........          48
Mercury or Galley-
   Mercury .......... 1 .. 1 ........... 4 ..        6
Marlin ............... 7 ...........                 7
Moon ................. 4  4  1 ...........           9
Nonpareil ...... 2 3 7 8 12 ..... 4 8 4 8 ..       56
Quittance ...... 2  6  7  4 ......... 2  4         25
Rainbow ........ 6 12  7  1 ..............          26
Scout .............. 4 .. 6 ...........             10
Swiftsure ...... 2 .. 5 12 8 .. 2 ...... 4 8 ..     41
Spy ................. 4  2  3 ...........            9
Swallow ............ 2  1 ... 2 .. 3 ..              8
Sonne ............... 1 .. 4 ...........             5
Triumph ........ 4 3 17 8 6 ..... 1 4 5 20 ..      68
Tremontana .............. 12  7  2 ...........      21
Tiger ............... 6 14 .. 2 ...........         22
```

Vauntguard ....... 4 14 11 2 ............... 31
Victory ........... 12 18 9 ......... 7 13 .. 59
Wastspight ...... 2 2 13 10 2 .............. 29

In all 42 Ships, &c.

* This List is attested by

JOHN CONYERS,
FRA⁵. GOFTON,  } Auditors of the Prest.

STEPHEN. RISLESDEN,
J. LINEWRAYE,
JOHN LEE,  } Officers of the Ordnance.
G. HEGGE,

† A Drumler.—This was an inferior sort of ship.

‡ In a Parenthesis is noted, "And one Spanish."

**1599**

### GUNS.
Description of several of the sorts of *Ordnance* mentioned in some of the early Lists.*

| Sorts of Ordnance. | Sir William Monson's account. | | According to some other accounts. |
| --- | --- | --- | --- |
| | Bore. | Weight of the Shot. | Weight of the Shot. |
| | Inches. | lb | lb |
| Cannon | 8 | 60 | 60 or 63 |
| Demi-Cannon | 6¾ | 33½ | 31 |
| Cannon Petro | 6 | 24½ | 24 |
| Culverin | 5½ | 17½ | 18 |
| Demi-Culverin | 4 | 9½ | 9 |
| Falcon | 2½ | 2 | 2 |
| Falconet | 2 | 1½ | |
| Minion | 3½ | 4 | 4 |
| Sacar | 3½ | 5½ | 5 |
| Rabinet | 1 | ½ | |

* See *Archæologia, vol. 6, p. 189; vol. 11, p. 170, and vol. 13, p.27.*— See also *Chambers's Dictionary.*

**1603**

An Account of the Royal Navy which the Queen left at her death, with the Number of Men, and Tonnage of the Ships.*

| Ships Names. | Burthen. Tons. | Mariners. | Gunners. | Soldiers. | Total No of Men. |
| --- | --- | --- | --- | --- | --- |
| Elizabeth Jonas | 900 | 340 | 40 | 120 | 500 |
| Triumph | 1000 | 340 | 40 | 120 | 500 |
| White Bear | 900 | 340 | 40 | 120 | 500 |
| Victory | 800 | 268 | 32 | 100 | 400 |
| Mer-Honeur (*or* Mary Honora) | 800 | 268 | 32 | 100 | 400 |

* *Entick.*

# James I 1603–1625

| Ships Names. | Burthen. Tons. | Mariners. | Gunners. | Soldiers. | Total No of Men. |
|---|---|---|---|---|---|
| Ark Royal† .......... | 800 | 268 | 32 | 100 | 400 |
| St. Matthew .......... | 1000 | 340 | 40 | 120 | 500 |
| St. Andrew .......... | 900 | 268 | 32 | 100 | 400 |
| Due Repulse‡ ........ | 700 | 230 | 30 | 90 | 350 |
| Garland ............. | 700 | 190 | 30 | 80 | 300 |
| Warspight .......... | 600 | 190 | 30 | 80 | 300 |
| Mary Rose .......... | 600 | 150 | 30 | 70 | 250 |
| Hope ............... | 600 | 150 | 30 | 70 | 250 |
| Bonaventure ......... | 600 | 150 | 30 | 70 | 250 |
| Lion ................ | 500 | 150 | 30 | 70 | 250 |
| Nonpareil ........... | 500 | 150 | 30 | 70 | 250 |
| Defiance ............ | 500 | 150 | 30 | 70 | 250 |
| Rainbow ............ | 500 | 150 | 30 | 70 | 250 |
| Dreadnought......... | 400 | 130 | 20 | 50 | 200 |
| Antelope ............ | 350 | 114 | 16 | 30 | 160 |
| Swiftsure ........... | 400 | 130 | 20 | 50 | 200 |
| Swallow............. | 330 | 114 | 16 | 30 | 160 |
| Foresight ........... | 300 | 114 | 16 | 30 | 160 |
| Tide ................ | 250 | 88 | 12 | 20 | 120 |
| Crane............... | 200 | 70 | 10 | 20 | 100 |
| Adventure........... | 250 | 88 | 12 | 20 | 120 |
| Quittance ........... | 200 | 70 | 10 | 20 | 100 |
| Answer ............. | 200 | 70 | 10 | 20 | 100 |
| Advantage........... | 200 | 70 | 10 | 20 | 100 |
| Tiger ............... | 200 | 70 | 10 | 20 | 100 |
| Tramontane ......... | 140 § | 52 | 8 | 10 | 70 |
| Scout............... | 120 | 48 | 8 | 10 | 66 |
| Catis‖ ....... | 100 | 42 | 8 | 10 | 60 |
| Charles ............. | 70 | 32 | 6 | 7 | 45 |
| Moon............... | 60 | 30 | 5 | 5 | 40 |
| Advice ............. | 50 | 30 | 5 | 5 | 40 |
| Spy................. | 50 | 30 | 5 | 5 | 40 |
| Merlin ............. | 45 | 26 | 5 | 4 | 35 |
| Sun................. | 40 | 24 | 4 | 2 | 30 |
| Synnet ............. | 20 | .... | ... | .... | .... |
| George, Hoy ........ | 100 | .... | ... | .... | .... |
| Penny-Rose, Hoy .... | 80 | .... | ... | .... | .... |
| | 17055 | 5534 | 804 | 2008 | 8346 |

In all 42 Ships, &c.

† *Named Ann Royal in 1608.*
‡ *Or Dieu Repulse, as spelt on several occasions, about this period.*
§ *See the Lists of 1604, and 1607.*
‖ *Or Cates.*

On comparing the preceding List with that, in 1578, it appears that in the last twenty-five years of Elizabeth, the Navy was almost doubled.
Before Elizabeth's time, the Navy, except in war, was not an expensive department. In her reign, the expence of it is stated to have amounted to £30,000 a year.

SOME alterations and additions had taken place in the King's Ships in the first year of this reign, as will be seen by the following List.

### 1604

"A List of the King's Ships and Pinnaces, with their respective Tonnages and Men, Anno Dom. 1603.*"

| Names. | Burthen. Tons. | Mariners. | Gunners. | Soldiers. | Total No of Men. |
|---|---|---|---|---|---|
| Elizabeth Jonas ........ | 900 | 340 | 40 | 120 | 500 |
| Triumph .............. | 1000 | 340 | 40 | 120 | 500 |
| Bear .................. | 900 | 340 | 40 | 120 | 500 |
| Victory .............. | 700 | 230 | 30 | 90 | 350 |
| Honour .............. | 800 | 268 | 32 | 100 | 400 |
| Ark................... | 800 | 268 | 32 | 100 | 400 |
| Due Repulse .......... | 700 | 230 | 30 | 90 | 350 |
| Garland.............. | 700 | 190 | 30 | 80 | 300 |
| Warspight ............ | 600 | 190 | 30 | 80 | 300 |
| Mary Rose ........... | 600 | 150 | 30 | 70 | 250 |
| Bonaventure .......... | 600 | 150 | 30 | 70 | 250 |
| Assurance ............ | 600 | 150 | 30 | 70 | 250 |
| Lion ................. | 500 | 150 | 30 | 70 | 250 |
| Defiance ............. | 500 | 150 | 30 | 70 | 250 |
| Rainbow ............. | 500 | 150 | 30 | 70 | 250 |
| Nonsuch ............. | 500 | 150 | 30 | 70 | 250 |
| Vanguard ............ | 500 | 150 | 30 | 70 | 250 |
| Dreadnought ......... | 400 | 130 | 20 | 50 | 200 |
| Swiftsure ............ | 400 | 130 | 20 | 50 | 200 |
| Antelope ............. | 350 | 114 | 16 | 30 | 160 |
| Adventure ............ | 250 | 88 | 12 | 20 | 120 |
| Crane................. | 200 | 76 | 12 | 12 | 100 |
| Quittance ............ | 200 | 76 | 12 | 12 | 100 |
| Answer............... | 200 | 76 | 12 | 12 | 100 |
| Advantage............ | 200 | 76 | 12 | 12 | 100 |
| Tramontane .......... | 140 | 52 | 8 | 10 | 70 |
| Charles .............. | 70 | 32 | 6 | 7 | 45 |
| Moon................ | 60 | 30 | 5 | 5 | 40 |
| Advice ............... | 50 | 30 | 5 | 5 | 40 |
| Spy.................. | 50 | 30 | 5 | 5 | 40 |
| Merlin ............... | 50 | 30 | 5 | 5 | 40 |
| Lion's Whelp ......... | 90 | 50 | 6 | 4 Rowers. | 60 |
| La Superlativa ... | | .... | 84 | 8 | 243 Rowers. | 335 |
| La Advantagia ... | | .... | 84 | 8 | 233 Rowers. | 223 |
| La Volatillia ..... | | .... | 84 | 8 | 233 Rowers. | 223 |
| La Gallarita ..... | | .... | 84 | 8 | 233 Rowers. | 223 |

(Galleys†)

* *Meaning 1603-4.—This List is taken from Pepys's Miscellanies, vol. 2, p. 129. Its date must have been in 1604 (New Stile) and probably in March, for the reasons mentioned at the end of the List.*
† *The total number of men for each of the three last Galleys, does not correspond with the particulars.*

| Mercury ....Galleon ... | 80 | 34 | 6 | 100 | 140 |
|---|---|---|---|---|---|
| George......Carvel.... | 100 | 10 | ... | .... | 10 |
| Primrose ....Hoy...... | 80 | 2 | ... | .... | 2 |
| A French Frigate ....... | 15 | 14 | 2 | .... | 16 |
| Disdain‡ ............. | .... | 3 | ... | .... | 3 |

In all 41 Ships, &c.

‡ *Mr. Phineas Pett mentions, that in January 1603–4, he was "ordered by the Lord High Admiral to build a vessel at Chatham with all possible speed, for the young Prince Henry to disport himself in above London-Bridge; her garnishing to be like the work of the Ark Royal, battlement-wise.—This little Ship was—In length by the-Keel ...........28 feet In breadth ..................12 I laid her keel the 19th January, and launched her the 6th March.—Set sail with her 9th March, and on 14th anchored right against the Tower, before the King's lodgings, his Majesty then lying there, before his riding through London. On 18th, anchored right against the Privy Stairs.—On 22d the Prince, with the Lord High Admiral, &c. &c. came on board, when we weighed and dropped down as low as Paul's Wharf, where we anchored: and there his Grace, with a great bowl of wine, christened the Ship, and called her by the name of the Disdain."—(MS. Life of Phinᵗ. Pett.)*

The five last Vessels in the List of 1604, appear to have been disposed of previous to Dec. 1607, at which period the Navy consisted of the following Ships.

### 1607

"Dec'. 1607."
"A Catalogue of all the King's Ships, with their respective Tonnages, and Men at Sea."

| Names. | Tonnage. | Men. |
|---|---|---|
| Elizabeth........................... | 900 | 500 |
| Triumph ........................... | 1000 | 500 |
| Bear............................... | 900 | 500 |
| Victory ........................... | 900 | 500 |
| Honour ........................... | 800 | 400 |
| Ark............................... | 800 | 400 |
| Repulse ........................... | 700 | 350 |
| Garland........................... | 700 | 300 |
| Warspight......................... | 600 | 300 |
| Mary Rose ........................ | 600 | 250 |
| Assurance ......................... | 600 | 250 |
| Bonadventure ...................... | 600 | 250 |
| Lion............................... | 500 | 250 |
| Nonsuch .......................... | 500 | 250 |
| Defiance .......................... | 500 | 250 |
| Vanguard.......................... | 500 | 250 |
| Rainbow .......................... | 500 | 250 |
| Dreadnought....................... | 400 | 200 |
| Swiftsure ......................... | 400 | 200 |
| Antelope .......................... | 350 | 160 |
| Adventure......................... | 250 | 120 |
| Crane ............................. | 200 | 100 |
| Quittance ......................... | 200 | 100 |
| Answer ........................... | 200 | 100 |
| Advantage ........................ | 200 | 100 |
| Tramontane ....................... | 140 | 70 |
| Lion's Whelp....................... | 90 | 60 |
| Charles ........................... | 70 | 45 |
| Moon.............................. | 60 | 45 |

| Advice ............................. | 50 | 40 |
|---|---|---|
| Spy................................. | 50 | 40 |
| Merlin.............................. | 50 | 40 |
| Superlativa ... ........................ | | 335 |
| Advantagia ... ........................ | | 223 |
| Volatilia ..... * ...................... | | 223 |
| Galarita...... ........................ | | 223 |

In all 36 Ships and Vessels.    14710   8174
*if each of the 4 latter Vessels was 100 Tons.*

\* *In the 11th vol. of the Archæologia, these Vessels are stated to have been of 100 tons each.*

MEMᵒ.—*This List is taken from Pepys's Miscellanies, vol. 2, p. 131, and vol. 5, p. 579, at the foot of which he says, "The foregoing are all the King's Ships, Pinnaces, and Galleys." By the List preceding this, it appears that the four last Vessels were large Galleys.*

### 1625

The accounts of the state of the Navy at the death of the King have varied exceedingly, and most of them have been very erroneous; making the number of Ships and Vessels to have been from 50 to 62, and their tonnage from 20 to 23,000 tons, whereas it appears by a report of the Commissioners appointed to examine into the state of the Navy, &c. in 1618,\* that there were then but 39 Ships and Vessels, as follows, whose tonnage amounted only to 14700 tons, viz.

### 1618

| | Tons. | |
|---|---|---|
| Prince Royal............................ | 1200 | |
| White Bear .......................... | 900 | |
| More Honour........................ | 800 | |
| Ann Royal .......................... | 800 | |
| Due Repulse ......................... | 700 | |
| Defiance ............................ | 700 | |
| Warspight........................... | 600 | |
| Assurance ........................... | 600 | |
| Vantguard........................... | 600 | |
| Red Lion............................ | 500 | |
| Nonsuch ............................ | 500 | |
| Rainbow ............................ | 500 | May be made Serviceable. |
| Dreadnought........................ | 400 | |
| Speedwell ........................... | 400 | |
| Antelope ............................ | 350 | |
| Adventure........................... | 250 | |
| Crane............................... | 200 | |
| Answer ............................. | 200 | |
| Phœnix ............................. | 150 | |
| Lion's Whelp........................ | 90 | |
| Moon............................... | 100 | |
| Seven Stars ......................... | 100 | |
| Desire............................... | 50 | |
| George, Hoy......................... | 100 | |
| Primrose, do. ........................ | 80 | |
| Eagle Lighter ........................ | 200 | |

\* *See Memoir on British Naval Architecture, by Ralph Willett, Esq. (Archæologie, vol. 11, p. 171.) And see Charnock.*

|  | Tons. |  |
|---|---|---|
| Elizabeth Jonas ................... | 500 or 900† | |
| Triumph ......................... | 1000 | |
| Garland.......................... | 700 | |
| Mary Rose ....................... | 600 | |
| Quittance ........................ | 200 | |
| Tramontane ...................... | 160 | Decayed and Unserviceable. |
| Primrose, Pinnace ................ | 30 | |
| Disdain .......................... | 30 | |
| Ketch............................ | 10 | |
| Superlative ... | 100 | |
| Advantagia ... (Galleys) | 100 | |
| Vollatilla ..... | 100 | |
| Gallerita ..... | 100 | |

|  | Total ..... | 14700 |
|---|---|---|
| 39 Ships, &c. | Or ....... | 15100 |

† *She was 900 Tons if she was the identical Ship that appears in preceding Lists; which, from her condition now, is highly probable.*

The aforesaid Commissioners recommend that the Navy should in future consist of the following Ships, and no more, viz.

**1618**

| Classes of Ships, &c. | Number. | Tonnage of each. | Total Tonnage. |
|---|---|---|---|
| Ships Royal ................. | 1 | 1200 | 1200 |
|  | 2 | 900 | 1800 |
|  | 1 | 800 | 800 |
| Great Ships................. | 3 | 800 | 2400 |
|  | 9 | 650 | 5850 |
|  | 2 | 600 | 1200 |
| Middling Ships............... | 6 | 450 | 2700 |
| Small Ships................. | 2 | 350 | 700 |
| Pinnaces ................... | 1 | 250 | 250 |
|  | 2 | 140 | 280 |
|  | 1 | 80 | 80 |
|  | 30 | .... | 17260 |

For which they assign these reasons among others, viz.

1st. —"This Navy will contain 3050 tons more than the Navy of Queen Elizabeth, when it was greatest and flourished most."

2d. —"As great a provision of long timber, planks and knees, will be required to supply these 30 Ships, as may conveniently be got in this time of great building and common devastations of woods in all places."

3d. —"These 30 Ships will require as many Mariners and Gunners as this kingdom can supply at all times, now traffick carrieth away so many and so far."

4th.—"The common building of great and warlike Ships by Merchants to reinforce the Navy, when need shall require, may well contain his Majesty's numbers and charge within these bounds."

It also appears by a report of the Commissioners appointed to enquire into the state of the Navy, &c. in 1624,* that the Navy then consisted of only 31 Ships and Vessels, of which the following is a List, viz.

**1624**

| | |
|---|---|
| Prince | Rainbow |
| Bear | Red Lion |
| Mer Honour | Entrance |
| Ann | Convertine |
| Dieu Repulse | Bonadventure |
| Defiance | Garland |
| Assurance | Antelope |
| Wastspight | Mary Rose |
| Nonsuch | Speedwell |
| Triumph | Dreadnought |
| St. George | Adventure |
| St. Andrew | Desire |
| Swiftsure | Phœnix |
| Victory | Charles |
| Reformation | Seven Stars |
| Vantguard | |

* *Pepys's Miscellanies, vol. 7. p. 203.*

As a further proof of the incorrectness of the generality of the statements mentioned page 49; as a corroborative proof of the accuracy of the reports respecting the Navy, in 1618 and 1624, as well as to shew what the Navy was just before His Majesty's death, I insert the following particular statement thereof, from the same authority as the aforesaid survey in 1618 is given.

A List of the Royal Navy, in 1624.

| Names. | Burthen. Tons. | No. of Pieces of Ordnance | Cannon Petro. | Demi-Cannon. | Culverines. | Demi-Culverines. | Sakers. | Minions. | Faulcons. | Port-pieces. | Fowlers. |
|---|---|---|---|---|---|---|---|---|---|---|---|
| Prince ......... | 1200 | 55 | 2 | 6 | 12 | 18 | 13 | .. | .. | 4 | .. |
| Bear .......... | 900 | 51 | 2 | 6 | 12 | 18 | 9 | .. | .. | 4 | .. |
| More Honour ... | 800 | 44 | 2 | 6 | 12 | 12 | 8 | .. | .. | 4 | .. |
| Ann .......... | 800 | 44 | 2 | 5 | 12 | 13 | 8 | .. | .. | 4 | .. |
| Repulse* ...... | 700 | 40 | 2 | 2 | 14 | 12 | 4 | .. | .. | 2 | .. |
| Defiance* ..... | 700 | 40 | 2 | 2 | 14 | 12 | 4 | .. | 2 | .. | .. |
| Triumph* ..... | 921 | 42 | 2 | 2 | 16 | 12 | 4 | .. | 2 | .. | .. |
| St. George* .... | 880 | 42 | 2 | 2 | 16 | 12 | 4 | .. | 2 | .. | .. |
| St. Andrew* ... | 880 | 42 | 2 | 2 | 16 | 12 | 4 | .. | 2 | .. | .. |
| Swiftsure* ..... | 876 | 42 | 2 | 2 | 16 | 12 | 4 | .. | 2 | .. | .. |
| Victory* ....... | 870 | 42 | 2 | 2 | 16 | 12 | 4 | .. | 2 | .. | .. |
| Reformation* ... | 750 | 42 | 2 | 2 | 16 | 12 | 4 | .. | 2 | .. | .. |
| Warspight* .... | 650 | 38 | 2 | 4 | 13 | 13 | 4 | .. | 2 | .. | .. |
| Vanguard* .... | 651 | 40 | 2 | .. | 14 | 12 | 4 | .. | 2 | .. | .. |
| Rainbow* ..... | 650 | 40 | 2 | .. | 14 | 12 | 4 | .. | 2 | .. | 4 |
| Red Lion....... | 650 | 38 | 2 | .. | 14 | 12 | 4 | .. | 2 | .. | 4 |
| Assurance ..... | 600 | 38 | 2 | .. | 10 | 12 | 10 | .. | .. | .. | 4 |
| Nonsuch ...... | 600 | 38 | 2 | .. | 12 | 12 | 6 | .. | 2 | .. | 4 |
| Bonadventure ... | 674 | 34 | .. | .. | 4 | 14 | 10 | 2 | .. | .. | 4 |

| | | | | | | | | | | | |
|---|---|---|---|---|---|---|---|---|---|---|---|
| Garland........ | 680 | 32 | .. .. | 4 | 12 | 10 | 2 | .. .. | | | 4 |
| Entrance....... | 580 | 32 | .. .. | 4 | 12 | 10 | 2 | .. .. | | | 4 |
| Convertine† .... | 500 | 34 | .. .. .. | 18 | 10 | 2 | .. .. | | | 4 |
| Dreadnought ... | 450 | 32 | .. .. .. | 16 | 10 | 2 | .. .. | | | 4 |
| Antelope....... | 450 | 34 | .. .. | 4 | 14 | 10 | 2 | .. .. | | | 4 |
| Adventure...... | 350 | 26 | .. .. .. | 12 | 6 | 4 | :. .. | | | 4 |
| Mary Rose ..... | 388 | 26 | .. .. .. | 8 | 10 | 4 | .. .. | | | 4 |
| Phœnix........ | 250 | 20‡ | .. .. .. .. | 12 | 4 | 2 | .. | | | 4 |
| Crane.......... | 250 | | .. .. .. | .. | .. | .. | .. .. | | | .. |
| Answer ........ | 250 | | .. .. .. | .. | .. | .. | .. .. | | | .. |
| Moon.......... | 140 | | .. .. .. | .. | .. | .. | .. .. | | | .. |
| Seven Stars..... | 140 | 14 | .. .. .. | 2 | 6 | 6 | .. .. | | | .. |
| Charles ........ | 140 | 14§ | .. .. .. .. | 2 | 6 | 4 | .. | | | .. |
| Desire.......... | 80 | 6 | .. .. .. .. | .. | .. | 2 | 4 | | | .. |

Total.... 19400

In all 33 Ships, &c.

The Navy left by Queen Elizabeth consisted of
..... 42 Ships, &c...17055 Tons
That of King James, in 1624, of............
31 or 33 ..... about 19400

Decrease in Number
of Ships........... 9 or 11
Increase in Tonnage ............. about 19400

\* *The Particulars of thr Ordnance do not correspond with the total.*

† *Spelt* Conventine *in the Archæologia.*

‡ *According to the particulars of the Ordnance, she carried 22 guns.*

§ *Only 12 specified in the particulars.*

MEM⁰.—*For a description of several of the sorts of the Ordnance in the foregoing List, see page 126.*

# Charles 1 1625–1649

### 1633

"A List of the King's Ships, Anno 1633.\*"

| "Established by the Lords of the Council for the measuring His Majesty's Ships, Whitehall.\*" | Length of the Keel. | Tons. | Highest Number of Men. | Guns. |
|---|---|---|---|---|
| "Great Ships.\*" | Feet | | | |
| Prince Royal.......... | 115 | 1187 | 500 | 55 |
| Mer Honour.......... | 112 | 828 | 400 | 40 |
| An: Royal............ | 107 | or 726 / 776 | 400 | 44 |
| Triumph ............. | 110 | 792 | 350 | 44 |
| St. George............ | 110 | 783 | 300 | 44 |
| St. Andrew........... | 110 | 764 | 300 | 42 |
| Dieu Repulse ........ | 108 | 876 | 300 | 40 |
| Defiance ............. | 104 | 751 | 280 | 38 |
| Vanguard ............ | 112 | 746 | 280 | 40 |
| Swiftsure ............ | 106 | 731 | 300 | 44 |

| | | | | |
|---|---|---|---|---|
| Rainbow ............ | 112 | 742 | 270 | 40 |
| Reformation .......... | 106 | 721 | 280 | 40 |
| Victory ............. | 106 | 702 | 300 | 40 |
| Warspight ............ | 97 | 810 | 250 | 36 |
| Charles ............. | 105 | 793 | 300 | 44 |
| H. Mari............. | 106 | 875 | 300 | 42 |
| James................ | 110 | 767 | 300 | 48 |
| Unicorn ............. | 107 | 512 | 250 | 49 |
| Leopard ............. | 103 | 698 | 250 | 36 |
| Red Lion............ | 103 | 619 | 250 | 40 |
| Nonsuch ............ | 88 | 610 | 250 | 38 |
| Assurance ........... | 104 | 621 | 250 | 34 |
| Convertine .......... | 96 | 567 | 250 | 34 |
| Bonadventure ........ | 96 | 552 | 200 | 32 |
| Garland.............. | 96 | 557 | 200 | 34 |
| Dreadnought ........ | 92 | 539 | 200 | 30 |
| Happy Entrance ...... | 96 | 528 | 200 | 30 |
| St. Dennis ........... | 104 | 512 | 200 | 38 |
| Antelope ............. | 92 | 321 | 180 | 38 |
| Mary Rose .......... | 83 | 287 | 120 | 26 |
| Adventure............ | 88 | 512 | 120 | 24 |
| Swallow............. | 103 | 186 or 136 | 250 | 36 |
| 1st Whelp ........... | 62 | 186 | 70 | 14 |
| 2d Whelp ........... | 62 | 186 | 70 | 14 |
| 3d Ditto............. | 62 | 186 | 70 | 14 |
| 4th Ditto ............ | 62 | 186 | 70 | 14 |
| 5th Ditto ............ | 62 | 186 | 70 | 14 |
| 6th Ditto ............ | 62 | 162 | 70 | 14 |
| 7th Ditto ............ | 62 | 186 | 70 | 14 |
| 8th Ditto ............ | 62 | 186 | 70 | 14 |
| 9th Ditto ............ | 62 | 186 | 70 | 14 |
| 10th Ditto ........... | 62 | 186 | 70 | 14 |
| Providence .......... | 58 | 89 | 30 | 8 |
| Expedition ........... | 58 | 89 | 30 | 8 |
| Henrietta† ........... | 52 | 68 | 25 | 6 |
| Madrid ............. | 52 | 68 | 25 | 6 |
| Roebuck ............ | 58 | 80 | 30 | 8 |
| Greyhound .......... | 58 | 80 | 30 | 8 |
| Swan..Frigate ........ | 40 | 60 | 10 | 3 |
| Nicodemus..Frigate ... | 40 | 60 | 10 | 3 |

In all 50 Ships, &c. — 23695 or 23595 — 9470 — 1430

\* *The words between the inverted commas are precisely as they are inserted in vol. 5, p. 267, of Pepys's Miscellanies, from whence the whole of this List is taken, except the spelling of the names, which is here modernized.—It does not appear where the distinction of* Great Ships *was meant to stop.*

† *Was built for a Pinnace.*

MEM⁰.—*This being the earliest List of the Navy I have met with, wherein any part of the Ships principal dimensions are inserted, it was thought advisable to insert them here. And it may be observed, that this is the first List in which any nice regard appears to have been paid to the tonnage of the Ships. Previous to 1633, the tonnage of almost every Ship seems to have been rather estimated than calculated, being inserted in even numbers.*

**1641**

Abstract of the Royal Navy when the Rebellion
broke out in 1641.

| Rates or Classes. | Nº | Burthen. |
|---|---|---|
| | | Tons. |
| 1st. | 5 | 5306 |
| 2d. | 12 | 8771 |
| 3d. | 8 | 4897 |
| 4th. | 6 | 2206 |
| 5th. | 2 | 600 |
| 6th. | 9 | 631 |
| Total...... | 42 | 22411 |

If this account is correct, and it has every appearance of being so, the Navy, owing to the circumstances of the times, must have fallen off in the latter part of the time that the King held the reins of government, as it consisted of 50 Ships and Vessels in 1633.* The only circumstance that creates any doubt in my mind on the subject is, the address of the House of Commons in the year 1641.

* *See the List of that date.*

# Commonwealth 1649–1660

WE come now to a very busy period of our Naval History, when we had to encounter with the greatest maritime power in Europe, and when our force had been considerably reduced; Prince Rupert having quitted the kingdom in the year 1648, with 25 Ships under his command, none of which ever returned.

On the 1st March, 1652, the Navy consisted of the following Ships.

**1652**

"A List of all Ships, Frigates, and other Vessels belonging to the State's Navy, on 1st March, 1651.*"

| Rates. | Names. | Length of the Keel. | Breadth. | Depth. | Tons. | Highest No of Men. | Guns. |
|---|---|---|---|---|---|---|---|
| | | Feet | Ft. In. | Ft. In. | | | |
| 1st. | Sovereign .... | 127 | 46: 6 | 19: 4 | 1141 | 600 | 100 |
| . | Resolution.... | 115 | 43: 0 | 18: 0 | 976 | 580 | 85 |
| . | Triumph ..... | 110 | 36: 0 | 14: 6 | 586 | 300 | 60 |
| 2d. | George....... | 110 | 36: 5 | 14:10 | 594 | 280 | 52 |
| . | Andrew ...... | 110 | 36: 5 | 14: 8 | 587 | 280 | 52 |
| . | James........ | 110 | 36:10 | 16: 2 | 654 | 280 | 52 |
| . | Vanguard .... | 112 | 36: 4 | 13:10 | 563 | 260 | 54 |
| . | Rainbow ..... | 112 | 36: 3 | 13: 6 | 548 | 260 | 54 |
| . | Victory ...... | 106 | 35: 0 | 15: 0 | 541 | 260 | 52 |
| . | Paragon...... | 106 | 35: 9 | 15: 8 | 593 | 260 | 52 |
| . | Unicorn...... | 107 | 35: 8 | 15: 1 | 575 | 260 | 50 |
| . | Fairfax....... | 116 | 34: 9 | 17: 4½ | 745 | 260 | 52 |
| . | Speaker ...... | 106 | 34: 4 | 16: 4 | 691 | 260 | 52 |
| . | Swiftsure ..... | 106 | 36: 0 | 14: 8 | 559 | 260 | 36 |

| Rates. | Names. | Length of the Keel. | Breadth. | Depth. | Tons. | Highest No of Men. | Guns. |
|---|---|---|---|---|---|---|---|
| | New Frigate building.... | ... | ..... | ..... | ... | ... | .. |
| 3d. | Garland...... | 96 | 32: 0 | 13:10 | 424 | 180 | 40 |
| . | Entrance ..... | 96 | 32: 2 | 13: 1 | 403 | 180 | 40 |
| . | Lion......... | 95 | 33: 0 | 15: 0 | 470 | 180 | 40 |
| . | Leopard...... | 98 | 33: 0 | 12: 4 | 387 | 180 | 40 |
| . | Bonadventure . | 96 | 32: 5 | 13: 5 | 479 | 180 | 40 |
| . | Worcester .... | 112 | 32: 8 | 16: 4 | 661 | 180 | 46 |
| . | Laurel ....... | 103 | 30: 1 | 15: 0 | 489 | 180 | 46 |
| . | Antelope, Frigate†.... | ... | ..... | ..... | 600 | 200 | 50 |
| 4th. | Tiger ........ | 99 | 29: 4 | 14: 8 | 442 | 150 | 32 |
| . | Advice ....... | 100 | 31: 2 | 15: 7 | 516 | 150 | 34 |
| . | Reserve ...... | 100 | 31: 1 | 15: 6½ | 513 | 150 | 34 |
| . | Adventure .... | 94 | 27: 9 | 13:10 | 385 | 150 | 32 |
| . | Phoenix ...... | 96 | 28: 6 | 14: 3 | 414 | 150 | 32 |
| . | Elizabeth ..... | 101½ | 29: 8 | 14:10 | 474 | 150 | 32 |
| . | Centurion .... | 104 | 31: 0 | 15: 6 | 531 | 150 | 34 |
| . | Foresight ..... | 101½ | 30:10 | 15: 5 | 513 | 150 | 34 |
| . | Pelican....... | 100 | 30: 8 | 15: 4 | 500 | 150 | 34 |
| . | Assurance .... | 89 | 26:10 | 13: 6 | 342 | 150 | 32 |
| . | Nonsuch ..... | 98 | 28: 4 | 14: 2 | 418 | 150 | 34 |
| . | Portsmouth, Frigate..... | 99 | 28: 4 | 14: 2 | 422 | 150 | 34 |
| . | Dragon ...... | 96 | 28: 6 | 14: 3 | 414 | 150 | 32 |
| . | President..... | 100 | 29: 6 | 14: 9 | 462 | 150 | 34 |
| . | Assistance .... | 101½ | 30:10 | 15: 5 | 513 | 150 | 34 |
| . | Providence ... | 90 | 26: 0 | 13: 0 | 228 | 120 | 30 |
| . | Expedition ... | 90 | 26: 0 | 13: 0 | 228 | 120 | 30 |
| . | Ruby ........ | 105½ | 31: 6 | 15: 9 | 556 | 150 | 40 |
| . | Diamond ..... | 105½ | 31: 3 | 15: 7½ | 547 | 150 | 40 |
| . | Sapphire ..... | 100 | 28:10 | 14: 5 | 442 | 140 | .. |
| . | Constant Warwick ... | 85 | 26: 5 | 13: 2 | 315 | 140 | 32 |
| . | Amity ....... | ... | ..... | ..... | ... | 140 | .. |
| . | Guinea, Frigate | ... | ..... | ..... | ... | 140 | .. |
| . | John......... | ... | ..... | ..... | ... | 120 | .. |
| . | Satisfaction ... | . | ..... | ..... | . | 100 | .. |
| . | Success....... | . | ..... | ..... | . | 150 | .. |
| . | Discovery .... | . | ..... | ..... | . | 120 | .. |
| . | Gilliflower.... | . | Not measured | . | 120 | .. |
| . | Marygold .... | . | ..... | ..... | . | 100 | .. |
| . | Fox.......... | . | ..... | ..... | . | 80 | .. |
| . | Convertine ... | . | ..... | ..... | . | 180 | .. |
| 5th. | 10th Whelp... | 62 | 25: 0 | 12: 6 | 180 | 60 | 18 |
| . | Mermaid ..... | 86 | 25: 1 | 12: 6 | 287 | 90 | 24 |
| . | Pearl ........ | 86 | 25: 0 | 12: 6 | 285 | 90 | 24 |
| . | Nightingale ... | 88 | 25: 4 | 12: 8 | 300 | 90 | 24 |
| . | Primrose ..... | 86 | 25: 1 | 12: 6 | 287 | 90 | 24 |
| . | Cygnet....... | ... | ..... | ..... | ... | 80 | .. |
| . | Star ......... | ... | ..... | ..... | ... | 70 | .. |
| . | Little President | ... | ..... | ..... | ... | 80 | .. |

| Rates. | Names. | Length of the Keel. | Breadth. | Depth. | Tons. | Highest No of | |
|---|---|---|---|---|---|---|---|
| | | | | | | Men. | Guns. |
| . | Warwick, Frigate..... | ... | ..... | ..... | ... | 90 | .. |
| . | May-flower, als. Fame‡.. | ... | ..... | ..... | ... | 60 | .. |
| . | Mary..Fly-boat........ | ... | ..... | ..... | ... | 80 | .. |
| . | Paradox...... | ... | ..... | ..... | ... | 60 | .. |
| . | Roebuck ..... | ... | ..... | ..... | ... | 70 | .. |
| . | Hector ....... | ... | ..... | ..... | ... | 70 | .. |
| . | Truelove ..... | ... | ..... | ..... | ... | 30 | .. |
| . | Golden Sun... | ... | ..... | ..... | ... | 60 | .. |
| . | Recovery..... | ... | ..... | ..... | ... | 70 | .. |
| . | Concord ..... | ... | ..... | ..... | ... | 70 | .. |
| . | Bryer ........ | ... | ..... | ..... | ... | 60 | .. |
| . | Swan ........ | ... | ..... | ..... | ... | 80 | .. |
| 6th. | Greyhound ... | 60 | 20: 3 | 10: 0 | 120 | 80 | 18 |
| . | Henrietta, Pinnace .... | 52 | 15: 0 | 7: 6 | 51 | 25 | 7 |
| . | Nicodemus ... | 63 | 19: 0 | 9: 6 | 91 | 50 | 10 |
| . | Drake.. } § .. | ... | ..... | ..... | ... | 50 | .. |
| . | Merlin . } .. | ... | ..... | ..... | ... | 50 | .. |
| . | Martin. } .. | ... | ..... | ..... | ... | 50 | .. |
| . | Scout........ | ... | ..... | ..... | ... | 30 | .. |
| . | Samuel ...... | ... | ..... | ..... | ... | 30 | .. |
| . | Fly.......... | ... | ..... | ..... | ... | 30 | .. |
| . | Spy.......... | ... | ..... | ..... | ... | 30 | .. |
| . | Heart........ | ... | ..... | ..... | ... | 60 | .. |
| . | Weymouth ... | ... | ..... | ..... | ... | 60 | .. |
| . | Minion ...... | ... | ..... | ..... | ... | 30 | .. |
| . | Hare, Ketch .. | ... | ..... | ..... | .. | 30 | .. |
| . | Eagle ........ | ... | ..... | ..... | ... | 40 | .. |
| . | Dove ........ | ... | ..... | ..... | ... | 30 | .. |
| . | Elizabeth..... | ... | ..... | ..... | ... | 50 | .. |
| . | Lilly ......... | ... | ..... | ..... | ... | 50 | .. |
| . | Peter of Waterford .. | ... | ..... | ..... | ... | ... | .. |
| . | Falcon ....... | ... | ..... | ..... | ... | 40 | .. |
| . | Mary, Frigate. | ... | ..... | ..... | ... | ... | .. |
| . | Galliot Hoy... | ... | ..... | ..... | ... | 40 | .. |
| . | Lady, Ketch .. | ... | ..... | ..... | ... | 24 | .. |
| Shallops to row with 20 Oars each | New building ... | ... | ..... | ..... | ... | ... | .. |
| | New ditto | ... | ..... | ..... | ... | ... | .. |
| Hulks. | Eagle, at Chatham ... | ... | ..... | ..... | ... | ... | .. |
| . | Fellowship, at Woolwich | ... | ..... | ..... | .. | .. | .. |
| . | New..buildg at Portsmth | ... | ..... | ..... | .. | ... | .. |

* 1652 New Stile.—This List is taken from Pepys's Miscellanies, vol. 5, p. 595.

† Building at Woolwich.

‡ Supposed to mean alias Fame.

§ Building.

# Abstract for 1652

| Rates. | Guns. | Number. |
|---|---|---|
| 1st. | 100 | 1 |
| | 85 | 1 |
| | 60 | 1 |
| 2d. | 54 | 2 |
| | 52 | 7 |
| | 50 | 1 |
| | 36 | 1 |
| | Guns not known. | 1 |
| 3d. | 50 | 1 |
| | 46 | 2 |
| | 40 | 5 |
| 4th. | 40 | 2 |
| | 34 | 9 |
| | 32 | 7 |
| | 30 | 2 |
| | Guns not known. | 11 |
| 5th. | 24 | 4 |
| | 18 | 1 |
| | Guns not known. | 15 |
| 6th. | 18 | 1 |
| | 10 | 1 |
| | 7 | 1 |
| | Guns not known. | 20 |
| Shallops......................... | | 2 |
| Hulks............................ | | 3 |
| | Total.... | 102 |

Estimates for the maintenance and support of the Navy were first laid before Parliament in the time of the Commonwealth; and the Protector procured an annual grant of £400,000 for the expence of the Navy, which at his death, in 1658, consisted of almost double the number of Ships to what there were at the commencement of the Civil Wars, as will be seen by the following account.*

* It may be proper to observe, in order to prevent mistake, that in the following Abstract, and in that of 1660, Sloops, and the small Vessels of inferior Classes, are included among the 6th rates, as the Sloops are in the Abstracts of 1688, 1697, and 1698; but that in after periods, Sloops, and the before-mentioned Vessels, are distinguished under the proper denominations.

## 1658

Abstract of the Ships and Vessels belonging to the Proctector and the Commonwealth, on 20th November, 1658.

| Rates or Classes. | Guns. | No of Ships. | Total Number of Guns. | Total Number of Men. |
|---|---|---|---|---|
| 1st. | 100 | I | | |
| | 80 | I | 250 | 1600 |
| | 70 | I | | |
| 2d. | 66 | I | | |
| | 64 | 4 | | |
| | 56 | I | 694 | 3930 |
| | 54 | 2 | | |
| | 52 | 4 | | |
| 3d. | 52 | I | | |
| | 50 | 10 | 776 | 4010 |
| | 46 | 2 | | |
| | 44 | 3 | | |
| 4th. | 44 | I | | |
| | 40 | 4 | | |
| | 38 | 3 | | |
| | 36 | 19 | | |
| | 34 | 6 | 1476 | 6630 |
| | 32 | 3 | | |
| | 30 | 3 | | |
| | 28 | 3 | | |
| 5th. | 34 | I | | |
| | 30 | 2 | | |
| | 28 | I | | |
| | 26 | 5 | | |
| | 25 | I | | |
| | 24 | 4 | 873 | 4080 |
| | 22 | 13 | | |
| | 20 | 9 | | |
| | 18 | I | | |
| | 16 | I | | |
| 6th. | 16 | I | | |
| | 14 | 5 | | |
| | 12 | 8 | | |
| | 11 | I | | |
| | 10 | 3 | 321 | 1660 |
| | 8 | 5 | | |
| | 6 | 8 | | |
| | 4 | 2 | | |
| | 2 | I | | |
| Hulks..................... | | 8 | ............. | |
| Building, force not known ...... | | 4 | ............. | |
| Total...... | | 157 | 4390 | 21910 |

Exclusive of the Guns and Men, for the four Ships building.

# Charles II 1660–1685

## 1660

Navy at the Restoration.

| Rates. | Number. | Burthen. |
|---|---|---|
| | | Tons. |
| 1st. | 3 | 4139 |
| 2d. | 12 | 10047 |
| 3d. | 15 | 10086 |
| 4th. | 146 | 21520 |
| 5th. | 37 | 8663 |
| 6th. | 41 | 3008 |
| Total, exclusive of Hulks* .......... | 154 | 57463 |

to which I think we may with propriety add eight Hulks, as none are included in this Abstract,† and as there was that number both in 1658, and 1675. This would give a total of 162 Ships and Vessels;‡ and as there were 157, only two years before, including those building, it seems highly probable that the preceding statement is perfectly correct.— Wishing however, in all cases not absolutely certain, to produce every collateral proof in my power, it may be proper to state, that when War was declared against the Dutch in February, 1665§ the English Fleet at sea, and ready for sea, consisted of 114 sail, besides Fireships and Ketches, which could not have been the case had the whole Navy, only four years before, amounted to but 65 Ships and Vessels,|| and there must have been some Ships building, or not equipped, exclusive of Hulks.—

* *Respecting Hulks, and the total tonnage of the Navy, see what follows the above Table.*

† *Several there must of course have been.*

‡ *The tonnage of which must have amounted to 62250 tons, at least, and probably to 62594 tons, as stated in* Columna Rostrata, *p. 251; and which may therefore be considered an accurate account of the tonnage.*

§ *This was the second Dutch War.*

|| *In October 1665, Lord Clarendon told the Parliament that the Naval and Military Stores were entirely exhausted.*

## 1675

On Thursday, 22d April, 1675, it was ordered by the House of Commons, "that Mr. Pepys do, on Saturday morning next, at ten of the clock, bring into the House a true state of the present condition of the Navy, and of the stores and provisions thereof.†" This was accordingly done on the day appointed: and the following is an abstract of the Navy, and the tonnage thereof, as stated by Mr. Pepys in the aforesaid account.

## 1675

Abstract of the Royal Navy on the 24th April, 1675.

| Rates of Classes. | Guns. | Number. | Burthen. |
|---|---|---|---|
| | | | Tons. |
| 1st. | 102 | I | 1416 |
| | 100 | 5 | 6954 |
| | 98 | I | 1102 |
| | 96 | I | 1328 |

| | | | |
|---|---|---|---|
| 2d. | 100 | 1 | 1004 |
| | 84 | 1 | 1038 |
| | 80 | 1 | 868 |
| | 78 | 1 | 1082 |
| | 75 | 1 | 906 |
| | 70 | 1 | 891 |
| | 68 | 2 | 1724 |
| | 56 | 1 | 866 |
| 3d. | 74 | 1 | 994 |
| | 72 | 1 | 859 |
| | 70 | 2 | 2044 |
| | 68 | 2 | 1790 |
| | 66 | 2 | 1967 |
| | 64 | 3 | 2228 |
| | 60 | 7 | 5612 |
| | 58 | 3 | 2199 |
| | 42 | 1 | 734 |
| 4th. | 60 | 1 | 666 |
| | 56 | 3 | 1852 |
| | 54 | 5 | 3163 |
| | 52 | 3 | 1652 |
| | 50 | 8 | 4479 |
| | 48 | 7 | 3744 |
| | 46 | 3 | 1438 |
| | 44 | 1 | 470 |
| | 42 | 2 | 651 |
| | 40 | 4 | 1652 |
| 5th. | 40 | 2 | 615 |
| | 34 | 2 | 562 |
| | 32 | 2 | 599 |
| | 30 | 6 | 1740 |
| | 28 | 3 | 764 |
| | 24 | 1 | 180 |
| 6th. | 20 | 1 | 141 |
| | 18 | 2 | 328 |
| | 16 | 1 | 182 |
| | 14 | 2 | 330 |
| | 8 | 1 | 90 |
| | 4 | 1 | 35 |
| Sloops . . . . . . . . . . . . . . . . . . | | 13 | 554 |
| Dogger . . . . . . . . . . . . . . . . . . | | 1 | 73 |
| Fireships . . . . . . . . . . . . . . . . | | 3 | 584 |
| Galley . . . . . . . . . . . . . . . . . . | | 1 | 260 |
| Ketches . . . . . . . . . . . . . . . . . | | 2 | 194 |
| Smacks . . . . . . . . . . . . . . . . . | | 5 | 57 |
| Yachts‡ . . . . . . . . . . . . . . . . . | | 14 | 1064 |
| Hoys . . . . . . . . . . . . . . | | 4 | 234 |
| Hulks . . . . . . . . . . . . . . . . . . | | 8 | 4628 |
| Total . . . . . . | | 151 | 70587 |

* See Pepys's Naval Minutes, p. 268.—The names, dimensions &c. of these 9 Ships, are given in the Appendix (No. 6).

† See Pepys's Miscellanies, vol. 5, p. 185.

‡ This is the first time that Yachts appear in this Collection. Mr. Pepys mentions that "in the year 1660, the Dutch gave his Majesty a Yacht, called the Mary; until which time we had not heard of such a name in England."

When the Parliament were assembled in February 1677, the King acquainted them with the decayed condition of the Navy, and asked money for repairing it. The House of Commons, the same session, voted £586,000 for building 30 Ships,* and strictly appropriated the money to that service. Estimates were given in of the expence, but it was afterwards found that they fell short near £100,000.† The King, in October, 1675, had likewise desired supplies for building of Ships, and £300,000 was then voted for that service, under very particular restrictions.

## 1678

It is a little surprising that historians should have so very much mistaken Mr. Pepys, as to assert, from his authority, that the Navy, in August, 1678, consisted only of the following Ships and Vessels; viz.

| Rates. | Number. |
|---|---|
| 1st. . . . . . . . . . . . . . . . . . . . . . . . . . . . . . . | 5 |
| 2d. . . . . . . . . . . . . . . . . . . . . . . . . . . . . . . | 4 |
| 3d. . . . . . . . . . . . . . . . . . . . . . . . . . . . . . . | 16 |
| 4th. . . . . . . . . . . . . . . . . . . . . . . . . . . . . . . | 33 |
| 5th. . . . . . . . . . . . . . . . . . . . . . . . . . . . . . . | 12 |
| 6th. . . . . . . . . . . . . . . . . . . . . . . . . . . . . . . | 7 |
| Fireships. . . . . . . . . . . . . . . . . . . . . . . . . | 6 |
| | 83 |

and 30 capital Ships building;—whereas, the numbers of which the whole Navy consisted, differed considerably from this statement; for the 83 Ships therein described, were those that were actually in sea-service: and besides that there are always some Ships lying up, in want of repair, it is impossible the whole Navy could at that time have been in sea-service, at so short a notice as four months, the period mentioned by Mr. Pepys respecting the 83 Ships under consideration.

* See a particular account of these Ships after the Abstract of 1685.——See also their names, dimensions, and establishments of men and guns, in Appendix (No. 6, and 28.)

† The Ships and their furniture cost £670,000.

## 1676

Abstract of the Royal Navy, in 1676.

| Rates or Classes | Guns | No of Ships | Burthen | Total Number of Guns | Men |
|---|---|---|---|---|---|
| 1st. | 100 | 4 | 10850 | 778 | 5925 |
| | 96 | 3 | | | |
| | 90 | 1 | | | |
| 2d. | 84 | 1 | 8372 | 666 | 4320 |
| | 82 | 2 | | | |
| | 80 | 1 | | | |
| | 70 | 3 | | | |
| | 64 | 2 | | | |
| 3d. | 74 | 1 | 16689 | 1298 | 7634 |
| | 72 | 1 | | | |
| | 70 | 5 | | | |
| | 66 | 1 | | | |
| | 64 | 2 | | | |
| | 62 | 4 | | | |
| | 60 | 6 | | | |

338

| Rates or Classes. | Guns. | No of Ships. | Burthen. | Total Number of Guns. | Men. |
|---|---|---|---|---|---|
| 4th. | 54 | 9 | | | |
| | 50 | 1 | | | |
| | 48 | 16 | | | |
| | 46 | 4 | 20995 | 1890 | 9200 |
| | 44 | 2 | | | |
| | 42 | 6 | | | |
| | 32 | 1 | | | |
| | 30 | 1 | | | |
| 5th. | 32 | 4 | | | |
| | 30 | 6 | 3236 | 364 | 1575 |
| | 28 | 2 | | | |
| 6th. | 18 | 1 | | | |
| | 16 | 6 | 1103 | 118 | 565 |
| | 4 | 1 | | | |
| Sloops | 12 | | 492 | 88 | 420 |
| Dogger | | 1 | 73 | ...... | ...... |
| Fireships | | 5 | 1049 | 38 | 205 |
| Galley | | 1 | 260 | ...... | ...... |
| Ketches | | 2 | 189 | 20 | 100 |
| Smacks | | 5 | 175 | ...... | ...... |
| Yachts | | 15 | 1163 | 90 | 316 |
| Hoys | | 3 | 168 | ...... | ...... |
| Hulks | | 7 | 4190 | ...... | ...... |
| Total.... | | 148 | 69004 | 5350 | 30260 |

Exclusive of the Guns and Men for the Dogger, Smacks and Galley,

Some decayed Ships and Vessels may certainly have been broken up, or otherwise disposed of, between the date of this Abstract and August 1678, as it was a time of peace, and as money was sparingly expended on the Navy after 1674, as before observed; still, however, on comparing the Ships from the 1st to the 6th rates inclusive and Fireships, in this Abstract, with those in sea-pay in August 1678, and making allowance for the Ships lying up in want of repair at that period, and for the other classes of Vessels, and the Hulks, all which are included in the said Abstract, it may be reasonably supposed that the Navy in August 1678, consisted of nearly, if not quite, as many Ships as in 1676.

**1677**

### ESTABLISHMENT OF GUNS AND MEN.

Proposed for the 30 *new Ships* to be built by act of Parliament, according to the opinion of the Navy Board, Officers of the Ordnance, and several Commanders, at a public meeting held at the Navy Office, humbly presented to His Majesty, in obedience to his command, the 16th May 1677.

| Guns | Rates 1st. | 2d. | 3d. |
|---|---|---|---|
| | No | | |
| Cannon | 26 | ...... | ...... |
| Demi-Cannon | | 26 | 26 |
| Culverines | | 28 | 26 | ...... |

| Guns | Rates 1st. | 2d. | 3d. |
|---|---|---|---|
| | No | | |
| Twelve-pounders | | | 26 |
| Sakers, Upperdeck | 28 | 26 | ...... |
| Forecastle | 4 | ...... | 4 |
| Quarter-deck | 12 | 10 | 10 |
| Three-pounders | 2 | 2 | 4 |
| | 100 | 90 | 70 |

MEMᵒ.—*It is supposed the Cannon were ....42 Pounders.*
*Demi-Cannon . 32*
*Culverines ......18*

| Men. | Rates 1st 100 Guns | 2d 90 | 3d 70 |
|---|---|---|---|
| | No | | |
| 8 to each Cannon | 208 | ...... | ...... |
| 6 ditto Demi-Cannon | | 156 | 156 |
| 5 ditto Culverin | 140 | 130 | ...... |
| 4 ditto 12-pounder | | | 104 |
| 3 ditto Saker | 132 | 108 | 42 |
| 2 ditto 3-pounder | 4 | 4 | 8 |
| The remainder of the Complements to consist of | 296 | 262 | 160 |
| | 780 | 660 | 470 |

The following is a particular account of the *Ordnance* required for the whole of the Royal Navy, on 1st January 1685, as appears by a List of the Navy, in the 11th vol. of Pepys's Miscellanies, p. 111, viz.

| | Fortified. No | Drakes No |
|---|---|---|
| Cannon of 7 | 192 | .. |
| Demi-Cannon | 994 | 66 |
| 24-Pounders | 346 | .. |
| Culverines | 993 | 211 |
| 12-Pounders | 1004 | .. |
| Demi-Culverines | 748 | 360 |
| Do.......do.....Cutts | 250 | .. |
| 8-Pounders | 282 | .. |
| 6-Pounders | 382 | .. |
| Sakers | 947 | 93 |
| Saker Cutts | 218 | .. |
| Minions | 118 | .. |
| 3-Pounders | 324 | .. |
| Falcons | 46 | .. |
| Falconets | 4 | .. |
| Rabinets | 3 | .. |
| Total.... | 6851 | 730 |

the whole of which are therein stated to have been in store, or on board the Ships except 40 twelve-pounders, and 15 Sakers, or Saker-cutts.*

*Both the List of the Navy, and the Abstract of the Ordnance inserted therein, are signed (at least the original ones were) by four persons.*

At what particular period, after January 1685, several of the before-mentioned species of Ordnance were changed, or when their names in general were changed I do not know; but in the year 1716, as appears by the following general establishment of Guns for the Navy, all are described by the respective weights of their shot, and by them only; as has been the practice ever since, with perhaps the single exception of the Carronades which have been pretty much used in the Navy, of late years.

## 1685

Abstract of the Royal Navy at the demise of Charles II. on 6th February, 1685.

| Rates or Classes. | Guns. | Number | Burthen. |
|---|---|---|---|
| | | | Tons. |
| 1st. | 100 | 5 | 12547 |
| | 96 | 4 | |
| 2d. | 90 | 10 | |
| | 84 and 80 | 3 | 17364 |
| | 70 .. 60 | 2 | |
| 3d. | 74 .. 70 | 31 | 38161 |
| | 66 to 60 | 8 | |
| 4th. | 54 .. 44 | 32 | 22680 |
| | 42 .. 30 | 13 | |
| 5th. | 34 .. 28 | 11 | 2977 |
| 6th. | 18 .. 4 | 8 | 1041 |
| Fireships .......................... | | 12 | 2288 |
| Sloops ............................ | | 4 | 210 |
| Yachts ............................ | | 19 | 1762 |
| Small Vessels ...................... | | 10 | 301 |
| Hulks ............................. | | 7 | 4227 |
| Total...... | | 179 | 103558 |

# James II 1685–1688

## 1688

Abstract of the Royal Navy on the 18th December 1688.

| Rates or Classes. | Number. | Burthen in Tons. | Force. Men. | Force. Guns. | Highest Value of Rigging and Sea-Stores for one Ship of each Class |
|---|---|---|---|---|---|
| 1st. | 9 | 13041 | 6705 | 878 | £5181 |
| 2d. | 11 | 14905 | 7010 | 974 | 4296 |
| 3d. | 39 | 37993 | 16545 | 2640 | 2976 |
| 4th. | 41 | 22301 | 9480 | 1908 | 2195 |
| 5th. | 2 | 562 | 260 | 60 | 1031 |
| 6th. | 6 | 932 | 420 | 90 | 634 |
| Bombs ......... | 3 | 445 | 120 | 34 | 634 |
| Fireships ....... | 26 | 4983 | 905 | 218 | 1031 |
| Ketches ........ | 3 | 243 | 115 | 24 | 391 |
| Smacks ........ | 5 | 89 | 18 | ............. | |
| Yachts ......... | 14 | 1409 | 353 | 104 | 550 |
| Hoys .......... | 6 | 480 | 22 | ............. | |
| Hulks .......... | 8 | 4509 | 50 | ............. | |
| Total.... | 173 | 101892 | 42003 | 6930 | ......... |

The number of Ships and Vessels at the commencement of this reign, was 179;* the decrease therefore is only six, notwithstanding the decayed state of the Navy at that time.

*See the List of 6th February 1685.*

# Gloria Britannica
## or the
## Boast of the British Seas.
## A.D. 1689 The Royal Navy of England

| No. | | Where Built. | By Whome. | Year. | L | B | D | Dr. | Tuns. | Peace abroad and at home | War home | abroad | Abroad and Peace in both | home |
|---|---|---|---|---|---|---|---|---|---|---|---|---|---|---|
| | **First Rates.** | | | | | | | | | | | | | |
| 9 | Britania | Chatham | Sir P Pet | 1682 | 146 | 47 | 19 | 24 | 1620 | 605 | 710 | 815 | 90 | 100 |
| | St Andrew | Woolwich | Byland | 1670 | 128 | 44.4 | 17.9 | 21.6 | 1338 | 510 | 620 | 730 | 86 | 96 |
| | Charles | Deptford | John Shish | 1667 | 128 | 42.3 | 18.3 | 21 | 1229 | 500 | 605 | 710 | 86 | 96 |
| | Royal Charles | Portsm | Sir Ant Deane | 1673 | 136 | 44.8 | 18.3 | 20.6 | 1531 | 560 | 670 | 780 | 90 | 100 |
| | Royal James | Portsm | Sir A Deane | 1675 | 132 | 45 | 18.4 | 20 | 1422 | 560 | 670 | 780 | 90 | 100 |
| | London | Deptford | Shish | 1670 | 129 | 44 | 19 | 20.6 | 1328 | 5.0 | 620 | 730 | 86 | 96 |
| | St Michael | Portsm | J Tippets | 1669 | 125 | 40.8 | 17.5 | 19.8 | 1101 | 430 | 520 | 600 | 80 | 90 |
| | Prince | Chatham | Mr P Pet. | 1670 | 131 | 44.4 | 19 | 21.6 | 1463 | 560 | 670 | 780 | 90 | 100 |
| | Soveraign | Woolwich | Mr P Pet. | 1637 | 131 | 48 | 19.2 | 23.6 | 1605 | 605 | 710 | 815 | 90 | 100 |
| | **Second Rates.** | | | | | | | | Tuns | | | | | |
| 16 | Albemarle | Harwich | Isaac Bets | 1681 | 142 | 44 | 18.6 | 18 | 1462 | 500 | 580 | 660 | 82 | 90 |
| | Coronation | Ports. | J Bets. | 1685 | 137 | 45 | 18.6 | 20 | 1475 | ,, | ,, | ,, | ,, | ,, |
| | Dutchess | Deptf | J Shish | 1679 | 137 | 45 | 18.3 | 19 | 1475 | ,, | ,, | ,, | ,, | ,, |
| | Duke | Woolw | Th Shish | 1682 | 142.6 | 45.2 | 18.9 | 20 | 1546 | ,, | ,, | ,, | ,, | ,, |
| | Ossory | Ports. | Betts | 1682 | 140 | 44.7 | 18.2 | 20 | 1300 | ,, | ,, | ,, | ,, | ,, |
| | French Ruby | Taken. | | 1666 | 112 | 38.2 | 16.6 | 18.6 | 868 | 350 | 435 | 570 | 72 | 80 |
| | St George | Deptf | Burrel | 1622 | 116 | 38 | 15 | 18 | 891 | 310 | 385 | 460 | 62 | 72 |
| | Katherine | Woolw. | Pet | 1664 | 124 | 41 | 17.3 | 20 | 1108 | 360 | 450 | 540 | 74 | 82 |
| | Neptune | Deptf | J Shish | 1683 | 124 | 41 | 17.3 | 20 | 1475 | 500 | 580 | 660 | 82 | 90 |
| | Rainbow | Deptf | Bright | 1617 | 114 | 38 | 15 | 17.6 | 868 | 270 | 335 | 410 | 54 | 64 |
| | Sandwich | Harwich | Betts | 1679 | 132 | 44.6 | 18.3 | 18 | 1395 | 500 | 580 | 660 | 82 | 90 |
| | Triumph | Deptf | Burrel | 1623 | 116 | 38 | 15.6 | 18 | 891 | 130 | 185 | 460 | 62 | 70 |
| | Vanguard | Portsm. | Furzer | 1678 | 126 | 45 | 18.2 | 18 | 1357 | 500 | 580 | 660 | 82 | 90 |
| | Victory rebuilt | Chat. | Ph. Pett | 1663 | 121 | 40 | 17 | 19 | 1029 | 350 | 440 | 530 | 72 | 82 |
| | Unicorn | Woolw. | Boat | 1633 | 120 | 37.6 | 15.1 | 17.4 | 823 | 270 | 335 | 410 | 54 | 64 |
| | Windsor Castle | Woolw. | J Shish | 1678 | 142 | 44 | 18.3 | 20 | 1462 | 500 | 580 | 660 | 82 | 90 |
| | **Third Rates.** | | | | L | B | D | Dr. | Tuns. | MEN. | | | Guns. | |
| 38 | Anne | Chatham | Ph Pett | 1678 | 128 | 40 | 17 | 18 | 1089 | 300 | 380 | 460 | 62 | 70 |
| | Berwick | Chat. | Ph Pett | 1679 | 128 | 40 | 17 | 18 | ,, | ,, | ,, | ,, | ,, | ,, |
| | Burford | Woolw | Th Shish | 1679 | 137.8 | 40.3 | 17.3 | 18 | 1174 | ,, | ,, | ,, | ,, | ,, |
| | Breda | Harw. | Betts | 1679 | 124 | 40 | 16 | 18 | 1050 | ,, | ,, | ,, | ,, | ,, |
| | Captain | Woolw. | Th Shish | 1678 | 138 | 40 | 17.2 | 18 | 1164 | ,, | ,, | ,, | ,, | ,, |
| | Defiance | Chat | Ph. Pett | 1675 | 117 | 38 | 16 | 17.6 | 881 | 270 | 345 | 420 | 60 | 70 |
| | Dunkirk | Wool | Burrel | 1651 | 112 | 34.4 | 14 | 17 | 662 | 210 | 270 | 340 | 52 | 60 |
| | Dreadnought | Blackwall | Johnson | 1653 | 116 | 34.6 | 14.2 | 16.6 | 732 | 215 | 280 | 355 | 54 | 62 |
| | Edgar | Bristol | Baily | 1668 | 124 | 39.8 | 16 | 18.4 | 994 | 370 | 290 | 445 | 62 | 72 |
| | Eagle | Ports | Furzer | 1679 | 120 | 40.9 | 17 | 18 | 1057 | 300 | 380 | 460 | 62 | 70 |
| | Elizabeth | 2 Blackw. | 2 Johnson | ,, | 132 | 40.6 | 16.6 | 18.6 | 1151 | ,, | ,, | ,, | ,, | ,, |
| | Essex | 1 Deptf. | 1 Castle | ,, | 124 | 40.3 | ,, | 18 | 1068 | ,, | ,, | ,, | ,, | ,, |
| | Expedition | Portsm | Furzer | 1678 | 120 | 40.9 | 17.6 | ,, | 1057 | ,, | ,, | ,, | ,, | ,, |
| | Exeter | Blackw. | Johnson | 1679 | 123 | 40.4 | 16.9 | ,, | 1070 | ,, | ,, | ,, | ,, | ,, |
| | Grafton | Wool | G Shish | ,, | 138 | 40.2 | 17.2 | ,, | 1184 | ,, | ,, | ,, | ,, | ,, |
| | Hampton Court | Deptf | Shish | 1678 | 131 | 40 | 17 | 18.6 | 1105 | ,, | ,, | ,, | ,, | ,, |
| | Harwich | Harwich | A Deane | 1674 | 123.9 | 39 | 15.8 | 17.6 | 993 | 270 | 345 | 420 | 60 | 70 |
| | Henrietta | Horslydown | Bright | 1653 | 116 | 35.7 | 14.4 | 17 | 781 | 215 | 280 | 355 | 54 | 62 |
| | Hope | Deptf | Castle | 1678 | 124 | 40 | 16.9 | 18.6 | 1058 | 300 | 380 | 460 | 62 | 70 |
| | Kent | Blackwall | Johnson | 1679 | ,, | 40.2 | 17 | 18 | 1064 | ,, | ,, | ,, | ,, | ,, |
| | Lenox | Deptf. | J Shish | 1678 | 131 | 39.8 | 17 | 18 | 1096 | ,, | ,, | ,, | ,, | ,, |
| | Lyon | Chatham | Apsly | 1640 | 108 | 35.4 | 15.6 | 17.6 | 717 | 210 | 270 | 340 | 52 | 60 |
| | Mary | Woolw. | Pett. | 1649 | 116 | 36.3 | 14.6 | 17 | 777 | 215 | 280 | 355 | 54 | 62 |
| | Monk | Portsm. | J Tippets | 1659 | 108 | 35 | 14 | 16 | 703 | 210 | 270 | 340 | 52 | 60 |
| | Monmouth | Chatham | Ph Pett. | 1666 | 118.9 | 37 | 15.6 | 18 | 856 | 255 | 320 | 400 | 58 | 66 |
| | Montague rebuilt | ,, | Pet | 1654 1675 | 117 | 36.6 | 15 | 17.4 | 829 | 215 | 280 | 352 | 54 | 62 |
| | Northumberland | Bristol | Pope | 1679 | 130 | 40.2 | 17 | 18 | 1115 | 300 | 380 | 460 | 62 | 70 |
| | Royal Oak | Deptf. | Shish. | 1674 | 125 | 40.6 | 18.3 | 18.8 | 1107 | 310 | 390 | 470 | 62 | 70 |

| Name | Yard | Builder | Year | L | B | D | Dr | Tons | | | | | |
|---|---|---|---|---|---|---|---|---|---|---|---|---|---|
| Plymouth | Wapping | Taylor | 1653 | 110 | 34.8 | 14.6 | 17 | 742 | 210 | 270 | 340 | 52 | 62 |
| Pendenis | Chatham | Ph Pett | 1679 | 128½ | 40 | 17 | 18 | 1093 | 300 | 380 | 460 | 62 | 70 |
| Restoration | Harwich | Ts. Betts | 1678 | 123½ | 39.8 | 17 | 18 | 1032 | ,, | ,, | ,, | ,, | ,, |
| Resolution | ,, | A Deane | 1667 | 120 | 37.2 | 15.6 | 17 | 885 | 270 | 345 | 420 | 60 | 70 |
| Rupert | ,, | ,, | 1665 | 119 | 37.2 | 15.6 | ,, | 832 | 255 | 320 | 400 | 60 | 70 |
| Stirling Castle | Deptf | T Shish | 1679 | 131 | 36.3 | 17.3 | 18 | 1114 | 300 | 380 | 460 | ,, | ,, |
| Suffolk | Blackw. | Johnson | 1680 | 132 | 40 | 16.6 | ,, | 1151 | ,, | ,, | ,, | ,, | ,, |
| Swiftsure | Ports. | A Deane | 1673 | 123 | 40.6 / 38.8 | 15.6 | 17.6 | 978 | 270 | 345 | 420 | 60 | 70 |
| Warspight | Blackw. | Johnson | 1666 | 118 | 38.9 | 15.6 | ,, | 742 | ,, | ,, | ,, | ,, | ,, |
| York | ,, | ,, | 1680 | 115 | 35 | 14.2 | 17 | 734 | 300 | 380 | 460 | 62 | 70 |
| Lyon rebuilt | Chatham | Taylor | 1658 | | | | | | | | | | |

**Fourth Rates.**  (44)

| Name | Yard | Builder | Year | L | B | D | Dr | Tons | | | | | |
|---|---|---|---|---|---|---|---|---|---|---|---|---|---|
| Adventure | Woolw | Pet | 1646 | 92 | 27.9 | 12 | 14 | 392 | 120 | 160 | 190 | 38 | 48 |
| Advice | ,, | ,, | 1650 | 100 | 31 | 12.9 | 15 | 544 | 150 | 200 | 230 | 42 | 48 |
| Antelope | ,, | Cary | 1653 | 101 | ,, | 13 | 16 | 560 | ,, | ,, | ,, | ,, | ,, |
| Assistance | Deptf | Johnson | 1650 | 102 | 32 | ,, | 15.6 | 550 | ,, | ,, | ,, | ,, | ,, |
| Assurance | ,, | Pet | 1646 | 89 | 27 | 11 | 13.6 | 340 | 115 | 150 | 120 | 36 | 42 |
| Bonaventure rebuilt | ,, | ,, | 1663 | 102.9 | 30.8 | 124 | 15.6 | 514 | 150 | 200 | 250 | 42 | 40 |
| Bristol | Ports. | T. Tippets | 1653 | 104 | 31.1 | 18 | 15.8 | 584 | ,, | ,, | ,, | ,, | ,, |
| Centurion | Ratcliff | Pet | 1650 | 104 | 31 | 13 | 16 | 531 | 150 | 200 | 230 | 42 | 48 |
| Charles Gally | Woolw. | ,, | 1676 | 114 | 28.6 | 8.7 | 12 | 492 | 220 | 220 | 220 | 32 | 32 |
| Constant Warwick | Ports. | J. Tippets | 1646 | | | | | | | | | | |
| rebuilt | | | 1666 | 90 | 28.2 | 12 | 12.8 | 379 | 115 | 150 | 180 | 36 | 42 |
| Crown | Rotherith | Castle | 1653 | 100 | 31.7 | 13 | 16 | 535 | 150 | 200 | 230 | 42 | 48 |
| Deptford | Woolw. | Th Shish | 1688 | | | | | | | | | | |
| St David | Woleston | Furzer | 1666 | 107 | 34.9 | 14.8 | 16.8 | 685 | 185 | 240 | 280 | 46 | 54 |
| Diamond | Deptf | Pet | 1651 | 105 | 31.3 | 13 | 16 | 548 | 150 | 200 | 230 | 42 | 48 |
| Dover | Shoram | Castle | 1654 | 100 | 31.8 | ,, | ,, | 530 | ,, | ,, | ,, | ,, | ,, |
| Dragon | Chat. | Godard | 1647 | 96 | 30 | 12 | 15 | 470 | 140 | 185 | 220 | 40 | 46 |
| Falcon | Woolw. | Pet | 1666 | 88 | 27.4 | 12 | 13 | 349 | 115 | 150 | 180 | 36 | 42 |
| Foresight | Deptf | Shish | 1650 | 102 | 31.1 | 12.9 | 14.6 | 522 | 150 | 200 | 230 | 42 | 48 |
| Greenwich | Woolw. | Pet | 1666 | 108 | 33.9 | 14.6 | 15 | 654 | 185 | 240 | 280 | 46 | 54 |
| Hampshire | Deptf | Peter Pet | 1653 | 101.9 | 29.9 | 13 | 14.5 | 479 | 140 | 105 | 220 | 40 | 46 |
| Happy Return | Yarmouth | Edgar | 1654 | 104 | 33.2 | ,, | 17 | 609 | 185 | 240 | 280 | 46 | 54 |
| James Gally | Blackw. | Deane | 1676 | ,, | 28.1 | 10.2 | 12 | 436 | 200 | 200 | 200 | 30 | |
| Jersey | Mauldm | Sterlin | 1654 | 102 | 32 | 13.1 | 15.6 | 556 | 150 | 200 | 230 | 42 | 48 |
| Kingfisher | Woodbridge | Pet | 1675 | 110 | 33.8 | 13 | 13 | 663 | 140 | 185 | 220 | 40 | 48 |
| Leopard | Deptf | Shish | 1658 | 109 | 33.9 | 15 | 17.3 | 645 | 185 | 240 | 280 | 46 | 54 |
| Mary Rose | Woodbridge | Munday | 1653 | 102 | 32 | 13 | 16 | 566 | 150 | 200 | 230 | 42 | 48 |
| Mordant | Deptf | Castle | 1681 | 110 | 31.1 | 15 | 12 | 663 | ,, | ,, | ,, | ,, | ,, |
| Mary Gally | Rotherith | Deane | ,, | | | | | | | | | | |
| St Alban | Deptf | Hardy | 1688 | | | | | | | | | | |
| Newcastle | Rotherh | Pet | 1653 | 108 | 33.1 | 13.2 | 12 | 628 | 185 | 240 | 280 | 46 | 54 |
| Nonsuch | Ports. | Deane | 1668 | 88.1 | 27.8 | 11 | 13 | 368 | 115 | 150 | 180 | 36 | 42 |
| Oxford | Bristol | Baily | 1674 | 109 | 34 | 15.6 | 17.8 | 670 | 185 | 240 | 280 | 46 | 54 |
| Phoenix | Portsm | Deane | 1671 | 90 | 28.6 | 11.2 | 13 | 389 | 115 | .150 | 180 | 36 | 42 |
| Portland | Wapping | Taylor | 1652 | 105 | 33 | 13 | 16 | 608 | 155 | 210 | 240 | 44 | 50 |
| Portsmouth | Portsm | Eastward | 1649 | 100 | 29.6 | 12.6 | 16 | 463 | 140 | 105 | 220 | 40 | 46 |
| Princess | Forest Deane | Furzer | 1660 | 104 | 33 | 14.3 | 16.6 | 602 | 185 | 240 | 280 | 46 | 54 |
| Reserve | Woodbridge | Pet | 1650 | 100 | 29.6 | 12.4 | 15 | 513 | 150 | 200 | 230 | 42 | 48 |
| Ruby | Deptf | Pet. sen. | 1651 | 105 | 31.6 | 13 | 16 | 539 | ,, | ,, | ,, | ,, | ,, |
| Swallow | Pitch House | Taylor | 1653 | 101 | 32 | 15 | 15.6 | 549 | ,, | ,, | ,, | ,, | ,, |
| Sweepstakes | Yarmouth | Edgar | 1666 | 97 | 28.8 | 11 | 13.8 | 376 | 115 | 150 | 180 | 36 | 42 |
| Tyger | Deptf | Pet | 1647 | | | | | | | | | | |
| rebuilt | ,, | Shish | 1681 | 99 | 29.4 | 12 | 14.8 | 453 | 120 | 160 | 190 | 38 | 44 |
| Tyger | Prize Algier | | 1678 | 112 | 33 | 12.8 | 15 | 649 | 150 | 210 | 230 | 42 | 48 |
| Woolwich | Woolw. | Pett | 1675 | 112 | 35.9 | 15 | 16.4 | 761 | 185 | 240 | 280 | 46 | 54 |
| Yarmouth | Yarm. | Edgar | 1653 | 105 | 33 | 13.3 | 17 | 608 | ,, | ,, | ,, | ,, | ,, |

**Fifth Rates.**

| Name | Yard | Builder | Year | L | B | D | Dr | Tons | | | | | |
|---|---|---|---|---|---|---|---|---|---|---|---|---|---|
| Dartmouth | Portsm | J Tippets | 1655 | 80 | 25 | 10 | 12 | 266 | 90 | 115 | 135 | 28 | 32 |
| Garland | Southamp | Furzer | 1654 | 81 | 24.6 | ,, | 11.6 | 260 | 85 | 110 | 130 | ,, | 38 |
| Guernsey | Waldwick. | Shish | ,, | 80 | 24 | ,, | 12 | 245 | ,, | ,, | ,, | ,, | 30 |
| Hunter | Dutch prize | | 1672 | 80 | 25 | 10.6 | 13.6 | 265 | ,, | ,, | ,, | ,, | ,, |
| Mermaid | Limehouse | Graves | 1651 | 76 | ,, | 10 | 12 | 286 | 90 | 115 | 135 | ,, | 32 |
| Norwich | Chatham | Pet | 1655 | 80'6 | 24.6 | 10.6 | ,, | 253 | 85 | 110 | 130 | ,, | 30 |
| Orange Tree | Algier. | | 1677 | 76 | 26.4 | 9 | 11 | 280 | ,, | ,, | ,, | ,, | ,, |
| Pearl | Ratcliff | Pet | 1651 | 86 | 25 | 10 | 12 | 285 | ,, | ,, | ,, | 28 | ,, |
| Richmond | Portsm | Tippets | 1655 | 72 | 23.6 | 9.9 | 11.6 | 211 | 80 | 105 | 125 | 26 | 28 |
| Rose | Yarmouth | Edgar | 1674 | 75 | 24 | 10 | 12.6 | 229 | ,, | ,, | ,, | ,, | ,, |

| No. | Where Built. | By Whome. | Year | L | B | D | Dr. | Tuns. | MEN. Peace abroad and at home | War. home | War abroad | GUNS. Abroad and Peace in both | home |
|---|---|---|---|---|---|---|---|---|---|---|---|---|---|
| Saphire | Harwich | Deane | 1675 | 86 | 27 | 11 | 13.2 | 333 | 90 | 115 | 139 | 28 | 32 |
| Swan | Bought of Capt Young. | | ,, | 74 | 25 | 10 | 11 | 246 | ,, | ,, | ,, | ,, | ,, |
| Success | Chatham | Taylor | 1657 | 85 | 25.6 | ,, | 12 | 294 | ,, | ,, | ,, | ,, | ,, |
| **Sixth Rates.** | | | | L | B | D | Dr. | | | | | | |
| Drake | Deptford | Peter Pett | 1652 | 38 | 18 | 7.8 | 9 | 146 | 45 | 65 | 75 | 14 | 16 |
| Fanfare | Harwich | Deane | 1655 | 44 | 12 | 5.6 | 5.6 | 33 | 18 | 25 | 30 | 4 | 4 |
| Francis | ,, | ,, | 1666 | 66 | 20 | 9.2 | 8.8 | 140 | 45 | 65 | 75 | 14 | 16 |
| Greyhound | ,, | ,, | 1672 | 75 | 21.6 | 9 | 8.6 | 184 | ,, | ,, | ,, | ,, | ,, |
| Lark | Blackwall | ,, | 1675 | 74 | 22.6 | 9.2 | 9 | 199 | 50 | 70 | 85 | 16 | 18 |
| Roebuck | Harwich | ,, | 1660 | 64 | 19.6 | 9.10 | 8.6 | 129 | 45 | 65 | 75 | 94 | 16 |
| Soudadoes | | T Shish. | 1673 | 74 | 21.6 | 10 | 9.6 | 188 | ,, | ,, | ,, | ,, | ,, |
| **Hulkes.** | | | | L | B | D | Dr. | | | | | | |
| Alphin | Dutch prize | | 1673 | 120 | 33.6 | 12 | 19 | 716 | 4 | 4 | 4 | | |
| America | Bought | | 1678 | 111 | 27.6 | 14.5 | 15.8 | 446 | 28 | 20 | 20 | | |
| Arms of Horne | ,, | | 1673 | 110 | 30.3 | 12 | 18 | 516 | 8 | 8 | 8 | | |
| Arms of Rotterdam | East India prize | | ,, | 119 | 39.6 | 18.9 | 18.6 | 987 | 7 | 7 | 7 | | |
| Elias | Dutch prize | | 1653 | 90 | 27 | 10 | 12.8 | 350 | 2 | 2 | 2 | | |
| Slothony | ,, | | 1665 | 112 | 36 | 17 | 18 | 772 | 7 | 7 | 7 | | |
| Stadthouse | ,, | | 1667 | 90 | 30.4 | 11.6 | 15 | 440 | 4 | 4 | 4 | | |
| **Fire Ships.** | | | | L | B | D | Dr. | Tuns. | | | | | |
| Anne & Christopher | bought | | 167½ | 76 | 25.5 | 10 | 11.6 | 261 | 40 | 40 | 45 | 8 | |
| Castle | ,, | | 167½ | 85 | 27 | 11 | ,, | 329 | ,, | ,, | ,, | ,, | |
| Eagle | Wapping | Taylor | 1654 | 85.6 | 25.6 | 10 | 12 | 295 | — | 45 | — | 12 | |
| Holmes | bought | | 1671 | 80 | 22.9 | 12.9 | 13.6 | 220 | — | 35 | — | 8 | |
| John & Alexander | ,, | | 1678 | 69 | 22 | 9.8 | 11 | 178 | ,, | ,, | ,, | ,, | |
| Peace | ,, | | ,, | 64 | 20 | 10 | 10.8 | 145 | 24 | 30 | 24 | 6 | 8 |
| Providence | ,, | | ,, | 66 | 22.4 | 9.9 | 10.6 | 175 | ,, | ,, | ,, | ,, | ,, |
| Sampson | ,, | | ,, | 78 | 24.1 | 10.8 | 12 | 240 | 40 | 40 | 45 | 8 | 12 |
| Sarah | ,, | | ,, | ,, | ,, | 10.1 | ,, | ,, | — | 20 | — | 4 | 6 |
| Spanish Merchant | ,, | | ,, | 79 | 26.9 | 10.6 | 11.6 | 250 | — | 36 | — | 6 | 8 |
| Ivanhoe | R. Page | | 1665 | 52 | 19.1 | 8.6 | 7.6 | 100 | 20 | 20 | 25 | 6 | |
| Young Sprag | bought of Sprag | | 1672 | 46 | 18 | 9 | 8.6 | 79 | ,, | ,, | ,, | 6 | |
| **Yatchts.** | | | | L | B | D | Dr. | Tuns. | | | | | |
| Anne | Woolw. | Pett | 1661 | 52 | 19 | 7 | 7 | 100 | 20 | 20 | 30 | 6 | 8 |
| Bezan | Given by the Duchess | | ,, | 34 | 14 | 7 | 3.6 | 35 | — | 4 | — | 4 | |
| Charlotte | Woolw. | Pet | 1677 | 61 | 21 | 9 | 8 | 142 | 20 | 20 | 30 | 6 | 8 |
| Cleaveland | Portsm | Deane | 1671 | 53 | 19 | 7.6 | 7.6 | 107 | ,, | ,, | ,, | ,, | ,, |
| Deale | Woolw | Pet. | 1673 | 32 | 13 | 5.8 | 5.8 | 28 | — | 4 | — | 4 | |
| Jimmy | Lambert. | Pett. | 1662 | 31 | 12.6 | 3.6 | 3.6 | 25 | ,, | ,, | ,, | ,, | ,, |
| Isle of Wight | Portsm | Furzer | 1673 | ,, | 12.6 | 6 | 6 | 23 | ,, | ,, | ,, | ,, | ,, |
| Katherine | Chatham | Pet. | 1674 | 56 | 21.4 | 8.6 | 7.9 | 135 | 20 | 20 | 30 | 6 | 8 |
| Kitchin | Rotherhith | Castle | 1670 | 52 | 19 | 8.6 | 8 | 103 | ,, | ,, | ,, | ,, | ,, |
| Mary | Chatham | Pett | 1677 | 66.6 | 21 | 8.9 | 7.6 | 166 | ,, | ,, | ,, | ,, | ,, |
| Merlin | Ratcliff | T Shish | 1665 | 53 | 19 | 6 | 7.4 | 109 | ,, | ,, | ,, | ,, | ,, |
| Monmouth | Rotherh. | Castle | ,, | 52 | 19. | 8 | 7.3 | 103 | ,, | ,, | ,, | ,, | ,, |
| Navy | Portsm | Deane | 1673 | 48 | 17 | 7.7 | 7.1 | 74 | ,, | ,, | ,, | ,, | ,, |
| Portsmouth | Woolw | Pet | 1674 | 57 | 19 | 7.4 | 7 | 133 | ,, | ,, | ,, | ,, | ,, |
| Queenbro | ,, | ,, | 1671 | 31.6 | 13.4 | 6.6 | 6 | 29 | — | 4 | — | 4 | |
| Richmond | Bought | | 1672 | 45 | 16 | 9 | 7.6 | 64 | 20 | 20 | 30 | 6 | 4 |
| Henrietta | Woolw. | T Shish | 1679 | 64.6 | 21 | 8 | 4 | 106 | ,, | ,, | ,, | 6 | 8 |
| Tubbs. | Greenw | Ph Pett. | 1682 | 62.4 | 21.2 | 10 | 8 | 142 | ,, | ,, | ,, | ,, | ,, |
| **Ketches.** | | | | L | B | D | Dr. | Tuns. | | | | | |
| Deptford | Deptf. | T. Shish | 1665 | 52 | 18 | 9.4 | 8.4 | 89 | 30 | 40 | 50 | 4 | |
| Quaker | Bought. | | 1674 | 54 | 18.2 | 9 | 9.6 | 80 | ,, | ,, | ,, | 10 | |
| **Hoyes.** | | | | | | | | | | | | | |
| Harwich | Gressingham | | 1660 | 38 | 16 | 8 | 8 | 52 | 5 | | | | |
| Lighter | Portsm | Deane | 1672 | ,, | 18 | 7.6 | 7.6 | 65 | 3 | | | | |
| Marygold | ,, | T Tippets | 1653 | 32 | 14 | 7 | 7 | 33 | 3 | | | | |
| **Smacks.** | | | | | | | | | | | | | |
| Bridget | Deptf | Shish | 1672 | 32 | 11.8 | 5.6 | 4.6 | 21 | 2 | | | | |
| Little London | Chatham | Pet | ,, | 26 | 11 | 5.8 | 4 | 46½ | ,, | | | | |
| Royal Escape | Bought | | 1660 | 30.6 | 14 | 7.9 | 7 | 34 | ,, | | | | |

| | | | | | | | | | | |
|---|---|---|---|---|---|---|---|---|---|---|
| Sheerness | Chat. | Pet | 1673 | 28 | 11 | 6 | 5.6 | 18 | ,, | |
| Shish | Deptf | T Shish | ,, | 38 | 11.4 | 4.6 | 4 | 24 | ,, | |

**Sloopes.**

| | | | | | | | | | | |
|---|---|---|---|---|---|---|---|---|---|---|
| Boneta | Woolw | P. Pet | 1673 | 61 | 13 | 5 | 4.6 | 57 | 10 | 4 |
| Chatham | Chat. | Pet | ,, | 57 | 12 | ,, | 4 | 50 | ,, | ,, |
| Dove | Deptf | Shish | 1672 | 40 | 10 | 4 | ,, | 19 | ,, | ,, |
| Emsworth | | Smith | 1667 | ,, | 13 | 4.9 | 5 | 39 | ,, | ,, |
| Experiment | Greenwich | Lawrence | 1673 | 35 | 11.6 | 6.4 | ,, | 24 | ,, | ,, |
| Hound | Chat. | Pet | ,, | 57 | 13 | 5 | 4.6 | 50 | ,, | ,, |
| Hunter | Portsm | Deane | ,, | 60.6 | 12 | ,, | ,, | 46 | ,, | ,, |
| Invention | ,, | ,, | ,, | 44 | 11 | ,, | 4 | 28 | ,, | ,, |
| Prevention | ,, | ,, | 1672 | 50 | 12 | ,, | 4.6 | 40 | ,, | ,, |
| Spy | Harwich | ,, | 1666 | 45 | 11 | 4.4 | 4 | 28 | ,, | ,, |
| Whipster Brigantine | Deptf | Shish. | 1672 | 58 | 14.6 | 5 | 4.6 | 64 | ,, | ,, |
| Woolwich | Woolw | Pet | 1673 | 61 | 13 | ,, | ,, | 57 | ,, | ,, |

Two Lyons  
Golden Horse  
Half Moon } Prizes from Barbary.  
Rose of Sally  
Rose of Algier  

Dumbarton } Argiles Prize.  
Heldenbergh } Monmouths Ship.

# Rates of Pay in 1689

| | †no. | 1. Rate. | no. | 2. Rate. | no. | 3. Rate. | no. | 4. Rate. | no. | 5. Rate. | no. | 6. Rate. |
|---|---|---|---|---|---|---|---|---|---|---|---|---|
| **Officers.** | | | | | | | | | | | | |
| Captain, daily | | 15s. | | 12s. | | 10s. | | 7s. 6d. | | 6s. | | 5s. |
| Lieutenant, daily. | | 3s. | | 3s. | | 2s. 6d. | | 2s. 6d. | | | | |
| | | | | | | | | | | | | |
| Master. Monthly. | | 7. 0.0 | | 5. 6.0 | | 4.13.8 | | 4. 6.2 | | 3.17.6 | | Cap. is Mast. |
| Mast Mate & Pilot. | 6 | 3. 6.0 | 4 | 3. 0.0 | 3 | 2.16.2 | 2 | 2.7.10 | 2 | 2. 2.0 | 1 | 2. 2.0 |
| Quarter-Master. | 4 | 1.15.0 | 4 | 1.15.0 | 4 | 1.12.0 | 4 | 1.10.0 | 3 | 1. 8.0 | 2 | 1. 6.0 |
| Quarter-Ma. Mate. | 4 | 1.10.0 | 4 | 1.10.0 | 2 | 1. 8.0 | 2 | 1. 8.0 | 1 | 1. 6.0 | 1 | 1. 5.0 |
| Boatswain. | | 4. 0.0 | | 3.10.0 | | 3. 0.0 | | 2.10.0 | | 2. 5.0 | | 2. 0.0 |
| Boatswains-Mate. | 2 | 1.15.0 | 1 | 1.15.0 | 1 | 1.12.0 | 1 | 1.10.0 | 1 | 1. 8.0 | 1 | 1. 6.0 |
| Yeomen of Sheets. | 4 | 1.12.0 | 4 | 1.10.0 | 2 | 1. 8.0 | 2 | 1. 8.0 | | | | |
| Gunner. | | 4. 0.0 | | 3.10.0 | | 3. 0.0 | | 2.10.0 | | 2. 5.0 | | 2. 0.0 |
| Gunner's Mate. | 2 | 1.15.0 | 2 | 1.15.0 | 1 | 1.12.0 | 1 | 1.10.0 | 1 | 1. 8.0 | 1 | 1. 6.0 |
| Quarter Gunner. | 4 | 1. 6.0 | 4 | 1. 6.0 | 4 | 1. 5.0 | 4 | 1. 5.0 | 1 | 1. 5.0 | 1 | 1. 5.0 |
| Carpenter. | | 4. 0.0 | | 3.10.0 | | 3. 0.0 | | 2.10.0 | | 2. 5.0 | | 2. 0.0 |
| Carpenter's Mate. | 2 | 2. 0.0 | 2 | 2. 0.0 | 1 | 1.16.0 | 1 | 1.14.0 | 1 | 1.12.0 | 1 | 1.10.0 |
| Ordinary or Crew.*‡ | 9 | 1. 6.0 | 6 | 1. 6.0 | 4 | 1. 5.0 | 3 | 1. 5.0 | 1 | 1. 5.0 | 1 | 1. 5.0 |
| Chysurgeon. | | 2.10.0 | | ,, | | ,, | | ,, | | ,, | | ,, |
| Chysurg. Mate. | | 1.10.0 | | ,, | | ,, | | ,, | | ,, | | ,, |
| Purser. | | 4. 0.0 | | 3.10.0 | | 3. 0.0 | | 2.10.0 | | 2.5.0 | | 2 .0.0 |
| Steward. | | 1. 5.0 | | 1. 5.0 | | 1 5.0 | | 1. 3.4 | | 1. 0.8 | | 1. 0.0 |
| Steward's Mate. | | 1. 0.8 | | ,, | | ,, | | ,, | | | | |
| Midshipmen. | 8 | 2. 5.0 | 6 | 2. 0.0 | 4 | 1.17.6 | 3 | 1.13.9 | 2 | 1.10.0 | 1 | 1.10.0 |
| Corporal. | | 1.15.0 | | 1.12.0 | | 1.10.0 | | 1.10.0 | | 1. 8.0 | | 1. 5.0 |
| Coxswain. | | 1.12.0 | | 1.10.0 | | 1. 8.0 | | 1. 8.0 | | 1. 6.0 | | |
| Trumpeter. | | 1.10.0 | | 1. 8.0 | | 1. 5.0 | | 1. 5.0 | | 1. 5.0 | | 1. 4.0 |
| Cook. | | 1. 5.0 | | ,, | | ,, | | ,, | | ,, | | 1. 4.0 |
| Armourer. | | 1. 5.0 | | ,, | | ,, | | ,, | | | | |
| Gunsmith. | | 1. 5.0 | | ,, | | | | | | | | |

Yeomen of Powder  
Cooks Mate  
Coxswains Mate } 1.4.0 in  
Swabber. } each Rate.  
Cooper  
Able Seaman  

Ordinary Seamen.  
Shifter. } 0.19.0  
Barber.  

Gromers at Sea    0.14.3  
Boy    0. 9.6

\* *This list is taken from a small book called* Gloria Britannica, *published by Thomas in 1689, and is not included in Derricks book.*  
† *Number carried per ship.*  
‡ *Carpenter's assistants.*

# William and Mary II
# 1688–1702 (Mary died 1694)

Abstract of the Royal Navy at the close of the War of the English Succession in September 1697.

| Rates or Classes. | Guns. | Number of Ships. | Number of Men to a Ship of each Class. |
|---|---|---|---|
| 1st. | 100 | 5 | 780 |
|  | 94 | 1 | 750 |
| 2d. | 96 | 1 |  |
|  | 94 | 1 | } 700 to 600 |
|  | 90 | 11 | } |
| 3d. | 80 | 15 | } |
|  | 70 | 23 | } |
|  | 68 | 1 | } 490 .. 380 |
|  | 66 | 3 | } |
|  | 64 | 1 | } |
| 4th. | 64 | 1 | } |
|  | 60 | 10 | } |
|  | 56 | 3 | } |
|  | 54 | 4 | } |
|  | 52 | 1 | } |
|  | 50 | 31 | } 365 .. 180 |
|  | 48 | 4 | } |
|  | 46 | 1 | } |
|  | 44 | 1 | } |
| 5th. | 44 | 4 | } |
|  | 42 | 1 | } |
|  | 40 | 1 | } |
|  | 36 | 2 | } |
|  | 34 | 4 | } |
|  | 32 | 21 | } 220 to 105 |
|  | 30 | 2 | } |
|  | 28 | 1 | } |
|  | 26 | 5 | } |
|  | Guns not known | 1 | } |
| 6th. | 24 | 18 | } |
|  | 18 | 3 | } |
|  | 16 | 2 | } |
|  | 14 | 1 | } 110 and under |
|  | 12 | 2 | } |
|  | 10 | 3 | } |
|  | Guns not known | 11 | } |
| Bombs | | 19 | 65 to 18 |
| Fireships | | 17 | 45 and 40 |
| Ketches | | 2 | 10 |
| Smacks | | 5 | ............ |
| Yachts | | 18 | 40 to 2 |
| Advice Boats* | | 5 | 50 and 40 |
| Brigantines | | 9 | 35 .. 30 |
| Tow Boats | | 2 | ............ |
| Machine Vessels | | 14 | 10 and 4 |
| Pinks | | 2 | 10 |

| | |
|---|---|
| Storeships | 5 | ............ |
| Hoys | 14 | ............ |
| Hulks | 11 | ............ |

Total.... 323

Many Ships and Vessels were disposed of, as usual, after the end of the War; and by the end of the ensuing year, the Navy was reduced to the following Ships.

*Advice Boats, so called, officially, are said to have been employed, for the first time, in 1692, before the battle off Cape La Hogue, in order to gain intelligence of what was passing at Brest.*

**1698**

Abstract of the Royal Navy on the 20th December 1698.

| Rates or Classes. | Number. |
|---|---|
| First | 6 |
| Second | 14 |
| Third | 45 |
| Fourth | 64 |
| Fifth | 34 |
| Sixth | 18 |
| Bombs | 13 |
| Fireships | 10 |
| Ketches | 2 |
| Smacks | 2 |
| Yachts | 13 |
| Advice Boats | 4 |
| Brigantines | 7 |
| Tow-boats | 2 |
| Pink | 1 |
| Storeships | 4 |
| Hoys | 16 |
| Hulks | 11 |

Total.... 266

**1702**

| Rates or Classes. | Number. | Burthen. |
|---|---|---|
| | | Tons. |
| First | 7 | 10955 |
| Second | 14 | 19447 |
| Third | 47 | 51988 |
| Fourth | 62 | 42940 |
| Fifth | 30 | 11469 |
| Sixth | 15 | 3611 |
| Bombs | 13 | 2105 |
| Fireships | 11 | 2956 |
| Sloops | 10 | 629 |
| Ketches | 2 | 132 |
| Smacks | 3 | 45 |
| Brigantines | 6 | 456 |
| Advice Boats | 4 | 339 |

| | | |
|---|---|---|
| Tow Boats.................... | 2 | 182 |
| Pink........................ | 1 | 89 |
| Storeships ................... | 3 | 911 |
| Yachts ...................... | 14 | 1371 |
| Hoys ....................... | 16 | 1177 |
| Hulks....................... | 12 | 8218 |
| Total.... | 272 | 159020 |

The Navy, at the King William's accession, consisted of

| | Ships. | Tons. |
|---|---|---|
| | 173 | 101892 |
| At his death......272 | | 159020 |
| Increase.. | 99 | 57128 |

which is an increase of more than half, both as to the number and the tonnage of the Ships.

# Anne 1702–1714

QUEEN ANNE had no sooner mounted the throne, than she declared her opinion for carrying on the preparations for war, which her predecessor had begun: and in May following, war was accordingly declared, both against France and Spain.

### 1703

The Navy sustained a considerable loss by the great storm which happened in November, 1703*, in which the following Ships, &c. were totally lost, viz.—

2d Rate ..Vanguard ..............In Chatham Harbour.
3d .......Resolution .............On the Coast of Sussex.
3d Rate ..Northumberland ....
Sterling Castle ......
Restoration......... On the Goodwin Sands.
4th ......Mary..............
Reserve...............At Yarmouth.
Newcastle .............At Spithead.
York ................At Harwich.
Bomb.....Mortar ...............On the Goodwin Sands.
Advice-boat, Eagle................On the Coast of Sussex.

and several other men-of-war were driven ashore, dismasted, and otherwise damaged.
The whole of the Ships named above, except the Vanguard, were in Commission; and the Queen immediately issued a proclamation, ordering, that all the widows and families of such officers and seamen as had perished by the storm in her Majesty's service, be entitled to her bounty in the same manner as if they had actually been killed in fight.†

* This was one of the most tremendous storms ever known in the history of the world.—It began about the middle of November, and did not reach its

greatest height until the morning of the 27th.—The Edystone Light-house was blown down at this time.—See the Rev. Robert Winter's Sermon, on 27th November, 1798, in commemoration of this storm.
† A fast was appointed in consequence of this storm.

### 1706

Abstract of the Royal Navy on the 13th December 1706.

| Rates or Classes. | Number. |
|---|---|
| First ..................... | 7 |
| Second................... | 14 |
| Third.................... | 47 |
| Fourth ................... | 61 |
| Fifth .................... | 35 |
| Sixth ................... | 27 |
| Sloops .................. | 8 |
| Brigantines .............. | 3 |
| Bombs .................. | 8 |
| Fireships ................ | 8 |
| Smacks ................. | 2 |
| Advice Boat ............. | 1 |
| Storeships ............... | 2 |
| Yachts .................. | 16 |
| Hoys ................... | 25 |
| Hulks................... | 13 |
| Total.... | 277 |

### 1708 and 1711

Abstracts of the Royal Navy on the 25th November 1708, and 21st July 1711.

| Rates or Classes. | Number on | |
|---|---|---|
| | 25th Nov'. 1708. | 21st July, 1711. |
| First........................ | 7 | 7 |
| Second...................... | 13 | 13 |
| Third....................... | 47 | 46 |
| Fourth...................... | 68 | 69 |
| Fifth........................ | 46 | 47 |
| Sixth ....................... | 27 | 44 |
| Sloops ...................... | 7 | 13 |
| Brigantines .................. | 2 | 2 |
| Bombs ...................... | 7 | 7 |
| Fireships .................... | 6 | 2 |
| Smacks ..................... | 2 | 2 |
| Advice-boats................. | 1 | 1 |
| Storeships ................... | 4 | 3 |
| Yachts ...................... | 16 | 18 |
| Hoys, Transports & Lighters .... | 25 | 25 |
| Hulks....................... | 13 | 14 |
| Total.... | 291 | 313 |

**1713**

Abstract of the Royal Navy, on the 17th April, 1713.

| Rates or Classes. | Number. |
|---|---|
| First . . . . . . . . . . . . . . . . . . . . . . . | 7 |
| Second . . . . . . . . . . . . . . . . . . . . . | 13 |
| Third . . . . . . . . . . . . . . . . . . . . . | 43 |
| Fourth . . . . . . . . . . . . . . . . . . . . | 70 |
| Fifth . . . . . . . . . . . . . . . . . . . . . . | 44 |
| Sixth . . . . . . . . . . . . . . . . . . . . | 30 |
| Sloops . . . . . . . . . . . . . . . . . . . . | 9 |
| Bombs . . . . . . . . . . . . . . . . . . . . | 6 |
| Fireships . . . . . . . . . . . . . . . . . . . | 2 |
| Storeships . . . . . . . . . . . . . . . . . . | 3 |
| Yachts . . . . . . . . . . . . . . . . . . . | 18 |
| Hoys, Transports and Lighters . . | 22 |
| Hulks . . . . . . . . . . . . . . . . . . . . . | 11 |
| Total. . . . | 278 |

**1714**

Immediately after the end of the war, many of the small Ships and Vessels were disposed of; but the numbers of the larger classes remained nearly the same until her Majesty's death, which happened in August 1714, at which time the Navy stood as follows:

**1714**

Abstract of the Royal Navy, at the death of Queen Anne, on 1st August 1714.

| Rates of Classes. | Guns. | Number. | Burthen. |
|---|---|---|---|
| | | | Tons. |
| 1st. | 100 | 7 | 11703 |
| 2d. | 90 | 13 | 19323 |
| 3d. | 80 | 16 | 47768 |
| | 70 | 26 | |
| 4th. | 60 | 19 | 51379 |
| | 50 | 50 | |
| Line. . . . . . . . . . . . . | 131 | 130173 |
| 5th. | 40 | 24 | 19836 |
| | 30 | 18 | |
| 6th. | 20 | 24 | 6435 |
| | 10 | 1 | 196 |
| Sloops . . . . . . . . . . . . . . . . . . . . . . | 7 | 869 |
| Bombs . . . . . . . . . . . . . . . . . . . . . | 4 | 597 |
| Fireship . . . . . . . . . . . . . . . . . . . . | 1 | 263 |
| Storeship . . . . . . . . . . . . . . . . . . . | 1 | 546 |
| Yachts . . . . . . . . . . . . . . . . . . . . . | 15 | 1521 |
| Hoys, Transports & Lighters. . . . . . . . | 13 | 1009 |
| Hulks . . . . . . . . . . . . . . . . . . . . . . | 8 | 5774 |
| Of 40 Guns and under. . | 116 | 37046 |
| Total. . . . | 247 | 167219 |

By this it appears, that although there were 25 Ships less at her Majesty's decease, than at her accession, there was an increase of tonnage in the Navy, of 8199 Tons.

**1716**

ESTABLISHMENT OF GUNS.

By Order of the King in Council, 6th July 1716, as proposed for the Ships of each Class by the Flag Officers, Comptroller, and Surveyor of the Navy, in lieu of the former Establishment, which had been found inconvenient.

| Classes of Ships. | Lower-deck. | | Middle-deck. | | Upper-deck. | | Quarter-deck. | | Forecastle. | |
|---|---|---|---|---|---|---|---|---|---|---|
| | No | Prs* | No | Prs | No | Prs | No | Prs | No | Prs |
| 100 Guns. . . . . | 28 | 42 or 32 | 28 | 24 | 28 | 12 | 12 | 6 | 4 | 6 |
| 90 . . . . . . . . . | 26 | 32 | 26 | 18 | 26 | 9 | 10 | 6 | 2 | 6 |
| 80 . . . . . . . . . | 26 | 32 | 26 | 12 | 24 | 6 | 4 | 6 | . . . . . . . . | |
| 70 . . . . . . . . . | 26 | 24 | . . . . . . . . | | 26 | 12 | 14 | 6 | 4 | 6 |
| 60 . . . . . . . . . | 24 | 24 | . . . . . . . . | | 26 | 9 | 8 | 6 | 2 | 6 |
| 50 . . . . . . . . . | 22 | 18 | . . . . . . . . | | 22 | 9 | 4 | 6 | 2 | 6 |
| 40 . . . . . . . . . | 20 | 12 | . . . . . . . . | | 20 | 6 | . . . . . . . . . . . . . . | | | |
| 30 . . . . . . . . . | 8 | 9 | . . . . . . . . | | 20 | 6 | 2 | 4 | . . . . . . . . | |
| 20 . . . . . . . . . . . . . . . . . . . . . . . | | | | | 20 | 6 | . . . . . . . . . . . . . . | | | |

*N.B.—This Establishment continued in force until 25th April 1743, the Establishment of 1733 having been suspended until that time. The Establishment of 1743 superseded the above, so far as respected the Ships ordered to be built subsequent to 1st January 1740.—(See MEMº. after the end of Table Nº 31.)*

\* weight of shot in pounds.

# George I 1714–1727

**1721**

Abstract of the Royal Navy, on the 19th April 1721.

| Rates or Classes. | Guns. | Number. |
|---|---|---|
| 1st. | 100 | 7 |
| 2d. | 90 | 13 |
| 3d. | 80 | 16 |
| | 70 | 24 |
| 4th. | 60 | 18 |
| | 50 | 46 |
| Line. . . . . . . . . . . . . | | 124 |
| 5th. | 40 | 24 |
| | 30 | 6 |
| 6th. | 24 | 8 |
| | 20 | 19 |
| Sloops . . . . . . . . . . . . . . . . . . . . . . . . . . . . . . . . . | | 6 |
| Bombs . . . . . . . . . . . . . . . . . . . . . . . . . . . . . . . . . | | 3 |
| Fireships . . . . . . . . . . . . . . . . . . . . . . . . . . . . . . . | | 3 |
| Storeship . . . . . . . . . . . . . . . . . . . . . . . . . . . . . . | | 1 |
| Hospital Ship . . . . . . . . . . . . . . . . . . . . . . . . . . . | | 1 |

Yachts .................................... 14
Hoys, Transports, & Lighters .............. 13
Hulks .................................... 7
_____
Of 40 Guns and under.... 105
_____
Total...... 229

No money was voted for the building or repairs of Ships for the last six years of his Majesty's reign; but some Ships were of course both built and repaired in the said time.—The Navy, however, upon the whole, declined in this reign, in a small degree, and consisted, at the death of the King, of the following Ships and Vessels.

Abstract of the Royal Navy at the death of George I. on 11th June 1727.

| Rates or Classes. | Guns. | Number. | Burthen. |
|---|---|---|---|
| | | | Tons. |
| 1st. | 100 | 7 | 12945 |
| 2d. | 90 | 13 | 20125 |
| 3d. | 80 | 16 | 21122 |
| | 70 | 24 | 26836 |
| 4th. | 60 | 18 | 16925 |
| | 50 | 46 | 33829 |
| Line............ | | 124 | 131782 |
| 5th. | 40 | 24 | 13801 |
| | 30 | 3 | 1264 |
| 6th. | 20 | 27 | 9760 |
| Sloops ......................... | | 13 | 1390 |
| Bombs ......................... | | 2 | 417 |
| Fireshipos ....................... | | 3 | 1057 |
| Storeship ....................... | | 1 | 546 |
| Hospital Ship ................... | | 1 | 532 |
| Yachts ......................... | | 12 | 1378 |
| Hoys, Transports & Lighters ........ | | 14 | 1216 |
| Hulks .......................... | | 9 | 7719 |
| Of 40 guns and under.. | | 109 | 39080 |
| Total......... | | 233 | 170862 |

The decrease in point of number, therefore, in this reign, is 14 Ships and Vessels; but there was an increase, as to tonnage, of 3643 tons.

# George II 1727–1760

**1730**

Abstract of the Royal Navy on the 1st December 1730.

| Rates or Classes. | Guns. | Number. |
|---|---|---|
| 1st. | 100 | 7 |
| 2d. | 90 | 13 |

| | Guns. | Number. |
|---|---|---|
| 3d. | 80 | 16 |
| | 70 | 24 |
| 4th. | 60 | 24 |
| | 50 | 40 |
| Line............... | | 124 |
| 5th. | 40 | 24 |
| | 30 | 1 |
| 6th. | 22 | 1 |
| | 20 | 28 |
| Sloops ................................... | | 13 |
| Bombs ................................... | | 3 |
| Fireships ................................. | | 3 |
| Storeship ................................ | | 1 |
| Yachts .................................. | | 12 |
| Smacks ................................. | | 2 |
| Hoys, Transports & Lighters ................ | | 17 |
| Hulks ................................... | | 9 |
| Of 40 Guns and under.... | | 114 |
| Total...... | | 238 |

*For further Dimensions of Ships, see pages 148 and 149.*

| Men. | Rates 1st 100 Guns. | 2d 90 | 3d 70 |
|---|---|---|---|
| 8 to each Cannon .............. | 208 | ............. | .... |
| 6 ditto Demi-Cannon .................. | | 156 | 156 |
| 5 ditto Culverin ................. | 140 | 130 | ....... |
| 4 ditto 12-pounder........................... | | | 104 |
| 3 ditto Saker.................... | 132 | 108 | 42 |
| 2 ditto 3-pounder............... | 4 | 4 | 8 |
| The remainder of the Complements to consist of............... } | 296 | 262 | 160 |
| | 780 | 660 | 470 |

**1742**

Abstracts of the Royal Navy on the 1st January 1739, and 25th June 1742.

| Rates or Classes. | Guns. | Number on 1st January, 1739. | Number on 25th June, 1742. |
|---|---|---|---|
| 1st. | 100 | 7 | 7 |
| 2d. | 90 | 13 | 13 |
| 3d. | 80 | 16 | 16 |
| | 70 | 24 | 25 |
| 4th. | 60 | 30 | 30 |
| | 50 | 34 | 34 |
| Line........... | | 124 | 125 |

348

| Rates or Classes. | Guns. | Number on | |
|---|---|---|---|
| | | 1st January, 1739. | 25th June, 1742. |
| 5th. | 44 | ........ | 24 |
| | 40 | 22 | |
| 6th. | 24 & 20 | 28 | 33 |
| | 10 | 1 | 1 |
| Sloops .............................. | | 15 | 19 |
| Bombs .............................. | | 3 | 14 |
| Fireships ............................ | | 3 | 11 |
| Storeships .......................... | | 1 | 3 |
| Hospital Ships....................... | | | 3 |
| Snow ............................... | | | 1 |
| Pink ............................... | | | 1 |
| Yachts ............................. | | 11 | 11 |
| Hoys, Lighters, and Transports ........ | | 13 | 15 |
| Hulks ............................. | | 7 | 10 |
| Of 44 or 40 Guns, and under........ | | 104 | 146 |
| Total.......... | | 228 | 271 |

In April 1743, the establishment of Ships Guns was altered, by order of the King and Council.

## 1743

### ESTABLISHMENT OF GUNS.

By Order of the King in Council, 25th April 1743, for Ships ordered to be built subsequent to the 1st January 1740.

| Classes of Ships. | Lower-deck. | | Middle-deck. | | Upper-deck. | | Quarter-deck. | | Forecastle. | |
|---|---|---|---|---|---|---|---|---|---|---|
| | No | Prs | No | Prs | No | Prs | No | Prs | No | Prs |
| 100 Guns.... | 28 | 42 | 28 | 24 | 28 | 12 | 12 | 6 | 4 | 6 |
| 90 ......... | 26 | 32 | 26 | 18 | 26 | 12 | 10 | 6 | 2 | 6 |
| 80 ......... | 26 | 32 | 26 | 18 | 24 | 9 | 4 | 6 | ......... | |
| 64 ......... | 26 | 32 | ......... | | 26 | 18 | 10 | 9 | 2 | 9 |
| 58 ......... | 24 | 24 | ......... | | 24 | 12 | 8 | 6 | 2 | 6 |
| 50 ......... | 22 | 24 | ......... | | 22 | 12 | 4 | 6 | 2 | 6 |
| 44 ......... | 20 | 18 | ......... | | 20 | 9 | 4 | 6 | ......... | |
| 20 ......... | | | | | 20 | 9 | ............... | | | |

*N.B.—This was the same Establishment as was settled by Order of the King in Council on January 1733, (but suspended until now) with an exception as to 50 Gunships, whose Establishment was then ordered as follows, viz.*

## 1744

Abstract of the Royal Navy, on the 31st December 1744.

| Rates or Classes. | Guns. | Number. |
|---|---|---|
| 1st. | 100 | 6 |
| 2d. | 90 | 13 |
| 3d. | 80 | 17 |
| | 70 & 64 | 26 |
| 4th. | 60 .. 58 | 31 |
| | 50 | 35 |
| Line............... | | 128 |

| 5th. | 44 | 30 |
|---|---|---|
| 6th. | 24 & 20 | 40 |
| | 10 | 1 |
| Sloops .................................... | | 33 |
| Bombs .................................... | | 13 |
| Fireships ................................. | | 3 |
| Storeships ................................ | | 4 |
| Hospital Ships ............................ | | 3 |
| Yachts ................................... | | 11 |
| Hoys, Lighters & Transports............... | | 17 |
| Hulks & Receiving Ships .................. | | 19 |
| Of 44 Guns and under.... | | 174 |
| Total...... | | 302 |

## 1745

In the year 1744 or 1745, a general complaint was made of the Ships in his Majesty's Navy, that their scantlings were not so large and strong as they should be; that they did not carry their guns a proper height above the water, (like those of other nations) that they were very crank, and heeled too much in blowing weather; and that they did not carry so great a weight of metal as the Ships of the enemy, whose batteries were said to be always open. In consequence of this, the Lords Commissioners of the Admiralty gave directions to the Flag Officers, the Surveyor of the Navy, and the Master Shipwrights of the dock-yards, to consult together,* and lay before them a scheme of dimensions and scantlings, and also a draught for a Ship of each class: and from these several draughts and schemes, their Lordships, in 1745, settled the dimensions for a Ship of each class.

*\* It appears by the report of the Flag Officers, that the establishment for building Ships, dated in 1719, had been for years discontinued.*

## 1748

Abstracts of the Royal Navy on the 26th May and 26th Nov'. 1748.

| Rates or Classes. | Guns. | Number on | |
|---|---|---|---|
| | | 26th May 1748. | 26th Nov. 1748. |
| 1st. | 100 | 6 | 6 |
| 2d. | 90 | 11 | 11 |
| 3d. | 80 | 11 | 11 |
| | 74 & 66 | 7 | 10 |
| | 70 .. 64 | 30 | 31 |
| 4th. | 60 .. 58 | 36 | 35 |
| | 50 | 39 | 34 |
| Line.................. | | 140 | 138 |
| 5th. | 44 & 40 | 44 | 42 |
| | 30 | ........ | 1 |
| 6th. | 30 | ........ | 2 |
| | 24 & 20 | 51 | 52 |
| | 10 | 1 | 1 |
| Sloops ................................. | | 35 | 30 |
| Bombs ................................. | | 10 | 10 |
| Fireships ............................. | | 3 | 4 |

| | | | |
|---|---|---:|---:|
| Storeships | | 2 | 2 |
| Hospital Ships | | 5 | 3 |
| Yachts | | 11 | 11 |
| Hoys, Lighters, & Transports | | 22 | 26 |
| Hulks | | 15 | 12 |
| | Of 44 Guns and under.... | 199 | 196 |
| | Total...... | 339 | 334 |

## 1749

Notwithstanding no money was voted by Parliament for building or repairing Ships, in any year of the preceding war, many Ships were built in the course of the war, and doubtless some were repaired.

Several old Ships and Vessels, and others not thought necessary to be retained in the service, were taken to pieces, sold, or otherwise disposed of, after the war; and on 1st January 1750, the Navy stood as follows.

## 1750

Abstract of the Royal Navy on the 1st January 1750.

| Rates or Classes. | Guns. | Number. |
|:---:|:---:|:---:|
| 1st. | 100 | 4 |
| 2d. | 90 | 10 |
| 3d. | 80 | 5 |
| | 74 | 7 |
| | 66 | 4 |
| | 70 & 64 | 31 |
| 4th. | 60 | 34 |
| | 50 | 31 |
| Line | | 126 |
| 5th. | 44 & 40 | 39 |
| | 30 | 1 |
| 6th. | 24 & 20 | 39 |
| | 10 | 1 |
| Sloops | | 32 |
| Bombs | | 5 |
| Storeship | | 1 |
| Hospital Ship | | 1 |
| Yachts | | 10 |
| Hoys, Lighters & Transports | | 17 |
| Hulks | | 10 |
| Of 44 Guns and under.... | | 156 |
| Total.... | | 282 |

A large sum was voted for building and repairing of Ships, for the year 1750; and every year, except one, throughout the peace, money was voted for the like services, greatly exceeding, on the whole, what had been granted in the last peace. A considerable number of Ships was therefore built and repaired in the course of the peace; and by the end of the year 1752, Six had been added to the number of those of the line of battle.

The following is an account of the numbers and tonnage of the Ships at the abovementioned period.

## 1753

Abstract of the Royal Navy on the 1st January 1753.

| Rates or Classes. | Guns. | Number. | Burthen. |
|:---:|:---:|:---:|:---:|
| | | | Tons. |
| 1st. | 100 | 5 | 9602 |
| 2d. | 90 | 13 | 21250 |
| 3d. | 80 | 7 | |
| | 74 | 6 | 65277 |
| | 66 | 3 | |
| | 70 & 64 | 31 | |
| 4th. | 60 | 34 | 69155 |
| | 50 | 33 | |
| Line | | 132 | 165284 |
| 5th. | 44 & 40 | 39 | 28813 |
| 6th. | 30 | 1 | |
| | 24 & 20 | 37 | 19129 |
| | 10 | 1 | |
| Sloops | | 34 | 8036 |
| Bombs | | 4 | 1104 |
| Storeship | | 1 | 678 |
| Yachts | | 10 | 1195 |
| Hoys, Lighters, & Transports | | 23 | 2037 |
| Hulks | | 9 | 8648 |
| Of 44 Guns, and under.... | | 159 | 69640 |
| Total...... | | 291 | 234924 |

The number of Ships, of each respective class, continued nearly the same as in the foregoing account, until the year 1755, in which year hostilities commenced against France. In May 1756, a declaration of war took place, previous to which, considerable additions had been made to the Navy, as will appear by the following account.

## 1755, 1756

Abstracts of the Royal Navy on the 1st January 1755, and 1st January 1756.

| Rates or Classes. | Guns. | Number on | |
|:---:|:---:|:---:|:---:|
| | | 1st Jany. 1755. | 1st Jany. 1756. |
| 1st. | 100 | 5 | 5 |
| 2d. | 90 | 13 | 13 |
| 3d. | 80 | 7 | 7 |
| | 74 | 6 | 13 |
| | 66 | 3 | 3 |
| | 70 & 64 | 33 | 32 |
| 4th. | 60 .. 58 | 34 | 36 |
| | 50 | 33 | 33 |
| Line* | | 134 | 142 |

*See Memo. at the foot of the list of October 1760, p. 139.*

| Rates or Classes. | Guns. | Number on | |
|---|---|---|---|
| | | 1st Jany. 1755. | 1st Jany. 1756. |
| 5th. | 44 | 38 | 38 |
| 6th. | 30 | 1 | 1 |
| | 24 & 20 | 38 | 44 |
| | 10 | 1 | 1 |
| Sloops ........................... | | 36 | 42 |
| Bombs ............................. | | 3 | 3 |
| Fireships ........................... | | | 2 |
| Storeship ........................... | | 1 | 1 |
| Hospital Ship ....................... | | | 1 |
| Yachts ............................. | | 11 | 11 |
| Hoys, Lighters & Transports .......... | | 24 | 25 |
| Hulks ............................. | | 9 | 9 |
| Of 44 Guns and under.... | | 162 | 178 |
| Total...... | | 296 | 320 |

The Ships built by the establishment of 1745, were found to carry their guns well, and were stiff Ships, but they were formed too full in their after part: and in the war which took place in 1756, or a little before, some further improvements in the draughts were therefore adopted, and the dimensions of the Ships were also further increased.

## 1757

### GUNS.

An Account of those carried on board the Ships of the several Classes, in the Year 1757 (particular Ships excepted).

| Classes of Ships. | Lower-deck. | | Middle-deck. | | Upper-deck. | | Quarter-deck. | | Fore-castle. | |
|---|---|---|---|---|---|---|---|---|---|---|
| | No | Prs | No | Prs | No | Prs | No | Prs | No | Prs |
| 100 Guns............... | 28 | 42 | 28 | 24 | 28 | 12 | 12 | 6 | 4 | 6 |
| 90................. | 26 | 32 | 26 | 18 | 26 | 12 | 10 | 6 | 2 | 6 |
| | 28 | 32 | 30 | 18 | 30 | 12 | .. | .. | 2 | 9 |
| 80................. | 26 | 32 | 26 | 18 | 24 | 9 | 4 | 6 | .. | .. |
| | 26 | 32 | 26 | 12 | 24 | 6 | 4 | 6 | .. | .. |
| 74 Large Class ...... | 28 | 32 | .. | .. | 30 | 24 | 12 | 9 | 4 | 9 |
| 74 Common Class .... | 28 | 32 | .. | .. | 28 | 18 | 14 | 9 | 4 | 9 |
| 70................. | 28 | 32 | .. | .. | 28 | 18 | 12 | 9 | 2 | 9 |
| 64................. | 26 | 24 | .. | .. | 26 | 12 | 10 | 6 | 2 | 6 |
| 60................. | 24 | 24 | .. | .. | 26 | 12 | 8 | 6 | 2 | 6 |
| | 26 | 24 | .. | .. | 26 | 12 | 6 | 6 | 2 | 6 |
| | 24 | 24 | .. | .. | 26 | 9 | 8 | 6 | 2 | 6 |

| Classes of Ships. | Lower-deck. | | Upper-deck. | | Quarter-deck. | | Forecastle. | |
|---|---|---|---|---|---|---|---|---|
| | No | Prs | No | Prs | No | Prs | No | Prs |
| 50 Guns.......... | 22 | 24 | 22 | 12 | 4 | 6 | 2 | 6 |
| | 22 | 18 | 22 | 9 | 4 | 6 | 2 | 6 |
| | 20 | 18 | 22 | 9 | .. | .. | 2 | 6 |
| 44 | 20 | 18 | 20 | 9 | .. | .. | 4 | 6 |
| 36 | .. | .. | 26 | 12 | 8 | 6 | 2 | 6 |
| 32 | .. | .. | 26 | 12 | 4 | 6 | 2 | 6 |
| 28 | .. | .. | 24 | 9 | 4 | 3 | .. | .. |
| 24 | 2 | 9 | 20 | 9 | 2 | 3 | .. | .. |
| 20 | .. | .. | 20 | 9 | .. | .. | .. | .. |
| Sloops Ship-rigged..14 | .. | .. | 14 | 6 | .. | .. | .. | .. |
| 12 | .. | .. | 12 | 4 | .. | .. | .. | .. |
| 10 | .. | .. | 10 | 4 | .. | .. | .. | .. |
| 8 | .. | .. | 8 | 3 | .. | .. | .. | .. |

*N.B.—The guns on board the Ships of foreign-built are not meant to be comprized in the above Account. The Sloops and small Classes of Ships carried Swivel-guns, (half-pounders).*

## 1762

### GUNS.

An Account of those carried on board the Ships of the several Classes, (particular Ships excepted) at the end of the War in 1762.

| Classes of Ships. | Lower-deck. | | Middle-deck. | | Upper-deck. | | Quarter-deck. | | Fore-castle. | |
|---|---|---|---|---|---|---|---|---|---|---|
| | No | Prs | No | Prs | No | Prs | No | Prs | No | Prs |
| 100 Guns............ | 28 | 42 | 28 | 24 | 28 | 12 | 12 | 6 | 4 | 6 |
| | 30 | 42 | 28 | 24 | 30 | 12 | 10 | 6 | 2 | 6 |
| 90................. | 26 | 32 | 26 | 18 | 26 | 12 | 10 | 6 | 2 | 6 |
| | 28 | 32 | 30 | 18 | 30 | 12 | .. | .. | 2 | 9 |
| 80................. | 26 | 32 | 26 | 18 | 24 | 9 | 4 | 6 | .. | .. |
| 74 Large Class ........ | 28 | 32 | .. | .. | 30 | 24 | 12 | 9 | 4 | 9 |
| 74 Common Class ..... | 28 | 32 | .. | .. | 28 | 18 | 14 | 9 | 4 | 9 |
| 70................. | 28 | 32 | .. | .. | 28 | 18 | 12 | 9 | 2 | 9 |
| 64................. | 26 | 24 | .. | .. | 26 | 18 | 10 | 9 | 2 | 9 |
| 60................. | 24 | 24 | .. | .. | 26 | 12 | 8 | 6 | 2 | 6 |
| | 26 | 24 | .. | .. | 26 | 12 | 6 | 6 | 2 | 6 |

| Classes of Ships. | Lower-deck. | | Upper-deck. | | Quarter-deck. | | Forecastle. | |
|---|---|---|---|---|---|---|---|---|
| | No | Prs | No | Prs | No | Prs | No | Prs |
| 50 Guns............. | 22 | 24 | 22 | 12 | 4 | 6 | 2 | 6 |
| 44................. | 20 | 18 | 22 | 9 | .. | .. | 2 | 6 |
| 36................. | .. | .. | 26 | 12 | 8 | 6 | 2 | 6 |
| 32................. | .. | .. | 26 | 12 | 4 | 6 | 2 | 6 |
| 28................. | .. | .. | 24 | 9 | 4 | 3 | .. | .. |
| 24................. | 2 | 9 | 20 | 9 | 2 | 3 | .. | .. |
| 20................. | .. | .. | 20 | 9 | .. | .. | .. | .. |
| Sloops rigged as Ships | | | | | | | | |
| 14............. | .. | .. | 14 | 6 | .. | .. | .. | .. |
| 12............. | .. | .. | 12 | 4 | .. | .. | .. | .. |
| 10............. | .. | .. | 10 | 4 | .. | .. | .. | .. |
| 8............. | .. | .. | 8 | 3 | .. | .. | .. | .. |

*N.B.—The guns on board the Ships of foreign-built are not meant to be comprized in the above Account. The Sloops and small Classes of Ships carried Swivel-guns, (half-pounders).*

**1702 to 1713 and 1755 to 1757**

### SHIPS.

An account of the highest prices ⅌ Ton paid for building *Ships* and *Sloops*, by Contract, in the following periods.

| In Queen Anne's War (1702-13). | | In 1755, 1756, and 1757. | |
|---|---|---|---|
| Rates or Classes. | Price ⅌ Ton. | Rates or Classes. | Price ⅌ Ton. |
| Gunships. | | Gunships. | |
| 90 . . . . . . . | £16 : 0 : 0 | . . . . . . . . . . . . . . . . . . . . | |
| 80 . . . . . . . | 12 : 0 : 0 | 74 . . . . . . . . | £17 : 2 : 6 |
| 70 . . . . . . . | 10 : 15 : 0 | 70 . . . . . . . . | 16 : 5 : 0 |
| 64 . . . . . . . | 9 : 10 : 0 | . . . . . . . . . . . . . . . . . . . . | |
| 60 . . . . . . . | 10 : 6 : 6 | 60 . . . . . . . . | 15 : 15 : 0 |
| 50 . . . . . . . | 9 : 3 : 0 | . . . . . . . . . . . . . . . . . . . . | |
| 42 . . . . . . . | 7 : 15 : 0 | 44 . . . . . . . . | 12 : 12 : 0 |
| 40 . . . . . . . | 8 : 7 : 6 | 36 . . . . . . . . | 12 : 12 : 0 |
| 32 . . . . . . . | 8 : 0 : 0 | 32 . . . . . . . . | 10 : 10 : 0 |
| 26 . . . . . . . | 6 : 5 : 0 | 28 . . . . . . . . | 10 : 10 : 0 |
| 24 . . . . . . . | 7 : 10 : 0 | 20 . . . . . . . . | 8 : 14 : 6 |
| Sloops . . . . . | 5 : 12 : 6 | Sloops . . . . . . . | 8 : 5 : 0 |

| | | | |
|---|---|---|---|
| 6th. | 30 .. 28 | 25 | 14730 |
| | 24 | 22 | 10831 |
| | 22 & 20 | 14 | 6057 |
| Frigates* . . . . . . . . . . . . . . . . . | 18 & under | 8 | 2498 |
| Sloops . . . . . . . . . . . . . . . . . . . . | 16 to 8 | 47 | 10361 |
| Bombs . . . . . . . . . . . . . . . . . . . . . . | | 14 | 4117 |
| Fireships . . . . . . . . . . . . . . . . . . . . . | | 8 | 2337 |
| Busses. . . . . . . . . . . . . . . . . . . . . . . . | | 3 | 242 |
| Storeships . . . . . . . . . . . . . . . . . . . . | | 2 | 1554 |
| Hospital Ships . . . . . . . . . . . . . . . . . | | 3 | 2791 |
| Yachts . . . . . . . . . . . . . . . . . . . . . . . | | 12 | 1518 |
| Hoys, Lighters, & Transports . . . . . . . . | | 33 | 2761 |
| Hulks . . . . . . . . . . . . . . . . . . . . . . . | | 12 | 11957 |
| Of 50 Guns and under. . . . | | 285 | 138275 |
| Total. . . . | | 412 | 321104 |

*\* Some Vessels of 18 guns and under, built about this period, were frequently denominated Frigates; but after a time, they were classed among the Sloops.*

# George III 1760–1820

**1760**

Abstract of the Royal Navy at the Accession of King George III, on 25th October 1760.

| Rates or Classes. | Guns. | Number. | Burthen. |
|---|---|---|---|
| | | | Tons. |
| 1st. | 100 | 5 | 9958 |
| 2d. | 90 | 12 | 20907 |
| | 84 | 1 | 1918 |
| 3d. | 80 | 7 | 11398 |
| | 74 | 28 | 45422 |
| | 70 | 11 | 15639 |
| | 68 | 1 | 1567 |
| | 66 | 3 | 4350 |
| | 64 | 24 | 31117 |
| 4th. | 60 | 35 | 40553 |
| Line. . . . . . . . . . . . . . . | 127 | | 182829 |

MEMᵒ.—*Previous to this it will be observed, that 50 Gunships are included in the number of those of the Line; but from about the years 1755 to 1756, they seem not to have been considered as Line of Battle Ships.*

| Rates or Classes. | Guns. | Number. | Burthen. |
|---|---|---|---|
| | | | Tons. |
| 4th. | 50 | 28 | 27348 |
| 5th. | 44 | 25 | 18623 |
| | 38 | 2 | 1887 |
| | 36 | 5 | 3655 |
| | 32 & 30 | 22 | 15008 |

**1762**

Abstract of the Royal Navy as it stood on the 3d November 1762.

| Rates or Classes. | Guns. | Number. |
|---|---|---|
| 1st. | 100 | 5 |
| 2d. | 90 | 15 |
| | 84 | 1 |
| 3d. | 80 | 7 |
| | 74 | 37 |
| | 70 | 11 |
| | 68 & 66 | 3 |
| | 64 | 30 |
| 4th. | 60 | 32 |
| Line. . . . | | 141 |
| 4th. | 50 | 24 |
| 5th. | 44 | 21 |
| | 38 | 2 |
| | 36 | 4 |
| | 32 | 32 |
| | 30 | 1 |
| | 24 | 1 |
| 6th. | 30 | 1 |
| | 28 | 22 |
| | 24 | 21 |
| | 20 | 13 |
| Frigates* . . . . . . . . . . . . . . . . . . . . . | 18 & under | 8 |
| Sloops . . . . . . . . . . . . . . . . . . . . . . . | | 49 |
| Brig . . . . . . . . . . . . . . . . . . . . . . . . . . . | | 1 |

*\* See Note above*

| Rates or Classes. | Guns. | Number. |
|---|---|---|
| Cutter | 18 & under | 1 |
| Bombs | | 14 |
| Fireships | | 11 |
| Busses | | 3 |
| Storeships | | 2 |
| Hospital Ships | | 2 |
| Yachts | | 12 |
| Hoys, Lighters, & Transports | | 34 |
| Hulks | | 12 |
| Of 50 Guns and under.... | | 291 |
| Total.... | | 432 |

From the year 1755 to 1762 inclusive, £200,000 was annually voted for the building and repairing of Ships; whereas in the preceding war, no money was ever voted for those services.

Twenty-six sail of the line, and Eighty-two smaller Ships and Vessels, including Hoys, Lighters, and Transports, were built in Merchants yards in the course of the war, which ended in 1762, or were building in those yards at the conclusion of the war: and Twenty-four sail of the line, and Twelve smaller Ships, were launched in the King's yards, between the declaration of war in 1756, and the proclamation peace in 1763.

On 3d November 1762, the following Ships were building, namely,

### 1762

| Guns. | In the | |
|---|---|---|
| | King's Yards. | Merchnts Yards. |
| Of 100 | 1 | ........... |
| 90 | 3 | ........... |
| 74 | 7 | 5 |
| 70 | 1 | ........... |
| 64 | 2 | 5 |
| Line.... | 14 | 10 |
| 50 | 1 | ........... |
| 32 | 1 | 2 |
| 28 | 1 | 2 |
| Sloops 14 | .......... | 2 |
| Of 50 Guns and under...... | 3 | 6 |
| Total.... | 17 | 16 |

### 1764, 1767, and 1771

Abstracts of the Royal Navy on the 24th October 1764; 25th March 1767; and 1st January 1771.

| Rates or Classes. | Guns. | Number on 24th Octr. 1764. | 25th Mar. 1767. | 1st Jany. 1771. |
|---|---|---|---|---|
| 1st. | 100 | 5 | 4 | 3 |
| 2d. | 90 | 12 | 13 | 14 |
| | 84 | 1 | 1 | 1 |
| 3d. | 80 | 5 | 5 | 3 |
| | 74 | 43 | 47 | 50 |
| | 70 | 10 | 10 | 9 |
| | 66 | 2 | 2 | 2 |
| | 64 | 29 | 29 | 32 |
| 4th. | 60 | 29 | 22 | 20 |
| Line................ | | 136 | 133 | 134 |
| 4th. | 50 | 22 | 19 | 10 |
| 5th. | 44 | 9 | 5 | 5 |
| | 38 & 36 | 4 | 4 | 4 |
| | 32 | 33 | 33 | 30 |
| | 24 | 1 | 1 | 1 |
| 6th. | 30 & 28 | 22 | 19 | 18 |
| | 24 to 20 | 26 | 24 | 19 |
| Sloops | 18 to 8 | 43 | 43 | 37 |
| Sloops on Survey | | 2 | 2 | 5 |
| Brig | | .... | .... | 1 |
| Cutters | | 38 | 34 | 30 |
| Bombs | | 7 | 7 | 7 |
| Fireships | | 2 | 2 | 1 |
| Schooners | | 6 | 7 | 10 |
| Storeships | | 2 | 3 | 1 |
| Hospital Ships | | 1 | 1 | ....... |
| Yachts | | 12 | 12 | 12 |
| Hoys, Lighters, & Transports | | 34 | 33 | 27 |
| Hulks | | 11 | 10 | 8 |
| Of 50 Guns and under.... | | 275 | 259 | 226 |
| Total.... | | 411 | 392 | 360 |

### 1775

Abstract of the Royal Navy on the 1st January 1775.

| Rates or Classes. | Guns. | Number. |
|---|---|---|
| 1st. | 100 | 4 |
| 2d. | 90 | 16 |
| | 84 | 1 |
| 3d. | 80 | 3 |
| | 74 | 57 |
| | 70 | 7 |
| | 64 | 32 |
| 4th. | 60 | 11 |
| Line................ | | 131 |
| 4th. | 50 | 12 |
| 5th. | 44 | 4 |
| | 36 | 3 |
| | 32 | 35 |
| 6th. | 28 | 24 |
| | 24 | 7 |
| | 22 & 20 | 13 |
| Sloops | 18 to 12 | 22 |
| | 10 & 8 | 16 |
| Sloops on Survey | | 6 |

| | |
|---|---|
| Cutters.................................... | 10 |
| Bombs .................................... | 2 |
| Fireship.................................. | 1 |
| Schooners ................................ | 7 |
| Storeship................................. | 1 |
| Yachts.................................... | 13 |
| Hoys, Lighters, & Transports .............. | 25 |
| Hulks.................................... | 8 |
| Of 50 Guns and under.... | 209 |
| Total.... | 340 |

The circumstances of the war with America rendered it necessary that a great number of Frigates, Sloops, and other small Vessels, should be employed. The Navy was therefore augmented very fast, from about the end of the year 1775, with regard to Ships and Vessels of those descriptions. The following statement will shew its progressive increase up to the breaking out of the war with France, in June 1778.

**1777 and 1778**

Abstracts of the Royal Navy on the 4th June 1977, and 24th June 1778.

| Rates or Classes. | Guns. | Number on | |
|---|---|---|---|
| | | 4th June 1777. | 24th June 1778. |
| 1st. | 100 | 4 | 4 |
| 2d. | 90 | 15 | 16 |
| | 84 | 1 | 1 |
| 3d. | 80 | 3 | 3 |
| | 74 | 55 | 59 |
| | 70 | 4 | 3 |
| | 64 | 35 | 37 |
| 4th. | 60 | 8 | 8 |
| Line............... | | 125 | 131 |
| 4th. | 50 | 17 | 21 |
| 5th. | 44 | 10 | 13 |
| | 36 | 2 | 2 |
| | 32 | 31 | 29 |
| | 28 | ....... | 4 |
| 6th. | 28 | 28 | 35 |
| | 26 | 1 | 1 |
| | 24 to 20 | 30 | 34 |
| Sloops ..................... | 18 to 14 | 42 | 51 |
| | 12 .. 8 | 16 | 19 |
| Sloops on survey ...................... | | 5 | 3 |
| Armed Ships........................... | | 3 | 2 |
| Brigs.................................. | | | 3 |
| Cutters................................ | | 15 | 24 |
| Bombs ................................. | | 4 | 4 |
| Fireships .............................. | | 1 | 3 |
| Schooners ............................. | | 13 | 10 |
| Storeships ............................. | | 4 | 11 |

| | | |
|---|---|---|
| Hospital Ships ......................... | 3 | 3 |
| Tender.................................. | | 1 |
| Yachts.................................. | 12 | 12 |
| Hoy, Lighters & Transports.............. | 24 | 24 |
| Hulks.................................. | 10 | 10 |
| Of 50 Guns and under.. | 271 | 319 |
| Total.... | 396 | 450 |

**1780 and 1782**

Abstracts of the Royal Navy on the 1st January 1780, and 1st January 1782.

| Rates or Classes. | Guns. | Number on | |
|---|---|---|---|
| | | 1st Jany. 1780. | 1st Jany. 1782. |
| 1st. | 100 | 4 | 4 |
| 2d. | 98 & 90 | 17 | 18 |
| | 84 | 1 | 1 |
| 3d. | 80 | 3 | 4 |
| | 76 | 1 | 1 |
| | 74 | 64 | 73 |
| | 70 | 2 | 3 |
| | 68 | ....... | 2 |
| | 64 | 42 | 45 |
| 4th. | 62 | ....... | 1 |
| | 60 | 9 | 9 |
| Line............... | | 143 | 161 |
| 4th. | 52 | 1 | 1 |
| | 50 | 19 | 22 |
| 5th. | 44 | 15 | 20 |
| | 40 | ....... | 2 |
| | 38 | 3 | 6 |
| | 36 | 6 | 16 |
| | 32 | 42 | 54 |
| | 30 | 1 | 1 |
| | 22 | ....... | 1 |
| 6th. | 28 | 34 | 29 |
| | 26 | 1 | 2 |
| | 24 | 16 | 13 |
| | 22 & 20 | 14 | 15 |
| Sloop..................... | 20 | ....... | 1 |
| Sloops .................... | 18 to 14 | 51 | 71 |
| | 12 .. 8 | 20 | 20 |
| Sloops ..................... Guns not known | | ...... | 3 |
| Sloops on Survey ...................... | | 3 | 3 |
| Xebeck ............................... | | 1 | ....... |
| Brigs.................................. | | 3 | 11 |
| Armed Ships........................... | | 2 | 4 |
| Transports ........................... | | | 6 |
| Armed Galleys ......................... | | 5 | 8 |
| Storeships............................. | | | 9 |
| Storeships (*not included above*).............. | | 6 | 4 |
| Cutters................................ | | 20 | 30 |

| Rates or Classes. | Guns. | Number on | |
|---|---|---|---|
| | | 1st Jany. 1780. | 1st Jany. 1782. |
| Bombs ................. | Guns not known | 4 | 4 |
| Fireships ........................... | | 18 | 17 |
| Schooners ........................... | | 11 | 11 |
| Hospital Ships ....................... | | 3 | 5 |
| Prison Ships ......................... | | 1 | 1 |
| Tenders ............................ | | 1 | 1 |
| Yachts ............................. | | 12 | 11 |
| Hoys, Lighters & Transports ........... | | 23 | 27 |
| Hulks .............................. | | 11 | 10 |
| Of 52 Guns and under.... | | 347 | 439 |
| Total...... | | 490 | 600 |

## 1783

It is scarcely necessary to mention that before the conclusion of the war, the Navy had been advanced to a much higher pitch than it had ever before reached. At the signing of the preliminaries of peace, it consisted of the following Ships and Vessels, exclusive of those not then registered, the number and classes of which are specified hereafter.

## 1783

Abstract of the Royal Navy as it stood on the 20th January 1783.

| Rates or Classes. | Guns. | Number. |
|---|---|---|
| 1st. | 100 | 5 |
| 2d. | 98 & 90 | 19 |
| | 84 | 1 |
| 3d. | 80 | 4 |
| | 76 | 1 |
| | 74 | 81 |
| | 70 | 4 |
| | 68 | 2 |
| | 64 | 49 |
| | 60 | 1 |
| 4th. | 60 | 7 |
| Line............... | | 174 |
| 4th. | 56 | 2 |
| | 52 | 1 |
| | 50 | 20 |
| 5th | 44 | 28 |
| | 40 | 2 |
| | 38 | 7 |
| | 36 | 17 |
| | 34 | 1 |
| | 32 | 59 |
| | 30 | 1 |
| | 22 | 1 |

| | | |
|---|---|---|
| 6th. | 28 | 33 |
| | 26 | 1 |
| | 24 | 11 |
| | 22 | 2 |
| | 20 | 12 |
| Sloops ...................... | 18 to 14 | 72 |
| | 12 .. 8 | 13 |
| Sloops on Survey ......................... | | 2 |
| Brigs.................................... | | 8 |
| Armed Ships & Vessels ................... | | 4 |
| Transports ..................... | | 7 |
| Galleys ...................... | | 6 |
| Storeships...................... | | 12 |
| Storeships (not included above) ............... | | 3 |
| Cutters................................. | | 28 |
| Bombs ................................ | | 4 |
| Fireships ............................. | | 17 |
| Schooners ............................ | | 6 |
| Lugger................................ | | 1 |
| Hospital Ships ......................... | | 5 |
| Prison Ship ........................... | | 1 |
| Tender................................ | | 1 |
| Yachts ............................... | | 11 |
| Hoys, Lighters, and Transports .............. | | 34 |
| Hulks................................. | | 10 |
| Of 56 Guns and under.... | | 443 |
| Total...... | | 617 |

The following Ships were building on the day the preliminaries of peace were signed.

## 1783

| Guns. | In the | |
|---|---|---|
| | King's Yards. | Merchts Yards. |
| Of 100 ...................... | 3 | ............ |
| 98 ...................... | 5 | ............ |
| 74 ...................... | 5 | 24* |
| 64 ................................. | | 5 |
| Line.... | 13 | 29 |
| 50 ...................... | 3 | ............ |
| 44 ................................. | | 13 |
| 36 ................................. | | 6 |
| 32 ................................. | 1 | 13 |
| 28 ................................. | | 9 |
| 24 ................................. | | 1 |
| Sloops of 16 ......................... | | 6 |
| Brigs................................. | | 2 |
| Fireships ........................... | | 4 |
| Of 50 Guns and under...... | 4 | 54 |
| Total.... | 17 | 83 |

* One of which was launched the next day, (21st January), being the last of the three 74 Gun ships presented by the East India Company.

**1786**

Abstract of the Royal Navy, on the 1st January 1786.

| Rates or Classes. | Guns. | Number. |
|---|---|---|
| 1st. | 100 | 5 |
| 2d. | 98 & 90 | 20 |
|  | 84 | 1 |
| 3d. | 80 | 5 |
|  | 76 | 1 |
|  | 74 | 70 |
|  | 68 | 1 |
|  | 64 | 43 |
| 4th. | 60 | 3 |
|  | Line................ | 149 |
| 4th. | 52 | 1 |
|  | 50 | 16 |
| 5th. | 44 | 25 |
|  | 40 | 1 |
|  | 38 | 7 |
|  | 36 | 15 |
|  | 32 | 48 |
| 6th. | 28 | 28 |
|  | 24 | 7 |
|  | 22 & 20 | 8 |

| | |
|---|---|
| Sloops rigged as Ships.................... | 27 |
| Brigs...................... | 15 |
| Nature of their rigging unknown........... | 2 |
| On survey............................. | 3 |
| Brigs................................. | 6 |
| Armed Transport......................... | 1 |
| Storeship.......................... | 1 |
| Galleys........................... | 6 |
| Cutters............................... | 27 |
| Bombs................................ | 2 |
| Fireships............................. | 9 |
| Schooners............................. | 4 |
| Yachts............................... | 11 |
| Hoys, Lighters & Transports............... | 32 |
| Receiving Ships......................... | 11 |
| Hulks................................. | 9 |
| Of 52 Guns and under.... | 322 |
| Total...... | 471 |

From the beginning of the year 1786, to that of the year 1789, no material interruption to the building and repairing of Ships took place.—Great progress therefore continued to be made therein, particularly with regard to Ships of the Line, to which preference had been mostly given throughout the peace, as the welfare of the country required, in bringing Ships forward in the King's Yards. In the course of the beforementioned period, however, sundry old Ships were disposed of; which left the number and tonnage of the Ships and Vessels of the respective classes, as follows.

**1789**

Abstract of the Royal Navy on the 1st January 1789.

| Rates or Classes. | Guns. | Number. | Burthen. |
|---|---|---|---|
|  |  |  | Tons. |
| 1st. | 100 | 6 | 13325 |
| 2d. | 98 & 90 | 21 | 40261 |
|  | 84 | 1 | 1918 |
| 3d. | 80 | 4 | 7847 |
|  | 76 | 1 | 120878 |
|  | 74 | 72 |  |
|  | 68 | 1 | 1934 |
|  | 64 | 40 | 55414 |
| 4th. | 60 | 2 | 2489 |
|  | Line............... | 148 | 244066 |
| 4th. | 52 | 1 | 17783 |
|  | 50 | 16 |  |
| 5th. | 44 | 23 | 20597 |
|  | 38 | 7 | 6691 |
|  | 36 | 15 | 13542 |
|  | 32 | 47 | 33120 |
| 6th. | 28 | 28 | 16697 |
|  | 24 | 7 | 3681 |
|  | 22 & 20 | 7 | 3068 |
|  | 10 | 1 | 512 |

| | | |
|---|---|---|
| Sloops........................... | 42 | 12870 |
| Brigs............................ | 6 | 1225 |
| Bombs........................... | 2 | 609 |
| Fireships........................ | 9 | 3821 |
| Storeships....................... | 2 | 1772 |
| Armed Vessel..................... | 1 | 220 |
| Tender.................... | 1 | 175 |
| Cutters.......................... | 23 | 3923 |
| Slop-Ship........................ | 1 | 300 |
| Yachts........................... | 11 | 1435 |
| Hoys, Lighters, & Transports........ | 33 | 3158 |
| Receiving Ships*.................. | 12 | 14131 |
| Hulks........................... | 9 | 10271 |
| Of 52 Guns, and under.... | 304 | 169601 |
| Total...... | 452 | 413667 |

* *Old Ships were selected in July 1783, and afterwards fitted, for the reception of Ships Companies and Stores during the time the Ships are in dock refitting. Previous to that period serviceable Ships, not in good condition, were made use of for the purpose, which did them considerable injury.*

**1787**

It will be proper here to mention some circumstances, which in the order of time might have been noticed before. In December 1787, it was directed, that in future, Ships lying up in good condition should have the works of their magazines and store-rooms completed, that by means of such advanced state of preparation for service at sea, they might be made fit to be commissioned at a short notice; it being thought, that from the practice which had been some time adopted, of making use of Airing Stoves, the said works might be done to the Ships, without injuring their frames. And in the preceding month, four Ships were ordered in future to be kept completely fitted for the reception of new-raised men; and one Hospital Ship; in order that the Artificers of the yards might, at the commencement of an armament, be entirely employed in bringing Ships forward for sea-service.

The good effects of using Copper Bolts under the load draught of water, having been satisfactorily proved, in Ships of 44 Guns and under; and it having been found that there was no possibility of guarding the iron bolts against the effects of the copper-sheathing,* it was ordered in November 1783, that in future Ships of all classes should be copper-fastened under the load draught of water.

It has been mentioned, that, before the beginning of the year 1789, great progress had been made in bringing Ships forward into good condition: and as the Navy had arrived at a much higher state of perfection in that respect by 1st January 1790, than it had ever attained before; and as an extensive armament took place a few months afterwards,† I will describe the state and condition of the Navy as it stood at that time.

The Sandwich of 90 Guns was the first 3 decked ship coppered in December 1779 and very few Ships of the Line were coppered until after that.

* In the course of the War which ended in 1783, Ships of every class were coppered.
† A war with Spain was expected.

An Estimate of the *Expence* of building a Ship of each Class in the King's yards (including Coppering and Copper Bolting), and providing them with Masts, Yards, Rigging, Sails, Anchors, Cables, and all other Boatswain's and Carpenter's Stores, to an Eight Months Proportion, according to the Prices paid for Timber, Hemp, and other Naval Stores, in August 1789.

| Ships of | Tons. | Rate ℔ Ton. Hull, including Coppering and Copper Bolting. | Rigging and Stores. | Amount of the Hull. | Masts and Yards. | Rigging. | Sails. | Anchors. | Cables. | Other Stores. Boatswains. | Carpenters. | Total of the Hull, Masts, and Yards. | Rigging, Sails, Anchors, Cables, and all other Boatswains and Carpenters Stores. | General Total. |
|---|---|---|---|---|---|---|---|---|---|---|---|---|---|---|
| | | £. s. d. | £. s. d. | £. | £. | £. | £. | £. | £. | £. | £. | £. | £. | £. |
| 100 Guns | 2220 | 24:10:0 | 4:19:0 | 54390 | 2220 | 2790 | 1220 | 1180 | 1880 | 1320 | 2600 | 56610 | 10990 | 67600 |
| 98 | 1920 | 23:10:0 | 5:5:0 | 45120 | 1920 | 2620 | 1140 | 970 | 1690 | 1270 | 2390 | 47040 | 10080 | 57120 |
| 80 new construction | 2020 | 20:10:0 | 4:16:0 | 41410 | 2020 | 2700 | 1200 | 960 | 1500 | 1150 | 2180 | 43430 | 9690 | 53120 |
| 74 | 1660 | 20:4:0 | 5:4:0 | 33530 | 1660 | 2550 | 1170 | 820 | 1300 | 1100 | 1690 | 35190 | 8630 | 43820 |
| 64 | 1390 | 19:10:0 | 5:7:0 | 27100 | 1390 | 2120 | 980 | 630 | 1150 | 1030 | 1520 | 28490 | 7430 | 35920 |
| 50 | 1050 | 18:0:0 | 5:10:0 | 18900 | 1050 | 1490 | 810 | 480 | 850 | 820 | 1320 | 19950 | 5770 | 25720 |
| 44 | 890 | 17:5:0 | 5:16:0 | 15350 | 890 | 1310 | 710 | 410 | 770 | 650 | 1310 | 16240 | 5160 | 21400 |
| 38 | 960 | 15:5:0 | 5:9:0 | 14640 | 960 | 1350 | 750 | 410 | 770 | 660 | 1290 | 15600 | 5230 | 20830 |
| 36 new construction | 900 | 14:17:0 | 5:7:0 | 13360 | 900 | 1220 | 730 | 350 | 730 | 600 | 1180 | 14260 | 4810 | 19070 |
| 32 | 700 | 14:13:0 | 6:6:0 | 10250 | 420 | 1140 | 680 | 280 | 660 | 560 | 1090 | 10670 | 4410 | 15080 |
| 28 | 600 | 13:10:0 | 6:12:0 | 8100 | 360 | 970 | 630 | 260 | 590 | 520 | 990 | 8460 | 3960 | 12420 |
| 24 | 530 | 13:0:0 | 6:6:0 | 6890 | 320 | 800 | 530 | 240 | 490 | 440 | 840 | 7210 | 3340 | 10550 |
| 20 | 440 | 12:18:0 | 7:4:0 | 5670 | 260 | 740 | 520 | 200 | 470 | 440 | 800 | 5930 | 3170 | 9100 |
| Sloop of | 300 | 12:3:0 | 8:3:0 | 3640 | 180 | 520 | 380 | 130 | 350 | 340 | 720 | 3820 | 2440 | 6260 |

N.B. Expences of this nature are subject to great fluctuations. Since these Estimates were formed, the permanent price of timber has been much advanced; and the prices of many other articles are at present much higher than they were.

**1790**

State and Condition of the Royal Navy on 1st January 1790.

| Rates or Classes. | Guns. | In good condition, in Ordinary. | At Sea, or in Commission for Sea-service. | In want of Repair. | Not surveyed. | Building or ordered to be built. | Repairing. | Total. |
|---|---|---|---|---|---|---|---|---|
| 1st. | 110 | .. | .. | .. | .. | I | .. | I |
|  | 100 | 3 | .. | .. | .. | I* | I | 5 |
| 2d. | 98 & 90 | 12 | 2 | 2 | .. | 4† | I | 21 |
|  | 84 | .. | .. | I | .. | .. | .. | I |
| 3d. | 80 | .. | .. | I | .. | 2 | I | 4 |
|  | 76 | I | .. | .. | .. | .. | .. | I |
|  | 74 | 37 | 12 | 13 | .. | 5‡ | 4 | 71 |
|  | 68 & 64 | 20 | 3 | 18 | .. | .. | .. | 41 |
| 4th. | 60 | .. | . | I | .. | .. | .. | I |
| Line | | 73 | 17 | 36 | .. | 13 | 7 | 146 |
| 4th. | 52 | .. | I | .. | .. | .. | .. | I |
|  | 50 | I | 5 | 8 | .. | I | I | 16 |
| 5th. | 44 | 14 | 6 | 2 | I | .. | .. | 23 |
|  | 38 | 3 | .. | 2 | .. | .. | 2 | 7 |
|  | 36 | 5 | 2 | 7 | .. | .. | I | 15 |
|  | 32 | 12 | 12 | 19 | .. | .. | 4 | 47 |
| 6th. | 28 | 11 | 10 | 7 | .. | .. | .. | 28 |
|  | 24 | I | 5 | I | .. | .. | .. | 7 |
|  | 22 & 20 | 2 | 2 | 3 | .. | .. | .. | 7 |
|  | 10 | .. | I | .. | .. | .. | .. | I |
| Of 52 Guns and under to 6th Rates inclusive§ .. | | 49 | 44 | 49 | I | I | 8 | 152 |

Sloops rigged as Ships . . . . . . . . . . . . . . . . . . . . . . . . . . . . . 30
Brigs . . . . . . . . . . . . . . . . . . . . . . . . . . . . 13
Brigs . . . . . . . . . . . . . . . . . . . . . . . . . . . . . . . . . . . . . . 6
Surveying Vessel . . . . . . . . . . . . . . . . . . . . . . . . . . . . . . . . I
Bombs . . . . . . . . . . . . . . . . . . . . . . . . . . . . . . . . . . . . . . 2
Fireships . . . . . . . . . . . . . . . . . . . . . . . . . . . . . . . . . . . . 9
Storeships . . . . . . . . . . . . . . . . . . . . . . . . . . . . . . . . . . . 2
Armed Vessel . . . . . . . . . . . . . . . . . . . . . . . . . . . . . . . . . . I
Tender . . . . . . . . . . . . . . . . . . . . . . . . . . . . . . . . . . I
Tenders . . . . . . . . . . . . . . . . . . . . . . . . . . . . . . . . . . . . . 4
Vessels rigged as Sloops . . . . . . . . . . . . . . . . . . . . . . . . . 2
Cutters . . . . . . . . . . . . . . . . . . . . . . . . . . . . . . . . . . . . . . 22
Slop-Ship . . . . . . . . . . . . . . . . . . . . . . . . . . . . . . . . . . . . I
Yachts . . . . . . . . . . . . . . . . . . . . . . . . . . . . . . . . . . . . . . 11
Hoys, Lighters, and Transports . . . . . . . . . . . . . . . . . . . . 53
Receiving Ships . . . . . . . . . . . . . . . . . . . . . . . . . . . . . . . . 13
Hulks . . . . . . . . . . . . . . . . . . . . . . . . . . . . . . . . . . . . . . . 9

Total of 52 Guns and under 332

General Total 478

* *This Ship was finished, but not launched.*
† *One of these was finished, but not launched.*
‡ *One of these was finished, but not launched.*
§ *It is not thought necessary to describe the condition of the lower classes.*

**1791**

| Guns. | Lying up. | At Sea, or in Commission for Sea-service. | Total. |
|---|---|---|---|
| Of 100. . . . . . . . . . | 4 | I | 5 |
| 98 & 90. . . . . . | 9 | 5 | 14 |
| 80. . . . . . . . . . | I | . . . . . . . . . . . | I |
| 74. . . . . . . . . . | 27 | 25 | 52 |
| 64. . . . . . . . . . | 19 | 4 | 23 |
| Total. . . . | 60 | 35 | 95 |

**1791**

By the end of February, the number of Ships of the line stated to be in good condition, including, as above, those at sea or in commission for sea-service, amounted to 98. This number was never exceeded, and most likely never will be; indeed eight of the said 98 Ships were found in May following to be in want of what is denominated in official language, a small, or very small repair, and were therefore struck off the list of Ships in good condition; and the number of Ships in that state continued to decrease from that time, as will be shewn further on, very many of those which had been built or repaired eight or ten years, being found to want repair faster than others were brought forward.* It also appeared on a thorough and complete investigation at this time, and from the experience of several years of peace, that such must ever be expected to be the case.

* *This had appeared in upwards of thirty instances previous to the end of May 1791.*

**1792**

State and Condition of the Navy on the 1st December 1792.

| Rates or Classes. | Guns. | In good Condition, in Ordinary. | At Sea, or in Commission for Sea-service. | In want of Repair. | Not surveyed. | Building or ordered to be built. | Repairing. | Total. |
|---|---|---|---|---|---|---|---|---|
| 1st. | 110 | .. | .. | .. | .. | 2 | .. | 2 |
|  | 100 | 5 | .. | .. | .. | .. | .. | 5 |
| 2d. | 98 & 90 | 11 | 2 | 2 | .. | 5 | I | 21 |
| 3d. | 80 | I | .. | .. | .. | 2* | .. | 3 |
|  | 76 | .. | .. | I | .. | .. | .. | I |
|  | 74 | 30 | 9 | 21 | .. | 3† | 6 | 69 |
|  | 64 | 16 | I | 22 | .. | .. | .. | 39 |
| 4th. | 60 | .. | .. | I | .. | .. | .. | I |
| Line | | 63 | 12 | 47 | .. | 12 | 7 | 141 |

* *One of which was finished, but not launched.*
† *One of which was finished, but not launched.*
N.B.—*Both these Ships were launched in 1793.*

| Rates or Classes. | Guns. | In good Condition, in Ordinary. | At Sea, or in Commission for Sea-service. | In want of Repair. | Not surveyed. | Building or ordered to be built. | Repairing. | Total. |
|---|---|---|---|---|---|---|---|---|
| 4th. | 52 | .. | .. | I | .. | .. | .. | I |
| | 50 | 2 | 5 | 7 | .. | 3 | 2 | 19 |
| 5th. | 44 | 8 | I | II | .. | .. | I | 21 |
| | 40 | I | .. | .. | .. | .. | .. | I |
| | 38 | 3 | I | 2 | .. | .. | I | 7 |
| | 36 | 7 | 2 | 3 | .. | .. | 2 | 14 |
| | 32 | 14 | 10 | 15 | I | 3 | 7 | 50 |
| 6th. | 28 | 3 | 7 | 15 | .. | .. | 3 | 28 |
| | 24 | .. | 3 | 2 | .. | .. | I | 6 |
| | 22 & 20 | I | I | 5 | .. | .. | .. | 7 |
| | 12 | .. | I | .. | .. | .. | .. | I |
| Of 52 Guns, and under to 6th Rates inclusive... | | 39 | 31 | 61 | I | 6 | 17 | 155 |

| | Total. |
|---|---|
| Sloops rigged as Ships ... | 30 |
| Brigs .......................... | II |
| Brigs............................. | 6 |
| Surveying Vessel ................ | I |
| Bombs .......................... | 2 |
| Fireships* ....................... | 9 |
| Storeships ....................... | 2 |
| Armed Vessel .................... | I |
| Tender .................... | I |
| Tenders.......................... | 4 |
| Vessels rigged as Sloops ......... | 2 |
| Cutters.......................... | 19 |
| Armed Schooners................. | 3 |
| Hospital Ship ................... | I |
| Yachts........................... | II |
| Hoys, Lighters, & Transports .... | 50 |
| Receiving Ships .................. | 16 |
| Hulks............................ | 10 |
| Total of 52 Guns, and under.... | 334 |
| General Total.... | 475 |

* Two of which were employed as Sloops.

**1792**

### GUNS.

An Account of those carried on board the Ships of the several Classes (particular Ships excepted) on the 1st October 1792.

| Classes of Ships. | Lower-deck. | | Middle-deck. | | Upper-deck. | | Quarter-deck. | | Forecastle | |
|---|---|---|---|---|---|---|---|---|---|---|
| | No | Prs | No | Prs | No | Prs | No | Prs | No | Prs |
| 110 Guns............ | 30 | 32 | 30 | 24 | 32 | 18 | 14 | 12 | 4 | .. |
| 100 .............. {| 28 | 42 | 28 | 24 | 28 | 12 | 12 | 12 | 4 | .. |
| | 30 | 32 | 28 | 24 | 30 | 18 | 10 | 12 | 2 | .. |
| | 30 | 42 | 28 | 24 | 30 | 12 | 10 | 12 | 2 | .. |
| | 28 | 42 | 28 | 24 | 30 | 12 | 10 | 12 | 4 | .. |

| Classes of Ships. | Lower-deck. | | Middle-deck. | | Upper-deck. | | Quarter-deck. | | Forecastle | |
|---|---|---|---|---|---|---|---|---|---|---|
| | No | Prs | No | Prs | No | Prs | No | Prs | No | Prs |
| 98 .............. {| 28 | 32 | 30 | 18 | 30 | 12 | 8 | 12 | 2 | .. |
| | 28 | 32 | 28 | 18 | 30 | 12 | 8 | 12 | 4 | .. |
| | 28 | 32 | 30 | 18 | 30 | 18 | 8 | 12 | 2 | .. |
| 90 .................. | 26 | 32 | 26 | 18 | 26 | 12 | 10 | 12 | 2 | .. |
| 80 .............. {| 30 | 32 | .. | .. | 32 | 24 | 14 | 9 | 4 | .. |
| | 30 | 32 | .. | .. | 32 | 24 | 14 | 12 | 4 | .. |
| 74 Large Class ....... | 28 | 32 | .. | .. | 30 | 24 | 14 | 9 | 2 | .. |
| 74 Guns..Common Class | 28 | 32 | .. | .. | 28 | 18 | 14 | 9 | 4 | 9 |
| | 28 | 32 | .. | .. | 30 | 18 | 12 | 9 | 4 | 9 |
| 64 ................. | 26 | 24 | .. | .. | 26 | 18 | 10 | 9 | 2 | 9 |
| 50 Common Class .... | 22 | 24 | .. | .. | 22 | 12 | 4 | 6 | 2 | 6 |
| 50 Small Class* ...... | 20 | 12 | .. | .. | 22 | 12 | 6 | 6 | 2 | 6 |
| 44................. | 20 | 18 | .. | .. | 22 | 12 | .. | .. | 2 | 6 |
| 40................. | .. | .. | .. | .. | 28 | 18 | 8 | 9 | 4 | 9 |
| 38................. | .. | .. | .. | .. | 28 | 18 | 8 | 9 | 2 | 12 |
| 36................. | .. | .. | .. | .. | 26 | 18 | 8 | 9 | 2 | 12 |
| 32 Large Class ....... | .. | .. | .. | .. | 26 | 18 | 4 | 6 | 2 | 6 |
| 32 Common Class .... | .. | .. | .. | .. | 26 | 12 | 4 | 6 | 2 | 6 |
| 28................. | .. | .. | .. | .. | 24 | 9 | 4 | 6 | .. | .. |
| 24 Guns .......... | .. | .. | .. | .. | 22 | 9 | 2 | 6 | .. | .. |
| 20................. | .. | .. | .. | .. | 20 | 9 | .. | .. | .. | .. |
| Sloops Ship-rigged ....... | 18 | .. | .. | .. | 18 | 6 | .. | .. | .. | .. |
| | 16 | .. | .. | .. | 16 | 6 | .. | .. | .. | .. |
| | 14 | .. | .. | .. | 14 | 6 | .. | .. | .. | .. |

* Only two Ships have ever been built of this Class.

N.B. It is not certain whether the 100 Gunships that appear by the foregoing account to have 42-pounders, have not had them exchanged for 32's; but they stand on the List of the Navy with their original Guns. The Guns on board the Ships of foreign-built, are not meant to be comprized in the foregoing account. The Sloops and small Classes of Ships carry Swivels (half-pounders) in addition to their Carriage-guns.

N.B. Since the year 1792, some alterations have taken place in the Guns of some of the Classes; and Carronades are now much used, but so unequally on board Ships of the same Class, that it is not possible to give a general statement of the Ordnance now in use.

**1793**

Abstract of the Royal Navy on the 1st September 1793.

| Rates or Classes. | Guns. | Number. | Burthen. |
|---|---|---|---|
| | | | Tons. |
| 1st. | 110 | 2 | 4664 |
| | 100 | 5 | 11000 |
| 2d. | 98 & 90 | 21 | 41125 |
| 3d. | 80 | 3 | 6232 |
| | 76 | 1 | 115763 |
| | 74 | 69 | |
| | 64 | 39 | 54067 |
| 4th. | 60 | 1 | 1285 |
| Line............... | | 141 | 234136 |
| 4th. | 52 | 1 | 21128 |
| | 50 | 19 | |

| Rates or Classes. | Guns. | Number. | Burthen. |
|---|---|---|---|
| | | | Tons. |
| 5th. | 44 | 21 | 18806 |
| | 40 | 1 | 1020 |
| | 38 | 14 | 13597 |
| | 36 | 14 | 12700 |
| | 32 | 53 | 37992 |
| 6th. | 28 | 29 | 17206 |
| | 24 | 6 | 3069 |
| | 22 & 20 | 6 | 2636 |
| | 12 | 1 | 406 |
| Floating Battery .................... | | 1 | 386 |
| Sloops rigged as Ships .............. | 42 | | 14400 |
| Brigs .............. | 11 | | 2939 |
| Brigs............................. | 6 | | 1225 |
| Surveying Vessel ................... | 1 | | 64 |
| Bombs ........................... | 2 | | 609 |
| Fireships ......................... | 9 | | 3820 |
| Storeships ........................ | 2 | | 1772 |
| Armed Vessel ..................... | 1 | | 123 |
| Tender ................... | 1 | | Not known. |
| Tenders .......................... | 4 | | 606 |
| Vessels rigged as Sloops ............. | 2 | | 84 |
| Cutters........................... | 18 | | 3254 |
| Armed Schooners................... | 3 | | 270 |
| Lugger.......................... | 1 | | 111 |
| Hospital Ship ...................... | 1 | | 1781 |
| Yachts ........................ | 11 | | 1450 |
| Hoys, Lighters & Transports.......... | 50 | | 4926 |
| Receiving Ships ................... | 16 | | 21092 |
| Hulks............................. | 10 | | 11618 |
| Of 52 Guns and under.... | | 357 | 199090 Exclusive of the Tonnage of one Tender |
| Total...... | | 498 | 433226 Exclusive of the Tonnage of one Tender |

## 1792 and 1793

| Guns. | In commission as fighting Ships. | |
|---|---|---|
| | 1st Decr. 1792. | 1st Sepr. 1793. |
| Of 100................................. | | 5 |
| 98 or 90 ............. | 2 | 8 |
| 80................................. | | 1 |
| 74.................. | 9 | 42 |
| 64.................. | 1 | 16 |
| Line.... | 12 | 72 |
| 50.................. | 5 | 6 |
| 44.................. | 1 | 13 |
| 40................................. | | 1 |
| 38.................. | 1 | 6 |

| Guns. | In commission as fighting Ships. | |
|---|---|---|
| | 1st Decr. 1792. | 1st Sepr. 1793. |
| 36.................. | 2 | 10 |
| 32.................. | 10 | 40 |
| 28.................. | 7 | 20 |
| 24.................. | 3 | 5 |
| 22 & 20............. | 1 | 3 |
| Of 50 to 20 Guns...... | 30 | 104 |
| Total.... | 42 | 176 |

## 1795, 1797, 1799, and 1801

Abstracts of the Royal Navy on the 1st January 1795, 1797, and 1799, and as it stood on the 1st October 1801.

| Rates or Classes. | Guns. | Number on | | | |
|---|---|---|---|---|---|
| | | 1st Jany. 1795. | 1st Jany. 1797. | 1st Jany. 1799. | 1st Octr. 1801. |
| 1st. | 120 | 1 | 2 | 2 | 2 |
| | 114 | ... | ... | 1 | 1 |
| | 112 | ... | ... | 1 | 1 |
| | 110 | 2 | 2 | 2 | 2 |
| | 100 | 5 | 5 | 5 | 5 |
| 2d. | 98 & 90 | 21 | 20 | 21 | 21 |
| 3d. | 84 | 2 | 2 | 2 | 3 |
| | 82 | ... | ... | 1 | 1 |
| | 80 | 5 | 4 | 7 | 8 |
| | 78 | 3 | 1 | 1 | 1 |
| | 76 | 1 | 1 | 1 | 1 |
| | 74 | 70 | 82 | 81 | 89 |
| | 72 | ... | ... | 2 | 1 |
| | 64 | 34 | 41 | 46 | 43 |
| 4th. | 60 | 1 | 1 | 3 | 1 |
| Line.............. | | 145 | 161 | 176 | 180 |
| 4th. | 56 | ... | 2 | 2 | 2 |
| | 54 | ... | 4 | 4 | 2 |
| | 52 | ... | ... | ... | 1 |
| | 50 | 17 | 16 | 15 | 15 |
| 5th. | 44 | 23 | 21 | 21 | 20 |
| | 40 | 1 | 4 | 7 | 7 |
| | 38 | 21 | 33 | 33 | 36 |
| | 36 | 20 | 24 | 33 | 43 |
| | 34 | ... | 2 | 3 | 3 |
| | 32 | 51 | 58 | 54 | 52 |
| | 30 | ... | ... | ... | 1 |
| 6th. | 28 | 26 | 26 | 27 | 26 |
| | 26 | ... | 2 | 2 | 2 |
| | 24 | 5 | 5 | 6 | 8 |
| | 22 & 20 | 8 | 9 | 13 | 14 |
| | 16 | 1 | 1 | 1 | 1 |
| Guns unknown | | ... | 1 | ... | ... |

| Rates or Classes. | Guns. | Number on | | | |
|---|---|---|---|---|---|
| | | 1st Jany. 1795. | 1st Jany. 1797. | 1st Jany. 1799. | 1st Octr. 1801. |
| Floating Batteries................. | | 2 | 2 | 2 | 2 |
| Sloops rigged as Ships............. | | 44 | 54 | 80 | 88 |
| Brigs ............ | | 16 | 42 | 38 | 44 |
| Sloops, nature of their rigging unknown ..................... | | 1 | 1 | 2 | 2 |
| Brigs............................ | | 6 | 5 | 2 | 1 |
| Armed Brigs ..................... | | ... | 2 | 3 | 2 |
| Advice Boats..................... | | ... | ... | ... | 2 |
| Surveying Vessels................. | | 1 | 1 | 1 | 1 |
| Bombs ......................... | | 2 | 2 | 14 | 13 |
| Fireships ....................... | | 8 | 7 | 13 | 7 |
| Fire Vessels ..................... | | 12 | 9 | 10 | 8 |
| Storeships ...................... | | 3 | 4 | 3 | 9 |
| Armed Vessels ................... | | 3 | 4 | 6 | 6 |
| Vessels rigged as Sloops ........... | | 2 | 1 | 1 | 1 |
| Armed Tenders .................. | | ... | ... | 1 | 2 |
| Tenders ........................ | | 4 | 4 | 4 | 4 |
| Cutters......................... | | 16 | 17 | 17 | 16 |
| Armed Schooners................. | | 3 | 5 | 5 | 6 |
| Galleots .................. | | 3 | 1 | 1 | 1 |

| Rates or Classes. | Guns. | Number on | | | |
|---|---|---|---|---|---|
| | | 1st Jany. 1795. | 1st Jany. 1797. | 1st Jany. 1799. | 1st Octr. 1801. |
| Schooners (exclusive of the above) ..... | | 5 | 3 | 2 | 3 |
| Luggers .......................... | | 1 | 1 | 1 | 1 |
| Hospital Ships .................... | | 2 | 2 | 2 | 3 |
| Prison Ships ..................... | | 1 | 3 | 4 | 8 |
| Gun Vessels* .................... | | 54 | 54 | 93 | 114 |
| Barge Magazines ................. | | 1 | 1 | 1 | 1 |
| Latteen Settee ................... | | ... | ... | ... | 1 |
| Yachts .......................... | | 11 | 11 | 11 | 11 |
| Hoys, Lighters & Transports ....... | | 55 | 60 | 63 | 67 |
| Receiving Ships .................. | | 16 | 15 | 16 | 17 |
| Hulks........................... | | 10 | 10 | 10 | 10 |
| Of 56 Guns and under.... | | 454 | 530 | 627 | 684 |
| Total.... | | 599 | 691 | 803 | 864 |

\* *Originally called* Gun Boats.

*N.B.—There were some Ships and Vessels in the service, at least in our possession, on the 1st October 1801, and perhaps at each of the other periods in the foregoing statement, that had not been registered on the list of the Navy, at those periods.*

# Dimensions of Ships, 1677–1745

An Account shewing the *Dimensions* established, or proposed to be established at different times, for building of Ships.

| Gunships 100 | Establishment of | | | | Proposed in | | Establishment of 1745 |
|---|---|---|---|---|---|---|---|
| | 1677. | 1691. | 1706. | 1719. | 1733. | 1741. | |
| | Ft. In. | | | | | | |
| Length on the Gundeck ............... | 165 : 0 | ...... | ...... | 174 : 0 | 174 : 0 | 175 : 0 | 178 : 0 |
| Of the Keel for tonnage | 137 : 8 | ...... | ...... | 140 : 7 | 140 : 7 | 142 : 4 | 140 : 6½ |
| Breadth extreme...................... | 46 : 0 | ...... | ...... | 50 : 0 | 50 : 0 | 50 : 0 | 51 : 0 |
| Depth in Hold ..................... | 19 : 2 | ...... | ...... | 20 : 0 | 20 : 6 | 21 : 0 | 21 : 6 |
| Burthen in Tons..................... | 1550 | ...... | ...... | 1869 | 1869 | 1892 | 2000 |

| Gunships 90 | | | | | | | |
|---|---|---|---|---|---|---|---|
| Length on the Gundeck ............... | 158 : 0 | ...... | 162 : 0 | 164 : 0 | 166 : 0 | 168 : 0 | 170 : 0 |
| Of the Keel for tonnage | ...... | ...... | 132 : 0 | 132 : 5 | 134 : 1 | 137 : 0 | 138 : 4 |
| Breadth extreme...................... | 44 : 0 | ...... | 47 : 0 | 47 : 2 | 47 : 9 | 48 : 0 | 48 : 6 |
| Depth in Hold ..................... | 18 : 2 | ...... | 18 : 6 | 18 : 10 | 19 : 6 | 20 : 2 | 20 : 6 |
| Burthen in Tons..................... | 1307 | ...... | 1551 | 1566 | 1623 | 1679 | 1730 |

| Gunships 80 with Three decks. | Establishment of | | | | Proposed in | | Establishment of 1745 |
|---|---|---|---|---|---|---|---|
| | 1677. | 1691. | 1706. | 1719. | 1733. | 1741. | |
| | Ft. In. | | | | | | |
| Length on the Gundeck | ...... | 156 : 0 | 156 : 0 | 158 : 0 | 158 : 0 | 161 : 0 | 165 : 0 |
| Of the Keel for tonnage | ...... | ...... | 127 : 6 | 128 : 2 | 127 : 8 | 130 : 10 | 134 : 10¾ |
| Breadth extreme | ...... | 41 : 0 | 43 : 6 | 44 : 6 | 45 : 5 | 46 : 0 | 47 : 0 |
| Depth in Hold | ...... | 17 : 4 | 17 : 8 | 18 : 2 | 18 : 7 | 19 : 4 | 20 : 0 |
| Burthen in Tons | ...... | 1100 | 1283 | 1350 | 1400 | 1472 | 1585 |

| Gunships 70 | 1677. | 1691. | 1706. | 1719. | 1733. | 1741. | 1745 |
|---|---|---|---|---|---|---|---|
| | Ft. In. | | | | | | |
| Length on the Gundeck | 150 : 0 | ...... | 150 : 0 | 151 : 0 | 151 : 0 | 154 : 0 | 160 : 0 |
| Of the Keel for tonnage | ...... | ...... | 122 : 0 | 123 : 2 | 122 : 0 | 125 : 5 | 131 : 4 |
| Breadth extreme | 39 : 8 | ...... | 41 : 0 | 41 : 6 | 43 : 5 | 44 : 0 | 45 : 0 |
| Depth in Hold | 17 : 0 | ...... | 17 : 4 | 17 : 4 | 17 : 9 | 18 : 11 | 19 : 4 |
| Burthen in Tons | 1013 | ...... | 1069 | 1128 | 1224 | 1291 | 1414 |

| Gunships 60 | Establishment of | | | | Proposed in | | Establishment of 1745 |
|---|---|---|---|---|---|---|---|
| | 1677. | 1691. | 1706. | 1719. | 1733. | 1741. | |
| | Ft. In. | | | | | | |
| Length on the Gundeck | ...... | 144 : 0 | 144 : 0 | 144 : 0 | 144 : 0 | 147 : 0 | 150 : 0 |
| Of the Keel for tonnage | ...... | ...... | 119 : 0 | 117 : 7 | 116 : 4 | 119 : 9 | 123 : 0½ |
| Breadth extreme | ...... | 37 : 6 | 38 : 0 | 39 : 0 | 41 : 5 | 42 : 0 | 42 : 8 |
| Depth in Hold | ...... | 15 : 8 | 15 : 8 | 16 : 5 | 16 : 11 | 18 : 1 | 18 : 6 |
| Burthen in Tons | ...... | 900 | 914 | 951 | 1068 | 1123 | 1191 |

| Gunships 50 | 1677. | 1691. | 1706. | 1719. | 1733. | 1741. | 1745 |
|---|---|---|---|---|---|---|---|
| Length on the Gundeck | ...... | ...... | 130 : 0 | 134 : 0 | 134 : 0 | 140 : 0 | 144 : 0 |
| Of the Keel for tonnage | ...... | ...... | 108 : 0 | 109 : 8 | 108 : 3 | 113 : 9 | 117 : 8½ |
| Breadth extreme | ...... | ...... | 35 : 0 | 36 : 0 | 38 : 6 | 40 : 0 | 41 : 0 |
| Depth in Hold | ...... | ...... | 14 : 0 | 15 : 2 | 15 : 9 | 17 : 2½ | 17 : 0 |
| Burthen in Tons | ...... | ...... | 704 | 755 | 853 | 968 | 1052 |

| Gunships 40 | Establishment of | | | | Proposed in | | Establishment of 1745 |
|---|---|---|---|---|---|---|---|
| | 1677. | 1691. | 1706. | 1719. | 1733. | 1741. | |
| | Ft. In. | | | | | | |
| Length on the Gundeck | ...... | ...... | 118 : 0 | 124 : 0 | 124 : 0 | 126 : 0 | 133 : 0 |
| Of the Keel for tonnage | ...... | ...... | 97 : 6 | 101 : 8 | 100 : 3 | 102 : 6 | 108 : 10 |
| Breadth extreme | ...... | ...... | 32 : 0 | 33 : 2 | 35 : 8 | 36 : 0 | 37 : 6 |
| Depth in Hold | ...... | ...... | 13 : 6 | 14 : 0 | 14 : 6 | 15 : 5½ | 16 : 0 |
| Burthen in Tons | ...... | ...... | 531 | 594 | 678 | 706 | 814 |

| Gunships 20 | 1677. | 1691. | 1706. | 1719. | 1733. | 1741. | 1745 |
|---|---|---|---|---|---|---|---|
| Length on the Gundeck | ...... | ...... | ...... | 106 : 0 | 106 : 0 | 112 : 0 | 113 : 0 |
| Of the Keel for tonnage | ...... | ...... | ...... | 87 : 9 | 85 : 8 | 91 : 6 | 93 : 4 |
| Breadth extreme | ...... | ...... | ...... | 28 : 4 | 30 : 6 | 32 : 0 | 32 : 0 |
| Depth in Hold | ...... | ...... | ...... | 9 : 2 | 9 : 5 | 11 : 0 | 11 : 0 |
| Burthen in Tons | ...... | ...... | ...... | 374 | 429 | 498 | 508 |

MEMO.—*Several Ships were built by the establishments proposed in 1733 and 1741. The establishment of 1745 was not generally adhered to for more than ten years, if so long; and there has been no establishment of the kind since.*

**1793 to 1801**

## SHIPS.

An Account of the *Increase* and *Decrease* of *Ships* of the Line, between the 1st January 1793 and 1st October 1801, when the Preliminaries of Peace were signed.

| Rate. | Guns. | In the Service on 1st Janr. 1793. | Added to the List of the Navy. | | | | Total added. | Disposed of. | | | | Total disposed of. | Registered on the List of the Navy, on 1st Octr. 1801. |
|---|---|---|---|---|---|---|---|---|---|---|---|---|---|
| | | | Built, building, or ordered to be built. | Bought from the India Company's Service. | Taken from the Enemy, or surrendered to us by them. | Converted from other Classes. | | Taken by the Enemy. | Taken to Pieces. | Lost. | Converted to other Classes. | | |
| 1st. | 120 to 100 | 7 | 2 | .... | 3 | .... | 5 | .... | .... | 1 | .... | 1 | 11 |
| 2d. | 98 & 90 | 21 | 3 | .... | .... | .... | 3 | .... | .... | 2 | 1 | 3 | 21 |
| 3d. | 84 to 80 | 3 | .... | .... | 9 | .... | 9 | .... | .... | .... | .... | ........ | 12 |
| | 78 | ...... | .... | .... | 3 | .... | 3 | .... | 2 | .... | .... | 2 | 1 |
| | 76 & 74 | 70 | 26 | .... | 8 | 1 | 35 | 3 | 3 | 7 | 2 | 15 | 90 |
| | 72 | ...... | .... | .... | 2 | .... | 2 | .... | .... | .... | 1 | 1 | 1 |
| | 64 | 39 | .... | 5 | 10 | .... | 15 | .... | 2 | 4 | 5 | 11 | 43 |
| 4th. | 60 | 1 | .... | .... | 2 | .... | 2 | .... | .... | .... | 2 | 2 | 1 |
| | Total...... | 141 | 31 | 5 | 37 | 1 | 74 | 3 | 7 | 14 | 11 | 35 | 180 |

N.B.—*Ships taken before 1st October 1801, but not registered till afterwards, are not included herein.*

## MEN.

Highest *Complements* established at several periods, and generally borne at others, (particular Ships excepted.)

| Classes of Ships. | As established in | | | | | | | Generally borne in | | |
|---|---|---|---|---|---|---|---|---|---|---|
| | 1677 | 1692 | 1706 | 1719 | 1733 | 1741 | 1745 | 1762 | 1783 | 1805 |
| 120 Guns | ... | ... | ... | ... | ... | ... | ... | ... | ... | 875 |
| 110 | ... | ... | ... | ... | ... | ... | ... | ... | ... | 837 |
| 100 | 780 | ... | 780 | 780 | 850 | 850 | 850 | 850 | 850 | 837 |
| 98 & 90 | 660 | ... | 680 | 680 | 750 | 750 | 750 | 750 | 750 | 738 |
| 80 | ... | 490 | 520 | 520 | 600 | 600 | 650 | 650 | 650 | 719 |
| 74 Large Class | ... | ... | ... | ... | ... | ... | ... | 650 | 650 | 640 |
| 74 Common Class | ... | ... | ... | ... | ... | ... | 600 | 650 | 600 | 590 |
| 70 | 460 | ... | 440 | 440 | 480 | 480 | 520 | 520 | 520 | ... |
| 64 | ... | ... | ... | ... | ... | ... | 470 | 500 | 500 | 491 |
| 60 | ... | 355 | 365 | 365 | 400 | 400 | 420 | 420 | 420 | ... |
| 50 | ... | ... | 280 | 280 | 300 | 300 | 350 | 350 | 350 | 343 |
| 44 | ... | ... | ... | ... | 250 | 250 | 280 | 280 | 300 | 294 |
| 40 | ... | ... | 190 | 190 | ... | ... | ... | ... | 300 | 320 |
| 38 | ... | ... | ... | ... | ... | ... | ... | 250 | 280 | 284 |
| 36 | ... | ... | ... | ... | ... | ... | ... | 240 | 270 | 264 |
| 32 Large | ... | ... | ... | ... | ... | ... | ... | ... | ... | 254 |
| 32 Common | ... | ... | ... | ... | ... | ... | ... | 220 | 220 | 215 |
| 28 | ... | ... | ... | ... | ... | ... | ... | 200 | 200 | 195 |
| 24 | ... | ... | ... | ... | ... | ... | 160 | 160 | 160 | 155 |
| 20 | ... | ... | 115 | 130 | 140 | 140 | ... | 160 | 160 | 155 |
| Large Sloops | ... | ... | ... | 100 | ... | ... | 110 | 125 | 125 | 121 |

N.B —*Flag-ships are allowed an additional number of men.*

The following Ships were building, or under orders to be built, on the day that the preliminaries of peace were signed,* and are included in the foregoing abstract, namely,

## 1801

| Guns. | In the | | Total. |
|---|---|---|---|
| | King's Yards. | Merch^ts Yards | |
| Of 120........... | 1 | ............ | 1 |
| 110........... | 1 | ............ | 1 |
| 100........... | 1 | ............ | 1 |
| 98........... | 4 | ............ | 4 |
| 74........... | 8 | 9 | 17 |
| 50........... | 2 | ............ | 2 |
| 44............... | | 1 | 1 |
| 38........... | 2 | ............ | 2 |
| 36........... | 4 | 3 | 7 |
| Sloops ........... | 1 | 1 | 2 |
| Yachts ........... | 2 | ............ | 2 |
| Total.... | 26 | 14 | 40 |

* *Peace of Amiens, concluded 1802.*

MEM°.—*In the course of the war, several very large 74 Gun ships were built pretty much after French models; but the Ships laid down of late have been of smaller dimensions.*

## 1793 to 1801

### SHIPS.

An Account of the *Increase* and *Decrease* of *Ships* under the Line, Sloops, and all other Vessels, between the 1st January 1793 and 1st October 1801.

| Rates or Classes. | Guns. | Built, taken, purchased, or converted from other Classes. | Taken, lost, sold, or otherwise disposed of. |
|---|---|---|---|
| 4th. | 56 | 4 | 2 |
| | 54 | 6 | 4 |
| | 50 | ....... | 4 |
| 5th. | 44 | 4 | 5 |
| | 40 | 6 | ....... |
| | 38 | 34 | 7 |
| | 36 | 41 | 10 |
| | 34 | 5 | 2 |
| | 32 | 21 | 18 |
| | 30 | 1 | ....... |
| 6th. | 28 | 8 | 10 |
| | 26 | 2 | ....... |
| | 24 | 5 | 3 |
| | 22 & 20 | 14 | 7 |
| 6th. | 12 | ....... | 1 |
| | 16 | 1 | ....... |
| Floating Batteries....................... | | 2 | ....... |
| Sloops rigged as Ships................... | | 86 | 24 |
| Brigs.................... | | 62 | 33 |
| Nature of rigg^g not known .......... | | 3 | 1 |

| | | |
|---|---|---|
| Brigs.................................. | 1 | 6 |
| Armed Brigs ......................... | 5 | 3 |
| Bombs ............................... | 12 | 1 |
| Fireships ............................. | 7 | 9 |
| Fire Vessels .......................... | 13 | 5 |
| Storeships ........................... | 7 | 2 |
| Advice Boats......................... | 2 | ........ |
| Armed Vessels ....................... | 6 | ........ |
| Tenders ......................... | 3 | 2 |
| Galleot ......................... | 1 | ........ |
| Vessel rigged as a Sloop ......................... | | 1 |
| Cutters............................... | 8 | 11 |
| Armed Schooners..................... | 5 | 2 |
| Schooners ........................... | 7 | 5 |
| Lugger............................... | 1 | ........ |
| Hospital Ships ....................... | 2 | ........ |
| Prison Ships ......................... | 7 | ........ |
| Gun Boats............................ | 131 | 18 |
| Barge Magazine ...................... | 1 | ........ |
| Latteen Settee ....................... | 1 | ........ |
| Yachts............................... | 3 | 3 |
| Receiving Ships ...................... | 6 | 5 |
| Hulks................................ | 2 | 1 |
| Total...... | 536 | 205 |

## 1803

Abstract of the Royal Navy as it stood on the 15th May 1803.

| Rates or Classes. | Guns. | Number. |
|---|---|---|
| 1st. | 120 | 1 |
| | 114 | 1 |
| | 112 | 1 |
| | 110 | 2 |
| | 100 | 5 |
| 2d. | 98 & 90 | 20 |
| 3d. | 84 | 3 |
| | 82 | 1 |
| | 80 | 8 |
| | 78 | 1 |
| | 76 | 2 |
| | 74 | 87 |
| | 72 | 1 |
| | 64 | 43 |
| 4th. | 60 | 1 |
| Line................. | | 177 |
| 4th. | 56 | 3 |
| | 54 | 2 |
| | 52 | 1 |
| | 50 | 14 |
| 5th. | 44 | 16 |
| | 40 | 7 |
| | 38 | 39 |
| | 36 | 43 |
| | 34 | 2 |
| | 32 | 50 |

| Rates or Classes | Guns. | Number. |
|---|---|---|
| 6th. | 28 | 24 |
| | 26 | 1 |
| | 24 | 6 |
| | 22 & 20 | 11 |
| | 16 | 1 |
| Sloops rigged as Ships...................... | | 83 |
| Brigs ...................... | | 43 |
| Nature of rigging not known ............ | | 2 |
| Armed Brig................................. | | 1 |
| Advice Boats............................... | | 2 |
| Surveying Vessel .......................... | | 1 |
| Bombs .................................... | | 12 |
| Fireships ................................. | | 4 |
| Fire Vessel ............................... | | 1 |
| Storeships ................................ | | 9 |
| Armed Vessels ............................ | | 6 |
| Vessel rigged as a Sloop ................... | | 1 |
| Armed Tenders ........................... | | 2 |
| Tenders ................................... | | 4 |
| Cutters.................................... | | 12 |
| Armed Schooners.......................... | | 5 |
| Galleot ................................... | | 1 |
| Schooners (exclusive of the above)............. | | 3 |
| Lugger.................................... | | 1 |
| Hospital Ships............................. | | 3 |
| Prison Ships .............................. | | 6 |
| Gun Vessels*.............................. | | 70 |
| Barge Magazine .......................... | | 1 |
| Latteen Settee............................. | | 1 |
| Yachts .................................... | | 11 |
| Hoys, Lighters & Transports ................ | | 63 |
| Receiving Ships ........................... | | 15 |
| Hulks..................................... | | 10 |
| Of 56 Guns and under.... | | 593 |
| Total...... | | 770 |

* Originally called Gun-Boats.

## 1803

In the year 1803, a 74 and a 36 Gunship were ordered to be built in the East India Company's docks at Bombay:* and it is expected that the building of Ships of War there, will be continued.† The Ships will be built with Teak Timber which is extremely durable.

Only very scanty supplies of Oak timber having been obtained for some time past for the dock-yards, and it being an article exceedingly wanted, the prices were much raised in the year 1802, and also in 1803.

* The Frigate (named the Salsette) is launched.
† Others have been since ordered to be built there.

## 1804

Orders were given in the course of this year to purchase six Ships in India to carry from 36 to 40 guns: and many Sloops and Gun Vessels were contracted for with private Ship-builders in this country.

The want of oak timber still continuing, a further advance was given to the Merchants, and other encouragements given them, this year, which had a good effect with regard to the supplies.

## 1805

Many Ships and smaller Vessels have been also contracted for in this year; and among them there are ten of 74 Guns. The Navy at the beginning of this year consisted of the following Ships and Vessels.

## 1805

Abstract of the Royal Navy, on the 1st January 1805.

| Rates or Classes. | Guns. | Number. |
|---|---|---|
| 1st. | 120 | 1 |
| | 114 | 1 |
| | 112 | 1 |
| | 110 | 2 |
| | 100 | 5 |
| 2d. | 98 & 90 | 18 |
| 3d. | 84 | 3 |
| | 82 | 1 |
| | 80 | 8 |
| | 78 | 1 |
| | 76 | 2 |
| | 74 | 87 |
| | 72 | 1 |
| | 64 | 43 |
| 4th. | 60 | 1 |
| Line............... | | 175 |
| 4th. | 56 | 5 |
| | 54 | 4 |
| | 52 | 2 |
| | 50 | 13 |
| 5th. | 44 | 20 |
| | 40 | 7 |
| | 38 | 45 |
| | 36 | 43 |
| | 34 | 2 |
| | 32 | 59 |
| 6th. | 28 | 27 |
| | 26 | 1 |
| | 24 | 5 |
| | 22 & 20 | 13 |
| Sloops rigged as Ships...................... | | 104 |
| Brigs ...................... | | 64 |
| Nature of rigging not known ............ | | 3 |
| Armed Brigs ............................... | | 2 |
| Surveying Vessel .......................... | | 1 |
| Bombs .................................... | | 19 |
| Mortar Boats ............................. | | 2 |
| Fireships ................................. | | 5 |
| Fire Vessels............................... | | 16 |
| Storeships ................................ | | 8 |
| Advice Boats............................... | | 2 |

| Rates or Classes | Guns. | Number. |
|---|---|---|
| Armed Vessels .......................... | | 7 |
| Tenders ...................... | | 2 |
| Galleot ......................... | | 1 |
| Tenders ................................ | | 4 |
| Cutters................................. | | 25 |
| Armed Schooners......................... | | 11 |
| Schooners ............................... | | 4 |
| Lugger.................................. | | 1 |
| Hospital Ships........................... | | 4 |
| Prison Ships ............................ | | 5 |
| Gun Vessels*............................ | | 125 |
| Barge Magazine ......................... | | 1 |

| Rates or Classes | Guns. | Number. |
|---|---|---|
| Latteen Settee............................ | | 1 |
| Yachts .................................. | | 11 |
| Gun Schooners ........................... | | 12 |
| Receiving Ships .......................... | | 15 |
| Hoys, Lighters, and Transports ............. | | 62 |
| Hulks................................... | | 11 |
| Of 56 Guns and under...... | | 774 |
| Total.... | | 949 |

*Originally called* Gun Boats.

# Appendix 4

# Further Abstracts of the Strength of the Royal Navy to 1983

**War-time January 1814**

| Rates or Classes | Guns | In commission | In ordinary | Total |
|---|---|---|---|---|
| Three-deckers | | | | |
| 1st. | 120 | 2 | — | 2 |
| | 112 | 2 | — | 2 |
| | 100 | 3 | — | 3 |
| 2nd. | 98 | 5 | 3 | 8 |
| Two-deckers | | | | |
| 3rd. | 80 | 1 | 4 | 5 |
| | 74 | 85 | 12 | 97 |
| | 64 | 1 | — | 1 |
| Total line | | 99 | 19 | 118 |
| 4th. | 56 | 3 | — | 3 |
| | 50 | 5 | 2 | 7 |
| 5th. | 44 | 2 | — | 2 |
| Single-deckers | | | | |
| (Frigates) | 44 | 1 | — | 1 |
| | 40 | 6 | 2 | 8 |
| | 38 | 51 | 6 | 57 |
| | 36 | 51 | 3 | 54 |
| | 32 | 12 | — | 12 |
| 6th. | 24 | 2 | 2 | 4 |
| Post-ships | 22 | 10 | — | 10 |
| | 20 | 13 | 2 | 15 |
| Sloops | 18 | 121 | 4 | 125 |
| | 16 | 54 | 1 | 55 |
| | 14 | 14 | — | 14 |
| | 10 | 28 | — | 28 |
| Gun-brigs | 14 | 3 | — | 3 |
| | 12 | 67 | 2 | 69 |
| | 10 | 1 | — | 1 |
| Cutters | 14 | 8 | — | 8 |
| | 12 | 8 | — | 8 |
| | 10 | 24 | — | 24 |
| | 8 | 2 | — | 2 |
| | 6 | 1 | — | 1 |

| | | | | |
|---|---|---|---|---|
| Bombs | 4 | 10 | — | 10 |
| | 8 | | | |
| & 2 mortars | | 8 | — | 8 |
| Total cruiser | | 500 | 24 | 524 |
| Troop-ships | — | 28 | — | 28 |
| Store-ships | — | 15 | — | 15 |
| Surveying-vessels | — | 3 | — | 3 |
| Advice-boats and Tenders | — | 4 | — | 4 |
| Grand total | | 654 | 43 | 697 |

At the beginning of 1820, four-and-a-half years after the end of the Napoleonic Wars, the Navy's peace-time strength was as follows.

**Peace-time, January 1820**

| Rates or Classes | Guns | In commission | In ordinary | Total |
|---|---|---|---|---|
| Three-deckers | | | | |
| 1st. | 120 | — | 5 | 5 |
| | 112 | — | 2 | 2 |
| | 108 | 1 | 1 | 2 |
| | 106 | 1 | — | 1 |
| | 104 | — | 6 | 6 |
| Two-deckers | | | | |
| 2nd. | 84 | — | 3 | 3 |
| | 80 | 1 | 5 | 6 |
| 3rd. | 78 | 2 | 6 | 8 |
| | 76 | 3 | 5 | 8 |
| | 74 | 6 | 58 | 64 |
| Total line | | 14 | 91 | 105 |
| 4th. | 60 | 2 | 1 | 3 |
| | 58 | 1 | 5 | 6 |
| Frigates | | | | |
| | 50 | 4 | 1 | 5 |
| | 48 | 1 | 5 | 6 |
| | 46 | 5 | 35 | 40 |

| | Guns | In commission | In ordinary | Total |
|---|---|---|---|---|
| | 44 | 1 | 1 | 2 |
| | 42 | 7 | 25 | 32 |
| 6th. | 32 | — | 2 | 2 |
| | 26 | 9 | 2 | 11 |
| | 24 | 5 | 3 | 8 |
| Sloops | | | | |
| | 22 | 1 | — | 1 |
| | 20 | 11 | 5 | 16 |
| | 18 | 23 | 41 | 64 |
| | 16 | — | 1 | 1 |
| | 14 | 1 | 3 | 4 |
| | 10 | 6 | 1 | 7 |
| Bombs | — | — | 5 | 5 |
| Gun-brigs | 12 | 6 | 8 | 14 |
| Cutters | 10 to 14 | 9 | 2 | 11 |
| Total cruisers | | 92 | 146 | 238 |
| Troop-ships | — | 1 | 6 | 7 |
| Store-ships | — | 5 | 5 | 10 |
| Discovery-ships | — | 2 | — | 2 |
| Surveying-vessels | — | 6 | 1 | 7 |
| Grand total | | 120 | 249 | 369 |

The next abstract is taken from the last year that the battle-fleet was a purely sailing one, 1845. The emphasis has shifted since 1820 to the employment of very large vessels in home and Mediterranean waters, and very small ones in distant parts.

### September 1845—The sailing navy

| Rates or Classes | Guns | In commission | In ordinary | Total |
|---|---|---|---|---|
| Three-deckers | | | | |
| 1st. | 120 | 3 | 10 | 13 |
| | 110 | 1 | 5 | 6 |
| | 104 | 2 | 5 | 7 |
| Two-deckers | | | | |
| 2nd. | 92 | 1 | 1 | 2 |
| | 90 | 2 | 1 | 3 |
| | 84 | 2 | 7 | 9 |
| | 80 | 4 | 2 | 6 |
| 3rd. | 78 | — | 5 | 5 |
| | 76 | — | 4 | 4 |
| | 74 | — | 3 | 3 |
| | 72 | 1 | 28 | 29 |
| Total line | | 16 | 71 | 87 |
| 4th. | 50 | 7 | 12 | 19 |
| 5th. | 46 | — | 3 | 3 |
| | 44 | 1 | 13 | 14 |
| | 42 | 4 | 22 | 26 |
| | 38 | — | 1 | 1 |

| | Guns | In commission | In ordinary | Total |
|---|---|---|---|---|
| 6th. | 36 | 3 | 1 | 4 |
| | 30 | — | 1 | 1 |
| | 26 | 11 | 9 | 20 |
| | 24 | 1 | 3 | 4 |
| Sloops | 22 | — | 4 | 4 |
| | 20 | 1 | 5 | 6 |
| | 19 | 1 | — | 1 |
| | 18 | 12 | 5 | 17 |
| | 16 | 17 | 6 | 23 |
| | 12 | 7 | — | 7 |
| | 10 | 7 | 6 | 13 |
| | 6 | 10 | 2 | 12 |
| Total sailing cruisers | | 82 | 93 | 175 |
| Survey-vessels | | 6 | — | 6 |
| Discovery-ships | | 2 | 2 | 4 |
| Troop-ships | | 3 | 1 | 4 |
| Total | | 109 | 167 | 276 |

### September 1845—The steam navy

It will be noted in this and subsequent abstracts from lists of the steam navy, that rating by numbers of guns becomes rather meaningless, as some sloops mount as many or more guns than some frigates. One reason was that the paddles took up so much room that an armament of a small number of large guns was preferred, and in the early frigates this was restricted to the upper-deck only. The other reason was that if a cruiser was a post-ship, that is to say a captain's command, then she had to be rated as a frigate, even if she had been a sloop before, and vice-versa.

| Class | Guns | In commission | In ordinary | Total |
|---|---|---|---|---|
| Paddle-frigates | 21 | 1 | — | 1 |
| | 16 | 2 | — | 2 |
| | 10 | — | 1 | 1 |
| | 6 | 1 | 2 | 3 |
| Screw-sloop | 11 | 1 | — | 1 |
| Paddle-sloops | 6 | 11 | 1 | 12 |
| | 5 | 3 | 1 | 4 |
| | 4 | 2 | — | 2 |
| Paddle-vessels | 6 | 1 | — | 1 |
| | 4 | 3 | — | 3 |
| | 3 | 6 | 1 | 7 |
| Steam cruisers | | 31 | 6 | 37 |
| Grand total, steam and sail | | 140 | 173 | 313 |

### September 1855

Ten years later, in the second year of the Russian War, the strength of the Navy is shown to be enormously increased, especially in the proportion of steamers. Indeed, as it was by then accepted that the battle-fleet must fight under steam, the sailing liners scarcely deserving of the name, and none of them went to the Baltic, where the Russian battle-fleet might have been encountered.

| Rates or Classes | | Guns | Number | | |
|---|---|---|---|---|---|
| | | | In commission | In ordinary | Total |
| Steam-assisted | { | 131 | 1 | — | 1 |
| Three-deckers | | 130 | — | 1 | 1 |
| 1st. | | 121 | 1 | — | 1 |
| | | 102 | 1 | — | 1 |
| | | 101 | 1 | — | 1 |
| Two-deckers | { | 91 | 6 | — | 6 |
| 2nd. | | 90 | 3 | — | 3 |
| | | 80 | 3 | 3 | 6 |
| 3rd. | | 70 | 1 | — | 1 |
| | | 60 | 9 | — | 9 |
| Steam line | | | 26 | 4 | 30 |
| Sailing | { | 120 | 4 | 4 | 8 |
| Three-deckers | | 116 | 1 | — | 1 |
| 1st. | | 104 | 1 | 4 | 5 |
| | | 102 | 1 | — | 1 |
| | | 101 | 1 | — | 1 |
| Two-deckers | { | 90 | 3 | 2 | 5 |
| 2nd. | | 84 | 4 | 6 | 10 |
| | | 80 | — | 7 | 7 |
| | | 78 | — | 6 | 6 |
| | | 72 | 1 | 6 | 7 |
| | | 70 | 1 | 2 | 3 |
| Sailing line | | | 17 | 37 | 54 |
| Total line | | | 43 | 41 | 84 |
| Steam-assisted cruisers | { | 51 | 2 | — | 2 |
| Screw-frigates | | 33 | 1 | — | 1 |
| | | 31 | 1 | — | 1 |
| | | 21 | 1 | — | 1 |
| Paddle-frigates | | 28 | 1 | — | 1 |
| | | 24 | 1 | — | 1 |
| | | 22 | 1 | — | 1 |
| | | 21 | 1 | — | 1 |
| | | 18 | 1 | — | 1 |
| | | 16 | 5 | — | 5 |
| | | 6 | 7 | — | 7 |
| Screw-sloops | | 21 | 1 | — | 1 |
| | | 20 | 3 | 1 | 4 |
| | | 17 | 5 | — | 5 |
| | | 14 | 6 | — | 6 |
| | | 11 | 1 | — | 1 |
| | | 9 | 4 | — | 4 |
| | | 8 | 5 | — | 5 |
| | | 6 | 1 | — | 1 |

| Rates or classes | Guns | Number | | |
|---|---|---|---|---|
| | | In commission | In ordinary | Total |
| Paddle-sloops | 8 | 1 | — | 1 |
| | 6 | 25 | 3 | 28 |
| | 5 | 2 | — | 2 |
| Screw-vessels | 4 | 5 | 6 | 11 |
| | 3 | 2 | — | 2 |
| Paddle-vessels | 5 | 1 | 1 | 2 |
| | 4 | 7 | 3 | 10 |
| | 3 | 13 | 4 | 17 |
| | 2 | 1 | 2 | 3 |
| Screw gun-boats | 2 | 18 | 52 | 70 |
| Mortars | — | — | 3 | 3 |
| Steam cruisers | | 123 | 75 | 198 |
| Sailing cruisers | 50 | 5 | 22 | 27 |
| Frigates | 44 | 1 | 7 | 8 |
| 5th. | 42 | — | 18 | 18 |
| | 40 | 2 | 3 | 5 |
| | 36 | 2 | — | 2 |
| 6th. | 26 | 5 | 7 | 12 |
| | 24 | 2 | — | 2 |
| Sloops | 18–22 | 3 | 6 | 9 |
| | 10–16 | 16 | 18 | 34 |
| | 3–8 | 14 | 11 | 25 |
| Mortars | — | — | 18 | 18 |
| Sailing cruisers | | 50 | 110 | 160 |
| Grand total | | 216 | 226 | 442 |

**September 1860**

For the sake of continuity the following abstract is still based on the number of guns carried in each class, although since 1856 a ship's rating depended entirely on the number of men she carried.

A measure of the continuing build-up of the Navy's strength, is that the battle-fleet in time of peace is larger than it was ten years previously in time of war.

| Classes | Guns | Number | | |
|---|---|---|---|---|
| | | In commission | In ordinary | Total |
| Steam-assisted Three-decker ships of the line | 131 | 1 | 3 | 4 |
| | 121 | 1 | 2 | 3 |
| Two-decker ships of the line | 101 | 3 | 3 | 6 |
| | 91 | 9 | 5 | 14 |
| | 90 | 8 | 7 | 15 |

| | | | |
|---|---|---|---|
| 86 | 1 | — | 1 |
| 81 | — | 1 | 1 |
| 80 | 4 | 6 | 10 |
| 70 | 1 | — | 1 |
| 60 | 8 | 1 | 9 |
| **Steam line** | **36** | **28** | **64** |

Sailing
Three-decker ships of the line

| | | | |
|---|---|---|---|
| 120 | 1 | — | 1 |
| 104 | 1 | — | 1 |
| 101 | 1 | — | 1 |
| Two-decker ships of the line 84 | 4 | 6 | 10 |
| 80 | — | 2 | 2 |
| 78 | 1 | 3 | 4 |
| 72 | 3 | 3 | 6 |
| 70 | 1 | — | 1 |
| **Sailing line** | **12** | **14** | **26** |
| **Total line** | **48** | **42** | **90** |

Screw-frigates

| | | | |
|---|---|---|---|
| 51 | 10 | 11 | 21 |
| 50 | — | 1 | 1 |
| 47 | 1 | — | 1 |
| 40 | 1 | — | 1 |
| 36 | 1 | — | 1 |
| 32 | 2 | — | 2 |
| 31 | 2 | 1 | 3 |
| 26 | 1 | 1 | 2 |
| 25 | 1 | — | 1 |
| 13 | 1 | — | 1 |
| **Screw-frigates** | **20** | **14** | **34** |

Paddle-frigates

| | | | |
|---|---|---|---|
| 28 | 1 | — | 1 |
| 22 | 1 | — | 1 |
| 18 | 1 | — | 1 |
| 16 | 4 | 1 | 5 |
| **Paddle-frigates** | **7** | **1** | **8** |

Sailing-frigate

| | | | |
|---|---|---|---|
| 50 | — | 18 | 18 |
| 44 | — | 8 | 8 |
| 42 | — | 15 | 15 |
| 41 | 1 | 4 | 5 |
| 36 | 1 | — | 1 |
| 28 | — | 1 | 1 |
| 26 | 2 | 10 | 12 |
| 24 | — | 2 | 2 |
| **Sailing-frigates** | **4** | **58** | **62** |
| **Total frigates** | **31** | **73** | **104** |

Screw-sloops

| | | | |
|---|---|---|---|
| 22 | 2 | 2 | 4 |
| 21 | 9 | 5 | 14 |
| 17 | 7 | 5 | 12 |
| 16 | 1 | — | 1 |
| 15 | — | 1 | 1 |
| 14 | 1 | — | 1 |
| 13 | 2 | — | 2 |
| 12 | — | 1 | 1 |
| 11 | 5 | 2 | 7 |
| 9 | 3 | 1 | 4 |
| 8 | 1 | 3 | 4 |
| 6 | 6 | 1 | 7 |
| 4 | 8 | 10 | 18 |
| **Screw-sloops** | **45** | **31** | **76** |

Paddle-sloops

| | | | |
|---|---|---|---|
| 21 | 1 | — | 1 |
| 12 | 1 | — | 1 |
| 8 | 2 | — | 2 |
| 6 | 18 | 12 | 30 |
| 5 | 2 | — | 2 |
| 4 | 1 | — | 1 |
| 3 | 2 | — | 2 |
| **Paddle-sloops** | **27** | **12** | **39** |

Sailing-sloops

| | | | |
|---|---|---|---|
| 22 | — | 1 | 1 |
| 20 | — | 1 | 1 |
| 19 | — | 1 | 1 |
| 18 | 1 | 4 | 5 |
| 16 | 1 | 7 | 8 |
| 14 | — | 4 | 4 |
| 12 | 2 | 15 | 17 |
| 8 | — | 3 | 3 |
| 6 | 1 | 3 | 4 |
| 4 | — | 1 | 1 |
| **Sailing-sloops** | **5** | **40** | **45** |
| **Total sloops** | **77** | **83** | **160** |

Screw gun-vessels

| | | | |
|---|---|---|---|
| 5 | 3 | 10 | 13 |
| 4 | 4 | 2 | 6 |
| 2 | — | 1 | 1 |
| 1 | 4 | — | 4 |
| **Screw gun-vessels** | **11** | **13** | **24** |

Steam vessels (paddle-wheel)

| | | | |
|---|---|---|---|
| 6 | — | 2 | 2 |
| 5 | 2 | — | 2 |
| 4 | 2 | 1 | 3 |
| 3 | 6 | 11 | 17 |
| 2 | 3 | 2 | 5 |
| 1 | 3 | — | 3 |
| **Steam vessels** | **16** | **16** | **32** |
| **Screw-Mortars** — | — | 3 | 3 |
| **Total cruisers** | **135** | **188** | **323** |
| **Grand total** | **183** | **230** | **413** |

**Iron-hulled warships built or purchased for the Royal Navy up to 1860**

| | 1841 | 1842 | 1844 | 1845 | 1846 | 1847 | 1849 | 1854 | 1855 | 1856 | Total |
|---|---|---|---|---|---|---|---|---|---|---|---|
| Screw-frigates | | | | | | | 4 | | | | 4 |
| Paddle-frigates | | | 1 | | | | | | | | 1 |
| Screw-sloops | | | | | 1 | | | | | | 1 |
| Paddle-sloops | | | 1 | | | | | | | | 1 |
| Screw gun vessels | | | | | 1 | | | | | | 1 |
| Paddle gun vessels | 3 | 2 | 1 | 5 | 2 | 3 | 3 | 3 | 3 | 2 | 27 |
| Armoured floating-batteries | | | | | | | | | | 3 | 3 |
| | | | | | | | | | Grand total | | 38 |

The purchases were all paddle gun vessels: one in each of the years 1844, 1847 and 1854, and two in 1855.

Although built as frigates, they were never commissioned as warships, but were converted into troopships. This was because of the unsatisfactory results of the firing tests made on the hull of the iron paddle-steamer *Ruby*, after the frigates were already ordered.

**September 1865**

| Class | Plan of armament | Guns | In commission Screw | In commission Paddle | In ordinary Screw | In ordinary Paddle | Total |
|---|---|---|---|---|---|---|---|
| The battle-fleet | | | | | | | |
| Sea-going ironclads (7 iron-built, 3 iron-cased) | Broadside | | 8 | | 2 | | 10 |
| Steam wooden line | | | | | | | |
| | | 121 | | | 1 | | 1 |
| | | 115 | | | 1 | | 1 |
| | | 107 | | | 1 | | 1 |
| | | 102 | 1 | | | | 1 |
| | | 97 | | | 1 | | 1 |
| | | 81 | 3 | | 7 | | 10 |
| | | 79 | | | 5 | | 5 |
| | | 78 | 2 | | 6 | | 8 |
| | | 76 | | | 2 | | 2 |
| | | 74 | 1 | | 1 | | 2 |
| | | 73 | 2 | | 2 | | 4 |
| | | 72 | 2 | | | | 2 |
| | | 71 | 1 | | | | 1 |
| | | 68 | 1 | | 6 | | 7 |
| | | 62 | | | 1 | | 1 |
| | | 60 | 2 | | | | 2 |
| Total line | | | 15 | | 34 | | 49 |
| Total battle-fleet | | | 23 | | 36 | | 59 |

| Class | Plan of armament | Guns | In commission Screw | In commission Paddle | In ordinary Screw | In ordinary Paddle | Total |
|---|---|---|---|---|---|---|---|
| Armoured coast-defence ships | Cupola central-battery | | 2 | | | | 2 |
| | | | | | | 1 | 1 |
| Iron floating-batteries | | | | | 1 | 2 | 3 |
| Cruisers Steam frigates | | | | | | | |
| | | 46 | 1 | | | | 1 |
| | | 40 | | | 1 | | 1 |
| | | 39 | 6 | | 8 | | 14 |
| | | 35 | 5 | | 5 | | 10 |
| | | 31 | | | 1 | | 1 |
| | | 30 | | | 2 | | 2 |
| | | 26 | 1 | | 1 | | 2 |
| | | 23 | 2 | | | | 2 |
| | | 21 | | 1 | | | 1 |
| | | 18 | | 1 | | | 1 |
| | | 16 | | 2 | | | 2 |
| | | 6 | | 1 | | 1 | 2 |
| Total frigates | | | 15 | 5 | 18 | 1 | 39 |
| Steam corvettes | | | | | | | |
| | | 22 | 1 | | | | 1 |
| | | 21 | 2 | | 3 | | 5 |
| | | 20 | 1 | | 3 | | 4 |
| | | 17 | | | 1 | | 1 |
| | | 16 | 1 | | | | 1 |
| | | 15 | | | 1 | | 1 |
| | | 14 | | | 1 | | 1 |
| | | 13 | 2 | | | | 2 |
| Total corvettes | | | 7 | | 9 | | 16 |
| Steam sloops | | 17 | 9 | | 1 | | 10 |
| | | 16 | | 1 | | | 1 |
| | | 15 | 1 | | | | 1 |
| | | 13 | 1 | | | | 1 |
| | | 11 | 6 | | | | 6 |
| | | 9 | 1 | | 1 | | 2 |
| | | 8 | | | 1 | | 1 |
| | | 7 | | 1 | | | 1 |
| | | 6 | 1 | 10 | | 3 | 14 |
| | | 5 | | | 1 | | 1 |
| | | 4 | 1 | | 1 | | 2 |
| | | 3 | | | 1 | 1 | 2 |
| | | 1 | 1 | | | | 1 |
| Total sloops | | | 21 | 12 | 6 | 4 | 43 |

**September 1865**—*continued*

| Class | Guns | In commission Screw | Paddle | In ordinary Screw | Paddle | Total |
|---|---|---|---|---|---|---|
| Steam gun vessels | | | | | | |
| | 5 | 16 | | | | 16 |
| | 4 | 11 | | 2 | | 13 |
| | 1 | 2 | | | | 2 |
| Total gun vessels | | 29 | | 2 | | 31 |
| Steam gunboats | | | | | | |
| | 2–4 | 26 | | 82 | | 108 |
| Steam paddle-vessels (iron) | | | | | | |
| | 6 | | | | 1 | 1 |
| | 3 | | 1 | | 1 | 2 |
| | 1 | | 1 | | | 1 |
| | None | | 5 | | | 5 |
| Steam paddle-vessels (wood) | | | | | | |
| | 5 | | 1 | | | 1 |
| | 4 | | | | 1 | 1 |
| | 3 | | 2 | | | 2 |
| | 2 | | 5 | | 1 | 6 |
| | 1 | | | | 2 | 2 |
| | None | | 12 | | 5 | 17 |
| Total paddle-vessels | | 27 | | 11 | | 38 |

168 in commission
172 in ordinary
——
Grand total 340
——

In addition to the fighting ships there were 6 iron screw troopships, 5 iron screw store-ships, 2 mortar vessels, and over 200 sailing ships. The latter were used by now only for harbour duties.

**September 1875**

| Class | Plan of armament | In commission | In ordinary | Total |
|---|---|---|---|---|
| The battle-fleet | | | | |
| Iron-hulled ironclads | Broadside | 7 | 3 | 10 |
| | Central-battery | 10 | | 10 |
| | Turret | 2 | | 2 |
| Wooden-hulled ironclads | Broadside | 1 | 8 | 9 |
| | Central-battery | 3 | 1 | 4 |
| Total battle-fleet | | 23 | 12 | 35 |
| Armoured coast-defence ships | Turret | | 8 | 8 |

| Class | Plan of armament | In commission | In ordinary | Total |
|---|---|---|---|---|
| Armoured floating-batteries | Broadside | 1 | 2 | 3 |
| Total armour | | 24 | 22 | 46 |
| Cruisers | | | | |
| Iron-hulled frigates | Broadside | 1 | 2 | 3 |
| Wooden-hulled frigates | Broadside | 8 | 6 | 14 |
| Paddle-frigates | Broadside | 1 | 2 | 3 |
| Iron-hulled corvettes | Broadside | 3 | 1 | 4 |
| Wooden-hulled corvettes | Broadside | 14 | 12 | 26 |
| Composite sloops | Broadside | 6 | | 6 |
| Wooden sloops | Broadside | 6 | 8 | 14 |
| Paddle-sloops | Broadside | 3 | 5 | 8 |
| Composite gun vessels | Central-mounted | 15 | 4 | 19 |
| Wooden gun vessels | Central-mounted | 14 | 5 | 19 |
| Iron paddle-vessels | Central-mounted | 2 | 2 | 4 |
| Composite paddle-vessels | Central-mounted | | 1 | 1 |
| Wooden paddle-vessels | Central-mounted | 5 | 4 | 9 |
| Iron gunboats | | | 21 | 21 |
| Composite gunboats | | 12 | 3 | 15 |
| Wooden gunboats | | 9 | 14 | 23 |
| Iron torpedo vessels | | | 1 | 1 |
| Total cruisers | | 99 | 91 | 190 |
| Grand total | | 123 | 113 | 236 |

Twenty-four steam liners are listed, some in commission for port duties; of non-combat ships, 15 were iron troop- and store-ships. All ships listed are screw unless stated to the contrary.

**September 1885**

| Class | In commission | In reserve | Total |
|---|---|---|---|
| Ironclads not rigged for sail | 7 | 1 | 8 |
| Ironclads rigged for sail | 14 | 12 | 26 |
| Coast-defence ironclads | 4 | 11 | 15 |
| Armoured cruisers | 3 | | 3 |
| Masted iron frigates | 1 | 2 | 3 |
| Second-class cruisers | 2 | 3 | 5 |
| Torpedo-cruisers | | 10 | 10 |
| Rams | 1 | | 1 |
| Paddle-frigates | 1 | 1 | 2 |
| Corvettes | 26 | 21 | 47 |
| Sloops | 21 | 5 | 26 |
| Gun vessels | 19 | 19 | 38 |
| Gunboats | 36 | 49 | 85 |
| Dispatch vessels | 8 | 5 | 13 |
| Grand total | 143 | 139 | 282 |

**The state of the Royal Navy's ironclad fleet in September 1885, including those ships discarded since 1860**

| | Construction | Armour-belt max. thickness | Armament Plan | Guns | Max. speed steaming (knots) | Rigged or not | In or out of commission | Launched | Com-pleted |
|---|---|---|---|---|---|---|---|---|---|
| *Warrior* | Iron | Iron 4½″ Teak backing 18″ | Broadside | 4 8″ M.L.R. 28 7″ M.L.R. | 14·3 | Rigged | Out | 1860 | 1861 |
| *Black Prince* | Iron | Iron 4½″ Teak backing 18″ | Broadside | 4 8″ M.L.R. 24 7″ M.L.R. | 13·9 | Rigged | Out | 1861 | 1862 |
| *Resistance* | Iron | Iron 4½″ | Broadside | 2 8″ M.L.R. 14 7″ M.L.R. | 11·8 | Rigged | Out | 1861 | 1862 |
| *Defence* | Iron | Iron 4½″ | Broadside | 2 8″ M.L.R. 24 7″ M.L.R. | 11·3 | Rigged | Out | 1861 | 1861 |
| *Hector* | Iron | Iron 4½″ | Broadside | 2 8″ M.L.R. 16 7″ M.L.R. | 11·5 | Rigged | In | 1862 | 1864 |
| *Valiant* | Iron | Iron 4½ | Broadside | 2 8″ M.L.R. 16 7″ M.L.R. | 11·5 | Rigged | Out | 1863 | 1868 |
| *Royal Oak* | Iron-cased on a wooden hull | Iron 4½″ | Broadside | (Originally) 11 7″ B.L.R. 24 68-pdrs. | 12·5 | Rigged | Sold Sept. 1885 | 1862 | 1863 |
| *Prince Albert* (coast-defence ship) | Iron-cased on a wooden hull | Iron 4½″ | Turret | 4 9″ M.L.R. | 12·5 | Not rigged | Sold March 1882 | 1862 | 1864 |
| *Royal Sovereign* | Iron-cased on a wooden hull | Iron 5½″ | Turret | 5 300-pdrs. M.L. | 11 | Not rigged | | 1857 | 1864 |
| *Caledonia* | Iron-cased on a wooden hull | Iron 4½″ | Broadside | (Originally) 10 7″ B.L.R. 8 100-pdrs. S.B. 12 68-pdrs. S.B. | 12·9 | Rigged | Sold Sept. 1886 | 1862 | 1865 |
| *Ocean* | Iron-cased on a wooden hull | Iron 4½″ | Broadside | (Originally) 24 7″ M.L.R. | 12·7 | Rigged | Sold 1882 | 1882 | 1866 |
| *Achilles* | Iron | Iron 4½″ Teak backing 18″ | Broadside | 12 9″ M.L.R. | 14·3 | Rigged | Out | 1863 | 1864 |
| *Research* (coast-defence ship) | Iron-cased on a wooden hull | Iron 4½″ Teak backing 19″ | Central-battery | (Originally) 4 100-pdrs. S.B. | 10·3 | Rigged | Sold 1887 | 1863 | 1864 |
| *Enterprise* (coast-defence ship) | Iron-cased on a wooden hull | Iron 4½″ Teak backing 19″ | Central-battery | 2 100-pdrs. 2 110-pdrs. B.L. | 9·9 | Rigged | Sold 1885 | 1864 | 1866 |
| *Favorite* (armoured corvette) | Iron-cased on a wooden hull | Iron 4½″ Teak backing 19″ | Central-battery | 8 100-pdrs. S.B. | 11·8 | Rigged | Sold March 1886 | 1864 | 1866 |
| *Lord Clyde* | Iron-cased on a wooden hull | Iron 5½″ Oak hull 31½″ | Broadside | (Originally) 24 7″ M.L.R. | 13·5 | Rigged | Sold 1875 | 1864 | 1866 |
| *Lord Warden* | Iron-cased on a wooden hull | Iron 4½″ Oak hull 31½″ | Broadside | 2 9″ M.L.R. 14 8″ M.L.R. 2 7″ M.L.R. | 13·5 | Rigged | Out | 1865 | 1867 |
| *Minotaur* | Iron | Iron 5½″ Teak backing 10″ | Broadside | 15 9″ M.L.R. 2 6″ B.L. | 14·5 | Rigged | In | 1863 | 1868 |

**The state of the Royal Navy's ironclad fleet in September 1885**—*continued*

| | Construction | Armour-belt max. thickness | Armament Plan | Guns | Max. speed steaming (knots) | Rigged or not | In or out of commission | Launched | Com-pleted |
|---|---|---|---|---|---|---|---|---|---|
| *Agincourt* | Iron | Iron 5½″ Teak backing 10″ | Broadside | 15 9″ M.L.R. 2 6″ B.L. | 14·75 | Rigged | In | 1865 | 1867 |
| *Northumberland* | Iron | Iron 4½″ Teak backing 10″ | Broadside | 7 9″ M.L.R. | 14·25 | Rigged | Out | 1866 | 1868 |
| *Bellerophon* | Iron | Iron 4½″ Teak backing 22″ | Broadside | 10 8″ B.L. 4 6″ B.L. 6 4″ B.L. | 14·17 | Rigged | Out | 1865 | 1866 |
| *Pallas* (armoured corvette) | Iron | Iron 4½″ Teak backing 22″ | Central battery | (Originally) 2 7″ B.L. 4 7″ M.L.R. | 13 | Rigged | Sold April 1886 | 1865 | 1866 |
| *Zealous* | Iron-cased on a wooden hull | Iron 4½″ Teak backing 30″ | Broadside | 20 7″ M.L.R. | 11·7 | Rigged | Sold Sept. 1886 | 1864 | 1866 |
| *Royal Alfred* | Iron-cased on a wooden hull | Iron 6″ Teak backing 30″ | Broadside | 10 9″ M.L.R. 8 7″ M.L.R. | 12·5 | Rigged | Sold 1885 | 1864 | 1867 |
| *Penelope* | Iron | Iron 6″ Teak backing 11″ | Central-battery | 8 8″ M.L.R. 3 5″ B.L.R. | 12·7 | Rigged | Out | 1867 | 1868 |
| *Hercules* | Iron | Iron 9″ Teak backing 12″ | Central-battery | 8 10″ M.L.R. 2 9″ M.L.R. 4 7″ M.L.R. | 14·7 | Rigged | In | 1868 | 1868 |
| *Monarch* | Iron | Iron 7″ Teak backing 12″ | Turret | 4 12″ M.L.R. 2 9″ M.L.R. 1 7″ M.L.R. | 15 | Rigged | Out | 1868 | 1869 |
| *Repulse* | Iron-cased on a wooden hull | Iron 6″ Teak backing and hull 31″ | Broadside | 12 8″ M.L.R. | 12·5 | Rigged | Out | 1868 | 1870 |
| *Captain* | Iron | Iron 7″ Teak backing 12″ | Turret | 4 12″ M.L.R. 2 7″ M.L.R. | 14·25 | Rigged | Foundered Sept. 1870 | 1869 | 1870 |
| *Audacious* | Iron | Iron 8″ Teak backing 10″ | Central-battery | 10 9″ M.L.R. 4 6″ M.L.R. | 13 | Rigged | In | 1869 | 1870 |
| *Invincible* | Iron | Iron 8″ Teak backing 10″ | Central-battery | 10 9″ M.L.R. 4 6″ M.L.R. | 13 | Rigged | In | 1869 | 1870 |
| *Iron Duke* | Iron | Iron 8″ Teak backing 10″ | Central-battery | 10 9″ M.L.R. 4 6″ M.L.R. | 13 | Rigged | In | 1870 | 1871 |
| *Vanguard* | Iron | Iron 8″ Teak backing 10″ | Central-battery | 10 9″ M.L.R. 4 6″ M.L.R. | 13 | Rigged | Sunk in collision Sept. 1875 | 1869 | 1870 |
| *Swiftsure* | Iron | Iron 8″ Teak backing 10″ | Central-battery | 10 9″ M.L.R. 4 6″ M.L.R. | 13·7 | Rigged | In | 1870 | 1872 |
| *Triumph* | Iron | Iron 8″ Teak backing 10″ | Central-battery | 10 9″ M.L.R. 4 6″ M.L.R. | 13·7 | Rigged | In | 1870 | 1873 |

| | Construction | Armour-belt max. thickness | Armament Plan | Guns | Max. speed steaming (knots) | Rigged or not | In or out of commission | Launched | Completed |
|---|---|---|---|---|---|---|---|---|---|
| *Sultan* | Iron | Iron 9″ Teak backing 12″ | Central-battery | 8 10″ M.L.R. 4 9″ M.L.R. 7 20-pdrs. B.L. | 14 | Rigged | In | 1870 | 1871 |
| *Devastation* | Iron | Iron 12″ Teak backing 18″ | Turret | 4 12″ M.L.R. | 13·8 | Not rigged | In | 1871 | 1873 |
| *Thunderer* | Iron | Iron 12″ Teak backing 18″ | Turret | 2 12·5″ M.L.R. 2 12″ M.L.R. | 13·4 | Not rigged | In | 1872 | 1877 |
| *Dreadnought* | Iron | Iron 14″ Teak backing 18″ | Turret | 4 12·5″ M.L.R. | 14 | Not rigged | In | 1875 | 1879 |
| *Alexandra* | Iron | Iron 12″ Teak backing 12″ | Central-battery | 2 11″ M.L.R. 10 10″ M.L.R. 6 13-cwt. B.L. | 15 | Rigged | In | 1875 | 1877 |
| *Temeraire* | Iron | Iron 11″ Teak backing 12″ | Open barbettes | 4 11″ M.L.R. 4 10″ M.L.R. 6 20-pdrs. | 14·6 | Rigged | In | 1876 | 1877 |
| *Inflexible* | Iron | Iron 24″ Teak backing 17″ | Turret | 4 16″ M.L.R. 6 20-pdrs. | 14·7 | Rigged | Out | 1876 | 1881 |
| *Ajax* | Iron | Iron 18″ Teak backing 18″ | Turret | 4 12·5″ M.L.R. 2 6″ B.L. | 13 | Not rigged | In | 1880 | 1883 |
| *Agamemnon* | Iron | Iron 18″ Teak backing 18″ | Turret | 4 12·5″ M.L.R. 2 6″ B.L. | 13 | Not rigged | In | 1879 | 1883 |
| *Belleisle* | Iron | Iron 12″ Teak backing 16″ | Central-battery | 4 12″ M.L.R. 4 20-pdrs. | 12 | Not rigged | In | 1876 | 1878 |
| *Orion* | Iron | Iron 12″ Teak backing 16″ | Central-battery | 4 12″ M.L.R. 4 20-pdrs. | 12 | Not rigged | In | 1879 | 1882 |
| *Superb* | Iron | Iron 12″ Teak backing 12″ | Central-battery | 16 10″ M.L.R. 6 20-pdrs. B.L. | 13 | Rigged | In | 1875 | 1880 |
| *Neptune* | Iron | Iron 12″ Teak backing 15″ | Turret | 4 12″ M.L.R. 2 9″ M.L.R. 6 20-pdrs. | 14 | Rigged | In | 1878 | 1881 |
| *Colossus* | Iron and steel | Compound 18″ Teak backing 22″ | Turret | 4 12″ B.L. 5 6″ B.L. | 16 | Not rigged | Fitting out | 1882 | 1886 |
| *Edinburgh* | Iron and steel | Compound 18″ Teak backing 22″ | Turret | 4 12″ B.L. 5 6″ B.L. | 16 | Not rigged | Fitting out | 1882 | 1887 |
| *Collingwood* | Iron and steel | Compound 18″ Teak backing 20″ | Open barbettes | 4 12″ B.L. | 16·8 | Not rigged | Fitting out | 1882 | 1887 |
| The Admiral class *Howe* | Iron and steel | Compound 18″ Teak backing 20″ | Open barbettes | 4 13·5″ B.L. 6 6″ B.L. | 17 | Not rigged | Fitting out | 1885 | 1889 |

**The state of the Royal Navy's ironclad fleet in September 1885**—*continued*

| | Construction | Armour-belt max. thickness | Armament Plan | Guns | Max. speed steaming (knots) | Rigged or not | In or out of commission | Launched | Completed |
|---|---|---|---|---|---|---|---|---|---|
| *Rodney* | Iron and steel | Compound 18″ Teak backing 20″ | Open barbettes | 4 13·5″ B.L. 6 6″ B.L. | 17 | Not rigged | Fitting out | 1884 | 1888 |

Of a total of 52 sea-going ironclads built since 1860, 39 survived in September 1885, 22 were in commission, 12 out of commission and 7 were fitting out.

**The battle-fleet at the time of the Diamond Jubilee, July 1897**

| Battleships, 1st class | Construction | Armour | Principal armament Plan | Guns (all breech-loading) | Max. speed (knots) | In or out of commission | Launched | Completed |
|---|---|---|---|---|---|---|---|---|
| *Collingwood* | Iron and steel | Composite 18″ Teak backing 20″ | Open barbettes | 4 12″ | 16·8 | In | 1882 | 1887 |
| The Admiral class of 5 | | | | | | | | |
| *Howe* | Iron and steel | Composite 18″ Teak backing 7″ | Open barbettes | 4 13·5″ 6 6″ | 17·5 | In | 1885 | 1889 |
| *Rodney* | Iron and steel | Composite 18″ Teak backing 7″ | Open barbettes | 4 13·5″ 6 6″ | 17·5 | In | 1884 | 1888 |
| *Anson* | Iron and steel | Composite 18″ Teak backing 7″ | Open barbettes | 4 13·5″ 6 6″ | 17·5 | In | 1886 | 1889 |
| *Camperdown* | Iron and steel | Composite 18″ Teak backing 7″ | Open barbettes | 4 13·5″ 6 6″ | 17·5 | In | 1885 | 1889 |
| *Benbow* | Iron and steel | Composite 18″ Teak backing 7″ | Open barbettes | 2 16·25″ 6 6″ | 17·5 | In | 1885 | 1888 |
| *Sans Pareil* | Iron and steel | Composite 17·75″ Teak backing 7″ | Turret | 2 16·25″ 1 10″ 12 6″ | 17·75 | In | 1887 | 1891 |
| *Trafalgar* | Iron and steel | Composite 20″ Teak backing 10″ | Turret | 4 13·5″ 6 6″ | 16·75 | In | 1887 | 1890 |
| *Nile* | Iron and steel | Composite 20″ Teak backing 10″ | Turret | 4 13·5″ 6 6″ | 16·75 | In | 1888 | 1891 |
| The Royal Sovereign class | | | | | | | | |
| *Royal Sovereign* | Iron and steel | Composite and steel 18″ Teak backing 18″ | Open barbettes | 4 13·5″ 10 6″ | 17·5 | In | 1891 | 1892 |
| *Empress of India* | Iron and steel | Composite and steel 18″ Teak backing 8″ | Open barbettes | 4 13·5″ 10 6″ | 17·5 | In | 1891 | 1893 |
| *Ramillies* | Iron and steel | Composite and steel 18″ Teak backing 8″ | Open barbettes | 4 13·5″ 10 6″ | 17·5 | In | 1892 | 1893 |
| *Repulse* | Iron and steel | Composite and steel 18″ Teak backing 8″ | Open barbettes | 4 13·5″ 10 6″ | 17·5 | In | 1892 | 1894 |
| *Resolution* | Iron and steel | Composite and steel 18″ Teak backing 8″ | Open barbettes | 4 13·5″ 10 6″ | 17·5 | In | 1892 | 1893 |
| *Revenge* | Iron and steel | Composite and steel 18″ Teak backing 8″ | Open barbettes | 4 13·5″ 10 6″ | 17·5 | In | 1892 | 1894 |

| Battleships, 1st class | Construction | Armour | Principal armament | Guns (all breech-loading) | Max. speed (knots) | In or out of commission | Launched | Completed |
| --- | --- | --- | --- | --- | --- | --- | --- | --- |
| | | | Plan | | | | | |
| *Royal Oak* | Iron and steel | Composite and steel 18″ Teak backing 8″ | Open barbettes | 4 13·5″ 10 6″ | 17·5 | In | 1892 | 1894 |
| *Hood* | Iron and steel | Composite and steel 18″ Teak backing 8″ | Turret | 4 13·5″ 10 6″ | 16·7 | In | 1891 | 1893 |
| *Barfleur* | Iron and steel | Composite and steel 12″ Teak backing 9″ | Barbettes with hoods | 4 10″ 10 4·7″ | 18·5 | In | 1892 | 1894 |
| *Centurion* | Iron and steel | Composite and steel 12″ Teak backing 9″ | Barbettes with hoods | 4 10″ 10 4·7″ | 18·5 | In | 1892 | 1894 |
| *Renown* | Steel | Steel 8″ | Barbettes with hoods | 4 10″ 10 6″ | 19·75 | In | 1895 | 1897 |
| The Majestic class | | | | | | | | |
| *Majestic* | Steel | Steel 6″ | Barbettes with hoods | 4 12″ 12 6″ | 18·3 | In | 1895 | 1895 |
| *Magnificent* | Steel | Steel 6″ | Barbettes with hoods | 4 12″ 12 6″ | 18·3 | In | 1894 | 1895 |
| *Prince George* | Steel | Steel 6″ | Barbettes with hoods | 4 12″ 12 6″ | 18·3 | In | 1895 | 1896 |
| *Victorious* | Steel | Steel 6″ | Barbettes with hoods | 4 12″ 12 6″ | 18·3 | In | 1895 | 1896 |
| *Jupiter* | Steel | Steel 6″ | Barbettes with hoods | 4 12″ 12 6″ | 18·3 | In | 1895 | 1897 |
| *Mars* | Steel | Steel 6″ | Barbettes with hoods | 4 12″ 12 6″ | 18·3 | In | 1896 | 1897 |
| *Hannibal* | Steel | Steel 6″ | Barbettes with hoods | 4 12″ 12 6″ | 18·3 | Fitting out | 1896 | 1898 |
| *Caesar* | Steel | Steel 6″ | Barbettes with hoods | 4 12″ 12 6″ | 18·3 | Fitting out | 1896 | 1898 |
| *Illustrious* | Steel | Steel 6″ | Barbettes with hoods | 4 12″ 12 6″ | 18·3 | Fitting out | 1896 | 1898 |

**Abstract of Units of the Royal Navy assembled at Spithead for Queen Victoria's Diamond Jubilee Review 26 June 1897**

| | 1st class | 2nd class | Total |
|---|---|---|---|
| Battleships | 15 | 6 | 21 |
| Cruisers | 15 | 29 | |
| | | 3rd class | |
| | | 9 | 53 |
| Sloops | | | 1 |
| Gunboats | | | 5 |
| Torpedo-gunboats | | | 19 |
| Gun vessels | | | 2 |
| Torpedo-gunboat-destroyers | | | 30 |
| Surveying vessels | | | 2 |
| Sailing brigs | | | 6 |
| | | Grand total | 128 |

**September 1907**

| | In commission | In reserve | Total |
|---|---|---|---|
| Battleships | 41 | 21 | 62 |
| Cruisers, 1st class | 45 | 2 | 47 |
| Cruisers, 2nd class | 31 | 5 | 36 |
| Cruisers, 3rd class | 11 | 5 | 16 |
| Scouts | 8 | | 8 |
| Torpedo-boat-destroyers | 146 | 1 | 147 |
| Torpedo-gunboats | 17 | 1 | 18 |
| Sloops | 9 | 1 | 10 |
| Gunboats | 6 | 2 | 8 |
| Coast gunboats | | 9 | 9 |
| Grand total | 314 | 47 | 361 |

**September 1914**

| | |
|---|---|
| Dreadnoughts | 25 |
| Battleships | 40 |
| Battle-cruisers | 9 |
| Cruisers | 48 |
| Light-cruisers | 74 |
| Destroyers and torpedo-boats | 334 |
| Torpedo-gunboats | 18 |
| Sloops | 10 |
| Gunboats | 5 |
| Submarines | 75 |
| Total | 638 |

**June 1897**

| | In commission | Out of commission | Total |
|---|---|---|---|
| Battleships, 1st class | 27 | 3 (fitting out) | 30 |
| Battleships, 2nd class | 6 | 6 | 12 |
| Battleships, 3rd class | 1 | 10 | 11 |
| Total | 34 | 19 | 53 |
| Cruisers, 1st class | 21 | 10 | 31 |
| Cruisers, 2nd class | 24 | 31 | 55 |
| Cruisers, 3rd class | 30 | 16 | 46 |
| Total | 75 | 57 | 132 |
| Sloops | 15 | 2 | 17 |
| Gunboats | 23 | 4 | 27 |
| Torpedo-gunboats | 19 | 13 | 32 |
| Gun vessels | 1 | 2 | 3 |
| Torpedo-boat-destroyers | 26 | 18 | 44 |
| Coast-defence ships | 3 | 11 | 14 |
| Coast-defence gun-boats | | 40 | 40 |
| Rams | 1 | | 1 |
| Torpedo vessel carrier | | 1 | 1 |
| Dispatch vessels | 2 | | 2 |
| Special-service vessels | 9 | 4 | 13 |
| Surveying vessels | 8 | | 8 |
| Grand total | 216 | 171 | 387 |

**November 1918**

| | |
|---|---|
| Dreadnoughts | 33 |
| Battleships | 31 |
| Battle-cruisers | 9 |
| Heavy cruisers | 19 |
| Old large cruisers | 10 |
| Light-cruisers | 67 |
| Old light-cruisers | 23 |
| Monitors | 36 |
| Destroyers | 527 |
| Torpedo-boats | 91 |
| Sloops | 113 |
| Torpedo-gunboats | 13 |
| Patrol boats | 100 |
| Minesweepers | 81 |
| Coastal motor boats | about 600 |
| Submarines | 164 |
| Aircraft carriers (with flight-decks) | 6 |
| Seaplane carriers | 7 |
| Total | 1750 |

**September 1939**

| | |
|---|---:|
| Battleships | 12 |
| Battle-cruisers | 3 |
| Cruisers (large) | 34 |
| Light-cruisers | 23 |
| Monitors | 3 |
| Aircraft carriers | 7 |
| Seaplane carriers | 1 |
| Destroyers | 164 |
| Minelayers | 1 |
| Escort vessels (ex-destroyers and sloops) | 44 |
| Minesweepers | 40 |
| Patrol boats | 7 |
| Submarines | 51 |
| Motor-torpedo-boats | 24 |
| Motor minesweepers | 2 |
| River gunboats | 23 |
| **Total** | **439** |

The battleships *Queen Elizabeth* and *Valiant* were under reconstruction at the outbreak of war. The *Valiant* was back at sea in December 1939, but the *Queen Elizabeth* was not ready until January 1941.

**April 1945**

| | In commission | In reserve | Total |
|---|---|---|---|
| Battleships | 10 | 3 | 13 |
| Battle-cruisers | 1 | | 1 |
| Aircraft carriers (Fleet) | 12 | | 12 |
| Aircraft carriers (Escort) | 39 | | 39 |
| Cruisers | 55 | 2 | 57 |
| Minelaying cruisers | 3 | 1 | 4 |
| Monitors | 2 | | 2 |
| Destroyers | 194 | 6 | 200 |
| Sloops | 48 | 1 | 49 |
| Frigates | 103 | 1 | 104 |
| Corvettes | 110 | 1 | 111 |
| Fleet minesweepers | 111 | 1 | 112 |
| Motor patrol, torpedo and gunboats | about 1000 | | about 1000 |
| Trawlers and drifters | about 550 | | about 550 |
| Motor minesweepers | 133 | 6 | 139 |
| **Grand total** | **about 2371** | **22** | **about 2393** |

**October 1950**

| | In commission | In reserve | Total |
|---|---|---|---|
| Battleships | 1 | 4 | 5 |
| Aircraft carriers | 9 | 12 | 21 |
| Cruisers | 16 | 10 | 26 |
| Minelaying cruisers | | 3 | 3 |
| Destroyers | 39 | 99 | 138 |
| Frigates | 52 | 78 | 130 |

| | In commission | In reserve | Total |
|---|---|---|---|
| Fleet minesweepers | 14 | 28 | 42 |
| Coastal minesweepers | 10 | | 10 |
| Submarines | 47 | 13 | 60 |
| Monitors | | 1 | 1 |
| Trawlers | 9 | 7 | 16 |
| River gunboats | 1 | | 1 |
| **Grand total** | **198** | **255** | **453** |

**January 1960**

| | In commission | In reserve | Total |
|---|---|---|---|
| Battleships | | 1 | 1 |
| Aircraft carriers (Fleet) | 5 | 4 | 9 |
| Aircraft carriers (Commando) | 1 | | 1 |
| Cruisers | 7 | 6 | 13 |
| Minelaying cruisers | 1 | 2 | 3 |
| Destroyers | 19 | 16 | 35 |
| Frigates | 72 | 45 | 117 |
| Coastal minelayers | | 2 | 2 |
| Fleet minesweepers | 3 | 20 | 23 |
| Coastal minesweepers | 38 | 29 | 67 |
| Inshore minesweepers | 9 | 16 | 25 |
| Submarines | 42 | 8 | 50 |
| Monitors | | 1 | 1 |
| Trawlers | | 9 | 9 |
| Motor-torpedo-gunboats | 2 | | 2 |
| **Grand total** | **199** | **159** | **358** |

**Autumn 1970**

| | In commission | In reserve | Total |
|---|---|---|---|
| Nuclear submarines (Polaris) | 3 | | 3 |
| Nuclear submarines (Hunters) | 4 | 1 | 5 |
| Aircraft carriers (Fleet) | 3 | 2 | 5 |
| Aircraft carriers (Commando) | 2 | | 2 |
| Cruisers | | 2 | 2* |
| Helicopter cruisers | 1 | | 1 |
| Guided missile destroyers | 7 | 1 | 8 |
| Anti-aircraft frigates | 4 | | 4 |
| Anti-submarine frigates | 47 | 11 | 58 |
| Aircraft direction frigates | 4 | | 4 |
| General purpose frigates | 7 | 3 | 10 |
| Destroyers (Radar pickets) | 2 | 16 | 18 |
| Submarines (Conventional) | 14 | 16 | 30 |
| Assault ships | 2 | | 2 |
| Coastal minesweepers | 36 | 28 | 64 |
| Inshore minesweepers | 3 | 3 | 6 |
| Motor-torpedo-gunboats | 3 | 6 | 9 |
| **Grand total** | **142** | **89** | **231** |

* One cruiser rebuilding as a helicopter cruiser

**Spring 1983**

| | |
|---|---|
| Nuclear submarines (Polaris) | 4 |
| Nuclear submarines (hunter killers) | 13 |
| Aircraft carriers | 3 |
| Guided missile destroyers | 14 |
| Guided missile frigates | 41 |
| Submarines (conventional) | 16 |
| Coastal minesweepers | 37 |
| Inshore patrol craft | 22 |
| Assault ships | 2 |
| Total | 152 |

# Appendix 5
# The Naval Surveyors From 1544

## Surveyors of the Navy

| | | |
|---|---|---|
| 1544–1545 William Brooke | 1654–1660 George Payler | 1765–1784 Sir John Williams |
| 1545–1549 Benjamin Gonson | 1660–1667 William Batten | 1778–1784 Edward Hunt |
| 1549–1589 William Wynter | 1667–1672 Thomas Middleton | 1784–1806 Sir John Henslow |
| 1589–1598 Henry Palmer | 1667–1686 John Tippetts | 1793–1813 Sir William Rule |
| 1598–1611 John Trevor | 1686–1688 Sir Anthony Deane[1] | 1806–1822 Sir Henry Peake |
| 1611–1618 Richard Bingley | 1688–1692 Sir John Tippetts | 1813–1831 Joseph Tucker |
| 1618–1625 Thomas Norrey | 1692–1699 Edmund Dummer | 1813–1832 Sir Robert Seppings |
| 1625–1628 Joshua Downing | 1699–1715 Daniel Furzer | 1832–1848 Sir William Symonds |
| 1628–1632 Thomas Aylesbury | 1706–1713 William Lee | 1848–1860 Sir Baldwin Walker, Bart, K.C.B. |
| 1632–1638 Kenrick Edisbury | 1715–1749 Jacob E. Ackworth | |
| 1638–1648 William Batten | 1716–1755 Joshua Allin | 1860–1863 Isaac Watts |
| 1648–1649 William Willoughby | 1755–1765 William Bately | 1863–1870 Sir Edward Reed, K.C.B. |
| 1649–1652 John Hollond | 1755–1771 Sir Thomas Slade | |

## Directors of Naval Construction

| | | |
|---|---|---|
| 1870–1885 Sir Nathaniel Barnaby, K.C.B.[2] | 1924–1930 Sir William Berry, K.C.B. | 1951–1958 Sir Victor Shepheard, K.C.B. |
| | 1930–1936 Sir Arthur Johns, K.C.B. | |
| 1885–1902 Sir William White, K.C.B. | 1936–1944 Sir Stanley Goodall, K.C.B. | 1958–1961 John Chapman, C.B. |
| 1902–1912 Sir Phillip Watts, K.C.B. | | 1961–1966 A. H. Harrison |
| 1912–1933 Sir Eustace Tennyson-d'Eyncourt, Bart. K.C.B. | 1944–1951 Sir Charles Lillicrap, K.C.B. | 1966–1968 C. E. Sherwin |

## Directors of Warship Design

| | | |
|---|---|---|
| 1968–1969 C. E. Sherwin | 1969–1976 N. Hancock | 1976–1977 L. J. Rydill |

## Directors of Ship's Design and Engineering

| | |
|---|---|
| 1977–1981 L. J. Rydill | 1981–1983 P. W. Jarvis |

## Director General Ships

1983 P. W. Jarvis

## Deputy Controller Ships

1983 P. W. Jarvis

## Chief Naval Architects

| | |
|---|---|
| 1979–1983 K. J. Rawson | 1983 K. Foulter |

[1] Was officially designated Commissioner of Current Business.
[2] Was D.N.C. only from 1875; between 1870 and 1872 he was a member of the Council of Constructors and from 1872 to 1875 was chief naval architect.

# Appendix 6

### Two Gun Establishments from

## 'A Sea-man's Grammar, With THE PLAINE Exposition of Smiths Accidence for young Sea-men, enlarged.'

### by Captain John Smith, 1627

(*a*) From the 1627 edition

**A Table of Proportion for the weight and shooting of great Ordnance.**

| | | *The names of the great Peeces.* | The height of the Peeces* | The weight of the peeces | The weight of the shot. | The weight of the powd. | The bredth of the ladle | The length of the ladle | 2400li. of powder makes of shot in a† | Shot point blanke in‡ | Shot randome in |
|---|---|---|---|---|---|---|---|---|---|---|---|
| | | | *Inches* | *Pound* | *Pound* | *Pound* | *Inches* | *Inches* | *Peece* | *Paces* | *Paces* |
| *These Peeces be most serviceable for battery, being within 80 paces to their mark, which is the chief of their forces.* | 1 | A Canon Royall. | 8 1/2 | 8000 | 66 | 30 | 13 1/4 | 24 1/2 | 80 | 16 | 1930 |
| | 2 | A Canon | 8 | 6000 | 60 | 27 | 12 | 24 | 85 | 17 | 2000 |
| | 3 | A Canon Serpentine | 7 1/2 | 5500 | 53 1/3 | 25 | 10 1/2 | 23 1/3 | 96 | 20 | 2000 |
| | 4 | A Bastard Canon | 7 | 4500 | 41 1/4 | 20 | 10 | 22 1/3 | 120 | 18 | 1800 |
| | 5 | A demy Canon | 6 1/2 | 4000 | 30 1/4 | 18 | 9 1/3 | 23 1/4 | 133 | 17 | 1700 |
| | 6 | A Canon Petro | 6 | 3000 | 24 1/4 | 14 | 9 | 23 | 171 | 16 | 1600 |
| *These Peeces be good and also serviceable to be mixt with the above Ordnance for battery to peeces being crost with the rest, as also fit for Castles, Forts and wals to be planted, and for defence.* | 7 | A Culvering | 5 1/2 | 4500 | 17 1/3 | 12 | 8 1/2 | 22 1/3 | 200 | 20 | 2500 |
| | 8 | A Basilisco | 5 | 4000 | 15 1/4 | 10 | 7 1/2 | 22 | 240 | 25 | 3000 |
| | 9 | A demy Culvering | 4 1/2 | 3400 | 9 1/3 | 8 | 6 1/3 | 21 | 300 | 20 | 2500 |
| | 10 | A bastard Culvering | 4 | 3000 | 7 | 6 1/4 | 6 | 20 | 388 | 18 | 1800 |
| | 11 | A Sacre | 3 1/2 | 1400 | 5 1/3 | 5 1/3 | 5 1/2 | 18 | 490 | 17 | 1700 |
| | 12 | A Minion | 3 1/4 | 1000 | 4 | 4 | 4 1/2 | 17 | 660 | 16 | 1600 |
| | 13 | A Faulcon | 2 1/2 | 660 | 2 1/4 | 2 1/4 | 4 1/4 | 15 | 1087 | 15 | 1500 |
| | 14 | A Faulcon | 2 1/3 | 800 | 3 | 3 | 4 1/4 | 15 | 800 | 15 | 1500 |
| *These Peeces are good and serviceable for the field, and most ready for defence.* | 15 | A Faulconet | 2 | 500 | 1 1/4 | 1 1/4 | 3 1/4 | 11 1/4 | 1950 | 4 | 1400 |
| | 16 | A Sarpentine | 1 1/2 | 400 | 1/3 | 1/3 | 2 1/2 | 10 | 7200 | 13 | 1300 |
| | 17 | A Rabonet | 1 | 300 | 1/2 | 1/2 | 1 1/2 | 6 | 4800 | 12 | 1000 |

* *The height is the bore.*

† *2400 lbs represents a last of powder, which was 24 casks of a 100 lbs each, cask and all. This column tables the number of charges to be got from a last of powder for each weight of gun.*

‡ *A pace in this context is 2½ feet, and this column and the end one show the ranges in straight trajectory and the extreme.*

(b) From the 1692 edition

## 86     *The Sea-mans Grammar.*

A Table wherein is deſcribed the *Names* of all ſorts of *Ordnance*, from the *Cannon* to the *Baſe*; Alſo the *Lengths, Breadths, Weights, Diameters*, &c. of Powder, Shot, Ladle, &c. belonging to each Peece.

| The Names of the several Peeces of Ordnance now in Uſe. | Diameter at the Bore (Inch 100 parts) | Weight (pound wight) | Long (Fe 100 parts) | The Load (poun 100 parts) | Shots Diameter (Inch 100 parts) | Weight of Shot (poun 100 parts) | Length of Ladle (Inch 100 parts) | Breadth of Ladle (Inch 100 parts) |
|---|---|---|---|---|---|---|---|---|
| Cannon. | 8.00 | 8000 | 12.00 | 32.50 | 7.50 | 58.00 | 24.00 | 14.75 |
| Demi Cannon, Extra. | 6.75 | 6000 | 12.00 | 18.00 | 6.62 | 36.00 | 22.75 | 12.0 |
| Demi Cannon, Ordi. | 6.50 | 5600 | 10:00 11:00 | 17.50 | 6.16 | 32.00 | 22.00 | 12.00 |
| Culvering, Extraordinary | 5.50 | 4800 | 10.00 12.00 13.00 | 12.50 | 5.25 | 20.00 | 16.00 | 10.00 |
| Culvering, Ordinary | 5.25 | 4500 | 12.00 | 11.37 | 5.00 | 17.31 | 15.00 | 9.50 |
| Culvering of the least ſize | 5.00 | 4000 | 12.00 | 10.00 | 4.75 | 14.90 | 14.25 | 9.00 |
| Demi-Culvering, Extraordinary | 4.75 | 3000 | 10.00 12.00 13.00 | 8.50 | 4.50 | 12.69 | 13.50 | 8.50 |
| Demi-Culvering Ordinary | 4.50 | 2700 | 10.00 | 7.25 | 4.25 | 10.26 | 12.75 | 8.00 |
| Demi-Culvering of the leſſer ſize | 4.25 | 2000 | 9.00 10.00 | 6.25 | 4.00 | 9.00 | 12.00 | 8.00 |
| Saker, Extraordina. | 4.00 | 1800 | 9.00 10.00 | 5.00 | 3.75 | 7.31 | 11.00 | 7.25 |
| Saker, Ordinary | 3.75 | 1500 | 9.00 | 4.00 | 3.50 | 6.00 | 10.50 | 6.75 |
| Saker of the leaſt ſize | 3.50 | 1400 | 8.00 | 2.27 | 3.25 | 4.75 | 9.75 | 6.50 |
| Minnion, Large | 3.25 | 1000 | 8.00 | 3.25 | 3.00 | 3.75 | 9.00 | 5.00 |
| Minnion, Ordinary | 3.00 | 750 | 7.00 | 2.50 | 2.92 | 3.25 | 8.50 | 5.00 |
| Faucon | 2.75 | 750 | 7.00 | 2.25 | 2.58 | 2.50 | 8.25 | 4.50 |
| Fauconet | 2.25 | 400 | 6.00 | 1.25 | 2.01 | 1.31 | 7.50 | 4.00 |
| Rabonet | 1.50 | 300 | 5.50 | 0.75 | 1.28 | 0.50 | 4.25 | 2.50 |
| Bale | 1.25 | 200 | 4.50 | 0.50 | 1.13 | 0.50 | 4.00 | 2.00 |

whole

\* *The load is the weight of the charge.*

# Appendix 7

# Flags and Pendants of Command and Distinction

## The Standard

From medieval times the royal standard had been used not only to identify the presence of the sovereign, but by his commanders at sea who represented him, and who flew it at the masthead; even the ships under his command wore little banners with the royal arms along their gunwales, and this practice persisted until the end of the sixteenth century. Thereafter the standard as a flag of command was restricted to the lord high admiral until Queen Anne withdrew the privilege on her accession in 1702.

A curious anomaly occurred during the Civil War when the Earl of Warwick was appointed lord high admiral by parliament in opposition to the king's wishes, there already being a lord high admiral in the person of the nine-year-old Duke of York, though substituted for by the Earl of Northumberland. Warwick took over the fleet and flew the standard. The situation culminated in 1648 when he faced the royalist fleet off the Dutch coast, with both he and Prince Rupert, who was by that time the royalist commander, flying the same standards. Paintings showing the Duke of York at sea following the Restoration in 1660 always show a plain royal standard without the duke's label, for it was the king's standard as lord high admiral, not his own arms that he flew. Indeed when the king was present in the fleet and not actually aboard the duke's ship, the latter had to strike his standard and hoist his other badge, the admiralty flag.

## The Admiralty Flag

This flag, a gold foul anchor horizontal on a red field, has hardly ever been seen at sea worn alone as a flag of command, though the sovereign flies it as well as the standard, formerly to indicate whence the board or person holding the office derived their title; though now since the formation of a unified defence council, by right of office, since the queen is again her own lord high admiral. Charles II and James II likewise held the office in their own person from 1673 until the Revolution of 1688, and James underlined the

point by putting a crown over the anchor, which for that brief reign, assumed an upright position.

## Admiral's Flags

The pattern of command flags does not become really clear until the middle of the seventeenth century, but with the organisation of the squadron system in the sixteenth century determined efforts were made to create a system. Thus in 1530 it was decreed that the lord admiral should fly the standard at the main and the flag of St George at the fore, and that all his squadron should wear the St George at the main. The admiral of the van squadron should fly a St George at the main and fore and that all his squadron should wear similar flags at the fore. The admiral of the rear, or wing squadron as it was called, flew a St George at his main and mizzen, and bonaventure-mizzen if his ship had one; his squadron also wore them at their mizzens and bonaventure-mizzens. This system with variations apparently lasted until the end of the sixteenth century, and in so far as the relative dignity of the mast-heads was concerned the precedence was to be permanent.

The reign of Charles I saw the introduction of different coloured flags and ensigns to identify the three squadrons of the fleet. The commander-in-chief, if he was not the lord high admiral, flew the union at the main and his squadron had red ensigns; the admiral of the van flew a blue flag and his squadron blue ensigns, and the rear squadron had white ensigns and the admiral a white flag. There was still only one admiral to a squadron.

In 1649, after the execution of Charles I, the council of state abolished the office of lord high admiral and designed a new Commonwealth standard which was to be used by the generals at sea. This had two shields, one with a St George's cross for England and one with a harp in a blue field for Ireland. These were set in a wreath on a red field. The admirals, for by the First Dutch War in 1652 there was more than one flag-officer per squadron, had a rather similar flag, the two shields being set on a gold field with a red border, and without the wreath. In 1658 this standard was dropped and replaced by Cromwell's standard, until his death a year later. This had the St George's cross in the first and fourth cantons, the St Andrew's saltire in the second, the harp for Ireland in the third, and on a shield in the middle, an argent lion rampart on a black field.

One innovation brought in early in the Commonwealth navy was the reversal of the colours for the van and rear squadrons; the van taking the white flags and ensigns and the rear the blue. This was an arrangement which was to remain permanent.

With the restoration of the monachy in 1660 the picture becomes much clearer. The fleet was, as before, divided into three squadrons, each with three flag-officers. The senior squadron was the red squadron which was in the centre of the fleet and all the ships in it wore the red ensign which was now established as the senior colour; the private ships had red pendants. The vice and rear admirals of the squadron flew red flags on the fore and mizzen masts respectively, but the commander-in-chief, who might have been expected to fly a similar flag at the main, in fact flew a union flag, or the royal standard if he was the lord high admiral. The admiral of the van squadron flew a white flag at the main, and the flags of his two subordinates, the pendants of private ships and the ensigns were also white. In the rear squadron the same arrangement pertained but all the flags were blue. Every ship in the fleet, and indeed every ship in the service wore a union flag as a jack at her sprit-topmast.

Outside the main fleet, a private ship on independent service wore a tricolour pendant; all these pendants had a St George's cross at the head. The broad-pendant of a commodore did not come in until the late seventeenth century, before which the practice when the senior captain commanded a squadron was for the junior captains to strike their pendants leaving only the senior one flying. In the English fleet pendants were always struck in a ship wearing an admiral's flag. This contrasted with the Dutch, who didn't differentiate their squadrons with colours, but used to fly pendants at the appropriate mastheads of all the ships in a squadron and even under the admiral's flags. They also often had one squadron wearing the multi-barred flags and ensigns called the double-prince.

In English squadrons serving abroad, such as the Streights Fleet, a more liberal use was made of the union flag until the end of the century, it being flown by the flag officer present. The first difficulty arose when the English stopped fighting the Dutch and began to fight the French, all of whose ships wore the white flags of the Bourbons. These were easily confused with those of the van squadron which led to the re-introduction at the beginning of the eighteenth century, of the flag of St George for the command flags of the white squadron, a large red cross being added to the ensigns as well. The flag of St George had been for some time the perquisite of the merchant service.

The distinctive plain broad red pendant, of what after the 1690s was to be called a commodore's, dates from an order to the senior captain in the downs in 1674. The rank of commodore has always remained a temporary rank, an acting flag-officer. In 1824 the rank was divided into first- and second-class commodores according to their responsibilities, the former having red or white pendants, the latter blue. In 1864 when squadron colours disappeared leaving only white ensigns and flags, the first-class commodores flew their pendants at the main and the second-class at the fore. With the passing of the masted navy, second-class commodores used their boat pendants which had a red ball in the upper canton. In 1958 the two classes went into abeyance, so that now there are just commodores and one would have thought that the pendant retained would have been the plain St George's pendant. Not so, the commodores retain the second-class pendant with the ball of difference, though there is now no senior rank to be different from. Another anomaly is the pendant of the R.N.R. commodores, which instead of being blue, is a plain blue cross on a white field; this has no place in the heraldry of command flags. It all reflects an increasing ignorance of the meaning of symbols in the service, and a resulting carelessness in their use. R.N.R. pendants should be plain blue.

To revert to the admiral's flags, in the seventeenth-century fleet an appointment as a flag-officer was rather an office than a rank, though once an admiral always an admiral. The idea of a rigid list of seniority among flag-officers, rising through dead mens' shoes, is an eighteenth-century innovation, and affected the squadron colours of the fleet in so far as they ceased to be ruled by their position in the fleet and took instead the colour of the flag-officer in command, whatever that might be according to his position on the flag-list. This produced situations where two or more squadrons might have the same colour, but in that case they were usually changed by arbitrary action of the commander-in-chief.

Lord Admiral's Standard 1588

Other Flag Officers 1588

Union Flag 1606 to 1801 and Admirals of the Fleet

Union Flag from 1801 and Admirals of the Fleet

Admiralty Flag from c. 1625, and Lord High Admiral's Flag from 1708

Generals at sea in the Commonwealth 1649 to 1658

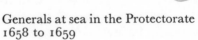

Generals at sea in the Protectorate 1658 to 1659

Other Commonwealth and Protectorate Flag Officers

Flag Officers of the White 1665 to c. 1692

Vice- and Rear-Admirals of the Red 1665 to 1864, and Full Admirals from 1805 to 1864

Flag Officers of the Blue 1665 to 1864

Flag Officers of the White c. 1700 to 1864, and Full Admirals from 1864

By 1805 there were 166 flag-officers on the active list, and in that year the rank of admiral of the red was introduced. The reasons for the abolition of the three colours in 1864 is set out in the section under ensigns; suffice to say that all flag-officers thereafter flew the flag of St George.

As with the commodores, the flag-officers in the late nineteenth century, when ships usually had only two and possibly only one mast, adopted their boat flags with enlarged balls in the cantons. These had two red balls, one in the upper and one in the lower canton for a rear-admiral, one ball in the upper canton for a vice-admiral, and none in an admiral's. The use of coloured or white balls in boat flags dates from the beginning of the eighteenth century and was designed to show a flag-officer's rank when flying his flag in the bows of his barge.

**Ensigns and Jacks**
The importance of the jack in the form of the union flag as being the sole perquisite of the king's ships, dates from shortly after the introduction of the sprit-topmast in large ships in the 1620s, which made it possible to rig a jack-staff on it. From that time, with a break during the Commonwealth and Protectorate, when another flag was used, the union flag at the jack-staff, and the wearing of a commissioning pendant, have denoted a naval vessel, though since the changes in design of headsails in the middle eighteenth century, which made it impracticable to wear them at sea, they are only worn in harbour or at anchor. For some reason the phrase 'union-jack' caught the public imagination and the flag is commonly known as the union-jack wherever it is found.

Ensigns were introduced into the navy in the second half of the sixteenth century and were usually striped. A painting of the return of Prince Charles with the fleet in 1623 shows the fleet with ensigns of blue, white and gold horizontal bars and with the St George's cross at the head. It was almost immediately after this, in 1625, that the navy apparently went over to red ensigns, which, being established as the first and senior ensign when squadronal colours were introduced in the middle of the seventeenth century, continues so to this day.

The three ensigns, red, white and blue, in that order, all carried a red cross of St George on a white field in the upper corner next to the staff. In 1707 the saltire of St Andrew was added after the Act of Union with Scotland so that it had the same form as the union flag of the day. Just before this the addition of the second cross of St George across the whole of the white ensign was made, for reasons already stated.

A further change to the union flag occurred in 1801, then a red saltire was added after the Act of Union with Ireland and this was included also into the union in the ensign. They thus assumed their final form, but only in the navy until 1864, when it was decided to have one flag for the merchant service, one flag for the navy and one flag for the naval reserve and other government services. The reasons were that the navy no longer needed squadron colours; tactics had changed, and it was found inconvenient and expensive to carry round three sets of colours. It was also stated that a clear distinction should be made between merchant ships and naval ships, both of which might be wearing red ensigns. As the two junior ensigns were peculiar to the navy and regarded as tactical colours, the protection of the senior and legal ensign was assigned to the merchant service, which had worn it from its beginning anyway. The next senior, the white, was taken by the Royal Navy, and the junior one, the blue, was given to the Royal Naval Reserve and was also to be used, possible defaced, by government vessels outside the service, such as the Post Office. Merchant ships too, if they had a sufficient proportion of reserve officers in their crews, were and are entitled to wear a blue ensign.

The ensign of a naval ship was always worn on an ensign staff until the introduction of the gaff boom, which protruded over the taffrail and could not swing if the ensign staff was in place. When it was in use, and by the end of the Napoleonic Wars it was always rigged, the ensign was worn at the peak. In harbour, however, it was generally put back on the ensign staff, and the tradition remains today that when at sea the ensign is worn at the peak, and at rest on its staff. There is, of course, a modern reason for wearing it at the peak at sea, since guns or rockets fired from turrets aft would be liable to blow it off the staff.

The size and more especially the shape of flags and ensigns has changed since the seventeenth century. The early ensigns were almost square being only one-and-a-quarter times their height in the fly. In the late Stuart navy this lengthened to one-and-a-half times the height and in a first rate measured 13½ feet by 18 feet. Correctly the length of a flag should be given in breadths, a unit of 9 inches. If there was an admiral aboard his flag measured 9½ feet by 13 feet, large by modern standards. If she was a private ship and wore a pendant; it was 96 feet long.

Early in the eighteenth century the proportion of the ensigns and jacks changed again to twice the length to the height, but flags and standards remained at one-and-a-half. The increase in the size of the ships during the century was reflected in the flags, so that by 1800 the largest ships wore ensigns of 30 breadths, or 22½ feet in the fly. Today the largest ensign issued is 22 breadths, or 16½ feet in the fly, and in general ensigns, flags and pendants are very much smaller.

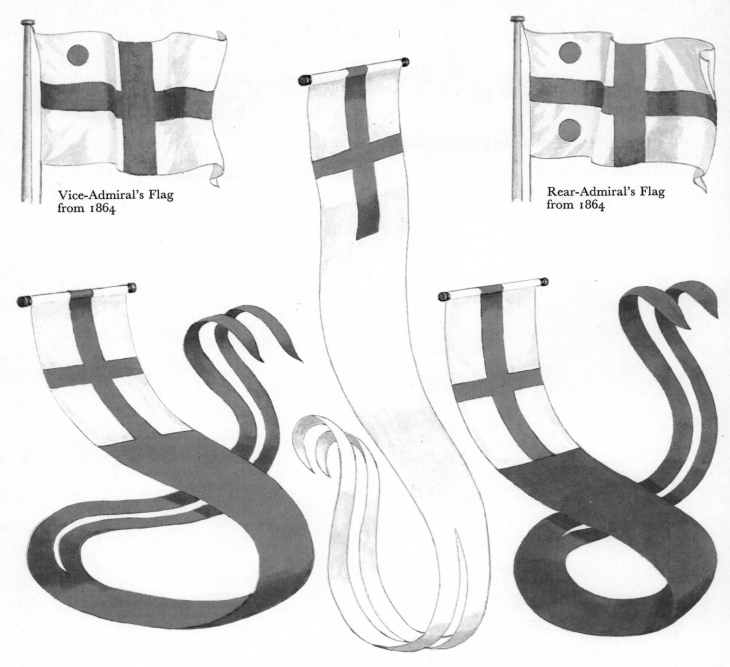

Vice-Admiral's Flag
from 1864

Rear-Admiral's Flag
from 1864

Red, White, and Blue Commissioning Pendants seventeenth century

Pendant of Independent Command
from 1660

Commissioning Budgee Pendant eighteenth century

Commodore's Broad Pendant 1697 to 1864
1st Class from 1824 to 1864

2nd Class Commodore's Pendant
1824 to 1864

1st Class Commodore's Pendant
1864 to 1958

2nd Class Commodore's Pendant 1864 to 1958
Commodore's Pendant from 1958

RNR Commodore's Pendant in
World War II, and since 1959

Ensign of c. 1623

# Appendix 8

# Types of shot and shell in use for smooth bore muzzle-loaders in first half of the nineteenth century

1 *Solid-shot*. This was the commonest type of projectile in use from the earliest times until the middle of the nineteenth century. Originally it was usually made of dressed stone, but by the seventeenth century iron shot was preferred. It was the only type of projectile that could be fired with any degree of accuracy, except at the shortest ranges, and being also aerodynamically the most efficient, and the heaviest, it carried further and struck harder on a hull than other shot.

2 *Spherical-shell*. This type of shell was in use in mortars from the seventeenth century, but although there were experiments with it in France in ordinary cannon from the beginning of the eighteenth century, it only went into general service with the fleets in the second quarter of the nineteenth century. The shell was loaded with a special shovel which ensured that the fuse was pointing outwards. On firing the flames engulfed the shell and ignited the fuse. In the mortar shells, where a certain latitude in the time between firing and the explosion was desirable, devices for lengthening the fuse were used. One was to have a series of holes in the detonator and a covered fuse led down to one of them, the lower the hole the longer the fusing time. The normal size of shell in the mid nineteenth-century fleet was 8 inches which corresponded to the 32-pounder.

As there were no fleet actions over this period the effectiveness of this type of shell on wooden hulls was never proven, and they did not entirely take over from solid shot, which still outranged it, as it was the heavier.

3 *Fagot-shot*. A cylindrical shot made up of six pieces of iron segmented like a cake, and ingeniously fitted together and bound. This was effective against rigging or personnel.

4, 5, 6, 7 *Chain-shot*. Before steam provided propulsion, a number of types of short-range projectiles were devised to slash through a ship's rigging and disable her. A favourite was chain-shot of which four types are shown here: Nos. 4 and 7 are of the ordinary sort with the balls a good deal smaller than the bore, so that they were very inaccurate. With No. 5 an effort has been made to make a shot that, though it would divide in flight, at its initial velocity when

placed together in the barrel, would fill the bore like solid shot. The neatest one is No. 6, where the chain is housed inside the two cups which fit together. This system, however, does entail a loss of weight compared to No. 5, which would make it less effective.

8, 9, 10 *Bar-shot*. Like chain-shot, this type again was mainly effective against rigging, but because it was rigid it would strike harder on a hull if it struck end-on. The drawings show two variations of the double-headed type, Nos. 8 and 9, and a multiple bar shot, No. 10. All flailed around during trajectory, so were most inaccurate except at point-blank range. In the French service the area around the bar was sometimes filled with an inflammable composition bound with linen soaked in brimstone; this would burst into flames on discharge.

11, 12 *Elongated-shot*. This was a development of the dumbell bar-shot in that it opened to nearly twice its original length by the outward pull of the two ends as it spun in the air. This gave it more chance of hitting something if it passed through the rigging.

13 *Case-shot or Canister*. A cylindrical tin full of ball-shot which scattered on being fired, and was used for clearing the enemy's deck. Canister was particularly favoured by the French.

14, 15 *Grape-shot*. Another anti-personnel shot; this is of a rather sophisticated type. More usual was a system of cording the balls together and putting the whole thing into a canvas bag, No. 15. It is not clear whether the tiered type also went into a bag.

Two types of shot which were seldom used in the service, but which were apparently used in the Merchant Service and by privateersmen, were langrage, which covered any old collection of bits of iron put in a bag, and star-shot which was formed by a number of hooked arms from a ring which splayed out on being fired. It was close to multiple bar-shot, but lighter.

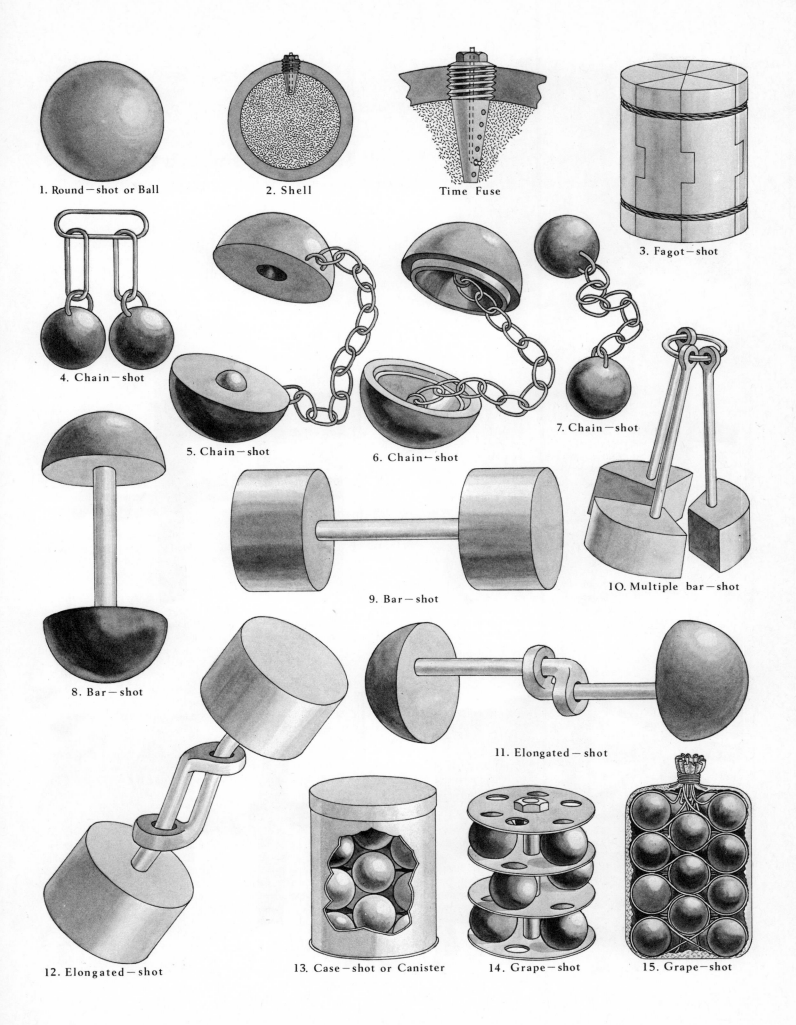

1. Round—shot or Ball

2. Shell

Time Fuse

3. Fagot—shot

4. Chain—shot

5. Chain—shot

6. Chain—shot

7. Chain—shot

8. Bar—shot

9. Bar—shot

10. Multiple bar—shot

11. Elongated—shot

12. Elongated—shot

13. Case—shot or Canister

14. Grape—shot

15. Grape—shot

Ensign 1625 to 1707

Ensign 1635 to *c.* 1695

Ensign 1635 to 1707

White Ensign 1707 to 1801

Red Ensign from 1801

Commonwealth Jack 1649 to 1660

# Glossary of Nautical Terms

**Amidships** — The middle of a ship between her stem and stern, or the middle between the sides when applied to the wheel.

**Balinger** — A large double-ended open boat with banks of oars, built as a fighting vessel in the Middle Ages.

**Beam** — The greatest breadth of a ship; but also, and originally, the name of the timber joining the sides of a ship and supporting her decks.

**Beat to quarters** — Until warships became too big for it to be practical, the men were called to action stations by a drum.

**Bend** — To knot one rope to another; also to bend a sail is to fasten it to its yard.

**Board** — Originally the moment of impact of one ship beside another, but later it meant to board and enter a ship, i.e. for men to go aboard.

**Bonaventure-mizzen** — The fourth mast abaft the mizzen found in some of the biggest late sixteenth- and early seventeenth-century ships.

**Bowsprit** — A large spar which points forwards, and in large vessels always upwards, from the bow over the ship's head.

**Brig and brig-sloop** — In nineteenth-century naval parlance a two-masted vessel square-rigged to topgallants on both.

**Brigantine** — In the same context as the brigs, a two-masted vessel square-rigged to topgallants on the fore, but fore-and-aft rigged on the main with a topmast.

**Broadside** — A ship's broadside was all the guns she could mount on one side or the other; also the discharge of the same.

**Bulkhead** — Vertical internal partitions between decks.

**Bulwark** — The side of ship from the deck to the gunwale.

**Cable** — The anchor rope or chain.

**Cannon** — The largest type of muzzle-loader, throwing a ball of about 30 to 60 pounds.

**Cannon-drakes** — A gun throwing a ball of cannon weight, but lighter and shorter in the barrel than a full cannon.

**Cannon-perier** — A chambered cannon throwing a stone shot of about 14 pounds in the late sixteenth century.

**Carrack** — The largest type of round-ship developed by the Portuguese in the fifteenth and sixteenth centuries, but also built in Northern Europe.

**Carriage** — (See Gun carriage.)

**Carronade** — (See page 63.)

**Chambered gun** — A gun-barrel in which the powder-chamber is of a different width to the ball or, in a breach-loader, was separate from the barrel.

**Channel** — Derives from chain-wale—broad, thick planks on a ship's sides down to which the shrouds are brought.

**Clinker-built** — Formerly called clincher-work, whereby a boat is planked so that the upper planks slightly overlay the ones below them.

**Coach** — In the seventeenth century the anteroom to the great cabin at upper-deck level, but in the eighteenth century an alternative name for the roundhouse, or the cabins at the after end of the quarter-deck.

**Cog** — A medieval double-ended round ship with a steering oar, thirteenth to late fourteenth century.

**Counter** — Just above the tuck and across the stern, it curves outwards under the stern-galleries.

**Crank** — Tender sided, incapable of carrying sail without the danger of overturning.

**Crossjack-yard** — Usually abbreviated to cro'jack, it was really the mizzen yard to which the mizzen topsail was brought down. It rarely had a sail bent to it.

**Culverin** A gun as long as a cannon but firing a lighter ball; a smaller version was called a demi-culverin.

**Cutter** A single-masted gaff-rigged vessel with more than one head-sail.

**Deck-head** The ceiling between decks, usually consisting of the underside of the deck above.

**Demi-cannon** A smaller cannon throwing an iron shot of 18 pounds (late sixteenth century).

**Dogger** A two-masted vessel, square-rigged on the mainmast, a lateen-sail on the mizzen, and with a stay-foresail and jib.

**Dolphin-striker** A spreader jutting downwards from the end of the bowsprit to provide a fulcrum for stays to the jibboom and flying-jibboom.

**Draught** A drawing of a ship's lines for building her.

**Driver** (See page 55.)

**Falcon** A small carriage gun throwing a ball of about 5 pounds.

**Falls** The stepped down decks aft in Elizabethan and early Jacobean warships.

**Fastening** The method by which the timbers in a ship are joined together.

**Filling** A method of giving a ship protection against the toredines (see page 59).

**Floor** The inside of a ship's bottom next to her keel for as wide as it is reasonably flat.

**Flush-decked** A vessel whose deck or decks run continuously from stem to stern without falls.

**Fly** The breadth of a flag from the staff to the end.

**Fo'c'sle** A shortened form of forecastle, which is the fore-deck and the area immediately beneath it at the forward end of the upper-deck.

**Frame** The ribs making the outer shape of a ship.

**Freeboard** The distance from the waterline to the lowest port-sill.

**Galleass** A type of galley with the addition of a broadside armament over or under her oars.

**Galleon** (See page 11.)

**Galley** A large-oared vessel.

**Grapple** An instrument for attaching one ship to another in action, it was a

kind of hook; also the act of attacking.

**Great ship** The development of the carrack type of large broad vessel with large superstructures.

**Gun carriage** A wooden structure on which rested the trunnions and breech of the gun barrel and which could be moved on four wooden trucks, or sometimes a slide.

**Gun-deck** The lowest deck above the orlop on which, in ships of the line, the heaviest battery was placed.

**Gunnade** A type of short barrelled cannon that replaced the carronade.

**Gunwale** The timbers along the tops of the bulwarks.

**Half-deck** The deck from the break of the waist aft; it came in the late seventeenth century to be called the quarter-deck, which formerly was the deck above and abaft it.

**Hermaphrodite brig** A name used in the first half of the nineteenth century for what was later known as a brigantine.

**Hold** The space between the floor and the lower-deck.

**Hoy** A single-masted vessel not unlike a cutter but lacking her long gaff and bowsprit.

**Jackstay** A rope or rod running along a mast or yard to which a sail can be bent.

**Jib-boom** An extension to the bowsprit.

**Jury** The word is put before any part of a ship's fittings which is doing temporary duty for the real article which has been carried away or damaged.

**Knee** A heavy angled piece of timber connecting a ship's side timbers with her beams, latterly made of iron.

**Liner** A mid nineteenth-century word for a ship of the line.

**Minion** A small carriage gun throwing a ball of about 4 pounds.

**Murderers** The smallest type of carriage gun throwing a ball of about 2 pounds.

**Nef** The development of the cog, having a hinged rudder instead of a steering oar.

**Oar-ports** Small square holes in the sides of the ship for the oars or sweeps. If located on the lower deck they were fitted with hinged port lids.

**Orlop** A series of platforms in the hold, developing in big ships to a light deck which carried the cable, cabins for some junior officers and the surgeons operating table.

**Paid off**    The act of de-commissioning a ship is known as paying off, because it used to entail paying the men and dismissing them. It also means when a ship's head has fallen off to leeward.

**Pay**    An alternative to painting a ship was to coat it with a type of varnish; this was called paying.

**Peak**    The upper corner of mizzen - sail supported by a lateen yard or a gaff.

**Pivot-gun**    A small gun mounted in the jaws of a metal shaft set in the gunwale so that it could be freely elevated or traversed.

**Primer**    A wafer containing gunpowder used at the touch-hole to fire the main charge.

**Private ship**    A ship in commission but not carrying a flag-officer.

**Quarters**    A ship's sides near her stern.

**Quarter-deck**    Originally the deck above and abaft the half-deck, but by the end of the seventeenth century it took the place of the half-deck and became the deck running from the after-end of the waist, and above it, to the stern.

**Race-built**    A sixteenth-century phrase for a low built galleon with very little superstructure.

**Raking**    Bringing a ship's broadside to bear on the bow or stern of another ship.

**Razee**    A ship that has had her hull altered by the removal of her upper decks is a razee.

**Recoil**    The backward movement of a gun resultant on the force of its discharge.

**Rifled**    Spiral grooving inside a gun barrel so that the bullet or shot leaves spinning, which keeps it pointing in the direction it is going.

**Roundhouse**    The cabin space at the after end of the quarter-deck, in naval parlance also called the coach.

**Royals**    The square sails above the top-gallants used in light weather.

**Rudder**    A flat framework hinged to the sternpost for steering the ship.

**Saker**    A small carriage gun throwing a ball of $5\frac{1}{2}$ pounds.

**Scuttles**    The naval term for porthole, which is used in the merchant service for the round glazed holes in a ship's sides and super-structures.

**Sheathing**    Protective layers over the main timbers of a ship's bottom below the waterline (see page 59).

**Sheer**    The longitudinal curve of a ship's decks or sides.

**Shipwright**    A man physically involved with the building or repairing of ships. In naval dockyards a senior one might also be a designer.

**Shrouds**    The standing rigging running from the mast-heads down and back to the channels on the ship's sides.

**Spanker**    The loose footed mizzen-sail that replaced the full lateen sail, being laced to the mast.

**Spar-deck**    A light deck in the form of a wooden grill supported on a stanchion above the upper, half and fo'c'sle decks, early seventeenth century.

**Sprit-topmast**    A small vertical mast stepped on the end of bowsprit, carrying a square sail, seventeenth century.

**Stay-sails**    Fore and aft sails bent to the stays.

**Step**    A block of wood with a hole in the top to take the heel of a mast. Hence a mast is stepped into its place.

**Stern-gallery**    A loggia at the after-end of the coach, and also of the great cabin in three-deckers, with a balustrade across the stern.

**Stern-walk**    An iron or steel structure, usually canopied, round the stern of a ship, the successor to the stern-gallery.

**Strike**    To remove or take down any part of the ship or her fittings.

**Sweep**    A large type of oar.

**Tackle**    A device of blocks and ropes for raising or securing heavy objects, or controlling guns, sails and yards.

**Taffrail**    Old spelling tafferel, the upper-most part of the stern between the two gunwales.

**Tender-sided**    A ship that heels over too easily and too far in a breeze.

**Tier**    The collective name for all the cannon mounted on one side of a ship's deck.

**Topgallant**    Used with the words masts, yards, sails, etc., denotes those

| | |
|---|---|
| | immediately above the topmasts, and below the royals, if any. |
| **Transoms** | The beams across the stern-post supporting the stern. |
| **Trebuchet** | A medieval machine for throwing stones, etc. A spar on a pivot was winched back against a heavy counter-weight. |
| **Troopers** | Ships adapted or designed for the conveyance of troops. |
| **Tuck** | The stern below the counter: in the seventeenth century round in English ships, square in Dutch and French Ships. |
| **Tumblehome** | To reduce the weight of a ship's topsides her beam was reduced from the gun-deck upwards. |
| **Weather gage** | To be to windward of another ship. |
| **Waist** | That part of the upper-deck between the quarter-deck and fo'c'sle. |
| **Wales** | Extra planking at certain levels of a ship's sides above the waterline. |
| **Whip-staff** | A stave attached to the tiller on a fulcrum for steering a ship (see page 58). |
| **Wolding** | The binding at intervals round a made-mast to hold it together (see page 56). |

# Bibliography

Bagnasco, Erminio. *Submarines in World War Two*. London, 1977.

Brassey, Sir Thomas. *The British Navy*. 5 vols. London, 1882.

*Brassey's Naval Annual*. 1887–1966.

Breyer, Siegfried. *Battleships of the World 1905–1970*. London, 1980.

Charnock, John, *A History of Marine Architecture*. London, 1800–02.

Clowes, William Laird. *The Royal Navy. A History from the Earliest Times to the Present Day*. 7 vols. London, 1897–1903.

*Conway's All the World's Fighting Ships 1860–1905*. London, 1979.

*Conway's All the World's Fighting Ships 1922–1946*. London, 1980.

Derrick, Charles. *Memoirs of the Rise and Progress of the Royal Navy*. London, 1806.

Dittmar, F. J. and Colledge, J. J. *British Warships 1914–1919*. London, 1972.

Douglas, Sir Howard. *Naval Gunnery*. London, 1821 and 1860.

Eardley-Wilmot, Captain S., R.N. *The Development of Navies During the Last Half Century*. London, 1892.

Eardley-Wilmot, Captain S., R.N. *Our Fleet Today, and its Development During the Last Half Century*. London, 1900.

Everett, Don. *The K Boats*. London, 1963.

Ffoulkes, Charles. *The Gun Founders of England*. Cambridge, 1937.

James, William. *Abstracts of the Royal Navy; Showing How It Stood, in Ships, Tons, and Classification at the Commencement of Every Year, from 1793 Inclusive*. London, 1820.

James, William. *The Naval History of Great Britain*. London, 1822.

Jane, Fred T. *The British Battle Fleet: Its Inception and Growth Throughout the Centuries*. London, 1912.

Jane, Fred T. *The Torpedo in Peace and War*. London, 1898.

*Jane's Fighting Ships*. Annual volumes 1898 to present.

Kemp, Lieut-Cdr. P. F., R.N. *H.M. Submarines*. London, 1952.

King, Chief Officer J. W., U.S.N. *The Warships and Navies of the World*. Boston, 1880.

Lavery, Brian. *The Ship of the Line*. vol I. London, 1983.

Lenton, H. J. and Colledge, J. J. *Warships of World War II*. London, 1972.

Lipscomb, Commander F. W. *The British Submarine*. Expanded edition. London, 1975.

Lyon, D. J. and H. J. *World War II Warships*. London, 1976.

Manning, Captain T. D., R.N.V.R. *The British Destroyer*. Putman, 1961.

March, Edgar, J. *British Destroyers, A History of Development 1892–1953*. London, 1966.

Marriot, John. *Fast Attack Craft*. London, 1978.

Morgan, William and Creuze, Augustin. *Naval Science*. London, vol I, 1827; vol II, 1829; vol III, 1831.

Openheim, H. *A History of the Administration of the Royal Navy and of Merchant Shipping in Relation to the Navy 1509–1660*. London, 1896.

Palmer, Norman. *Aircraft Carriers, a Graphic History of Carrier Aviation and its Influence on World Events*. London, 1969.

# BIBLIOGRAPHY

Parkes, Oscar. *British Battleships, 'Warrior' 1860 to 'Vanguard' 1950*. London, 1957.

Poolman, Kenneth. *The Catafighters and Merchant Aircraft Carriers*. London, 1970.

Preston, Antony and Major, John. *Send a Gunboat, a Study of the Gunboat and its Role in British Policy 1859–1904*. London, 1967.

Preston, Anthony. *Battleships of World War I*. London, 1972.

Raleigh, Sir Walter. *Excellent Observations and Notes, Concerning the Royal Navy and Sea-Service*. London, 1650.

Raven, Alan and Roberts, John. *British Cruisers of World War Two*. London, 1980.

Reed, E. J. *Our Ironclad Fleet, Their Qualities, Performance and Cost*. London, 1869.

Reed, E. J. *Shipbuilding in Iron and Steel: a Practical Treatise*. London, 1869.

Robertson, F. L. *The Evolution of Naval Armament*. London, 1921.

Schomberg, Captain Issac, R.N. *Naval Chronology; or a Historical Summary of Naval and Maritime Events; from the Time of the Romans, to the Treaty of Peace 1802*. London, 1802.

Smith, John. *The Sea-man's Grammar and Dictionary*. London, 1692.

Sueter, Commander Murray F., R.N. *The Evolution of the Submarine Boat, Mine and Torpedo*. London, 1907.

U.S. Senate. *Report of Chief Officer J. W. King, United States Navy, on European Ships of War and Their Armament, Naval Administration and Economy, Marine Constructions and Appliances, Dockyards, etc. etc*. Washington, 1877.

# Index

*Cerberus* (1868) 113, 117, 127
*Ceres* (1917) 211
*Ceylon* (1942) 218, 223
*Chailey* (1952–8) 245
*Challenger* (1902) 195, 196
*Chameleon* (1942–4) 244
*Chamois* (1896–1901) 230
*Chamois* (1942–3) 244
*Champion* (1878) 141
*Champion* (1915) 209, 211
*Chance* (1942–3) 244
*Chanticleer* (1942–5) 247
*Chaplet* (1943–5) 239
Chapman 62
*Charger* (1894–5) 229
*Charity* (1943–5) 239
Charles I 20, 22, 25
Charles II 27, 28, 59
*Charlestown* (1917–20) 237
*Charlock* (1942–4) 251
*Charon* 48
*Charybdis* (1892) 193, 221
*Charybdis* (1940) 224
*Charybdis* (1968) 254
*Chaser* (1941–2) 272
*Chatham* (1911) 205, 206
*Chawton* (1952–9) 245
*Cheam* (1918–19) 243
*Chediston* (1952–9) 245
*Cheerful* (1896–1901) 230
*Cheerful* (1942–4) 244
*Chelmer* (1903–5) 230
*Chelmer* (1941–3) 251
*Chelmsford* (1916) 243
*Chelsea* (1917–20) 237
*Chelsham* (1952–8) 245
*Cheltenham* (1916) 243
*Chepstow* (1916) 243
*Chequers* (1943–5) 239
*Cherwell* (1903–5) 230
*Chesapeake* 81
*Chester* (1915) 210, 212
*Chesterfield* (1917–20) 237
Chevalier de Martino 158
*Cheviot* (1943–5) 239
*Chevron* (1943–5) 239
*Chichester* 41
*Chichester* (1955) 254
*Chiddingfold* (1940–2) 238
*Chiddingfold* (1983) 240, 299
*Chieftain* (1943–5) 239
*Chilcompton* (1952–9) 245
*Childers* (1943–5) 239
Childers, Hugh 117
*Chillingham* (1952–8) 245
*Chilton* (1952–9) 245
*Chivalrous* (1943–5) 239
*Christopher* (1912–13) 231
*Chrysanthemum* (1917–18) 242, 246
*Chrysanthemum* (1940–2) 251
*Churchill* (1917–20) 237
*Churchill* (1968) 289, 291
*Cicala* (1915) 147
*Cicero* (1918–19) 246
*Circe* (1892) 228
*Circe* (1942–4) 244
*Clacton* (1940–2) 244
*Clarbeston* (1952–9) 245
*Clare* (1917–20) 237
*Clarkia* (1940–2) 251
*Clematis* (1915) 246
*Clematis* (1940–2) 251
*Cleopatra* (1878) 141
*Cleopatra* (1915) 208, 221
*Cleopatra* (1940) 224
*Cleopatra* (1964) 254
*Cleveland* (1940) 238

*Clinton* (1942–4) 244
*Clio* (1900) 145
*Clonmel* (1918–19) 243
*Clover* (1940–2) 251
*Clyde* (1934) 286
*Clydebank* (1940–2) 244
Coast Defence Ships 110, 113, 129
Coastal Craft 293
Coastal Motor Boat 293, 297
*Cobham* (1952–8) 245
*Cobra* (1899) 230
*Cochrane* (1905) 201, 204
*Cockade* (1943–5) 239
*Cockatrice* (1912–13) 231
*Cockatrice* (1942–4) 244
*Cockchafer* (1915) 147
*Codrington* (1929) 43, 236
Cog 4
Cog Type Ships, English 6
Coles, Captain Cowper 107, 110
Collier, Commodore Sir George 80
*Collingwood* (1882) 121, 122, 123
*Collingwood* (1908) 162, 163
Collingwood, Admiral Lord 58
*Colne* (1903–5) 230
*Colombo* (1918) 211
*Colony* (1939) 216, 218, 221, 223
*Colony* Class (1939–42) 223, 251
*Colossus* (1882) 121, 122
*Colossus* (1910) 162, 163
*Colossus* (1943) 268, 272
*Coltsfoot* (1940–2) 251
*Columbine* (1940–2) 251
*Columbine* 51, 54, 83
*Combatant* (1942–3) 244
*Comet* (1822) 75
*Comet* (1867–81) 147
*Comet* (1910–11) 231
*Comet* (1931) 236
*Comet* (1943–5) 239
*Comfrey* (1942–4) 251
*Commerce de Marseille* 44, 64, 72
*Commonwealth* (1903) 159
*Comus* Class (1878) 135, 141
*Comus* (1914) 208
*Comus* (1943–5) 239
*Concord* (1916) 211
*Concord* (1943–5) 239
*Condor* (1898) 145
*Conflict* (1894–5) 229
*Coniston* (1952–9) 245
*Conn* (1942–4) 253
*Conqueror* (1881) 128, 130
*Conqueror* (1911) 167
*Conqueror* (1969) 289, 291
*Conquest* (1878) 141
*Conquest* (1915) 208
*Consort* (1943–5) 239
*Constance* (1880) 141, 149
*Constance* (1915) 211
*Constance* (1943–5) 239
*Contest* (1894–5) 229
*Contest* (1912–13) 231
*Contest* (1943–5) 239
Constitution 80, 82
*Convolvulus* (1917–18) 246
*Convolvulus* (1940–2) 251
*Cooke* (1942–3) 253
*Coquette* (1896–9) 230
*Coquette* (1942–4) 244
*Cordelia* (1881) 141
*Cordelia* (1914) 208
*Coreopsis* (1917–18) 246
*Coreopsis* (1940–2) 251
*Coriander* (1940–2) 251
*Cornel* (1942–4) 251
*Cornflower* (1915–16) 246

*Cornwall* (1902) 199
*Cornwall* (1926) 200, 214, 216
*Cornwallis* (1901) 153, 154
*Corunna* (1945) 239
Corvettes 50, 54, 83, 133, 134, 141, 242, 248, 250, 251
Corvettes, Screw 85
*Cosby* (1942–3) 253
*Cossack* (1885) 144
*Cossack* (1907–9) 230, 235
*Cossack* (1937) 237
*Cossack* (1943–5) 239
*Cotillion* (1917–18) 243
*Cotswold* (1917) 243
*Cotswold* (1940) 238
*Cottesmore* (1917) 243
*Cottesmore* (1940) 238
*Cottesmore* (1982) 299
*Cotton* (1942–3) 253
*County* Class 213, 214, 215, 216, 257, 260
*Courageous* (1916) 178, 183, 185, 186, 222, 262, 267
*Courageous* (1970) 270, 291
*Courier* (1942–4) 244
*Coventry* (1917) 209, 211
*Coventry* (1974) 259
Coventry, Sir William 29
*Coverley* (1917–18) 243
*Cowdray* (1940–2) 238
*Cowslip* (1917–18) 246
*Cowslip* (1940–2) 251
*Cradley* (1952–8) 245
Cradock, Admiral 179, 200
*Craigie* (1918–19) 243
*Crane* (1896–1901) 230
*Crane* (1942–5) 247
*Cranham* (1952–8) 245
*Cranstoun* (1942–3) 253
*Creole* (1943–5) 239
*Crescent* (1892) 191, 198
*Crescent* (1931) 236
*Crescent* (1943–5) 239
*Cressy* (1899) 197, 199
*Crichton* (1952–9) 245
*Cricket* (1915) 147
Crimea War 1854–5 24, 97, 252
*Crispin* (1943–5) 239
*Crocus* (1915–16) 246
*Crocus* (1940–2) 251
*Crofton* (1952–9) 245
*Cromarty* (1940–2) 244
*Cromer* (1940–2) 244
*Cromwell* (1943–5) 239
Cromwell, Oliver 26
*Croome* (1917) 243
*Croome* (1940–2) 238
*Crossbow* (1945) 239
*Crown* (1943–5) 239
*Croxton* (1916) 243
*Croziers* (1943–5) 239
Cruisers 214, 215
Cruisers, Armoured 197, 204
Cruisers, Belted 200, 204, 219, 220, 223, 224
Cruisers, Guided Missile Light 257
Cruisers, Helicopter 259
Cruisers, Iron & Steel Masted 131
Cruisers, Light 205, 207, 208, 211, 212
Cruisers, Mastless Steel 191
Cruisers, Mine Laying 219
Cruisers, Protected 192, 193, 194, 195, 198, 199
Cruisers, Washington Treaty 213
*Crusader* (1907–9) 230
*Crusader* (1931) 236
*Crusader* (1943–5) 239
*Crystal* (1943–5) 239
*Cubitt* (1942–3) 253

*Trailer* (1941–2) 272
*Tralee* (1918–19) 243
*Traveller* (1937–45) 290
Trawlers 295
Trawlers, Admiralty 245
*Tremadoc Bay* (1944–5) 253
*Tremendous* (1811) 67, 68
*Trenchant* (1916) 233
*Trenchant* (1937–45) 290
*Trent* (1876) 145
*Trent* (1941–3) 251
*Tresham* (1952–8) 245
*Trespasser* (1937–45) 290
*Triad* (1937–45) 290
*Tribal* Class 230, 235, 237, 254, 256, 257
*Tribune* (1891) 193
*Tribune* (1918–19) 233
*Tribune* (1937–45) 290
*Trident* (1937–45) 290
*Trillium* (1940–2) 251
*Trinidad* (1918–19) 233
*Trinidad* (1940) 218, 223
*Tring* (1918–19) 243
*Tristram* (1917) 233
*Triton* (1937) 280, 290
*Triumph* (1870) 106, 107, 114, 149
*Triumph* (1903) 143, 159, 160, 201
*Triumph* (1937–45) 290
*Triumph* (1944) 268, 272
*Trojan* (1918–19) 233
*Trollope* (1942–3) 253
Tromp, Marten 26, 59
*Trooper* (1937–45) 290
*Troubridge* (1942) 238, 253
*Trouncer* (1942–3) 272
*Truant* (1918–19) 233
*Truant* (1937–45) 290
*Truculent* (1916–17) 232
*Truculent* (1937–45) 290
*Truelove* (1942–5) 244
*Trump* (1937–45) 290
*Trump* (1951–6) 290
*Trumpeter* (1942–3) 272
*Truncheon* (1937–45) 290
*Truncheon* (1951–6) 290
*Truro* (1918–19) 243
*Trusty* (1918–19) 233
*Trusty* (1937–45) 290
*Tryphon* (1918–19) 233
Tsushima, Battle of 155
*Tuberose* (1917–18) 246
Tucker, Joseph 73
*Tudor* (1937–45) 290
Tudors 3
Tudor Navy 10
Tudor ship design 15
*Tulip* (1916–17) 246
*Tulip* (1940–2) 251
*Tumult* (1918–19) 233
*Tumult* (1942) 238
*Tuna* (1937–45) 290
*Turbulent* (1918–19) 233
*Turbulent* (1937–45) 290
*Turbulent* (1982) 292
*Turpin* (1937–45) 290
*Turpin* (1951–6) 290
*Turquoise* (1918–19) 233
Turret-ship 103
Turret-ship, armoured 108, 109, 121
Turret-ship, iron-built 110
*Tuscan* (1918–19) 233
*Tuscan* (1942) 238
*Tweed* (1876) 145
*Tweed* (1941–3) 251
*Tyler* (1942–3) 253
*Tynedale* (1940) 238
*Tyrant* (1916–17) 232

*Tyrian* (1861) 89
*Tyrian* (1918–19) 233
*Tyrian* (1942) 238

*Ulleswater* (1916–17) 232
*Ultimatum* (1940–3) 290
*Ulster* (1917) 233
*Ulster* (1942) 238, 253
*Ultor* (1940–3) 290
*Ulysees* (1917) 233
*Ulysees* (1943) 238, 253
*Uganda* (1941) 218, 223
*Umbra* (1940–3) 290
*Umpire* (1917) 233
*Umpire* (1937–41) 290
*Una* (1937–41) 290
*Unbeaten* (1937–41) 290
*Unbending* (1940–3) 290
*Unbroken* (1940–3) 290
*Undaunted* (1860) 69, 83, 85, 100
*Undaunted* (1937–41) 290
*Undaunted* (1943) 238, 253
*Undine* (1917) 233
*Undine* (1937–41) 290
*Undine* (1943) 238, 253
*Union* (1937–41) 290
*Unique* (1937–41) 290
*Unison* (1940–3) 290
*United* (1940–3) 290
*Unity* (1912–13) 231
*Unity* (1937–41) 290
*Universal* (1940–3) 290
*Unrivalled* (1940–3) 290
*Unruffled* (1940–3) 290
*Unruly* (1940–3) 290
*Unseen* (1940–3) 290
*Unshaken* (1940–3) 290
*Unsparing* (1940–3) 290
*Unswerving* (1940–3) 290
*Untamed* (1940–3) 290
*Untiring* (1940–3) 290
*Upholder* (1937–41) 290
*Upright* (1937–41) 290
*Uproar* (1940–3) 290
*Upshot* (1943–4) 290
*Upstart* (1940–3) 290
*Upton* (1952–9) 245
*Urania* (1943) 238, 253
*Urchin* (1917) 233
*Urchin* (1937–41) 290
*Urchin* (1943) 238, 253
*Ure* (1903–5) 230
*Urge* (1937–41) 290
*Ursa* (1917) 233
*Ursa* (1943) 238, 253
*Ursula* (1917) 233
*Ursula* (1937–41) 290
*Urtica* (1943–4) 290
*Usk* (1903–5) 230
*Usk* (1937–41) 290
*Usk* (1941–3) 251
*Usurper* (1940–3) 290
*Uther* (1940–3) 290
*Utmost* (1937–41) 290

*Vagabond* (1943–4) 290
*Valiant* (1863) 94, 102
*Valiant* (1914) 166, 168
*Valiant* (1963) 168
*Valiant* (1963) 289, 291
*Valerian* (1915–16) 246
*Valentine* (1917) 233
*Valentine* (1943) 238
*Valhalla* (1917) 233
*Valkyrie* (1917) 233
*Valorous* (1917) 233
*Vampire* (1917) 233

*Vampire* (1943–4) 290
*Vancouver* (1917) 233
*Vandal* (1940–3) 290
*Vanessa* (1918) 233
*Vanguard* 46
*Vanguard* (1835) 70
*Vanguard* (1870) 106, 114
*Vanguard* (1909) 162, 163
*Vanguard* (1944) 176, 177, 178
*Vanity* (1918) 233
*Vanoc* (1917) 233
*Vanquisher* (1917) 233
*Vansittart* (1918–19) 234
*Varangian* (1940–3) 290
*Variance* (1943–4) 290
*Varne* (1943–4) 290
*Vectis* (1917) 233
*Vega* (1917) 233
*Vehement* (1917) 233
*Veinticinco de Mayo* 268
*Veldt* (1943–4) 290
*Velox* (1902) 230
*Velox* (1917) 233
*Venetia* (1917) 233
*Vendetta* (1917) 233
*Venerable* (1899) 154
*Venerable* (1943) 268, 272
Venetians 10
Venetian ships 11
*Vengeance* (1899) 154
*Vengeance* (1944) 268, 272
*Vengeful* (1943–4) 290
*Venomous* (1918–19) 234
*Venturer* (1943–4) 290
*Venturous* (1917) 233
*Venus* (1895) 194
*Venus* (1943) 238, 253
*Verbena* (1915–16) 246
*Verbena* (1940–2) 251
*Verdun* (1917) 233
*Verity* (1918–19) 234
*Vernon* 41
*Veronica* (1915) 246
*Veronica* (1940–2) 251
*Versatile* (1917) 233
*Verulam* (1917) 233
*Verulam* (1943) 238, 253
*Vervain* (1940–2) 251
*Veryan Bay* (1944–5) 253
*Vesper* (1917) 233
*Vestal* (1898) 145
*Vestal* (1942–4) 244
*Vetch* (1940–2) 251
*Veteran* (1918–19) 234
*Viceroy* (1917) 233
Vickers-Maxim 205
*Victor* (1912–13) 231
*Victoria* (1859) 23, 65, 69, 93, 149
*Victoria* (1887) 124, 126
*Victoria and Albert* 151, 155
Victoria, Queen 66, 111, 138
*Victorious* (1895) 154
*Victorious* (1939) 266, 271
*Victorious* (1950–8) 274
*Victory* (1737) 34, 35, 36, 38, 39, 40, 44
*Victory* (1765) 85
*Victory* (1803) 68, 69, 72, 97
*Vidette* (1918) 233
*Vigilant* (1896–1901) 230
*Vigilant* (1942) 53, 238
*Vigo* (1945) 239
*Vigorous* (1943–4) 290
*Viking* (1907–9) 230
*Viking* (1943–4) 290
Viking ships 3
*Vikrant* 268
*Ville de Paris* 36, 44